# WILLIAM PLUMER'S MEMORANDUM OF PROCEEDINGS IN THE UNITED STATES SENATE, 1803–1807

THE MACMILLAN COMPANY
NEW YORK    BOSTON    CHICAGO
ATLANTA    SAN FRANCISCO

MACMILLAN & CO., Limited
LONDON  BOMBAY  CALCUTTA
MELBOURNE

THE MACMILLAN CO. OF CANADA, Ltd.
TORONTO

# WILLIAM PLUMER'S
# MEMORANDUM OF PROCEEDINGS
# IN THE UNITED STATES SENATE

## 1803-1807

EDITED BY

## EVERETT SOMERVILLE BROWN, Ph.D.

UNIVERSITY OF MICHIGAN

New York
THE MACMILLAN COMPANY
London: Macmillan & Company, Limited
1923

# PREFACE

WILLIAM PLUMER of New Hampshire merits the recognition of historical students along with those other pioneer diarists of the United States Senate, William Maclay of Pennsylvania and John Quincy Adams of Massachusetts, for Plumer's *Memorandum* is an almost daily record of sessions in the Senate from October 17, 1803, when Congress convened in special session to consider the treaty and conventions with France respecting the purchase of Louisiana, until the close of his term in March, 1807.

William Plumer was born at Newburyport, Massachusetts, in 1759, but moved with his parents to Epping, New Hampshire, in 1768. After a liberal education he engaged in the practice of law, but soon entered politics and rose to the position of presiding officer of the New Hampshire house of representatives and later, of the senate. He was a member of the State constitutional convention in 1791–1792; served as United States senator from December 6, 1802 to March 3, 1807; and was governor of his State for the terms of 1812–1813 and 1816–1819. As presidential elector in 1820, Plumer cast the single vote against James Monroe, not, as has so often been stated, to protect Washington's fame as the only President to receive the unanimous electoral vote, but to draw attention to his friend John Quincy Adams, for whom he voted, and as a protest against what he regarded as the wasteful extravagance of the Monroe Administration.

The later years of Plumer's life, until his death in 1850, were devoted to literature. His election as first president of the New Hampshire Historical Society was a recognition of his labors in the historical field. For many years he harbored the ambi-

vii

tion of writing a history of the United States and employed every opportunity to collect materials toward that end. In his *Memorandum,* Plumer relates his conversations with Thomas Jefferson, John Quincy Adams and Albert Gallatin, to whom he unfolded his plan and whose advice he sought. He also tells with what painstaking care he tried to gather a complete set of early government documents. A small fragment in the Manuscript Division of the Library of Congress attests to the fact that Plumer at least started to write his history but he was forced to give it up. He then devoted himself to biographical sketches of distinguished Americans and left a mass of materials on the subject.

The *Memorandum* is but a small part of Plumer's collection, yet it forms a distinct unit and is therefore published with but little reference to his other records. Only a few extracts from the *Memorandum* were printed by William Plumer Junior in his *Life of William Plumer.* The younger Plumer remarks that Senator Plumer's reports and discussions of the secret debates in the Senate " belong to the history of the country, rather than of the individual, and are therefore not quoted here." Senator Plumer's account of the debate on the Breckinridge Bill for the government of Louisiana (1804) — failure to report which was deplored by Henry Adams as a serious gap in the parliamentary history of the Union — was printed in the *American Historical Review* in January, 1917 (Vol. XXII, 340–364). This portion of the *Memorandum* formed the basis of Chapter VII in my *Constitutional History of the Louisiana Purchase.*

The journal here reproduced is in the Manuscript Division of the Library of Congress. The editor first used it in the summer of 1916. At that time the second part of the manuscript, covering the period from November 5, 1804 to March 3, 1805, was missing. It was located in the State Library in Concord, New Hampshire, and has since been transferred to the Library of Congress. The New Hampshire State Library contains a large amount of valuable Plumer material, especially letters. There is also a smaller quantity in the library of the New Hampshire Historical Society at Concord.

Various references are made by Plumer to his method of taking notes. In most cases he took abbreviated notes during the debates and then wrote them out at length at night. Occasionally the diary went untouched for several days and was brought up to date at a sitting. Although the style is fairly uniform, it is possible to detect parts of the *Memorandum* which were more hurriedly written than others, or which were not revised. Plumer himself calls attention to this fact.

In editing the *Memorandum* the form of the original text has been followed as closely as possible, even as to spelling and punctuation. A few entries have been omitted, as also the appendices. The latter contained copies of documents and letters now easily available in print. The division of the manuscript into three volumes is here preserved as Parts I, II and III.

Lack of complete detailed official records of the debates in the Senate during the period covered by Plumer, and a careful comparison of his journal with the *Memoirs* of John Quincy Adams and the *Annals of Congress,* force one to the conclusion that Plumer's *Memorandum* is an invaluable source for early American history. On the personal side, his descriptions of Thomas Jefferson, James Madison, James Monroe, John Quincy Adams, Albert Gallatin, John Marshall, Aaron Burr, George Clinton, Henry Clay, James Wilkinson, John Randolph of Roanoke, and a host of lesser lights, retouch our dim portraits of early political leaders who are, in Plumer's own words, " rapidly hasting to oblivion."

EVERETT SOMERVILLE BROWN

ANN ARBOR, MICHIGAN
    May, 1922.

# PART I

MEMORANDUM: PROCEEDINGS OF CONGRESS,
1803–1804

# PART I

*Memorandum of the proceedings of Congress particularly of the Senate, from October 17, 1803, to March 27, 1804. With an Appendix. Written by* WILLIAM PLUMER *for his own use.*

## October 17, 1803.

The President (Jefferson) convened Congress this day, it being three weeks sooner than the time established by a law of the last session. This meeting was occasioned by the treaty & conventions with France relative to Louisiana.[1] A quorum of both Houses met.

Nathaniel Macon of North Carolina, an honest man, possessed of a common share of candor, integrity & moderate talents, but a real democrat, was speaker of the House of Representatives the last Congress. He was now returned a member of the present House. The most bitter & zealous democrats were dissatisfied with his conduct as Speaker in the last House. They charged him with favoring the federal members. They now gave their votes to Genl Varnum of Massachusetts for Speaker, but the federalists uniting with the more moderate democrats re-elected Macon, who had 76 Votes, Varnum 30 & Dawson[2] one.

The Presidents message was this day communicated to both Houses of Congress.[3] He informs them that France had by a treaty & conventions ceded Louisiana to the United States.

---

[1] This is the reason given by Jefferson in a letter to Thomas Randolph, July 15, 1803, in *Jefferson Papers*, Coolidge Collection, Massachusetts Historical Society Library.

[2] John Dawson, representative from Virginia.

[3] Text of the message in Richardson, *Messages and Papers of the Presidents*, I, 357–362; *Annals of Congress*, 8 Cong., 1 sess., 11–15.

*That when these shall receive the constitutional sanction of the Senate, he will without delay lay them before the House of Representatives. That the ceded country is vastly extensive, fertile & will prove highly useful to the United States.* No language could be more improper for a President than this — & no one in this Country ever before assumed it. He not only publicly pledges himself to ratify the treaties if the Senate should advise thereto, but takes it for granted that the Senate will sanction them. As far as his influence can extend this is destroying the freedom of opinion in the Senate on that subject.

In the same style he has taken the liberty of recommending *what communications its proper for the Members to make to their constituents.* Are the members to be restrained in the free expressions of their own sentiments to their friends!

Mr. Dawson, in the House, offered a resolution to amend the Constitution, by making it the duty of the Electors to *designate* their votes for President & Vice President.

The treaty and two conventions with France purporting to be a cession of Louisiana to the United States, were communicated to the Senate, & read. The instructions to Livingston & Munroe our ministers at the Court of France & their Correspondence with the Secy of State were also laid before the Senate, & were partly read.[4] The treaty & Conventions were ordered to be printed for the use of the Senators under an injunction of secrecy.

### Oct. 18.

The Senate finished the reading of the Instructions to said ministers, & their correspondence with the Secy of State, relative to the subject.

The documents accompanying treaties are not printed but are open to the inspection of the Senators.......

---

[4] Text of the treaty and correspondence in *American State Papers,* II. *Foreign Relations,* II, No. 182, pp. 506–583.

### Oct. 19th.

Printed copies of the Treaty & Conventions were given to each member of the Senate. They were read a second time — & a desultory debate thereon.

### Oct. 20.

The Treaty & Conventions were read the third time, & a resolution offered to advise the President to ratify them. Mr. Wells [5] moved, & Mr. Hillhouse [6] seconded a resolution requesting the President to communicate to the Senate a copy of the Journal of our ministers at Paris during the time the negotiation was pending, and of the papers containing the title that France had acquired to Louisiana. The democratic Senators negatived the resolution; affirming, with unblushing front, that the information was unnecessary.

The treaty & Conventions with France are dated April 30, 1803 and each are to be ratified within six months from the date.

The treaty is designed to be considered as containing the cession of Louisiana. The 1st Convention is to provide for the payment to be made by the United States for that territory. And the second convention is a provision to allow certain sums to be deducted from the purchase sum to be appropriated by the United States to the payment of certain claims that our people have against the French nation. The treaty contains a stipulation that each of these Instruments " shall be ratified in the same form, & in the same time, & jointly." It is difficult to assign a reason why these three should not have been included in one Instrument.

By the first article of this treaty it appears that by the treaty of St. Idelfonso [7] Oct 1, 1800, " the king of Spain *promised* & *engaged* to cede to the French Republic, six months after the

---

[5] William H. Wells, senator from Delaware.
[6] James Hillhouse, senator from Connecticut.    [7] San Ildefonso.

*full and entire execution of the conditions & stipulations herein* relative to his royal highness the Duke of Parma [son of the Spanish King] [8] the colony or province of Louisiana, with the same extent as it now has in the hands of Spain, & that it had when France possessed it; & such as it should be after the treaties subsequently entered into between Spain & other States." What those conditions & stipulations to be performed by France to Spain were, doth not appear. The Senate were not indulged with a view of that treaty. The Spanish minister, in the name of his King has entered a protest against our ratifying the treaty. And alledges that the conditions & stipulations of the treaty of St Idelphonso have never been performed on the part of France — & that this treaty is founded in the *breach* of faith on the part of that nation.

The treaty of St Idelphonso is not a *cession* of Louisiana to France, but a *promise* to cede it six months *after* certain conditions & stipulations should be fully & entirely *executed.* And in the 4th article of the present treaty, the Commissary to be sent by France to Louisiana to give our agent possession thereof, is authorized to receive from the Spanish officers " the said country & its dependencies, in the name of the French Republic, if it has not been already done." So that at that time the actual *cession* had not then followed the Spanish *promise to cede;* or if it had the French government had then no knowledge of it. The fact is, we know that there has not even now been a delivery of it to France. The Spainards are yet in the quiet possession of that country.

How does France cede this territory to the United States? She does it by the foregoing recital, and " in pursuance of the Treaty (of St Idelphonso) particularly the third article, the French Republic has an incontestible right to the domain & to the possession of the said territory." Then follows a clause describing the cession and is said, " as fully & in the same manner as they

---

[8] Brackets appear in the original manuscript.

have been acquired by the French Republic *in virtue* of the above mentioned treaty concluded with his Catholic majesty." This is a simple *quit claim* of the right that France acquired by *that treaty*, & by *that only* to the territory. If Spain has not given a good title to France, this treaty has given none to us. The treaty does not contain a single covenant or assurance that the French title was good and that they will guarantee the Country to the United States.

For this naked quit claim, the first Convention stipulates that the United States shall create a stock of eleven million two hundred & fifty thousand dollars bearing a present interest of six pr Cent per annum payable half yearly in Europe. The principle to be paid in fifteen years after the ratification in annual payments of not less than three millions each. The stock to be delivered to the French government in three months after the ratification & possession given of Louisiana. The second convention provides that the United States shall pay at their Treasury, sixty days after the exchange of the ratification, to certain Americans, to whom the French nation were indebted, a sum not exceeding three million seven hundred & fifty thousand dollars — making in the whole fifteen million of Dollars. To this sum add compound interest at the rate of six pr Cent for the term of fifteen years, & it will then amount to Thirty five million nine hundred forty eight thousand two hundred sixty five Dollars. A sum nearly equal to half our national debt.

What are the limits & extent of Louisiana — what number of inhabitants, exclusive of the numerous hostile tribes of Indians, it contains — or what grants & of how much land have been made by either the Spanish or French government — are important inquires, & of which we have no correct information.

The second article provides that " In the cession made by the preceeding article are included the adjacent islands belonging to Louisiana, all *public* lots & squares, *vacant lands*, & all *public* buildings, fortifications, barracks, & other edifices which are not *private* property." What portion of this territory is *vacant land* we cannot determine; nor doth it appear from the Treaty that any provision is made by which our government can hereafter ascertain at *what time* grants were made by the Spanish or French governments to their *favorites,* who may hereafter claim any portion of those lands. The documents to be delivered respect the jurisdiction not the right of the soil. The article, like all the other parts of the treaty, is very cautious, & is expressive of the Art of French diplomatic skill. The words are, " The archieves, papers & documents, relative to the *domain & sovereignity* of Louisiana & its dependencies, will be left in the possession of the Commissiaries of the United States, and copies will be afterwards given in due form to the *majestrates & municipal officers, of such of the said papers as may be necessary to them."* Can we therefore say, as some gentlemen have, that the sale of the *vacant lands* will command a much higher price in the market than the territory cost us!

We have already, without Louisiana, more uncultivated lands than we can sell. Our territory was before this treaty too extensive, our settlements too sparse, for the security of our government. Our republican government derives its authority & momentum from the frequent meetings of the mass of the people in town & county assemblies. An extension of the body politic will enfeeble the circulation of its powers & energies in the extreme parts. A piece of our coin, an eagle, may be extended to the size of a coach wheel, but its beauty & use will be destroyed. If the bed of the *North River* was ten times as wide as it is, that noble stream, would lose both its force & usefulness. The testimony of history and the very nature of things unite in declaring that a republican government established over a large extensive country cannot long exist. And I am confident that the ratification of this treaty & the possession of that immense territory will hasten the dissolution of our present government. We must form different empires, & the form of our governments will then result more from the circumstances of the times in which the change is effected, than the will of the people or the fitness & propriety of the measure.

The third article stipulates, that " the inhabitants of the ceded territory shall be *incorporated in the Union* of the United States, & admitted as soon as *possible,* according to the principles of the *federal* constitution, to the enjoyment of *all* the rights, advantages & immunities of *citizens* of the United States; & in the mean time they shall be maintained & protected in the free enjoyment of their liberty, property, & the religion which they possess." What could induce Bonaparte to insist on this people's being incorporated into the Union? He has never discovered a strong attachment to the rights of any nation, or to that of any individual — & he has never had any connection with these people. Did he expect, that their admission would create an influence in his favor in the Councils of our nation. What could induce our Ministers to agree to an article in direct opposition to the spirit & genius of our Constitution?

The constitution of the United States was formed for the express purpose of governing the people who then & thereafter should live within the limits of the United States as then known & established. It never contemplated the accession of a foreign people, or the extension of territory. It is introduced with these appropriate terms, " We the *people* of the *United States* in order to form a more perfect union, establish justice, insure domestic tranquility, provide for the common defence, promote the general welfare, & secure the blessings of liberty *to ourselves & our posterity,* do ordain & establish this constitution for the *United States* of America."

I know authority is given to Congress to make *new States;* but this authority, from the very language which gives it, is necessarily limited to the territory then within the boundaries of the United States. The words are, " New States may be admitted by the *Congress* into this Union; *but* no new State shall be formed or erected within the jurisdiction of any other State; nor any state be formed by the junction of two or more states, or parts of states, without the consent of the Legislatures of the States concerned, as well as of the Congress." Art. 4. Sect. 3. It was a fact well known & perfectly understood by the Convention, who formed the constitution, that the treaty of Peace of 1783 with Great Britain, established the limits of the United States. That within those limits there were large portions of territory that did not of *right* belong to any *one* of the States. It was equally as well known that it might prove expedient to divide a large state into two or more states; or to form a new state out of parts taken from two or more of the old states. And the provisions in the constitution for the admission of new States into the Union, is predicated upon, & extends to these cases, *only*.

The constitution is in its form as well as in its nature a *federative* government. It may be fitly compared to a company in trade consisting of several partners. And with as much propriety might a *new* partner be admitted, & the *firm* of the company changed, without the consent of each of the old partners, as to admit a new State, formed from without the limits of the original territory, into the Union, without the previous consent of each State. For such admission might not only effect the relative interest of a particular State, but destroy the prosperity & endanger the peace & security of the Union. To elucidate this, I will state a case. Suppose the four British American colonies, at the north, to wit, Upper Canada, Lower Canada, Nova Scotia & New Brunswick contain ten million of inhabitants, attached from both habit & principle to a monarchal government. Suppose the British King should by treaty cede them, as Louisiana is, to the United States. Could the President & Senate, with propriety, ratify such a treaty, & admit them into the Union? And if admitted would they not immediately change both the forms & the principles of our government? Would not the influence and votes of the *old* states be controuled & negatived by the *new?* If we can admit Louisiana, why not the British provinces, why not the *terrible* Republic of France itself! The principle is the same, and applies with equal propriety to the one case as to the other. I have been told that a proposition was once made to annex Rhode-Island to Connecticut. The former complained that it would destroy their weight & influence. The celebrated *Roger Sherman* then proposed to change the proposition & annex Connecticut to Rhode Island. But the latter considered this as in fact annexing them to Connecticut. Louisiana, is of itself a *world.* Mr. Jefferson says it contains as much territory as that of the United States. That its soil is remarkably fertile — its climate highly salubrious — its rivers large & numerous — & that it is in every respect calculated to produce wealth & population. Such a country incorporated into the United States, must inevitably in the nature of things, have a powerful tendency to divide & sever the United States. I have said, & I again repeat the observation, that the existance of our government depends on public opinion. Admit this western world into the union, & you destroy with a single operation the whole weight & importance of the eastern states in the *scale* of politics. That portion of your *present* Union is inhabited by a hardy brave race of men. They know their importance, they know their rights, they feel the high rank that they are entitled to hold in the Union — and they have too much pride tamely to shrink into a state of insignificance. Adopt not the ruinous measure that will precipitate them to erect a seperate & independent Empire.

If the President & Senate can by treaty purchase new territory & stipulate that it shall be incorporated into the Union, without the previous consent of each of the *old* States — why may they not by treaty, *sell* a State, & sever it from the union, without its consent?

If the President & Senate can by treaty purchase territory &

stipulate that it shall be incorporated into the Union, it is in fact reducing the House of Representatives to the alternative of either making the appropriations for the purchase, or exposing the Union to the charge of breach of faith & violation of treaties.

But it is *Congress,* not the President & Senate, that can in any case whatever, constitutionally admit a *new state* into the Union. To this object, the *treaty-making powers* cannot from the nature of our government extend.

The constitution authorizes Congress " to establish a uniform rule of naturalization." This they have done by law. But the treaty stipulates that the inhabitants of Louisiana " shall enjoy *all* the rights, advantages & immunities of citizens of the United States." Does the treaty repeal the law upon this subject? Does it suspend the operation of the law as it respects that people? I shall be told that this law never extended to that country. Agreed. But the instant that you incorporate this territory into the Union you naturalize all its inhabitants who till then are foreigners. By the act of incorporating them into the Union, you naturalize a whole people by a single operation. And this if done, must be in *direct opposition* to that principle of *uniformity* which the constitution requires on this subject, & which Congress have by law established. And here also arises another proof that the Constitution was not formed to govern a people living without the limits of the United States as established when that constitution was made.

The constitution explicitly declares, That " no person except a natural born citizen, or a citizen of the United States, at the time of the adoption of this constitution, shall be eligible to the office of President." But the treaty stipulates " that the inhabitants of the ceded territory shall enjoy *all the rights, advantages & imminuties* of citizens of the United States." Suppose the territory & its inhabitants should be tomorrow incorporated into the Union — Would an inhabitant of Louisiana be elegible to the office of President?  Certainly not — for though born in that country — He would not be a natural born citizen, nor was he a citizen of the United States at the time your constitution was adopted.  At that period he lived without the United States, and at that time he was a foreigner, & owed allegiance to a foreign nation.  You cannot therefore fulfil the stipulations of the treaty — you cannot enable " the inhabitants of the ceded territory to *enjoy all* the rights, advantages & immunities of citizens of the United States."  The important *right* of being eligible, & being elected, to the high office of President of the United States cannot be conferred on an inhabitant of the ceded territory.  Here again we have another proof, that the constitution never contemplated the acquisition of new territory by treaty — that it was not formed for such an event.

The constitution declares that " all duties, imposts, & excises shall be *uniform* throughout the United States."  But the treaty admits the ships of France & Spain, to the exclusion of all other nations, for twelve years, into that territory, without subjecting their ships to the foreign extra duty of 44 Cents pr ton, & ten per Ct on the duty payable on their cargoes, as our law made in pursuance of the constitution & agreeably to this principle of *uniformity*, require.  Thus a *preference* is given to the *port* in that country — & the inhabitants of the adjacent states are thereby enabled to procure the articles of consumption without being subject to the extra duty — on foreign ships & their cargoes, which the citizens of other States are compelled to pay.  This *preference* established by the treaty, is in express words prohibited by the constitution.  It declares that " no *preference* shall be *given* by *any* regulation of commerce or revenue to the ports of one state over those of another." [9]  But gentlemen may say that New Orleans is a *port without* the United States.  But if that is admitted, do they not thereby admit the great objection

---

[9] Article, I, section 9, clause 6.

in all its force, to wit, that our constitution is not predicated upon the principle of acquiring foreign territory & incorporating it into the Union.

I have no doubt but that the United States may in their own defence, or in support of their commerce, conquer & hold a country. They may purchase a country by treaty & hold it. They may establish a military or colonial government in the country thus obtained. But it cannot be admitted as a State into the Union without the previous consent of each State first obtained.

So sensible were the Democrats that the treaty was unconstitutional, that Mr. *Taylor* [10] one of the Virginian senators, declared in debate in the Senate, " That he would, like an attorney who exceeded the authority delegated to him by his client, vote to ratify the treaty, *& throw himself upon the people,* & request the States so to amend the Constitution as to admit Louisiana into the Union."

If some articles, if particular stipulations, in the treaty, are unconstitutional, how can we ever fulfil them? And if we fail of preformance in one article on our part, is it not at least a doubtful question whether France will be bound by the treaty. May not this hereafter serve as a pretext to that nation to declare war against us, & attempt the conquest of that country.

The free navigation of the Mississippi is of great importance to the United States. To this, & to a deposit at New Orleans, we had a clear & indisputable title, secured to us by a treaty with Spain.[11] That right was the last year violated by the Spaniards. We ought to have maintained that right at the point of the bayonet. We ought to have taken possession of New Orleans & held it as a pledge for their performing their stipulations — & till they had indemnified us for the losses we sustained by their breach of faith. New Orleans was then weak, feeble & incapable of resistance. A single regiment on appearing

---

[10] John Taylor.
[11] Treaty of 1795, negotiated by Thomas Pinckney.

& demanding possession would have obtained it without loss of blood.

No demand has been made, that we are informed of, on Spain, for the insult offered us, or reparation for the injury she has done us, in violating our treaty rights. We have an Executive whose measures are better calculated to invite insults than to resent them. An Executive better calculated to drain our Treasury than to maintain the honor & glory of the nation. For such a President Mr. Monroe was a fit Minister. In his *Vindication*,[12] that he published soon after he was recalled from France by Genl Washington, he expressed his anxiety to furnish France with money. He has now gratified his wishes. And Bonaparte has sold his claim to a Country that he never possessed — & which the British nation, but for this treaty, would in a few months have taken. The United States are now doomed to pay a large sum for a vast wilderness world which will I fear prove worse than useless to us. To keep the possession, if we can obtain it, an army must be raised & supported there — A form of government made, & a long train of officers appointed to execute it. Though this must draw monies from the commercial States, particularly the eastern portion of the Union, without their deriving any advantages from it, it will encrease the patronage, & enrich the minions, of the Executive.

I am informed from high authority that the First Consul has sold the stock that we are to create to pay for the purchase of this country to the British House of Baring & Co & Hope & Co. at a discount of twenty two & a half pr cent. This House is established at London & Amsterdam. One of the House, a Mr. Baring, I saw here yesterday.

The Senate have taken less time to deliberate on this important treaty, than they allowed themselves on the most trivial Indian contract. The rules of the Senate require a treaty to

---

[12] *A View of the Conduct of the Executive,* in *Writings of James Monroe* (Hamilton, ed.), III, Appendix, 383–457.

be read three times, & not more than once in a day. Its probable that it is owing to this rule, that the final question was not decided the first day we met — & the first time we ever heard the Instrument read.

Previous to the question being taken, Peirce Butler, a senator from South Carolina, stated That after the vote of ratification was decided, he would bring in a resolve, requesting the President to open a new negociation with the first Consul to obtain his consent to dispose of Louisiana, or exchange it with Spain for the two Florida's.[13]

This resolution is improper in every respect. The treaty when ratified will be complete. The first Consul will then have no claim to that country or its Inhabitants. And if the stipulations to incorporate is to be regarded, a right is vested in those inhabitants, that cannot be lawfully withheld.

The question was taken on the resolution to advise the President to ratify the Treaty & Conventions. Thirty one senators were present. General Dayton with twenty three democrats voted in favor of the resolution, & the seven federal senators against it.[14]

Mr. Butler's resolution was then read, and ordered to lie on the table.

How far this treaty, by admitting the ships of France & Spain into the ceded territory on an equality with our own shipping, for twelve years, will affect the carrying trade of the eastern & commercial states, time will, I fear, to our great injury demonstrate.

Dewit Clinton [15] offered a resolution to amend the Constitution of the United States, directing the Electors to designate their votes for President & Vice President. Ordered to lay on the table.

---

[13] For the text of Butler's resolution, see Senate *Executive Journal* (printed in 1828) I, 450.

[14] For the resolution and vote, see *ibid.*, 450.

[15] Dewitt Clinton, senator from New York. Text of the resolution in *Annals of Congress*, 8 Cong., 1 sess., 16–17.

*Oct. 21, 1803.*

Mr. Clinton's resolution was ordered to be printed.

*Oct. 22.*

Clinton's resolution was printed & laid on our tables. To this resolution two objections were made. I. That it involved an absurdity, in supposing that after the *designation* was established two candidates could have an equal number of votes, & each have a *majority* of all the Electoral votes. The second objection was that if designation is established, a majority ought to be required in the choice of the Vice President. Bradley moved & Clinton seconded to strike out that part of the resolve that related to two candidates have each of them the majority of votes for President. This motion prevailed.

Bradley [16] then moved to amend the resolution so as to make a majority of the votes of all the Electors necessary to the choice of the Vice President.

Clinton said this was introducing a new & important principle into the Constitution; but he thought it was both just & necessary.

Mr. Butler moved an amendment, which provided that no man should hold the office of President for more than eight successive years — & that for the next four years he should not be eligible — & after the last term had elapsed he should not hold that office but for four years only.

It was moved that the resolution & the amendments proposed be referred to a Committee. In favor of the reference it was urged that amendments to the constitution was a subject of the first importance, & required much deliberation — That though the resolution as first proposed had received the approbation of the Legislature of New York & had in two successive years been by them recommended to Congress — and though the mover of

---

[16] Stephen R. Bradley, senator from Vermont.

it (Mr. Clinton) in the Senate had declared that he had often contemplated the subject & often examined the resolution, yet in the course of a few hours discussion, he had seconded & voted in favor of amending it — & had advocated the Omission of an important principle which his resolve did not include.

This was strenuously opposed by Clinton, Cocke,[17] Saml Smith [18] & Wright,[19] upon the ground that this motion was made only for *delay.*

Mr. Wright said that a few years since the same resolution, in substance, was brought up from the other House (the Representatives) to the Senate.[20]   But a majority of the Senate, being then federalists, & they knowing they could reject it, did not request a Committee to examine it; but after suffering it to lay two or three days on the table rejected it.   This appears from the journals of the Senate, which I now have in my hand.   Federalists are now a small *minority,* & they want to *rule* us.

Mr. Hillhouse said the gentleman is incorrect — for the journal that he has quoted, shows that the resolution he has mentioned was bro't up to the Senate on the very day, on which Congress adjourned — They had no time to commit, & little to deliberate on the subject.

Mr. Wright apologized by saying — That ten or twenty pages was included in the Journal between the notice of the resolve being brought to the Senate and their decision thereon: & from thence he inferred that several days had lapsed.

The motion for a committee prevailed by a majority of one vote.

Mr. Brown [21] the president pro tem. of the Senate decided, That the rules & course of proceeding in the Senate did not re-

---

[17] William Cocke, senator from Tennessee.
[18] Samuel Smith, senator from Maryland.
[19] Robert Wright, senator from Maryland.
[20] See Ames, *The Proposed Amendments to the Constitution of the United States,* in *Annual Report* of the American Historical Association, 1896, II, 77–78.
[21] John Brown, senator from Kentucky.

quire that a resolution, in which the concurrence of the other House is necessary, should be read three times on different days in the Senate.

### Sunday Oct. 23.

The Committee on Clinton's resolution, of whom he was one, met this day formed their report, included Butler's amendment in it, but in the form of a seperate resolution; had it printed, & this evening sent it to each Senator at his lodging. One principle cause of this great precipitancy, proceeds from Clinton's being appointed Mayor of the city of New York, & his being obliged to leave the Senate early this week.[22]

### Oct. 24.

In casting my eye over the Presidents message to Congress of the 17th of this month, speaking of the cession of Louisiana he says, " The provisional appropriation of two millions of dollars, to be applied and accounted for by the president of the United States, intended as a part of the price, *was considered as conveying the sanction of Congress to the acquisition proposed.*" What duplicity & hypocrisy is this man guilty of! He knew, very well knew, that he himself, though not by written message, recommended the last session, to make this appropriation, not for the purchase of Louisiana, but for the express & limited purpose of purchasing the island of New Orleans, & the two Florida's. The report of the secret Committee of the House of Representatives of the 11th February 1803 — which its well known, was drawn up by Mr. Madison, the Secretary of State, a copy of which Mr. Jefferson received at that time, contains the reasons & principles that induced Congress to pass the law making that appropriation. That report does not contemplate the purchase of Louisiana but New Orleans & the Florida's or

---

[22] Dewitt Clinton was appointed mayor of New York by his uncle, Governor George Clinton. He held the office until 1815, with the exception of the years 1807–1809 and 1810–1811.

a part of them. The report itself will in a day or two be made public.

The very instructions given by the President to our ministers, Livingston & Monroe, did not authorize 'em to purchase Louisiana, but only New Orleans & the Florida's.

The ministers apologize for having exceeded their authority — The Sec'y of State replies, the President notwithstanding approves of the measure.

I very well remember of Mr. Jefferson's asking me one day last winter in the Library what were the objections that the Senate had to the bill for appropriating the two million of Dollars? I then replied, That one objection I had, was that the bill did not *express* the *object* to which the money was to be applied — And that tho' I as a senator, knew what was contemplated, yet from the *law itself,* I could not discover it. He said, "I know that very well, & I also know what the *secret* intention of Congress is." But now it seems notwithstanding all this, Mr. Jefferson informs Congress, that this appropriation made for the express, though secret, purpose, of purchasing the Florida's & New Orleans, *sanctions* the purchase of Louisiana, an object not then contemplated either by him or Congress.

Clinton's resolution, to amend the Constitution, as reported by the Committee, was taken into consideration by the Senate.

Mr. Dayton, moved, & Mr. Tracey [23] seconded, the motion to strike out of the report, all that related to the Vice President, so as to take the opinion of the Senate on the question of abolishing the office of Vice President.

Mr. Dayton said, no heir apparent ever loved his father — A jealousy must, from the very nature of things, exist between the President & Vice President. The constitution requires the Electors to vote for two men for President — from this very circumstance they will select two characters highly respectable. If the report is accepted the inducements to look for a very

---

[23] Uriah Tracy, senator from Connecticut.

respectable man for Vice President will be removed — The advantages arising from the 2d office will in a great measure cease, but the evils attending the election of both will be encreased.

*Mr. Clinton.* This motion is made to effect procastination. — I am, however, myself *rather* in favor of the *principle*.

*Mr. Dayton.* The gentleman from New York (Mr. Clinton) is more disposed to arraign gentlemen's motives, than to answer their arguments.

*Mr. Clinton.* The language & declarations of the gentleman from New Jersey (Mr. Dayton) is *unfounded* — 'tis *untrue*. I never arraign the motives of any man.

*Mr. Nicholas.*[24] I am opposed to the motion, because it will prevent the amendment from being ratified previous to the next presidential election.

Several gentlemen declared they had not made up their opinions upon the subject — that they wanted time.

*Mr. Butler* said it was unreasonable to compel gentlemen to vote on a subject who had not had time to form their opinions — he therefore moved to postpone the consideration of Mr. Dayton's motion to Wednesday.

*Mr. Cocke* was opposed, because delay would prevent its being sent in season to the State Legislatures. The legislature of Tennessee is now in session — They meet but once in two years — & if we delay this business a few days that legislature will rise — & all will be lost.

*Mr. Wright.* I am against the postponement — because I do not know what is the opinion of the people, whether they wish a Vice President or not. I am myself rather inclined to be in favor of abolishing the office. But it is the duty of each senator to feel the pulse of the State he represents, & as soon as he knows what the public opinion is, to carry it into effect — We know people demand the *designating principle* — I am for it.

---

[24] William Cary Nicholas, senator from Virginia.

*Mr. Jackson.*[25] I am in favor of postponement — I shall, I hope, always vote in favor of postponing business, whenever a single senator says he wants time to make up his mind, unless imperious necessity demand a prompt decision — I am not for doing business on horseback.

*Mr. Hillhouse.* The motion to abolish the office of Vice President is of importance — it requires deliberation. If the President dies, resigns or is incapable, the Vice President succeeds him for the remainder of the term. We generally elect a President who is advanced in years — he may die before the four years expire. In one State, in the course of a few years, two governors, who were elected only for one year, died before the year expired, & the lieutenant governor exercised the functions for the remainder of those years. I am not prepared to give my vote — There are many reasons for & against the measure — I wish further time to investigate the subject before I am obliged to decide.

*Mr. Worthington.*[26] I have not made up my mind upon the motion respecting the Vice President, but I shall vote against it — I do not wish the subject discussed. I am for the designating principle only, and therefore shall vote against a postponement.

*Mr. Saml Smith.* What a dreadful situation we were in at the last presidential election — It was carried into the other House, & we were on the eve of a civil war. From the information we have had from our constituents we are prepared to establish the designation principle; but not to adopt the amendment proposed by the gentleman (Mr. Dayton) from New Jersey. I believe every senator has made up his mind — Delay is the object of some gentlemen.

The question for postponement was taken & lost, ayes 15, nays 16.

---

[25] James Jackson, senator from Georgia.
[26] Thomas Worthington, senator from Ohio.

*Mr. White.* If the majority are so assuming as to press a hasty decision I must be excused from voting.

*Mr. Wright.* It is very extraordinary that the minority should wish to govern the majority.

*Mr. Tracey.* I hope we shall decide with moderation — Warmth & passion ill accord with the dignity of a deliberate body. I hope my honorable friend from Delaware (Mr. White) will not persist in his request to be excused from voting on this question — I think he had better move for a postponement till tomorrow. And I trust the majority will consider that minorities have their rights, & that it behoves majorities to decide with reason & propreity.

*Mr. Cocke.* A delay will prove a denial of justice — Delay will defeat us.

*Mr. Adams.*[27] I am in favor of designation — I shall vote for it. But I am willing to own that I have not contemplated this subject in all its relations & consequences. I now see & feel that if we establish the *designating principle* some measures must be taken respecting the Vice President, at least as to the mode of choice. I have long & frequently contemplated the original question, that of designation, & I approve of it; but I have not sufficiently attended to all its consequences. I am not prepared to say whether the mode of choosing the Vice President must be changed, or the office abolished. One or the other must be done. Without a decision as to the Vice President we can decide nothing definitively as to the President. I want time — I think it necessary I should have it.

*Mr. McClay.*[28] If the designating principle as reported by the Committee is adopted no *new* principle will be introduced into the constitution. I think the Electors, will after this amendment, pay as much attention to select a respectable man for the office of Vice President, as they have heretofore done.

---

[27] John Quincy Adams, senator from Massachusetts.
[28] Samuel Maclay, senator from Pennsylvania.

*Mr. Brackenridge.*[29]   I am in favor of the *designating principle,* & against all other amendments. If I was to propose such amendments to the constitution as I myself wish, I would reduce the term for which senators hold their seats in this house. It is too long — tis antirepublican. But I am *now* only for changing the principles of electing the President, because the people are prepared for that, & wish it.

*Mr. White.*[30]   Every gentlemen who has spoken has convinced me that the Senate are not prepared for a vote on the merits of the question. I therefore move that it be postponed till tomorrow.

*Mr. Clinton.*   I demand the yeas & nays on the postponement.

*Mr. Plumer.*[31]   I have heard much complaint against the *omnipotence* of a British parliament. But I now witness the overbearing precipitate spirit of a triumphant majority in the American Senate. I think the temper of the House ill accords with that cool dispassionate investigation which the high importance of the subject demands. The amendment affects the rights of a great & encreasing nation, & ought not to be decided but with great caution & after mature deliberation. I am therefore in favor of postponement.

*Mr. Anderson.*[32]   I never knew a postponement denied, when requested on an amendment to an important bill. Shall we deny it when amendments are to be made to the constitution, the supreme law of the land? If amendments are to be made to the constitution, its best to make them at once & not at different times.

*Mr. Jackson.*   I agree with the gentleman from Tennessee (Mr. Anderson). The call for yeas & nays never deter, but rather makes, me, more decided. I do not court or fear popularity. I *will* vote for the postponement.

---

[29] John Breckinridge, senator from Kentucky.
[30] Samuel White, senator from Delaware.
[31] William Plumer, senator from New Hampshire.
[32] Joseph Anderson, senator from Tennessee.

*Mr. Cocke.* I am against the motion — & hope gentlemen will not in a *pet* reject the designating principle. Vermont legislature is now in session — they are in favor of the resolution, but will in a few days adjourn, & not meet again till next October. Delay will therefore defeat us.

*Mr. Butler.* The proceedings of Senate this day has alarmed me — I fear for my country — I want time to state my fears & apprehensions — I think I shall vote against the motion of the gentleman (Mr. Dayton) from New Jersey; but I owe it to him, to Senate, & to myself, to do it, if at all, after mature deliberation. I am inclined to think I shall vote for the report of the committee — but I have not made up my mind — I want time for reflection. I am not to be hurried by such adventitious circumstances as either the meeting or adjourning of State legislatures.

*Mr. Saml Smith.* Nothing retards deliberation so much as motions for postponement. We might have heard the arguments today, & decided the main question tomorrow.

*Mr. Dayton.* Some gentlemen form their opinion in the Senate from debate — others in their chambers — but all who act correctly require time for investigation. The rough, indecorous, abusive & unmanly language of the gentleman from New York (Mr. Clinton) merits & shall receive from me, a reply in another place, in another time, & in a manner which the respect I have for the decorum of this House now prevents.

Mr. White moved an adjourned — carried by a majority of two.

### House of Representatives.

In the House, Mr. Griswold of Connecticut, moved " That the President of the United States be requested to cause to be laid before them a copy of the treaty between the French Republic & Spain of Oct. 1, 1800, together with a copy of the deed of cession from Spain executed in pursuance of the same treaty conveying Louisiana to France, (if any such deed exists;)

also copies of such correspondence between the government of the United States & the government or Minister of Spain, (if any such correspondence has taken place) as will show the assent or dissent of Spain to the purchase of Louisiana by the United States — together with copies of such other documents as may be in the department of State, or any other department of this government tending to ascertain whether the United States have, in fact, acquired any title to the province of Louisiana by the treaties with France, of the 30th April 1803."

A division of the question was called for — and a vote taken on the following words, " Resolved That the President of the United States be requested to cause to be laid before this House, a copy of the treaty, between the French republic & Spain, of the 1st October 1800."

The House was equally divided, 59 yeas & 59 nays — the Speaker declared himself in the affirmative. The remainder was rejected — That part of the resolution that was agreed to, was amended, & then rejected, yeas 57, nays 59.

When the Federalists were in power, the democrats (upon the British treaty [33]) called upon the Executive for papers, not to ascertain what the treaty contained, but to ascertain whether it was the *best* treaty that could be made — and to enable them to decide whether it was best to make the necessary appropriations to carry it into effect. Then they considered the denial of the papers, as a refusal of useful & necessary information — & as evidence that the Executive was under the influence of monarchal principles. But now the request for papers & information, made not for the purpose of examining the goodness of the bargain, but to know *what title we have acquired to Louisiana,* is *now* considered as useless, dangerous, & an encroachment on the perogatives of the Executive.

John Randolph Jr of Virginia is evidently the leader of the Democrats in the House. The manner in which he exercised

---

[33] Jay's Treaty.

this authority today, was very disgusting, & excited my indignation. Profuse in censuring the *motives* of his opponents — artful in evading their arguments, & peremptory in demanding the vote — sitting on his seat insolently & frequently exclaiming *I hope this motion will not prevail* — or when it suited his views, *I hope this will be adopted.*

### Tuesday Oct. 25.

Last evening after the Senate adjourned Mr. Dayton sent a note by the doorkeeper to Mr. Clinton demanding an explanation of what he had said of him that day in the Senate. Mr. Clinton sent by a friend a message to Mr. Dayton proposing that they should both of them make mutual concessions. Dayton peremptorily insisted on an answer to his note. But at eleven O Clock in the evening he sent a challenge by Maj P. Butler of South Carolina to Mr. Clinton, authorizing Mr. Butler to accept of such concessions from Mr. Clinton, if he proffered any, as would be satisfactory to a man of honor — If such should not be offered Mr. Butler was to agree with Mr. Clinton on the time place & weapons necessary to end the dispute. On Mr. Butler's informing Mr. Clinton of Mr. Dayton's determination, Mr. Clinton readily agreed that he would write a letter to Mr. Dayton, the purport of it was *That Mr. Clinton did not mean, in the smallest degree, to insinuate anything against the verasity of Mr. Dayton — & that he (Clinton) owed it to him, (Mr. Dayton) & to the Senate, to make this public apology in the Senate, & that had he not been under the necessity of leaving this city, he should have personally made in the Senate from his seat this concession & apology for his conduct.* Mr. Clinton wrote two letters of this purport to Mr. Dayton, one of which was to be delivered to Mr. Wright & to be by him read publickly in the Senate, & the other to be delivered to Mr. Dayton. Mr. Butler declared, in behalf of Mr. Dayton, that this was satisfactory. Mr. Clinton then delivered the two letters, to his friend Mr. Wright, who accompanied Mr. Butler to Mr. Dayton's lodgings, — stated the proceedings & delivered one of the letters to Mr. Dayton, who declared he was satisfied — And Mr. Wright this morning read the other letter publickly in the Senate.[34]

Clinton is appointed mayor of the city of New York, an office worth from eight to ten thousand dollars pr annum, which he has accepted, & resigned his seat in the Senate. His absence will not be the subject of regret to a single member of the Senate. He is a man of violent passions, of a bitter vindactive spirit, — unfeeling — insolent — haughty — & rough in his manners.

Mr. Wright moved to postpone the consideration of the report of the committee upon the subject of amendment to the Constitution — declaring that the importance of the subject required *further time* — Carried.

On the motion of Mr. Wright, made the 22d instant " That the Senate now proceed to the election of a Secretary & other officers of the Senate." The Senate refused to proceed to the consideration thereof — fifteen being in favor of proceeding, & sixteen against it.

### Wednesday Oct. 26.

The Senate passed the bill to enable the President to take possession of Louisiana & for the temporary government thereof.

This bill vests in the persons whom the *President* shall appoint, all the military, civil & judiciary powers exercised by the existing government of Louisiana, unto the end of the present session, unless Congress shall sooner establish a temporary government for that country.

The constitution provides that " Congress may by law vest the appointment of such inferior officers as they think proper in the President alone; in the Courts of law, or in heads of

---

[34] *Cf.* J. Q. Adams, *Memoirs,* I, 266. This episode is not mentioned in the *Annals of Congress.*

Departments." But by this bill the appointment of all the officers, *superior* as well as *inferior,* are vested in the President *alone.* And this authority will be exercised by him at a time when the Senate will be in session. Had such a bill been passed by federalists, the Democrats would have denounced it as *monarchal;* but when enacted by the *exclusive friends* of the people, it is pure *republicanism.* —

The bill passed yeas 26, nays 6.

### *Thursday Oct. 27.*

Samuel Alleyne Otis Esq has been Secretary of the Senate from the first commencement of the government under the present constitution. He was elected secretary in 1789, & as the senate are a permanent body, he has held the office from that time under that election. At the last session a resolve was brought forward in the senate, at near the close of the session, that the senate should at the commencement of this, proceed to the election of a Secretary — that motion was then negatived 15 to 7. But as the democrats at this session have received an accession of numbers in the senate, & as Mr. Otis is a federalist, it was now determined to remove him from office, by electing another man. Mr. Otis for some years has employed a Mr. *Way* [35] to do the printing for the Senate. He has done it with great dispatch, accuracy & integrity. William Duane,[36] the Irish fugative, came to Mr. Otis at the commencement of this session & threatned the secretary that he should be removed unless he would give him the printing business. Mr. Otis very well knew that Duane could command votes in the senate, & to retain the Office, he withdrew the business from Mr. Way (an industrious well deserving man) & gave it to Duane. Strange as it may seem, it is a fact, that this Duane, this foreigner — this printer of news papers, has a very con-

---

[35] Andrew Way and George Way, printers.
[36] Editor of the Philadelphia *Aurora.*

siderable influence in both Houses of Congress. And I will venture to say, that his influence with Mr. Jefferson, is greater than that of all the democrats of New Hampshire united. The President dare not refuse his requests — because he fears Duane, if offended, would *write him down.* He is an unprincipled wretch, but he has talents. —

The last evening, the democratic senators met in caucus, to determine who should succeed Otis as Secretary. Some of them were in favor of John Beckley (a foreigner) who is now Clerk of the other House. Mr. Wright said that Col. Chambers of Maryland had received encouragement that he should have the office, & that one of his sons should be first clerk in the office under the Colonel. Another senator insisted on a different candidate — Jackson, Bradley & one or two more, declared they would support Otis — And it was said that Otis had now made a good disposition of the printing, & that he ought not to be removed.

Mr. Wright this day brought forward in the Senate his resolution to proceed to the election of Secretary & other officers of the senate.

The Senate postponed the further consideration thereof, untill the first monday of October next. Seventeen voted in favor of postponement, and fourteen against it.

### Friday the 28th.

The Senate spent all the day in debate on Mr. Butler's resolution of the 20th, which is to request the President to open an negotiation with Bonaparte to obtain permission to sell, or exchange, a part of Louisiana. The debate was almost intirely managed, both for & against the resolution, by the democrats. No decision was had on the resolution.

The House of Representatives sent us a resolve to amend the Constitution — It passed in that house, yeas 88, nays 31.

General Dayton (the senator from New Jersey) informed me

that he was at New Orleans in April & May last — That he was then informed directly from the Spanish officer that they were determined not to yield the possession of that country to the French Prefect — That the Spainards had in a formal manner come to the resolution of maintaining their possession of it by arms — That their regular force was then something less than five hundred troops — & that their fortifications were then in a ruinous state. —

### Saturday, 29th.

The Senate, after long debate, agreed to the amendments made by the House to the bill authorizing the President to take possession of Louisiana & for the temporary government thereof. By this law the President is authorized to employ any part of the army & navy of the United States, and a detachment of the militia not exceeding eighty thousand men to enable him to take and hold the possession of that country. And to defray the expenses thereof, a sum is appropriated not exceeding one million five hundred thousand dollars. From this measure being considered necessary, it appears that administration are apprehensive that Spain will not voluntarily give us possession of the *purchased* territory. —

### Monday the 31st.

" The senate unanimously resolved, that the members thereof, from a sincere desire of shewing every mark of respect due to the memory of the honorable Stevens Thompson Mason, deceased, late a member therof, will go in mourning for him one month, by the usual mode of wearing a crape round the left arm."

Mr. Mason died the last spring aged 45. At the time of his death he was a senator from the State of Virginia. His memory is rendered *famous* by his *publishing* the British treaty [37] before

---

[37] Jay's Treaty.

it was ratified, & while it was pending in the Senate. This he did by delivering up the copy of it, contrary to the injunction of secrecy injoined on him by the *then* implied rules of the senate, his duty, and his oath. He was a man of talents — & at the last session was evidently the leader of the Democrats in the Senate. His *moral* qualities were never *burthensome* to him. —

Mr. Brackenridge moved That the Senators should wear a like *badge* of mourning for the late Samuel Adams (of Massachusetts) & Edmond Pendleton (of Virginia) deceased, for the like term.[38] The debate on this resolution took up nearly the whole of the day. It was opposed upon the ground That other men equally as eminent, patriotic & useful as these had died without receiving such a tribute of respect from the Senate — That if we extend the precedent further than to those who die members of Congress, or have been Presidents &c it will be extremely difficult to establish a rule beyond which we may not pass. Every member of Senate who is so unfortunate as to lose a friend or connection may make a similar motion — The senate may be divided in sentiment upon the merits of the character for whom it proposed to mourn. This will necessarily produce a discussion in which the *feelings* of the friends of the deceased may be wounded; — & that perhaps *more* than by the *loss* they mourn. — That if these resolves are thus extended, from the power of precedent, they will become frequent, & from that very circumstance, lose much of their force in exciting good & great actions.

The resolve however passed, yeas 21, nays 10.

### Thursday Nov. 3d.

The Senate passed the bill for creating the eleven million two hundred & fifty thousand dollars stock for the payment of

---

[38] Adams and Pendleton were members of the First Continental Congress but not of the Federal Congress.

Louisiana. To this bill my much esteemed friends Tracey, Hillhouse, Pickering,[39] White & Wells, were opposed. Their opposition was made on the ground that the treaty was unconstitutional — That it is a meer naked quit claim from a nation that has neither a legal or equitable title to the territory in question — That if appropriations must be made, it is not necessary we should make them untill we know whether quiet possession will be had — And that this information can be had within six weeks — & that will be in season to pass the necessary laws.

I voted in favor of the bill. The President & senate, the only tribunal established to make treaties, have declared this Instrument to be a treaty. My vote, while sitting as a member of the Senate in their Executive capacity, was against advising the President to ratify — In that case I differed from the majority — but that question is settled so far as it affects the Senate — & the faith of the nation is pledged to make the necessary appropriations. And I do not feel myself at liberty to with-hold the necessary appropriations — A large majority of the Senate have, contrary to my opinion, declared the Instrument a treaty — By that opinion I am now bound so far as to make the necessary appropriations. That treaty is now a *law* to me as a *senator* as far as it is to me as a *man*. And on an incidental question, as making appropriations, I think I am not at liberty to with-hold my vote upon the ground either that the treaty is unconstitutional, or its a bad bargain. Those questions as they relate to the Senate, are definitely settled. A Judge of the supreme Court & a district Judge make a Circuit court — they disagree upon a question of law — The cause is to be continued — The next term another of the Judges of the Supreme Court goes into the same Circuit if he differs also in opinion with the District Judge upon the same question, notwithstanding the later has not changed his former Opinion he is bound by the Opinion of the two supreme Judges, & must aid in carrying that

---

[39] Timothy Pickering, senator from Massachusetts.

opinion into execution. This was the law under the first statute establishing the Judiciary of the United States. These rules are founded in the reason & fitness of things. They result from that principle of subordination & order that is essential to the very existence of government. I do not say that the ratification of the treaty has made it a constitutional treaty, if its articles are in violation of the Constitution. It cannot have such an effect — But its ratification has bound the government to carry it into effect so far as they have authority so to do. Perish the eleven millions of stock; but preserve the *faith* of the nation. Nor do I contend but that cases may arise respecting the rights of individuals under this treaty in the Courts of law, in which the constitutionality of the treaty may be questioned. And there may be cases in which it may become the duty of the Judges, if that is their opinion, and if the nature of the case require it, to declare the treaty to be repugnant to the constitution.

I am also *now* ready to pass the law. I am willing that the President should decide whether he receives such possession of the Country as will justify him in delivering the stock to the assignees of France. He must be responsible for the measure. I will give him the same authority as I would do were he the man of my own choice.

This circumstance of differing in opinion from my friends, in whom I have the highest confidence, & with whom I have been in habits of thinking & acting, gave me much *uneasiness*.

The bill passed, twenty six yeas, five nays.

### Friday the 4th.

Mr. Dayton moved, & Mr. Butler seconded the motion, That the Senate should take into consideration the amendment to the Constitution. Mr. Butler demanded the reason why gentlemen who ten days since pressed a speedy decision of this question — who then declared they had made up their minds & were ready to vote, *now* refused to go into a consideration of the subject. The majority gave no answer. The motion was negatived — yeas 12, nays 19.

### *Thursday the 10th.*

Mr. Butler again renewed the same motion; which was also negatived.

### *Monday the 14th.*

Mr. Wells (from Delaware) renewed the same motion, & that we *now* proceed to take the subject into consideration. On this motion a long & very spirited debate ensued. The democrats were pressed to state their reasons for refusing to consider of the propriety of their own resolution. Taylor, Cocke & Wright were compelled to say, in their own defence, that the reason of their being averse to considering the subject now, was because they could not obtain the votes of two thirds of the Senators present. The motion was negatived, yeas 9, nays 22. Adams & Pickering voted in the negative.

### *Wednesday 16th.*

Mr. Wright moved That the resolution reported by the Committee, & the resolution brought up from the other House on the subject of amending the Constitution should be the order of the day for monday next. Carried by a majority of one vote.

The democrats were very averse to the making both resolutions the order of the same day.

### *Friday 18th.*

While the Senate were sitting in their Executive capacity, on the nomination of Abraham Bishop for collector for the port of New Haven in Connecticut, objections were made to his appointment, on the ground of his *immoral character*. Mr. Wright in express words, observed to the Senate, " That honesty &

capacity were not *yet* requisite qualifications for office — That the great object that we ought *now* to keep in our constant view is to place *Democrats* in office." Every man present, except the federalists, voted in favor of Bishop's appointment.

### Monday Nov. 21, 1803.

The "Act for the further protection of the seamen & commerce of the United States"—was debated. Mr. Wright moved to add a proviso to the bill, "That free ships should make free goods." Note the design of the bill was to authorize the President to declare *War* against the Emperor of Morrocco.[40] The debate continued all day — no decision of the question.

### Tuesday 22d.

The same question under consideration.

Mr. Wright said he had three great authorities in his hand which were in point to prove the doctrine he contended for, & which he would now read. He then read a few sentences from one of Genl Washington's proclamations — a passage from one of Mr. Jefferson's letters — & also from Mr. Pickering's, written whilst he was Secretary of State. Each of these authorities, in the very paragraph's he read, contradicted the doctrine he advocated — Mr. Wright then said, "I beg leave to differ in opinion from the authorities I have read."

Mr. Adams (Massachusetts) said, "he had examined the proposition of amendment offered to the bill, & he was opposed to its principles. As to the authorities that the gentlemen from Maryland (Mr. Wright) has read, I differ with him — Genl Washington's opinion was against the doctrine that Mr. Wright now contends for — & Mr. Jefferson's opinion was directly in favor of it. *And I am very much embarrassed when two such high respectable authorities as Washington & Jefferson*

---

[40] A similar opinion was expressed by John Quincy Adams: *Memoirs*, I, 273.

*differ in opinion to determine which of the two are the most respectable.*

Mr. Hillhouse, said, I am opposed to the proposed amendment — This nation ought to be the last on earth to agree to such a principle. Our commerce is valuable & extensive — The existence of our public faith & of our government itself is dependent on the revenue derived from that commerce — A large portion of your citizens, living, depends on trade. If we were involved in a war with England our little navy is insufficient to protect our trade. We cannot send troops to attack Great Britain, or her possessions — We must defend ourselves by attacking her commerce on the seas — Our privateers & letters of Marque are our *militia* moving on the *water* — Let this principle be established, & in time of war, much of the trade of our enemy may be secure in neutral bottoms. Suppose we should be at war with Spain, & the probability is now great, would it be prudent to adopt a principle, that would permit that nation to send her wealth from America in British vessels out of our reach? No nation who has adopted such a principle ever regarded it in time of war. Interest governs nations more than abstract principles. These, if adopted, may perplex, but cannot benefit us.

The question not decided — The bill referred to a select committee.

The amendments to the Constitution debated, but no vote taken thereon.

### Wednesday 23d.

The amendments to the constitution under consideration.

A debate arose whether any amendments to the amendment to the constitution could be made unless two thirds of the Senate vote in favor of those provisional amendments.

Whereupon Mr. Brown the president pro. temp. proposed the following question of order to be decided by the Senate — *viz.*

"When an amendment to be proposed to the constitution is under consideration, shall the concurrence of two thirds of the members present, be requisite to decide any question for amendments, or extending to the merits, being short of the final question?"

The opinion of the Senate was taken on this question, & determined in the negative by a majority of *one* vote. And so its determined that a bare majority is sufficient to amend a resolution that cannot be passed with less than two thirds. Mr. Adams was the only federal member who voted in favor of this rule. When a bill is under consideration, every section at the second reading is passed in detail by the major vote; & no amendment whatever can obtain but by the same majority that is requisite to pass the bill itself at the third reading. And why should not the same two thirds be requisite to amend this resolution that is necessary for its final passage? The principle is the same. The design of the constitution is to render it difficult to attain amendments — its security is hedged around by making the assent of two thirds of both Houses of Congress, & three fourths of the State Legislatures, necessary to obtain a change in any case.

The rule now established will be found in practise to be attended with difficulties. A bare majority may now add to, or take from, an amendment, such parts thereof, as will change the very *principles* of the original resolution — & thereby prevent two thirds of the senators from voting in favor of it. —

Several amendments were made to the resolution.

### Thursday 24.

The amendment to the constitution under consideration.

After a long debate upon questions of order, the Senate reconsidered their several votes of yesterday amending the original resolution as reported by the committee — And restored the resolution to the same form as it was first reported.

A part of the report was struck out, & a new sentence, copied from the words of the constitution, was incorporated into the amendment.

*Mr. Bradley* moved to amend the report so as that a majority of all the Electoral votes should be necessary to the choice of the Vice President — And that if no candidate have such majority, then the Senate shall from the two highest numbers on the list elect the Vice President.

*Mr. Wright,* I know it is impossible to preserve all the *rights* of the *small states;* but I am for doing as little *violence* to the constitution as possible. I wish that in case the Electors should not compleat the choice of Vice President, that the Senate should finish it, voting by States, as the House of Representatives do, in case the Electors do not choose a president. This would conform the amendment to the spirit of the Constitution.

*Mr. Bradley,* The States are *equally* represented in the Senate; they are not so in the other House. If the Senate vote by States in choosing a Vice President — & if a majority of all the States are necessary to a choice, — if five States should be divided — it would be in the power of two or three Senators absolutely to prevent the choice of a Vice President.

Bradley's motion was agreed to by a majority.

The report of the Committee was in case no person had a majority of all the Electoral votes for President, then the House of Representatives should elect the President from the *five* highest candidates. Yesterday the word *five* was struck out & the word *three* inserted.

Mr. Tayler (of Virginia) moved to strike out the word *three* & leave it *blank,* that gentlemen might have an opportunity of considering & debating what number it should be filled with — declaring at the same time that he should move to have it filled with the word *three.*

The motion for striking out was carried.

### Friday 25.

The amendment to the constitution was postponed on account of the illness of Mr. Anderson, who was unable to attend the Senate. The Virginia senators opposed the postponement.

Mr. Adams gave notice to the senate, That in case of no choice of President by the Electors, if the amendment confined the House of Representatives to the *three* highest candidates, he should vote against the resolution in chief.

*Mr. Wright,* Last monday, I gave notice to the Senate, that I should this day move an amendment to the " Act for the further protection of the seamen & commerce of the United States " — declaring, " That free ships should make free goods;" but I will not trouble the senate on the subject — for the " *Cabinet* have settled the question that it is *now* improper to introduce such a principle into the bill."

## Monday 28th.

The amendment to the constitution postponed to tomorrow.

## Tuesday 29th.

The bill brought up from the other House for the repeal of the *bankrupt Law* was read the second time. The opposers of the bill moved to have it referred to a select committee — The friends to the bill contended that the Bankrupt law ought to be repealed, & that this was correct & needed no amendment. The motion did not prevail.

The resolution to amend the constitution was resumed. The debate was confined to the following paragraph, to wit, " The person voted for as President having a majority of votes of all the Electors appointed, shall be the President: & if no person have such majority, then from the . . . highest on the list of those voted for as President, the House of Representatives shall choose the President — "

The motion was to fill the blank with the word " *five.*"

*Mr. Cocke.* I am in favor of sending such an amendment to the State Legislatures as they request whether I approve of it or not in all its parts. They request the *designating principle* — Let us send them *that.*

*Mr. Tayler.* The introduction of the classification of States, *large & small*, into debate, has a tendency to produce a spirit of *rivalry*, & that will produce corruption.

The carrying the election of the President into the House of Representatives, & there compleating it by ballot from *five* candidates will produce the same pernicious effects as carrying an election into a diet or mob.

It has a direct tendency to bribery & corruption, & that to monarchy.

It will create alarm in the large States; & throw the election into the hands of small States; & small States will be corrupted.

Your Electors will nominate, but the representatives of the small States will in fact become themselves the real Electors.

The greater number of candidates you allow the House of Representatives to choose from — the more you extend & multiply the evil — For the candidates will always be equal to that number.

I think there is a very material difference between the number three & five — I am in favor of the first, & against the last.

*Mr. Dayton,* The constitution is founded on the idea of a classification of States. This is evident in all its parts, particularly, in the equal representation of each State in this House — which is so guarded as to prevent its ever being a subject of amendment.

*Mr. Jackson,* I am for filling the blank with *three,* and not *five.* At the last presidential election the fifth candidate, Mr. Jay,[41] had but one electoral vote. The House of Representatives might have chosen him for President. If they had, it would have thrown the country into a civil war. I will never give that House the power of choosing a man President who has but one vote.

There may not be five candidates on the list, & then there

---

[41] John Jay.

can be no choice made by the House; but I think there is no danger but that there will be three.

It is improper — its wrong, to talk, in this House, of great & small States. It is exciting & creating jealousies that ought not to exist.

*Mr. Wright,* The Constitution is a compact between great & small States. It was the work of mutual concession. — I do not wish to injure the rights of small states — I am willing to fill the blank with *five.*

*Mr. Nicholas,* I am in favor of the doctrine of amendments — And if I thought we could obtain a better constitution, I would freely vote to expunge every letter of our present constitution from the book.

I am for filling the blank with *three* — & will never consent to have it filled with *five.*

What would have been the impression, on the people, if Jay, who had but one vote, had been chosen by the House, President? The people would never have submitted to such a usurpation!

This amendment has been demanded by the Legislatures of New Hampshire, Vermont, South Carolina, & Tennessee. Can it be said to be a measure that the large States are anxious for?

*Mr. McClay,* The intention of the constitution is that the people, not the House of Representatives, should choose the President. This amendment is designed to secure that right to the people. That intention may be better answered by. filling the blank with three than five; for the House will then be obliged to choose a President that has more votes than if their right was extended to five.

The filling the blank with three cannot effect the rights of small States. A rich man has more at stake than a poor man: & so has a large state than a small one. Large States will protect & defend small states. I think we ought to consider the question upon principle, and not in relation to small & large States.

*Mr. Adams,* My vote on the Resolution itself will depend altogether upon the number with which the blank is filled. If it be filled with *five* I shall vote for it; but if with *three* I shall vote against it. I am the representative of a large State, & it does not become me to be the champion of the small states. But I must say that filling the blank with three, will be excluding the candidates from the small States from the House — & may materially affect their rights. I am therefore bound to vote against the amendment, if three is added, although I approve of the designing principle. Why do not the senators of the small States come forth as the champions of the rights of their own States?

*Mr. Cocke,* I prefer three to five — tis immaterial which is added — I will vote for the resolution with either.

*Mr. Franklin,*[42] I wish the vote could be taken — we shall I fear spin out the debate till after the Legislature of North Carolina rises, for they will not set longer than till Christmas.

*Mr. Cocke,* It is very easy for small states to coaleze — easier than for *big* states to swallow them up — *big* states cannot unite so well as small.

*Mr. Dayton,* I am the representative of a small State — I claim the rights of a small State — but my claim will be rejected by the power of an over bearing dominant majority. What candid man who has witnessed our debates & proceedings for days past, when our requests are denied, our reasonings are sneered at, can call upon Gentlemen to step forth the champions of small states. We have been told by the Gentleman from Virginia (Mr. Taylor) that it is the interest of small states not to provoke the large States. I heard such a voice in the old Congress under the confederation; but we laughed at it — because we knew our vote was equal. I heard such a voice in the Convention that formed this constitution, but we laughed at it because we knew we were equal. But I now fear the threat —

---

[42] Jesse Franklin, senator from North Carolina.

because it seems that several of the senators from small states appear disposed to surrender the rights of the small states to the claims of the large.

By filling the blank with three you give power to the large States exclusively to nominate & choose your President.

*Mr. Cocke,* I hope we shall not lose sight of the designating principle — The Legislature of my State are unanimously in favor of it.

*Mr. Wright,* I rise meerly to say, That the account that is given in the newspaper called *The Washington Federalist* of my speech of a few days since, *is a lie.* I hope that account was not written by a senator. Sir, if I knew who wrote it, I would, indeed I would, call him to an account.

Now I am *up,* I will say I am for the designating principle. I will vote for the resolution if the blank is filled with any number from three to twenty — The people demand it.

*Mr. Jackson,* I fear Sir we shall too often vote by States, and not as the senators of the Union. Tis time to loose sight of local interests & local prejudices — We must rise above them.

Why talk of the rights of small States being injured by this amendment? Have not the small states always voted for a man to be President who lived in a large State?

I know the office of President is important — but he is responsible for his actions. He can do no Executive business without the consent and advice of this House — Nothing upon the subject of finance without the aid of the other House. Why then fear his power or influence.

I am the representative of a small state, but I am in favor of the motion — because I know that large states are jealous· of each other — they are hostile to each others claims. Five is the number in the constitution from which the President & Vice President are to be selected in case of no choice by the Electors. By confining the House to three from whom they must choose the president, & the senate to two candidates from whom we must choose the vice president we make the amendment conform to both the spirit & letter of the constitution.

*Mr. Taylor,* I am pleased with the argument of the gentleman from Georgia (Mr. Jackson) — it is correct.

If the Electors do not chuse a President, the Representatives from the small States, from the smallness of their numbers, will be most liable to corruption. It is of great importance to those states to remove temptation from their representatives as far as possible — & preserve their morals — Its therefore the interest of small states that the blank should be filled with *three* & not with *five.*

The motion to fill the blank with the word *five* was negatived, yeas 12, nays 19.

It was then moved to fill it with the word *three,* & prevailed yeas 21, nays 10.

And the resolution as amended was ordered to be printed & to be laid on our tables tomorrow morning.

### *Wednesday 30th.*

The resolution was not printed, though sent in season to Duane for that purpose. I have strong reasons for believeing that it was intimated to Duane that it would be advisable not to print it.

*Mr. Wright* read a resolve that was passed by the Legislature of Massachusetts in the year 1800 requesting their senators & representatives in Congress to use their influence to obtain an amendment establishing the designating principle.

*Mr. Adams,* It is my duty to pay the greatest respect to the Legislature of the State I represent; but these instructions have much less influence on me than if they came from the present Legislature. I know the legislature of Massachusetts, this, & the last, year, were not anxious for a change in the constitution — it excites little interest in that State.

I am in favor of designating the votes for President & Vice

President, & to affect this with as little change in the constitution as possible.

The constitution contains two great leading principles — a *popular* & a *federative* principle. The House of Representatives is founded on the *popular* principle — Its numbers are apportioned to the population of the several states, except in the southern states, where to population is added a species of property, that of slaves. The Senate is founded on the *federative* principle — here each State is equal — because here state sovereignty is represented. In the choice of President & Vice President the popular & the federative principles are combined. Each state has a number of Electors equal to the number of its senators and Representatives. But if the Electors fail in making a choice, the house of Representatives compleat the election, not on the popular, but on the federative, principle, voting not by numbers, but by States. This resolution affects the federative rights of all the States, & is a violation of the federative principle itself.

It is in the power of the Senators from the small states to prevent this amendment — It is in the power of the Legislatures of those states to do it. — If they think it beneficial to them they will ratify it. The resolution originated with Vermont, a small State.

*Mr. Saml Smith,* It was the intension of the Constitution that the *people* should elect the President & Vice President. But such is the defects of the constitution that its intention, without amendment, cannot be carried into effect. A combination of little more than a fifth of the Union can carry the election of those officers into the House of Representatives — & the same combination can there elect them President. Nine of the States have only 32 representatives — & the other states have 110, & yet the 32 representatives from the nine States can elect. The former House that compleated the last presidential election was *incorruptible* — I know they were — I was a member of it. Future Houses may not be so, foreign & domestic influence — bribery and corruption may creep in — This discrimating principle is designed to prevent the choice being carried into the House.

The debate continued till half past three — The majority declared it was their intention to have the final question decided this day. But at four oclock they became apprehensive lest their arbitrary conduct in pressing a speedy decision might furnish a pretext to some of their party, who were not very cordial to the resolution, to vote against it, to secure these they ordered it printed, & adjourned. —

### *Thursday December 1.*

*Mr. Adams* moved to add the following to the resolution, to wit, " And in case the House of Representatives shall not within . . . days, effect the choice in manner aforesaid, & there be a Vice President duly elected, the sd. Vice President shall discharge the powers & duties of the President of the United States: — But if the office of Vice President be also vacant, then the sd powers & duties of President of the United States, shall be discharged by such person as Congress may by law direct, untill a new election shall be had in manner already prescribed by Law."

This motion was postponed.

*Mr. Taylor* made the following motion, " Provided, That whenever the right of choosing a President shall devolve upon the House of Representatives, the Vice President shall act as President, in case they fail to make such choice, in like manner as in the case of the death or resignation of the President.—"

*Mr. Wright,* If this motion prevails, I will at all events, be the consequence what it may, vote against the resolution itself. This will give the power to the Senate to elect a man President for whom the people never gave a single vote.

This declaration alarmed the majority.

*Mr. Saml Smith,* The *argument* of my colleague (Mr. Wright) is *conclusive.* I therefore move that the two motions be printed, & that we adjourn. Carried.—

## Friday 2d.

The Senate agreed that the motion of Mr. Taylor should be withdrawn.

Mr. Taylor then made the following, *viz.* " And if the House of Representatives shall not choose a President, whenever the right of choice shall devolve upon them, before the fourth day of March next following, then the Vice President shall act as President, as in the case of the death or other constitutional disability of the President."

*Mr. Wright.* I rise to second this motion — I think it a necessary & important amendment.—

The debates on amending the resolution continued till half past twelve oClock.— when the amendments being finished — the resolution was read, and a motion made to adopt it. Mr. White spoke against, & Mr. Cocke in favor of it.

*Mr. Plumer,*[43] Mr. President, I have generally contented myself with expressing my opinion by a silent vote; but as I am the Representative of a *small* State, & as this important question materially affects the rights of those States, I request the indulgence of the Senate to a few observations on this subject.

The Constitution has established but two methods in which amendments can be effected; & each of these are *guarded with great care & peculiar caution.*

If *two thirds* of the several State legislatures apply, Congress *shall* call a Convention to *propose* amendments; & the amendments proposed by that Convention, when ratified by the Con-

---

[43] Plumer's speech is reported here at much greater length than in the *Annals of Congress.* This is the one important exception to Plumer's rule not to deliver extended addresses in the Senate.

ventions of *three* fourths of all the States form a part of the
Constitution. If this mode is adopted, *Congress* have nothing
to do but to ascertain the fact whether the necessary number of
States require a Convention. If the necessary number require
it, Congress *shall* call it — The language of the Constitution is
imperative — it does not give Congress any discretion upon the
subject — it only gives them the authority, & makes it their
duty, to summon a Convention. That Convention when assembled will then have the sole authority of *proposing* amendments, if any should by them be thought necessary. These
amendments when formed & proposed are not to be sent either
to the State legislatures who requested the Convention, nor
to Congress who called it; but to a Convention chosen by the
people in each State. These State conventions will have the sole
& exclusive power of approving or rejecting the amendments.
The State legislatures can only *apply* to Congress for a Convention, & Congress can only call it — Neither Congress or the
State Legislatures, can instruct that Convention what amendments are requisite, or dictate to the State conventions either to
ratify or reject the amendments proposed by the General Convention. These two kinds of Conventions have each a check
upon the other — each have particular authority delegated to
them. It is the province of the General Convention to propose
the amendments, but not to ratify them. It is the duty of the
State Conventions not to propose amendments, but only to
decide on such as are proposed to them.

The other method of making amendments, (and on which we
now practicing) provides, That if *two thirds* of both houses of
Congress *deem it necessary* to *propose* amendments, and *three
fourths* of the State Legislatures *ratify* them, they are valid.

A vote of a *majority* in each house of Congress is insufficient
to propose an amendment; & the ratification of a *majority* of the
State Legislatures are alike unavailing. It was the design of
the Constitution to guard against innovation; & in the very

article that makes provision for amendments, its existance is secured & prolonged by the unanimnity that is requisite to obtain those amendments. In the first instance it renders it necessary for *two thirds* of both Houses of Congress to concur before an amendment can even be *proposed* to the consideration of the State Legislatures. This term *two thirds* of both houses of Congress includes *two thirds* in *number* of all the members of each house that all & each of the States have a right to send to Congress, & not barely two thirds of those who may happen to be present & vote on the question.

This construction, is not only conformable to that care & caution with which the Constitution is guarded against innovation, but is supported by both the letter & spirit of the instrument itself. Let me for a moment request the attention of the Senate to this point. The very *description* that the Constitution has given of the Senate is a proof of the position I contend for. It is contained in these laconic, but expressive, terms — " The Senate of the United States shall be composed of *two senators from each state* — " (Art. I. Sect. 3.) Not that a majority of the Senators make the Senate, but two senators from each state in the Union compose the Senate.

In Article I. sect. 5. It is declared that " a *majority* of each *house* shall constitute a *quorum* to do business." What is the construction, & what has been the practise upon this clause? It has, on all occasions, been one & the same — All have agreed that the word *majority* here implies a *majority* of *all* the members that all the States have a right to elect — & that the words cannot be satisfied without this extension. And if majority is extended so as to include a majority of all the members, I can see no reason why the term *two thirds* when used indefinitely, does not in fact include a full *two thirds* of *all* the members of each house in like manner.

I beleive it will be found on a careful examination that the term *two thirds* as applied to either house, by the Constitution, includes two thirds of the whole number composing the House, unless the terms are particularly qualified. In case of Impeachments, " no person shall be convicted without the concurrence of *two thirds* " but its immediately added " of the *members present.*" (Art. I. Sect. 3.) The president " shall have power, by & with the advice & consent of the Senate, to make treaties, provided two-thirds of the *Senators present* concur "— (Art 2. Sect. 2.). " The yeas & nays of the *members* of either House on any question, shall, at the desire of one-fifth of *those present,* be entered on the Journal." (Art I. Sect. 5.). These *exceptions* prove the general rule — And in these cases last mentioned it was necessary that there should be exceptions, because the business to which they refer requires prompt decision.

Where a bill or resolve has received the Presidents *veto,* it cannot pass into a law unless *two thirds* of each House after considering the Presidents reasons against it, are in favor of it. (Art. I. Sect. 7.) Here the term *two thirds* is unqualified by any thing that precedes or follows it. And if a bill or resolve is so exceptionable as that the Chief Majestrate of the Nation objects to its becoming a law it is fit & proper that it should be approved by *two thirds* of the whole Legislature.

And in the same section the Constitution provides that when the House of Representatives compleat the choice of a President, they shall vote by States, & they cannot have a *quorum* for this purpose or compleat the Election unless *two thirds* of the States are actually represented, & vote in favor of one of the candidates. At the last presidential election it was considered by both parties that the *two-thirds* here spoken of was a full *two thirds* of *all* the States in the Union.

If the concurrence of *two-thirds* of all the members composing the Senate were not necessary to propose an amendment, it would follow that twelve senators, (the representatives of six States) when only a quorum is present, might propose an amendment contrary to the opinion & against the will of twenty two senators — And that the vote of these twelve who are in fact but little more than *one* full *third* of the Senate, should be considered as constitutionally performing the act that required the concurrence of *two thirds*.

" The Congress, whenever two thirds of both Houses shall *deem it necessary,* shall propose amendments to the Constitution — " The amendments must originate here & not in the State legislatures. They have nothing to do till after Congress have formed & proposed the amendments to them; & then, but not before, its the exclusive right of the State legislatures either to ratify or reject them. Congress, & the State Legislatures, are, as it respects this subject, distinct tribunals, and each have a check & controul upon the acts of the other.

The State Legislatures have no authority to apply to Congress for a particular amendment. Their right of application is confined to requesting a Convention — it does not extend to the power of requesting that Congress would propose a particular amendment to them that they may ratify it. This would preclude the discussion of the amendment in Congress, & supercede investigation in the State Legislatures when the same amendment should be returned to them for their decision — It would effectually destroy one of the checks established by the constitution to preserve its permanency & security.

Nor have the State Legislatures any authority whatever, to instruct their Senators & Representatives in Congress, upon this subject. Their instructions are the assumption of authority not delegated to them by the people — Tis a usurpation of power, not the exercise of a right — tis an unwarrantable attempt to create an undue influence over the deliberations of Congress on a subject that the Constitution has made it their exclusive right freely to discuss & to decide in such manner as *they deem necessary*.

I do not say but that State Legislatures may on some subjects instruct their Senators & Representatives in Congress.

But that is a question that is unnecessary now to decide. I only say, that in this case, it is highly improper that those who are to ratify the amendments, should instruct Congress what amendments are fit & proper to be proposed to *themselves* (the State Legislatures) for their approbation. As well might a petite jury instruct a grand jury to indict a particular man for a particular offence, & then decide definitely on the bill. This mode of proceeding, is pre-judging the question before its proposed by that body who alone have the constitutional right of moving it. 'Tis *judging before the time* — tis creating prejudice & barring the mind against enquiry. If these instructions are obligatory, we are mere machines — & our votes on this important question must be governed not by the propriety of the measure, or the conviction of our own judgments, but by the sovereign mandates of State Legislatures.

I trust honorable gentlemen have too much discernment, to believe these instructions are obligatory on them; & too much independence, to suffer them to have any influence on their votes — And that we shall not vote in favor of the resolution unless we ourselves *deem it necessary.*

Several gentlemen on the other side of the House have said they do not consider these Instructions as obligatory; but as the State Legislatures require us to propose the amendments and as we have no authority to ratify them — its fit & proper we should gratify those that *created us,* as our act is not definitive. The instructions of the State legislatures are to induce us to propose the amendments, & those Legislatures when deliberating on the question of ratifying them, are to be influenced in their decision by the information, that two-thirds of all the Senators & Representatives in Congress assembled, & who have the best means of discovering the defects in the constitution, have *deemed these amendments necessary.* Unauthorized instructions are then to influence Congress to *propose* amendments — & State Legislatures are to be influenced to ratify them because Congress *has proposed them.*

An honorable gentleman from Maryland (Mr. Samuel Smith) observed the other day, *That the Legislature of New Hampshire had some years since instructed their senators & representatives in Congress to vote for this amendment.* Permit me, Sir, to inform that honorable gentleman that his statement is *not correct* — And I will add, that there is not *one* State Legislature in the Union whose instructions imbraces all the amendments contained in the resolution on your table. I very well know, Sir, that the legislature of New Hampshire did some years since pass a resolve instructing their senators, & requesting their representatives, in Congress, to obtain such an amendment to the constitution as should oblige the Electors *to designate their vote for President & Vice President;* but those instructions did not direct that in case the House of Representatives when the choice should be carried into that House, failed of electing a President by the 4th day of March, that then the Vice President, if any such there should be — & if none, that the Senate should elect a man who had not a single Electoral vote for President, to act as President for four years — but this is one of the amendments contained in the present resolution.

I respect the Legislature of my State; but I am confident that this subject was not understood in all its relations to the constitution — it was not fully investigated & discussed — it passed without that due consideration & thorough investigation which the high importance of the subject demanded. I may be allowed to say this with some degree of confidence, for I was a member of that Legislature & voted in favor of that resolve. For myself I am willing frankly to own that I did not then understand the subject; & that if I had, I should not have voted as I did. I think it more noble and dignified for a man, when convinced of his errors to renounce them, than to persist in them against the conviction of his own judgment.

It is my duty to exercise my own judgment, & form the most

correct opinion on the subject that I am able — & to vote accordingly. My seat in this House may be of little consequence to my constituents, it is still less to me. But while I am here it is of importance to me to judge & decide correctly.

We have been repeatedly told That the *people* require this amendment. 'Tis very easy to make such a declaration, & equally as difficult to prove it. We have no evidence of the fact. When & where have the *people* assembled, & expressed their opinions, & who has collected their votes, on this subject? Have the tables of your State Legislatures been loaded with petitions from the people requesting them to apply to Congress to call a Convention to propose amendments? No such thing is pretended. Are you to consider the noisy declamation of a few restless turbulent scribblers in the news papers as evidence of the *public will?* Or will you resort to the clamours of a rabble assembled in taverns over their cups? In vain, Sir, will you resort to either of these impure & incorrect sources to obtain evidence of the *public opinion,* on this subject. In an elective government, a few men may raise a clamour in favor of a *change* in the government, & urge the very ferment they have raised, as evidence of the voice of the people. I do say, Sir, that the *public* have not expressed their opinion on this subject — that no regular means have been taken to collect that opinion. And the question returns to this point — Are *two-thirds* of the Senate convinced that the peace prosperity & security of the Union renders these amendments *necessary.* If we are not thus convinced we are bound to reject the resolution.

But I think, Sir, had the great mass of the people clearly & unequivocally expressed their opinion in favor of this resolution, that would not be obligatory upon the Senate. We are not sent here for the purpose of registering the public opinion — our duty is to obtain the best information we can & act according to our judgments. The *people* themselves established this Constitution, & they gave to Congress the sole & exclusive *right* of proposing amendments to the State Legislatures. We ought to exercise these *rights* without being influenced by the opinion of others. This is the only proper way of obeying the voice of the *people*. The *people* established the constitution, & by virtue of it elected the members of Congress. Congress pass laws in conformity to that constitution — The Executive appoint Judges to carry those laws into effect. What should we say if an attempt was made to influence the decisions of those judges in a cause pending before them? Would not every man say it was highly improper — And is it not equally so in this case?

I have said that the Constitution has provided for amendments, but with *great caution*. In some cases they cannot, in the nature of things, be ever obtained. They are not subject to amendment — For example, the equal representation of each State in this House cannot be abbridged but with the consent of the State itself. This prohibition is contained in the article (the 5th.) that gives the right of amendments in an express proviso, " that no State, without its own consent, shall be deprived of its equal suffrage in the Senate."

The forms & *modes of proceeding* established by the Constitution may be amended; but its *principles* cannot, without violence, be changed. In support of this idea permit me to cite two sections in the fourth article oˆ the constitution.

" New States may be admitted by the Congress into this Union; but no new state shall be formed or erected within the jurisdiction of any other State; nor any state be formed by the junction of two or more States, without the consent of the Legislatures of the States concerned, as well as of the Congress.

" The United States shall guarantee to every state in this Union, a *republican form of government;* & shall protect each of them against invasion; & on application of the legislature, or of the Executive (when the legislature cannot be convened) against domestic violence."

Will any man pretend, that it is in the power of two thirds of Congress with the assent of three-fourths of the State Legislatures, materially to change these articles? Can they, for example, so amend, the first article, as that New Hampshire & Massachusetts, shall, without their individual consent, be formed into ten seperate & independent states? Or can they determine that a part of Massachusetts & a part of New Hampshire shall constitute a new state without the previous consent of those States.

Or Can two-thirds of Congress & three-fourths of the State legislatures so far alter & amend, the article last quoted, as to establish a monarchal government in the State of Virginia, even if that state consent to the change? And thereby endanger the very existance of the other states. Can they so amend the article, as to destroy the faith of the nation, that is pledged, to guarantee to each state a republican form of government, & to protect it against invasion & domestic insurrection or violence?

The reason why amendments cannot be made in these & other articles, is, that it would change the *principles*, & destroy the *substance* of the constitution. That instrument is a compact formed by each state with the whole — & is founded in the express consent and actual agreement of each individual state. And its *principles* cannot be changed or its substance impaired without the consent & express approbation of each state. A change in the *principles* of the constitution, either by abolishing particular parts of it, or by introducing *new principles* into that important instrument, may operate as a dissolution of the Union. The states dissenting from the *change* would be no longer bound by the compact. The principles of the confederacy being changed without the previous consent of the *partners* to that confederacy, is in fact a virtual dissolution of the Union. Are honorable gentlemen prepared to go thus far — are they willing to introduce a *new order of things*, & establish different *forms* of government on *new principles*.

I was very much surprised the other day to hear the honorable gentleman from Virginia (Mr. Nicholas) say " That if he *thought* he could obtain a better constitution he would freely vote to expunge every letter of our present constitution from the book." Do gentlemen consider how dangerous the experiment is, to tamper with a constitution that binds such variant & jarring interests together! What would the gentleman from Virginia, say, if an Eastern senator should move to expunge from the Constitution those parts of it that relate to *slavery*. Would he not tell us that those clauses in the Constitution relative to slaves & the apportionment of direct taxes cannot be changed till the year 1808?

I think the specious term of *Amendments* will be fully satisfied by applying it to *forms & proceedings* without extending it to the *principles & substance* of the constitution. The necessity of this restriction will appear more evident when we consider the almost insuperable difficulty there is of establishing an elective efficient government in a country so extensive as ours is, & where the interests, habits & manners are so variant.

This constitution, as the illustrious band of patriots who formed it say, " is the result of a spirit of amity, & of that mutual deference and concession which the peculiarity of our political situation rendered indispensible." It was formed & established at a time when the rage of *party* had infused little, if any, of its baneful influence into society. And even then, I doubt, whether it would have been established, had not the idea of *common danger,* operated with great force, on the public mind, in favor of an efficient government. Just before that period *insurrection* appeared in one state, & *rebellion* had raised its hostile banners in another.

In an elective government much depends on public opinion. And it is of great importance that the constitution in such a country should be stable & permanent — & considered as the standard to regulate that opinion. By introducing *new prin-*

*ciples* into your constitution, will you not insensibly infuse a spirit of fickleness & love of novelty into the *public mind?* Will not one change prepare the way, & lay the foundation, for another?

A constitution perpetually changing, can never long command the veneration or esteem of any people. It is better, to submit to partial evils, & inconveniences, resulting from its imperfections & defects, than to yield to the rude & dangerous experiment of innovation. How many *new* constitutions has the French nation established since the formation of ours? And each of those constitutions was considered by them as preferable to the one it preceeded. And what has been the result of their frequent changes? Has not that ill fated nation at last, grown weary of change & sick of liberty, consented to establish a system of government more arbitary & despotic than that of any other in Europe? A government, in which all law, virtually emanates from the *will of the First Consul.* Ought we not to profit by their errors, & studiously avoid the rocks and quick sands on which that *terrible Republic* have suffered shipwreck; & not attempt amendments to our constitution, unless imperious necessity demand it!

There is another circumstance that ought not to escape our attention. By introducing this amendment into the constitution we shall not now probably perceive all the relative, but necessary changes, that a *new principle* will make in the system. We may, perhaps, remedy an ideal & partial evil, but introduce a real one in its place.

When the resolution to amend the constitution was first introduced into the Senate by the honorable gentleman from New York (Mr. Clinton) he told us, *That it was the result of much deliberation — That it had been two years under the consideration of the Legislature of that State — That he had himself paid much attention to it — & that he thought the resolution was well matured.* And yet, Sir, that resolution contained a gross absurdity, on the face of it — to wit, although the Electors were bound to designate their votes for President & Vice President, yet that two men for the *first* office might have A majority of all the Electoral votes, & neither of them be chosen. This is a fact that in the nature of things can never happen.

The Resolution that was this session passed by the House of Representatives on this very subject, & now lays on your table, effectually destroys all qualifications requisite for a Vice President. Had that resolution passed, a *foreigner* would have been eligible for that office. Indeed, it is but a few days, since, that we discovered that our own resolution was liable to the same objection.

Since the designating principle has been under discussion in this House, we have added *new & important principles* to the Resolution. We have declared, *That if a President shall not be elected by the fourth day of March following the time of Election, that the Vice President shall act as President for the four years — That a majority of all the Electoral votes shall be necessary for a choice of Vice President — & That if the Electors fail of choosing him a majority of the Senate shall from the two highest numbers on the list elect the Vice President.*

These *errors*, (for such the Senate has considered them) have been discovered, & corrected. Do not our proceedings on this subject, show, that when men have a *particular object* in view, they are apt to confine their attention only to the *means* necessary to attain that object, without extending their views of the same subject to other objects equally as important. Will honorable gentlemen, say, that they are able to *mark with precision* all the changes that this resolution will make in the constitution. Other men, not ourselves, must construe this amendment — they must build on the foundation that we establish.

In an elective government, the choice of a First Majestrate, is not only a very important election; but I am confident, in all large republic's, it has ever been found one of the most perplexing & difficult parts of government, to fix & establish the principles & modes of his election. I have been repeatedly assured, by several gentlemen who formed our Constitution, that this very subject embarrassed them more than any other — That various systems were proposed, discussed, & rejected — That the Convention were on the point of rising without being able to agree on a system to elect this high officer — That at last the principles contained in the constitution was adopted, upon a full conviction that they were less exceptionable than any others that they were able to devise. These principles that have hitherto, proved so safe and beneficial in practise, we are now called to abandon.

The Constitution of the United States is in its nature & principles a complex system. It is formed on *popular* & *federative* principles; & these in various cases are mixt & combined the one with the other. 'Tis a government of the *people*, & a government of the *States*. The *people* of each State elect their Representatives to Congress; the States as states, by their legislatures, elect their senators. The State Legislatures themselves either elect the Electors of the President & Vice President, or they authorize & establish the manner in which the people shall exercise that right. The citizens have their rights — & the States as States have their rights — & tis the design & object of the Constitution to secure to each of them the free & full exercise of their respective rights. When either the *people*, the *States*, *President*, or Congress exercise these *rights*, in the manner prescribed by the constitution, then the *public will* — the voice of the *people* — is pronounced by the constitutional organ.

Each State is entitled to a number of Electors of President & Vice President equal to the whole number of Representatives & Senators that they are entitled to send to Congress. In apportioning to each State, the number of Electors, both the *popular* & *federative* principles operate. The *popular*, on which the principle of representation is established; & the federative, on which an *equal* number of Senators are chosen from each State, without any reference whatever to the population of the States. These Electors are to meet in each State in the Union, on the same day, & to give their votes for two men qualified to be President of the United States. They have no authority to vote for one man to be President, & the other to be Vice President; but to vote for two men to be President. Hence it is that our constitution contains no qualifications whatever for the Vice President, as such; the qualifications requisite of age, citizenship & residence, are as President. If one of the Candidates have a majority of all the Electoral votes he is President, & the next highest candidate is Vice President. So that till the President is elected the Vice President, is not known. But if no one candidate is elected to the office of President by the Electors & there should be more than one candidate who had a majority, & equality of the Electoral votes, then the House of Representatives should immediately elect one of them two for President. But if no person have such majority then the House are from the five highest on the list to elect the President. But in completing the Choice, the votes are to be taken by States, each state having one vote; a quorum is to consist of a member or members from two-thirds of the states — & a majority of the whole is requisite. And the choice, in this case, is finally decided upon the *federative* principle.

What system can be devised, that will so effectually secure the elective right in the people, & at the same time so powerfully guard against the views & designs of the ambitious? An intriging, ambitious, aspiring man finds the difficulties he has to encounter, *doubled* — for he must enter the list not against one rival but against two. If he forms combinations — & to strengthen these, promises his aid to make a popular character Vice President, those very votes may render his favorite his rival, & defeat his own views by placing his friend in the Presidential chair. This complex system, wisely established by the

Constitution, is a guard & security to the small States against
the large — It gives them their relative weight & importance
in the election — by encreasing the difficulties of the large States
agreeing upon two men being voted for as President, each large
State, from local or other circumstances will feel a preference
to the one candidate over the other. And if *parties* exist, & in
a government like ours they must exist, this system will afford
grounds to hope, that each of the two great parties, will succeed
in the election of one of those high officers. And if both succeed,
that success will tend to moderate the rage of party, & check
the too sanguine views of the party that is most predominant.

We are now called upon to destroy this complex system, &
to establish a *new & simple* principle, not congenial with the
principles of the Constitution; but A principle that will materially affect the relative interest & importance of the smaller
States. The Electors are each to vote only for one man as
President & one as Vice President — This will enable the most
ambitious candidate to consentrate his whole force to a single
point, & with greater ease secure his election. None but those
who are inhabitants of large States can ever hope to prove successful candidates. The power & influence of the President of
the United States is now a flattering object to ambition. As we
encrease in wealth & population the office will encrease in importance. The President will always bring into office with him
a large portion of the habits manners & prejudices of the State
to which he belongs. And it can not be denied that the local
situation, and wealth of one State, may, & often does, create
an interest in favor of that state in relation to particular objects,
which are injurious to the interests of an other state. The
interests of agricultural & commercial states are varient. Hence
the violent struggle, in the last Congress, on the part of many
of the friends to agriculture, to repeal, & of the united efforts
of the friends to Commerce, to continue, the *discriminating
duties.* The former conceived that the produce of their lands

would command a higher price in the market if foreign shipping were admitted into our ports subject to only the same duties as own ships are. The Mercantile States considered the repeal of the extra duties on foreign shipping as a ruinous measure to their navigation.

This amendment will materially injure the *small* states — It gives increased power to the powerful — & it weakens the feeble —it takes from them what *they seem to have.* The whole number of Electoral votes are one hundred seventy six, eighty nine is a majority. Four states & a half, may, against the will of twelve states & a half, elect the President.

Massachusetts gives 19 votes
New York.......... 19
Pennsylvania ...... 20
Virginia ........... 24
           ————
making .......... 82
           7 The half of North Carolina
           ————
           89.

Can such a change, tend to conciliate & strengthen the Union? Is it not calculated to create jealousy, produce fear & alarm? The same spirit that impels gentlemen from some of the *large* States, to urge the adoption of this resolution, & exclude the agency of the small states in the election of the President — have induced them to reduce the number from whence the House is to compleat the election from *five* to the *three* highest candidates on the list. Why is the number reduced, but for the purpose of wholly excluding the candidates from the small States, from the office? Gentlemen know very well if the House were authorized to elect from the *five* Candidates, a small State might have one of its citizens elevated to the Presidency — for in compleating the choice in that House the vote of Delaware is equal to that of Virginia. The specious, but fallacious, reason assigned for this change is, that it will oblige the House to elect the President from one of the three highest candidates in whose favor the will of the *people* is most fully expressed. If this be the principle on which the change is made why not confine the House to the *two* highest candidates? Why give them any agency in the business — why not say, at once, that the person who has the highest number of Electoral votes shall be the President?

I may be told that the *large* States are not, and never will be, united in *one party*. Most gentlemen who speak of the large states have confined that number to Massachusetts, New York, Pennsylvania & Virginia. And what, Sir, are the present state of parties in those States. Do not gentlemen on the other side of the House consider the three last states as united in one party — And is there not a powerful minority in Massachusetts — Look at the Representatives from that state in the other House, & out of seventeen members you will find seven of them whose political sentiments accord with the dominant party. But Massachusetts will not long remain a large State; the District of Mayne [44] will soon become a new State — That indeed is large in territory, but a considerable portion of it, from its inhospitable climate, will probably long remain unpeopled. The states east of Pennsylvania, in point of population, will soon become stationary. Those west & south of it, with the exception of Delaware, are large in territory, & increasing in population. To these, add Louisiana, which is a world of itself — & the west & southern states, will, on all occasions, decide the election just as they please.

I know the *present* state of parties cannot long continue — other parties will & must succeed them. And I request honorable gentlemen, not to confine their views to the present pros-

---

[44] Maine became a State in 1820 as part of the Missouri Compromise.

pects, but to extend them to another state of things — to posterity, for whom, as well as ourselves, we are legislating.

There is another point of view in which this resolution, if adopted, will prove injurious to the nation. I mean as it respects the election of the Vice President. He will no longer be voted for as President of the United States, but as President of the Senate — he will be elected *to preside over forms in this House*. He will have less dignity, & be less respectable — This will be the unavoidable consequence of the change. In electing a *subordinate officer,* men do not, they will not, seek for, or require, those qualifications which they deem requisite for *supreme* command.

This office will become a meer sinecure — It will be brought as *change* to the markett, & exposed to sale in your Elections, to procure votes for the President. It will be an article of traffic, & the subject of barter in your most important Elections. Will not this resolution afford a fit opportunity to an artful, ambitious & unprincipled candidate, living in one large state, to contract with a man of moderate but popular talents, in another large state, that he shall be Vice President in case he will use his influence & procure votes for him to be President. Men can easily be found whose pride will be flattered, & whose ambition is bounded by this second office. And they will be sought for in the large States, because a citizen of a small state could not procure but a few votes for the Presidency, even if he could obtain all the Electoral votes of his State.

Will the aspiring candidate for the Presidency, will his friends, or his favorites, aid the election of a man of talents, probity & extensive popularity, to the office of Vice President? No. They are not insensible, that such a man called to the second office, may prove a dangerous & successful rival for the first. Their policy will be to fix on a man of moderate talents — a man better fitted for a *tool*, than qualified for a *rival*. The Presidency of the United States, will in a few years of prosperity, become an object highly flattering to the pride of ambition — It will be sought for with avidity. With encreasing wealth, & encreasing population, the torrent of bribery & corruption will swell upon us — it will influence our elections — it may direct them. Will foreign nations feel no interest in them — will they remain inactive spectators of the election of a man to this high office, whose politics may deeply affect their interests? In such a state of things can you beleive it would be desirable for a President to have a man raised to the second office in the government whose integrity would reproach him, & whose talents would obscure the lustre of his fame. No, Sir, like the jealous *Turk*, he would not wish to behold the painful sight of *genius so near to the throne.*

This resolution, to me, appears calculated to create corruption, increase intrigue & invigorate lawless ambition.

But there is a still further evil attending the election of the Vice President — He is not only to be the creature of the President — but he is to give to some one of the large States an encreased weight of influence in this House. He will have a casting vote in all cases in which the Senate are equally divided [45] — A circumstance which on very important subjects, has happened oftener than those not intimately acquainted with our proceedings are aware of. On all questions of order, & they are sometimes of importance, his decisions are final & conclusive. The order & dispatch of business very much depends on the ability & talents of the presiding officer. Small indeed, would the compliment be, to say his influence here would be less than that of a common senator. Thus, in fact, the large State, to which he belonged, would virtually have a third senator in this House. The resolution appears, in every point of view, calculated, to give strength to the strong & to enfeeble the weak.

The Vice President, is *exofficio* President of the board of

---

[45] In this connection, see Henry Barrett Learned, " Casting Votes of the Vice-presidents, 1789–1915," in *American Historical Review*, XX, 571–576.

Commissioners of the Sinking Fund. — And in the case of a failure of choice of President, or of his death, removal, resignation or inability, this officer, *thus chosen,* is placed at the head of your government, & that, perhaps, for near four years.

In the southern states, the *blacks* are considered as property & entitle the States in which they live to *sixteen* additional Representatives in the other House, & to a like number of Electors of President & Vice President.

By this resolution, you destroy the *complex system* of election, — a principle which gives weight & influence to the small states, & to the eastern portion of the Union, & still retain the right, in consequence of your slaves, to the extra number of Electors & Representatives. Why should property (for such you consider *slaves*) give an increase of Electors to one portion of the Union, but in other states property is not all considered.

In Massachusetts & Vermont there are no slaves — in Connecticut & Rhodeisland there are but few. In New Hampshire, by the last Census, there appears to be eight; but this is an error made by the Marshall. There are no slaves in that state — the principles of slavery are abhorant to the genius of its laws — Freedom is not there dependent on the colour & complexion of the skin — it extends to all persons.

Examine the census — see in what states this partial, unequal & unjust right is given —

In New Hampshire there are returned 8 slaves
    Rhode island .................. 380
    Connecticut .................... 951
    New York ................... 20613
    Pennsylvania ................ 1706
    New Jersey ................. 12422
    Delaware .................... 6153
    Maryland .................. 107707
    Virginia ................... 346968
    North Carolina ............ 133296

South Carolina .............. 146151
Georgia ..................... 59699
Kentucky ................... 40343
Indiana Territory ............. 135
Ohio ........................ 3489
Tennessee .................. 13584

---

making in the whole .............. 893605 slaves. And yet, strange & inconsistent as it may appear, in those very states where slaves are most numerous, the people are most vociferous for *liberty & equality.*

I again repeat the observation, for the remark is worthy of repetition, why should *property* give Electors & Representatives to one portion of the Union, & none to the other? Why should the four states of Maryland, Virginia, North & South Carolina be entitled for their slaves to more than thirteen Electors & Representatives, while all the wealth of New England does not give them a single vote, even for the choice of one of those officers? all the slaves give sixteen Representatives & Electors & are more than equal to the vote of four whole states.

Rhode Island chooses 2 Representatives & 4 Electors.
Delaware ........ 1 ................ 3
Ohio ............ 1 ................ 3
Tennessee ....... 3 ................ 5
New Hampshire.. 5           —
Vermont ........ 4          15
               —           —
          16.
           —

Thus it appears that the negro Electors exceed those of four states, & their representatives are equal to those of six states. With propriety & truth it may be said that a constitution establishing such *unequal rights* was the work of *compromise.* And will honorable gentlemen who enjoy these *unequal priveledges* by their votes here, & those of their State Legislatures at home, render this *inequality* still greater? There is a point in *sufferance* to which men will submit; but beyond *that,* even cowards, will be desperate, if not brave. What the effect this inequality — this change in our constitution, will produce in New England time alone will unfold. The people of the eastern states are a brave hardy race of men — they are not insensible of their rights — and they have too much pride to be reduced tamely to a state of insignificance.

For the injury this amendment will inflict on the small states, & on the eastern states, for the increased weight of influence it gives to the southern & western states at the expence of the former, what equivalent rights do you give to the small States, or to the eastern portion of the Union? You give them none — you do not even pretend it.

Can such a measure be right — is it founded in good policy — will it cement the Union of the United States?

Honorable gentlemen have told us that this constitution was the work of compromise & that the *large* states conceded many of their *rights* to the *small* states for the sake of establish it. To prove this bold assertion we have been told that the vote of Delaware in the other House, when the election of President is carried into that house, is equal to that of Virginia — & that the vote of that same small state in the Senate is on all occasions equal to that of the largest State in the Union — That the Senate, thus unequally constituted, has not only a negative upon the legislative proceedings of the other House, but the sole & exclusive right of deciding upon treaties, & appointments to office. — I admit these facts; but they fail of proving the declaration. To decide this point we must recur to the government, & actual state of things, that existed previous to the establishment of the constitution. Under the Confederation all the States were *equal* — Congress then voted by *States,* on every question,

& each State whether represented by *few* or by *many* delegates had but *one* vote. All laws, resolves, & treaties were decided, & all appointments were made, by the then Congress, upon this principle. The states then assembled upon the principle of perfect *State equality* — no preference was then given to any one State in consequence of either their wealth or population. State soveignity was equal — the vote of a small State was equally as important & necessary as that of a large one. This was the government that then existed. And if any State *inequalities* now exist in our Constitution so far they are departures from the principles of the original confederation. That system of government was formed to enable the United States to maintain their Independence — It was in many of its principles defective — it was weak & feeble, not on account of its principle of *State equality*, but because it did not give authority to Congress to legislate on many important & necessary subjects, nor give them the power on other subjects, of executing their own resolves. The idea of *common danger*, during the revolutionary war, supplied the want of power. With a state of peace, the idea of common danger ceased to operate — The government was found too weak & feeble — &, in most respects, inadequate to answer the great objects of government. Congress, & even the mass of the people, were fully sensible of this. A Convention was called to form a new system. — In this convention the states again met on the principle of *State equality* — they again voted by States.

But here a new & more efficient system of government was necessary to be established. The members from each State were zealous for & jealous of, the rights of each State. But consessions were necessary, & without them an efficient government could not be formed. And in this contest for power & authority, where small & large States were struggling with each other, was it to be expected that the weak would triumph over the strong, or the small over the great? The result of that contest fur-

nishes the answer.   And whoever will take the trouble of reading
the constitution of the United States, will find in every instance
in which State inequalities exist, they are all in favor of the
*large,* & against the *small* States.   Hence it is that we find each
State represented in the other House according to its population;
& the votes of that House determined not by States, but by
a majority of the individual members of it.   Hence it is that
the Electors of President & Vice President are apportioned to
each State according to its population, with the addition of two
to each state.   And hence it is that the powerful States of the
South have an encrease of Representatives & Electors for their
slaves, while the property of the eastern States give them none.
The fact is that the small states conceded a portion of their
rights, & the large & powerful States thereby became more
powerful.   And now the *large* states wish for further inequality.
And if the representatives of the small states consent to grant
their request they will obtain it — And when obtained, however
injurious it may prove to the small states, they will be unable,
under this constitution, to regain their present constitutional
rights.

I have a further objection to this amendment — It does not
appear to me calculated to remedy the evil complained off.
Gentlemen say the design of the amendment is to prevent the
*evils* that occurred at the last presidential election — to prevent
the choice being carried into the other House.

The evils, if evils they were, that attended that election, have
been greatly exaggerated — & in consequence thereof, have made
an undue impression on the public mind.

Two men had an equal number of all the Electoral votes, &
that number was a majority, but being equal there was no choice.
This was an extraordinary event — it was a casualty that can
seldom happen.   But what were the dreadful consequences that
ensued?   Were they followed with tumult, riot, or blood — was
the government dissolved — No such thing.   The election was

carried into the other House — they did their duty in a peaceable & quiet manner — & fourteen days before the new president could enter on the duties of his office they compleated the election.[46]

But honorable gentlemen, on a former day, enquired what would have been the consequence if that House had refused to elect one of the five candidates? Let me answer this question by asking another, What if either House should refuse to pass appropriation laws? could your government exist without them. I will state a stronger case, suppose a majority of the state legislatures should refuse to pass the necessary laws to choose Electors — could you then have a President? If a majority of the State legislatures should refuse to elect Senators — could your government continue? These are evils that may happen, but we are not to presume them. I believe that if another House of Representatives should be placed in similar circumstances, as that of March 1801 was, they would provide the United States a President.

It is not correct to say, that we are to presume men clothed with necessary power will abuse that power. It is possible they may — but against that possible abuse it is almost impossible to provide a remedy that will not be equally as fatal as the abuse itself.

If the resolution prevails, it will not prevent the evil — it will encrease it. It is true that neither of the candidates sent into that House can be elected Vice President. But if the state of parties, in the nation, should be nearly equal, or if the parties themselves should divide in their candidates, there will be no choice by the Electors — And the House must then ultimately decide from the three highest numbers. But the probility is, that men of different politics, of opposite parties, will be carried into that house — & the House will then have a very different case from what they had in 1801 — then they had to decide only

---

[46] For an interesting account of the balloting in the House, see Margaret Bayard Smith, *The First Forty Years of Washington Society*, 21–25.

between two men of the *same party*. And will the parties in the House be disposed to agree as readily when each party has one of their own favorites on the list — As we increase in wealth & population the office of President will become more important — Men of ambition will seek it with greater avidity — And in porportion to the importance of the office so will the difficulty encrease in the House in compleating the election. You have by this resolution provided that in case the House do not elect the President by the fourth of March, then the Vice President shall act as President. This provision, appears to me, to destroy, in a great measure, the responsibility of the House, as it respects the election. It forms an excuse for their not agreeing — for if they do not agree, there will be no interregnum — the Vice President becomes President — & perhaps he will be the favorite of the minority in that House — It encreases the means of intrigue — for the Vice President & his friends have only to prevail on the minority not to yield for a few days — not to vote for a man whom they do not wish to elevate to office, & he will then be Chief majestrate. This provision has a direct tendency to destroy the *designating principle* itself: because a man who had not a single Electoral vote for President may against their will obtain that office.

Under every view of this resolution that I am capable of considering it, it appears to me calculated to give power to the strong & weaken & enfeeble the small, states — That it will lessen & destroy the respectability of the office of Vice President — And that it will not remedy, but encrease, the evil, it was designed to prevent. I therefore hope the Constitution, which has been declared *the world's best hope* will not be impaired — & that the *successful tide of experiment* we now enjoy will not be interrupted by the rude hand of innovation.

I thank the Senate for indulging me with so much of their time — & shall give my vote against the resolution on your table.

The debate continued upon the resolution without an adjournment through the whole of the day & evening. Mr. Tracey delivered a very able & ingenious argument against it. Between nine & ten oClock at night the vote was taken, yeas 22, nays 10.

The President pro. temp. declared that the resolution had passed by a constitutional majority; Mr. Tracey suggested that 22 senators was not *two thirds of the* Senate. Mr. Brown, the President pro. tem. observed that as it was a constitutional question, he requested the opinion of the Senate upon the question whether the resolution was passed by the constitutional majority. A desultory conversation ensued — but no vote was taken. It was said by some, That this was a constitutional question — That it was well known What number of members composed the Senate — That the journals would show how many voted for & against it — & that a declarative vote would conclude nothing.

Mr. Butler's motion, for rendering the President ineligible after a certain number of years, was not decided. A majority of the Senate said they would not connect it with this resolution.

### *Monday 5th.*

A motion was made, " That a Committee be appointed to prepare a form or forms of government for the territory of Louisiana."

*Mr. Adams,* I am opposed to the motion. Congress have no authority to establish any form of government whatever in that country without the express consent of the inhabitants thereof first had & obtained. — We must amend the constitution before we can legislate for that country — And it is our duty to amend it without delay.

The motion prevailed, & a committee was appointed.

### *Tuesday 6th.*

The bill to *establish salaries* was read a second time.
*Mr. Bradley,* I move to raise the salary of the Postmaster

General from three thousand dollars to four thousand pr annum. The duties of that officer are greatly encreased — He is frequently obliged to write all night till one oClock in the morning. He is a great man, his duties & *patronage* are great — & if his salary is not raised it will not be possible to retain him in office; & it will be difficult to find his *equal.*

*Mr. John Smith* (of Ohio) The postmaster General has wrote *two quires* & *three sheets* of paper in one day in his office; & I think his salary ought to be five thousand dollars pr annum.

Bradley's motion prevailed.

The bill " to divide the Indiana territory into two seperate governments," was read a third time & passed.[47] The new territory is named the " North western Territory " — each of them contain about 4000 souls exclusive of Indians — the inhabitants of the later are principally Frenchmen.

### Thursday 8th.

A bill, to repeal the *bankrupt Law* was read a second time. The debate continued till four oClock in the afternoon, but no decision.

*Mr. Wright,* The existance of the British nation depends on the existance of their bankrupt law. Merchants govern that kingdom. Our State Legislatures are partial — they ought not to be entrusted with passing bankrupt laws. The laws of the State extend only to the people living in the state — America is a commercial people, our bankrupt law is designed to aid creditors, & to prevent our merchants starving in goals. The constitution authorizes us to make such a law. This law cost the United States two hundred thousand dollars to pass it & It contains sixty four sections, & therefore ought not to be repealed.

*Mr. Burr,* the Vice President, presides in the Senate with great

---

[47] The bill was defeated in the House by the close vote of 59 to 58; *Annals of Congress,* 8 Cong., 1 sess., 1042.

ease, dignity & propriety. He preserves good order, silence — & decorum in debate — he confines the speaker to the point. He has excluded *all* spectators from the area of the Senate chamber, except the members from the other House. A measure which contributes much to good order.

### Friday 9th.

On the second reading of the " bill to authorize the sale of the Frigate General Green, & a further addition to the naval armament of the United States —" Mr. Hillhouse said, That for two years he had observed a disposition in the majority on all occasions to encrease the power & authority of the President — That by this bill he is vested with the sole authority of appointing the officers of the two additional vessels of war without the advice or consent of the Senate — It may be right & proper to enlarge his powers & encrease his patronage. On this suggestion, the words giving the President the authority to appoint was striken out.

The bill for the repeal of the bankrupt law passed to a second reading.

*Mr. Adams* agreeably to his motion of the 25th of November requested, " That a committee be appointed to enquire whether any, & if any, what further measures may be necessary for carrying into effect, the treaty, between the United States & the French Republic, concluded at Paris on the 30th April, 1803, whereby Louisiana was ceded to the United States."

*Mr. Adams* said, My object in making this motion is that a Committee should be appointed to report an amendment to the Constitution. I am in favor of the treaty although it is made in direct violation of the Constitution, & I think it my duty to move for the appointment of a committee to report such amendments to the constitution as will make it conform to the treaty. The third article of the treaty is a stipulation that cannot be carried into effect without amending the constitution — The faith of the nation is pledged, & we must alter the constitution. A treaty is the supreme law of the land — the treaty making powers are unlimited. A treaty opposed to a particular law cannot be carried into effect till that law is repealed. Most treaties require appropriations — these cannot be made but by a law passed by both houses of Congress. This treaty is *now very popular,* & now is the favorable moment to effect a change in our Constitution, so as to enable us to maintain the faith of the nation.[48]

*Mr. Wright,* I am opposed to the motion, for the Constitution itself declares, *that treaties are the supreme law of the land,* & therefore no change in the constitution is necessary. Not more than six or seven senators think the treaty unconstitutional, & they are mistaken. But if it is unconstitutional no *after act* can make it constitutional.

*Mr. White,* I am clearly of the opinion that the treaty is a violation of the constitution — But I see no propriety or necessity of altering the constitution — I am not for incorporating Louisiana into the Union, but governing it as a colony.

*Mr. Cocke,* The treaty-making power is *unlimited* & it *ought to be so* — We have ratified the treaty, & thereby have said it is a constitutional treaty, and that is enough — The committee is unnecessary.

*Mr. Brackenridge,* If the treaty is unconstitutional, it is not prudent to stir the question, much less to decide it. I know that greater, wiser, & better men than I am, are divided in opinion upon this question. I will not give an opinion upon it. Tis a long and tedious process to obtain amendments to our constitution — they must be sent to seventeen states. If amendments to the constitution are necessary it will take much time to obtain them — we cannot effect them before the time we are bound to pay the purchase sum, which will be due in three months after the ratification of the treaty — If we attempt

---

[48] *Cf.* J. Q. Adams, *Writings,* III, 20, footnote.

amendments & fail, we shall be placed in a worse situation than we are now in.

*Mr. Anderson,* The treaty, according to my view of the subject, is strictly constitutional. We are bound to admit that people *into the Union according to the principles of the federal constitution.* If by that constitution we cannot admit them, we violate no promise. And if by the constitution we can incorporate them into the Union, & do not, then we violate our faith. I do not therefore, in either case, at present see any necessity of appointing a committee.

*Mr. Pickering,* I did think, & still am of the opinion, that the treaty is unconstitutional; but I think a committee ought to be appointed to make enquiry & report. There are men of talents & information, at New Orleans, who know & will demand the rights secured to them by this treaty.[49] An act of Congress is not competent to secure those rights — it requires a change in the constitution. The treaty is ratified, laws are passed to enable the Executive to take possession of that country, & appropriations are made to pay the purchase sum. I am *now* for holding that Country, and for that purpose, I think we must amend our constitution. The committee may be ordered to make their report in *private,* & the debate may be had with *closed doors.*

*Mr. Dayton,* The treaty is in no part unconstitutional — & a committee is unnecessary.

*Mr. Hillhouse,* Our constitution will not permit us to receive that country & its inhabitants into the Union as a component part — But the treaty provides that we shall — 'Tis a right vested in them — tis a part of the consideration on which the cession is founded. If we do not make provision to effect this object, the treaty will be void *in toto,* as much so as if we had

---

[49] Edward Livingston and Daniel Clark were two of the Americans in New Orleans to whom allusion is made. For Livingston's part in the movement for a greater degree of self-government for the new territory, see Brown, *Constitutional History of the Louisiana Purchase,* 149–160.

neglected to create the stock to pay for the territory. Tis a difficult thing, but we have pledged the faith of the nation to that people, & we must remedy the difficulty. We are bound to incorporate them into the union. We cannot under that treaty govern them as a Colony. If the Constitution is not altered, we ought not to part with the purchase sum. For if we do not on our part fulfill every article, the whole is void — France may for our breach of faith take the country & hold the stock.

*Mr. Baldwin*,[50] I am not for anticipating remedies for cases that may hereafter occur. If that people demand rights, I will hear & examine their claims — &, if they are just, will provide for them.

The motion was negatived — Adams, Pickering & Hillhouse, *only* voted in the affirmative.

The resolution of the Senate of the 2d instant, for amending the constitution, was this day decided in the House of Representatives. 83 voted in favor of a concurrence, 42 against it. The speaker declared himself in the affirmative.

Bishop,[51] Clay,[52] Eustis,[53] Elliot,[54] Hoge,[55] Seaver[56] & Varnum,[57] democratic members, voted with the minority. They were opposed to the resolution, 1, Because, that in case there should not be a choice of President by the Electors the house would be confined to the *three* highest candidates. 2d. That if the House should not choose a President before the 4th of March the Vice President would act as President — which will make a man President whom the Electors never voted for as such. 3d. That the Vice President acting as President has a

---

[50] Abraham Baldwin, senator from Georgia.
[51] Phanuel Bishop, representative from Massachusetts.
[52] Joseph Clay, representative from Pennsylvania.
[53] William Eustis, representative from Massachusetts.
[54] James Elliot, representative from Vermont.
[55] John Hoge, representative from Pennsylvania.
[56] Ebenezer Seaver, representative from Massachusetts.
[57] Joseph B. Varnum, representative from Massachusetts.

direct tendency to prevent the House from choosing the President — It will be an inducement & justification to the House not to compleat the choice, & is in effect a destruction of the designating principle. 4. The resolution is ungrammatical, vague, ambiguous & uncertain.

The debate has engaged the attention of the House for four days, & has been conducted, on the part of the Federalists, with great ability. Roger Griswold,[58] Dana[59] & Huger,[60] distinguished themselves — particularly the former.

### *Monday 12th.*

Mr Butler's resolution of the 27th of Oct. as an amendment to the constitution was considered to wit, " That no person who has been twice successively elected President of the United States, shall be eligible as President, untill foûr years shall have elapsed: but any citizen who has been President of the United States, may after such intervention, be eligible to the office of President for four years, & no longer." This resolution was negatived yeas 4, nays 25.

The House of Representatives returned us, the Resolve of the 2d for amending the constitution, with their concurrence, enrolled. Mr. Tracey moved That the committee of enrolled bills be directed to present said resolution to the President of the United States for his approbation.

This motion was strenuously opposed on the ground, That the resolution had been already passed by *two-thirds* of both houses of Congress — That this negative would therfore be unavailing — That in proposing amendments to the Constitution, the President of the United States has no authority to act — he is excluded from all agency in the business — The words of the article are, " *The Congress,* whenever two-thirds of both Houses

---

[58] Roger Griswold, representative from Connecticut.
[59] Samuel W. Dana, representative from Connecticut.
[60] Benjamin Huger, representative from South Carolina.

shall deem it necessary, shall propose amendments to the constitution."

It was said in answer to these objections, That the provision of the constitution was explicit, " Every order, *resolution* or vote to which the concurrence of the Senate & House of Representatives may be necessary (except on a question of adjournment) shall be presented to the President of the United States; & before the same shall take effect, shall be approved by him, or being disapproved by him, shall be *repassed* by two-thirds of the Senate & House of Representatives." If a bill or resolve is passed by both houses unanimously, still it must be sent to the President for his approbation, and if he disapprove it, it must be *repassed* by two-thirds of both House before it can take effect.

It is said, *The. Congress* shall propose amendments — And so the Constitution says *All legislative powers shall be vested in a Congress — & The Congress shall have power to lay & collect taxes — regulate commerce — declare war — raise armies &c* (Art. 1. Sect. 1. & Sect. 8). Upon the same principle therefore that you exclude the President from an agency in this amendment to the constitution; you may with equal propriety exclude him from either approving or disapproving of every bill or resolve that is passed by the two Houses.

As to precedents in this case I believe they are against the motion — but it is to be observed that, they are precedents established without debate, or without a particular attention to the subject — & therefore they prove nothing. The motion was negatived, yeas 7, nays 23.[61]

A resolve was brought up from the House of Representatives for the concurrence of the Senate, " That the President

[61] No report of this debate is given in the *Annals of Congress;* nor does J. Q. Adams mention it in his *Memoirs.* It is the generally accepted interpretation of the Constitution that the President's signature is not necessary to an amendment; Ames, *Proposed Amendments to the Constitution,* 295–296.

of the United States be requested to transmit to the Executives
of the several States, copies of the article of amendment proposed by Congress, to be added to the constitution of the
United States, respecting the election of President & Vice
President."

The Vice President was requested to Determine whether this
resolve could pass without having three several readings on
different days. He observed, " That when a resolve partakes
of the nature of a bill, it must then have three readings on
different days; but this resolution is not of a legislative
nature, tis merely a directory to the President — one
reading only is therefore necessary." The Senate concurred.
A question then arose, whether it was necessary for the Vice
President to sign this last resolution, or whether the attesta-
tion of the Secretary was sufficient. The Speaker of the House
had doubts upon the subject but had signed it — several
senators expressed their opinion agt. the Vice President signing it — no vote was taken, & the Vice President, declared he
should not sign it, as he tho't it improper.

In the course of the debate  Mr. Wright rose & said, " That
Mr. Otis our secretary had a few days since, at the request
of Mr. Griswold a representative from Connecticut, given him
(Griswold) a copy of the vote of the Senate on the 2d instant
relative to the resolution for amending the constitution, tending to falsify the record itself. And that the certificate went
to prove that that resolution had not passed by a constitutional
majority of two-thirds of the Senate, & thereby giving the *lie*
direct to our resolve— That this improper conduct of the Secretary had occasioned the House of Representatives to debate
two days upon the question, & that in a very improper & indelicate manner as it respected the honour & dignity of the
Senate " —

The Vice President called Mr. Wright to *order* — declared
his observations were very *improper & indecent*.

The Secretary rose to explain — but the President would not permit him. —

## Tuesday 13th.

After the minutes of yesterday were read the President said He was desirous that the Senate should proceed for a few moments to *Executive business.* A motion was made, & the spectators were excluded from the gallery, & and the doors closed. He then read the following letter — *viz* " To the Vice President and Senate of the United States.

" The Secretary of the Senate respectfully calls to their recollection a charge made yesterday against him in very harsh terms by Mr. Wright in his place with having been guilty of indelicate conduct towards the Senate in certifying a paper with a view of falsifying their proceedings.

Not less surprised than shocked at the charge, which he denies, he prays an investigation of his conduct on the subject. If found guilty he will patiently submit to censure, — If innocent he trusts the honorable Senate will exculpate him from the charges.

Which is respectfully submitted by their Most humble servant Saml A Otis — Dec. 13, 1803."

The President then read a copy of the certificate which the Secretary gave to Mr. Thatcher,[62] (for he gave none to Mr. Griswold), which was nothing more than a copy of the Journal of the Senate, which is published every week, & contained the yeas and nays upon the resolution of the 2d instant for amending the constitution. The President then stated the words used by Mr. Wright yesterday, & observed that they were improper & highly reprehensible. Mr. Wright rose with great spirit, & wished to know whether it was the wish of the President, or of the Senate, to support the Secretary against a member of the Senate — That what he said yesterday he had

---

[62] Samuel Thacher, representative from Massachusetts.

a right to say, & he would now justify. But upon the President & several of the Senators expressly declaring the conduct of the Secretary not only just but fit and commendable, Mr. Wright said, " I did not mean yesterday to be understood as questioning the veracity of the Secretary, or his propriety of conduct." Mr. Otis then rose & said Mr. Wrights explanation was satisfactory. And here the matter ended.

The bill to repeal the *bankrupt Law* was read a third time.

*Mr. Brackenridge,* The principles of the bankrupt law are unjust — Men in trade, are to be discharged from their promises without fulfilling them — husbandmen & planters are not to be releived. But traders must be released from their contracts against the consent of their creditors. The effect of this law has been an encouragement to fraud — It has proved expensive — Scarse an instance, has occured of a dividend being made of the bankrupts property to his creditors — or one worth receiving. This Law has unjustly taken suits, between citizens of the same state, from the State Courts, & carried them improperly into the Courts of the United States. — The law is in its nature calculated to encourage an unwarrantable spirit of speculation — in which if the merchant succeeds he may make his fortune — if he fails, it is at the expence of his creditors, & a commission of bankruptcy will forever release him from their demands — & enable him to commence business again. — The penalties of this law are too mild — but if they were as severe as the extroadinary nature of the case requires, the temper, habits & manners of the people, would never execute them. This law was a law of *experiment,* it was designed to continue for a little more than five years; but *experience* demands its repeal. — The great majority of the other House who voted in favor of its repeal is strong evidence that the law is obnoxious to the *public mind.*

*Mr. Saml Smith,* If we pass this law, the states may pass bankrupt laws more injurious than the one we repeal. I know the law is defective — but why not mend it. Gentlemen from agricultural States, say it aids fraud — their opinion is founded on report only — Gentlemen from commercial cities, who are most acquainted with the subject, are in favor of the law — they know that it is in favor of creditors. Merchants may have their property plundered from them by belligerent powers — In the last European war, Great Britain & France took from our merchants property to the amount of more than ten million of dollars — This law aided them under their misfortunes. I knew a man, last session, vote for the reduction of the Marine Corps, who did not know the difference between a Marine & a seaman — This may be the case with some who will vote for the repeal of this law.

The people do not require the repeal of this law — there is not a single petition for it. All nations have bankrupt laws. I should be glad to extend this law to Farmers; but I know they could not exist under it — it would render the law more unpopular. Great Britain is an *agricultural* nation, but they have a bankrupt law — they are wise in aiding commerce. Lands in Virginia are not by their laws subject to the payment of debts; this law makes them so — & that may be the cause why the Virginians discover so much anxiety for the repeal. The repeal of this law will be fatal to merchants. — Under state bankrupt laws, foreign creditors who act as agents to the bankrupt, will hold the monies they have collected to pay themselves, to the exclusion of the creditors here. I know the law is defective — amend it — make the assent of three-fourths of all the creditors necessary to the bankrupts having a certificate — let no bankrupt have the benefit of the law unless he pays twenty-five pr Cent on his debts — subject the property which he may afterward receive from legacies or descent — but do not repeal the Law.

*Mr. Cocke,* I may be the man who did not know the difference between the Marine & seaman; but I am not the man who beleived the Marine corps ought not to be reduced, & who because it was popular to reduce it, voted last session against my own conscience — The Gentleman from Maryland (Genl Smith) knows that I am not the man — but *he* well knows who voted so last session — Sir, Nathan said to David *thou art the man.*[63] I do not know much of commerce, but I know that this law has occasioned much fraud — it has done more evil than good. If this law is so necessary for merchants, why does the gentleman from Maryland (Mr. Smith) consent to limit it only to those merchants who can pay one fourth of their debts — This would be doing business by the halves — & humanity by quarters.

*Mr. S. Smith,* I move that the further consideration of this repealing law be postponed to the 2d monday of December — If this motion prevails we shall then have time to amend the law complained off.

*Mr. Wright,* Whenever bankrupt laws are necessary, Congress must pass them — they are always necessary, & therefore we ought not to repeal this. Planters & Farmers have no interest or concern with this law — it does not affect them. In a state of society we have a right to absolve debtors from their contracts against the will of the creditor. — In Virginia lands & slaves are not liable to pay debts — they ought to be, & this law makes them so. —

*Mr. Venable,*[64] I did not intend to have risen on this subject but as I am the only senator from Virginia that is present, and as the laws of that state have been misrepresented, I think it my duty — Our laws relative to lands & slaves are now what they were at the first settlement of our country. Slaves, are in all cases, subject to the payment of debts. Our lands, are not, it is true, in the first instance, liable to the payment of debts — When a judgment is rendered against a man

---

[63] II Samuel, XII, 7.
[64] Abraham B. Venable.

— he cannot alienate his lands till that judgment is satisfied — If the judgment is not cancelled by a certain period, if the debtor's lands are of a certain value, or afford so much rent — a certain annual portion of the income of the land is subject to pay the judgment; but the fact, generally is, that the debtor, rather than have the precept extended on the profits, sells a portion of the land & pays the Judgment. But the lands in Virginia are principally in the hands of Planters — traders or merchants own little real estate in Virginia.

I do not so much fear any extensive mischief resulting from Insolvent laws passed by state legislatures — If they pass imperfect unequal laws, it will be their own citizens who will feel their ill effects — & they will soon correct the evil, by electing members who will repeal the obnoxious law. If the states pass *expost facto laws, or laws impairing contracts,* the Courts of law will protect creditors against the operation of such laws.

Motion for postponement lost, yeas 13, nays 17.

It was then moved, That the bill for the repeal of the Bankrupt law should pass.

*Mr. Butler,* This law, both in its principles & effects is unjust and unequal, & has occasioned much fraud. Insolvent laws only releases the person of the debtor from confinement, but this discharges both person & property. The merchant who has obtained the property from the Planter or Farmer is freed from his contract — but the planter & farmer who suffers by the bankruptcy of the merchant is held in prison & his property sold at auction.

Motion prevailed, yeas 17, nays 12.

### Wednesday 14

The Senate passed a bill for the sale of the Frigate General Greene — & to authorize the President to purchase or build 2 vessels of War to carry not exceeding sixteen each, & appropriates the sum of $50,000. The reason assigned for the sale of the Frigate was that she is old & not worth repairing. —

The " Act fixing the salaries of certain officers " — was read. The Senate added one thousand Dollars to the salary of the Post Master General & two hundred & fifty to that of the Assistant Post Master, more than what the House had given them. The salaries to all the officers, except those two, are the same as was allowed by the temporary law of March 2d 1799.[65] A motion was made to strike out of this bill the following sentence, — " which said several compensations were *established* by the Act passed the 2d March, 1799." It was contended that these words were not only unnecessary but useless & improper.

To this Brackenridge, Bradley, Saml Smith & Wright, were much opposed — They said if this clause was not retained in the bill, the great body of the people would beleive that the Democrats in Congress had *raised* the salaries — That though such reports could not effect senators who held their seats for six years — yet without such a clause in the bill, it could not pass the other House — It would cost many of those members the loss of their seats — & therefore if the motion prevails here, it will prevent the passage of this bill in that House — That on the subject of salaries it is not only improper to consult the people; but in fact they are *incapable* of judging. —

Consistency, is not, I know, a trait in democracy! When it suits there purpose — when unanswerable arguments are opposed to democrats, then our ears are stunned with the *people*, the *sovereign people* demand it — the *public will* is in its favor — & we must bow submissive. But these same men, when they pursue measures to which they conceive the *public mind* is opposed, then tell us, that the people are *uninformed* — they are a *rabble incapable of judging* — & good legislators will not consult them.

The motion was negatived yeas 9, nays 17. —

In the House of Representatives, the Committee of Ways &

---

[65] See *Statutes at Large*, I, 729–730.

Means made a report on Mr. Eppes [66] motion " relative to the
expediency of discontinuing the office of Commissioner of Loans
in the several States." The report was, " that it is inexpedient
to discontinue the office." John Randolph Jr the chairman of
the Committee was opposed to the report — Gallatin, the Secretary of the Treasury, & indeed the President himself, were in
favor of the measure of discontinuance. The House after spending two days in debate, disagreed to the report of the Committee
yeas 58, nays 55, so that the original motion is yet undecided.
It was designed to discontinue the loan offices in the states, &
have their business done by Clerks at the Treasury here. The
interest & instalments to be paid to the stock holders at some
bank in each state, where there are banks — & in the two states
in which there are no banks, by some officer of the United States
in those States — The transfer of the stock to be made only at
the Treasury — & the books to be closed against transfers from
21 to 28 days preceeding the end of each quarter. This measure
is, in my opinion, in direct violation of the contract made by
the United States with the stockholders. The law of Augt 4,
1790,[67] which is the law creating the stock, & of course makes
the contract, expressly provides that there shall be a Commissioner of Loans in each of the *then* States — that the interest
& instalments should be paid, & that transfers of the stock be
made, at those several offices. If these offices were discontinued,
the difficulty & delay it would occasion in making transfers
would injure the credit of stock. Transfers are now made with
ease & dispatch — Men in trade find their stock very convenient
to deposit for loans of money from banks & individuals. If
the right of making the *transfer* in each state may be destroyed
by the government, the debtor, without the consent of the
creditor, why may not, on the same principle, other parts of
the contract be changed — Why not oblige the creditors to send

---

[66] John W. Eppes, representative from Virginia and son-in-law of
President Jefferson.

[67] See *Statutes at Large,* I, 138–144.

to Washington or Europe for their interest & instalments — why not reduce the rate of interest?  The whole number of stockholders are **14236** — Some of these are meerly nominal & hold the stock in trust for foreigners — A large portion of the debt is in fact due to the people of the Eastern states. — It is true the sum standing on the Loan office of Pennsylvania is large; but the fact is that at the time when Congress sat at Philadelphia, foreigners interested indirectly in our domestic debt, had their subscription made at that loan office.

### Thursday 15.

The " Act fixing salaries " was read a third time.

A motion was made to strike out the words, " Which said several compensations were established by the act, passed the 2d March **1799**."

*Mr. White,* These words are *useless* in the bill — If they are retained, it will be conclusive evidence to me, that *the majority* are afraid to take the responsibility of this law upon themselves — This is a pitiful miserable subterfuge — I did think honorable gentlemen had too much spirit to resort to it. —

*Mr. Saml Smith,* We wish to retain this clause, to prevent newspaper calumny — to prevent designing men from rendering us odious — by publishing lies — Tis our duty to guard the morals of the people — We do it by publishing a fact *viz* — that these salaries are the same as the *federal administration* established in **1799**.

*Mr. Dayton,* These words, then, are to be considered as the *apology* for passing this Act — This is the first time I have known the Senate of the United States stoop to the meaness of an *apology* — an *apology* for passing a law — If an apology is necessary for adopting the salaries granted by the federalists to some of your public officers — what excuse will you make for the additions you have made for the salaries of the Post office department.

*Mr. Adams,* I am in favor of retaining the words as part of the bill, & shall vote against the motion for striking them out. The law of March 1799 was passed by a Federal Congress — Those salaries were then opposed by several gentlemen who now belong to the present majority. The present majority by retaining these words in this bill, do thereby bear honorable testimony that the Federalists were correct in passing the law March 1799 granting salaries.

The motion for striking out was lost yeas 11, nays 16.

The bill then passed, with the amendments, yeas 22, nays 5.

In opposition to the final passage of the bill, it was said, That the salaries established by this bill were too high compared with the salaries granted, to other officers. That the salary given to the Vice President, the second officer in the government, is only $5000 pr annum — That this bill gives the same salary to the Secretary of the Treasury — & to the Secretary of State — That the Chief Justice of the United States has only $4000, & each of the assistant Justices of that Court $3500 pr annum. That the office of Judge of the Supreme Court is as important & requires men of as much talent & integrity, & is more expensive & fatiguing than either of the Secretaries.

That these salaries to the Secretaries are more than $13, per diem for the year —That members of Congress receive only $6. pr diem & that on an average for not more than 135 days in the year, making pr annum $810. This sum little more than actually supports them while here — Its true they have fees for travelling, but that is considered barely as a compensation for the expence &c of the Journey — And were gentlemen to come here in their own Carriages & with their own servants, as they ought, the whole sum received, would not defray their expences while attending Congress. The time we are here effectually deranges our business for the rest of the year. Members of Congress ought to be men of talents, & if the salaries in this bill are right our own pay is inadequate.

In 1799, Several gentlemen who now urge the passage of this bill, were then opposed to the same salaries. The expence of living was then as high as it is now — & the duties of some of the officers were greater then than they are now, particularly that of the Attorney General, who then had duties to perform under the British treaty, that do not now exist.

Mr. Gallatin, Secy of the Treasury, was then a member of the other House — He then reasoned against the salaries — declared they were extravagant — that to grant them was a profusion of public money — That in republican governments salaries ought to be moderate & granted with a sparing hand — This was the language of the Secy Treasury when acting as a member of the other House in 1799 — & his vote on that subject is recorded on their Journals.[68] But now, strange to tell, this very Gentleman & his friends, think these salaries are moderate, & ought to be granted not indeed for two or three years, but established by a permanent law.

### Executive business.

The Vice President read to the Senate the nomination made by the President of the United States of a man from Maryland to be Commercial agent at a foreign port. Mr. Wright rose and said he knew the Candidate to be honest, capable & faithful — The vote passed in his favor — Just as the Vice President was taking the question on the nomination of another candidate for another office, Mr. Wright said, He beleived he owed it to the Senate to inform them, " That the gentleman whom We had just appointed Consul or Commercial agent was a little *deranged in his mind.*" One of the Senate enquired of the Vice President what Mr. Wright had said — Mr. Burr replied, " Mr. Wright wishes the Senate to decide whether *derangement* disqualifies a man for office." The appointment was reconsidered.

---

[68] *Journal of the House of Representatives,* 5 Cong., 3 sess., (1798–1799, reprint of 1826), IV, 452–453, 499–501.

### Saturday 17.

The Certificates for the payment of Louisiana are now printing — They are payable to Baring & Co. & Hope & Co. — And
a few of them to their assignees who are Americans — They are
to be signed by the Register of the Treasury only. There are
to be 5000 Certificates of different denominations, from one
hundred dollars to six thousand — They are printed on 100
Rheams four quire & four sheets of paper — & the work is very
handsomely executed. —

### Monday 19.

The Vice President immediately after his arrival here this
session, excluded all persons from the area of the Senate chamber, except members of the other House. This prevented much
noise, & contributed much to the orderly dispatch of business.
But some of the Senate were dissatisfied with the rule —

Mr. Wright (who had two daughters in the City) made the
following motion, " That no person be admitted on the floor of
the Senate Chamber, except members of the House of Representatives, foreign ministers, & the heads of departments; *unless
introduced by a member of the Senate.*"

After long debate, the words *underscored* were struck out, &
the following subjoined, " And judges of the supreme & district
Courts of the United States."

It was then moved to add, " and the ladies." This last motion
produced a long & animated debate, in which Dayton, White
& Wright were eloquent in their arguments in favor of the
admission of the ladies — They contended that their presance
gave an animation to debate, that is not only pleasing but necessary — & had an irresistable power of polishing the speakers
arguments & softening their manners — This was opposed by
Adams, Baldwin & Hillhouse who contended that their admission introduced noise & confussion into the Senate — that several
senators frequently left their places — & that debates were

protracted to arrest the attention of the ladies — but That if ladies wished to attend they might take seats in the gallery, a part of which was now fitted up in a style elegant & convenient.

The motion was negatived, yeas 12, nays 16.

It was then moved to add to the motion, "the governors & councellors of the respective states, & the representatives of the state legislatures." This was also negatived yeas 13, nays 15.

The question was then taken upon the resolution as amended, & rejected, yeas 7, nays 21.

The debate on this subject has taken up nearly the whole day. —

### *Wednesday 21.*

A Convention between the King of Spain & the United States for the Indemnification of Losses, dated August 11, 1802, with the accompaning documents were read.[69]

This Convention was laid before the Senate at the last session, and was then opposed on various grounds, but principally, 1. Because it did not make any provision for indemnities to our Citizens for the losses they suffered by the sale of their ships and merchandize in Spanish Ports by French Consuls. — And 2d Because Spain in direct violation of her treaty with us of Oct. 20, 1795 had denied us the right of Deposit at New Orleans — which denial was just cause of war — & without redress for that injury & insult, it was then probable, war would ensue.

Every democrat in Senate then voted to ratify this Convention, & every federalist voted against it —

The vote respecting the ratification was then reconsidered, & the consideration of the subject postponed. —

And this day the President of the United States again sent us the Convention for our further consideration & the message & documents following.[70] — . . .

---

[69] See *American State Papers,* II. *Foreign Relations,* II, 475–483.

[70] The President's Message of December 21, 1803 and accompanying documents, copied into his *Memorandum* by Plumer, are omitted here.

## *Thursday 22d.*

Mr. Bradley moved the following resolution, " That the message & documents communicated by the President of the United States to the Senate on the 21st instant be referred to a select committee to consider & report whether any & if any what further proceeding ought to be had by the Senate in relation to the message or the *disclosures* made by the same." Ordered to lie on the table.

The object of this resolution was to devise means to direct the Attorney General to prosecute those lawyers who had given their answer to the " Abstract question " as related page 246,[71] as intermedling with a negotiation then pending with Spain. It was declared to be an offence against the " Act for punishment of certain crimes therein specified," passed Jany 30, 1799, commonly called the *Logan Act*. This law subjects a person to fine and imprisonment, who shall, without permission of the Government of the United States, carry on any correspondence or intercourse with any foreign Government, or officer or agent thereof, with an intent to influence the measures or conduct of such government in relation to any dispute with the United States, or to defeat their measures, or who shall counsel advise aid or assist in any such correspondence.[72]

This law was passed with a view to prevent such conduct as Dr. Logan, (now one of the Senators from Pennsylvania) was then guilty off. The Dr. at that time, without any authority from the United States, had undertaken a voyage to France & actually opened a correspondence with the French government relative to our controversy with that country.

Bradley said this law was drawn by Mr. Rawle, one of the gentlemen who had signed the paper in question, & that it

---

[71] The page reference is to a section of Plumer's manuscript omitted here; see footnote 70. The document referred to was dated at Philadelphia, November 15, 1802; see *American State Papers, II. Foreign Relations,* II, 605.

[72] See *Statutes at Large,* I, 613.

would be right he should be one of the first suffers under the law, he himself drew with a view to punish Dr. Logan. In this Bradley is incorrect — for Roger Griswold Esq of Connecticut, informed me that he himself drew the Act, & that Rawle had nothing to do with it.

*Mr. Wright,* I move that the consideration of the Spanish Convention be postponed to a distant day — The last session when the vote was taken on this convention, perceiving it would not be approved by two-thirds of the senators present, I then voted against my conscience, against the treaty, that I might bring myself within the rule of moving for a reconsideration — I effected this — I must now be absent — & I think I have a right to indulgence on this subject.

The House yesterday informed us that they would not agree to the encrease of salaries we had granted to the Postmaster Genl & Assistant Post Master —

Bradley, Jackson & Wright contended that the Senate ought to insist upon our amendments — They considered the Post office as all important, & that Granger [73] of all other men was the best qualified for the officer.

*Mr. Brackenridge,* The office of Comptroller of the Treasury is of more importance — there is much more responsibility attached to it — His salary is lower than the one we have voted to the postmaster general — & there is much greater reason for raising his salary than that of the Postmaster General — I am therefore in favor of receding from our amendment.

The Senate voted, That they insist on their amendments, asked a conference & appointed Bradley & Jackson managers.

### Thursday 29.

The managers aforesaid reported, That they had met the managers appointed on the part of the House of Representatives, but they could come to no agreement.

---

[73] Gideon Granger, Postmaster General from 1801 to 1814.

It was then moved, " That the Senate adhere to their amendments " — yeas 17. nays 7. Notice of this resolution was then given to the House — Mr. John Randolph Jr then made report from the Managers appointed by the House — assigning their reasons to the House for not agreeing with the Managers appointed by the Senate — *viz* " That the amendments in question go to raise the salaries of the Post Master General, & his assistant, from $3000, & $1700, respectively, to $4000, & $2000. The committee are of the opinion that it would be inexpedient to concur with these amendments for the following reasons —
" 1. That the office of Post Master General, of very *inferior* consequence to that of Comptroller of the Treasury, would thereby be compensated by a salary superior to that of the Comptroller, & superior, in proportion to the duties of Post Master General, to the compensation of all the other great officers of the State, when the duties of those officers are taken into consideration. " 2. Because the Assistant Postmaster General is, in fact, but the Chief Clerk of that department; because his duties are of a nature *very inferior* to those of the chief Clerk of the department of State, in whom a high confidence is necessarily reposed, the abuse of which might prove incalculably detrimental to the best interests of the government. The present emoluments of the Chief Clerk of the department of State are $1850 per annum; & the proposed amendment would give to that officer, *merely ministerial,* a greater compensation. The same observation might be extended to the Chief Clerk of the Treasury Department." The House disagreed to the amendment of the Senate, yeas 71. nays 22.

Mr. Granger has for sometime discovered a restless uneasy mind. His office does not admit him as a Member of the Cabinet [74] — The secretaries of State, Treasury, Navy & War, with the Attorney-General compose the privy Council — indeed its

---

[74] It was not until 1829 that the Postmaster General became a member of the President's Cabinet.

said, on some occasions, the latter is not always admitted. To elevate his rank the Post master Genl, has sought to obtain an encrease of salary, failing in this he has uttered some unguarded expressions against *Virginia encroachments* — but these he will meanly retract, and renew his labours to diseminate democracy thro' the medium of his office.

*January 3, 1804.*

*Tuesday 3d.*

It was moved that tomorrow the Senate should form themselves into a Court of Impeachment, & take an Oath as prescribed by the Constitution, Art. 1. sect. 3. [75]

*Brackenridge & Maclay* were opposed, on the ground that the oath ought not to be taken by the senators untill after the House of Representatives had exhibited the articles of Impeachment to the senate. The motion prevailed yeas 15 nays 13.

It was moved that the following should be the form of the Oath to be taken by each senator, " I . . . solemnly swear (or affirm as the case may be) that in all things appertaining to the trial of the impeachment of John Pickering, Judge of the district court of the District of New Hampshire, I will do impartial justice, *according to Law.*"

*Mr. Cocke* I move to strike out the words " according to law " & insert in lieu of them " to the United States & John Pickering." My reason for this motion is that if the Senators take the Oath proposed, it will then be incumbent on the House of Representatives to prove that John Pickering has committed an offence against *law,* & that perhaps they cannot prove — for I understand the Judge is deranged — & *I know of no law that makes derangement criminal* — The motion was lost no man voting in favor of it except the mover.

---

[75] *Cf. Senate Doc.,* No. 876, 62 Cong., 2 sess. *Extracts from the Journal of the United States Senate in all cases of Impeachment presented by the House of Representatives, 1798–1804,* pp. 17–34.

## *Wednesday 4th.*

Mr. Adams offered the following resolution, " That any senator of the United States, having previously acted & voted as a member of the house of Representatives, on a question of Impeachment, is thereby disqualified to sit & act, *in the same case,* as a member of the Senate, sitting as a Court of impeachment." [76]

The impeachment of John Pickering was voted by the House of Representatives March 2d 1803, *Mr. Bayley,*[77] *Mr. Condit* [78] & *Mr. Samuel Smith* were then members of that house, & voted in favor of the impeachment as appears by the Journal — they are now senators.

*Mr. Brackenridge,* I am opposed to this resolution — those gentlemen as members of the House of Representatives are now dead, they live & act in a different capacity as senators.

*Mr. Jackson,* If these are excluded, we establish a precedent that may on some future occasion exclude so many of the senators, as that two-thirds of those who may be present and sit in Judgment cannot be induced to *convict* the accused.

*Mr. Baldwin,* If the trial should last as long as Hasting's [79] it may happen that nearly all the senators may be in the situation of those gentlemen — Impeachments are not like indictments — or is the House & Senate to be compared to Grand & petit jurors — Senators are like Judges — & it is no challange to a judge that he has formed an opinion & even promulgated that opinion.

*Mr. Adams,* The case stated by the gentleman (Mr. Baldwin) will probably never happen.  The cause of justice & humanity require that those who voted the accusation should not decide

---

[76] *Cf.* J. Q. Adams, *Memoirs,* I, 283.
[77] Theodorus Bailey, senator from New York.
[78] John Condit, senator from New York.
[79] The impeachment trial of Warren Hastings before the House of Lords covered the years from 1788 to 1795.

it. It is improper & very indelicate that Judges who have given an opinion in a particular cause should afterwards sit in judgment in that cause. Jurors may be challanged — but judges cannot. If it could have been in the power of the *Accused* to have bro't this question before the Senate, I should not have done it — I will have a decision of it by the senate — I think it important.

The consideration of the resolution was postponed — & all the senators present, including those three, were sworn.

On the right hand of the Vice President seats were assigned for the Managers of the Impeachment — Notice was given to the House of Representatives that the Senate were ready to receive the articles of Impeachment. The Managers appeared at the bar of the Senate, & informed that they were then ready to exhibit said articles. The Vice President then directed the Sargent at Arms to conduct the Managers to their seats — In a few minutes, Mr. Nicholson,[80] the chairman rose, & all the managers with him — he then read the articles of Impeachment — dld. them to the President, & declared that the House prayed process against the Accused. The president informed him that the Senate would take order thereon, & give due notice thereof to the House; — & then the Managers withdrew.

The impeachment consists of four Articles —

1. Art. states that George Wentworth the surveyor of New Hampshire arrested the ship Eliza & two cables — that a libel was filed agt them before the said Judge — that the said Judge without E. Ladd the owner producing any certificate from the Collector & naval officer that the duties was paid, delivered said ship & cables to said Ladd.

*2d Article* — That at a District Court holden by said Judge Nov 11, 1802 Joseph Whipple the Collector libeled said ship &c because certain goods had been unladen therefrom contrary to law — That said Judge with an intent to defeat the claim of

---

[80] Joseph H. Nicholson, representative from Maryland.

United States refused to hear testimony of witnesses to prove said libel, but contrary to his trust & duty as a Judge gave up said ship &c to said Ladd — in violation of the Laws.

3 Article, That in said suit at said Court the said Judge refused an appeal to the next Circuit Court.

4 Article, That said Judge at said Court was intoxicated & used prophane & indecent language.

### Thursday 5th.

I dined this day with President Jefferson — I was at his house near an hour before the other gentlemen — Speaking of the impeachment of Pickering, I observed I had no doubt that the judge was *insane*, & asked him whether insanity was good cause for impeachment & removal from office. He replied, " If the facts of his denying an appeal & of his intoxication, as stated in the impeachment are proven, that will be sufficient cause of removal without further enquiry."

I then observed to him that I understood the House of Representatives were then debating the question whether a Committee should be raised to enquire into the expediency of impeaching Judge Chase of the Supreme Court — He replied, *I have heard so,* & asked me what facts had been stated — I answered I had not been in the House during the day — Just at this moment Mr. Harvie, his private secretary, returned from the Capitol. The President asked him what particular part of Judge Chase's conduct had been referred to as the ground of Impeachment. Mr. Harvie said " He understood the case of Cooper." — The President, turning round to me said, " There are three cases to which I suppose the House would refer, Fries, Cooper & Callender [81] — But the conduct of Judge Chase was, perhaps the most extro-

---

[81] John Fries, James T. Callender and Thomas Cooper. Fries was tried and sentenced to be hanged because of leadership in the " house or window tax" insurrection in Pennsylvania. He was pardoned by President John Adams. Thomas Cooper was tried for libel under the Sedition Act.

adinary in the trial of Callender — He there refused to admit Col Taylor, late one of your senators, as a witness for Callender, because he could not prove the whole of the case. — This business of removing Judges by impeachment is a *bungling way."*

### Saturday 7th.

On the 5th John Randolph Jr made the following motion in the House of Representatives, to wit, " Resolved, That a Committee be appointed to enquire into the official conduct of Samuel Chase, one of the associate justices of the Supreme Court of the United States, & to report their opinion, whether the said Samuel Chase hath so acted in his judicial capacity, as to require the interposition of the constitutional power of this House." [82]

It was moved that this resolution should lie on the table, as is the usual course of business — It was urged that it was an important subject — that members desired time to investigate it — to examine precedents — but this was denied. The debate continued till a late hour of the day — & has been debated every day till this evening — the resolution was amended by adding the name of " Richard Peters district judge of the district of Pennsylvania " & has now passed 81 to 40, & a committee of seven appointed, of whom Mr. Randolph is chairman. The Committee are not confined to any *specific charge.* This is similar to the French *denouncing* a victim & like them his condemnation will follow of course.

The removal of the Judges, & the destruction of the independence of the judicial department, has been an object on which Mr. Jefferson has been long resolved, at least ever since he has been in office. In his first message to Congress, Dec. 8, 1801,[83] he insinuated, *That the state legislatures had the principle care of our persons, property & reputation —* He was explicit, *That*

---

[82] For the Senate record of this impeachment trial, see *Senate Doc.,* No. 876, 62 Cong., 2 sess., 35–60.

[83] See Richardson, *Messages and Papers of the Presidents,* I, 326–332.

*the Judiciary of the United States was too expensive & that it required reform.* To prove that there were too many Judges he had previously required from the Clerk of each District the number of actions that been entered on their docketts — these he communicated to Congress. In the same session, Congress passed the Act repealing the Law that established the Circuit Court — by this single operation all those Judges, without the slightest accusation were removed from office — an office which the Constitution expresly guaranteed to them *during good behavior.* At the last session Mr. Jefferson told me that the Constitution ought to be so altered as that the President, on application of Congress should have authority to remove any Judge from office. This business of *amending* the constitution is found to be a tedious process — the good work of *reform* cannot be delayed — The president & his Cabinet agree that impeachment conviction & removal from office is necessary — A triumphant majority in each House are devoted to their views & will carry them into effect.

The doctrine is now established in the House that a specific charge against a Judge is not necessary to institute an enquiry into his official conduct. A committee of enquiry is said to be a harmless measure — some vote for it, who are not prepared to vote an impeachment — not perceiving that when the Committee have collected exparte testimony & reported an impeachment — that then they will be under a kind of necessity to impeach. —

I was surprised to find Mr. Eppes, the son in law of the President, in debate in the House on this subject — state the very ideas of Jefferson — the very same that he mentioned to me in private conversation. — Mr. Eppes said in the House " It will always be sufficient for me to vote an enquiry, for a member to declare he considers an enquiry necessary — I shall consider it a duty — I believe, that in the Commonwealth of Virginia, but one sentiment prevails, as to the conduct of Judge Chase on this occasion " (the trial of Callender) " viz that it was *indecent & tyrannical*. In the course of the trial he refused to allow a witness on the part of the prisoner to be examined, because the witness could prove the truth of a part only, & not the whole of the words laid in the indictment. By a system of conduct *peculiar to himself* he deprived the prisoner of the aid of Council — I do not mention these circumstances as *hearsay evidence*, but as facts, which I am induced to *beleive* can be established by legal testimony."

When the Judges of the Circuit Court were removed by the repeal of the law in 1802, then was the time for the Judges of the Supreme Court, to have taken their stand against the encroachments of Congress & of the Executive. That Court ought to have declared the repealing law unconstitutional — they ought to have refused to have held Circuit Courts — & the Judges of the Circuits ought to have continued to have held their Courts the repeal notwithstanding. But unfortunately there was then a diversity of opinion in the Supreme Court upon this subject —

### Monday, 9th.

More than two-thirds of the Senators present voted to advise the President to ratify the Convention with Spain.

A Committee was appointed on Bradley's motion of the 22d of December, p. 271 [84] of which he is chairman.

### Tuesday 10th.

Mr. Adams introduced the following resolutions, *viz.* 1. "Resolved, That the people of the United States, have never, in any manner delegated to this Senate, the power of giving its legislative concurrence to any act for imposing taxes upon the inhabitants of Louisiana, without their consent.

2. "Resolved that by concurring in any act of legislation

---

[84] Page 94 of this volume.

for imposing taxes upon the inhabitants of Louisiana without their consent, this Senate would assume a power, unwarranted by the Constitution & dangerous to the liberties of the people of the United States.

3. " Resolved, That the power of originating bills for raising revenue, being exclusively vested in the House of Representatives, these resolutions be carried to them by the secretary of the Senate: that whenever they think proper they may adopt such measures as, to their wisdom may appear necessary & expedient, for raising & collecting a revenue from Louisiana."

Mr. Adams moved that they should be taken up in the usual course of business, be postponed till tomorrow, be printed & laid upon the table. This was refused.

Mr. Adams urged there adoption — read several paragraphs from the declaration of Independence — & the Journals of Congress of 1774 & 1775 to prove that they were the very principles on which the American revolution was founded.[85]

Dayton, Nicholas & Jackson, considered them as being alarming, destructive — more fatal than Pandora's box — & therefore that a decision ought to be immediate — They did not however point out any particular evil that would result from them.

My objections to them were, that the resolutions are meer abstract propositions, not connected with any business immediately before the senate — & that a vote in favor of them, in the present form, would in fact conclude nothing.

They were rejected yeas 4, nays 22.

The Members of Congress are furnished by the Government with stationary — It has been said that some of the southern gentry who are in the habit of writing circular letters to their constituents, have had those letters printed on the paper they received from the public — To prevent this, & to encourage *economy, the catchword* of the sect. *Mr. Early* [86] made the fol-

[85] Cf. *Writings of John Quincy Adams* (Ford ed.), III, 25–30; *Memoirs,* I, 286, footnote.

[86] Peter Early, representative from Georgia.

lowing little pitiful motion in the House, which they adopted —
" Resolved, That in future, the stationary used by the members
of this House shall be drawn by an order entered by each member in a book to be provided for that purpose, & kept by the
*doorkeeper*, & in no other manner."

### Wednesday 11th.

In the Senate, " An act for the punishment of certain crimes
against the United States," was read the third time. The object
of this bill is to punish those who on the high seas wittingly &
wilfully destroy or attempt to destroy any ship, vessel &c.

Two instances of fraud of this kind, the one in Massachusetts
& the other in Georgia, but particularly the former, was the
occasion of this bill. The owner (Peirpoint) of the ship had her
& the cargo insured for more than ten times their value — He
then agreed with the captain that he should as soon as he had
got out at sea bore holes through the vessel & sink her — this was
done, & the seamen but narrowly escaped with their lives.

The penalty to this offence is by this bill, *Death* — Logan &
Worthington contended that the principles of humanity were
endangered by this penalty — they moved to strike out the
words *and shall suffer death* — their object was to insert
*banishment — or perpetual imprisonment*. Motion lost yeas
7, nays 20. — Bill passed.[87]

### Thursday 12th.

### Court of Impeachment —

*Mr. Brackenridge*, We ought now to authorize the House of
Representatives, & Judge Pickering to take out subpona's for
witnesses returnable the 2d of March, the time when he is
ordered to appear.

*Mr. Hillhouse.* It is said the Judge is *insane* — suppose his
friends should plead *that* — are the House now prepared to say

---

[87] Approved, March 26, 1804; see *Statutes at Large*, II, 290–291.

what evidence is necessary — or even whether any — on their part.

*Mr. Anderson,*[88] The appearance day ought to be considered as the day of trial, & witnesses should then attend — I do not think insanity cause of impeachment or even of inquiry.

*Mr. Nicholas,* The day of appearance ought to be the day of trial, & Pickering ought to be furnished with subpona's for witnesses the sametime that he is summoned.

The form of a subpena was made — it was directed to the marshall of the State in which the witnesses lived.

*Mr. Venable,* I think the marshall is not bound by law to serve precepts issuing from the Senate.

*Mr. Tracey,* On this point there can be no doubt — The Senate is now acting as a *Court* under the highest authority, the constitution — one of the incidents of a Court is to issue process — The law has defined the duty of marshalls — reads it. —

*Vice President,* I observe the subpena is to be issued by me where no *discretion* is given to act — why not therefore require it of the Secretary? It is directed to the marshall — I see no necessity of this — Subpena's ought to be directed to the witnesses, not to the officer — the party may serve it, & prove the service by affidavit.

## Saturday 14th.

The Senate passed " An Act giving effect to the laws of the United States, within the territories ceded to the United States, by the treaty of the 30th April 1803 between the United States & the French Republic; & for other purposes " — with amendments.[89] This bill originated in the House —

I think there is a great impropriety in thus hastily extending such a body of Laws as this act extends to the inhabitants of

---

[88] Joseph Anderson, senator from Tennessee.
[89] See *Statutes at Large*, II, 251–254.

Louisiana who are not only ignorant of our laws, government, & usuages under them, but a large portion of them wholly unacquainted with our language.

### Monday, 16th.

*The bill erecting Louisana into two territories.* —

*Mr. Worthington,* moved to amend the 4th section so as that the Legislative Council should be authorized to elect a deligate to Congress with the right to debate but not vote.[90]

*Mr. Brackenridge,* I approve of the motion — it will be the means of conveying useful knowledge to Congress.

*Mr. Saml. Smith,* This is going as far as we can at present to satisfy the third article of the treaty [91] — This will be placing that country on the same footing as the other territorial governments [92] — & from this delegate we shall derive much information.

*Mr. Dayton,*[93] I am opposed — The legislative Council itself will be better able by their memorials to represent the actual state & wants of that country than their agent.

*Mr. Jn. Smith,*[94] I think the amendment is necessary & important.

*Mr. Pickering,*[95] No man will undertake to say, Louisana is incorporated into the Union, it is therefore absurd to admit a delegate from that country to debate in our national councils — That is a purchased province, & as such we must govern it.

---

[90] The fourth section of the bill made provision for the appointment and powers of the legislative council. It is quoted in the Senate *Journal,* 8 Cong., 1 sess., (1803), 143.

[91] The third article of the Louisiana Treaty provided that the inhabitants of the ceded territory should be incorporated in the Union of the United States and admitted as soon as possible to the enjoyment of the privileges of citizenship, and that in the meantime they should be protected in the enjoyment of their liberty, property and religion.

[92] Referring to statutory provisions for delegates from the Mississippi and Indiana territories.

[93] Jonathan Dayton, senator from New Jersey.

[94] John Smith, senator from Ohio.

[95] Timothy Pickering, senator from Massachusetts.

*Mr. White,* I cannot consider that territory as a part of the Union — The legislative council are to be created by the President, & shall they be vested with the power of choosing a delegate to Congress, & who will in fact be the representative of the President — 'Tis wrong.

*Mr. Jackson,* I am opposed to the motion — The people of that country ought not to be represented in Congress. It is too soon.

*Mr. Anderson,* If this amendment does not obtain, I must vote agt. the section — What tax that people without their being represented!

*Mr. Worthington,* What danger can arise from this measure — the delegate can only debate not vote.

*Mr. Bradley,* This delegate will be the representative of your President not of that people — I am surprised to find an advocate for such doctrine — Is the Executive to be represented in the other House — If he can have one delegate to represent him, why not fifty?

*Mr. Dayton,* The motion is unconstitutional — The constitution has provided only for the representation of States, & no man will pretend that Louisiana is a State. It is true by the confederation provision was made for delegates from territories — & our constitution has provided *that all contracts and engagements entered into before its adoption shall be valid* (Art. 6th) but no man will have the hardihood to say that Louisana was included in that engagement.

*Mr. Adams,* I was pleased with this motion — but the objections arising from the Constitution, & from the Delegate's being the representative of the Executive & not of that people — compels me *reluctantly* to decide against it.

*Mr. Cocke,* Gentlemen confound things — this man will not be a representative but a delegate — The government of Louisana has been compared to other territorial governments, as Mississippi — but this is wrong. This is an original system, founded on new principles — it is unlike anything in Heaven, in earth or under it — we must therefore reason from itself & not compare it with others — for myself I admire it. What part of the Constitution shall we violate by this amendment — none. This delegate will not be a constitutional representative, the objection is therefore not solid. I know *that* people are ignorant, but ignorant people will always elect learned and wise men to represent them, they know the necessity of it. — I love & venerate these people — *they live in the west.*

*Mr. Brackenridge,* This amendment is no infringement of the constitution — This officer will not be a representative, for he cannot vote — he will be a delegate, & can only deliberate — He will have no legislative power.

*Mr. S. Smith,* There is nothing in the constitution that precludes the senate from admitting delegates on this floor from the old territories & what is there that can restrain us from admitting Louisiana to send a delegate to the other House? There can be no danger that the delegate will mislead or impose upon the House.

The motion failed yeas 12 nays 18.

### Tuesday, 17th.

The motion to extend the trial by jury in all criminal prosecutions in that territory was lost [96] yeas 11, nays 16.

### Wednesday, 18th.

Samuel Smith's bill, " for the further protection of the seamen of the United States " was debated, but no decision. The real object of this bill is not the security of our seamen, but to afford such protection to foreign seamen that are aboard our merchant-men, as will preclude the nation to which they be-

---

[96] The bill provided for trial by jury, " in all cases which are capital." The motion was to strike out the words " which are capital; " Senate *Journal,* 8 Cong., 1 sess., (1803), 148.

long from retaking them. This measure is to aid merchants
in the southern states in obtaining seamen, to the injury of
the seamen of the eastern states. The provision is in general
terms, but it is designed, & can in fact operate only, against
the British nation, whose people speak our language.

'Tis a clear principle established by the law of nations, that
each nation has an unquestionable right to take their own subjects out of the merchant-ships of any other nation, whenever the Government of a nation judges it necessary to demand
the aid & service of its subjects.

### Thursday 19th.

The same bill debated — but no decision had. —

Passed the bill with amendments " Making appropriations for
the military establishment of the United States for 1804 " — The
appropriations in this law amount to $863351..9. —

### Monday 23d.

The Vice President being absent — after seven repeated trials
John Brown was elected President pro. temp. of the Senate. The
senators from Virginia & others set up Mr. Franklin from North
Carolina — & had not several of the Federalists voted for
Brown, Franklin would eventually have been chosen. I continued my vote for Mr. Tracey — my wish was that the dominant party should themselves decide the election, for every such
event tends to divide & weaken them. The most *violent* censure the moderation of Mr. Brown, & were mortified at his
election.

### Tuesday 24th.

*The bill for the government of Louisana —*

*Mr. Jackson,* The inhabitants of Louisana are not citizens of
the United States — they are now in a state of probation —
They are too ignorant to elect a legislature [97] — they would
consider jurors as a curse to them.

---

[97] The amendment under discussion provided for popular election of
the legislative council; *ibid.,* 156.

*Mr. Maclay* Those people are men and capable of happines — they ought to elect a legislature & have jurors.

*Mr. Saml. Smith,* Those people are absolutely incapable of governing themselves, of electing their rulers or appointing jurors. As soon as they are capable & fit to enjoy liberty & a free government I shall be for giving it to them.

*Mr. Cocke,* The people of that country are free — let them have liberty & a free government — This bill I hope will not pass — it is tyrannical.

*Mr. Nicholas,* I approve of the bill as it is — I am opposed to giving them the rights of election, or the power of having jurors. We ought not *yet* to give that people *self-government.* As soon as it is necessary I will give my assent to that Country's being admitted as a state into the Union.

*Mr. Anderson,* Several gentlemen of the Senate, I am sorry to say it, appear to have no regard for the third article of the treaty — they seem opposed to freedom. This bill has not a single feature of our government in it — it is a system of tyranny, destructive of elective rights — We are bound by treaty, & must give that people, a free elective government.

*Mr. Pickering,* That people are incapable of performing the duties or enjoying the blessings of a free government — They are too ignorant to elect suitable men.

*Mr. Jackson,* Slaves must be admitted into that territory, it cannot be cultivated without them.[98]

*Mr. Brackenridge,* I am against slavery — I hope the time is not far distant when not a slave will exist in this Union. I fear our slaves in the south will produce another St. Domingo.

*Mr. Franklin,* I am wholly opposed to slavery.

*Mr. Dayton,* Slavery must be tolerated, it must be estab-

---

[98] Comparison of the original bill, amendments, and amended bills preserved in the Senate files shows that the Senate at this point began the consideration of an amendment which extended to the new territory the act of February 28, 1803, forbidding importation of slaves into States which prohibited their importation.

lished in that country, or it can never be inhabited. White people cannot cultivate it — your men cannot bear the burning sun & the damp dews of that country — I have traversed a large portion of it. If you permit slaves to go there only from your States, you will soon find there the very worst species of slaves — The slave holders in the United States will collect and send into that country their slaves of the worst description.

*Mr. John Smith*, I know that country — I have spent considerable time there — white men can cultivate it. And if you introduce slaves from foreign Countries into that territory, they will soon become so numerous as to endanger the government & ruin that country. I wish slaves may be admitted there from the United States — I wish our negroes were scattered more equally, not only through the United States, but through our territories — that their power might be lost. I can never too much admire the deep policy of New England in excluding slavery — I thank God we have no slaves in Ohio. —

*Mr. Franklin*, Slavery is in every respect an evil to the States in the south & in the west, it will, I fear, soon become a dreadful one — Negro insurrections have already been frequent — they are alarming — Look in the laws of Virginia & North Carolina made for the purpose of guarding against & suppressing these rebellions, & you will learn our dangers. —

A private letter from Gov. Claiborne, now at New Orleans, to the Secy of State, was communicated by the President to Congress — some passages of the letter was covered with paper — it being an *original* the President requested it to be returned — which was done. From this letter it appears that the Spanish Government in that territory has been very corrupt & wicked — That civil suits were pending that were commenced twenty years since — That persons were found in prison who had lain there ten or twelve years without having a trial. — He says that the people in general are very ignorant & incapable of receiving the blessings of a free government. — And he advises, the raising &

sending some regular troops there, least after the novelty of the present state of things is past, they should prove troublesome.[99]

### Wednesday 25th.

### Bill for the government of Louisiana —

### Question relative to slavery —

*Mr. Bradley,* I am in favor of extending slavery to that country, because it is a right they claim, & by the treaty we are bound to grant it to them — but I think that in this bill we had better say nothing on that subject.

*Mr. Hillhouse,* Negroes are rapidly encreasing in this country — there encrease for the ten years ending with the last census was near two hundred thousand. I consider slavery as a serious evil, & wish to check it wherever I have authority. Will not your slaves, even in the southern states, in case of a war, endanger the peace & security of those states? Encrease the number of slaves in Louisiana, they will in due time rebel — their numbers in the district of Orleans, are now equal to the whites [100] — Why add fuel to this tinder box, which when it takes fire will assuredly extend to some of your states — Why encrease the evil at a distant part of your territory — which must necessarily require a standing army to protect it? If that country cannot be cultivated without slaves, it will instead of being a paradise prove a curse to this country, particularly to some of the states in its vicinity.

*Mr. Bradley,* I am in favor of establishing a form of general, not particular, government — we ought not to descend to particu-

---

[99] See Richardson, *Messages and Papers of the Presidents,* I, 367; Rowland, *Official Letter Books of W. C. C. Claiborne,* I, 322–329.

[100] Hillhouse probably meant the district consisting of the island of New Orleans, with its immediate dependencies. In that case the numbers, according to statistics which had been supplied by Jefferson (*American State Papers. Miscellaneous,* I, 384), were 25,000 whites, 25,000 blacks.

lars — We are incompetent to that — they are too distant from us, & we are ignorant of their wants, their habits & manners. Congress is an improper body to make municipal laws — we have abundant proof of this in our legislation for this district in which we sit — our laws here are very imperfect & insufficient.

*Mr. Adams,* Slavery in a moral sense is an evil; but as connected with commerse it has important uses. The regulations offered to prevent slavery are insufficient, I shall therefore vote against them.

*Mr. Dayton,* I do not wonder at the sentiments of the gentleman from Connecticut, (Mr. Hillhouse) for he has been opposed to everything that relates to Louisiana — he appears to me to wish to render this bill as bad as possible; but I am surprised that gentlemen who are friendly to that country, wish to prohibit slavery — it will bar the cultivation & improvement of that extensive territory. The lives of white people are shorter there than in any of our states, & the labor of slaves more necessary. An elective government & trial by jury would be a curse of that people; but slavery is essential to their existence.

*Mr. Hillhouse,* I do not understand the doctrine nor censures of the gentleman from New Jersey (Mr. Dayton) — The constitution is by him winked out of sight — that admits of a republican government & no other. We must apply the constitution to that people in all cases or in none — We must consider that country as being within the Union or without it — there is no alternative. I think myself they are not a part or parcel of the United States.

*Mr. John Smith.* I have traversed many of the settlements in that country — I know that white men labour there — they are capable of cultivating it — Slaves ought not to be permitted to set their feet there. Introduce slaves there, & they will rebel — That country is full of swamps — negroes can retire to them after they have slain their masters. This was in fact the case not eighteen years since — they rose, slew many, & fled to the morasses.[101] Will you encrease their number, & lay the necessary foundation for the horrors of another St. Domingo? If slaves are admitted there, I fear, we shall have cause to lament the acquisition of that country — it will prove a curse —

*Mr. Jackson.* The treaty forbids this regulation. It will depreciate your lands there fifty pr cent. I am a Rice-planter — my negroes tend three acres each pr man — I never work them hard, they finish their stint by one or two oClock, & then make three shillings pr diem to themselves. I know that a white man cannot cultivate three acres of rice, & yet Georgia is not so warm as Louisiana. You cannot prevent slavery — neither laws moral or human can do it — Men will be governed by their interest, not the law — We must keep the third article of the treaty always in view.

*Mr. Anderson.* On the ground of the interest of the Western states the admission of slaves into Louisiana ought to be opposed — it will prove a curse to us. By the constitution slavery is criminal — All the States, except South Carolina, have passed laws against the importation of Slaves.[102]

*Mr. White.* I think it unfortunate that whenever this question is stirred, feelings should be excited that are calculated to lead us astray. I have entertained the hope that Congress would on all occasions avail themselves of every mean in their power to prevent this disgraceful traffick in *human flesh*. There is nothing in the treaty that guarantees to the people of that Country the *power*, I will not say *right*, of holding slaves. 'Tis our duty to prevent, as far as possible, the horrid evil of slavery — & thereby avoid the fate of St. Domingo. Nothing but the interposition of Heaven, an unusual thunder-storm, prevented the slaves, only two years since, from destroying Richmond in

---

[101] Possibly the reference is to the abortive attempt at insurrection in Pointe Coupée parish in 1795, *eight* years before.

[102] By successive enactments from 1787 to 1803, South Carolina had, like the other states, forbidden the importation of slaves, but these laws had been repealed, December 17, 1803, and the trade reopened.

Virginia.[103] That, & other states are obliged annually to make many severe & expensive provisions to protect & guard the lives of the masters & their families against the violence of the slaves.

It is said that Louisiana cannot be cultivated by *white men* — May not this proceed from the very circumstance of their having slaves — Let white men be accustomed to the culture of that country, & they will, I believe, find they are able to bear the fatigue of it. We may by use, by long habit, be brought to bear heat & fatigue as well as blacks. We boast of liberty & yet in the very bosom of our Country, establish slavery by law. Examine the state of this Union — In the Eastern States where slavery is not suffered, their lands are highly cultivated — their buildings neat, useful & elegant — & the people are strong, powerful & wealthy. But as you travel south, the instant you arrive to where slavery is, you find the lands uncultivated, the buildings decaying & falling into ruins & the people poor, weak & feeble — This is not the effect of climate — for our southern climates are more favorable than the eastern and the northern.

*Mr. Bradley,* I am opposed to slavery in the eastern states; but the resolution under consideration admits the principle of slavery, & therefore I shall vote against it.

*Mr. White,* I shall vote for it not because I wholly approve of it, but because I think it as favorable towards people of colour as anything we can now obtain.

*Mr. Saml Smith,* I am at a loss to know why the gentleman from Massachusetts (Mr. Adams) has so often considered & declared himself as the exclusive advocate for constitutional rights. — I am against this motion — The people of that country wish for African slaves, & we ought to let them have a supply — We have a constitutional right to prohibit slavery in that country, but I doubt as to the policy of it — I shall vote against

---

[103] The reference is to Gabriel's Insurrection, September, 1800.

the motion. — We are bound to provide for the support of the clergy of that country.

*Mr Hillhouse,* The gentleman from Vermont (Mr. Bradley) is opposed to slavery — To prove his opposition he declares he will vote against the resolution, which is designed to limit slavery to those who are in the country — & if he prevails in his opposition, the consequence will be that the people of Louisiana will have the liberty of importing slaves not only from the United States, *but also directly from Africa.* If that country cannot be cultivated without slaves, let slaves hold it — or let it remain a wilderness forever. Those are the real friends of liberty who extend it to others, as well as to themselves.

*Mr. Israel Smith,*[104] The provision proposed, is insufficient — it will rather encrease than prevent slavery. I am opposed to slavery but as Congress cannot prohibit it effectually till 1808 — & as there are many slaves in Louisiana, I think the change proposed will be too sudden — that it will operate as an encouragement to South Carolina to import slaves[105] — I am therefore opposed to doing anything upon the subject at the present.

No vote taken on the subject —

Since the absence of Mr. Burr, Duane has been almost a constant attendant in the area of the Senate chamber — not as a stenographer — no other person has been admitted as a spectator, members of the other House excepted.

### Thursday 26th.
### Government of Louisiana — Slavery —

*Mr. Hillhouse,* I have been accused of being unfriendly to this territory — & of having made the motion now under discussion not from a regard to that country or its inhabitants but to embarrass the measures of government. I was opposed

---

[104] Israel Smith, senator from Vermont.
[105] See note 102.

to the ratification of the treaty, but as that is past, I am bound to act in relation to that country upon such principles as to me appear correct & calculated to promote the general interest of the Nation.  And I hope I shall never find it necessary to adduce evidence to prove the sincerity of my disposition or the truth of my declaration.  It has been said on this floor that I am an *Eastern-man.*  I am so, but *while* I am the representative of a State which is *yet* a member of the *Union,* I hope I shall have as much influence as if I was a *southern man.*  I did not expect *so soon* to hear on this floor the distinction of *eastern & northern, & southern, men.*  Has it indeed come to this — are we to be designated by a *geographical line!*

The question was on the following motion, to wit.

" That it shall not be lawful for any person or persons, to import or bring into the said territory, from any part or place without the limits of the United States, or to cause or procure to be so imported or brought, or knowingly to aid or assist in so importing or bringing, any slave or slaves; & every person so offending & being thereof convicted, before any court within the said territory, having competent jurisdiction, shall forfeit & pay, for each & every slave, so imported or brought the sum of . . . . dollars, one moiety for the use of the United States, & the other moiety, for the use of the person or persons who shall sue for the same; & every slave so imported or brought, shall thereupon become entitled to & receive his or her freedom " —

Note, This amendment was presented by Mr. Hillhouse.[106]

*Mr. Jackson,* Slavery must be established in that country or it must be abandoned.  Without the aid of slaves neither coffee or cotton can be raised.  My interest is to prevent slavery in that country, because that will prevent its settlement, & thereby raise the value of estates in Georgia — but my duty is in this opposed to my interest, & that of my State.

---

[106] Senate *Journal,* 8 Cong., 1 sess., (1803), 160–161.

I think it would be for the real interest of the United States to have an end to slavery in this country; but we cannot get rid of them.

I am against the prohibition — let those people judge for themselves — the treaty is obligatory upon us.

I dislike the traffic in human flesh — but we must decide not on the morality but policy of the case.

The present time is an improper time to prohibit the importation of slaves into that country — our government is not yet established there.

Slaves in America are generally well fed clothed & taken care of — our interest obliges us to do it — they live better than if they were free — they are incapable of liberty.

*Mr. Dayton,* These very debates will encrease the *hopes* of slaves. You are about to prohibit African slaves from that country — & to admit the worst slaves — such as the southern planters wish to sell. — I say admit slaves for slaves must cultivate Louisiana — white people cannot subsist there without them.

The faith of the nation, is by the treaty, pledged to that people, that their rights shall be secured to them — one of their rights is slavery.

It is of importance that we should raise our own sugar — that we can do if we have slaves. —

*Mr. Bradley,* The prohibiting slaves in that territory from Africa, & admitting them from the States, will encrease, not lessen, slavery. Each State can till 1808 import slaves from Africa, & by this law the slave states may send their vicious slaves to Louisiana.

*Mr. Brackenridge,* I have no hesitation in saying, That the treaty does not in the smallest degree authorize that people to hold slaves — much less does it pledge the faith of the Union to support this unjust, unnatural traffic. When I look at the Census, I am alarmed at the encrease of slaves in the southern states. I consider slavery as an evil — & am for confining it within as small a compass as possible.

*Mr. Bradley,* I am against slavery — but this provision is insufficient, & I shall vote against it. If the States holding slaves, require it, I will go as far as they wish in abolishing slavery, for I am an enemy to it. But that time is not yet come — the public mind is not ready for it — & I think we had now better do nothing upon the subject.

*Mr. Samuel Smith,* I am sorry this proposition is brought before the Senate — I am against slavery — but I shall vote against this proposition — & I fear it will therefore appear that I am in favor of slavery — Yet let it be remembered, that although I am a slave holder, I declare I disapprove of slavery.

*Mr. Franklin,* My wish is to prohibit slaves altogether from that country, except those carried thither by actual settlers from the United States — but I dispair of obtaining such a vote in Senate — I will vote for such a prohibition as I can obtain.

I have no objection to sending a frigate to Charlestown to prevent the landing of slaves from Africa imported by South Carolina — & *frittering those nefarious traders to pieces.*

*Mr. Jackson,* Gentlemen from the north & the east do not know that *white men* cannot indure the heat of a vertical sun — they cannot cultivate & raise a crop of rice — negroes are necessary for that country. It is as impossible to prevent the importation of them into that country as to move the sun into the moon — Human power & invention cannot prevent it. Within less than a year 10,000 slaves have against law been imported into South Carolina & Georgia.[107] 'Tis in vain to make laws upon this subject. Slaves directly from Africa are preferable to those who have been long in this country

---

[107] See the statements of Lowndes of South Carolina and Mitchill of New York in the House debate of February 14, 1804; *Annals of Congress,* 8 Cong., 1 sess., 992–1000.

or even to those born here. I am sorry that the constitution of Georgia prohibits slavery.[108]

*Mr. Pickering,* When this subject was first brought up I was favorably inclined to the admission of slavery in that territory — but the discussion has convinced me that it will be bad policy indeed to admit slaves there — that it will entail upon their posterity a burthen they will be unable to bear or remove — & that slaves are unnecessary there — white people can cultivate it — I therefore approve of the resolution.

*Mr. Bradley* This resolution supports slavery therefore I shall vote against it, although it is bro't forward by those who wish to destroy slavery. The Constitution of Vermont declares all men free — I have sworn to support it, & I will.

*Mr. Israel Smith,* I am opposed to this resolution, because it will not prevent slavery — I am opposed to slavery; but I think no law can prevent or destroy it — the law will be useless & therefore I shall vote against it. If a law was made to prohibit the use of cyder in New England, where it is now used in every family, could you carry it into effect. — This is the case of slaves in that country — We cannot till **1808** pass any effectual law against slavery — South Carolina has opened its ports for the importation of slaves from Africa, & this she has a *right* to do.

The people of Louisiana ought not to be subject to much change in government, laws, or habits at present — They are not yet bound to us by any ties — This resolution will estrange them from us — it will oppress them — It cannot be carried into effect — It will give encouragement to the States in **1808** to resist any laws we may then constitutionally make to abolish slavery. I therefore hope we shall *now* do nothing relative to slavery.

*Mr. Samuel Smith,* I wish I could prevent the taking of the

---

[108] The constitution of Georgia, 1798, art. IV, sect. 11, prohibited, not slavery, but the future importation of slaves into that State from Africa or any foreign place.

yeas and nays when the Senate are sitting in Committee of the whole — I dislike it — it is absurd.[109] —

*Mr. Jackson,* It is now more than half past three P. M. & I move for an adjournment — Refused. — He then said, It is unfair for a *majority* thus to press the subject.

The question was then taken on the amendment (page 316.) [110] & prevailed, yeas 21 nays 6.

We passed the Act making Appropriations for the Navy of the United States for 1804 — The sums appropriated by this law amount to $650,000. —

*Mr. Bradley,* As tomorrow is to be a day of festivity on account of the acquisition of Louisiana, I move that the Senate adjourn to Monday next —

Negatived —

After the senate was adjourned, he said, with great passion that he would not on the morrow either attend the Senate or the feast.  He kept his word. —

### House of Representatives.

In the bill giving effect to the Laws of the United States within Louisiana, the question was whether Natchez should be a port of entry as it stood in the bill.  Mr. J. Randolph was violently opposed to the motion to strike it out.  Several of the leading democrats differed from him in opinion, & considered his opposition as imprudent — & the debate was by many of the party considered as a mere question respecting his *personal influence* — & they with great spirit resolved to shew their independence & voted against him — The motion prevailed yeas 84, nays 40.[111]  Some of the democrats in the hearing of federalists said that *Randolph was assuming & very arrogant & that*

---

109 See J. Q. Adams, *Memoirs,* I, 292–293.
110 Page 118 of this volume.
111 The vote is given in *Annals of Congress,* 8 Cong., 1 sess., 950, but there is no report of the debate.

*they hated him.* His manners are far from conciliating — Many of the party dislike him — & on trifling measures they quarrel with him, but on all measures that are really important to the party they unite with him. He is *necessary* to them — they know it — he knows it — & they dare not discard him. These frequent quarrels may eventually sour their minds against him, & prevent a reunion — A *few* of them consider themselves as *personally* injured by him, they will probably never *cordially* unite with him — but at present, with the majority of them its like the bickerings of lovers who contend but afterwards unite with greater zeal.

### Friday 27th.

Few senators attended — at 12 oClock we adjourned to Monday. —

The democratic members of Congress gave a feast this day at Stelle's Hotel in celebration of the accession of Louisiana. Three pieces of cannon were bro't up from the Navy yard & placed on Capitol Hill, & were discharged at twelve oClock & after dinner. The President Vice President & Heads of Departments were invited & dined as guests.

After the President & Vice President retired, this toast was given " The President of the United States " — & accompanied with three cheers. The next toast " The Vice President," few cheered him, & many declined drinking it, particularly Macon, Randolph, Nicholson &c. Genl Varnum one of the Vice Presidents of the day was requested to give a volunteer, he gave " The union of all parties "; This was ill received — some refused to drink it. Mr. Nicholson, another Vice President, gave " The tempestuous sea of Liberty, may never be calm." — some of the company would not swallow this. — Mr. Adams, Mr. Dayton & Mr. Huger, federalists were of the party. A number of the guests drank so many toasts that in the night they returned to their houses without their hats.[112]

---

[112] See J. Q. Adams, *Memoirs,* I, 293.

## Monday 30th.

Mr. Hillhouse moved the following amendment, to the Louisiana bill —

" That no male person bro't into said territory of Louisiana, from any part of the United States, or territories thereof, or from any province or colony in America, belonging to any foreign prince or state, after the . . . . day of . . . . next, ought or can beholden by law to serve for more than the term of one year, any person as a servant, slave, or apprentice, after he attains the age of 21 years; nor female in like manner, after she attains the age of 18 years, unless they are bound by their own voluntary act, after they arrive to such age, or bound by law for the payment of debts, damages, fines, or costs. *Provided,* that no person held to service or labor in either of the States or territories aforesaid, under the laws thereof, escaping into said territory of Louisiana, shall by anything contained herein, be discharged from such service or labor, but shall be delivered up in the manner prescribed by law." [113]

*Mr. Hillhouse,* I am in favor of excluding slavery from that Country altogether — Every slave increases the necessity of a standing army — Every slave weakens the power of the militia — The *distance* from the States encreases the necessity of excluding slavery there.

*Mr. Bradley,* made a few observations in support of the amendment.

It was rejected yeas 11, nays 17. —

*Mr. Hillhouse* then offered the following amendment,

" That it shall not be lawful for any person or persons, to import or bring into the said territory, from any port or place within the limits of the United States, or cause to, or procure to be so imported or bro't, or knowingly to aid or assist in so importing or bringing, any slave or slaves, which shall have

---

[113] See Senate *Journal,* 8 Cong., 1 sess., (1803), 164–165.

been imported, since that day . . . . into any port or place within the limits of the United States, from any port or place from without the limits of the United States; & every person so offending & being thereof convicted, before any court within the said territory, having competent jurisdiction, shall forfeit & pay for each & every such slave, so imported or bro't, the sum of . . . . dollars one moiety for the use of the person or persons who shall sue for the same." [114]

*Mr. Hillhouse*, observed this was but a part of the system necessary to be adopted.

*Mr. Dayton*, South Carolina has now a constitutional right to import slaves from Africa — she is in the exercise of that right — and this amendment impairs it. —

*Mr. Hillhouse*, It does, & justly.

*Mr. Jackson*, It is unfortunate that we have slaves; but having them we cannot with safety or policy free them. A very few *free negroes* in Louisiana would revolutionize that country. In Georgia we prohibit men from manumitting their slaves [115] — One free slave is more dangerous where there are slaves than a 100 slaves. I will join to *export* all the slaves.

*Mr. Hillhouse*, I beleive slavery is a real evil; but I am sensible we must extinguish it by degrees — It will not do to attempt to manumit all the slaves at once — Such a measure would be attended with serious evils — These slaves are men — they have the passions & feelings of men — And I believe if we were slaves, we should not be more docile, more submissive, or virtuous than the negroes are.

*Mr. Nicholas*, Free men of *colour* have a very ill effect upon slaves — they do much more mischief than strangers conceive of. —

[114] The amendment presented at this time by Hillhouse, (Senate *Journal*, 166), embraces both this text and that which appears at the beginning of the next day's proceedings.

[115] A Georgia act of 1801 made manumission illegal unless accomplished by an act of the legislature; Cobb, *Digest*, 983.

*Mr. Adams,* The general complaint against gentlemen from the eastern States has been that they have discovered too much opposition to slavery. I am opposed to slavery; but I have in this bill voted against the provisions introduced to prohibit & lessen it. I have done this upon two principles, 1. That I am opposed to legislating at all for that country — 2. I think we are proceeding with too much haste on such an important question.

*Mr. Bradley,* I abhor slavery — I am opposed to it in every shape — *He that steals a man & sells him ought to die* [116] — I will on every occasion vote against slavery — I am very sorry the question is *now* called up, — I have done everything I could to prevent it — but since gentlemen, (& many of them from Slave States) will stir the question, I am prepared & will on all occasions vote against slavery.

The amendment was adopted, yeas 21, nays 7.

### *In the House of Representatives —*

On the question to bring in a bill " to discontinue the office of Commissioner of loans in the several States " — Mr. John Randolph Jr said he should on this question vote against the resolution & doing it he should vote against the conviction of his own mind, & for the sake of gratifying his friends from Massachusetts, (Eustis & Varnum) New York (Mitchell) & Pennsylvania (Clay). Gregg of Pennsylvania complained that the gentleman was *partial* to his friends — that in *one* state he preferred one gentleman to all the residue of the delegation. Some of the members whispered, That Randolph's conduct was a display of weakness exhibited to preserve his popularity. The motion was negatived, yeas 52, nays 58.[117] — Administration is alarmed on the subject. —

---

[116] Exodus, XXI, 16.
[117] See *Annals of Congress,* 8 Cong., 1 sess., 952–959.

## Tuesday 31.

### Bill relating to Louisiana —

Motion to strike out the following words from the amendment to the bill —

"And no slave or slaves shall directly or indirrectly be introduced into said territory, except by a person or persons removing into said territory for actual settlement, & being at the same time of such removal *bona fide* owner of such slave or slaves; & every slave imported or bro't into the said territory, contrary to the provisions of this act, shall thereupon be entitled to, & receive his or her freedom. " [118]

*Mr. Bradley,* I am opposed to this paragraph, because it admits the doctrine of slavery to be just — it is like a law regulating theft or any other crime, I shall therefore vote to expunge it. — I really consider slavery as a moral evil — as a violation of the laws of God — of Nature — of Vermont.

*Mr. Nicholas,* The gentleman from Vermont (Mr. Bradley) has surprised me by his extraordinary conduct — for several days he spoke & voted with his friends who advocated slavery — but yesterday & today he has avowed other sentiments & changed his vote — He is now become vociferous for emancipation — Is he apprehensive the restriction will prevail — Is he afraid of finding his name on the journal against the vote — Why this unaccountable change?

*Mr. Bradley,* I have not changed my sentiments — I was unwilling to have the question stirred — I was desirous of shutting my eyes against the subject — but since I am compelled to act, I will vote in favor of *liberty.*

*Mr. Jackson,* If this law with these amendments passes you destroy that country — you render it useless — You will excite alarms in the minds of Frenchmen — you will render a standing

---

[118] See note 114.

army necessary. I again say that country cannot be cultivated without slaves — it never will.

*Mr. John Smith,* I am willing to admit slaves into that country from the U. S., because slaves are already there, but I am unwilling to admit them from Africa — You cannot prevent slaves going there from the United States, I know this is an evil, but it is an evil they will have.

*Mr. Saml Smith,* When the prohibition of slavery was first introduced into this bill I was much alarmed. I foresaw it would take up time — that it would create alarm & even endanger the peace & security of these States holding slaves — especially when the subject is debated in the other House — & those debates published in Newspapers. God knows that I am not friendly to slavery, although I own slaves & live in a state where slavery is established by law. I am unwilling to think much less to speak on this subject. This bill if passed into a law cannot be carried into effect — the people of that country will not submit to it. It will render a standing army necessary — In the year 1808 we may then effectually legislate on the subject — the constitution will then admit of it, & our navy will then enable us to carry it into affect. American slaves carried into Louisiana will prove adders that will sting that people to the heart. — The report of your debate in this Senate on this subject will reach that country in twelve days, & I fear will produce a rebellion — Our troops there are few & feeble, & will be unable to prevent it.

*Mr. John Smith,* If the slaves now in the southern States continue to encrease in 20 or 30 years those States will be compelled to call on the eastern and western states to aid them against their rebellious slaves.

*Mr. Franklin,* We cannot wink this subject out of sight — if we leave it, it will follow us. We must make laws against slavery, unless we mean to aid the destruction of our southern States, by laying the foundation for another St. Domingo.

Slavery is a dreadful evil — we *feel* it in North Carolina — we can emancipate — I am for restraining foreign importation, but to proceed no further.

*Mr. Brackenridge,* We can make laws to prevent slaves, & we can carry those laws into effect — if we cannot do this our power is too feeble to govern this nation — We must not despair — we must act. We are legislating for a great country — for an important section of the nation. In doing this I will not for a moment attend to its immediate effects, whether it will lessen or encrease sugar, or other articles — No Sir, I extend my views to posterity. It is of importance that our first acts of Legislation should be correct. Can it be right to extend & foister slavery into that country?

I think it good policy to permit slaves to be sent there from the United States. This will disperse and weaken that race — & free the southern states from a part of its black population, & of its danger. If you do not permit slaves from the United States to go there, you will thereby prohibit men of wealth from the southern States going to settle in that country.

It has been said by the gentleman from Vermont (Mr. Bradley) *that liberty cannot exist with slavery.* This is not correct — *it* exists in those states who have slaves — Our constitution recognizes *slavery* — it does more it expressly *protects it.*

*Mr. Nicholas.* One State only, South Carolina, can now import slaves — & that is a *right* derived not from Congress, but from the constitution — it is a mere temporary right. The people of Louisiana cannot therefore complain of partiality in Congress because we deny them the liberty of importing foreign slaves — It is no more than what we long since denied to the Mississippi & Ohio territories. We are now making a form of government for Louisiana, not establishing a common & ordinary law — I am for prohibiting the people of that country from importing slaves from foreign countries, & leave it optional with the government of Louisiana, when they have one, to prohibit it from the United States also, if they should think best.

*Mr. Adams,* I do not like either of the amendments that have been offered, but if I must vote for either it will be to retain the words moved to be struck out — If I must vote it will be in favor of liberty.  The Constitution does not recognize *slavery* — it contains no such *word* — a great circumlocution of words is used merely to avoid the term *slaves.*

*Mr. Venable,* I know the constitution does not contain the *word* slave — but it admits the *thing* & protects it — & Congress have uniformly acted accordingly.

The question for striking out was lost, yeas 13, nays 15.*

\* It is obvious that the zeal displayed by the Senate from the Slave States, to prohibit the foreign importation of Slaves into Louisiana, proceeds from the motive to raise the price of their own slaves in the markett — & to encrease the means of disposing of those who are most turbulent & dangerous to them.

### *In the House of Representatives.*

On the question *that the postmaster general's salary be $3500.*

*Mr. Lucas.* I am opposed — this sum is too much — All that is necessary in a postmaster general is mechannical talents, honesty & constant industry.  If the present officer has high talents they are *surplusage,* & for that surplusage we ought to make no allowance.  This officer is not of the privey Council of State — He cannot be considered as a candidate for either the presidency or vice presidency — He is at little expence in entertaining company —

In committee of the Whole House the motion prevailed, but on taking the vote in the House by yeas & nays it was rejected, yeas 53, nays 66.[119]  This difference in the vote proceeded from a fear of offending the sovereign people.  This entering the yeas & nays has an astonishing effect, on fools & knaves.

Mr. Lucas is a member from Pennsylvania, & is the **same**

---

[119] See *Annals of Congress,* 8 Cong., 1 sess., 962.

man who brought forward the impeachment against the celebrated Judge Addisson.[120]   Lucas is a frenchman — speaks
very broken English — is a man of some talents & information — he frequently speaks in the House. He lately observed, that Mr. Gallatin by his complaints & blustering had
raised himself to an important & lucrative office — & he
thought the same means prudently & steadily pursued would
produce the same effect.

### *Wednesday [Feb.] 1.*

*Bill for the government of Louisiana* — It was moved by
Mr. Hillhouse to amend it by adding the following, —

" And no slave or slaves shall directly or indirectly be introduced into the said territory, except by *a citizen of the
United States*,[121] removing into said territory, for actual
settlement, & being at the time of such removal *bona fide*
owner of such slave or slaves; & every slave imported or
brought into the said territory, contrary to the provisions of
this act, shall thereupon be entitled to, & receive his or her
freedom."

*Mr. Jackson*, I move to postpone the further consideration
of this amendment to September.

*Mr. Hillhouse*, This being an amendment to a bill it cannot
be postponed unless the bill is postponed with it.

*The President*,[122] The motion is not in order — it cannot be
recd.

*Mr. Wright*, The owners of land in that country who do not
live there ought to have liberty of sending their slaves to
cultivate their own land but not to sell their slaves there.

---

[120] See McMaster, *History of the People of the United States*, III,
154–157.

[121] The words which Plumer has underlined are the new matter, sub-
stituted for " person or persons."

[122] Senator John Brown of Kentucky. See page 110.

It is wrong to reproach us with the *immorality of slavery* — that is a crime we must answer at the bar of God — we ought not therefore to answer it here — for it would be unjust that we should be punished twice for the same offence.

I am against admitting *foreign slaves,* because the state of Maryland has declared it *wrong.*[123]

*Mr. Jackson.* This amendment does not authorize foreigners who may go to settle in that country to carry their slaves with them, I am therefore on this ground opposed to the amendment. The great object we should have in view should be the settlement of that country — Our interest is to admit Englishmen there as soon & as fast as possible.

*Mr. Hillhouse,* I hope foreigners will not be permitted to settle in that *distant* country — It is seldom, that any but the *worst* of men leave their own to settle in a foreign country.

*Mr. Jackson,* I am not afraid of such evils. The *friends of liberty only will come* — let us encourage the settlement of that country as much as possible — It is dangerous to exclude foreigners. The very best of men will flee from Europe — for liberty exists only in this country — Bad men are afraid to come here — they are encouraged to stay at home. I *trust the present Congress are not apprehensive of having too many Jacobins in this Country.* The government & the Congress were five years ago afraid of Jacobins — I hope we are not like them.

*Mr. Pickering,* I am very willing that foreigners should be admitted to settle in that country — for I beleive before we purchase that we had territory in the United States sufficient for *us* & *our* posterity to the thousandth generation. I am willing that in Louisiana oppressed humanity should find an assylum, & that the patriots of no country should there find a Country in which no restraints should be imposed upon them.

It was then moved to strike out of the amendment the words

---

[123] Maryland act of 1796, c. 67.

*citizen of the United States* & insert *person.* The motion was lost yeas **13** nays **14.**[124]

The question was then carried on the amendment, yeas **18,** nays **11.**

*Mr. Jackson* If you establish a regular government there, you will destroy the western States, by the strong inducements you will hold out to people to settle Louisiana. The cession will prove a curse — why invite people to settle it now — it is too soon — 50 or 100 years hence will be soon enough. By exposing these immense tracts of uncultivated lands to sale you will encourage bribery. I was offered half a million of acres to hold my tongue in the Georgia speculation — *I* had *virtue* to resist the temptation.[125]

The settlement of Louisiana will destroy the value of our lands — It will effect what I very much deprecate a *seperation* of this Union.

How great, how powerful, was Spain before she acquired South America — Her wealth has debased & enervated her strength. If you establish a regular government in Louisiana, that will be settled — you cannot then prevent it — & if settled, such is the enterprising spirit & avaricious disposition of Americans that they will then soon conquer South America, & the rich mines of that country will prove our ruin. A military government ought to be established in upper Louisiana — that would prevent settlement — I would pay those Americans who are now there for their lands if they would quit them.

*Mr. Cocke,* I am glad Georgia has one uncorrupt man, & I rejoice that he is a Senator — I trust we have many such in the nation — I am ready to vote — The debate on this bill has been so long that I have already lost the benefit of much of it, for I have really forgotten it. I can throw no new light — I call

---

[124] This motion does not appear in the Senate *Journal* (1803).
[125] In 1796 Jackson was the leader of the "Anti-Yazoo Party" in the Georgia house of representatives, having resigned his seat in the United States Senate in order to conduct the contest.

for the question — We must give that people a rational government.

*Mr. Worthington,* The government contemplated by this bill is a military despotism, & I am surprised that it finds an advocate in this enlightened Senate. The gentleman from Georgia (Mr. Jackson) talks of a *seperation* — Sir, the *western states* will not seperate unless the *eastern States* by their conduct render it absolutely *necessary.*

## Thursday 2d.

### Government of Louisiana —

*Motion to strike out the 8th section of the bill.*[126]

*Mr. Hillhouse,* I am against the establishment of an arbitrary government in that country — It has been said it is best to establish such government in that country as will prevent its settlement — I wish gentlemen to consider, that by the treaty the rights of the inhabitants of that country are guaranteed to them — Look at documents now on your tables, by them it appears that much of those vacant or uncultivated lands are granted to Spaniards — And you must give to them such a government as they can live under, or you will not protect them in the enjoyment of their rights as you have by your treaty stipulated. — You must give that people a practical government — not like our own, for they are unacquainted with it — a military government would be too arbitary — I would not give them a trial by jury, because they are not used to it — but I would give them the liberty of having trial by jury whenever they are able to express their desire of it by their own legis-ture [sic] & to make laws regulating that mode of trial. —

---

[126] The eighth section of the original bill, with slight modifications, is quoted in the Senate *Journal* (1803), 174. It relates to the government of the portion of the Louisiana cession north of the territory of Orleans, and provides for rule by a governor having the executive and judicial powers exercised by the former governors of the province.

*Mr. John Smith,* The establishment of a Military government is at war with the third article of the treaty — with the letter & spirit of your constitution — which knows no other government than that of Republicanism. That country is now ours — & it will be utterly impossible, by any law you can pass, to prevent people from emigrating to & settling in that country. Reference is frequently made to the documents that the President has sent us respecting that country — Those documents are incorrect — I know of three large settlements in that country that are not even named in these papers — We know but little of that Country.

*Mr. Cocke,* Give that country a Jury. — I know we can pre- it. The only way to govern that country safely is to govern ment — I prefer a *bad* one to a good one *for them* — because a bad one will make them contented, they have been used to it. The only way to govern that country safely is to govern it justly — Let them have their old laws & ancient customs, except a trial by jury & that they *should have.* Too much wisdom is painful — it conjures up too many evils — I fear we are too wise to do good. Our way is plain, it is the old way — but I am really afraid we are fond of projects — novelties. Our fears are chimerical — We should be bold & resolute. Tell that people you shall have justice, but you shall obey the laws. I have taken up much of your time, but coming from the westward, I have frequently been urged to tell my opinion — no arbitrary — no military government will do — we must give them a free government. We talk too much of the ignorance of that people they know more than what you think they do — they are not so plagay ignorant. —

*Mr. Jackson* Rome flourished while she confined herself within proper bounds — but she extended her limits too far — when she gratified her insatiable thirst for lands — the northern hordes overwhelmed & destroyed her — I fear this will be our case in the *south.* I never wish to see our people go beyond the Mississippi. We ought not to give them such a government as will afford them protection in their settlements. If you permit the settlement of that country, you will depreciate the value of your public lands & destroy the western states. I know the President approves of this eight section.

*Mr. Anderson,* This 8th section is a military despotism — its unconstitutional — its opposed to the spirit & genius of our constitution. The only power we have to legislate for that country is derived from the constitution — & we must give them a republican government — we can give them no other.

There never existed on earth a free Republican Government untill the present government of the United States.

This section establishes the former laws & government of Spain in that Country — & what those are we know not.

I know the settlement of Louisiana will materially injure Tennessee — it will injure all the western states — still we must give them a constitutional government. I am for preventing the settlement of that country by law, & I think our laws may be executed.

There is now about 8000 inhabitants in Upper Louisiana — more than two-thirds of them are Americans — most of them have emigrated from Virginia — they understand & will demand their rights.

If the President of the United States now approves of this 8th section — & should it be adopted, I will venture to say he will soon have more cause to repent of it.

*Mr. Dayton,* I ask the gentleman (Mr. Anderson) where, & in what part of the Constitution does he find any authority to legislate for that Country — The constitution gives us no authority on the subject — We derive our power & right from the nature of government — That Country is a purchased territory & we may govern it as a conquered one.

A military government is the best & the only government you can prudently & safely establish in Upper Louisiana. A strong efficient government is essential. — I hope we shall prevent the settlement of Upper Louisiana, not only for the present, but forever — If that country is settled — the people will seperate from us — they will form a new empire — & become our enemies.

I beleive we may induce the Indians on this side to remove to the other side of the Mississippi — & this will be a great & useful thing to us.[127]

This section of the bill is important & will I hope be retained.

*Mr. Wright,* I am in favor of the section, The constitution requires that the governments of States should be republican, but not so of territorial governments — The Territorial governments in this Country are not, or is it necessary they should be, republican — none of them have the power to elect representatives.

To extend the trial by jury to that country would be a denial of Justice — they live too remote from each other to derive any benefit from it.

*Mr. Samuel Smith,* This 8th section embraces a country in which there are settlements 800 miles distant from each other. A governor & three Judges cannot regulate their affairs. This section of the bill is in principle republican — we ourselves are their Legislators & the Commandants are only our agents.

*Mr. Pickering,* I think we are in an error in applying the Constitution to that country — it does not extend there. But we are bound by the treaty to extend protection to the people of that country, & secure to them their rights & priveledges. We must consider & govern them as a colony.

Laws will never be sufficient to prevent the settlement of that country — If people find their interest in settling it, your prohibitions will prove unavailing.

---

[127] See Miss Abel, " History of Events resulting in Indian Consolidation West of the Mississippi," in *Annual Report* of the American Historical Association for 1906, I, 241–249.

*Mr. Brackenridge,* I do not feel any constitutional difficulty as to the form of government — I am for giving them such a system as to me appears best — The provisions contained in this 8th section are arbitary — there is no legislative authority given to that people — I am opposed to the section.

*Mr. Nicholas,* I am glad the section gives no legislative authority — that country needs none — I am inimical to change — Do as little for that people as possible — Let them have & enjoy their old laws & customs.

*Mr. Wright,* I would have such a despotic government in the Upper Louisiana as should absolutely prevent people from settling it. I would remove those who are now settled there, if I could — but at all events I would let no more go there.

*Mr. Cocke,* I will always give a good government when I can — I will not do evil meerly because I have the power of doing so — The question —

The question was then taken & the 8th section was struck out — yeas 16. nays 9.

*See Journal of Senate p. 174.*[128]

### *Friday 3d.*

*The bill for the government of Louisiana under consideration.*[129]

*Mr. Jackson,* I have high authority for saying it is the intention of our government to take effectual measures to induce all the Indians on this side of the Mississippi to exchange their lands for lands in upper Louisiana.[130] I think it a prudent & practicable measure — & that is one reason why I wish to pre-

---

[128] Page reference to the original edition (1803).

[129] Debate was apparently on an amendment not mentioned in the Senate *Journal* but preserved in manuscript in the Senate files, giving Upper Louisiana a territorial government of the simplest form, with its own governor, secretary, and judges, and with legislative power vested in the governor and judges. This amendment is endorsed "Breckinridge."

[130] For Jefferson's course in the matter see Miss Abel, *loc. cit.*

vent the establishment of a civil government in that territory. In the name of God have we not land enough for a settlement without this! I would buy up the title of those who have already gone there. The Indians would have gone there before this had not the Spaniards have prevented them. The Indian wars have cost us millions of dollars — & much blood — They are bad dangerous neighbors. There are already many Indians there — if you establish a civil government — if you permit settlers — you will find the expense of that government immense — it will render the purchase a curse.

*Mr. Worthington,* The Indiania Territory is as good soil & situation as Upper Louisiana. There has been settlers in the former for 100 years, & a civil government established for some time — that government has not encreased settlers — And in *all* the Indiana Territory there are not now more than 7000 souls.

*Mr. Nicholas,* I hope the Upper Louisiana will not for many, very many years, be admitted as a State or States — New Orleans, perhaps must soon be admitted as such.

*Mr. Jackson,* I move to annex Upper Louisiana to the Indiana Territory.

*Mr. Brackenridge,* I have little objections to this.

*Mr. Hillhouse,* The governments, laws, customs, manners & habits of the two countries are in direct opposition to each other. The regulations of the one cannot be established in the other — You cannot immediately effect such a change.

*Mr. Saml Smith,* I approve of the measure — It will lessen the number of offices & of course expence — I know it will estop slavery there,[131] & to that I agree.

*Mr. Wright,* This is a new proposition, but I am in favor of it — it will lessen expence — I would unite the two territories governmentally but not territorially.

*Mr. Hillhouse* Both of those Countries have seperate *rights,*

---

[131] By provision of the Ordinance of 1787.

& by this regulation you will impair them both. The ordinance establishing the Indiana Territory created certain rights which are vested in the inhabitants of that territory. The people in Louisiana have their *rights* & we have by treaty guaranteed to them the enjoyment of those rights. If these territories are united who will legislate for them — Must they be governed by different laws — This union will make one of the territories a mere colony to the other.

*Mr. Wright.* They must be governed by different laws.—

*Mr. John Smith.* I cannot wholly approve of the motion I think there is might in the argument of the gentleman from Connecticut (Mr. Hillhouse) — But I will accord with the majority. I should be better pleased if a part of Upper Louisiana was annexed to the Mississippi Territory.

*Mr. Venable.* I approve of the principle, but wish it modified. It is not yet settled that Louisiana is a part of the United States — I would not therefore annex the two territories together; but I would extend the authority of the government of the Indiana territory to the territory of Upper Louisiana.

### *Tuesday 7th.*

*The bill for the government of Louisiana* —

The debates on this bill was principally confined to the question whether people of *colour* should be necessarily disqualified & excluded from serving on juries. — Excluded — Democrats in general voted in favor of exclusion.

### *Wednesday 8th.*

*Same Bill.*

The amendment to annex the upper Territory of Louisiana to Indiana, was withdrawn.

Mr. Nicholas offered an amendment authorizing the officers of the Indiana Territory to govern the Upper District of Louisiana — & establishing the existing laws of Louisiana in that district.[132] — Adopted.    Act as amended ordered to be printed.

The democratic senators held a Caucus last evening in which they settled the principles of the bill — & agreed to the same in the Senate without any debate.[133]

## Thursday 9.

The British Convention respecting boundaries under consideration — All the democrats except those from Vermont voted to expunge the 5th article — carried — voted unanimously to advise to the ratification of the remainder.[134]

## Tuesday 14

The House sent us a bill to reduce the *Marine Corps* [135] — The question of its passing to a second reading was negatived by a silent vote 8 yeas, 18 nays.    This was a humiliating decision to Jefferson, Nicholas, Leib [136] & others — They were taken by surprise — Brackenridge turned pale — It has been an object with the President to destroy Col. Burrows the Commandant of this Corps & to reduce their numbers — Repeated, but unavailing, attempts have been made at this & former sessions to reduce the corps, & have them commanded by an officer of an inferior grade to that of Lt. Col. Commandant. — Col. Burrows is the favorite of Mr. Burr — he is suspected of federalism — crimes that appear of a deep dye in the mind of Jefferson. —

---

[132] This amendment, in manuscript, is in the Senate files, and also appears in the bill as amended (and in the statute) as sect. 12.

[133] Some amendments offered on subsequent days appear in the Senate *Journal,* but Plumer records no debates respecting them.

[134] See Senate *Executive Journal* (printed 1828), I, 463–464; *American State Papers,* II.    *Foreign Relations,* II, 584–591.

[135] The bill provided for reduction of the officers of the Marine Corps to one captain and twelve lieutenants, and empowered the President, at any future period, when in his opinion it might be necessary, to augment the number of officers so as not to exceed those at present authorized by law.    The House *Journal* (1801–1804), vol. IV, 579, reports the bill as having passed the Senate.    The Senate *Journal* (1803, p. 195), reports that the bill was lost, thus supporting Plumer's statement.

[136] Michael Leib, representative from Pennsylvania, reported the bill favorably from the committee to whom it had been referred.

'Tis more than a year since any vacancies have been filled in this corps though several have happened — *Rank* is dear to military men — more so than pay — But this studied, unprecedented, neglect while it shews the *meanness* of the President, has not been able to drive several officers of merit from the service of their country.

The salary bill — the same as established in 1799 passed — to continue 3 years & more, yeas 20, nays 8.[137]

### Thursday 16th

*Louisiana bill.* Salaries to the officers — Governor of Orleans Mr. Jackson, Mr. Dayton, Mr. Saml Smith & Mr. Logan [138] reasoned in favor of $8000 pr annum — 7 only voted for it. Mr. Brackenridge & John Smith for $6000. 12 voted for it. Mr. Olcott,[139] Franklin & Cocke for $5000. 18 voted for it — carried —

The salary to the Secretary $2000
Three Judges each              2000
District Judge                 2000
Attorney                        600
Marshall                        200

The members of the Legislative Council each to have four dollars pr diem while attending the Council.

In the course of the debate, Jackson & Samuel Smith observed " That the people must be governed more by pomp, parade & shew than by reason — that splendid retinue & armed men are more convincing than arguments.

### Friday 17.

*Louisiana bill.*

*Mr. Stone.*[140] There are near 900000 slaves in the U. S. &

---

[137] The salary bill was not passed until the next day, February 15; see Senate *Journal* (1803), 197–198.

[138] George Logan, senator from Pennsylvania.

[139] Simeon Olcott, senator from New Hampshire.

[140] David Stone, senator from North Carolina.

they are worth $200,000,000. Slaves are property — The rights of property are by the Constitution guaranteed & why should the holders of this kind of property be prohibited from sending & selling their slaves in Lousiana?

*Mr. McClay.* That country was purchased to serve as an *outlet* for the U. S. — to admit slaves there will defeat that object.

*Mr. Jackson* It has been proposed to prohibit South Carolina from sending slaves into Louisiana, because she imports slaves from Africa. She has a right to do it — If you pass this prohibition you will offend that State — & I venture to say very serious consequences will follow — I will speak plain — offend her & she will reject the amendment to the Constitution — & if she rejects it, it will never be ratified.

Some people laugh at the provision that the bill contains authorizing the President to make an exchange of lands in Louisiana with the Indians for their lands on this side of the Mississippi. Let me tell such, that this is a favorite measure of the President's — he has assured me so — He has, this week, informed me that sixteen of the Cherokee Chiefs have already agreed to pass over to Louisiana & relinquish their lands on this side of the Mississippi.

### Saturday 18th.

*Bill for the government of Louisiana.*

*Mr. Adams,* This bill is to establish a form of government for the extensive country of Louisiana. I have from the beginning been opposed to it — & I still am. It is forming a government for that people without their consent & against their will.

All power in a republican government is derived from the *people* — We sit here under their authority.

The people of that country have given no power or authority to us to legislate for them — The people of the United States could give us none, because they had none themselves. The treaty has given us none, for they were not parties to it — it was made without their knowledge. To pass this bill is an encroachment on their rights — its a commencement of assumed power — its establishing a precedent for after Congress's destructive of the essential principles of genuine liberty.

The first territorial Ordinance under the Confederation was made by the then Congress without any legal authority — but the Constitution afterwards sanctioned it.

This bill contains arbitary principles — principles repugnant to our Constitution — The legislative Council are to be appointed by the Governor, who is a creature of the President's — not elected by the people.

The judges are to legislate — make laws & expound them — this is of the essence of tyranny.

In the other territorial governments, even in the departure from liberty, there is a reverence for it — for it provides that when its inhabitants are encreased to a certain number they shall elect a representative.

This bill provides that the officers shall be appointed by the President *alone* in the recess of the Senate — why this departure from the Constitution.

The Judicial officers are to be appointed for a term of years only, & yet the bill is not limited. The constitutional tenure for judicial officers *is during good behavior.*[141]

The first thing Congress ought to have done in relation to that Country, should have been to propose an amendment to the Constitution, to the several States to authorize Congress to receive that Country into the Union — we ought to have applied to the inhabitants of Louisiana to recognize our right to govern them. This we ought to have done, & there is no doubt that the States & that territory would have given the authority before the next session.

---

[141] *Cf. American Insurance Co. v. Canter* (I Peters, 546) for a different interpretation.

The 3rd article of the treaty pledges the faith of the Nation to the inhabitants of that country that we will protect their persons, religion property & rights; but we have taken no measures to ascertain there numbers, religions or rights.

We have not the necessary information to pass a law containing the great fundamental principles of government — we know little of that people or Country — In thus passing this bill we commit an act of practical tyranny.

The bill contains incongruous articles — establishment of courts — juries — numerous laws — prohibition of slavery etc.

This is a Colonial system of government — It is the first the United States have established — It is a bad precedent — the U. S. in time will have many colonies — precedents are therefore important.

The governor's appointing & proroguing the Council is an act of tyranny.

Tis too soon to extend the trial by jury to that Country — There are serious inconveniences attending this mode of trial —& those people have not laws, customs or habits to correct those evils. Extending juries to them in their present condition, will, I fear, excite opposition to the institution itself. There present mode of trial is *summary* no jury — a single judge decides. Trial by jury & delay are synomymous — by introducing it you establish new principles. What is meant by *vicinage* in that country? In law books it has a definite & precise meaning — it is confined to a County — There you have no Counties. Is it to extend thro' the whole country — Will it not give too much power to the judge — & will it not be burthesome & even oppressive to compel people from distant parts of that extended world (for such I may call it) to attend Courts of law as grand and petit jurors! The District court is to sit once in three months, & the Supreme Court once every month — the call for jurors will therefore be frequent.

The governor & judges of the Indiana territory are to govern

Louisiana — will they not govern it in an arbitary manner —
will they not consider it as a colony to them? [142]

The bill passed yeas 20 nays 5.[143]

### In the House

*Mr. Eppes* moved the appointment of a Committee to enquire & report whether the monies drawn on account of the
*Marine Corps* have been faithfully applied.

*Dr. Leib* moved, That the Committee on Ways and Means
be directed to inquire into the expediency of abolishing the
office of Lt. Col. Commandant of that *Corps.*

Mr. Bradley [144] of the secret Committee made a Report in
favor of a prosecution of those Lawyers who gave their opinion,
as stated p. 246 [145] provided the Atty Genl should think it expedient. Motion made to print the report — a majority
ordered it printed but under the injunction of secrecy.

### Wednesday 28th.[146]

The bill " Further to protect the Seamen of the United States "
— under consideration —

*Mr. Nicholas,* I am authorized to say that at no period of our
Government has there subsisted so cordial a friendship between
the government of this Country & that of the Government of the
United Kingdom of Great Britain as at this time, the news
paper publications to the contrary notwithstanding. At this
time there is a friendly negotiation now pending between the
two nations, & it is of importance that it be not interrupted.
But I have no hesitation in saying that if this bill passes that
harmony will be destroyed, & in a short time we shall be neces-

---

[142] *Cf.* J. Q. Adams, *Memoirs,* I, 295, where only a brief mention is
made of this speech.
[143] Approved March 26, 1804; see *Statutes at Large,* II, 283–289.
[144] In the Senate.
[145] Page 94 of this volume. See note 71.
[146] Wednesday, February 29.

sitated to build & equip ships of war & raise an army — This bill is a virtual declaration of war — If the injury or insult offered to us renders war necessary let us in a bold manly tone declare it against the offending nation, not agt the ship whose commander may by an act, perhaps unauthorized, offend us. I see nothing in the conduct of Great Britain hostile to us, I therefore move that the further consideration of this bill be postponed to Dec. next.

## *Thursday 29.*[147]

The debate on Mr. Nicholas's motion continued most of the day. Most of the Democrats evidently wished that the motion should prevail — even Saml Smith, the mover of the bill, although he vociferated loudly against the postponement & voted agt it — yet he discovered a wish that the motion should prevail —

Bill postponed — i. e. lost.

This debate on the part of the Democrats was designed solely for the News papers & the gallery — S Smith procured Duane to take the debates & to publish them.

As soon as Mr. Burr saw Duane in the Area of the Senate chamber he directed the door keeper to order him to the stenographer's table or to leave the Chamber instantly — Duane reluctantly complied. —

## *March 2d 1804.*
### *High Court of Impeachment.*

United States vs John Pickering District Judge of the District of New Hampshire, impeached by the House of Representatives of high crimes & misdemeanors.

I have already stated the purport of the articles of Impeachment, p. 281.[148]

---

[147] Thursday, March 1.
[148] Pages 99–100 of this volume.

Mr. Adams called up his resolution offered Jany 4th to exclude those Senators from sitting as Judges on the trial of the Impeachment who had previously acted & voted as members of the House of Representatives on the question of Impeachment.

John Smith of New York, who was one of the Senators alluded to modestly requested to be excused from voting on this resolve — Excused.  Saml Smith another of the Senators declared That a false sense of delicacy should never prevent him from doing his duty — he had voted as a Member of the House in favor of the impeachment — & he was determined to act and vote as a Senator upon the trial unless a majority of the Senate excluded him — And he should now vote himself against the resolution.

The motion was lost ays 8, nays 20.

A resolution was reported by the Committee of whom Mr. Tracy was chairman — " That all motions made by the parties or their Council, should be addressed to the President of the Senate — And after the parties are heard upon such motion, the Senate shall retire to the adjoining Committee room for consideration, if one third of the Senate request it — but all decisions shall be public by ayes & noes in open Court without debate."

It was said that this rule would destroy the dignity of the Court, by retiring to a chamber to consider of every question that may occur — That it ought to be public in the presance of the parties witnesses & spectators — That if it was necessary for the Court to have a private consultation it would be more dignified that the Court should remain in their own chamber, & direct the parties witnesses & spectators to withdraw.

To this it was said in reply, That all questions of order were to be decided by the President; but questions of a different nature would probably arise, e. g. questions relative to the admission of testimony &c that the Court must decide — That it was probable there would be a diversity of opinion — That this would occasion altercation & a degree of warmth in the Mem-

bers which would not comport with the honor & dignity of so
high a Court — That a court consisting of thirty four Members
ought to retire — to consult together & derive aid from a free
expression of each other's opinions — That it would require much
time & create much dissatisfaction to turn so many people out
of the Senate Chamber — Area, & gallery — but the Court
could any time retire with ease & dispatch — That the British
House of Lords sat in Westminister Hall on the trial of Warren
Hastings — & that in the course of that trial, that House, who
are punctilious as to their dignity, retired to their own house
to consult on motions, questions &c fifty three several times. —

It was further objected That this rule would preclude Members from giving their reasons on the final question, as it was to
be by ayes & noes *without debate.*

It was said, That this rule would not exclude a member from
giving his reasons, but only prohibited him from combating the
reasons & opinions of those who preceded him.

Others contended that it was designed, & ought, to preclude
the members of the Court from giving the reasons on which they
formed their opinions — for if they were not excluded from stating the grounds of their opinions it would be impossible to prevent discussion — Judges would publicly contend agt each other
— & those who had once given their opinion would be precluded
from reply — This would occasion numerous interruptions, explanations declarations that they were misunderstood — & confusion — That in a Court so numerous, after the judges had
advised & consulted with each other, the decision ought then to
be public & declared by a simple aye or nay of each Judge.

The resolution was adopted, 16 for, 15 against it.

*Mr. Tracey* moved, That each member of the Court should
be at liberty, if he pleased, after the Judgment was rendered to
enter his opinion with his reasons on the record. He observed
that this would be the only correct mode of perpetuating the
opinion of the Judges, & establishing precedents on the principles on which the decisions were formed.

This was rejected — 12 only voted in favor of it.

The Court was opened at One OClock, the articles of impeachment, the summons to Judge Pickering to appear, & the return upon the same were read, & the return being attested by the oath of the Sargent at arms, the Secretary was directed to inform the House of Representatives that the Senate organized as a Court of Impeachments was ready to proceed upon the impeachment of John Pickering in the Senate Chamber.

The Managers on the part of the House of Representatives accompanied by most of the House attended, The managers were introduced into seats prepared for them, but the other members were not well accomodated — the Speaker of the House had a particular seat assigned him. — After a pause — the President of the Senate directed the crier to call Judge Pickering — he was called three times but came not whereupon his nonappearance was entered of record.

The President' then observed that he had a letter from Robt. G. Harper Esq inclosing a petition from the son of Judge Pickering addressed to the Court — These he directed the Secretary to read —

The petition stated, That the Judge was & for near three years had been in a state of insanity, incapable of doing any act that required the exercise of reason — That the decree in the case of the Eliza, though not the result of reflection, was conformable to law & equity — and that from indisposition of body & mental derangement he was utterly unable, at this inclement season of the year to attend this Court — & prayed for a postponement. —

Mr. Harper stated in his letter, that he was desirous of appearing, as the Council of Judge Pickering's son not as the Council of the Judge — That the Judge from bodily infirmity & total derangement of mind was then wholly incapable of appearing before the Court, of making a defence, or of giving authority to any person to appear for him — That he was furnished with testimony to prove these facts — & requested to be admitted to appear in support of the petition.

These papers were accompanied by sundry affidavits to support the facts stated in the petition but which were not then read — The President enquired if Mr. Harper was in Court, & invited him to a seat within the bar, upon which he made the following address —

Mr. President,

Before I proceed to address this Honorable Court in the case now before it, I think it proper to repeat explicitly what is stated in the letter just now read, that I do not appear as the council, agent, or attorney of Judge Pickering, nor by virtue of any authority derived from him — he being in a state of absolute and long continued insanity, can neither appear himself nor authorize another to appear for him. I present myself to this honorable Court, at the request of Jacob S. Pickering, son of Judge Pickering, on whose part I have preferred a petition, stating his father's insanity, & praying that time may be allowed for collecting & producing compleat proof of this melancholy fact. This application for a postponement I am prepared to support by depositions now in my possession — And it is also my intention, if permitted, to make a further application on the part of Judge Pickering, for compulsary process to compel the attendance of such witnesses as it may be necessary to produce in proof of the fact of insanity, or for an order to take their depositions in writing on interrogatories, & notice to the prosecutors.

It rests with this honorable Court whether it will receive such an application, & hear council so appearing in its support, & this decision I beg leave to request.

*Vice President,*

It is my opinion, Sir, that you may be heard — & as no objection is made, you will consider yourself at liberty to proceed.

*Mr. Harper,*

May I be allowed to ask, Sir, whether my thus appearing will be considered as in any manner binding on Judge Pickering, or as precluding or affecting any defence which it may hereafter be judged proper to make on his part. If it be so considered, I must decline appearing, for I repeat that I have no authority or power to bind him in any manner whatever.

*Vice President,*

I do not suppose that your appearance under such circumstances, & for such a purpose, could be considered as binding or injuriously affecting Judge Pickering —

Mr. Harper was about to enter upon the subject, when Mr. Nicholson, on the part of the managers arose & objected to the whole of the proceeding.

The objection was supported by Mr. Rodney,[149] Mr. G. W. Campbell,[150] Mr. Randolph, & Mr. Early (managers) upon the ground that untill the party accused shall appear either by himself or Council, & put in a plea, no proceedings could be had in the case, except such as might have it for their object to compel an appearance, & that no person could be allowed to apply to the Court and address it in this case, unless he appeared as the Agent or attorney of Judge Pickering, or as an *Amicus curiae.*

*Mr. Rodney,*

Mr. President, I rise to make a few observations on this case, in addition to those which have fallen from my colleagues who have preceded me; & to submit to the consideration of this Court remarks which have suggested themselves to my mind, on the application made, at the present stage of this business.

I understand the President as having declared that agreeably to the rules of proceeding adopted by the Senate, no person can be heard in this case but the accused, or his agent or counsel.

---

149 Caesar Augustus Rodney, representative from Delaware.
150 George Washington Campbell, representative from Tennessee.

I beleive I have correctly understood what was expressed — (the Vice President nodded assent) I also understand the gentleman who appears on this occasion, as clearly & explicitly stating, that he does not appear as the counsel of Mr. Pickering, nor does he wish it so to be understood. That gentleman has informed us in a very fair & candid manner of the only character in which he does appear, & has assumed very properly & correctly the only ground upon which he wishes to stand. He has in positive terms disavowed the idea of his being the agent or Counsel of the accused, because he has protested agt Mr. Pickering's being affected by any act done by him. On this single ground then, I respectfully submit whether it would be proper to hear the gentleman under these circumstances, & whether it be not manifest that he does not come within the rules laid down by the Senate for the government of this high court of Impeachment.

But if the gentleman is to be heard on this subject in the anomalous character in which he appears, with a view of postponing the proceedings of this Court, it will first be necessary for the Court to decide that the case is properly before them agreeably to the rules which have been established. If no appearance in person or by attorney has been entered, unless proceedings have been had which they shall consider tantamount to an appearance, there is no cause regularly in Court, & it would be idle for any person to talk of postponing the consideration of that which really was not before the Court. A question of this kind must, from the nature of it, ever be incidental to the principle or main question. When a writ is in Court according to the rules of the court, a motion for postponement may with propriety, if the circumstances justify it, be made. This must always be a subsequent consideration, after the Court are in full possession of the Case. Agreeably to the correct course of proceeding in ordinary courts, untill bail & appearance, there can be no case in court. The party has no day given him, because he is till this takes place, considered to be out of Court; nor would any counsel, tho' duly authorized, be heard in his behalf. There has in this case then, been no appearance in person or by agent or counsel. The accused has made default, & no agent or attorney has been recorded for him. Surely then his default should be first recorded, & if the court consider that after his having been duly served, & making default, they will proceed to a hearing & determination of the principle question, it will then be proper to listen to those which are necessarily incidental. It will be at this stage of the business competent for the court, if at all, to hear the gentleman. But I am decidedly of the opinion, there is no period at which it will be proper so to do, unless he claims this right as the agent or counsel of the accused. In that capacity he has a right to be heard — & in that capacity alone. Our constitution has wisely secured to every man this priveledge, & I would not deprive the humblest object in the community of this inestimable benefit. I flatter myself, therefore, that this honorable court will adhere strictly to the rules which they have prescribed for themselves, & that they will for these reasons, & those which have been assigned by my colleagues, refuse the present application.

*Mr. Nicholson*, then observed, The Respondent was defaulted — that there was no appearance — no pleading — no issue joined or tendered — & demanded why the House of Representatives were notified to attend the trial unless the accused had appeared & answered.

The Vice President, replied, The House was notified that the Court was open, & untill they, or the Managers in their behalf, attended, the court could not know whether there would be an appearance on the part of the accused.

After the managers had concluded, the Vice President declared that as an objection was made to the appearance of Mr. Harper he should not decide the point but would refer it to the court.

Mr. Harper asked, whether it would be proper for him in that stage of the business to offer anything in reply to the objections of the Managers? The Vice President answered that in his opinion it would not.

As the Vice President was proceeding to put the question whether the application of Jacob S. Pickering should be received, & counsel & testimony heard in support of it — a motion was made that the Court should retire to their chamber for consultation — More than one third of the Senators rose in favor of the motion — it was therefore carried. —

Mr. Nicholas, in a low, but indignant voice, asked Mr. Brackenridge, who sat near me, " shall we obey the order of the Senate & retire? " Brackenridge replied, " We must."

The Court retired to the Committee room — spent more than an hour — the debate was animated — the opinions various.

Nicholas, Venable, Brackenridge & Logan contended that the Judge was defaulted — that his default must be recorded, & therefore Mr. Harper could not be heard upon the petition of the son.

Bradley, Hillhouse, Olcott, Wright & Israel Smith contended, That in England, in all courts of Law, where a suggestion is made, that a man accused of a crime, is insane, the first process of the Court is to direct a jury to try the suggestion — if insanity is found, the court proceed no further — but if not found, they then direct the respondent to plead. That in this case we can have no jury — we ourselves must first hear & try the suggestion of insanity, before we can proceed in the trial of the impeachment — That if the Accused is found to be insane, he is incapable of action & utterly unable to appoint an attorney or agent to represent his case in this Court — If he was, in fact, in a state of insanity when the Sargent at Arms left the summons with the judge, he has in that case had no notice of the trial, & of course, the Court, can have no jurisdiction of the Case — for without notice given to the accused, no trial can be had — If the Accused is insane he is incapable of being defaulted — he can, in that state, be guilty of no laches or fault — We are therefore bound on such a suggestion as is now made to enquire & decide.

Mr. Tracey moved That the Court return to the Senate Chamber & that the Vice President be requested to give notice that no decision is yet made upon the question by the Court, but that in due time a decision will be made & notice thereof shall be given — Carried — adjourned to tomorrow 10 OClock —

Yesterday it appeared that a majority of the Senate only wanted proof of Pickering's insanity to convince them of the propriety & necessity of removing him from office; but today, Bradley, Wright, Cocke, Jackson & Anderson not only doubt, but some of them have explicitly declared that " it is a gross absurdity to convict a man of high crimes & misdeamenors who is *insane.*" This is an embarassing case to the Democrats, but still I fear just principles will not restrain them from removing the Accused from office.[151]

### *Saturday 3d.*

This morning while the Senate were sitting in their Legislative capacity Mr. Nicholas moved *That the doors be closed* — Carried — He then moved that the Minutes of the proceedings of the Court on yesterday be read — carried — From the minutes it appeared, *That John Pickering was called — That Mr. Harper immediately presented a letter inclosing a petition from Jacob S. Pickering stating that the Accused was insane — That the Managers objected to Mr. Harper's being heard — And that the President informed them the Court would take time to consider of the objection & give them due notice of their decision.*

Mr. *Brackenridge,* The minutes are incompleat — they ought

---

[151] Neither in J. Q. Adams *Memoirs* (I, 297–299), nor in 62 Cong., 2 sess., *Sen. Doc.* 876 (*Extracts from the Journal of the United States Senate in All cases of Impeachment*) is there so full an account of this day's proceedings as is given by Plumer.

to state that John Pickering did not appear — The notice of Jacob S. Pickering's application & of Harper's letter & appearance, are, I think, surplusage, & ought to be expunged from the minutes.

*Mr. Adams,* From the suggestion it appears that John Pickering is incapable of appearing or of being defaulted — An insane man can no more appear in Court or be defaulted than a dead man — The suggestion of Harper & of Jacob S. Pickering are proper — The minutes of the Court should be more particular — it ought to state that the Managers objected to Mr. Harper's appearing in support of the petition of the son of the Accused — & that the Court to determine that objection retired.

*Mr. Wright,* I think differently — we ought not to encumber our records with anything of the kind — We must determine whether Harper shall be permitted to appear in manner & form as he requests.

*Mr. Tracey,* This is a mere minute or journal of proceedings — it ought to state facts correctly — when the trial is through the record will be made up by the order & under the inspection of the Court, or the President — I do not therefore see why we should take up more time upon these minutes than merely that they should contain a plain statement of facts.

*Mr. Brackenridge,* I am of a different opinion from the gentleman from Connecticut (Mr. Tracey). In all the Courts in which I have practised, the clerk each morning read the proceedings of the Court of the day preceding — & these are always corrected (if necessary) & then signed by the presiding Judge. This is the mode adopted by the House of Lords in Great Britain. From these proceedings thus stated we ought to furnish the House of Representatives with such official copies as may be necessary. I can see no reason why a concise statement of the appearance & request of Mr. Harper should not be entered on the minutes — We may hereafter have occasion to refer to it — it may be considered as proof of an important fact.

*Mr. Hillhouse,* All courts keep minutes — these are not records — they ought to be correct — for from them the record must be made up. The minutes ought to be corrected — they ought to state, *that after John Pickering was three times called he did not appear, & then the suggestion of Harper & the petition of Jacob S. Pickering.*

*Mr. Adams,* I move that a Committee of three be appointed, who shall every morning inspect & correct the minutes of the proceedings of the preceeding day, subject to the order of the Court.

*Mr. Anderson,* I think the minutes ought not to proceed further than that John Pickering was called & did not appear — The suggestion of Harper & the petition of Jacob S. Pickering ought not to be admitted on the minutes — they may remain on file.

*Mr. Jackson,* I agree with the gentleman from Tennessee (Mr. Anderson). I think Mr. Harper ought to have appeared as the Counsel of Judge Pickering & as such have entered up a plea of *not guilty,* & under that plea offered evidence of the insanity of the accused. Insanity is here a bar to all proceedings on an Impeachment — Why did not the son bring the Judge here that we might see him. I am inclined to think that I shall never agree to hear Mr. Harper. How shall we get rid of the Judge? Must we first amend the Constitution — I fear we must — I am not however certain.

*Mr. Israel Smith,* These are mere minutes — we shall make them too prolix — why appoint a Committee — why not leave the business to the Secretary under the direction of the President.

*Mr. Jackson,* The friends of Judge Pickering might, and ought, to have deceived him — & under a deception obtained a resignation from him — Why have they not brought him here — I am afraid all our Judges will be *mad* — The other House is now impeaching another Judge (*Chase*).

*Mr. Hillhouse* We are sitting here not to devise how we can get rid of a Judge, but as Judges under oath to try a public officer accused of having committed high crimes and misdemeanors.

*Mr. Nicholas,* I think a Committee necessary, but we must ourselves first amend the minutes of yesterday.

The Court amended the minutes of yesterday.

*Mr. Jackson* I move that the suggestion of Mr. Harper & the notice of the petition of Jacob S. Pickering be erased from the minutes.

*Mr. Tracey,* These are real facts, & I think ought to remain on the minutes. I have no objection to have this erased & have a more concise entry made — As that it was suggested by Jacob S. Pickering that John Pickering is insane & that his son the said Jacob requested to be heard by Counsel.

*Mr. Jackson,* Young Mr. Pickering ought to have sworn to his petition. The depositions that Mr. Harper states he wished to read, I am told were never sworn to. No dilatory plea is ever received till after it is sworn to.

*Mr. Wells,* If we erase this suggestion, we bar enquiry as to the fact of insanity — If the Judge was insane no process has been served upon him — his mind has received no notice — We must meet this enquiry — If we make the erasure, our journal will speak a language variant from the facts.

*Mr. Hillhouse,* Suppose the Judge had come here to make his defence, & in this city became insane — what should we do upon a suggestion being made of the fact — must we not ascertain it?

*Mr. Franklin,* I do not see that the suggestion on our minutes can avail anything — The suggestion of insanity is made — the managers deny it. We must then decide the question — but I do not know how. There is a difference between lunacy & insanity — the latter may, perhaps, be cause of impeachment.

The Court then ordered the minutes to be amended — [Before

I leave the city I will obtain a copy of the Minutes as amended, & add them to the Appendix.] [152]

A Committee of three was appointed to direct and assist the Secretary in making up the minutes.

*Mr. Wright,* I move that Robert Goodloe Harper Esq be assigned as Counsel for John Pickering, & that under the plea of not guilty he be allowed to give insanity in evidence.

This motion did not receive a second.

It was then moved, " Will the Court hear evidence & counsel respecting the Insanity of John Pickering upon the suggestion contained in the petition of Jacob S. Pickering & the letter of Robert Goodloe Harper? "

*Mr. Hillhouse,* If the Respondent is insane he is incapable of moral· action — is not answerable for any action — He is totally incapable of constituting an attorney or pleading himself. The suggestion of insanity is properly before us, let the Managers make answer to it — This must be done before the trial can proceed.

*Mr. John Smith* (of Ohio) The constitution knows nothing of lunacy or insanity. If the facts are proved as stated in the Impeachment he ought to be removed from office — His insanity is no excuse — Why was he not brought here — I have heard no good reason assigned.

*Mr. Tracey,* The gentleman from Ohio asks why the Judge is not brought here — The petition states that. he cannot be bro't but at the hazard of his life. Mr. Harper says that he has depositions to prove this fact, I wish to hear him & them. But if the Senate have agreed that an insane man can be *convicted* of high crimes & misdemeanors, they will act consistant in refusing to hear Mr. Harper & his testimony. When the powers of reason & the sense of right & wrong are destroyed in any mind, that man can commit no crime. I will not say an insane man may not be removed from office, but I say he

---

[152] Brackets appear in the original manuscript.

cannot be convicted of crimes. We are now a Court, bound by rules & restricted by principles, & within these we must act. Innocence is to be presumed by all Courts, untill guilt is proved.

*Mr. Brackenridge,* I do not wish to act as the Advocate of the United States or of the Accused. We have adopted rules & I am willing to be bound by them. The accused has been summoned but has not appeared. What course shall we now persue? I think the proceedings here must be the same as in a Court of criminal jurisdiction — And in such a Court a lawyer circumstanced as Mr. Harper is could not be heard. The plea must be not guilty, & if insanity is proved, & is a defence, it will avail; but the question of insanity cannot be decided but only upon the plea of not guilty. I am not yet prepared to say insanity is a defence. I am against hearing Harper, because he is not the Counsel of the judge but of the son, who is not the counsel of the father. I think we ought now to ·inform the other House of the state of facts as to the impeachment — And if they then demand a trial, I will hear them, & I will hear counsel for the accused — but not on the petition at this time.

*Mr. Adams,* You cannot possibly have any trial at this time, whether the accused be insane or not. He has made no appearance either by himself or Attorney — your record says that when he was called he came not. Your same record states the reason why he did not appear — that he was incapable of coming — & that if present he would be incapable of pleading, because he is insane — These are allegations made by his son, & by his Counsel proof of the facts are tendered. Under these circumstances you cannot have a trial — you can have but one party. You require a man to plead for another who is incapable of appointing a representative, & who in fact is no longer a man. Will you consider his non-Appearance as a default — as a confession of the truth of the articles of Impeachment? Will you permit the Managers to proceed & prove the charges,

& will you then hear evidence that at the time when the acts were done the Accused had no mind — was in a state of insanity. A Court of Law never proceeds in this manner — They would ascertain the fact of insanity before they would suffer a trial, default, or a motion for judgment.

*Mr. Cocke*, I think we ought to settle the question whether John Pickering shall be tried — & what evidence is admisable. There is no proof of his insanity — it is only suggested. The Constitution says that a judge shall receive a compensation for *his services*. If this judge from any cause whatever fails to render *services*, he ought to have no compensation — for the omission of services are *criminal* — I hope I am *understood* — I am for proceeding with the trial on monday. —

*Mr. Bradley*, It has been said by the gentleman from Kentucky (Mr. Brackenridge) That a man charged in a court of law with murder, who is insane, may by his friends appear & plead not guilty, & that under that plea insanity has been proved, & if a defence, it has been received as such. The gentleman is mistaken both in his law & fact. In all capital offences the plea cannot be made by counsel, it must be by the person accused. I know that a lunatic or insane person who commits a crime, *after* his reason is restored, may plead not guilty & under that plea give his *former* insanity in evidence. But no Court of Law ever received an attorney or plea from an insane man, because all courts have considered him as incapable of moral action. — But when insanity has been suggested the Court have always taken notice of it — ascertained the fact, & if found, stayed all proceedings.

*Mr. Wright*, If I was *now* bound to decide it would be against the question, because the petition is not accompanied with affidavits. Why did not the petitioner prove the Accused to be insane before a Judge of Probate in that State & have a guardian appointed for him? If he is in fact insane he is as an infant & must be considered as under our guardianship. We ought to assign him counsel & proceed & try him — The admitting counsel for the son is in fact admitting the insanity of the father.

*Mr. Hillhouse,* Mr. Harper assured us that he had affidavits, the only question is shall he have an opportunity of reading them. The suggestion of insanity must be proved, Mr. Harper says he is ready to prove it as far as the present state of the Accused & the shortness of notice will permit.

At 4 OClock adjourned, without the question being decided.[153]

### Monday March 5, 1804.

The Court met with closed doors —

The president (Mr. Burr) informed the Court that he had received a letter from Mr. Harper enclosing certain affidavits to prove the insanity of the Judge — & certain letters from Mr. Sherburne the district attorney of New Hampshire relative to his former character, requesting that they might be laid before the Court.

*Mr. Nicholas,* I object to their being read.

*Mr. White,* It has been stated that the petition of Young Mr. Pickering ought not to be read, because it being in the nature of a dilatory plea, & is not accompanied by affidavits — I hope this letter & the depositions enclosed in it will be read.

*Mr. Logan* We have been led into an error by considering this Court as a court of *criminal jurisdiction,* & Judge Pickering as a *criminal.* This is a *court of enquiry only.* — If the Judge is *insane,* whether it be by *the act of God,* or his *own imprudence,* is immaterial — for in either case he is incapable of discharging the duties of a Judge — And being unable to do his duty, & a complaint being made to us, it is our duty to remove him.

*Mr. Jackson,* I have now an *authority* to prove that under the plea of not guilty insanity may be given in evidence. It

---

[153] *Cf.* J. Q. Adams, *Memoirs,* I, 299–300.

is the *New Annual Register* giving an account of Hatfield's case. [He read the case — not in point — He then proceeded to say,] [154] That Harper ought to be admitted as the Counsel of the Judge, not of the son, & plead not guilty — then offer evidence of his insanity, & argue its effect upon the process & proceedings.

Motion was made that Mr. Harper's letter be read.

*Mr. Wright*, It is improper to read the letter in the absence of the Managers.

*Mr. Bradley*, The letter ought to be read, & the Court will then decide whether they will take any notice of it or not — & whether its necessary to give information of it to the managers.

The motion was rejected, ayes 14, nays 15.

*Mr. Wright*, I voted in the negative — I hope our journal will not include any account of Mr. Harper's letter of this day or our vote thereon. (See Appendix p. 48 minutes of this day.) [155]

*Mr. Bradley*, An insane man cannot appoint an attorney — he cannot be tried during his insanity. A lunatic may in his lucid intervals plead & be tried, & under the general issue may prove his lunacy — But no man while in a state of insanity was ever required to plead, much less ordered to trial.

*Mr. Stone*, It is suggested that Judge Pickering is now in a state of insanity — I therefore move the decision of the following questions, 1. Will the Court hear evidence of Judge Pickering's insanity, he not being in Court? 2 Will the Court hear councel on that evidence, the Judge not being present.

*Mr. Wright* If a criminal is insane the Court will ascertain the fact by inspection, or by a jury; but in civil cases the trial goes on. This is a civil case, we may therefore remove this judge from office, his insanity notwithstanding. I am willing to hear the petition & also to hear Mr. Harper; but I think its

---

[154] Brackets appear in the original manuscript.
[155] The Appendix referred to was not copied. It follows the report of Pickering's trial of March 5, 1804, as given in *Sen. Doc.* 876, *loc. cit.*

best to try insanity & guilt both at once under the plea of not guilty.

John Smith (of Ohio) The presumption is that all men are sane till proved otherwise — The non appearance of the judge is but another word for his default — I think we ought to consider him as defaulted, & that default as a confession of his guilt — I have been against hearing Harper, because he is not the attorney of the Judge — & untill the Court assigns councel for the accused I doubt as to the propriety of hearing Mr. Harper in the character in which he appears.

The question was taken, Will the Court hear evidence & Councel on the petition of Jacob S. Pickering? On this question the Senate divided ays 15, nays 14.

*Mr. Cocke* I will not consent to hear councel for Jacob S. Pickering — he is not a party — & this would be creating a defendant.

*Mr. Worthington,* moved to strike out the word *Counsel.*

*Mr. Bradley,* How will you hear evidence without counsel? Will the witnesses volunteer, or the affidavits present themselves.

This process must be considered either as a civil suit & the non appearance of the accused as a confession that the charges against him are true; or the Court will proceed & hear evidence in support of the articles — & if the evidence thus produced is unsatisfactory, say the Respondent is not guilty. This mode is unprecedented. Or we may adopt a third method of proceeding — The Judge was summoned but has not appeared — Let a Capias be issued against him — He is, if sane, subject to punishment, for contempt of court in not appearing when requested — If brought in by a Capias we may bring him to trial. I never will consent in future to any other process against a person impeached but that of Capias — Had a capias issued in this case we should have avoided many difficulties.

But if the Accused is in fact insane, he has never had any

kind of notice of this process — he is as ignorant of the whole charges & trial as his horse.

Motion in *B. R.* are frequently made in behalf of the friends of insane persons, but never by persons who derive any authority from the person insane.    [He then read some case inpoint from Burrow's Reports.] [156]

I am therefore for hearing Jacob S Pickering by counsel — I trust we are not *yet* arrived to that state of things in which it is necessary to suppress evidence or refuse to hear counsel — And I trust we are not afraid of being mislead by fact or reasoning.

*Mr. Wright,* We have power to try John Pickering's impeachment, but not authority to try Jacob S Pickering's petition. If the Judge appears by himself or his Counsel & pleads his insanity, we must hear him & determine upon his plea.

*Mr. Plumer* The amount then is, that if a man suggested to be *insane* will do a *sane* act, such as disproves his insanity, appoint an Attorney, we will then hear him upon the question of insanity.    I live in the neighbourhood of the Accused — I have long lived in habits of intimacy with him — I have seen him frequently — & I have not the smallest doubt in my mind as to his being in a state of confirmed insanity.

The question was then stated, Whether the Court will hear evidence & counsel on the suggestion of Judge Pickering's insanity on the petition of Jacob S. Pickering & the letter of Mr. Harper?

*Mr. Brackenridge,* In England, in capital cases, the evidence of insanity is given under the *general plea.*

[Reads from Hale's pleas of the Crown.] [157]

But even there, I am willing to own, there are many instances in which where insanity is suggested, the fact is first ascertained before trial — if the suggestion is made after trial, judg-

---

[156] Brackets appear in the original manuscript.
[157] Brackets appear in the original manuscript.

ment is suspended — & if after judgment the judgment is arrested, till the fact is established. But this Court have power only to try the impeachment upon a plea to its merits. We cannot compel the attendance of the accused — We cannot operate upon either his person or property — We cannot inspect him to know whether insane or not — Our jurisdiction is limited. If the Judge does not appear we must notify the managers, & they must prove the truth of the articles before we can convict. We cannot consider the non appearance of the Accused as a default. Nor do I think we can hear this petition or letters but on the trial — then I will agree to hear them.

*Mr. Anderson,* What we have heard from British law writers does not apply to us — We cannot do impartial justice unless we hear both sides.

*Mr. Wright,* If it should appear that the Judge is insane, that will not decide the impeachment — we can remove from office the insanity notwithstanding — His not discharging the duties of a Judge is good cause of conviction & removal altho' he is not guilty of any corruption or improper conduct in office. In England insanity ends the trial, but not so in this Court.

*Mr. Dayton,* I will not say what effect the proof of insanity will or ought to have in this case, because that would be prejudging the cause — But at all events we must hear the evidence to know whether the suggestion of insanity be true — We cannot avoid this enquiring — stern justice demands it of us.

*Mr. Wells,* If the accused after pleading, becomes insane the trial must be stayed — for an insane man cannot be convicted of an offence. You have at your bar received a suggestion that the accused is insane — you have admitted that suggestion on your record, & you are now told that evidence is *now* ready to be produced to prove the truth of that suggestion — can you therefore refuse to hear that evidence?

*Mr. Hillhouse,* There seems to be a difference in opinion — some say that insanity is good cause for impeachment & removal — To such I say, admit Mr. Harper to offer his evidence to prove the insanity, & your case is made. My own opinion is that we are bound to enquir into the truth of the suggestion, & that if insanity is proved, we can proceed no further. But it is a fact we must investigate — The insanity may have happened since the notice was given, & in that case if we attempt a trial, there can be no defence —

*Mr. Pickering,* Suppose your Sargent at Arms had found the Accused chained in a *mad-house* & had on the process returned the fact, would you in that case proceed against the unfortunate Judge? His son now appears, by his councel, at your Bar suggest insanity, & tenders evidence to prove it —Will you refuse to hear this evidence! If insanity is proved you cannot convict — for in that case the accused is not a moral agent & therefore not accountable for any action.

*Mr. Israel Smith,* Our jurisdiction would, in this particular case, be excluded, unless the summons giving notice to the Accused, had been served upon him. The service of notice gives the Accused a day in Court, & that service gives to the court jurisdiction in the particular case. In this case there is no Appearance — but a friend, a natural friend, a son, has suggested the insanity of the accused — We must hear evidence upon this point. If we do not hear the evidence our proceeding will be as if no summons had issued, or had issued & not been served. If insanity is proved, I think we cannot convict — Insanity does away guilt, & puts an end to conviction.

*Mr. Venable,* If this insanity is voluntary — if it proceeds from an immoderate use of ardent spirits, it is no excuse; but if it is the visitation of God, it is *another thing.*

*Mr. Israel Smith,* If the insanity is temporary the trial must be postponed till it is removed — if it is perpetual, that puts an end to the process — the trial cannot proceed.

The doors were then opened, and the question last stated, was taken without debate, & passed yeas 18, nays 12.

The Secretary was ordered to notify the House of Representatives, that at 12 oClock tomorrow, the Court of Impeachments, holden for the trial of John Pickering, will be open & ready to proceed to bisiness in the Senate chamber.

## *Wednesday March 7.*[158]

The bill " making appropriations for the support of government, for the year 1804 " — passed the senate with amendments. This bill appropriates the sum of $1,012,274.51.

## *March 8 & 9.*[159]

*Mr. Tracey* then submitted the following resolution,

Resolved, as the opinion of the Court that the proceedings on the articles of impeachment, exhibited by the House of Representatives against John Pickering be postponed to the . . . . day of . . . next.

*Mr. Tracey,* When notice issued for the appearance of the accused I then thought that notice was sufficient — I will not now say it was insufficient — but from the course of these proceedings I have my doubts. My object is to postpone the subject to the next session — & then decide whether a capias against the accused shall issue.

The Managers refused to hear anything upon the petition of Jacob S. Pickering, & they ought *ergo* in their examination of the witnesses to have confined themselves to the articles of impeachment — but they have not done this. All that they have said upon the insanity of the accused is extraneous — at least, it is irregular.

Can any man say that this has been a fair impartial trial? There has been no appearance — no trial — a man cannot be

---

[158] Plumer's entries for March 6 and 7 on the Pickering trial are almost verbatim copies of the report as found in *Annals of Congress,* 8 Cong., 1 sess., for these dates. They are omitted here.

[159] Plumer's report of Pickering's trial on March 8 and 9 is the same as the *Annals of Congress* except for the section here added.

tried who does not appear — the whole proceedings have been exparte. I am at present unwilling to decide — If the cause is continued to the next session, we must either appoint a Guardian for the Accused, or issue a capias to bring in his body. At present, I feel strongly inclined, to think, that in cases of impeachment, the most regular course of proceeding will be to issue a capias to compell the personal attendance of the Accused. During the time I have been a member of the Senate I have never been so much embarrassed as I have been & still am in this trial. I have heard much, very much, improper testimony — I did not object to it, because I was unwilling to dictate, & because I thought such evidence would have no effect — but I fear I was mistaken.

*Mr. Cocke,* I am against postponement — A delay of Justice is a denial. I think Pickering has had a fair trial — He is insane, & his insanity is the effect of drunkenness — that drunkenness is a crime — is a wrong — & that he ought not to take advantage of that. I am prepared for convicting & removing him from office.

*Mr. Nicholas,* The personal appearance of the accused is altogether unnecessary.

*Mr. Adams,* I am in favor of postponement — because there has been no trial. We have heard the suggestion of insanity — We have heard the managers introduce much improper evidence — We have seen & heard witnesses testify who ought to have been cross-examined — because on one side of the question they appeared as *unwilling* witnesses. No member of the Court could object, because the rules of the Court precluded the objecting member from stating his objections.

I have said that we have heard much improper evidence — for example we have heard witnesses testifying respecting Judge Pickering's *general character as to sobriety.* This is the first time I have ever heard such testimony admitted in any Court as to the character of the accused — It is right to examine witnesses in certain cases as to the general character of a witness — but even then that examination must be confined to the general reputation of the witness as to *veracity only* — no Court has ever extended the rule, even thus restricted, to a *party* to a suit. We have not only partially enquired what the character of the Accused is as to *sobriety;* but we have instituted an enquiry into the *causes* of *his disease.* This inquiry we have made from strangers, & at the same time have refused to hear the opinion of his family phisician.

Witnesses say that he was insane at the time when the offences charged to have been done were committed, other witnesses say not. Mr. McClary contradicts in express language the testimony of Livermore — I want information to decide who of the witnesses are most credible.

It does not appear to me that judge Pickering has had any notice of this process — for if he is insane he could have none. The managers do not offer any evidence to prove his sanity — but on the contrary his present insanity is proved by the testimony of the witnesses whom I know are entitled to full credit. To call therefore such an order, notice of a trial, is solemn mockery. Justice demands a postponement.

*Mr. John Smith* (of Ohio), I am against postponement — I feel for the unfortunate judge — but the honor & glory of our government require a decision. The weight of evidence is against him — Intemperance produced his insanity, & not the latter the former — on this ground I shall vote against the resolution.

*Mr. Hillhouse,* We are prejudging — Had the Accused been represented here the case would no doubt have worn a different aspect — I say this from what happens in all cases. The reason of his non appearance is declared from good authority to be *Insanity.* The government of the United States is now on the high road of Experiment — what effects as a precedent, our decision in his case will have, ought to induce us to act with caution.

We can direct another Judge, say the District Judge from the District of Mayne, to act as Judge in New Hampshire — And the salary can never be considered as an object to the United States.

Can we lay our hands on our hearts & say, if this case was our own, it has been a fair trial. Those that think so will vote against the postponement.

Can any one of us say the Accused was sane at the time of the notice being served?

There has been no trial — In all cases of insanity, as soon as that appears — the trial ceases — because there is no moral agent remaining to try.

The affidavits all say that the Accused is insane — incapable of attending here — these are not contradicted — can you therefore say there has been a fair impartial trial? — you cannot.

If he was insane at the trial of the libels mentioned in the impeachment, & sane now, he can be tried & give that insanity in evidence in excuse of his conduct. But if he was sane then, & is insane now, we cannot proceed to try him.

In all courts I have ever seen, motions for continuances under circumstances like these always prevail. The insanity, & the utter inability of the Accused, to attend here at this time, cannot be questioned.

This unfortunate man through a long life of usefulness has acquired a fair title to fame, & will you now by your votes fix eternal infamy upon him & his family!

The question was taken, & the resolution was rejected — ays 10, nays 20.

*Mr. Nicholas,* moved, That the Secretary be directed to acquaint the House that the Court of Impeachment will on Monday next at twelve OClock pronounce Judgment on the articles of Impeachment exhibited by them against John Pickering. —

Ordered to lay on the table. —

Mr. John Brown one of the Senators from Kentucky said to be inclined to vote against convicting of the Accused; but being a Democrat, & unwilling to offend his party, obtained leave of absence for the residue of the session.

### *Saturday March 10th.*

The Vice President thinking it of importance to *himself* to be at New York to make arrangements to support his claim to be elected as Governor of that State, abruptly left the Senate.[160] Mr. Franklin of North Carolina was elected President Pro. temp.

Mr. White then submitted the following resolution

Resolved, That this Court is not at present prepared to give their final decision upon the articles of impeachment preferred by the House of Representatives, against John Pickering, district Judge for the District of New Hampshire, for high crimes & misdemeanors, the said John Pickering not having appeared, or been heard by himself or by counsel, & it being suggested to the court by Jacob S. Pickering, son of the said John Pickering, that the said John Pickering at the time of the conduct charged against him in the said articles of Impeachment, as high crimes & misdemeanors, was & yet is insane, which suggestion has been supported by the testimony of two members of the Court, & by the affidavits of sundry persons, whose integrity & veracity is unimpeached; & it being further suggested in the said petition, that at such future day as the Court may appoint, the body of the said John Pickering shall be produced in court, & further testimony in his behalf, which would enable the Court to judge for themselves as to the insanity of the said John Pickering, & to act more understandingly in the premises; but that the said John Pickering owing to bodily infirmity could not be brought to court at present, at so great a distance

---

[160] For Burr's nomination, see McMaster, *History of the People of the United States,* III, 49–50.

& at this inclement season of the year without imminent hazard of his life.

*Mr. Nicholas*, Mr. Wright & other gentlemen, objected to the resolution as not being in order.

*Mr. Anderson* asked if it would be in order to move an amendment to it.

*Mr. Adams* said he should object to any amendment to it, as by the rule of Court a gentleman had a right to a vote upon any specific proposition he might please to submit, connected with the trial.

Mr. White called for the reading of the rule — Read.

A motion was made that the galleries be closed — but the motion was lost.

*Mr. Anderson* then moved that the resolution submitted by the gentleman from Virginia (Mr. Nicholas), yesterday be taken up as being entitled to be acted upon first.

The president pro. tem. declared that the resolution of the gentleman from Delaware (Mr. White) was fairly before the Court, & must be disposed of in some way before anything else could be taken up.

A motion for postponing the further consideration of it was then made — but withdrawn.

On motion of Mr. Dayton the galleries were cleared & the doors closed.

*Mr. White*, There has been no trial — no appearance no plea — no defence whatever on the part of the Accused — Our proceedings scarcely deserve the name of a *Mock-trial.*

*Mr. Nicholas* vociferated, order, order, order — I will not submit to hear our proceedings called by the degrading name of a mock trial.

*Mr. White*, Mr. President, I am in order Sir — & while I have a seat in this body I will act & speak *my opinion* with freedom. If any gentleman's *feelings* are wounded I am the innocent cause of it. I have spoken the truth — and I assure the gentleman from Virginia (Mr. Nicholas), I wish not to offend him, or any other member of this Court; but if truth gives offence he must bear it. I did say, & I again repeat it, our proceedings upon this impeachment are not evidence of a regular trial — they are wholly unlike it — they are farcical — a mere *mock trial.* If the gentleman is offended at this declaration, I assure him, I shall not retract it — they are words of truth & soberness. If in this I have offended him, I am willing & ready to give him satisfaction at any time & place he will please to name. I assure him he shall again & again hear this language — he shall hear it within & without these walls — & the nation shall hear it.

*Mr. Saml Smith,* The testimony of Mr. Livermore is in itself contradictory — & Mr. McClary the Marshal expressly contradicts & denies what Mr. Livermore deposed.

*Mr. John Smith of Ohio.* I thought I understood one of the gentlemen from New Hampshire (Mr. Plumer) to say, that in his opinion, the insanity proceeded from the intemperance of the Accused.

*Mr. Plumer,* I am sorry the gentleman so understood me — he wholly misapprehended what I deposed — I stated facts — I observed that Judge Pickering, during a long & useful life, lived in habits of temperance & sobriety — that I never once heard of his intemperance till after that of his insanity. And I have no hesitation in saying that I fully beleive that his hypocondriac complaints produced the delirium & insanity — & that his insanity caused his intemperance — that the later was the effect & consequence of the former — Though I have no doubt that his insanity & the consequent intemperance, acted afterward mutually as cause & effect upon each other.

*Mr. Adams,* If proceedings like ours were had in a Court of law, I have no hesitation in saying, it would be considered as a *Mere Mock-trial.*

*Mr. Nicholas,* I hope this resolution will not be permitted to be entered even on our minutes — that it will never see the public light — It is not correct — it does not contain all the facts.

*Mr. Venable,* Although the Accused has not appeared, yet the trial cannot be considered as exparte. If the trial has been irregular, it has been so only in favor of the Accused. The petition of Jacob S. Pickering ought to have been sworn to by himself — but it was not — It is true other witnesses have sworn to the same facts — & he ought to have done it, & this neglect of his is sufficient excuse for the Senate in refusing a decision on his petition.

*Mr. Wright.* We have heard the Accused — Did we not record his default? Yet after this did we not hear Mr. Harper? he indeed said, he did not appear as Counsel for the Judge — but for my part I heard him as the Counsel of the Judge, & not of the son, his declaration to the contrary notwithstanding. Mr. Harper ought to have attended the trial — I really thought he would. If judge Pickering was now here as mad as Bedlam it would make no difference — I would remove him — he holds his office during good behavior — Madness surely is not good behavior.

I have had different ideas of the nature of this process. The first day I thought it criminal, the second day, mixt both criminal & civil; but I am of opinion it is altogether a civil process.

*Mr. Logan.* The accused is now unfit to be a judge, & it is of no consequence to me how he became so — I shall vote for his conviction & removal.

*Mr. Nicholas,* If this resolution is not passed, I shall object to its being recorded.

*Mr. Jackson,* moved the previous question, *viz.* " shall the main question be now put."

*Mr. White.* Whatever question is taken on this subject, I hope will be yeas & nays; & that the resolution and the manner in which it is disposed of, may be seen and understood.

*Mr. Anderson,* then moved to amend the resolution by striking out the words " not having been heard by himself or by council." — & all after the words, " was and yet is insane," to the end of the resolution. —

But this motion for amendment was not seconded.

At three OClock the doors were opened — and Mr. Anderson moved that the resolution should lie on the table. On this question the yeas and nays were required — but the motion of Mr. Anderson's was withdrawn.

The question was then taken by yeas & nays upon the resolution as at first submitted — yeas 9, nays 19 — so it was negatived.

On the motion of Mr. Nicholas, the resolution he yesterday submitted for notifying the House of Representatives, that the Court would be prepared to pronounce judgment on monday next was taken up & passed, yeas 20, nays 9. —

Mr. Bradley found it convenient to be absent from the Court this day — And Mr. Stone fled the question.[161]

## *Tuesday 13th.*

Mr. John Randolph & Mr. Early two of the Members of the House of Representatives appeared at the bar of the Senate, & impeached the sd Chase of high crimes & misdemeanors, & informed that the House of Representatives would in due time, exhibit particular articles of impeachment against him, & make good the same — And also demanded that the Senate should take order for his appearance to answer to the said Impeachment.

The House appointed a Committee to prepare & report Articles of Impeachment against the said Chase; & authorize them to send for persons, papers & records.

---

[161] Plumer's report for March 12 follows the *Annals of Congress* and is omitted here.

## *Wednesday 14th.*

The Senate ordered their Secretary to inform the House of Representatives, that they will take proper order upon the Impeachment of judge Chase, & will give them due notice thereof.

Ordered, That the Secretary of the Senate do wait on the President of the United States, & present to him a copy from the records of the Senate, while sitting as a court of impeachments, of the judgment pronounced by them on the 12th instant, removing from office, John Pickering, district judge of the district of New Hampshire.

## *Monday 19th.*

On saturday Mr. Wright bro't into the Senate a bill for the temporary removal of the seat of government of the United States from the city of Washington to the city of Baltimore — it passed to a second reading. This day he himself moved that the further consideration of said bill be postponed to the first monday of May next — yeas 3, nays 24.

The question was then taken, shall this bill be read a third time, yeas 9, nays 19. —

I voted in favor of this bill, because the accomodations in this city for Congress are very bad and inconvenient — & little prospect of their being better.

## *Thursday 22d.*

The President of the United States nominated to the Senate John Samuel Sherburne to be District Judge of the District of New Hampshire *vice* John Pickering removed by the Senate — & Jonathan Steele to be district attorney for New Hampshire.

## *Saturday 24th.*

The Senate advised to the foregoing appointments. Thus is the man who advised & promoted as far as he was able the impeachment of Judge Pickering, rewarded by being appointed his successor. And Mr. Steele another of the witnesses is raised from Clerk of the Court to Attorney of the District.

Mr. Ellery moved that the Senate sit tomorrow, sunday; Armstrong, Ellery & Samuel Smith were the only senators who voted in favor of it. —

The Senate, refused, to print the record of the proceedings of the Senate, sitting as a Court of Impeachments on the impeachment of John Pickering.

### Monday 26th.

The Committee of the House reported articles of Impeachment against judge Chase — The House ordered them printed for the use of the members of the both Houses, & directed the clerk to transmit to each member of both Houses a copy thereof.

The baker of the Navy erected an oven, & having made a barrel of flour into a loaf he baked it, and called it the *Mammoth-loaf*. This loaf was laid on a bier & covered with white linnen was borne on the shoulders of men, & was this day carried to the Capitol & lodged in a Committee room near adjoining to the Senate Chamber. A large surloin of roasted beef, & casks of wine, cyder and whiskey were provided & deposited in the same place. At twelve O Clock the Chamber was crouded with people of all classes & colors from the President of the United States to the meanest vilest Virginia slave. Mr. Jefferson took his jack knife from his pocket & cut & eat of the beef & bread & drank of the liquors. He compared this drunken frolic to the sacrament of the Lords supper. This motley collection made so much noise & uproar as to disturb the Senate, Mr. Franklin the President Pro. tem. sent Mathers, the sargent at arms, to command silence. He returned & informed the president (Franklin) that they would neither keep silence or disperse. The President then communicated the fact to the Senate; several of the senators approved the measure, requested that the room be cleared, & the liquors & provision instantly removed from the Capitol, & all the Senate concurring, Mathers soon effected it.

At this time, in the Capitol, was seen people, with large prints caricaturing Mr. Wright, for attempting to remove the seat of government. This senator was represented as crouching under the weight of the Capitol resting on his feeble back, with this label in his mouth, " Damn it, it will not move." Some other senator's who voted for the measure were on the print. Mr. Wright fearing insult from the rabble came into the senate with a pair of large horse pistols loaded, determined to defend himself, & if a fair opportunity presented, to take vengence on his libellers. In the *afternoon,* the gallery of the Senate was crouded with the *sovereign mob.* General Jackson [162] in the midst of a speech observing it, turned from the President, & said, " Citizens of Columbia, if ever you are again guilty of the like, you shall be punished — I will inflict it — The navy shall be brought up & kill you outright."

The Senate passed the bill (yeas 20, nays 5) entitled, " An act further to protect the commerce and seamen of the United States, against the Barbary Powers." The object of the bill is to increase the revenue — it levys an additional duty of two & a half per Centum, on goods wares & merchandize imported into the United States after the 30th day of June next. The pretext assigned for this measure is the war with Tripoli — that paltry regency has captured the frigate Philadelphia. The war that will be carried on with that power will not be expensive. The duties that this act will produce to the treasury will be nearly nine hundred thousand dollars pr annum. A sum that will be necessary to pay the interest on the stock created for the purchase of Louisiana!

---

[162] Senator James Jackson was an officer in the Revolutionary army.

## Tuesday 27th.

The Senate passed a bill entitled " An act for imposing more specific duties on the importation of certain articles, & also for levying & collecting light money on foreign ships or vessels." 'Tis said that the light money is designed to equalize our duties with those in Great Britain — And that the changing the ad-volorem duties to specific, is reducing the system of revenue to more certainty & great ease.  But the fact however is, that this act will give an encrease of Revenue to the treasury, of about one hundred thousand dollars annually.  These are the methods the present administration have adopted to raise new taxes.

The bill for appropriating $50000, to be laid out on the public buildings & roads in the City of Washington, passed.

Congress this day adjourned to the first monday in November next.

Note, Mr. Steele not being appointed District Judge, refused to accept the office of District attorney for New Hampshire. And Mr. Sherburne, appointed Richard Cutts Shannon Clerk of the Court — this was the reward of the third witness. — [163]

[163] The Appendix which followed contained copies of documents which are available in print.  Reference has already been made to a number of them

# PART II

MEMORANDUM: PROCEEDINGS OF CONGRESS,
1804–1805

# PART II

*Memorandum of the Proceedings of the second session of the Eight Congress commencing Nov. 5th 1804 & ending March 3d 1805 — with an Appendix containing Extracts & minutes from the Executive Journals of the Senate — & a variety of other papers — Collected by* WILLIAM PLUMER *for his own private use.*

## Nov. 7, 1804.

This day the Senate made a quorum for the first time this session.[1] Mr. Burr, the Vice President, appeared and took his seat in the Senate the very first day of the session. It has been unusual for the Vice President to take his seat the first day of the session. But this man, though indicted in New York & New Jersey for the murder of the illustrious Hamilton, is determined to brave public opinion.[2] What a humiliating circumstance that a man Who for months has fled from justice — & who by the legal authorities is now accused of murder, should preside over the first branch of the National Legislature!

I have avoided him — his presence to me is odious — I have merely bowed & spoken to him — Federalists appear to despise neglect & abhor him. The democrats, at least many of them, appear attentive to him — & he is very familiar with them — What line of conduct they will generally observe to him is yet uncertain.

---

[1] The Senate convened on November 5 but adjourned for want of a quorum. The same was true of the following day.

[2] The duel between Burr and Hamilton was fought July 11, 1804. Hamilton died the next day. Burr was indicted by the Grand Jury in the County of New York for sending the challenge, and a charge of murder was made against him by the Grand Jury of Bergen County, New Jersey; see J. Q. Adams, *Memoirs*, I, 314–315.

185

## *Nov 8. 1804.*

This day the President of the United States sent his message
to the two houses of Congress.[3]  It is, perhaps, more empty &
vapid, & wrapt in greater obscurity than any of his preceding
messages.  I know that this is saying much; but in *this*, such
is the generality of his expressions, & the ambiguity of his style,
that they will admit of different interpretations, & be appli-
cable to events that may hereafter happen, as will best suit
his crooked policy.  I do not mean to analize this production.
I shall on this, & on any other subject, I may mention, set
down, as I have leisure & inclination a few ideas — & state a
few facts — such as may in some future leisure moment contribute to my information & amusement.  I write this for
*myself*, not others — The style will be incorrect — but it will
preserve to me the remembrance of certain Opinions & facts.

In this message the President says, " While noticing the
*irregularities* committed on the ocean by *others*, those on our
own part should not be omitted, nor left *unprovided for."*  What,
are we to *provide for irregularities!*  " Complaints ", continues
he, " have been received, that persons residing within the United
States, have taken on themselves to arm merchant vessels & to
force a commerce into certain ports & countries in defiance of
the laws of those countries.  That individuals should undertake
to wage private war, independant of the authority of their
country, cannot be permitted in a well ordered society.  Its
tendency to produce aggresion on the laws and rights of other
nations, & to endanger the peace of our own, is so obvious, that
I doubt not you will adopt measures for restraining it effectually in future."

Into what *ports & countries is this trade forced?*  Is it on
the Spanish coast? is it the trade carried on by South Carolina,
& from other States, to the coast of Africa? or is it the trade

---

[3] See Richardson, *Messages and Papers of the Presidents,* I, 369–373.

to St Domingo?   To each of these, many of the merchants are
in the habit of arming their vessels.   And to either of them
will the paragraph apply, & be fully satisfied.   Those, however,
who pretend to be in habits of intimacy with the President, say
that he meant the trade with St Domingo.   That he thought it
necessary to make a peace offering to the emperor of France,
though at the expence of the rightful commerce of the United
States.

Let us bestow a few moments attention to the *right* which our
merchants have to maintain trade with the island of St Domingo.
Let us state facts & principles that apply to the case.

It is difficult to draw the distinction, at the threshold, between
a revolution & a rebellion.   The issue often decides & gives both
character & name.   Success stamps it a revolution, subjugation
marks it rebellion.   But a neutral nation ought not to undertake
to decide between the government of another nation, & the
opposers of that nation.   When a party is strong enough to
oppose the government & laws, it is a civil war.   Civil war dis-
solves the bands of society.   The two parties must be considered
as two bodies — as two societies.   They stand in relation to
other powers, as two nations who engage in a contest.   And the
common laws of war ought to be observed by each to the other
— & by all neutral nations to them.   A foreign nation has no
authority to decide between them.

The island of St Domingo was formerly a colony of France,
composed of white & black population.   The blacks were the
slaves of the whites.   An insurrection took place, & after a
violent contest, the blacks were by the government of France
declared to be free.   They are then a part of the community.
Another insurrection takes place, & this colony attempts a
seperation from France, & aims at independence.   The government of France attempts to subdue them — the colony opposes
— & the French are obliged to wage war against them.   They
are therefore two independent parties; & there is no power on

earth to judge between them.   The island is no longer a province of France, for french laws have there no longer any binding force.   The trade of the island is governed by laws of its own government — & the laws of France have no more influence or efficacy there, than those of the United States.   The island therefore must be treated as under the law of nations.[4]

St. Domingo, in the view of all the world, must be considered, not as a province of France, but as an independent State, with whom any nation has a right to traffick.   An anonymous, but able, writer, in the Gazette of the United States of Nov 3, 1804, says, " Every State is the sole judge of the propriety, & regulations of commerce on her part.   A state of war may produce other rights in another nation.   But these rights do not take away or destroy the rights of a neutral trading with one of the belligerents.   They may subject the property in the exercise of those rights to danger, but the rights may be exercised without violation of the law of nations.   To elucidate this point & apply it.   France & St Domingo are two independent parties engaged in a war.   The United States are neutral to both.   The citizens of the United States have an indisputable right to carry on commerce with either of the belligerents.   The property engaged in the commerce is exposed to condemnation, if the property is contraband of war, if there be a breach of an existing blockade, or if there be a denial of the right of search. But this is the mere risque of the individual engaged in the trade, & the trade itself is free & open, subject to those risques.   The government is not to be considered as interfering between the belligerents by this commerce of its individuals; the commerce itself should not be restrained by the neutral government unless for political reasons of its own; & the failure of that government to restrain such commerce, was never considered as a departure from strict neutrality.

---

[4] After the capture of Toussaint l'Overture by the French, the blacks renewed their struggle under Jean Jacques Dessalines. The French evacuated the island in November, 1803. Independence was declared and in October, 1804, Dessalines proclaimed himself emperor.

"From these observations I think it evident, on general grounds, that our citizens are not engaged in an unlawful trade with the island of St Domingo, & that our government has no call upon it, on the principles of good faith & natural law, to interfer with the trade."

No power but France can consider that island as in a state of rebellion; & even that nation must treat her in the existing war, as entitled to all the rights of an independent *warring* state. For one nation has no right to judge another.

During the American struggle for Independence, did not the *merchants* of France, of Holland, & of other nations, trade with the United States? And was this trade of the merchants, considered as an interference of the government of those nations, with the controversy between Great Britain and the United States? Certainly not. Let trade be free, but let the government preserve that faith which both policy & justice require. Let not Congress, nor the Government, interfere with the trade of individuals, & there will be no cause of war against us from France.

Our Merchants have traded to St Domingo — Our government has never once intimated to them that that trade was unlawful — or that they ought not to arm their vessels in carrying it on. — On the contrary our Merchants have at our Custom houses cleared out their vessels for that island, when they were known to be fully armed & manned. Not a single Collector has refused, or even hesitated, to give them a Clearance. Will our government now, from a servile fear of offending the French Emperor, admit the principle, & declare, that trade unlawful, & thereby expose our innocent merchants to ruin!

Speaking of the establishment of a district & port of entry on the waters of the Mobile in Louisiana, giving offence to Spain, the President, says, that *the object was misunderstood on the part of Spain — & that the explanation sent to Spain, & the instrument establishing the port & district will satisfy them.* Mr. Jefferson, the last session, publickly declared, & to me personally said, " that the whole of West Florida was included in our purchase of Louisiana " — And the act of Congress of the last session providing for the government of that country, recognizes West Florida — It authorizes the President to *erect the shores, waters & inlets of the bay of Mobile, & of the other rivers, creeks, inlets & bays, empting into the gulph of Mexico, " east " of the said river Mobile, & west thereof to the Pascaguola inclusive, into a seperate district for the collection of duties on imports & tonnage.* Observe the *consistent* conduct of the President — in his proclamation of the 30th of May last establishing & designating this port — Does he assert our right to West Florida — No — he makes use of language capable, & I beleive intended, to convey, at least to the court of Madrid, an idea that the United States did not claim West Florida. After he had recited the *italized* paragraph aforesaid he says, " I do hereby decide, that all the above mentioned shores, waters, inlets, creeks & rivers, lying *within the boundaries of the United States,* shall constitute and form a seperate district, to be denominated, *The District of Mobile;* & do also designate Fort Stoddert *within the district aforesaid,* to be the port of Entry & delivery for the sd district."

Charles Pinkney's convention with Spain, to which the Senate the last year advised the President to ratify, is not ratified by the government of Spain.[5]

The President says, " that the objections which had been urged by that government, (Spain) against the *validity* of our title to the country of Louisiana, have been *withdrawn;* its exact limits however remaining still to be settled between us." One would be led to suppose, from this sentence, that the court of Madrid fully acknowledges the *justice & legality* of our claim to that country. Mr. Jefferson's information on this subject, is derived from a letter from Cevallos, the Spanish minister of

[5] See *American State Papers,* II. *Foreign Relations,* II, 475–483.

State, to Charles Pinckney our minister of that Court, dated Feby 10, 1804, & from a letter from the Marquiss of Casa Yrujo, the Spanish minister here, to our Secretary of State, dated May 15, 1804.[6] Cevallos says, " his majesty has tho't fit to renounce his opposition to the alienation of Louisiana made by France, *notwithstanding the solid reasons on which it is founded*" — The Marquiss says, " The *explanations which the government of France has given* to his Catholic Majesty, concerning the sale of Louisiana to the United States, & the amicable dispositions on the part of the king my master towards these states; have determined him to abandon the opposition, which at a prior period, & *with the most substantial motives*, he *had manifested against that transaction*." This is not an acknowledgement of our title — it is at most, but waiving their opposition to it, accompanied with a solemn explicit declaration, that, their objection to our claim is founded on *solid reasons*. Mr. Jefferson well knows, that the ground on which the government of Spain refused compensation for the *illegal condemnations* of our shipping & of our commerce in their ports, was on the express declaration *That the Spanish nation were compelled by the strong arm of the French Republic to permit those adjudications to be made — that Spain could not prevent them, & therefore was not answerable to our merchants*. And even in this case, the Marquiss is careful, to assign as the reason, why Spain abandoned her opposition to our claim to Louisiana, *that the government of France has given such explanations to his Catholic majesty as induced him to do it*. At a future, & more propitious period, Spain may renew her *well founded opposition* to our title — she may then claim that country, & alledge that her present abandonment ought not to operate against her, for that she was compelled to the measure by the irresistable arm of France — & not being her voluntary act, it cannot bind her.

---

[6] The letters from Cevallos and Casa Yrujo are not in the *American State Papers* with the correspondence on this subject.

The last year the President had much to say respecting the immense value of the *salt mountains* of Louisiana. Time has made him silent on that subject. But now we are told of there being many *rich lead mines* in that country. Baits like these are well calculated to keep alive the expectation of the credulous, & draw their attention from the immense debt we owe for that country.

He recommends the encreasing the number of *Gun-boats* as the best means of guarding & securing our harbours & seaports. But we are surprised to find him, in his enumeration of there advantages, saying, they will prove " an *obstacle* to naval enterprize." — But he might say this, with greater propriety than that they would " be manned by the *militia* of the place." They will prove an *obstacle to Naval enterprize* — yes, this whimsical phylosophic President is expending that money in building these boats that are incapable of sailing on the rough sea or of being of use to us, instead of building ships of the line & frigates to defend our national honor, & the commerce of our country. — This ardour for gun-boats is like his idle plan for *dry docks*. His gun boat No. 1. is now safely on shore in a *corn field* in the south.[7]

He informs us that the receipts at the treasury for the year ending 30th September last, amounts to $11,500,000 — & that during that time they have paid $3,600,000 of the principle of the public debt — And that the probable receipts of the ensuing year will be sufficient to meet all the current demands of that year. To inform the *people* that we have a *full treasury* is grateful to them. But he takes care to insinuate that this is owing to his *prudence & oeconomy* — when in fact it is the effect, the product, of federal laws & federal regulations. Yes the great *increase* of our population & wealth, must necessarily encrease our revenue, while the laws & regulations upon the

---

[7] See McMaster, *History of the People of the United States,* III, 195–197.

subject of revenue established by the preceeding administrations, are suffered to remain. But why is the President altogether silent respecting our *brave seamen* who for a year have been close prisoners in Tripoli? Why has the crew of the Phila-delphia, been suffered thus long to remain, not only in a state of captivity, but of *actual slavery,* with the barbarous Tripoli-tans?[8] Not for the want of money to redeem them, — for we are told the treasury is full. Why are we amused with stories of wild land purchased of the Indians — of building gun-boats & no care, no attention paid to these suffering seamen? Is the President's regard for the welfare & prosperity of our navy, & of our commerce, to be found, in his gasconading professions? And does he in fact, mean, that his *guns boats* shall, while he presides over the nation, prove real *obstacles to naval enter-prize?*

### Saturday 10th.

Went in company with several of my friends, to pay a cere-monious visit to the President of the United States. Some of the Federalists think we ought not to visit him, because he acts more as the head of a faction, than that of the nation. I shall visit him, & of course intend, when invited, to dine with him. He is President, & we must acknowledge him such. These are visits & dinners of ceremony. Beside, I have a curiosity, which is gratified, by seeing & conversing with him. I gain a more thorough knowledge of his character, & of his views, & those of his party — for he is naturally communicative.

I found the President dressed better than I ever saw him at any time when I called on a morning visit. Though his coat was old & thread bare, his scarlet vest, his corduroy small cloths, & his white cotton hose, were new & clean — but his linnen was much soiled, & his slippers old — His hair was cropt & powdered.

---

[8] The *Philadelphia* was captured on October 21, 1803.

His conversation was vapid — mere common place observations on the weather — crops and sickness of particular districts. From these he went into an elaborate defence of Horseracing — he said it was an effectual means to improve the breed of horses — That nineteen out of 20 of the horses that were bredd for the race would not answer that purpose — that these nineteen proved excellent horses for the saddle & for the carriage, & the twentieth only answers for the turf. That all people will have their amusemants — that horse racing is less injurious to the people than playing at cards or dice as the Bostonians do. In the latter case a man is frequently ruined by a single game of cards, or throw of the dice — but not so at horse raising — it requires several races to sweep a man's property, & that gives time for reflection.

He observed that the last year the Senate adjourned over the races, on the pretext of having their wall mended — What will now be the excuse? Mr. Hillhouse replied, we can next week adjourn to have our Chamber fitted to try Judge Chase on the Impeachment now pending in the House. The President hung his head — silence ensued — the state of the weather became the topic of conversation — Tarried about half an hour.

### Monday 12th.

The President of the United States nominated James Monroe now our Minister at the Court of London, as Minister plenipotentiary & Envoy extraordinary to the Court of Madrid, for the purposes mentioned in a former nomination, in which, Monroe was, with Charles Pinckney, appointed jointly — but which appointment is rendered void by the intended return of said Pinckney.

What, notwithstanding all that is said in the Message, respecting Spain, being at peace with us, is a Minister plenipotentiary & envoy extraordinary to be sent to that nation?

I have no doubt that Pinckney has insisted on terms that the

Spanish nation will not grant — that he has informed that Court that an appeal to arms must decide the controversy between the two nations — He could stay no longer — But Mr. Jefferson sends Monroe from England to tell Spain we have thought better of it — Give us peace on the best terms you can afford — At all events give us peace — We will relinquish our claims for spoilation on our commerce — we will abandon most of Louisiana with the mountains of salt & rich lead mines if you will consent to give us what *we now own,* West Florida! This is the humble language of the Philosophic American Court. And I shall not be surprised to find, that our Administration, under the idea of *establishing "the exact limits" of Louisiana* should relinquish the greater part of that Country & receive in exchange West Florida — & we paying, as the ballance of that exchange, to our own subjects, a sum adjudged equavalent to the Spanish spoilations on our commerce!

### *Thursday 15th.*

This is the third day this week that the Senate have adjourned without making a quorum. The clock in the Senate Chamber has been moved forward half an hour beyond the true time— a majority of the Senate Democrats appeared anxious to attend the horse races — The Vice President was in the chair precisely at 11 OClock, by the Senate clock, & observed *we shall have no quorum, it is best to adjourn.* — I have myself no objections to adjourning thus early, because the less business is done by Congress the better it will be for the Union — I have never attended the horse races.

### *Friday Nov 16, 1804.*

At 11 OClock AM. the Senate met — Mr. Bradley moved that we now go into the consideration of Executive business — Carried. The gallery was cleared & the doors closed — He then said my object in making the motion was that it might appear from the journal that we do some business — that object is attained — I therefore move that the Senate now adjourn to monday next — Carried.[9]

### Saturday 17th.

There is a standing rule of the Senate that extracts shall not be *furnished* from the Executive records of the Senate.[10] These journals are never published — they remain in the office of the Secretary of the Senate, & any member of the Senate has access to them at any time. For two or three days I have been reading in the first volume in the Senate chamber & taken minutes therefrom. To day I received a note from Mr. Otis the Secretary informing me that one of the Senate had complained to him of my having those journals out of the office — & advising me to read them in his office in future. I fear I shall be unable to compleat my object — altho' I now examine them in the Secretary's office — Formerly Mr. Burr the Vice President carried them to his lodging; & Mr. Ross one of the senators did the same — But the times are changed, & I am one of a small minority.

From the information received from New Hampshire & Massachusetts it appears probable that in both those States the democratic list of Electors for President & Vice President will prevail; & that in Massachusetts a majority of the members for the ninth Congress from that State will be democratic. A few days will give us conclusive information on these points. I have no doubt myself that the democratic ticket, in Massachusetts, for Electors has prevailed — & I think it probable that a majority of the Representatives for the next Congress from that State will be also democratic. From the little information, I have received, from New Hampshire, I am strongly

---

[9] J. Q. Adams in his *Memoirs* (I, 315) notes: "The races at length are finished, and the Senate really met this day." Adams criticized the Senate's action on Bradley's motion.

[10] Rule XXXIX.

inclined to beleive that State has elected democratic Electors of President & Vice President. Many of the federalists in New Hampshire, said if they chose Federal Electors their votes would be lost, for Mr. Jefferson would be re-elected as President, & Mr. Clinton be elected as Vice President — & that the votes of New Hampshire would not avail. This single circumstance, I am confident has prevented many from attending the meeting's. If the federalists have prevailed in that State, their vote will be unavailing — they have gained nothing — but if they have been unsuccessful they have lost much. This Democratic Victory will not only tend to mark the character of the State as democratic, but it will discourage many federalists — it will add to the number of democrats, & will, I fear, render them triumphant at the March elections. I consider New Hampshire & Massachusetts in fact as revolutionized — their next governors & legislatures will be democratic. The state of parties has been progressing to this point for a long time. In New Hampshire all that federalists could do in our legislature was to have the people choose the Electors by a general ticket, for a majority of our legislature are democratic. But in Massachusetts a majority of their legislature were federal — they had on a former occasion passed a law authorizing their Legislature to choose the Electors — & they ought to have done it now. Imprudently they authorized the people to do it — unnecessarily they multiplied the business of town meetings, & the federalists have now discovered what they ought to have known long ago that their honesty & integrity is not a match for the wiles & subtilties, deceit & falshood of democrats.

Delaware has a federal Governor & legislature & her representative & senators for the Ninth Congress are federal. She has chosen federal Electors.

Connecticut has a federal governor, legislature, & all her members to Congress, & her Electors, are federal. The Democrats in that State are clamouring with the people because

they have no _written State constitution_. This I think is a
fortunate circumstance for the federalists of that state, if
they improve it. It presents them with an opportunity to
withdraw, in a great measure, their opposition to the measures
of the general government, & fix the attention of the people
to their own immediate local interests — To the necessity of
continuing men in office, who will preserve inviolate their
present constitution, form of government, laws & institutions.
And to avoid men who wish to innovate upon a system, &
institutions, under which they, & their Ancestors, have lived for
more than 140 years, in peace & prosperity.[11]

But in New Hampshire our Democrats do not propose to
change our laws, much less our constitution — They wish to
turn federalists out of office, & get into place themselves &
introduce innovations imperceptibly. The only rallying point
we have is against the abuses of power & the ruinous measures
of the general government — The domination of Virginia, &
the degradation of New Hampshire — The inequalities & injustice of the present measures. These are it is true solid
grounds, whereon to rest our defence — Yet what chance have
we to succeed. A mania has seized the public mind — Few men
have talents to investigate the measures & conduct of administration— few indeed, have the talents requisite to investigate,
or the means to know & understand the principles of government — still fewer, have the inclination to make that investigation, & to communicate the result to the people — 'Tis
unreasonable — tis absurd — to expect a whole people should
be statesmen — you may as well expect every man to be a
watchmaker. — Mankind are naturally credulous — the unblushing assurance with which a democrat retails lies, gains
more credit with the multitude, than the truth.

In this state of things, what measures ought the Federalists

---

[11] The Connecticut charter of 1662 was the basis of government
until the adoption of a State constitution in 1818.

in Congress to pursue, what line of conduct ought they to observe? I think myself, federalism can never rise again. — The democrats in New England, aided by the whole force of the general government will, & must prevail — They will have a triumphant majority. This is my opinion, & if this is correct — I think it is best for us, in Congress, to be silent — Debate none — move no amendments — when we are required to vote, then vote, for, or against, the measure, as to us appears right. Always act our own opinions. But if we debate, our debates will not convince either a democrat here, or at home — but our silent votes would alarm them here — they would more sensibly feel their responsibility — irration from us would cease — they would divide among themselves — & sooner produce a state of things more favorable. —

If the March elections in New Hampshire should terminate in favor of democracy — I shall then consider federalism as down to rise there no more. And that the most prudent course, not only as it respect myself as an individual, but as it respects the public weal, will be for me, to observe a *total silence upon politic's*. Attend no town meetings — By this means opposition will cease, & the rage of party be no more. For 'tis opposition that supports party — And if party rage can be quieted — we may thereby save our constitution, laws, tribunals & altars, — & preserve those steady habits & manners that are our security. The general government may then desist from their war against our institutions.

My sentiments respecting the government of the United States is not changed. I am still a federalist — I still consider the great leading measures of the federalists as being correct. But I beleive federalism is too pure a government for the people — That it presupposes more knowledge & virtue in the mass of the people than they really have. That the present democratic system flatters the vanity, the follies, & vices of the people — that it deceives them — & arms the worst passions in man against men of talents integrity & property — & thus supports itself.[12]

These are the impressions that arise in my mind from the most thorough view I am able to take of the present situation of my country — & the government over it. I freely own, that I feel gloomy — though I have long contemplated such a state of things. I am determined not to form resolutions hastily — but I am more & more convinced of the necessity of talking but little myself on the subject — hear & weigh the opinions of others but give none myself except where absolutely necessary. I do not think I shall feel much difficulty in this, unless it be to restrain myself. My taciturnity will seldom offend the company with which I may be — for most men are fonder, of speaking than of hearing others. At all events, I will write more for myself, & less to others, than I did the former sessions. And what I write on politic's shall be with caution. As I do not see a rational prospect of doing good, I think it would be imprudent unnecessarily to expose myself.

I feel no disposition to shrink from my duty — much less to court the dominant part. The latter I can never do — to such a party, so long as I am what I am, & they remain what they now are, I never can or will unite.

### Tuesday 20th.

Yesterday the President nominated, & to day the Senate advised to the following appointments —

James Bowdoin of Massachusetts as Minister plenipotentiary from the United States to the Court of Madrid.

William Lyman, of Massachusetts, to be Naval officer & Inspector of the Port of New Orleans.

George W. Erving, of Massachusetts as Secretary of Legation to Spain.

---

[12] Although Plumer is pessimistic over the political outlook, there is no trace here of the extreme measures suggested in some of his letters; see Plumer, *Life of William Plumer*, 285 ff.

Franklin Wharton, of Pennsylvania, now a major, to be Lt. Col. Commãdant of the Marine Corps, in the room of Col. Burrows resigned.

Since the prevalence of democracy in Massachusetts, the administration appear determined to heap appointments upon their friends in that State.

### Thursday 22d.

The Senate passed the bill appropriating $70000, for carrying into effect the treaty of amity, commerce & Navigation with Great Britain.

### Friday 23d.

This day while I was in the Secretary's office, reading & taking a *few* minutes from the Executive Journal of the Senate, Mr. Otis came to me in much haste & great fear — & said, " Sir, you have taken minutes — you will injure me — & complaint will be made by one of the Senators to the Senate against you — I fear — I hold my office at the will of violent men ". — I asked him who had complained of my conduct — He declined to name any one — but I was satisfied to whom he alluded. I shut the book, informed him I would now desist. I went into the senate chamber and conversed with Baldwin & Worthington upon the subject separately — & informed them that I had taken minutes &c. Baldwin replied I had done nothing improper — & that the rule of the Senate was *only to prohibit the Secretary from furnishing extracts* — not the senators from taking minutes to aid their memory — & that he had done it frequently himself. — Worthington said every senator had a right to read those records, & that his honor would prohibit him from making an improper use of them — & that all he feared was, that possibly incorrect statements might be published from them & the public mind be mislead — That for his own part he really wished, these journals were printed & published — I assured him I should publish no book — & since it gave offence

I should take no further minutes — He said he was *not dis-satisfied* with my conduct. But I know the man, *his smiles are the smiles of deceit*. What course these men contemplated I know not. It may be that they wished to make me desist from reading those journals, least I should obtain the knowledge of certain facts which if promulgated would injure them. They will not prevent my reading — & tho' I shall take no minutes — I will read them with that attention that shall so impress the contents on the tablets of my memory, as to enable me at my chamber to make such minutes as I may on some future day have occasion to use. It is possible that some of them contemplated a different proceedure — that they would con-sider me as violating one of the Rules of the Senate — & for that violation, a triumphant majority would expell me, & give to our democratic Legislature an opportunity of sending a man of different politic's. But I cannot beleive, blind & prejudiced as party spirit renders men that they are prepared for such a course. Such is the state of things that at present I can do little service to my country in my present station; but I dare not at present resign it. I would not by improper or imprudent conduct forfeit my seat; but if I could honorably retire to private life — to the bosom of my family — my friends & my study — I would do it cheerfully.

Another reason, & perhaps the only one that influences the democratic senators respecting my taking these minutes may be, a pretext to quarrel with Mr. Otis, that they may bring in one of their tools to be Secretary. Since writing the foregoing, I am inform'd that Worthington told one of the Secretary's Clerk's that *he ought to have prohibited me from having access to those journals.* A pretty fellow indeed!

### Saturday 24th.

I have received a pamphlet entitled "Republican Address to the Electors of New Hampshire on the choice of Electors of

President & Vice President." This pamphlet was industriously circulated among the Democrats in that State a few days previous to the Meetings on the 5th of this month. I have no doubt it had influence on many of them, & with the personal applications of those who distributed it, induced them to attend & vote at the Meetings. It is written for the avowed purpose of answering the pamphlet published in that State under the signature of *Impartialis*.[13] But it is mere rant and declamation, & what is worse it contains many falsehoods. It is destitute of fact & argument. It had not, on that account, however, I presume, the less effect on the sovereign people. It attributes Impartialis to my pen; & whilst it contains much scurrility & abuse, it ascribes the success of the federal ticket for representatives to the ninth Congress from New Hampshire, to my pamphlet. I do not repent the publication, though by democrats, at home & abroad, I am much abused & villified. To a few friends I have owned myself the author — to enimies I have neither owned or denied it. It has met with the approbation of some men of talents literature & science — It has been republished in many news papers in several of the States. And if it will serve as an index, to direct inquisitive minds to investigate the several subjects it mentions, my labour will not be in vain.

### Monday 26th.

I am now satisfied with the course Administration and the democratic members of Congress, intend to pursue in relation to Mr. Burr. I never had any doubts of their joy for the death of Hamilton; my only doubts were whether they would manifest that joy, by carressing his murderer. Those doubts are now dispelled — Mr. Jefferson has shewn more attention & invited Mr. Burr oftener to his house within this three weeks than ever he did in the course of the same time before. Mr. Gallatin,

---

[13] *Cf. ibid.,* 311–316.

the Secy of the Treasury, has waited upon him often at his (Burr's) lodging — & on one day was closetted with him more than two hours. The Secretary of State, Mr. Madison, formerly the intimate friend of Genl Hamilton, has taken his murderer into his carriage rode with him — accompanied him on a visit to M. Terreau the French Minister. Mr. Giles, of Virginia, the ministerial leader in the Senate, has just drawn up a paper addressed to Governor Bloomfield of New Jersey — stating in explicit terms that the late duel between Hamilton & Burr was a fair duel — & that the latter killed the former fairly —& that Burr who only killed his antagonist in a fair duel was *not guilty of murder,* & requesting that the Governor would direct a Nolle prosequi to be entered on the indictment now pending in that State. I have not seen the Address It was not shewn to New England Senators — It was presented to Mr. White of Delaware, who declined signing it — It was signed by many, if not all, of the Democratic senators present, & I presume by General Dayton.[14] Whether a similar address was presented to Gentlemen of the House I know not. — The Democrats of both Houses are remarkably attentive to Burr — And I presume, nothing but the votes of the last winter Caucus, prevent them from again electing him to the office of Vice President. What office, they can, or will, give him, is uncertain — They know the man, & will not choose to trust him unnecessarily. Duane, in his Aurora, has declared in his favour.

Paid a visit to the Navy yard — was surprized to find how fast our little navy is rotting in the mud of the Potomac. Shipping laid up in the harbours of the eastern states will endure much longer & be in a situation much more convenient to the Ocean then they are here. Saw the keels of two Gun boats — As the means of naval defence they will to us be altogether unavailing — As a mean to waste public money, divert the attention of the sovereign people from the necessity of building

---

[14] *Cf.* J. Q. Adams, *Memoirs,* I, 317–318.

a Navy — & gratify the whims of the *Chief* — they will have a powerful effect.

The frigate General Greene is rotten in many of her timbers. The Secretary of the Navy has ordered her to be cut down & to be moored near the wharf, & a roof like that of a house to be built over her. She is to be a store ship to contain salted provisions & the cables & rigging of other ships. It seems to me as the Navy Yard is large & land cheap it would have been better to have built a permanent store on the land.

Within a few days Genl Turreau the Imperial Minister from the Emperor of France arrived here. He appears in great splendor — is very attentive to dress & equipage. It is said on high authority, that previous to his audience, he dispatched his Aid, who now acts as his Secretary, to Mr. Jefferson to know what was the *Court-dress*. I cannot learn what the answer was — but if it comported with truth — It was, as is described, page 17.[15]

On the very first day of the sessions John Randolph moved for the appointment of the standing Committees of the House. — The motion prevailed, & the Speaker appointed them. The names of those members who appear & take their seats on the first day of the session are entered on the Journals — & the other members are entered as they appear. The Speaker said it was a rule to appoint no man on a Committee whose name was not previously on the Journals of the session in which he was appointed. Among the committees thus appointed, was that of *Ways & Means.* Mr. Randolph was again of that Committee & chairman. Mr. Roger Griswold had been several years of that committee, & the thorough knowledge that he possesses of the state of our finances, rendered him a highly useful & important member. Randolph knew his talents, & respected him, notwithstanding Mr. Griswold's federalism — & anxiously wished his aid as a member of that committee. In

---

[15] Page 193 of this volume.

a private conversation with the Speaker, he said Griswold must be appointed of that Committee, & that he would move to encrease the number.  The Speaker told him that would not avail — for he could not appoint two men from the same State on one Committee.  Randolph then used his influence to induce Mr. Davenport, who is from Connecticut, to request the House to excuse him from serving on that Committee.  He did not, indeed apply personally to Davenport — but he did by the agency of one of his friends.  This application wounded the pride of Davenport — it conveyed to him an idea that he was not qualified for the station — and of course he would not request to be excused.

On the same day the Committee of *Claims* was appointed. John C. Smith a federalist from Connecticut was of the first named & appointed on this Committee.  He had been chairman of that committee for several years.  On the 6th day of this month Mr. Smith moved, & the House excused him from serving on that Committee.  Mr. Saml W. Dana from the same state was appointed of the same Committee in Mr. Smith's stead. It had from long use become one of the fix'd Rules of the House for the man first named to be chairman of the Committee. And it has been generally understood that in case of the chairman being absent, or being excused from the committee, that the second man on the list shall of course succeed as Chairman.  The business of Chairman of a standing committee is very arduous & attended with much labour.  His duty is to call the Committee together, draw up the report in writing, which frequently is prolix & argumentative — And in the House he must support & defend the Report.  David Holmes of Virginia was the second on this committee, & ought according to former usage to act as Chairman.[16]  But its evident that the Democrats considered him as unequal to the task.  The com-

---

[16] For the personnel of the committee, see House *Journal,* (1804–1807; reprint of 1826), V, 5; *Annals of Congress,* 8 Cong., 2 sess., 678.

mittee were summoned together — the first question was a motion from one of the democratic members to choose a Chairman. Mr. Dana remonstrated against it, as being a violation of long established usage, & as calculated to wound the feelings of the man who of right was now chairman. After several meetings the Committee voted that Mr. Dana should be their chairman. He told them he should not accept the appointment. They then requested him to move the House to excuse him from the Committee. He replied he had no objection to serving on the committee, tho' he was willing to be excused. He was the man *last* appointed, & it was not his lot to do the duty of the *first*. After flattering & threatning to no purpose, they pursued another course.

Nov. 20th A motion was made in the House, to add a new rule to the standing rules & orders of the House — " That each of the committees of this House be empowered to appoint a Chairman, by plurality of votes, in all cases where the first named member of the Committee shall be absent, or excused by the House." Referred to a Committee.[17]

On the 22d the Committee reported, " That the member first named on such of the standing & select committees of this House, shall be the chairman thereof; & in case of his absence, or of his being excused by the House, *the committee shall then appoint the member, by a majority of votes, who shall be their chairman.*" Mr. R. Griswold, moved to strike out the words in italics & insert in lieu thereof, " the member next named on such committee, shall be chairman; & in like manner, shall the senior member present of such committee, be the chairman, in case of the absence of the chairman, or in case he shall be excused by the House." The amendment was lost ayes 45, nays 56; & also the report of the committee ayes 50, nays 60.[18]

---

[17] See House *Journal*, V, 18–19; *Annals of Congress*, 8 Cong., 2 sess., 692.

[18] *Cf.* House *Journal*, V, 20–21; *Annals of Congress*, 8 Cong., 2 sess., 697–698.

On the 23d a rule was moved, "That committees, in all cases, shall choose their own chairman; & it shall be incumbent on the person so chosen to serve, unless he be excused by the House." This was disagreed to. The House, after long debate established the following rule — "That the first named member of any committee appointed by the Speaker, or the House, shall be the Chairman; & in case of his absence, or being excused by the House, the next named member, & so on as often as the case shall happen, unless the committee shall, by a majority of their number, elect a chairman." [19]

The Committee of Claims held several meetings & the democratic members elected Mr. Dana chairman — declaring at the same time that Mr. Holmes should not have that office. Mr. Dana requested to be excused, but they would not consent. He has not yet accepted — but I presume he will — for should he peremptorily refuse they might expel him from the House. —

### Tuesday 27th.

This day, in company with Mesrs. Pickering, Hillhouse & Olcott, paid a visit of ceremony to General Turreau, the imperial minister from France. He was not dressed in his Court dress, but decent-booted — hair powdered & Cued — He is 48 years of age middle sized — top of his head bald. Speaks but little English — he told me that its only four weeks since he began to learn our language — He has certainly made great proficiency for the time. He was as social as the knowledge of our language would permit — Inquisitive as to the organization & operations of our government. He is not so pleasant or agreeable as M. Petition [20] — His countenance indicates a ferocious disposition & an obstinate fixed determination of mind. His Aid, who acts as his Secretary, was in full military dress.

---

[19] *Cf.* House *Journal,* V, 22; *Annals of Congress,* 8 Cong., 2 sess., 699.

[20] Pichon.

General Varnum, a member of the House from Massachusetts, handed me a letter from Boston, by which it appears that the democratic list of Electors has prevailed by a majority of between 3 and 4000. "Thus," said he to me, in an insulting tone, "the Republicans of Massachusetts have triumphed, notwithstanding the great exertions of the New England monarchists, & the clamour, raised by them, against Virginia domination. The county of Essex is the head quarters of Monarchy, yet even there we have obtained a majority of the votes." He, and several of his party, discovered much bitterness of spirit & insolence.

In the morning, half an hour before the Senate met, I was in the Senate Chamber, & half a dozen senators were present, & General Bradley read aloud to them, in my hearing, a most insolent abusive attack upon me, as being the writer of Impartialis. Bradley appeared much pleased with the abuse — Worthington looked malignant, & spoke contemptuously — I made no reply. — I will pursue the steady path of duty unmoved by their scurility. —

*Wednesday Nov. 28, 1784.*[21]

The House of Representatives when Congress first came to this city sat in the Library room. The *round House*, commonly called the *Dutch Oven*, was built by Mr. Jefferson. This cost $10000 — This year it has by his order been pulled down, and the south wing of the capitol is now building on the spot where the Dutch oven stood. The Representatives now hold their sessions in the Library room — That room had been fitted up at an expence of $700. It is too small a room to accomodate the House. The library is removed at the expence of 3 or $400. to a small adjoining chamber. Most of the houses erected in the neighborhood of the Navy yard, were built & are in-

---

[21] 1804.

habited by the mechannic's who work there. Few new buildings of any magnitude have been erected within the city this year.

### Thursday 29th.

The House have this day debated upon a bill " To regulate the clearance of armed vessels." [22] This bill is designed to prevent armed merchant vessels from receiving clearances from the Custom House, unless the owner will give bond " Not to commit any depredation, outrage, unlawful assault, or violence against the vessels, citizens, subjects, or territory of any nation in amity with the United States." But this is not to extend to vessels bound to the Mediterranean, or beyond the Cape of Good Hope. It authorizes the Collector of any Port, if he has evidence that any vessel is armed or arming in such port, to " detain such vessel untill the case is submitted to the President of the United States, who is authorized to cause such vessel to be disarmed, or to order a clearance to be granted, as he shall judge proper." This is vesting the President with a very extensive discretionary power!

The real design of the bill is to restrain the trade of our merchants to St. Domingo — altho' that place or even the West Indies is not named. Dr. Eustis, the chairman of the select Committee, who reported the bill, observed to that committee that it would not answer to prohibit that trade. But that we must do something to keep up an appearance of friendship for Napolean. That the French Minister has arrived here no doubt charged with complaints upon this subject — And that our Administration think it best to anticipate his demands, & pass a law upon the subject.

I do not myself approve of the law — 'tis too vague — too uncertain— it contains no definition of what is an *unlawful trade*.

---

[22] Approved, March 3, 1805; see *Statutes at Large,* II, 342–343.

## *Friday 30th.*

The President nominated to the Senate W. C. C. Claiborne[23] to be governor of Orleans; Thompson J. Skinner to be Marshall, & Benjamin Austin to be Loan officer, of Massachusetts. Thus Massachusetts democracy is rewarded. The deserving & highly meritorious Bradford whose office of Marshall expires in December is not renewed but Skinner is to be removed from the Loan office the duties of which he did not understand, to make room for that vile contemptible Austin, better known in Boston by the names of *Old South* & Honestus. Signatures he assumed in the Chronicle. He has shed ink with profusion in support of democracy.

## *Monday Dec. 3d.*

To day I shall dine with the President of the United States. His cards of invitations are unlike those of former President's — their's issued in the name of *The President of the United States.* The following is the form established by Mr. Jefferson. — "*Th: Jefferson* requests the favor of Mr. Plumer to dine with him on monday next at half after three, or at whatever later hour the *house* may rise. The favor of an answer is *asked.*" It is *Th: Jefferson* not the *President* of the United States that invites — & yet were he not the President I presume I should not be invited. Having a curiosity to know what induced Mr. Jefferson to adopt such a form, I enquired of Mr. Giles, one of the Senators from Virginia. He replied, " That the President meant it should be considered more as the invitation of a private gentleman, than of that of the President. For if he invited as President he must take the list &

---

[23] William Charles Cole Claiborne, governor of Mississippi Territory, 1801–1803; appointed provisional governor and, in 1804, governor of Orleans Territory, which office he held until 1812; elected first State governor of Louisiana; elected to the United States Senate in January, 1817, but died in November of that year.

invite all the members of both Houses of Congress as they stand
on it. But his present mode will not oblige him, either to
invite gentlemen of different politic's at the same table; or to
invite at any time those members who for the hour together
*abuse him in speeches in Congress,* as some gentlemen do."

I have myself no doubt of this being the true grounds of his
adopting the present form. And the last session there were
gentlemen, who tho' they called upon him, were not invited
to dine with him — as Roger Griswold, John Rutledge,[24] & I
beleive one or two others. It is true these gentlemen *reasoned*
against some of Mr. Jefferson's favorite measures — & their
arguments made his recommendations appear rather ridiculous.
And this manly yet decent conduct is styled by him abuse.
Such a line of conduct as this in Mr. Jefferson has a tendency
to restrain the freedom of debate in Congress. It is on that
account, I think, highly improper — It discovers a littleness of
mind unworthy of the President of the United States. As
President — he ought never to act toward an individual as if
he knew what was said for or against him or his measures.

To day Mr. Hillhouse of the Senate, myself, & eight federal
members of the House, his two sons in law,[25] (both members of
the House) and his private secretary formed the company. He
was well dressed — A new suit of black — silk hose — shoes —
clean linnen, & his hair highly powdered. His dinner was elegant & rich — his wines very good — there were eight different
kinds of which there were rich Hungary, & still richer *Tokay*
— for this last he informed me that he gave a *guinea a bottle*
(little more than a quart). — There were also exposed on the
table two bottles of water brought from the river Mississippi,
& a quantity of the Mammoth cheese.[26] This cheese, was one

---

[24] John Rutledge, senator from South Carolina.
[25] Jefferson's sons-in-law, John W. Eppes and Thomas Mann Randolph of Virginia.
[26] *Cf.* McMaster, *History of the People of the United States,* II,
604-605.

made by some Democrats in Massachusetts two three years since, & presented to Mr. Jefferson. It weighed 1200 lb. & is very far from being good.

His table furnished a great variety of pies, fruit & nuts.

He performed the honors of the table with great facility — He was today reserved — appeared rather low spirited — conversed little — he is naturally very social & communicative.

One thing I have always noticed when dinner is announced — he directs the company to walk, & he is the last that enters the dining room.

### Wednesday 5th.

'Tis now more than a month since we have been in session, & day by day, when in the Senate Chamber, have I attentively watched the conduct of Aaron Burr. After the minutes of the preceeding day have been read — the little business before us dispatched — he would leave the chair — come to some one Senator, & intimate in strong terms that it was best to adjourn — & sometimes request a senator to move an adjournment — & in a few moments he was gone — He appears to have lost those easy graceful manners that beguiled the hours away the last session — He is now uneasy, discontented, & hurried.— So true it is, "Great guilt never knew great joy at heart." What course he will take after the 3d of March is very uncertain — He can never I think rise again. But surely he is a very extraordinary man, & is an exception to all rules. — No man is better fitted to brow beat or cajole public opinion. And considering of what materials the mass of men are formed — how easily they are gulled — & considering how little restraint laws human or divine have on his mind is impossible to say what he will attempt — or what he may obtain.

### Thursday 6th.

The democrats in Connecticut sometime the last summer in consequence of notice from Pierpont Edwards assembled at

New Haven to agree & form an address to the people of that
State upon the utility & necessity of forming a written constitution.[27]   This self created body consisted of members from
more than ninety towns.  Four of them were Justices of the
Peace.  They recommended to the people to have a constitution & form of government established — intimating that their
present government was a usurpation.

The General Court of that State in November last cited
those justices to appear & shew cause why they should not
be removed from office.  The Justices appeared & were heared
by themselves & Council — The Court removed them from
Office.  Major Judd was one of these Justices — He died a
very few days after — Since his death a pamphlet has been
published in his name as an Address to the people of that
State.  The pamphlet is written with great art & much apparent candour.  The preface asserts that Judd corrected the
proof sheets on his death bed.  This address & the death of
Judd connected with it is calculated to make an impression on
the minds of common people very unfavorable to the existing
government of that State.  My friends from that State assure
me that Judd was unable to produce such an artful address —
that it was written by some other person.  This Mr. Judd was
an officer in the revolutionary war — was a lawyer — & supported a tolerable fair Character.  The democrats now say he
died a martyr to the cause of liberty.

I think myself that these removals were impolitic.  In Connecticut Justices of the peace are appointed by their Legislature & hold their commissions for one year only.  These
commissions would have expired next May — & then the Court
might omit them.  These removals are considered by the warm
friends of the Court as *strong* measures.  To me they are
evidence of the weakness of the government — just as con-
vulsionary fits are of the unfortunate patient who is afflicted

[27] See note 11.

with them. In a royal or aristocratic government, I should think it highly prudent to remove that man from office who insinuated that the authority under which he acted was a usurpation. But in such a feeble government as we have, all things are not expedient that are lawful.

The friends of the present government in that State, contend that they have a Constitution. That in support of this dec̃on [declaration] they are obliged to say the charter from King Charles the 2d of England — & on agreement made a few years after that charter between the people of two or three towns, is the Constitution of Connecticut. This was not only unnecessary — but I think improper. By this dec̃on they have given a kind of licence to the democrats to say what they are now publishing in exulting language — The Federalists of Connecticut are Monarchists — they declare the constitution of the State is a *royal* charter *granted* by a British King more than 140 years since. Instead of resorting to this charter or to the agreement made by an association of a few towns, for their temporary security, in times when Connecticut were two independent governments — the federalists ought to have asserted that they have a free republican constitution more permanent than that of any other State in the Union. That it consists of the common or unwritten law— of principles — usages, & of customs held sacred for more than a century — That the revolutionary war made few changes in it — That like that of other countries, for example Great Britain, it has not a *written* constitution. And that the mere circumstance of a constitution & form of government being agreed to by the people and enrolled on parchment will never secure to a people their just rights. A paper constitution is a feeble barrier against the encroachments of the ambitious, or the intrigues of demagogues.

I think present appearances augur a change in the government of Connecticut.

## Friday 7th.

The Managers on the part of the House of Representatives attend this day at the Bar of the Senate & exhibit articles of Impeachment against Samuel Chase one of the Associate justices of the Supreme Court of the United States.[28]  The House of Representatives did not adjourn.  There are eight articles — The first charges the judge with arbitrary, oppresive & unjust conduct, in the trial, (in April & May 1800 at Philadelphia) of John Fries indicted for treason, (1st.)  In delivering an opinion in writing, on the question of law, tending to prejudice the jury against Fries case before his counsel was heard in his defence. (2) In restricting his counsel from recurring to certain English authorities, & statutes of the United States.  And (3) in preventing his counsel from addressing the jury on the law, & endeavoring to wrest from the jury the right of determining the law.  In consequence of which Fries was unjustly condemned to death.

### Article II.

That, in May 1800 at Richmond in Virginia, in the trial of James Thomas Callender for a libel, the judge prompted by a similar spirit of persecution & injustice, & with intent to oppress & procure the conviction of Callender, over-ruled the objection of John Basset one of the jury, who wished to be excused from serving on the trial, because he had made up his mind, as to the publication from which the words, charged to be libellous, in the indictment, were extracted — that Basset did serve & was one of the Jury by whose verdict Callender was convicted.

### Article III.

That he refused to admit the evidence of John Taylor, a material witness for Callender, pretending he could not prove

---

[28] For a full report of the trial of Associate Justice Chase, see *Annals of Congress*, 8 Cong., 2 sess., 81–676.

the truth of the whole of one of the charges, in the indictment, altho' that charge contained more than one fact.

## IV.

That his conduct during the whole course of the trial was marked by manifest injustice, partiality & intemperance. — (1) In compelling the prisoners counsel to reduce to writing, & submit to the inspection of the Court, the question they meant to propound to said Taylor. (2) In refusing to grant Callender a continuance, to procure witnesses — (3) In using unusual, rude & contemptuous expressions to his counsel. (4) In repeated & vexatious interruptions of said counsel. (5) In an indecent solicitude for the conviction of the accused.

## V.

That he awarded a capias agt. the sd Callender & not a summons, as by the law of Virginia he ought to have done.

## VI.

That he adjudged Callender to be tried at the same term in which he was indicted contrary to the laws of Virginia.

## VII.

That at a Court held at New Castle in Delaware, June 1800, he refused to discharge the Grand jury when the foreman informed him they had found no bills or had any to make — He replied there was a seditious printer in Wilmington — & authoritatively enjoin it on the District Attorney to procure a file of the News papers printed by sd printer.

## VIII.

That in May 1803, at Baltimore in Maryland, in a charge to the Grand jury, he delivered an intemperate & inflammatory political harangue, to excite the fears & resentment of the jury

& the people of Maryland agt. their State government & constitution — That he endeavoured to excite the odium of said jury & of the people of Maryland agt the government of the United States, by delivering opinions, highly indecent, extrajudicial and tending to prostitute the high judicial character with which he was invested to the low purpose of an electioneering partizan.

Note all the federal members of the House of Representatives, with a few of the Democrats, voted against each of the Articles.

### Monday 10th.

The Senate ordered a summons to issue requiring Judge Chase to appear before them at their chamber on the second day of January next to answer to said Impeachment. The summons to be served at least 15 days before the return day.

For several days past I have discovered an unusual degree of concern & anxiety in the leading democratic members of the senate. They frequently retire two or three at a time into Committee rooms, or in the lobby — If a federalist approaches 'em, then either avoid him, or immediately change the subject of conversation. I have been unable to ascertain the cause of this anxiety; but it is certain, both, that they are greatly embarrassed on some subject they deem important, & that they are divided in opinion. There are two or three things, I think, are troublesome to them. The Spaniards are collecting their forces near that part of West Florida adjoining Louisiana. The administration have for more than a year given out that West Florida belongs to us, & was included in the treaty of France to us of the last year. This construction was one that tended to add to the popularity of the purchase of Louisiana. The construction is unsound, & the Administration by their conduct, tho' contrary to their news paper declarations, admit it — for they were not to deliver to France the stock in payment for the ceded country untill actual possession was given —

Possession was given of Louisiana, but not of Florida — yet on that possession, the admōn delivered the stock to the French agent — & thereby virtually acknowledged that the country ceded did not include West Florida. To go to war for it, would expose 'em to the charge of imprudence in delivering the stock before possession was obtained. To raise troops to obtain it, will not only drain the treasury, but they fear it may look like raising a *standing army,* terms which they have rendered odious to their own creatures. They have sent as many of the *few* troops there as can be sent — But what are they to do — the spaniards are fortifying — are troops to oppose them?

2d. Tis now a considerable time since the President nominated Wm. Charles Cole Claiborne to be governor of Orleans. The office is important & requires a man of talents, information, & efficiency. He has not those qualities — The democrats in the Senate have not yet suffered the question to be taken whether they will advise to his appointment. Some of them are zealously opposed to him — others say 'tis enough, the President has nominated him. [The fact was tho I did not then know it — president originally intended the Marquiss La Fayette for that office.] [29]

3d. They fear the talents of Burr. He appears now friendly to them — Some office must be given him — what office can that be, that he will accept, & not injure them?

4th I have lately been informed that Hawkins [30] a Commissioner to the Creek Indians has concluded a treaty with them for the purchase of lands in Georgia, for which he has engaged the United States shall pay them $200,000. By the act of cession from Georgia, the United States engage to extinguish the Indian claims to the lands lying within that State

---

[29] Brackets appear in the original manuscript.

[30] Benjamin Hawkins was appointed Indian agent for all the tribes south of the Ohio River by President Washington in 1796 and held the office until his death in 1816.

" as early as the same can be peaceably obtained on reasonable terms." This treaty the President has not yet laid before the Senate, & it is doubtful whether he will — Its existance is denied — but I know the fact — & I know its the opinion of some Democrats that the compensation promised is enormous, & of course that the treaty ought to be rejected.

### *Tuesday December 11, 1804.*

The Senate advised to the appointment of Mr. Skinner to be Marshall, & Benja. Austin Junr to be Loan officer, of Massachusetts.

Previous to the question being taken for advising to the appointment of Mr. Austin, Mr. Franklin of North Carolina, requested that the senators from Massachusetts would give some information respecting his character & qualifications for office — For unless he could obtain information that he could rely upon he could not give his vote. Mr. Adams said he " *knew* Mr. Austin, but should say *nothing* of him." [31]

Mr. Ellery of Rhode Island, said, Mr. Austin was a man of extraordinary talents, & a most respectable character.

Almost every democrat voted in his favor.

The nomination of Mr. Claiborne to be governor of Orleans, on motion of Mr. Anderson was postpned.

The president nominated William Lyman of Massachusetts to be Consul at the port of London.

### *Wednesday Dec. 12, 1804.*

The question was this day taken in the Senate upon the nomination of Mr. Claiborne to be governor of Orleans, & without debate was agreed to. The opposition to this appointment was a few days since very strong; but in a private caucus it was resolved by the democrats to agree to it. After the Senate

---

[31] *Cf.* J. Q. Adams, *Memoirs* I, 320. Adams' statement is almost identical with Plumer's.

was adjourned the Vice President observed at the fire that the Senate had agreed to advise to the appointment of Claiborne when not a single Senator beleived he was qualified for the office. And Genl Bradley, said that the President's dinners had silenced them — & that Senators were becoming more servile.

Upon the nomination of Wm. Lyman to be Consul at London, Saml Smith required recommendations of his ability & character. Mr. Giles of Virginia, Dr. Mitchel of New York, & Genl Bradley of Vermont, spoke much in his favor. The senators from Massachusetts were silent. The nomination was agreed to by the usual majority.

The last year the documents sent by the President to Congress gave a flattering account of an immense mountain of salt in Louisiana.[32] — This year the documents accompanying the message amuses us with lead mines; but is altogether silent upon the subject of Salt. The President at his own house in a very serious manner at his own table a few days since observed to Col. T. Pickering that up the Missouri there was a very extensive plain, — covered with salt — that when the people scraped it off, the next morning it would be covered again with salt two inches deep. That it was called the sacred plain — that there the most hostile tribes of Indians met in peace & perfect security. Upon Mr. Pickering's enquiring whether the salt accumulated only in the night following the day on which the plain had been *scraped* — the President appeared confused, said he could not tell — but that he had no doubt of the existance of such a salt plain.

### Friday 14th.

The President by a Confidential message laid the treaty with the Creek Nation of Indians, the instructions to the Commissioners & correspondence, before the Senate.[33] All treaties are

---

[32] See *American State Papers, Miscellaneous*, I, 346.

[33] See Senate *Executive Journal* (printed in 1828), I, 477–478; *American State Papers*, IV. *Indian Affairs*, I, 690–693; McMaster, *History of the People of the United States*, II, 631–633.

considered by the Senate with closed doors — All treaties are printed under an injunction of secrecy for the use of the Senate. Mr. Brackenridge moved to have the message, Instructions & correspondence printed with the treaty subject to the usual injunction. Saml Smith opposed it — the motion prevailed, ayes 13, nays 10.

### Saturday 15.

Some days since I requested to have the Gentlemen who are now attending Congress as agents from Louisiana in support of the Memorial from that Country, invited to dine with us. Mr. Pickering in behalf of the Club invited them, & to day they dined with us. Their names are Derbigny, Sauve & Destrehan.[34] They are all frenchmen — the two first speak our language fluently. They are all gentlemen of the first respectability in that country. Men of talents, literature & general information — Men of business, & acquainted with the world. I was much gratified with their company — they have little of French flippery about them — They resemble New England men more than the Virginians.

Sauve is the eldest — he has lived in that Country 21 years. He was a merchant, but is now a planter. He had this year 150 acres of sugar cane. He has a wife & four children.

Destrehan is a native of that place but was educated in Paris — He can speak very little of our language. He has a wife & six or eight children. He has a fine promising son who has accompanied him hither. He was a merchant, but is now a planter — & has this year 200 acres of sugar cane. He says it will take 60 negroes to manage it — & that his ground generally produces on an average by the acre one hogshead of sugar weighing 1200 ℔ & a hogshead of molasses.

Derbigny is the youngest — He has lived in that country fourteen years — & has a family. He is a man of science — of real

---

[34] Pierre Derbigny, Jean Noel Destréhan, Pierre Sauvé. For a copy of the Memorial, see *American State Papers, Miscellaneous*, I. 396–399.

talents & very general information for his age. He is very shrew'd — converses with ease & great propriety.

They complain in decent but firm language of the government that Congress established over them at the last session. They say nothing will satisfy that people but an elective government. That under the Spanish government they paid only six per Cent duty upon their imports & exports; & the whole charge of their religion & government was then supported by the Crown. That the duties they now pay are greater than what they then paid — & are themselves beside obliged to support their religion & internal government. So that they now pay more for public uses than when they were subjects of a royal government, & enjoy less real liberty. That Claiborne, their present governor, is unable to speak a word of French, the language that is most generally used in that country. That the proceedings in the courts of law are in a language that most of the people do not understand — That they have in many instances been convicted of breaches of laws the existance of which they were ignorant. That Claiborne is incompetent to discharge the duties of Governor.

That the President had selected some very respectable men whom he has appointed members of the legislative Council. That out of these all except three have positively declined the appointment. That no man who wishes to enjoy the friendship & esteem of the people of that country can accept of an office under the existing system of government.

They say that they have visited Mr. Jefferson — that he has not made any enquires of them relative either to their government, or the civil or natural history of their country — That he studiously avoided conversing with them upon every subject that had relation to their mission here.

They say that the city of New Orleans is situated on the banks of the Mississippi — that those banks are from one hundred to a 120 feet deep — And that a considerable part of the city is in danger of being under-mined by the stream — the land being sandy. That it will require immense expence to secure the town — that they must either sink rafts covered with rocks on the bank next to the city, or cut down the bank on the opposite side of the river.

That the country around the city & for a very considerable distance up the river is very good land for the width, on an average, of three quarters of a mile from the river — that beyond that distance from the river much of the land is a sunken swamp. That there is in the Country a considerable tract of good upland. That they speak, in common language, of mensuration by the acre, not by the mile — That is by the square side of the acre.

### Monday 17th.

After the Senate had sat near *one hour & a half*, Mr. Burr while sitting in the chair, addressed himself to the Senate, & observed that there was some business not yet disposed off, but as it was not pressing — & as it was inconvenient for him to sit any longer this day, he should be gratified by an adjournment. The Senate on motion of Mr. Brackenridge immediately adjourned.

### Wednesday Dec. 19. 1804.

This day the Secretary laid printed copy's of the treaty with the Creek nation, & documents accompanying it, as is stated p. 68, [35] on our tables.

The President's message to the Senate, accompanying this treaty is dated the 13th of this month. The treaty was signed, Nov 3d 1804, on the part of the United States by Benjamin Hawkins, & on that of the Creeks by Hopoie Micco,[36] their Speaker & Select*men.*

The Indians relinquish certain lands in the forks of Oconee & Ockmulgee rivers &c within the State of Georgia — And the

---

[35] Pages 221–222 of this volume.
[36] See note 30.

United States are to pay to said Nation $200,000. in stock bearing an interest of six per Cent per annum, payable half yearly at the factory of the United States on the frontiers of Georgia. This stock to be payable to the Secretary of War in trust for that nation.

Col. Hawkin's letter to the Secretary of War inclosing the treaty is of the same date. He says, he informed the Indian Chief when he agreed to the treaty, that *the purchase sum was too large, & that it was not unlikely that the treaty would not be ratified.* Speaking of the quantity of land obtained by this treaty, he says, "We have acquired somewhat more than two millions of acres, half of which is unquestionably the best land in this Country. I have done the best I could in this transaction, & I beleive a delay to another year would not have benefited us, & it would have greatly inconvenienced the views of Georgia, who have an undoubted right to these lands whenever they can be obtained at a reasonable price, & the one given, in my opinion, is far from being unreasonable."

The first instructions are of April 12, 1802, & are to James Wilkinson, Benjamin Hawkins, & Andrew Pickens Esqrs commissioners to that nation.

The second, May 5, 1803, to James Wilkinson, Benjamin Hawkins & Robert Anderson Esqrs.

The third, April 2d 1804, is to Hawkins alone. He is authorized, "to make a treaty with the aid of General David Meriwether,[37] who is directed to meet you at said Council." — Again, "General Meriweather not having an appointment as Commissioner, should not prevent his opinion having as full weight in any transaction at the proposed conference, as it would have, if he had received an appointment as a Commissioner. You will nevertheless consider yourself responsible for whatever you agree to. It is desirable that the most perfect harmony

---

[37] General David Meriwether, representative from Georgia, December 6, 1802 to 1807; appointed commissioner to the Creek Indians in 1804.

should prevail between General Meriwether & yourself." —
And again, "You will let the Chiefs know that general Meriwether has been particularly requested by the President of
the United States, to attend with you for the purpose aforesaid."

These instructions were seigned by H. Dearborn secy of War.

The constitution of the United States expressly declares, That
"No Senator or Representative shall, during the time for which
he was elected, be appointed to *any* civil office under the
authority of the United States, which shall have been increased
during such time; & no person holding *any* office under the
United States, shall be a Member of either House during his
continuance in office." Art. I. sect. 6. And yet this very *David*
was at that time a member of Congress — a Representative from
the State of Georgia. But mark the duplicity — the pitiful
evasion! The General is not appointed to an office — he is
not a commissioner — he is only an agent to do the duty of an
officer. His opinion is to have as much effect as if he was
formally appointed a Commissioner. Col. Hawkins is to act
in harmony with him — & the Colonel must let the Chiefs know
that the General attends at the particilar request of the President.

The land thus purchased is not to be the property of the
United States, but that of Georgia. By the agreement made
by the Commissioners of the United States with those from
Georgia, dated April 24, 1802, that State cedes to the United
States the jurisdiction & soil of certain lands that it claimed.
And the United States in consideration of that cession agree
to pay to the State of Georgia out of the first net proceeds of
the ceded lands $1,250,000 — to quiet certain claims to the
ceded lands — & "to extinguish for the use of Georgia as early
as the same can be peaceably obtained on *reasonable terms* the
Indian title to all the other lands within the State of Georgia."
This agreement was to be obligatory on the United States unless

Congress should within six months from the date thereof repeal the law authorizing the same. April 26th 1802, the President laid this agreement before Congress; & they adjourned on the third day of May to the first monday of December then next. By this means the agreement became obligatory on the United States — And thus Georgia obtained from the Union $1250000 in cash, & the Indian titles extinguished to immense tracts of land. And all this is done because she claims this extended territory under an ambiguous charter from a British king, executed at a time when the limits & extent of the country was unknown to the British government, & when it was actually in the rightful possession of hostile & independent nations of Indians.

The United States appear to be bound to extinguish the Indian titles within the limits of Georgia — but they are to do it *peaceably*, & as soon as it can be done on *reasonable terms*. We are told, in these documents, that the Indian title to the country of Tallassee has once been purchased of the Indians by the State of Georgia. Others say the Indians were deceived by the fraudulent conduct of the Georgian commissioners, & that the United States ought not to countenance it. The only question that must govern my decision, is *are these terms reasonable* — At present they do not appear to me so. —

William Hoge a member of the House of Representatives of the United States from Pennsylvania, not being elected as a member of the ninth Congress resigned his seat in the present Congress — & assigned his losing the confidence of his constituents as the cause of his resignation. This man was a democrat, but by no means so violent as most of them are. He dared at the last session to vote agt. the amendment to the Constitution; & on some other questions he left the dominant party. A democrat more violent, is elected in his district, against him, for the next Congress. The district elected his brother John Hoge, a decided zealous federalist to supply his place in this Congress. A petition was prefered against him, requesting that he should not be admitted to hold his seat, because they alledged the district had not due notice of the time of holding the Election. It appears that William's letter of resignation to the Governor was dated 15th of last October — That the governor of Pennsylvania issued a writ of election to supply the vacancy on the 22d day of the same month, directing the election to be holden on the 2d day of November last, eleven days after the date of the writ — That the writ was brot by the mail to the County of Washington where the election was to be holden on the 30th of October, & by him proclaimed the next day. The day of Election was the same on which Electors of President & Vice President were chosen in that State. The governor issued his writ by virtue of the 2d section of the 1st article of the Constitution of the United States. The legislature of Pennsylvania have not passed any law directing the time place & manner of holding elections to supply such vacancies. Dr. Leib & others were violently opposed to this election; but a large majority of the House of Representatives this day decided in favor of John Hoge's holding his seat.

His brother William Hoge was one of the Men who signed the petition against him. John told me he had not spoken to his brother for this eight years. —

This John Hoge is an intimate friend and correspondent with Mr. Ross [38] & Judge Addison.

### Thursday 20th.

The senate were engaged to day in establishing rules for the trial of Impeachments.[39] One of the rules provided that in case the accused on being called did not appear his default should be

---

[38] Probably James Ross, senator from Pennsylvania from 1794 to 1803.

[39] *Cf.* J. Q. Adams, *Memoirs*, I, 321. The report of the trial in the *Annals of Congress* has no record of the discussion of this date.

recorded.  Genl Bradley moved to add to this rule, That such default should be considered as a full confession of the facts stated in the articles of Impeachment.

In the course of the debate on this motion Mr. Giles travelled out of his way to observe — That there were certain offences which when charged by the House against an officer, & when those facts thus charged were found against him by two thirds of the Senate — the Senate would then have no discretion left — they must remove the officer from office.  But as the judges were created not for their own emolument but to advance the public good: therefore tho' a judge may act honestly, yet he may commit such errors as will endanger the peace of the community — if he persists in those errors, he must be impeached convicted and removed from his office.  The President is by the constitution (Article 2 sect. 3d) obliged to " take care that the laws be faithfully executed " — He proceeds in discharge of this duty — directs an officer to perform certain things — the officer obeys — a suit is brought against him — And a Judge decides against the measure directed by the President — declares it illegal — In this, & all other cases where the judge, though honest & upright, commits such errors, & persists in the repetition of them — The House may impeach & the Senate convict & remove from office.  Error in a Judge, without his being guilty of a high crime or misdemeanor, is cause for impeachment.  This is discretionary — All that is necessary is for a majority of the House to accuse & two thirds of the Senate to agree to that accusation.  This is the mode the constitution has devised to remove a man from office — & it may be done without any guilt in the officer removed — meer error — or what partakes still less of the nature of the crime, mere *inability* to discharge the duty of an office is sufficient cause to justify removal.  The Senate are not bound to know the cause of that inability, whether it proceed from the misconduct or misfortune of the accused — or from the Act of God.  It is

enough to know that the inability exists — that the officer does
not perform his duty & that the public are injured thereby.
The judgt. of the Senate, the last session, in the case of Judge
Pickering, is a proof of my position. In the trial of an Impeachment we do not sit as a Court but as a Senate. I admit,
we sit not in a legislative, but a judicial capacity. But we
have no criminal jurisdiction — tis merely civil — our judgment
is confined to removal from office, & to disqualification to hold
office. And if the Accused has, in fact, committed Crimes he
is to be further dealt with in the courts of Law; & by them
to be punished for those crimes.

*Mr. Brackenridge.* Our proceedings in the case of impeachments ought not to be compared to defaults in civil suits. In
civil actions in Courts of law, the paper declared on in many
cases is prima facie evidence of the demand — & the default
confesses it. Not so in the case of an impeachment. The
House of Representatives is the Grand jury of the Nation —
the impeachment is their accusation — & the non appearance
or default of the accused, is not proof — is not an acknowledgement, of the truth of that accusation. If the accused de-
murs to the Impeachment, & the Senate decide on the pleadings
against him — He will have then a right to plead over — &
should he then be defaulted — the facts stated, or a principal
part of them must be proved — we are never to presume them
true — they must be proved so before we can convict the Accused.

The Senate adjourned without any decision on Mr. Bradley's motion — but he previous thereto in great anger retired
from the Senate.

This doctrine of Mr. Gile's if reduced to practice at once
destroys the independence of the judiciary, & renders them
dependant on the will of the President. 'Tis a rapid stride of
despotism — 'tis making the Judiciary the mere creature &
tool of the Executive & legislature. It is an observation I

have heretofore made, that the Constitution of the United States is an excellent piece of composition. That it is remarkably explicit & concise. — The doctrine it establishes & the rules it prescribes on the subject of Impeachments will illustrate this. The subject is mentioned five times only in the Constitution.

The 1st, designates who shall have the power of impeaching — " The House of Representatives shall have the *sole* power of Impeachment." Art. I. Sect. 2d.

2d. Who shall have the power of trying impeachments. — " The Senate shall have the *sole* power to try all impeachments. When sitting for that purpose, they shall be on oath or affirmation. When the President of the United States is tried, the Chief Justice shall preside; & no person shall be convicted without the concurrence of two-thirds of the members present." Article I. Sect. 3d.

The 3d What Judgment the Senate shall render in case the Impeachment is supported. " Judgment in cases of impeachment shall not extend further than to removal from office, & disqualification to hold & enjoy any office of Honor, trust or profit under the United States: but the party convicted shall nevertheless be liable & subject to indictment, trial, judgment & punishment, according to law." Art. I. Sect. 3d.

These paragraphs give authority to the House to impeach & the Senate to try, & defines what judgment in case of conviction shall be given. But neither the offences or offenders who are the subjects of impeachments are even mentioned.

The 4th place in which the subject is mentioned, defines both the persons who are subjects of impeachment, & the *crimes* for which they are liable to be impeached. " The President, Vice President, & all civil officers of the United States, shall be removed from office on impeachment for, & conviction of, treason, bribery, or other high crimes & misdemeanors." Art. 2d sect. 4.

*The President, Vice President & all civil officers* are liable to be impeached — A man must hold one of those offices or he is not the subject of impeachment. A private man can not be impeached or an officer in the army or navy. A senator of the United States is not liable to an impeachment. This was determined by the Senate in the case of William Blount, a senator from Tennessee, who was impeached in 1789, & on that principle was acquited.[40]  And of course a member of the other House of Congress cannot be impeached. Each house may expell a Member; but the House cannot impeach or the Senate try a member of the National Legislature. Because a seat in Congress is not a *civil office*.

The 5th place in the Constitution in which impeachments are mentioned excludes the impeached from a trial on the impeachment by a jury. " The trial of all *crimes,* except in cases of Impeachment, shall be by jury." Art. 3d. Sec. 2.

It is only for " treason, bribery or *other* high crimes & misdemeanors ", that any of these public officers can be impeached, convicted & removed from office. *High crimes & misdemeanors* are requisite to give the senate jurisdiction in cases of impeachment. And unless these are alledged with sufficient certainty in the impeachment, & proved on the trial there can be no conviction & removal. Incapacity in the officer is a misfortune, but no cause of impeachment. There can be no principle of law better known, or that is more clearly founded in the reason & fitness of things, than That a Judge is never to be punished for an error of judgment — To impeach convict and remove a judge from office, for having formed an erroneous opinion, & honestly acting agreably to that opinion, is a doctrine pregnant with ruin to the Judiciary. It is of all other doctrines the most dangerous — It is only accusing a judge of having formed & delivered erroneous opinions — & the senate, may find him guilty of a mistake, & he must be punished for his error by loss of office & disqualification to hold any other in future. And

---

[40] See 62 Cong., 2 sess., *Sen. Doc.,* No. 876, pp. 5–15.

what still renders this more absurd, is that the Accused is to be tried by men as liable to err in judgment & to form opinions as erroneous as those for which he is impeached. But the constitution authorizes the one house to impeach, & the other to try, civil officers is *only* in case they have committed *high crimes & misdemeanors*. No other authority is given but in those cases, & it is a principle explicitly declared in the 9th & 10th amendments to the Constitution, that nothing shall be taken by implication — & that the powers not given by the people & States to Congress, are reserved & still retained by the people or by the States.

This impeachment is the third [41] under the Constitution of the United States. The practise has been for the Senate to issue a summons to the accused. This practise may have been regular & most proper in the cases that have occurred; but I am strongly inclined to think that in case the President were impeached for Treason that a capias should issue & he be taken into custody — otherwise he might continue his traiterous conduct to the ruin of the government. For I do not think a Court of law could with propriety proceed & try him for high treason untill after he was found guilty by the Senate & removed from office. There is a manifest impropriety in a court of law indicting & trying the first Majestrate of the Nation as a common Malefactor — a traitor — & in effect suspending the functions of his high office — whilst the Grand Inquest of the Nation have not seen cause to accuse him of any crime. ————

*Friday 28th.*

The bill to prevent arming Merchant vessels was read in the Senate a 2d time & referred to a Committee. Immediately after it was read Dr. Mitchell presented the Memorial from the Chamber of Commerce from the city of New York stat-

---

[41] The first trial was that of William Blount; the second, Judge John Pickering.

ing reason why our merchant men ought not to be prohibited from arming their vessels bound to the West Indies — & praying that the bill might not pass into a law. The Dr. moved that the Memorial might be printed, yeas 12 nays 13. As this document which is far more important than many that are printed cannot be bound up with the State papers of this session it will make No 10 in the Appendix to this volume.[42]

## *Monday 31.*

The President laid before Congress a letter from Richard OBrien, our late Consul at Algiers giving an account of certain transactions before Tripoli.

By these accounts it appears " we have lost 45 brave men — that Commodore Barron with the frigates arrived too late to end the affair this year — That our force there was only adequate to *irritate* Tripoli, but will not be adequate to reduce it to American terms, & obtain our fellow citizens."

Here two or three reflections arise to our view.

1st. It is now near four years since this war was commenced against Tripoli — It began a few months after Mr. Jefferson was appointed President. It is his war.

2d. He has himself declared in one of his messages to Congress, that in relation to the prosecution of this War, he " has sent the *least possible* competent force." This he makes a merit of — and boast that he thereby promotes oeconomy. I am far from being the advocate for a profusion of public money. I do verily beleive that the federal administration was too profuse of money. It was their greatest error. But I think it *bad policy, & base wickedness,* for a President to send brave men where they must inevitable be destroyed for the want of an adequate force. Had he sent a sufficient number of men & ships it would have been expensive — it might have endangered his reputation for oeconomy & lessened his

---

[42] Appendix of Plumer's manuscript not copied here.

popularity with the rabble but would most probably have saved the lives of deserving men.  He ought to have sent something more than a sufficiency — enough to inspire the Men with confidence — to guard against accidents — & to insure success.

3d.  It was near three months after it was resolved to send out Commodore Barron before the frigates under his command could be got out on the Ocean.  They then lay at this place — Materials to repair the ships and rigging — carpenters & other mechanic's were at a great distance.  This delay occasioned the loss of the season — A loss of near, or quite, half a million of dollars.  How wretched the policy to have our little navy laid up in this stream, to rot at such a distance from the Ocean. The Navy will remain here as long as the government does. This single consideration, were there not many others, would determine my mind upon the subject of removing the Government of the US. from this dreary place, & against voting to appropriate any more money to be expended here for erecting public buildings.

### Tuesday Jany 1. 1805.

The disagreeableness of the weather, my ill health — the sickness of George W Livermore Esq of Holderness New Hampshire — & the necessity of providing him better accomodations — prevented me from calling upon the President, as is usual on this day for most members of Congress to do.  Indeed a small excuse was sufficient to prevent me.

### Wednesday 2d.

The Senate for several days have held their sessions in the Committee room.  This has been done to make some preparations in their Chamber for the trial of Judge Chase.  Our tables & chairs have been removed.  Two rows of seats have been built on each side of the Vice Presidents chair, & these seats have been all covered with red baize.  Small dining chairs have been sat where our chairs used to stand, to accomodate the members of the other House. At twelve OClock the Senators took their seats on the *red* benches in the Senate Chamber. The House of Representatives did not adjourn but very many of the members attended. The Managers, as such, did not attend, but several of them were present. The Senators have not taken the oath prescribed by the Constitution.

The Vice President was authorized to make the necessary arrangements & accomodations for the trial. He very readily undertook it. — Just before we took our seats there was an arm chair sat in a suitable place for the Judge, but the Vice President privately directed it to be taken way by the Seargeant of Arms — & I heard him say — *let the Judge take care to find a seat for himself.*

One of the Stenographers was preparing a place to take minutes of the proceedings; but Mr. Burr told him he need not do it — he might remember all that would be said — for he should take care that Mr. Chase would make no speech to day.

The Court was opened by proclamation. The secretary read the Seargeant of Arms return of serving the Summons upon judge Chase, & swore him to the truth thereof. Proclamation was then made for the Judge to appear & make answer. He came & bowed to the President & the Court. He then moved that a seat should be assigned him. Mr. Burr in a very cold formal insolent manner replied he presumed the Court would not object to his taking a seat. Mr. Mathers [43] brought him the Arm chair. The Judge sat down — I whispered to Mathers & told him he ought to bring the Judge a small table. He replied he was forbid doing it — such was Mr. Burr's order. —

The Judge arose & very respectfully addressed himself to the President & to the Court — holding several papers in his hands. He did not proceed to utter scarse a single sentence

---

[43] James Mathers, Sergeant at Arms of the Senate.

before Mr. Burr interrupted him, & enquired of him if that (the paper) was his answer to the impeachment, & if it was it must be filed & the Senate would dispose of it. The judge replied it was not his answer — He was about to address the Court to grant him till the first day of the next session to make answer to the articles of Impeachment. Mr. Burr told him to proceed — The Judge proceeded — Mr. Burr again interrupted him — & closed his observations by saying he would not again interrupt him unless some one of the Court objected to the proceeding in that manner — But not a single senator accepted of Mr. Burr's intimation — & he once more interrupted the Judge before he closed his address. The Judge read his address — I believe every word of it was on paper.

The Judge said he did not think a simple denial of the charges contained in the Impeachment was a sufficient answer. He thought there ought to be a full & particular answer in writing to each article — that this would enable the managers to come prepared to support the charges & to comprehend the defence — That the duty he owed to himself, his family, & the world made it requisite that his answer should contain his defence — at least the principles on which it was founded — That since the charges have been exhibited against him he has, owing to his ill state of health & the shortness of the notice been unable to procure & instruct council in his case — That his ill health render it peculiarly necessary that he should have the aid of Council well instructed — That it is four years or more since the supposed offences were committed — That they are stated to have happened in three different states — That he is charged with violating a law of Virginia that he never heard existed untill he found it stated in the Impeachment — That he could not procure the necessary information and witnesses for trial this session. That he *knew* he was not guilty — that a consciousness of his innocency made him anxious to hasten the trial; but that a regard to his reputation, more dear than the honor or the emoluments of the high office he held, convinced him of the great necessity of having more time to plead & prepare for the trial in such a manner as the justice & high importance of the case demended.

The Judge conducted himself with great propriety — There were indeed some few expressions that some thought too much resembled the bitter & acrimonious language of some part of the Impeachment.

It is indeed a humiliating scene to behold an *aged man, a Judge,* of the Supreme Court of the United States — A man who from 1796 has held very high responsible offices in the nation — discharged the duties of them with integrity — bro't to trial as a criminal — Arraigned before a Court, the president of whom is a fugative from Justice — & stands indicted as a MURDERER!

The Judge was affected — tears suspended his voice for a moment or two — he soon recovered.

After he had made his motion & assigned his reasons in support of it — the Vice President requested him to reduce it to writing. He did it at a corner of the Secretary's table — For no table was assigned him  It was a simple request that the Court would give him till the first day of the next session to make his answer & to prepare for his trial. The Vice President then informed him that the Senate would again meet tomorrow at twelve OClock. The Court retired to the committee room — & there continued an informal debate untill a late hour. Israel Smith was in favor of notyfying the Managers of Judge Chase's motion, that they might be heard thereon.

*Vice President.* The House of Lords decide all preliminary questions without admitting managers — They do not appear but on the trial.

Giles, Brackenridge, Anderson & others were in favor of not being sworn untill after the issue was actually joined. A large majority decided that the Members should be sworn tomorrow morning immediately after the court is opened & before *any decision* is made.

Mr. Giles said, He did not like the term *Court*. Our *business* is judicial but our *name* is that of a Senate — & I am unwilling to be entangled with the *rules* of Courts — They are troublesome.

The conduct of Mr. Burr to Judge Chase during the proceedings of the day has been very rude and highly reprehensible. These violent measures in Mr. Burr may, & I beleive are, adopted with a view to ingratiate himself with the Admōn. — In this he will, I presume fail — He has merited the contempt & indignation, (two qualities rarely united) of many. Mr. Anderson, of the Senate, told me the treatment was indecorous & rude, & he would never again sit as a Judge where the Accused should be thus treated.

### Thursday 3d.

The Senate met in the Committee room. The Vice President received a letter from Judge Chase inclosing his affidavit. It was read — He states, That he cannot procure the evidence necessary for him to make his answer & be prepared for his trial so as to finish the same at any time previous to the 5th of March next.

*Mr. Pickering* moved to add at the end of the Oath to the Members of the Court the words — " So help me God." Negatived.

*Mr. Giles*, I do not know that any plea or issue is necessary — The impeachment may be tried without it. In the case of Judge Pickering tried last session, there was no pleadings. If we are to receive a plea it will waste time — the Managers also must have time to reply — Mr. Chase to rejoin — there will be rejoinders & surrejoinders — rebutters & surre-butters — & never an end. We had better dismiss the Impeachment — have the constitution so amended as that the President may on the application of Congress remove an officer from office.

*Mr. Bradley* I would give Judge Chase till the first day of February to file his answer — & have the business in such a train as the trial might commence with the next session. There is no Court under Heaven but what gives time — requires an answer in the nature of a plea — even in Chancery — and there must be a replication. Destroy the forms of proceeding & you endanger the rights of Man. Delay is unavoidable, unless you mean to have a Mock trial.

*Israel Smith,* I am clearly of opinion that as soon as the answer of Judge Chase is given the issue will then be closed. We ought not to allow the Managers to reply.

*Mr. Giles,* Courts of Law do not ever give the Respondent time to plead — he is obliged to plead instanter.

*Mr. Adams,* Some of the British precedents in the trials of Impeachments are founded in injustice — & we ought never to follow them further than they are consonant with law justice & equity. Their house of Commons have less authority than our House of Representatives. Yet the Commons have a right not only to reply to the answer of the Accused in writing, but to demand & have time to make their replication. In Turkey the *forms* of law, which the gentleman from Virginia (Mr. Giles) complains off, are disregarded. That government has advantages — but no wise man can wish to live under it. There is as much dispatch as the gentleman wishes. The accused is informed in the same day of the Accusation, trial, sentence & execution.

*Mr. Tracey,* exposed in strong terms Mr. Giles's opinions — as being wild absurd & illegal — & as resembling the French revolutionary tribunal.

*Mr. Hillhouse,* In the trial of impeachments we sit as a court of criminal jurisdiction — We are to try *crimes* & that without a jury — We are the only Court in the land that can do it. See Constitution Art. 3. Sect. 2. And when we convict an Accused officer we remove him from office & declare him incapable of holding any office in future. The President may pardon other criminals — Yes Sir he may pardon even a MURDERER; but he cannot pardon the man whom we convict. His political death is eternal. See Constitution Art. 2. Sect. 2. We are *ergo* a Court of the highest criminal jurisdiction in the Nation — Our judgment affects the political existence of the Accused — they reach his reputation — dearer than life. We ought *ergo* to give reasonable liberal time to the accused. The other House have taken a year to collect the evidence barely to impeach him. Shall we say the Judge shall immediately make his answer & produce his witnesses instanter — One of the very charges against him is that he as a judge refused to give Callender a term to prepare for his trial on an Indictment as the law of Virginia required him to do. Judge Chase has had only 15 days notice of this impeachment — the time you give a man to answer to a suit before a Justice. He says he cannot be ready within two months. Will you deny him — It is not true that Courts of law refuse to give the accused time to plead — So far from it the Courts are obliged to assign them Council, least they should be ignorant of their own rights.

*Mr. Dayton,* The time for trial, but not the time to make answer, ought now to be fixed.

*Vice President* All our proceedings in this room are irregular — but necessary — they prepare gentlemen to vote in the other room.

Note Yesterday during the debate in the Committee room the Vice President would not permit the members of the House to attend; but to day he admitted them.

The Court was opened in the Senate Chamber & the Members thereof were sworn & affirmed.

The question was taken to give the Judge till the first monday of December next to make his answer & prepare for his trial. This was negatived, 12 only voted in favor of it. The time assigned for the answer & trial is the 4th day of February next.

Messrs Adams, Bradley, Dayton, Hillhouse, Olcott, Pickering, Plumer, Tracey & White voted against it.

The Members of the House generally attended — Judge Chase was at the fire side.  As soon as the decision was declared the Vice President ordered the Secretary to furnish the House with a copy of it — & one to Judge Chase if he applied for it — But said not a word to the Judge tho' known to be within the Chamber.

### Friday 4th.

In the House of Representatives, sometime since pending the debate upon the bill " to regulate the clearance of armed merchant vessels " Mr. Eppes, the son in law of Mr. Jefferson, in a speech he made in Congress, declared " That the American merchants are not fit to be trusted with arms, more than *highwaymen* are with pistols." Is this the degraded abandoned character of our Merchants!  I have been, & still am, in the habit of considering the great body of them, as men deserving the esteem & confidence of the nation.

On the 28th of last month an incident happened in the House of Representatives that merits notice.  On the question of whether the engrossed bill to " amend the charter of the town of Alexandria " should pass — Mr. Larned of Massachusetts voted in the affirmative.  The state of the vote was reported by the Clerk to be ayes 55, nays 52.  A resolve relating to other business was passed.  Mr. Larned after this rose & stated to the House, " That he had intended to vote against, and not for the passing of the said bill — & requested that his name might be erased from the yeas & placed with the nays."

The Speaker decided, That after any question taken by yeas & nays, or otherwise, had been finally determined, & so stated from the Chair, no member could be permitted to change his vote on such question, unless by the unanimous consent of the members present.  From this decision an appeal was made to the House — & the Speaker's decision was confirmed.

In the early part of the debate *John Smilie,* a member from Pennsylvania — said, " *sound principles* induced him to object against Mr. Larned having liberty to amend the minutes. It is the *principle* —the danger of such a *precedent* — & not the *effect* the change will have on this bill." Had Mr. Larned changed his vote, & then the Speaker voted in the negative as it was intimated he would — the bill according to the state of the vote, as reported by the Clerk, would have been lost. Before the debate closed, the Clerk informed the House that his former report, was not correct — that the yeas were in fact 55 & the nays only 51. & that the change of Mr. Larned's vote could not effect the bill. Soon after this Mr. Smilie rose, & unmindful of the *principle* or of the *danger of the precedent,* said, " The minutes were not correct as to Mr. Larned — they were contrary to his real intentions — that he hoped an opinion would not ever prevail in the House that the word of any Member was to be scrupled — & that rules that were made to promote justice should compel us to let our Journals contain a known falsehood."

---

## Saturday 5th.

Judge Chase's address to the Senate was this day published in the Washington Federalist. It does honor to him — the more I examine it — the more I approve of it. It is too valuable to be trusted to the Journals of the *day* — I shall therefore transcribe it into my Appendix. See No. 12.[44]

Mr. Eppes a few days since speaking of the Black government of St. Domingo — said — " He would venture to *pledge the Treasury of the United States,* that the Negro government should be destroyed."

---

[44] Appendix not copied here. For the speech, see *Annals of Congress,* 8 Cong., 2 sess., 92–97.

## Tuesday 8th.

Mr. Burr appears irritated at some things published in the Washington Federalists — & observations that are frequently made, censuring him for not providing Judge Chase with a chair, & for interrupting him on the 2d instant. To day in the Senate chamber at the fire side in conversation upon the subject, instead of regreting what he had done — He said, " In Great Britain when an officer is impeached, & Appears before the House of Lords — instead of having a Chair the Accused falls on his knees & rises not till the Lord Chancellor directs him." I doubt the fact — but if true would Mr. Burr wish to see such servitude — ! Is this plain republicanism?

## Thursday 10th.

In the course of the debate, in the Senate this day, upon the bill " to regulate the clearance of armed vessels " Dr. Mitchell said, The bill was brought into the other House in consequence of a complaint from the French Minister to our Executive against our people for trading at St. Domingo.

When the Dr. rose the 2d time he observed that the French Minister had not a serious objection to the American's trading at that island — for he offered *passports for sale* to our merchants who wished that trade.

*Genl Jackson,* said, He was in favor of prohibiting the trade to St Domingo altogether — He beleived the self created emperor of *Hayti* must be subdued — That the peace & security of both America & Europe demanded it — We ought to be cautious how we trust our Merchants with arms.

*Mr. Brackenridge,* We must consider St Domingo as a Colony of France — as a colony in rebellion against its parent state — Our trade to that island aids those rebels — sound policy requires us to restrain our citizens from trading there — & that is the design & object of this bill. ———

It seems that the French Minister wishes to make a purse from the sale of passports to American merchants to trade to St Domingo — as the Spanish Minister did some years since in granting permits to trade at the Havannah. It is a fact a passport was sold by Turreau a few weeks since to a merchant at New York. That we should pass this law to gratify France — to enable her minister to levy a contribution on our merchants — is a degradation to which I hope we shall not submit.

*Friday Jany 11, 1805.*

The Senate renewed the debate of yesterday. —

*Mr. Jackson,* Our armed merchant vessels are in fact *armed floots* — They will fight those who oppose them, & thereby involve the nation in a war. I wish to prohibit the trade to St. Domingo — I am willing to go "*whole lengths*". The present *usurped* government of that unfortunate island must be destroyed. The trade of our Merchants to that place is a *forced trade,* & it ought not to exist. The President has said this in his *message.*

*Mr. McClay,* The design of this bill is to restrain the trade with St. Domingo — All must agree that this trade is illegal — is unfair — & being so these restraints cannot injure the fair trader.

*Mr. Baldwin,* Merchants do all their business by figures — If they can make a trade profitable & pay the penalties, they will pursue their enterprize in direct violation of the laws of their country — Gain governs & directs them in all they do. The design of this bill is *only* to regulate our trade to St. Domingo. 'Tis a law to regulate a mere domestic temporary trade. A portion of this trade is now carried on from our ports by foreigners, who are induced to do it not only from a prospect of gain, but feel interested in the events of the European war. This circumstance ought to induce us to increase the penalties. — I have no doubt this restriction will injure some of our merchants.

Those who have capitals can procure the security required — those who have small capitals or none, & have reputation, can find sureties. But the security of the nation demands this caution — as much so as the policy of our laws do that he who is Treasurer of the nation shall procure sureties in millions. In both cases honest worthy industrious poor men may suffer — but we cannot help it. —

*Mr. Pickering,* The advocates for this bill say it is designed only to regulate the trade to St. Domingo. There is nothing in the bill that thus restricts it — But if that is the object intended, we ought in the bill to avow it — We ought first to decide whether that trade is unlawful — If unlawful prohibit it — but if lawful why restrain our merchants from arming in defence of their lives & property against the pirates, buccaneers & marauders who now infest those seas — villains who do not pretend to act under the authority of any nation.

*Mr. Mitchell,* The authority to be given by the first amendment to the President of the United States to order & establish rules for the government of this trade, arises from the great facility with which a law of this kind may be evaded. He will by this clause be authorized to remedy these defects as soon as they are discovered. He is the first & great conservator of the peace of the Nation. I am confident he will exercise this high prerogative with *sound discretion,* & for the good of the nation.

If we had a navy it would be wrong to suffer our Merchant vessels to *arm* — but our maritime weakness renders it *necessary*.

### Saturday 12th.

Yesterday morning the House of Representatives were informed of the death of James Gillespie one of the representatives from the State of North Carolina. After they had resolved to go into morning for him & appointed a committee from the members of that State to superintend the funeral & make the necessary arrangements the House adjourned. The Committee gave informal notice to the Senate of the event, the time & place of the funeral, & an invitation to attend.

To day at 12 OClock a majority of Congress attended at the house were Mr. Gillespie died. Biscuit & cheese, wine & brandy, in great abundance was on the tables in each room & chamber. After taking some refreshment the corpse was put into a hearse drawn by a span of white horses. This was preceeded by a carriage in which were the two Chaplins of Congress Revd Mr. Balch & another. Then followed the carriage with the Speaker & members from North Carolina — after them other carriages with other members; there were about 20 carriages containing near 100 members — a considerable number walked — The corpse was buried north of but in George Town.

The Members from North Carolina, the Secretary of the Senate, the Clergy present, the Clerk of the House & the Sargeant of Arms of the House had each of them white Scarfs on. Each scarf contained about three yards of fine India Cotton It was thrown over one shoulder & the two ends were tied together under the right arm near the hand with black ribband — a bow of black ribband & one round the cloth was placed upon the left shoulder. Each of these & all of the members of the House wore black crape on their right arms. The Senators had no mourning on.

The coffin was an elegant mahogany one well polished — there were plate at the top & round the edges — It was lined with white muslin. In the grave was a white coffin made of pine — into this the coffin containing the corpse was put & then a man went into the grave & put a board over it & nailed it.

As soon as this was done the Revd Mr. Balch made a very neat elegant concise address to those who attended at the Grave. He discanted on the mortality of man — the certainty of death — the certainty of another life — the necessity & utility of religion — the consolation it afforded in the hour of death to those whose lives conformed to its precepts. He said not a syllable upon the character of the deceased. There were no prayers — 'tis not usual on such occasions in this place.

The expence of the funeral is defrayed principally, if not all, by the United States. The Carriages were all furnished by the Committee. The price of the coffin was $35. The *liberty* of burying for a stranger in that grave yard is $8. —

Mr. Gillespie was in his 64 year. He was in a decline when he left home. He has indulged very freely this winter in the use of whiskey. I am assured from good authority that during the last week of his life there was not a single day but what he was in a state of intoxication. He has left no wife but a number of children.

### Monday 14th.

The bill — relating to the *clearance of armed vessels* — under consideration in the Senate.

*Mr. Giles.* I beleive there is not a gentleman present who is *hardy enough* — I recall the expression — not one who would think it good policy, to say that St. Domingo is independent — If not independent it follows that she is a colony of France. And it is all-important to us that we should take such measures in relation to our trade to that devoted island as will be approved off by the government of that great nation. There are only two things that we can do, either prohibit the trade altogether — or restrain & regulate our armed merchant vessels — I am in favor of the last.

The Minister of that nation is now waiting the result of our deliberations on this subject.

I think there is a necessity of authorizing the President to issue from time to time, as he shall judge necessary, *instructions* to the commanders of our armed *merchant vessels*. This will enable him to *supply* the *defect* in the law, if our practise should discover any.

### Tuesday 15th.

Mr. Burr absented himself from the Senate — He yesterday informed us that he was under the necessity of being absent a few days — but that at all events he should return again previous to the 4th day of next month. Joseph Anderson was elected as president pro-tem. of the Senate — He had 16 votes.

Yesterday Mr. *Ellery* moved & the Senate resolved That they would go into mourning, by wearing a crape round the left arm, for one month, for Samuel J Potter late one of the senators from Rhode Island. Note, Mr. Potter died last July, & Mr. Ellery who was his colleague has been with us in session more than two months, & *now* makes the motion for mourning.

It is principally owing to the influence of this same Mr. Potter had that this very Ellery was not this winter re-elected a Senator. Those who know the character of Ellery will never beleive that he moved the resolution from a respect to the memory of the deceased — 'Tis the offspring of hypocrycy!

These resolves are designed as a tribute of respect & esteem for the memory of the dead. They are becoming of little consequence, from the indiscrimate use that is made of them. Mr. Potter was a man who in Rhode Island was made Lt. Govr & then Senator in Congress; but he was intemperate. The Members of both houses of the National Legislature have now the habiliments of Mourning for the loss of two of their members, both of whom were intemperate.

### Wednesday 16th.

Levi Lincoln the Attorney General of the United States resigned his office on the first day of this month — There is no persom yet nominated as his successor. I enquired this day of Mr. Wright Who was to be the man — he replied he could not tell — " The Admõn were anxious to obtain a man of talents

& informations, for that the time was not distant when persons might *possibly* be indicted for treason." ——

### Monday 21st.

Mr. Logan one of the senators from Pennsylvania asked liberty to present a memorial from the yearly meeting of the people called Quakers assembled at Philadelphia from the states of Pennsylvania, Delaware, Maryland &c  He stated that the Memorial was drawn in decent and respectful language — That the Memoralists considered negro slavery as an evil — & both moral & political — & requesting that Congress would soon restrain its encrease as far as the principles of the Constitution will permit.

Mr. Bradley, Jackson, Cocke, Wright & Samuel Smith opposed its being read with great zeal & vehemence. —

Mr. Adams, Bayard, Hillhouse, Logan Maclay, Franklin, & Pickering advocated the propriety & necessity of receiving & *hearing* the petition.

Its opponents contended that the Quakers were not interested in the question of slavery, for they had no slaves — & *ergo* they had no right to petition — That in the southern states slavery was legal — that every petition like this, if received by Congress, tended to depreciate the value of their slaves — That it would render their slaves uneasy, useless & rebellious to them. — Would produce the scenes of St Domingo in our own land.

Its advocates said That all the eastern & middle states were greatly interested in the question of preventing as far as they constitutionally can prevent, the increase of slavery — for the owners of every five slaves have a voice in consequence of those slaves equal to any three of the most respectable white men in the nation in the election of Representatives to Congress or Electors of President & Vice President.  That this is a real grievance — that it is considered by all New England as a grievance  That Massachusetts has offered  a resolution to amend the constitution upon this particular [45] — That an important resolution on this subject is now on our tables. —

Mr. Bayard observed, That the southern states ought not to complain of the eastern & middle States for wishing to prevent the further encrease of slaves — For he would Venture to say that all the plagues of Egypt united were not equal to the plague that slavery will eventually prove to the southern States.

The question for receiving the petition was yeas 19, nays 9. It was read — A motion was then made to refer it to the Committee appointed on the Louisiana Memorial [46] — On this the Senate were equally divided 14 & 14 & so the motion was lost.

Mr. Wright in the course of the debate very unjustly said that the motive that induced the gentlemen from the northern States to advocate the cause of the negroes proceeded from *envy* — They were obliged to till their own land, & could not bear to see southern men have their's tilled by slaves.

This is a question that agitates the southern men. Genl Jackson said to day in debate that if the slaves were manumitted their lands would fall 75 pr Ct. That white people could not till their low lands.

All the New England senators except Bradley voted in favor of receiving the petition — & indeed all east of Maryland, with the further exception of John Smith of New York.[47]

This very subject of Negro slavery will I am convinced eventually produce a division of the United States.

---

[45] See Ames, *The Proposed Amendments to the Constitution of the United States,* 45-46. The resolution was introduced by Senator Pickering of Massachusetts, December 7, 1804; *Annals of Congress,* 8 Cong., 2 sess., 21.

[46] See note 34.

[47] J. Q. Adams, whose later career was so largely associated with the reading of petitions in the House of Representatives on the subject of the abolition of slavery, remarked (*Memoirs,* I, 336) that the petition presented by Logan was " very warmly debated for about three hours." He did not give details of the debate. For information concerning slavery petitions at this time, see Locke, *Anti-Slavery in America, 1619-1808,* pp. 143-156.

## *Tuesday 22d.*

On reading the bill making appropriations for the support of the naval establishment for the present year, Mr. Moore of Virginia objected to one Item as exceeding the sum that would probably be necessary. Genl Smith replied, That the want of a sufficient appropriation for the last year, the Naval Expedition against Tripoli has failed — & rendered another necessary — For the President had not money enough appropriated to enable him to equip a sufficient force.

Why was not a larger sum appropriated — The fact was the President was consulted — the sum was declared by him adequate — Federalists have never objected to appropriations for the Navy. It was a love for the *popularity of the day* that determined the President as to the quantum of expence in that expedition. In this he has sported with life & treasure in a way & manner that sound discretion will not justify. And instead of *saving* cash has *squandered* it — & must now prepare for another campaign.

General Jackson speaking upon the treaty with the Creek Nation said, That the State of Georgia had exported 17,000,000 ℔ of cotton in one year that was raised in that state.

## *Tuesday 25th.*

The State of South Carolina has not yet assessed any part of their proportion of the Direct Tax that was raised under the administration of Mr. Adams. The Senate have this day passed a bill to provide for the completing the valuation of lands &c in that State.[48] This law authorizes the Secretary of the Treasury to complete the valuation — & it appropriates $13593..23 to that object. It is *now probable* that in the course of this year the valuation may be completed, & the tax perhaps as-

---

[48] Approved January 30, 1805; see *Statutes at Large*, II, 311-313.

sessed. Extents in the eastern states have long since issued agt. those Collectors who neglected to pay their taxes. This is unequal!

In the course of the debate upon the bill to establish rules for the regulation of the Army — Mr. White moved to add a rule authorizing the Officer who is impowered by law to discharge soldiers from the service, to all such soldiers as are honorably discharged their regimentals. Mr. Bayard objected — He said that the clothing belonged to the soldier & the officer had no more controul over it than he had over the soldiers wages.

Mr. White replied — that was his opinion — but this very winter a soldier afflicted with Rheumatism was discharged a few days since in this city and the officer would not allow him to have his coat & pantaloons.

*Genl Dayton* This soldier I personally know — He has honorably & faithfully served the United States 16 years. A few days since he complained to me that having ruined his health in the service of his Country he was now without his consent discharged from service, & deprived of a coat and pantaloons to wear in this cold weather. The poor fellow's statement interested my feelings — I wrote to Col. Wharton requesting information — He returned me an answer in writing, & complained that the orders he had received from the Department of War compelled him to deprive the unfortunate sufferer of clothing he very much needed. And a very few days since Col. Wharton paid me a visit & speaking of this transaction he said, with tears in his eyes, " The peremptory orders of his Superior obliged him to perform this hard act." The Secretary of War [49] conceives that the Act of Congress requires such conduct. His opinion is unlike that of others.

I voted against the motion — from a thorough persuasion that there is nothing in the law that will warrant such a construction — & from a full conviction that measures will be taken

---

[49] General Henry Dearborn of Massachusetts.

to remedy the evil in future. As well might Genl Dearborn deprive such unfortunate soldiers of their wages — of their very shirts — & turn them naked to the inclement skies as wrest their coat & pantaloons from them. With pitiful meanness — yet this is called *Oeconemy!*

Mr. Wright moved, but could not find a senator to second his motion, to strike out the article respecting giving or receiving challenges for duels.

### Saturday 26th.

Mr. Brackenridge, on the bill relating to the jurisdiction of Courts, said, That there were now more than 300 suits depending in the District Court in Kentucky — That many of them respected titles of land — many are suits in Chancery — & that in many of the suits the costs exceed the damages. The suits respecting the titles to lands have been occasioned by the lands being sold for the payment of taxes.

### Tuesday 29th.

The Senate negatived a nomination made by the President of a man to be Consul to St Domingo — upon the full conviction of his being disqualified. Mr. Smith of Maryland objected to the appointment upon the ground of his being a subject of Great-Britain — & his reputation not being good. He sd our *Consuls* in general are disgraceful.

The Senate spent the day in debate upon the treaty with the Creek nation of Indians, mentioned page 68 [50] — but no vote was taken thereon. —

*Dr. Mitchell,* I am sorry our Government has established the practise of making treaties with the wandering hords of Savages — We have given them rank as soverign nations, & introduced the solemnities of treaties with them. Much better

---

[50] Page 219 of this volume.

would it have been for us to have adopted the simple but efficacious practise of Gov Penn the first proprietary of Pennsylvania, of acquiring the Indian claim to lands by mere bargain & sale.

If we can collect the President's opinion of this treaty, from the message that accompanies it, he is not favorable to its ratification.

The idea of creating $200000 of irredeemable stock — of entailing this debt with six pr Ct interest pr annum to distant posterity, is an evil — I wish to avoid.

The price is too high — 'tis unreasonable — We can never expect to purchase other lands from other tribes without giving the same price as for this. The prcceedent will be dangerous!

I do not beleive that Col. Hawkins has acted fairly in this transaction — He is too much in the interest of this tribe to negociate to advantage for us — He is their agent — the documents proove it. And 'tis a fact that he himself has prevented their Chiefs from coming here.

Look at the map of the United States — see what immense tracts of country the Indians yet own — this tract is triffling compared with it.

We have not money to spare for such a purchase —

I am for rejecting the Treaty & inviting the Chiefs to come here & make a new one.

*Mr. Hillhouse,* I am an advocate for preserving peace with the Indian tribes — 'Tis good policy to purchase their lands — to pay for them by Annuities — Tis more humane & less expensive than War — In this mode the treaty is the best security for their good behavior, for as the annuity depends solely on the treaty, if they violate it, the annuity is then forfeited. But this treaty destroys that security — it is to create stock which our faith is pledged to perform the payment. When the United States revolted from Great Britain, she declared & considered us as Rebels — the State of Maryland had then stock in her

Bank — that nation sequestered it during the War, but has since with good faith paid the same with interest. We cannot by a law say that in case the Indians violate this treaty the Stock shall be forfeited — We are but one of the contracting parties, & have no authority to annex such a condition to the contract.

This Stock, I have no doubt, is requested at the motion of some white man — it did not originate with the Indians. But this has no doubt led them to enquire into the nature of our stocks, & they will consider it like our common stock transferable at the pleasure of the Owner. If we do not consider it so — & they request a transfer, & we refuse, it will cause discontent, & war.

If we set this example other tribes will require stock, or make war. Tripoli now makes war with us, because she says we do not pay her *so much* tribute as we pay to her neighbors.

I do not think that our Convention with Georgia binds us to ratify this treaty — because the terms & conditions of this treaty are not reasonable — Because the original design & meaning of the Convention with Georgia was that the United States should not be obliged to pay that State money from our Treasury, but only out of the sales of those lands that she ceded to us — We have yet received no Money from those lands — none I beleive has been sold. —

*Mr. Wright* — moved to strike out of the treaty all that related to *stock* and lieu thereof to insert an annuity of . . . . dollars.

*Mr. Baldwin,* I hope the amendment will not prevail — for the Creeks will never agree to it. Georgia has a just claim upon the United States to have this Indian title extinguished — & she never will rest satisfied till it is done — The faith of the Union is pledged for its performance.

*Mr. Wright* withdrew his motion.

*Mr. Jackson* If this treaty is rejected, Georgia will obtain possession of the land by force of arms — This will involve the United States in a war with those Indians which will subject the Union to greater expence than the treaty.

*Mr. Hillhouse,* This threatening language does not terrify me, nor will it influence me to vote for the treaty.

*Mr. Jackson,* The U. S. have exercised over Georgia acts that are both tyrannical & unconstitutional — They have arbitarily & unjustly deprived that State of the whole county of Tallassee — a county containing four million & a half acres of land. Scarsely had the Royal government established itself in Georgia before it greatly extended our limits — but Congress has against our wills & without right deprived us of immense tracts of lands. We have received little advantage from the Union, but have suffered much loss.

I do not mean to threaten — but I say if the Indian title is not extinguished to those lands — war is unavoidable — We are so circumstanced — so surrounded by the savages — have so many bad men — we cannot prevent it.

I beleive the Creeks will soon leave the United States — The President has informed me that 200 of their warriors have gone to explore Louisiana — & the President has the authority to make the necessary exchange of lands with them.

The rejection of this treaty is depriving Georgia of many advantages — it is denying us of population that would give us three more Representatives in the other House. The land contained in that treaty is the most valuable of any in the State — it is capable of yielding annually 50,000,000 ℔s of cotton.

The stock mentioned in the treaty I am confident will not ever be transferred — I wish to God it was not in the treaty.

*Mr. Pickering,* 'Tis a wise provision in the Constitution that prohibits an individual State from making a treaty with the Indians. The local interests of a State, had they power to treat, might induce them to pursue such unjust measures as would commit the peace of the Union. The Articles of Confederation also prohibited States from forming treaties with the Indians, except those Indians who lived within the State & were *subject* to the laws of the State.[51]  The treaty formed by Georgia with the Indians prior to our Constitution, but under the Confederation, for the purchase of the County of Tallassee was made without authority, & *ergo* is void.  But I have been informed from the most correct authority from Mr. Pickens [52] of South Carolina that that treaty was founded in fraud — that the Indians were grossly imposed upon.  The commentary of the Indians upon that treaty was a long, bloody, & expensive war — In which the United States was obliged to interfere at the loss of much blood & treasure.  Mr. Pickens had the means of knowledge — He was then & afterwards a Commissioner to treat with Indian tribes — He is a gentleman of talents and unquestionable integrity.  I have myself been a Commissioner to various Indian tribes — I have ever found them faithful, scrupulously so, to all their contracts.  I well remember of requesting certain tribes the Six nations, to grant the right of way to the United States, & of my offering them a large annuity They said they would not dispose of an inch of land.  But while I was on my passage to their Country I met with a treaty that Great Britain had made with the same Nations for a right of way four miles wide, & part of the same course that I wished to obtain.  This treaty was made previous to the Revolution — I accidently found it in a British Magazine.  I mentioned to the Chiefs that they had forty years before that time granted the way thus far to the British king & that we were his successors & entitled to the way.  They replied they know the way thus

---

[51] By Article IX the treaty-making power was given to Congress, as well as the power of " regulating the trade and managing all affairs with the Indians, not members of any of the States, provided that the legislative right of any State within its own limits be not infringed or violated."

[52] Probably Andrew Pickens, who rose to the rank of brigadier general in the Revolutionary army; served in the campaign against the Cherokee Indians in 1782; and was a member of the House of Representatives from 1793 to 1795.

far was ours, & that they never should object to our having
it — But not an inch further would they grant.

I know the US. are bound to Georgia to extinguish the Indian
claims to certain lands as soon as the same can be done on
*reasonable terms:* I think these conditions are *not reasonable,*
& *ergo* must vote against ratifying this treaty as it now is — I
wish it modified, & *ergo* renew the motion made by Mr. Wright.

*Mr. Bayard.* The President might have rejected this treaty
without laying the same before the Senate — & should two
thirds of us now advise him to ratify it, he would not be bound
to comply with our advice — & our opinion ought be given freely
& independent of & uninfluenced by his.

I am opposed to the amendment — I like the treaty better
as it is than I should if amended agreeable to the motion. I
like stock better than annuities because its transferable — &
when transferred may be redeemed.

Under the Confederation a State could not treat with an
Indian tribe, unless that tribe was in subjection to the laws of
that State. The Creeks never were subject to the laws of
Georgia — they have ever been an independent nation — The
treaty therefore of Georgia with the Creeks for the purchase of
Talassee was never valid — But that treaty & that question
have no relation to the business before us.

By the Convention with Georgia the US. have pledged the
faith of the nation to that State to extinguish the Indian claim
to the lands in question as soon as it can be done on reasonable
terms. It is now near three years since the negociation has
been pending. Our Agent reports these are the most favorable
terms on which the lands can be obtained — that in his opinion
delay will not be favorable to us — The value of an article is
what it will bring — & that common price is the *reasonable price*
— And if this is the best bargain that we can make I am for
ratifying it — And unless proof is adduced of fraud, & I can see
none, I think myself bound to ratify it. It is too late for me

to enquir whether the US. made a good or bad bargain with Georgia — The faith of the nation is pledged to extinguish the Indian title to these lands — & if the purchase was a million of dollars & the land could not be had for less I would advise the President to ratify the treaty & fulfill our contract.

*Mr. Saml Smith,* I am for ratifying the treaty as it is. The price is too high — but when we have ratifyed it we shall have no more money in the Treasury. The Creeks will establish the price of land for themselves, the Choctows & all the other nations — None will sell under this price — the effect will be that we shall buy no more land — & we shall need no more for a century.

*Mr. Israel Smith,* I am for the amendment. The annuity will be a pledge for the good behavior of the Indians — Stock can be transferred, annuities cannot. The price I think is unreasonably high, & if the amendment is not adopted I shall vote against the treaty.

*Mr. Dayton,* I am of the opinion that we cannot obtain a better treaty — I shall vote agt. all amendments, & risque the question of ratification.

*Mr. Giles.* I beleive this stock will be unalienable & irredeemable. I beleive our Agent was more anxious to create it than the Indians — This treaty is an experiment of Col. Hawkins upon this point. The Indians will prefer money to stock. Annuities are not transferrable none ever have been transferred. Stocks never have been introduced into Indian treaties — Annuities have— & we have ever experienced there good effects — I am *ergo* in favor of the amendment. I fear to adopt new & untried principles — It will be dangerous.

The various arguments I have heard this day on the subject has had great influence on my mind — I sometimes feel inclined to ratify — at other times I doubt — I hesitate — I am willing to own I am not yet prepared to vote on the final question.[53]

---

[53] On this debate, see J. Q. Adams (*Memoirs,* I, 340), where only a brief mention is made of the difficulty of arriving at a satisfactory conclusion.

## *Wednesday 30th.*

This day a memorial was presented to the Senate from a number of Militia Officers & other very respectable gentlemen from the State of Tennessee — It states that Col. Butler of the US. army is again arrested for the trivial crime of not cropping his hair in compliance with the orders of General Wilkinson — & requests that Congress will pass some law upon the subject — particularly preventing such orders from operating upon the Militia in case they should ever be called into actual service.[54]

There is now a Committee of the Senate upon the bill for establishing rules for the government of the Army. It was moved to refer this Memorial to that Committee. The motion was violently opposed by Mr. Dayton, Giles S Smith and others — And supported with great ability by Mr. Bayard, Adams, Hillhouse Pickering & others. The Motion prevailed yeas 16 nays 15. This debate took up the whole day. Mr. Giles declared that soldiers & subordinate officers ought never to *think* — that they were bound to yield passive obedience & non-resistance in all cases whatever to the command of their superiors.

I am really pleased with Mr. Bayard — he is certainly a man with great talents — prompt & ready on every question. I have yet seen no man in Congress whose resources are so great. He is a host.

## *Thursday 31st.*

The treaty with the Creek nation under consideration.

*Mr. Tracey,* I see no reason for the amendment — If it prevails you will subject the US. to as much expence & inconvenience as if you reject it — The Indians will feel as much uneasiness & dissatisfaction at this amendment as at its being

[54] *Cf. ibid.,* I, 340–341.

rejected — But by amending it in the manner proposed you only change the *mode* of payment; but you in fact establish the sum & inevitably fix the price — If this amendment prevails I will vote against the treaty.

*Mr. Adams,* I am agt. the amendment — Indeed I think amendments to treaties imprudent. By making them you agree to all the treaty except the particular you amend — & at the same time you leave it optional with the other party to reject the whole. This is unequal. — When amendments are made by one party, they generally produce discontent & jealousy in the other contracting party. I beleive there has not been an instance in which the US. have made a conditional ratification to a treaty but has proved injurious to us. Three instances now occur — *Viz.* the two last treaties with Great Britain — Mr. Jay's [55] & Mr. King's [56], the last is suspended by that nation — & the treaty with France.[57] —

*Mr. Pickering* — I withdraw my motion — the reasoning of the gentlemen, & my own reflection upon the subject convince me it ought not to prevail.

The motion was then made to advise the President to ratify the treaty.

*Mr. Cocke,* I was of the Senate when Col. Hawkins who made this treaty was first appointed a Commissioner to treat with Indians. I was then directed by the instructions from the State of Tennessee to oppose his appointment. I had *no* confidence in the man then, & I have *less* now. I opposed him but in vain — The Senate thought I was then rude. — He is in fact an Indian Chief — the treaty & documents shew it I really

---

[55] Jay's Treaty, 1794.

[56] The convention negotiated by Rufus King was communicated to the Senate on October 24, 1803. The Senate having given its consent on the condition that the fifth article should be expunged, the ratifications of the respective Governments were never exchanged. For the text of the convention, with accompanying correspondence, see *Annals of Congress,* 8 Cong., 2 sess., 1235–1255.

[57] The Convention of 1800 with France.

consider this treaty as made by Benjamin Hawkins for the use of Benjamin Hawkins — I do not like the idea of introducing *stock* into Indian treaties — Indians know nothing of it. I think a new treaty may be made with that nation, & if Hawkins has nothing to do with it & is not even permitted to attend, this land may be purchased for one tenth of this sum.

*Mr. Brackenridge,* It is with great reluctance I am compelled to say, I must vote agt. this treaty — A better bargain I am confident can be made — The price very much exceeds the expectations of the Executive the documents prove this —

The sum promised in this treaty exceeds all that we have paid for all the treaties we have yet made with all the Indian tribes. I do not mean in this to include any of the Annuities we have paid to the Indians; but only the sums paid at the making of the treaties.

The land in question is but a small tract to which Indian titles extend. To obtain those lands at this rate will drain your treasury — it will be insufficient —

The State of Tennessee contains 200,000 of acres — the Indians claim one half of it — The half they claim divides that state in such a manner, as obliges us to have two district federal courts in that State — & the State is compelled to have two district & seperate treasurers. These Indian Claims must soon be extinguished. These Indian lands in Tennessee are valuable they are surrounded by cultivated fields — Will you by this enormous sum establish a price porportionately high for these other more valuable Indian lands? Prudence forbids it.

I will only add that in the State of Kentucky the Indian claims Cover 300000 of acres.

*Mr. Bradley.* If I beleived the stock was transferrable I should vote agt the treaty — but beleiving it not transferable — that it is irredeemable, & the price reasonable I shall therefore vote for the ratification.

*Mr. Giles* I know Col. Hawkins — he is a man of strict

integrity & inviolable honor — I know he has some strong peculiarities — he is from principles of friendship strongly attached to the Indians — This however does not render him the less suitable to treat with them — He may have estimated their rights too high.

I beleive the stock is negociable, & if I did not so beleive I would vote for the treaty. The President in his message considers it so, & his opinion will govern the Treasury department in this particular.

*Mr. Dayton* — I have known Col. Hawkins from childhood — we were classmates at Princeton College — He was proverbial for frankness, integrity & correct judgment.

*Mr. Pickering,* I have long known him — he is a fair amiable character.

I beleive there is not less than 100,000,000 of acres of land in the US. which the Indians claim. To extinguish their claims to all these lands at the rate of this treaty would cost us $10,000,000 — To this we must add the immense tracts claimed by them in Louisiana.

This purchase compared with former treaties is enormous — is far from being reasonable.

*Mr. Saml Smith,* This land is fit for the cultivation of cotton — its very favorable to it — Cotton will be the staple of our country. We must export it, instead of specie, to China.

*Mr. Bayard,*[58] There is nothing on the face of this treaty that casts the slightest imputation on the character of Col. Hawkins — but the reverse — Had he been a cunning designing fraudulent man would *he* have sent you the information that the Indians considered him as their Agent? It is peculiarly necessary that the Indians should have a confidence in the man that negociates with them. In their state of society they substitute this confidence for the reasoning that prevails in well informed civilized Courts.

---

[58] James Asheton Bayard, senator from Delaware; later one of the commissioners who negotiated the Treaty of Ghent with Great Britain.

I think the only question for us to decide, is this a good bargain? Have we solid grounds to beleive if we reject it We can obtain the lands on terms more favorable? I do not myself think we have. The commission has been pending three years & these are the best terms that during that period could be obtained — We give less than ten cents pr acre — We sell none of our own under two dollars. The Creeks are the most civilized of Savages — they know the price at which we sell land — they know that we are under obligation to Georgia to procure this land — reject this treaty & is it not probable they will demand a higher price? The President has assured us they have a greater aversion to sell land than any other tribe.

### Friday Feby 1.

*Treaty with the Creeks under consideration.*

*Mr. Adams.* The arguments for & against the treaty are equally strong — they neutralize each other.

It is reduced to a question of feeling — feeling as it respects the State directly & immediately interested. I ask myself what should I do was Massachusetts situated as Georgia is? What line of conduct should I expect from other senators? My first feelings were in favor of ratifying, & the arguments for & against ratifying being equal, my feelings still govern me, & induce me to vote for the treaty.

Those who know more of the lands than I do, say they are more valuable than any we have ever obtained from the Indians — I am bound to beleive them; We cannot ergo compare this price with the former.

I am inclined to beleive this Stock is not transferable — because it is not in the name of the Nation but in that of its agent to their use. Estates in trust are in their nature transferable. If the owner is under no legal disability the trustee may transfer. The Chiefs of this Nation are unable to make the transfer. It can be done only by the Nation — to obtain this consent will be difficult, & *ergo* probably will not be effected.

I really wish to see the treaty modified — I am in favor of ratifying it, & requesting the President to negociate further.[59]

Note, Yesterday, for the first time I saw the whole number of Senators, 34, present together in the Senate Chamber.

### Saturday Feby 2d 1805.

*Treaty with the Creek nation under consideration.*

*Mr. Moore.*[60] I have no doubt a better treaty can be obtained — The state of the Creeks is such they must have money from the US. — Their wants encrease & return with every returning season.

The Convention with Georgia embarrasses me — The faith of the US. is pledged to extinguish the Indian claim — I should have no hesitation, therefore, in voting for this treaty were not Stock introduced into it. — I totally disapprove of it — it is transferrable — Annuities are better — their annual wants will be gratified by annual payments — The stock they will squander — they will sell it.

*Mr. Adams,* I shall vote for the ratification, & if it prevails, I shall then move a resolution requesting the President, previous to his ratifying it to negociate with the Creeks to change the stock to an Annuity.

*Mr. Pickering,* The Creeks well know the difference between the Stock & annuities. By virtue of a former treaty, still in force they receive from us an Annuity of $4000. They know that if they receive this stock they can receive the interest annually as long as they think proper & when they please sell the principal. There remains no doubt therefore of the Indians actually knowing the difference between Stock & Annuities.

Our public stock is in its nature transferrable — & to prevent that standing to the credit of States from being so, negative words were necessary & are introduced into the law. The provisions of

---

59 *Cf.* J. Q. Adams, *Memoirs,* I, 342.
60 Andrew Moore, senator from Virginia.

our laws relative to transfers generally extend to the mode & manner, not to the right, of making transfers.

Indian tribes act by their Chiefs — They can obtain the authority to make a transfer with as much ease as to receive the interest due on the stock.

If this price is reasonable will not Georgia demand of us to extinguish at the same rate the Indian claim to the County of Tallassee, & the rest of the lands in that State? Are gentlemen prepared for this?

*Mr. Sumpter,*[61] The stock is transferrable — 'tis more tis irredeemable — A permanent debt is a serious evil — it is a national curse.

Genl Meriweather has assured me that he was notified to meet the Indians — that he met them once — & found them friendly. That previous to the meeting of Congress, Col. Hawkins informed him the Chiefs would repair to this city — in consequence of this he sat out to take his seat in Congress at the meeting of Congress — And the first information he received on the subject was that the treaty was formed — And that he beleives a much better one can be made. I am of the same opinion.

I fear if this treaty is ratifyed, it will have a pernicious influence upon all after treaties. I am unwilling to vote against it, but a sense of duty compels me.

Mr. Brown [62] moved to strike out all the resolution after the word Resolved, & insert, that the further consideration thereof be postponed to some time next December, & that the President in the meantime be requested to renew the negociation to obtain the land for a less sum & to change the stock into an annuity. A division of the question was called for — first to determine on striking out.

The rules of the Senate requiring the question of striking

---

[61] Thomas Sumter, senator from South Carolina.
[62] John Brown, senator from Kentucky.

out to be in these words " shall the words stand " that is the words in the original resolution.

The yeas were Baldwin, Dayton, Giles, Hillhouse, Jackson, Mitchell, Pickering, Plumer, John Smith of N. Y. Stone & Tracey — eleven.

The nays were, Adams, Anderson, Bayard, Brackenridge, Brown, Cocke, Condit, Ellery, Franklin, Gaillard, Logan, Maclay, Moore, Olcott, Israel Smith, Samuel Smith, Sumter, White, Worthington, & Wright.   20.

There not being two thirds of the senators present the motion for striking out did not prevail.

The question was then taken upon advising & consenting to ratifying the treaty — the yeas were Mr. Adams, Bayard, Baldwin, Dayton, Gaillard, Giles, Jackson, Logan, Samuel Smith, Tracy, White and Wright.   12.

The nays were Anderson, Breckenridge, Brown, Cocke, Condit, Ellery, Franklin, Hillhouse, Maclay, Mitchell, Moore, Olcott, Pickering, Plumer, Israel Smith, John Smith New York, Stone, Sumter & Worthington, 19.

Bradley, Howland & John Smith of Ohio each of them avoided the question.

---

The House of Representatives have this week been engaged in debate upon the report of the Committee of Claims upon the Memorial of the purchasers of lands in Georgia.  The Committee reported, a state of facts & recommend " That three Commissioners be authorized to receive propositions of compromise & settlement, from the several companies or persons, having claims to public lands within the present limits of the Mississippi Territory, & finally to adjust & settle the same in such manner as in their opinion will conduce to the interest of the United States: Provided, that in such settlement, the commissioners shall not exceel the limits prescribed by the Convention with the state of Georgia." [63]

---

[63] See *Annals of Congress,* 8 Cong., 2 sess., 1024–1033.

John Randolph has pronounced two or three very bitter & very personal phillippic's on this subject. He is violently opposed to the report — His speeches were too personal — his allusions to brothel-houses & pig stys too course & vulgar — his arraigning the motives of members charging them with peculation, bribery, & corruption, were insufferable — He lashed demo's & feds indiscrimately — He treated no man that was opposed to him with either respect or decency. The Speaker [64] ought to have called him to order — for his conduct was insufferable; but the Speaker dared not offend him.

Eliott,[65] replied with great spirit & retorted with propriety. Randolph affects to despise him.

Jackson of Virginia in an open direct manner repelled Randolph's argument, & in course language accused Randolph of being guilty of improper, indecent conduct & using base abusive language.

Mr. Root of New York made an able speech — directly attacked Randolph — said severe & offensive things of him.

Mr. Dana, the chairman of the Committee considered himself obliged to speak — three of his committee had spoken in opposition to the report — to wit Holmes,[66] Bedinger[67] & Sandford.[68] Mr. Dana's speech did much honor to his head & heart — The argument was logical, the wit chaste but poignant — the language elegant & the allusions to the black guardian of Randolph were severe — the satire keen — yet manly & gentlemanlike.

Mathew Lyon of famous memory[69] — turning to Randolph

---

[64] Nathaniel Macon of North Carolina.
[65] James Elliot, representative from Vermont.
[66] David Holmes, representative from Virginia.
[67] George Michael Bedinger, representative from Kentucky.
[68] Thomas Sandford, representative from Kentucky.
[69] Matthew Lyon, representative from Kentucky, gained considerable notoriety in 1797 by his refusal to accompany the other members of the House to pay their respects to President John Adams. In the following year (1798) he fought with Griswold of Connecticut on the floor of the House. He was convicted under the Sedition Act.

thanked God for giving him the face & the heart of a man, not that of an ape or monkey & said that the post master general & himself had been *belied* in that House. For this he was called, & justly, to order. The Speaker directed him to sit down. He complied — Soon after rose again — Bryan [70] & others objected to this as being out of order — The Speaker decided he was in order & might proceed — from this Lyon's accusers appealed & the House approved of the decision of the Speaker.

I never witnessed so much rage & indignation in a deliberative assembly before. Had the gallery applauded — or any little unfavorable incidents happened — it appeared the House would have been at logger-heads.

Yesterday the question was taken upon the report, & adopted yeas 65 nays 58. Every man from New England, except Seaver of Massachusetts & Olin of Vermont, voted in the affirmative.

The distinction of federalist & democrat did not appear to have any influence. The eastern democrats seemed to forget their opposition to the federalists — They both unite as men — & they act as the Inhabitants of free, not *slave*, States. Randolph in vain invoked the aid of party — eastern demo's would not rally under his banners. —

For more than a month the old party spirit of federalists & democrats has subsided in Congress particularly the Senate — I fear the trial of Judge Chase will too much revive it.

Mr. Randolph sent his friend Mr. Bryan to Mr. Root to request an *explanation.* Mr. Root very sternly replied — it was a subject on which he would not converse — If Mr. Randolph wished to communicate anything, it must be in writing — & he should return a prompt answer — such a one as the necessity of the case & the fitness of things required. —

Mr. Randolph after Mr. Dana had ended his speech & before the House adjourned walked across the chamber & requested

---

[70] Joseph Bryan, representative from Georgia.

Mr. Dana to accompany him to the Committee room. He there enquired if he intended by what he had said in the House to accuse him of calumny? Mr. Dana replied He tho't the decorum of debate forbid him arraign any gentleman's motives — He owed it to himself & to a sense of propriety to say that he never intended, in debate, to charge any member with calumny. Mr. Randolph asked him if he would tomorrow make such a decõn publickly in the House? Mr. Dana replied, that was a proposition he would consider off. The next morning Mr. Dana was called into the Committee room by Mr. Bryan, the friend of Randolph. Mr. Bryan asked Mr. Dana if he would make the decõn in the House as he had promised Mr. Randolph? Mr. Dana replied he had made no such promise — but least Mr. Randolph should think one was implied & mistakes should in future arise, whatever communications take place between us they must be in writing.

Two or three times after this Mr. Bryan called Mr. Dana into the Committee room & Mr. Dana refused to converse with him unless in the presance of Mr. Roger Griswold his friend. Mr. Bryan asked him if he would answer a letter in case Mr. Randolph should send him one? Mr. Dana replied that would depend upon the nature of the letter — if it was such a one as a gentleman ought to receive he would certainly answer it, & that directly. —

If Mr. Randolph wishes a duel, why decline sending a challenge to either Eliott, Root or Jackson — each of whom, its publickly said, would accept it. Why attempt to practise on Genl Dana? does he think this gentleman living in Connecticut dare not accept a challenge — Mr. Dana has nerves —

What course Mr. Dana will take in this business I can not yet determine — whether he will accept a challenge, should one be given, or lay it on the Speaker's table — or pursue some other course — he thinks it improper at present for him to say — But he has made up his mind — & from my knowledge of the man, I have no doubt he will act with propriety.

Mr. Randolph's intention is obvious — It is to awe the freedom of debate — it is to silence his opponents. The constitution has provided, " That for *any speech* or debate in either House, the members shall not be *questioned* in any other place." [71]   If a man says any thing improper he must at the time be called to order — He may be silenced by the House — he may be censured — he may, if two thirds think proper, be expelled.   I have no doubt should Mr. Randolph challenge any member, & information be given to the House, & a motion made to expell him, a majority would be found who would vote for his Expulsion but not two thirds.   At this time he is unpopular.

Randolph, Nicholson & Rodney, the three champions of southern democracy, with Eppes & Thomas Man Randolph, the Presidents two sons in law, are in the *minority.*

---

The Mint of the United States for the year 1804 has cost us $14,027..28 more than what we received from it — as appears by the report from the Director of that establishment.

### Sunday 3d February 1805.

Between three & four OClock this afternoon Mr. Joseph Bryan one of the Representatives from Georgia called upon Mr. Dana at our lodgings.   Mr. Dana requested him to walk into the Hall — he declined, saying he could not, for he had company waiting for him at the door.   He then handed Mr. Dana a letter, saying it was from Mr. Randolph, & that he would call for an answer at eight OClock this evening.   Mr. Dana replied, That this was a day on which it was not customary for him, or the people of the State he had the honor to represent, to transact business — that he should return no answer whatever to day — but that tomorrow he would attend to the business. — Mr. Bryan bowed & walked off — he appeared to be much agitated

---

[71] Article I, section 6.

— Mr. Dana was calm & collected. This all took place publicly, in Capt Coyle's entry, in the presance of most of the boarders — I was a witness to the whole proceeding.

Mr. Randolph in his note said that Mr. Dana in the debate of last friday had wounded his feelings — And he requested that Mr. Dana would give him satisfaction commensurate to the injury — & requested him to recall to his consideration an after conversation.

Mr. Bryan did not call upon Mr. Dana at eight OClock or at any other time this night.

## *Monday 4th.*

Mr. Dana this morning returned a note to Mr. Randolph in which Mr. Dana informed him that he had perfect recollection of the conversation he wished him to recall to his consideration — & very plainly intimated that he had no concessions to make.

This note Mr. Randolph shewed to several of his friends — sneered at it — And while the House was in session went to the window near Mr. Dana, called out to him to come — Mr. Dana sat in his seat, Randolph went to him & in loud boisterous language Told Mr. Dana to *take care of himself, for he would be revenged on his person* — This was taking Mr. Dana by surprise — but he replied *Ah! have you come to this — I am ready for you.* This was in the hearing of the Speaker — but he is the friend of Randolph!

Men of the turf, whom Mr. Dana has consulted, such as Mr. Bayard, Dayton, White & others, say that Mr. Randolph's proceeding has been altogether improper, & that Mr. Dana is not bound by the laws of honor to accept of a challenge from Randolph —

I presume that Mr. Randolph expected by this last attack to take Mr. Dana by surprize & induce him to make the humiliating concessions in the House he demanded — Or that Randolph expected Mr. Dana or his friends would complain to the House of a breach of priveledge — & then he would be bound to keep the peace — & so his affair of honor would end in *fumo.*

Mr. Burr this day took his seat in the senate — During his absence he has I beleive travelled no further east than Philadelphia. There he was met by Mr. Bloomfield, the governor of New Jersey. What arrangements were made relative to the indictment now pending in that State agt Mr. Burr for murder — does not yet appear. The seconds of Hamilton & Burr have both been convicted in New York for being the bearers of challenges, & they are disfranchised in that state for the term of twenty years.

At a few minutes previous to One OClock the senate repaired to their Old chamber — The galleries & area was crouded with anxious spectators — The House did not formally adjourn — but being informed of the hour of our meeting — the Speaker & members attended — the Managers took their seats — Judge Chase was called & appeared — a seat was assigned for him & his council. He informed the Court that Mr. Harper,[72] Mr. Martin [73] & Mr. Hopkinson [74] were his council. They each of them were directed by the President to take the seats that were previously assigned for them.

The President asked the Judge if he were now ready to make his plea & answer to the articles of Impeachment & proceed on the trial.

The Judge replied he had his answer, but from the shortness of notice that Was allowed him it was imperfect — but he supposed he must now deliver the answer — & abide by the same. — He then requested in writing that he & his Council

---

[72] Robert Goodloe Harper, representative from South Carolnia, 1795 to 1801, moved to Baltimore, Maryland, where he attained eminence at the bar.

[73] Luther Martin was one of Maryland's delegates to the Federal Constitutional Convention. He opposed the Constitution and refused to sign it.

[74] Joseph Hopkinson of Philadelphia is perhaps best known as the author of the national song, " Hail Columbia."

might read this answer — The court decided he should — The Reading took up two hours & a half — It is a very able answer indeed — I shall not attempt to analize it — It was written on two quires of paper — & will I presume be printed. [75] —

Mr. Randolph, the chairman of the Managers, then rose & enquired whether this was the Answer of the Accused — He was told by the President it was. Randolph then requested that the Managers might be furnished with a copy thereof to be laid before the House. Mr. Burr informed him the Court would take it into consideration & in due time return their answer to the House.

The Senate then returned to their other chamber — ordered the Secretary to furnish the House with a copy of the Judge's answer.

### Tuesday 5th.

In debate this day upon the bill for the clearance of armed vessels — Genl Smith said, It appeared to him that our Executive were more anxious to restrain & fetter our commerce lest our merchants should by some means injure the French government, than they were to demand from France the millions they had wantonly robbed from our Merchants.

The Senate by a large majority ordered the Secretary to procure printed copies of Judge Chase's answer delivered yesterday.

### Wednesday 6th.

*Bill for the clearance of armed vessels. —*

*Mr. Giles,* If this bill, or one nearly similar, does not pass, we shall very soon be involved in a state of actual war.

I scarse ever meet with a member of the Administration, but he expresses his anxious wishes that this bill may pass. —

The Vice President has discovered in the course of this week an unusual share of impatience — He is very fretful & peevish.

---

[75] Chase's answer is given in full in *Annals of Congress,* 8 Cong., 2 sess., 101–150.

There is a further observation relative to the bill aforesaid I ought not to omit — In the course of the discussion, Genl Smith moved to strike out certain words, & add in others in their stead. He said the words he wished to add, were what he had copied from a statute of Great Britain.

*Mr. Giles,* I am in favor of the motion. This regulation is taken from the law of as wise a nation as any on earth — it has been tested by experience, & no doubt, approved by legal adjudications — I am therefore in favor of it.

A few words more respecting Mr. Dana &c. On monday morning when he went to the house he met Mr. Bryan, & very civilly asked him if he expected to receive an answer to Mr. Randolph's note delivered on sunday. Mr. Bryan replied He did not, & that if Mr. Dana had one for Mr. Randolph he might carry it to him himself. Mr. Dana then sent his note by his friend Roger Griswold. —

Mr. Dana has every day attended the House & has expected Mr. Randolph would insult him by spitting in his face, kicking pulling his nose striking him with a horse whip, or some such method. Mr. Dana had been prepared to receive such insult, not indeed tamely — but in such a manner as to cause the haughty Virginian to repent of his folly & insolence. Mr. Dana has carried weapons of defence in his pocket — a pistol with a spring bayonet — his friends have been near him — to see that the adherents of Randolph should not join in the assult. — But all has been quiet — It is surprizing how far this man, like the cowardly Robesspiere has awed the freedom of debate. The stand which Mr. Dana has made is a noble one & he now, on every principle, has the *vantage* ground.

### Thursday 7th.

The House of Representatives sent us notice that they had agreed upon a replication to the answer of Judge Chase to the articles of Impeachment — & that their Managers were directed to bring them to the Senate. After debate the Senate at two OClock went into the Court room & notified the House that they were then ready to receive said replication. The Managers, but not the House, appeared — Mr. Randolph read the replication, which was very concise, but conceived in very bitter, indecent, & abusive language.[76] Judge Chase was not present, or called — Mr. Hopkinson, one of his councel, sat in his seat during the time it was read — & afterwards rose & moved the Court that judge Chase might be furnished with a copy of the replication, & time to consider of the same. The Vice President replied that on his applying to the Secretary, he would receive a copy thereof. The Court then adjourned tomorrow 12 OClock — And the members retired to the Secretary's office to transact legislative business.

### Clearance bill, under consideration.

*Mr. Wright,* The British nation is superlatively wise in the *science* of Commerce. She sends convoys to protect her merchantmen — & in particular instances encourages their arming themselves.

This bill if it passes will make all our merchants as pusillanamous as Quakers.

A stranger coming into the Senate would be led, from our debates, to beleive that Great Britain and France have legitimate councel within these walls, who are advocating their interest against the United States.

*Dr. Mitchel,* I have no doubt that three fifths of all the seamen who navigate American vessels from New York, are in fact British subjects. It is true they get American protections — these can be purchased for a dollar a piece — & these seamen swear for each other. We have made too much ado on account of the British ships taken American seamen from our mer-

---

[76] For the text, see *ibid.,* 151.

chantmen. I have no doubt that nineteen out of twenty whom they have taken were in fact British subjects — & according to the laws of that country were lawfully impressed. The fact is our young men are too proud for seamen — our merchants are obliged to employ foreigners — or negroes.

The Senate passed a bill appropriating $50000 to ascertain & adjust the titles to Lands in the Territory of Orleans, & the district of Louisiana.

Yesterday Mr. Randolph reported from the Managers to the House of Representatives a replication to Judge Chase's answer. Mr. Dennis moved to strike out of the report the following words — " That the said Samuel Chase hath endeavored to cover the high crimes & misdemeanors, laid to his charge, by *evasive insinuations, & misrepresentation of facts;* that the said answer does give a gloss & colouring, *utterly false & untrue,* to the various criminal matters, contained in the said articles." The motion was negatived by a large majority.

### *Friday 8th.*

At twelve OClock the Court met in the Senate Chamber. Mr. Randolph requested that the names of the witnesses whom the Managers had directed to be summoned should be called. It was done — He then moved the Court to postpone the trial untill tomorrow alledging that they were not now ready. Mr. Harper agreed to the request — The names of the witnesses summoned by the Judge were called over. The court then adjourned.

Printed copies of Judge Chase's answer & the replication on the part of the House of Representatives were laid on our tables.

The Senate passed the bill for the support of the Military establishment of the United States for 1805. It appropriates the sum of $943,950..79. for that purpose.

Mr. Burr is remarkably testy — he acts more of the tyrant — is impatient & passionate — scolds — he is in a rage because we do not sit longer. —

## Saturday 9th.

At twelve OClock The Court met — Mr. Randolph the Chairman of the Managers addressed the Court — He said, It was to the *manner* in which the judge delivered his opinion in the case of *Fries viz* before the solemn argument of councel was heard — & in *writing* — to the *intent,* not to the opinion itself — for that may be correct — is the cause for which he is this day accused.

The Court & the world were entirely ignorant what John Taylor's testimony would prove at the time that Judge Chase rejected it.

The Judge required the questions to the witnesses to be reduced to writing — It does not become me to question so high an authority as that of the Respondent — I know that is not the practise in Virginia, the state where he then was. — 'Tis not the practise of Chief Justice Marshall.

His rudeness to Callender's counsel was intolerable — It must be tried by the common sense of mankind. I do not know that it is an offence that is indictable — nor perhaps is, drunkeness, or prophanity on the bench.

The laws of Virginia required that Callender should have been summoned, not taken by a Capias. This law extends to all cases not capital. If it be said, this mode is giving the Accused an opportunity to escape. What then — It will be a favor to the Commonwealth to have the Offender go into voluntary exile.

Trials at common law are contra-distinguished from trials at Maritime law.

It is impossible to place the 7th article of the Impeachment on stronger ground for us than the Judge in his answer has done.

As a Judge he had no authority to address a Grand jury upon political subjects.

Because other judges have done the same, that is no excuse for him.

He has said That in the case of Fries — of Callender &c the district judges — agreed in opinion with him, & gave the same judgt. as he did. The answer to this is, That the accused is a Man of extraordinary talents & of unusual legal information — But these judges who were associated with him, were men of *inferior* temper, &, perhaps, of as *inferior intellect* — They tamely submitted to the mandates of his arbitary will.

We do not charge the judge with a general anxiety to convict offenders, but only in particular cases & those of *very questionable nature.*

His official conduct is a tissue of judicial tyranny.

The mercy of the late President (Adams) prevented the blood of the innocent Fries, of a wretched widow & of helpless orphans, from crying to the throne of Grace for vengeance against the man now arraigned at your bar. The late President by that single act atoned for many of his faults: for mercy like charity covereth a multitude of sins.

Mr. Randolph made many observations upon Murder. He endeavored to liken it to high treason — He labored this point. In this he was unfortunate — for *malice prepense* is essential to the crime of murder — but treason consists only of *overt acts,* which may be committed by a person influenced by the purest of motives — love to liberty, & the most inviolable attachment to one's country.

This speech is the most feeble — the most incorrect that I ever heard him make.

He was immoderate in his enconiums on his father in law, Dr. Tucker.[77] He traduced the accused — He vilified other judges — He insulted one of the Judges of this Court (Mr. Adams) by unnecessarily abusing his father — & he grated the ears of Mr. Burr by a dissertation on *murder.*[78]

---

[77] St. George Tucker, to whom reference is made, was Randolph's step-father.

[78] For the text of Randolph's speech, see *Annals of Congress,* 8 Cong., 2 sess., 154–165.

Two witnesses were then examined — William Lewis & Alexander James Dallas by Mr. Nicholson one of the Managers.

*Mr. Lewis* said, That the only cause of his withdrawing from the defence of Fries, was that he might be of greater use to him afterwards.

That he thought the President would be more likely to pardon a man thus convicted, than he would if convicted after being defended on the trial by council.

*Mr. Dallas,* We thought it good policy to withdraw from his defence — we thought it would operate as a reason with the Executive for a pardon.

A question was proposed by Mr. Randolph to a witness & objected to by Mr. Harper. Mr. Bayard requested that it might be reduced to writing it was done. One of the Rules of the Senate require that all questions may be reduced to writing at the pleasure of the President, & shall be whenever any one senator require it.[79] 'Tis curious that this very circumstance of obliging a party to reduce questions to a witness to writing is one of the very offences for which the Senate are now trying Judge Chase. See Article 4th of the Impeachment.

### *Monday 11th.*

The Court met at 12 OClock. Mr. Lewis was cross-examined by Mr. Harper, i.e. a single question only was asked him.

The managers then examined Edward Tilghman, Wm. S. Biddle, William Rawle & George Hay. The testimony of Mesrs Tilghman & Rawle were very particular correct & impressive. Their candour & intelligence was highly honorable to their hearts as well as heads. The evidence of the three first gentlemen as to the first article of the impeachment, to which their testimony only related, of itself presents a full & solid justification to Judge Chase. It indeed shews the frailty, or in other & more correct words, the imprudence, but not any imputation

---

[79] Rule XVIII of the Rules of Procedure and Practice in the Senate when Sitting on Impeachment Trials.

of a crime in the Judge.   The three first gentlemen are Philadelphia lawyers.

George Hay is a Virginian lawyer — his testimony related to the trial of Callender.   He discovered a disposition to aid the managers — a willingness to testify that was not commendable — His testimony amounted to less than I expected from his introduction.   He very unguardedly declared that it was not Callender for whom he felt on the former trial concerned — but the *cause* in which Callender was engaged.

After Hay had made an introduction — he said he should from the paper he held in his hand refresh his memory as to the facts — This paper he said was transcribed by his *clerk* from a *printed account* of Callender's trial — which was not originally *written by himself*.   To this paper Mr. Harper objected — yeas 16, nays 18. —

At half past 4 OClock motion for adjournment Senate equally divided — Vice President decided agt. adjournment —

My real indisposition obliged me to leave the Senate immediately after the vote was declared.   Mr. Tracy & Mr. Dayton did the same.   The Court sat half an hour longer & then returned to the Secys room.   Mr. Burr immediately called to order & said he tho't himself obliged to require tomorrow morning an apology from the three gentlemen who withdrew from Court — their conduct was improper & indecent.   Mr. Hillhouse said he thot it highly improper that gentlemen of the Senate should be censured in their absence — He had no doubt that their want of health rendered their absence necessary.   Gentlemen were not obliged to tarry so long in the House as to injure their health.[80]

*Mr. Stone,*   I shall never consent to be confined to my seat but by the express vote of the Senate — no other authority will bind me there.

*Mr. Bayard* made some pointed observations —

---

[80] *Cf.* J. Q. Adams, *Memoirs,* I, 350.

The conduct of Mr. Burr is really extraordinary! What, cannot a judge of a Court retire from Court peaceably & quietly without being censured by him — especially when those retiring still leaves a large majority!

I presume I shall hear no request for an explanation tomorrow. My answer will not please him.

This man seems inclined to act the tyrant — What can be his motive now — He can neither intimidate his enemies, or flatter his friends, to any purpose.

A few days since he insolently said to the Senate he had thoughts of removing their chairs & desks & having seats. He was told the Senate would not consent to it.

On friday he sent a message to Mr. Key to inform him he must not appear as counsel with his loose coat on. Mr. Key took it off. The next day Rodney one of the Managers wore his — no notice taken of it. Mr. Pickering, observed to him he was unwilling to see gentlemen controuled in their dress — ill health might render great coats necessary. Mr. Key appeared with his on to day.

Mr. Burr has for this few weeks assumed the airs of a *pedagogue* — & rather considered the senators as his scholars than otherwise. I am unable to divine his motive. — It may be he acts according to his nature having nothing to hope by disguise.

### Tuesday 12th.

At half past 12 OClock the Court met — The Managers finished the examination of Mr. Hay — John Tayler, Philip Norbonne Nicholas, John Thompson Mason, & John Heath were also sworn & examined as witnesses in support of the Impeachment. The testimony of this day proves not wilful crimes but the want of that caution & prudence which enables men to ward off & avoid much difficulty.

Hay discovered much zeal in testifying, & an anxiety to represent Judge Chase in the most disagreeable & criminal point of view, he was able — He quite over-acted his part.

John Tayler (formerly senator in Congress) I have no doubt substantially stated facts as they appear to him at this distance of time. His representation of Chase was a natural one, & must so appear to those acquainted with him. Tayler is a cunning, designing metaphysical man.

Mr. Nicholas is Atty General of Virginia — Is quite a young man — appears of considerable talent but not a profound lawyer — discovered much more candour & firmness of mind than *Hay*.

John Tomson Mason, was formerly District Atty for this District. He is a man of a strong mind. He now, at the request of the Secretary of the Treasury, is acting Attorney General of the United States. A very large fortune has descended to him by the death of two of his uncles — He is therefore retiring from the practise. He will not accept the office of Attorney General of the United States.

John Heath is a Virginia lawyer — was formerly a representative in Congress — Appears a man of moderate talents — Gave his testimony cooly — but, I cannot assign reasons, yet I was unable to give credence to his testimony.

The gentlemen of the Virginia Barr appear at great disadvantage compared with the Barr of Pennsylvania, judging by the specimen we have had these three days — both as to the qualities of the head & heart — both as to matter & manner — & both as to natural & acquired talents & information. None but lawyers have yet been sworn.

I have taken very full notes of the testimony. It is on file, except the testimony of saturday.

Mr. Randolph has a tedious circuituous method of asking questions — they are often imperative.

Mr. Key was so indisposed as to be unable to attend Court this day. Mr. Lee [81] late Attorney general of the United States supplied his place.

The Court retired a little before 4 OClock.

Just as the time for adjourning to tomorrow was to be put in

---

[81] Charles Lee.

the Secretary's office — Mr. Burr said he wished to inform the Senate of some irregularities that he had observed in the Court. Some of the senators as he said during the trial & while a witness was under examination walked between him & the Managers — Others eat apples — & some eat cake in their seats.

Mr. Pickering said he eat an apple — but it was at a time when the President had retired from the chair. Burr replied he did not mean him — he did not see him.

Mr. Wright said he eat cake — he had a just right so to do — he was faint — but he disturbed nobody — He never would submit to be schooled & catechised in this manner.

At this instance a motion was made by Bradley, who also had eaten cake, for an adjournment — Burr told Wright he was not in order — sit down — The Senate adjourned — & I left Wright & Burr scolding.

Really, *Master Burr*, you need a ferule, or birch, to enforce your lectures on polite behavior!

### Wednesday Feby 13th 1805.

A warm debate but of short continuance arose in the Senate whether the Galleries of the Senate Chamber should be open during the time that the two Houses of Congress should be in Convention counting the votes of the Electors for President & Vice President.

On the former occasion they were shut, as appears by the Journals of the Senate.[82]

It was said that times might come in which it would be dangerous to admit the people into the galleries — that they might endanger the lives of the Members of Congress — Over-awe their proceedings — That the people could derive no benefit from being present — That a precedent was established, & ought not now to be departed from of excluding spectators from the gallery.

---

[82] See Senate *Journal,* 6 Cong., 2 sess., (1800), 66–70. *Cf.* J. Q. Adams, *Memoirs,* I, 351.

The motion to admit the people prevailed by the majority of one vote.

At twelve OClock the Senate met in their Chamber — in a few minutes, the Sargeant at Arms with the Mace entered the Chamber followed by the Speaker & the members of the House of Representatives. After they had taken the seats previously provided for them — the Vice President broke the seals of the Electoral returns & handed them to the tellers (one of whom was appointed by the Senate & the other two by the House) & they read the returns & made out a list of the votes. The whole number of Votes were 176 of these Mr. Jefferson had 162 & Charles Cotesworth Pinkney 14 for President — George Clinton had 162 & Rufus King 14 for Vice President. The states of Connecticut & Delaware & two Electors in Maryland voted for Pinkney & King. After the Tellers had made their report Mr. Burr simply declared That Thomas Jefferson was elected President & George Clinton Vice President of the United States.

The two Houses then retired to their respective chambers.

The return of the votes from Georgia was very incorrect — & from Ohio was absolutely inadmissable — In the latter case it was not stated *that the Electors voted by ballot.* Had any one member insisted on the votes being rejected, it would have been a question involving serious difficulties. The Constitution has not provided a tribunal for settling the returns of Electors — no law of Congress is passed on the subject. Suppose different returns from different Electors is made from one State what tribunal shall decide which of the two shall be received. Will the two Houses settle it in Convention? The constitution gives them in that capacity no such power. Will they by law settle such questions in their two seperate Houses? A law must be previously passed.[83]

---

[83] This is an interesting prediction of the dispute which arose over the election of 1876 and of the passage of the Presidential Count Act of 1887.

At 40 Minutes past two the Court met in the Senate chamber.

Mr. Lee as Councel for Judge Chase cross examined Mr. Heath who was sworn yesterday.

The Managers swore John Triplet — His testimony related to the trial of Callender.

Judge Chase requested that John Bassett, whose family was sick might be examined. The Managers agreed. Bassett was sworn — He was the Juror who is mentioned in the Impeachment. His testimony was much in Chase's favor. He did not serve agt. his will.

Court adjourned at 20 Minutes past four OClock.

### *Thursday Feby 14, 1805.*

Mr. Bayard called up his resolution that at any time when the Senate withdraw from their Judicial chamber the rule may be so far amended as to allow each Senator if he please to speak *once* upon the question that may be stated previous to its being decided.

Saml Smith moved to limit the time that each member should speak, to five minutes only. Mr. Cocke seconded that motion.

Mr. Bayard said he had no arguments to offer on this extraordinary resolution, he rose only to request it might be decided by ayes & nays.

Mr. Smith immediately rose & said he withdrew his motion.

The resolution was negatived — ten only voting in favor of it. Mr. Giles, who strenuously opposed it voted in the affirmative.

At twelve OClock the Senate went into their Judicial chamber — The following witnesses were examined, on the part of Judge Chase, Edmond Randolph — & on the part of the managers, George Read, James Lee, John Crow, John Montgomery, Samuel Harrison Smith & John Stevens — They also again called up John Thomson Mason, & re-examined him. —

*Edmond Randolph* is the man that was formerly Secretary of

State & Attorney General of the United States. He is a public defaulter — the correspondent of Fauchet [84] — & by whom he obtained the name of *Floor Merchant.* I was disappointed in the man — my impressions were unfavorable. But in his testimony he discovered good sense & great candour.

*George Reed* is the District attorney of Delaware. He discovered much formality — He had studied his Deposition & had as fully committed it to memory as ever a presbyterian clergyman did his sermon — or an Episcopalian his prayer. His testimony was verbatim with his deposition taken last year.

*John Montgomery,* is of Maryland — he swore he was not a lawyer — but discovered considerable knowledge of law. He was very *formal* — He had I am certain taken great pains to draw up his deposition & then commit it entirely to memory — When he was interrupted he would begin where the interruption was repeating the same words again — He was several times called to repeat the last *section* — which he did verbatim. He is a member of the Maryland legislature. This is the man who made so much opposition to Gov Mercer — This is the man who drew the bills & exerted himself so effectually to break down the independence of the Judiciary of Maryland — & introduce the right of *universal suffrage* in their election. He is a bold, daring, aspiring man — And I think will yet shew his love of liberty & equality by acts of tyranny.

*Samuel Harrison Smith,* is the editor of the National Intelligencer. His nerves failed him — he stated that the sum of all he could say was contained in an affidavit he gave last winter to the Committee — & he requested & obtained liberty to read a printed copy of it which he had compared with the original.

Mr. Randolph read the copy of the Judgt against John Fries — & the copy of the Judgt vs Callender. The last was read to

---

[84] For the Randolph-Fauchet episode, see Lodge, *George Washington,* II, 191–201. A defence of Randolph is made by Conway, *Edmund Randolph.*

prove that the Court directed a warrant or capias to arrest Callender.

Mr. Nicholson stated that they had nine absent witnesses whom they should hereafter wish to examine.

At four OClock the senate retired to their Legislature Chamber — where they passed the law making appropriations for the support of government the present year. The sum thus appropriated is $1,373,973..47.

The Senate adjourned at five OClock.

## *Friday 15th.*

Met in Judicial chamber 15 minutes past 12 OClock.

Waited 15 minutes for the Managers.

After they had called the list of witnesses called yesterday, & none answered —

The President informed the judge that he might proceed in his defence.

Mr. Harper rose & addressed the Court stating the evidence they intended to offer in the defence. This statement was concise & logical — It occupied half an hour. They then examined the following witnesses Mr. Ewing,[85] Edward J Coles, William Meredith, Luther Martin, Mr. Winchester & William Marshall. Mr. Rawle was also again called, & asked a single question

Mr. Ewing & Cole are both lawyers.

Mr. Meredith, is a young but very intelligent lawyer — He is from Pennsylvania.

Mr. Martin is the Attorney General of Maryland — & possesses much legal information.

James Winchester, is the District Judge of that state. He is one of those men whom Mr. Randolph has denominated *weak in temper & intellect.* He discovered mind, information & candour in his testimony.

---

[85] Samuel Ewing.

William Marshall, is & has long been Clerk of the Circuit Court of the United States in the District of Virginia. He is brother to John Marshall the present Chief Justice of the United States. This man has been, & yet is a practising lawyer. In his testimony he discovered a strong clear discriminating mind — a retentive memory — his answers were both prompt & lucid — Their was a frankness, a fairness & I will add a firmness that did him much credit. He was Clerk of the Court & present during the trial of Callender. His testimony was of itself, so far as relates to the 2d, 3d, 4th, 5th & 6th articles of the Impeachment, a complete defence for the accused — unless it can be destroyed.

A question was proposed by Mr. Harper to Mr. Marshall requesting to know what judge Chase had said respecting democrats being on the jury who were to try Callender. Mr. Randolph objected — because it would be only the declaration of the Accused —

Mr. Harper said, He hoped the Managers would not insist upon their objection — for one of the articles charged the Judge with having oppressed Callender — And they had endeavored to prove the Judge attempted to pack a Jury — & had offered evidence of what the Judge had said upon this point.

The Managers withdrew their objection.

Mr. Cocke then renewed the objection — He said he would not be bound by the agreement of the parties. After spending ten minutes in reducing the question to writing &c Mr. Cocke withdrew the motion. The witness was proceeding, when Mr. Wright renewed it & he & Mr. Cocke voted to preclude the witness from answering, & the other 32 senators voted for the witness to answer

At three OClock we returned to our legislative chamber — From thence we went into the Secretary's chamber where we partook of a cold collation with brandy & porter that the Vice President had previously provided for the occasion.

We in a few minutes after proceeded to legislation & sat till 20 minutes after six in the evening.

## Saturday 16th.

At 10 OClock the Senate met in their Judicial chamber & the following witnesses were sworn & examined on the part of Judge Chase, David Meade Randolph, John Marshall, Edmund Lee, . . . Chevally,[86] Col. Gamble,[87] Philip Grouche,[88] & David Robinson.

David Meade Randolph was a Military officer in the revolutionary War — was appointed Marshall by both Washington & Adams in Virginia. He was marshall at the time of Callenders trial. His testimony was clear concise candid & intelligent.

John Marshall is the Chief Justice of the Supreme Court of the United States. I was much better pleased with the manner in which his brother testified than with him. The Chief Justice really discovered too much caution — too much fear — too much cunning — He ought to have been more bold — frank & explicit than he was. There was in his manner an evident disposition to accomodate the Managers. That dignified frankness which his high office required did not appear. A cunning man ought never to discover the arts of the *trimmer* in his testimony.

Edmond Lee, a Virginia lawyer.

David Robertson, a Virginia lawyer — has been in the practise about 17 years. He is remarkable for the accuracy with which he writes short hand — He published an account of the trial of Callender — most of which he read as his testimony.

The gentlemen of the Virginia bar appear unable to state with precision what are the cases in which a summons, not a

---

[86] John A. Chevalier.
[87] Robert Gamble.
[88] Philip Gooch.

capias, issues in the first instance agt persons indicted. It seems, from the current of their testimony, that a summons only issues agt those whose only punishment cannot exceed a fine. But even to this there has been exceptions. Discretion has been used. If their law & practise is thus little known, even by their most eminent lawyers — It is not surprising that Judge Chase should not know their law in this particular. — He could not be accused of a breach of it, with an intent to injure Callender.

At three OClock we returned to our Legislative chamber where we continued till six.

### *Monday 18th.*

At 15 minutes past ten met in the Judicial Chamber.

Six of the witnesses who have been formerly sworn were re-examined — And the following witnesses were sworn, & examined, on the part of the Judge. —

*Gunning Bedford Esq.* the District Judge of Delaware. He appeared to be very fair & candid, but not a man of strong mind.

*Nicholas Vandike* [89] *Esq* Attorney General of the State of Delaware. He is a young gentleman — candid, prompt & intelligent.

*Archibald Hamilton Esq* A young gentleman of the law of the State of Delaware — correct decisive & intelligent.

*John Hall*

*Samuel Moore,* He peremptorily declined stating a private confidential conversation he had with Mr. Reed the District Attorney of Delaware respecting his testimony. He said he never would submit to disclose a confidential communication.

Neither party pressed him — And the Senate would not interfere. Note Mr. Moore is a federalists & Mr. Reed a democrat. He is a husbandman — he affirmed.

---

[89] Nicholas Vandyke.

*William H. Winder Esq.* Is a young gentleman of the law from Maryland. I was much pleased with him. He discovered talents, candor & intelligence.

Judge Chase's councel read passages from the law of the US. establishing Courts Sections, 14, & 29. Vol. I.

Gilberts Law of Executions, pages 307, 308, 313.

2 Dallas's Reports 335, 341.

Judge McKean's charge to the Grand jury in Pennsylvania in Nov 1797.

And Col. Montgomery's virulent account of Judge Chase's Charge to the Grand Jury at Baltimore in May 1803.

At three OClock the Senate retired to their Legislative Chamber.

Past the bill "providing for the government for the territory of Orleans." This gives to that District the second grade of Territorial government. I voted against it because it provides that when they shall have sixty thousand free Inhabitants they shall be admitted as a State into the Union upon the footing of the original States. This provision appears to me unconstitutional. I think we cannot admit a new partner, formed from without the limits of the United States, into the Union without the previous consent of each partner composing the firm first obtained.

### Tuesday Feby 19, 1805.

Met in our Judicial chamber at 15 minutes past ten. Five of the former witnesses were called up & re-examined.

The following new witnesses were called by Judge Chase & sworn — Thomas Chase — his son. Candid. —

Philip Moore, Clerk of the District & Circuit Courts of Maryland. A Democrat but very candid & fair.

Walter Dorsey, a Judge in Maryland — candid, frank & intelligent.

John Purviance, Nicholas Brice, James Boyle, & William

McKinnin,[90] all of them lawyers of Baltimore — Men who testified with great apparent candour, & men of good understanding.

John Campbell, a member of Congress from Maryland — & who was foreman of the Grand Jury at the Circuit Court held at Baltimore May 1803. A very amiable well informed sensible man.

William Cranch one of the Judges of the District Court of the District of Columbia. A very honest worthy good man.

Mr. Harper then read, or rather stated the charge of W. H. Drayton Chief Justice of South Carolina to a Grand jury in that State in 1776. *Ramseys history of South Carolina.*[91]

A letter from the Executive of Pennsylvania to the Judges of the Supreme Court of that State in 1785. *American Museum Vol. I.*[92]

Judge Iredell's charge to the Grand jury in Pennsylvania 1799. *Carpenter's Report trial of Fries.*

Chief Justice McKean's Charge to Grand jury in Pennsylvania in 1797 — Porcupine's libels. *Gazette of the United States for Nov 1797.* See Exhibit No. 7.[93]

Gov Claiborne's Address to the legislative Council at Orleans. *National Intelligencer.*

List of particular grand juries. —

The Managers called up one witness.

Thomas Hall.

They also presented a list of certain Grand Jurors.

Mr. Harper read a short address from Judge Chase requesting as a favor, that in consequence of his ill health — a severe attack of the gout — his personal attendance might be dispenced with.

Granted, not as a matter of favor but of *right.*

Mr. Randolph in behalf of the Managers requested that they

90 William McMechin.
91 Ramsay's *History of South Carolina*, I, 103.
92 *American Museum*, I, 228.
93 See *Annals of Congress*, 8 Cong., 2 sess., 306.

might have untill tomorrow to digest, colate, & arrange the testimony.

Granted — The Counsel for the Judge said they should not consent; but did not wish to oppose it.

At a little past one OClock the Senate returned to their legislative chamber.

### *Wednesday 20th 1805.*

At half past ten met in the Judicial Chamber.

The managers called up Philip Stewart who was sworn & examined.

Mr. Dayton moved to have all the witnesses discharged from further attendance — To this the Managers objected although they declared they did not intend further to examine. Motion lost 15 senators only voting in the affirmative.

At 11 OClock Mr. Early, one of the Managers rose & addressed the Court upon the articles of Impeachment and the evidence adduced. He closed his address at 40 Minutes past 12 OClock. — Much declamation & little argument.[94]

The parties agreed, & all the witnesses were then discharged from further attendance.

Mr. George Washington Campbell arose & addressed the Court upon the charges, the testimony, & the law period. He unfortunately read two cases from *Bacon's Abridgement* & *Jacob's Law Dictionary* — both of which were pointly against him — The latter book is seldom admitted as an *authority.*

At 15 minutes past two he requested the Court would indulge him with a short delay — he wished till tomorrow — for he said he felt very unwell.[95]

The Court retired for half an hour.

Met again.

Mr. Early moved the Court for time till tomorrow alledging that Mr. Campbell was too unwell to proceed.

---

[94] See *ibid.,* 312–329.
[95] *Ibid.,* 330–343.

Mr. Campbell pressed it as a favor — said he was sick — & he would condense his observations so as to take up little time tomorrow.

The Court retired.

The speech of Mr. Campbell was feeble indeed — his law was incorrect — his statements confused — & his concessions fatal to his cause. He was much embarrassed — He had copious notes — they confused him — He is a disagreeable speaker — Most of the Members of the other House left the Chamber, & a large portion of the spectators, the gallery — long before he sat down. I do not wonder at his illness, for he drank nine tumblers of water during his speech.

The Senate proceeded to Legislative business. On the passage of a bill to a second reading, to amend the law relative to the collection of the Direct Tax. Mr. Brackenridge said, That one full third of all the lands in the State of Kentucky had been sold for the payment of that tax — That the sales were fraudulent — that the time was near expiring for the redemption of those lands — That although the Supervisor was innocent yet such was the ferment in that State, that it was with difficulty that the people were restrained from burning his buildings & the assessments & proceedings of the Collectors — That the Insurance Company in that State had come forward & offered to pay all the redemption money, & trust to the honor of the owners of the land to repay them — And that the purchasers at the Auctions of these lands had withdrawn from the State to prevent a tender to be made to them.

John Smith of New York brot in a bill extending the law to *Aaron Burr* of having the priveledge of sending & receiving all letters & packages free of postage for & during his natural life.

### Thursday 21st.

The Senate met in the Judicial chamber at half past ten. Mr. Campbell rose again — & continued his speech for an hour. His argument, if it deserves that name, was very feeble indeed — & the manner was as disgusting as the reasoning was weak. A large majority, both yesterday & to day, Of the other House, left their seats — & the gallery seats soon became nearly vacant.

Neither Mr. Early or Campbell were confined to particular articles but each of them wandered through the whole Impeachment.

Mr. Clark a 3d Manager followed Mr. Campbell. Mr. Clark was concise — he occupied the floor only eight minutes.

Mr. Hopkinson, the junior Councel, for Judge Chase, then rose, & addressed the Court — He confined his argument entirely to the first article of the Impeachment. His argument continued three hours & a half. It was very luminous — very logical — strongly fortified by legal authorities. It was one of the most able arguments I ever heard delivered on any occasion. It was sententious — the reasoning strong & clear — the narrative correct & succinct — & the manner impressive. The House & both galleries were crouded — & as a proof of his eloquence silence pervaded every part — the listless spectator found his passions attacked & his understanding illumined. Of 100 ladies in the gallery two or three only left their seats — altho' it was after three OClock when he sat down.

Mr. Hopkinson has done ample justice to Judge Chase character as it relates to the trial of Fries — He has done much honor to himself. Judge Chase heard this young able lawyer (say of 35) three years since argue a cause before him — it made such an impression on his mind that as soon as he was summoned to answer to this impeachment — he sent & requested the aid of Mr. Hopkinson.

Mr. Key then rose, & said it was his lot to address the Court — he did not wish delay — but his ill health would absolutely prevent his proceeding at that late hour.[96]

The Court retired.

---

[96] See *ibid.*, 344–394, for addresses here noted.

## *Friday 22d.*

Mr. Key on the 2d 3d & 4th Articles of the Impeachment addressed the Court, in a speech that occupied near three hours & a half in which he displayed much legal information — a thorough acquaintance with his case — & intimate knowledge of human nature. His argument was forcible — logical & legal — but not so impressive as was that of Mr. Hopkinson. An uncommon & numerous audience listened with mute attention to his argument.

This gentleman is one of the Circuit Judges who was removed from office by Congress repealling the law in 1801 establishing the Circuit Courts of the United States.

He volunteered in this defence for Judge Chase.

At two Oclock the Court retired for half an hour to the Secretary's office — partook of a cold collation.

At half past two the Senate returned — Mr. Charles Lee formerly Attorney General of the United States rose & as Council for Judge Chase addressed us for two hours upon the 5th & 6th Articles of the Impeachment. He discovered talents & information. He is not a pleasing speaker. He wants energy & manner but his argument will certainly read well.[97]

At half past four OClock we returned to our Legislative Chamber — We passed the bill for the clearance of Armed Vessels. On this subject there was considerable debate. Mr. Wright was the last speaker. He has uniformly opposed the bill in every stage — & in the speech he last made he explicitly declared that he considered it as being unconstitutional. As soon as he sat down the question was taken of its passing, & both he & Samuel Smith voted in favor of it — Yeas 20 nays 8.

---

[97] *Ibid.,* 394–429.

*Friday 22 Feby* [98]

. . . . . . . . . . . . . . . . . . . . . . . . . . . . . . . . . . .

This is the birthday of the late illustrious President Washington. Ever since his death the Federalists in Congress have celebrated it. They, with the distinguished characters who happen to be here, have dined with splendor together — drank pointed & elegant toasts discharged cannon — had music & balls. This festival has been a kind of rallying point. This year, I began early with my friends, to convince them of the impropriety & impolicy of the measure. That it had a direct tendency to encrease & strengthen the state of parties in New England — An evil much to be deprecated — That we ought to endeavor to amalgamate — that our interest was one — & the *slave states* had interests & views inimical to ours — That the celebration would have an ill effect upon the pending trial of Judge Chase — for there are senators who for the veriest trifles may be brought to vote against him. By prudent firm and decided conduct I have prevented a festival — I do believe it might have injured us — I am sure it could do us no good. — And as the federalists found we could not unite — they did not meet at all.

*Saturday 23d. 1805.*

. . . . . . . . . . . . . . . . . . . . . . . . . . . . . . . . . . .

Mr. Martin continued his argument till near 5 OClock, & then observed he was much fatigued — that he had eat nothing — That he should be obliged if the Court would grant him till monday.

---

[98] Plumer's journal from February 22 to February 28 is concerned largely with notes of his own, based upon the addresses made in the Chase trial. Since the report of the trial for these days is to be found in full in *Annals of Congress,* 8 Cong., 2 sess., (394–664), only Plumer's personal comments on the trial and his discussions of other matters are here reproduced.

The Court retired — to their Legislative Chamber & adjourned. —

It was the recommendation of Mr. Burr to sit tomorrow — but the question of adjournment was taken and carried too suddenly to meet the other question.

Mr. Martin really possesses much legal information & a great fund of good humour — keen satire & poignant wit. He is far from being a graceful speaker. His language is often incorrect — inaccurate, & sometimes is too low. But he certainly has *talents* — & from 27 years close application, & much practise, he has acquired much knowledge of the principles of law, the rules of Court & forms of practise.

At the time when the gallery was fitting up for this trial in the Senate Chamber, I then thought the expence unnecessary; but I now own my mistake. A vast many people daily attend, & without the new gallery many hundreds of them could not have been accomodated so as to hear the arguments. Many of these people are from distance places — the arguments have informed them — & through them much information will be communicated to many others who have not been present — & have & will, in fact, make an impression favorable to the accused.

Mr. Early, said, today, he was weary of the cause & intimated his regret, that the impeachment was ever brought forward. This was said to a friend of mine. And I beleive he spoke the language of the majority of the House — still I think as the work has commenced it will end in the removal of the Accused from office.

### Monday February 25, 1805

. . . . . . . . . . . . . . . . . . . . . . . . . . . . . . . . . . . . . . . .

Note Mr. Randolph said when he moved for the admission of Mr. Holmes [99] as a witness this day — that he felt no

---

[99] Hugh Holmes, former Speaker of the Virginia House of Delegates.

anxiety whether he was sworn or not for he "thanked God that the Impeachment did not depend upon the testimony of witnesses." . . . . . . .

Mr. Harper's argument of this day was an able correct argument— it discovered more of the lawyer — was more prudent & cautious than I expected. It did honor to his head & heart.

The Judge has really discovered talents & knowledge of mankind by the prudent selection he has made on this occasion.

His Counsel have stated the evidence with very great accuracy.

### Tuesday 26th Feby 1805

. . . . . . . . . . . . . . . . . . . . . . . . . . . . . . . . . . . .

At half past six Mr. Rodney stated to the Court that he was unable to proceed — "that his *knees* (these were his words) failed him" — the Court then adjourned.

Mr. Nicholson & Mr. Rodney have attempted to enter into as minute a detail of the evidence as if they were addressing a jury. It is a fact they well know that a considerable number of the Court have taken very large notes of the testimony.

These two gentlemen have discovered a degree of low cunning & mean-ness I did not expect. During the whole examination — & during the arguments of the Councel of the Respondent they frequently said they beleived the written opinion of the Judge in the case of Fries was correct — that it was only the *time & the manner of delivering it,* that they thought wrong — But to day, they have in closing the cause, & after the Judge's councel were precluded from reply, declared they thought the opinion itself was wrong, & argued to prove that point.

Mr. Nicholson was told when he offered a new authority that the Councel would have an opportunity to reply. He said then I will not read it — But *I will state the substance of it!*

I was not prepared to expect such things from the Managers appointed by the Representatives of the Nation.

*Wednesday Feby 27, 1805*

. . . . . . . . . . . . . . . . . . . . . . . . . . . . . . . . . . . . . . . . .

The Senate unanimously resolved that they would on friday next at 12 OClock pronounce judgment on the articles of Impeachment.

Mr. Randolph certainly was *correct* when he said his argument would be *desultory* if by argument he meant what he *uttered.* —

The word *argument* I think inapplicable to his performance. — it is too dignified for such a feeble *thing.*

After he sat down — he threw his feet upon the table — distorted his features & assumed an appearance as disgusting as his harangue.[100]

The Senate retired to their legislative Chamber — and sat till past six OClock.

The bill freeing from postage all letters & packetts to & from Aaron Burr during his life was taken up & read.

A considerable debate ensued —

It was moved to postpone it to the next session  This motion was lost.

Mr. Adams moved to strike out the words Aaron Burr & so amend the bill that it should extend to all Vice Presidents after the term of their service should expire.

Genl Dayton said the bill was designed to be personal — the name of Aaron Burr was in the bill — had it been general at the first he should have been satisfied — but that name being in — to strike it out would wear the appearance of dislike to the man — the bill is designed as a mark of approbation of his conduct & a compliment to him.

*Genl Jackson* said he was opposed to having the bill a general one — We might hereafter have a Vice President to whom it would be improper to grant this priveledge. —

---

100 *Cf.* J. Q. Adams, *Memoirs*, I, 359.

Mr. Pickering & Mr. Hillhouse advocated the postponement on the indelicacy of the situation of having Mr. Burr in the chair.

I called for the yeas & nays — on the question of its passing to a 3d reading — ayes 18 nays 9.

Mr. Adams voted in the affirmative.[101]

Mr. Burr said he was apprehensive that tomorrow he should be afflicted with pain in the head & should be unable to attend.

### Thursday 28th

Mr. Burr was absent — chose Mr. Anderson as President pro. tem. —

The bill for franking as aforesaid under consideration.

*Mr. Hillhouse.* This bill introduces a new principle into our law — it extends a peculiar priveledge to an individual whose rank in office does not upon the principle of any former law entitle him to have it. We have extended this priveledge only to three persons Mr. Washington & Mr. Adams both of whom have been Presidents, & to Mrs. Washington after the death of her illustrious husband — but we never extended it to a Vice President. The precedent once established must always be followed. In every point of view I dislike it. It is establishing a priveledged order — it is conferring an exclusive right on a particular class — & in what it may end no one can say — The Knights of the Garter was an order of knighthood that rose from a trivial cause. In France the legion of Honor is established — & will prove in fact an establishment of Nobility. The post office produces a revenue to the government — this is a draw back upon it — It may be to a large amount. It is well known that in Great Britain the priveledge of franking is greatly abused by the Members of Parliament — We are not more virtuous than they.

---

[101] J. Q. Adams in his *Memoirs* (I, 360), refers to " a long and extraordinary debate " on this subject but does not go into detail.

The Vice President is an ambitious man — he aspired to the Presidency — disappointed ambition will be restless. You put arms into his hands to attack your government — He may disseminate seditious pamphlets, news papers & letters at the expence of the very government he is destroying.

You declare this bill to be personal — you have refused to extend it to Vice Presidents generally. You are at the time of every Vice Presidents leaving the office — to make inquest into his character — & if the rage of party — or the interest of his friends or other causes uniting can prevail he is to be pensioned for life — if not he is to be stamped with being less deserving than his predecessors — This principle of personal merit forms a solid objection in my mind to the provisions of this bill. I cannot approve of the conduct of Aaron Burr. He has during his holding the second office in the government of the nation descended from the high dignity of his station to commit an Act, a violation of law for which the constitutional tribunals of his country say he ought to submit to trial. Under these circumstances I am bound by a duty I owe my country to oppose the passage of this bill.

*Genl Dayton,* I am sorry to find a gentleman with whom I have been in the habit of acting oppose the passage of this little paltry bill — Had that gentleman began earlier to respect the opinion of the people perhaps he & I should not now be in a small feeble minority. I approve of the bill — I think it a mark of approbation that is due to merit. The allusion of the gentleman from Connecticut, to a late affair is *cruel.* I will say no more.

*Mr. Hillhouse,* When in power, when strong in numbers that gentleman (Mr. Dayton) knows I often differed from him — The Journals of Congress will in some instances attest the fact — his recollection will furnish him with many other instances. In things immaterial I always go with my friends, but in principles & in important acts I must always follow the result of my own mind.

*Mr. Wright* — The secret is now out — The reason why gentlemen oppose this bill is because Mr. Burr has fought a duel & killed a man. Duelling is not only necessary but is lawful. The first duel I ever read of was that of David killing Goliah — " Our *little* David of the Republicans has killed the Goliah of Federalism — & for this I am willing to reward him." Duelling is more honorable than the wounding of the reputation of a man by the tomahawk of slander.

*Mr. Adams,* Had I been a member of Congress when the bills granting this priveledge were pending I should have voted against them. I do not like this bill — had it been to all future Vice Presidents I would given it my support — I do not say I shall vote against it as it is.

*Mr. Pickering,* I am opposed to this bill. I will not undertake to justify or condemn former Congresses in the precedents they have established. But neither of them apply to this bill — this is a new precedent — And the next Congress may as well extend the principle to Ex-senators as we carry it to the Vice President.

President Washington during an eight years war was commander in Chief of your armies — He had formed extensive correspondence — this was encreased in consequence of being 8 years President of the United States — The postage on these letters would have been a heavy tax even on his wealth. As he served in the army only for his country & his fame, he received no pecuniary reward — the support of his table — his actual expenditures — was the only charge his country paid for his unpararelled services.[102] Hence on his retiring from the Presidential office his Country passed the law freeing all letters & packages to & from him carried in the mail from postage. This precedent thus established under peculiar circumstances was after his death extended to his relict Mrs

---

[102] See *George Washington's accounts of expenses while commander-in-chief of the Continental army, 1775–1783,* reproduced in facsimile, with annotations by John C. Fitzpatrick (1917).

Washington. It was found that her postage was $100. pr Month. And on Mr. Adam's retiring from office the precedent set was pursued in his favor. First precedents are made under peculiar & strong circumstances .& then they are extended to other & very different cases. This ought to render us cautious how we establish them.

The reasons for now establishing a new precedent does not appear to me a strong one.

There is no officer in the government so well paid as the Vice President, if his services are compared with his salary. In four years he has received from the government $20000 — & I doubt whether he has attended during the whole of that term more than one year. It is not considered that he is under any obligation to keep a table for members of either House or for strangers any further than Senators. His duty consist in presiding over this House — he has no other duties or connection with the government — except that of Commissioner of the sinking fund — a duty that involves not a single days consideration in each year — for the report of the Secy of the Treasury is in fact the report of the board.

This bill, if it passes, makes Mr. Burr a pensioner for life, & that without consideration. His services have been amply remunerated. The extent of this grant is unknown — it embraces all letters & packetts carried to & from him — To what amount this will tax your post office revenue can not be ascertained. There is no restriction — he may sell the right of franking to commercial houses — And in the city of New York alone it may give him a fortune. I know of one Commercial House who annually pay more than $1500 postage.

The right of franking to members of Congress is restricted in point of time & of weight — to the session of Congress & 20 days after, each packett not exceeding two ounces. This priveledge is founded upon the idea of our station requiring us to transmit & receive information to & from our numerous Constituents. Our compensation is also inadequate to the services & sacrifices we make in the discharge of our duty.

As there is no evidence of extraordinary services having been rendered by this man — And no evidence of extraordinary merit — And considering his late fatal conduct on the Jersey shores which has inflicted a wound on our country which even the lenient hand of time for ages cannot heal — I shall therefore vote against the passage of this bill.

*Mr. Sumter,* The extraordinary circumstances of the case induced me to vote for the bill in favor of General Washington & Mrs. Washington. Like circumstances did not happen in the case of Mr. Adams late President of the United States, I therefore did vote against that law. I shall not vote for this it is a tax on the government of the Country that the existing circumstances of the case will not warrant. We ought to talk less, & practise more, of public oeconomy. I do myself think this will be a dangerous precedent. I wish gentlemen to understand me that the conduct of Mr. Burr has no influence on my mind — My opposition has nothing to do with his personal conduct.

*Mr. McClay,* Thought the bill was unconstitutional, because it tended to render duties not uniform, & cited the first clause of the 8th section of the first article of the Constitution of the United States — And he considered *duties* as a term that included *postage.*

*Mr. Jackson,* It appears to me that the principal objection to this bill arises from the personal encounter that took place in July on the Jersey shore. This can form no objection in my mind — It ought not in that of any honorable gentleman.

The question was then taken, & the bill passed yeas **18** nays **13.** All the senators from New England were in the negative except Mr. Adams, Bradley & Israel Smith.[103]

---

[103] The yea and nay vote is given in *Annals of Congress,* 8 Cong., 2 sess., 66.

*Friday March 1, 1805.*

The House of Representatives on reading said bill resolved by a large majority that the same should *not* be read a second time.[104]

At 11 OClock Mr. Bayard moved That after the Senate should meet in their Judicial chamber, that the President of the Senate should call upon each senator by name upon each article of Impeachment being read & propound the following question " Mr. A. what say you, is Samuel Chase Esq guilty or not of *high crimes & misdemeanors* as charged in the article last read? " And that each senator as thus called shall rise in his place & answer *guilty,* or *not guilty.*

To this motion there was much opposition — It was contended that in the trial of Judge Pickering the form of the question was simply " Is J. P. *guilty* as charged in the Article last read — " & that, that was a precedent from which we ought not now to depart.

The motion prevailed yeas 17, nays 16. —

At half past 12 OClock the Senate met in their Judicial Chamber — The area & both of the galleries were crouded with anxious spectators. Many ladies were present — Silence pervaded the Court. After the Court had sat in silence a few moments — the usual proclamations were made — The President sat silent — & Mr. Tracy, who for several days had been confined to his chamber & even bed, was bro't to the Capitol & led to his seat. The appearance of a very sick man in the Senate added to the solemnity of a proceeding, which the great importance of the trial, had previously given it.

At the end of two hours the votes of the Court were collected and on each article stands

---

[104] The bill was read the second time and ordered to be committed to a Committee of the Whole House on the first Monday of the following December; see *House Journal,* (1804–1807), 157.

| Articles | Guilty | not guilty. |
|---|---|---|
| 1 | 16 | 18 |
| 2d | 10 | 24 |
| 3d | 18 | 16 |
| 4 | 18 | 16 |
| 5 | 0 | 34 |
| 6 | 4 | 30 |
| 7 | 10 | 24 |
| 8 | 19 | 15 |

The following senators voted not guilty upon each and all of the articles, Mr. Adams, Bayard, Bradley, Dayton, Gaillard, Hillhouse, Mitchell, Olcott, Pickering, Plumer, Israel & White — 15. Smith, John Smith of New York, John Smith of Ohio, Tracy,

Mr. Anderson voted guilty upon the 1st, 2, 3, 4 & 8th articles — & not guilty upon the residue.

Mr. Baldwin upon articles, 1, 3, & 8th guilty, not guilty of the others.

Mr. Breckenridge upon the 1, 2, 3, 4, 6, 7 & 8th guilty, & upon the other not guilty.

Mr. Brown upon the 1, 3, 4, & 8th guilty, others not guilty.

Mr. Cocke on the 1, 2, 3, 4, 6, 7 & 8th guilty, the *other* not guilty.

Mr. Condit on the 1, 2, 3, 4 & 8th guilty, the others not guilty.

Mr. Ellery on the 1, 2, 3, 4 & 8th guilty, the others not guilty.

Mr. Franklin on the 1, 3, 4, 7, & 8th guilty, the others not guilty.

Mr. Giles on the 2, 3, 4 & 8th guilty the others not guilty.

Mr. Howland on the 1, 2, 3, 4, 6, 7, & 8th guilty, the *other* not guilty.

Mr. Jackson, 3, 4, 7 & 8th guilty, the others not guilty.

Mr. Logan, 1, 3, 4, & 8th guilty, the others not guilty.

Mr. Maclay, 1, 2, 3, 4, 6, 7, & 8th guilty, the *other* not guilty.

Mr. Moore, 1, 2, 3, 4 & 8th guilty, the others not guilty.

Mr. Saml Smith, 3, 4, 7 & 8th guilty, the others not guilty.

Mr. Stone, 1, 4, 7 & 8th guilty, the others not guilty.

Mr. Sumter, 1, 2, 3, 4, 7 & 8th guilty, the others not guilty.

Mr. Worthington, 1, 3, 4, & 8th guilty, the others not guilty.

Mr. Wright, 1, 3, 4, 7 & 8th guilty, & on the others not guilty.[105]

Mr. Burr then rose & with great perspicuity stated the result & observed — " There not being a constitutional majority on any one article, it becomes my duty to pronounce that Samuel Chase Esq is acquitted on the articles of Impeachment exhibited agt. him by the House of Representatives."

The Court then adjourned sine die. —

There was great order & regularity observed during the whole of the trial.

The Gallery was perfectly silent — though from their countenances they *appeared* not only satisfied but highly *gratified.*

Mr. Burr has certainly, on the whole, done himself, the Senate & the nation honor by the dignified manner in which he has presided over this high & numerous Court.

The House of Representatives with their Speaker as well as the Managers have day by day attended the trial. They did not adjourn but appointed a Chairman & resolved themselves into Committee of the Whole — & when the Court retired from the Judicial chamber the House of Representatives returned to their Chamber & the Chairman reported to the House that progress had been made. —

Mr. Randolph appeared chagrined & much mortified at the result.

---

[105] On the votes, see *Annals of Congress,* 8 Cong., 2 sess., 664–669; J. Q. Adams, *Memoirs,* I, 362–364.

And this day in the afternoon he rose & pronounced in the House a violent phillippic against Judge Chase & against the Senate — & concluded with offering a resolution proposing an Amendment to the Constitution of the United States — That the President of the United States *shall* on request from a majority of each House of Congress remove any Judge from Office [106] — Mr. Nicholson moved an amendment to which Mr. Randolph assented — authorizing the Legislature of any State at any time to recall its senators from Congress. —

Mr. Eliott said he would not move — but he would state whether it would not be advisable to propose to the people to revoke the Constitution in toto —

Mr. Randolph & Nicholson were very warm & passionate in the debate — The angry passions were all roused & in full activity — A motion at length was made that the resolution & amendment be postponed to December & in the mean time that they be printed — prevailed by a large majority.

Administration disapproved of this violent measure.

### Saturday 2d.

Mr. Jefferson nominated & the Senate advised to the appointment of Robert Smith (now Secy of the Navy) to be Attorney General of the United States — & *Jacob Crowninshield!* of Salem Massachusetts, to be Secretary of the Navy.

It is now well understood that the late pending trial of Judge Chase is the cause why an Attorney General has not for more than three months past been nominated to the Senate. Had Judge Chase been removed there is no doubt that Mr. Smith would have succeeded him — Nicholson been created Atty General & Crowninshield to the office he now holds.

The removal of Judge Chase was deemed an imprudent measure — public opinion so far as it could be collected was

---

[106] For the text of the resolution and the action taken thereon, see *Annals of Congress*, 8 Cong., 2 sess., 1213–1214.

decidedly opposed to the measure. In this case a great point is gained in favor of the Constitution. A prosecution commenced with the rage of party has been arrested — & to the honor of the Accused his political foes his enemies have acquitted him.

At two OClock Mr. Burr informed the Senate that he should now take leave of the Senate. His address was very correct & elegant & the sentiments very just.

He said he hoped That the constitution of the US would never be destroyed but he would venture to predict that if such an unfortunate event should ever take place, on this floor it would meet with its last & most noble defence — Here it would draw its last gasp. — This house is the last portion of the people, the last branch in the government that will abandon it.

As to his conduct in office — he said he had with great care endeavored to know no party — no friend or political enemy — He had acted with promptitude & decision — that he thought this more correct although he might thereby sometimes err — than a wavering undecisive conduct — which would stamp ignorance on him & produce confusion & insubordination in the Senate. He had in that promptitude no doubt sometimes wounded the feelings of an individual senator — on these occasions, which he trusted were few, he never had suffered any explanation at the time because the animation of the moment always rendered it improper. He was proud to say that during the four years he had presided he had never seen a single senator but what appeared anxious to support the authority of the Chair. That it was with great consolation he could review his official conduct & with conscious pride could say he had not degraded the dignity of that Chair which he now resigned to his successor. For each individual senator he entertained & felt a spirit of friendship, & he trusted that the regret on parting was mutual.

He bowed & retired — several shed tears very plentifully.[107]

Mr. Anderson was again re-elected President pro. tem. Mr. White moved, & the Senate unanimously passed a resolution expressing their approbation & thanks to Mr. Burr for the ability talent & impartiality with which he had discharged his official duties.

Mr. Saml Smith & Mr. White were appointed to present the same to Mr. Burr.

The business not being compleated at seven OClock in the evening, the Senate adjourned to tomorrow 10 OClock AM. —

I ought to observe that to day on the bill sent from the House providing for the payment of Witnesses &c summoned on the part of the United States in the case of Judge Chase's impeachment. — The Senate so amended it as to include the payment of Judge Chase's witnesses. It was done upon the principle that in the trial of Judges — truth is the only object — the subpena's do not distinguish who required the attendance of any particular witness, they were therefore bound to attend — & now if the Judge is unable or unwilling they must return without pay — And if a Judge is to be subject to this cost an impeachment in most cases will be certain ruin to the Accused however innocent he may be. The amendment was rejected by a great majority of the House; but the bill is not yet returned to the Senate.

### Sunday 3d.

I here, as the session is now closing, observe that the preceding sheets have been written in great haste — some of them I have never read — after I wrote them the style & composition is *ergo* in many places incorrect. Facts I have stated & that correctly. —

The Amendments to the bill last mentioned came to the Senate — We agreed to adhere & appointed Managers Mr.

---

[107] *Cf. ibid.*, 71; J. Q. Adams, *Memoirs*, I, 365–367.

Giles & Bradley.  The former made a very handsome speech, declaring his first determination to support the amendments of the Senate at all events.

The House appointed Randolph, Nicholson and Early as their managers, or if you please, conferees.  The Conferees of the two Houses met.  Mr. Giles enquired if they were disposed to make any concessions Randolph replied none.  Giles said they were desirous of adopting such measures as would restore & preserve harmony to the two houses — That the Senate considered their amendment of too much importance to be abandoned — That they were willing to take the whole responsibility of the measure on themselves, by adding a preamble to the bill, stating that the Senate had issued the subpena's to the witnesses in such general terms as did not distinguish those summoned on the part of the Accused from those summoned at the request of the United States, & therefore did not leave any witness at liberty to demand payment previous to his attendance.  Randolph said they would not consent to the smallest alteration in the bill as it passed the House.  Mr. Early approved of the amendment made by the Senate.  The Conferees reported to each house their disagreement.  The Senate unanimously voted to insist upon their amendment — & gave notice thereof to the House.  The House refused to recede, & the bill was lost.  Mr. Randolph then moved A resolve directing the Speaker to pay the witnesses summoned on the part of the United States out of the contingent fund of the House — but they could not make a quorum.  He moved for a call of the House — This was opposed upon the principle that previous notice must be given, & that before the Sargeant at Arms can arrest an absent member & compel his attendance — the House must establish forms of process & the Speaker must issue warrants agreeable to such form.

It was then agreed to read over the names of the Members — It was done — A quorum was found — Mr. Randolph then again proposed his resolution — a division was required — & it was found there was not a quorum. This was the result of several trials. Mr. Randolph said this was a trick — Genl Varnum replied it was a measure they resorted to to prevent a trick — to prevent an application of the contingent fund to a purpose to which it was never appropriated. Whenever it was necessary to receive messages from the President or Senate the House made a quorum — but not on any other subject. After repeated attempts the resolve was abandoned — & at nine OClock P.M. Congress adjourned *sine die.*[108]

At 11 OClock in the evening I took my seat in the Mail stage & travelled all night & at three OClock P.M. on the 4th I arrived at Baltimore. In the course of an hour after the President's inaugural speech was handed about the streets. I have no doubt that it was printed long before I left Washington & was bro't to Baltimore in the same stage that brought me. Mr. Smith[109] ought not to have[110] stated that it was delivered to both Houses of Congress — There was not a quorum of either House in Washington. —

The President says, *his Conscience tells him he has on every occasion acted up to the declaration contained in his former inaugural speech.* In that address he explicitly condemned political intolerance — declared all were federalists, all were republicans — Yet in a few days after that, he removed many deserving men from office, because they were federalists. And in his answer to the remonstrance of the New Haven Merchants he considers himself as the head of a *party*, more than of the nation — & declares that its necessary, to remove federalists from office to make room for Republicans — & that when a sufficient number of the latter are appointed it will then be time to enquire whether candidates for office are honest, faithful

---

[108] *Cf. Annals of Congress,* 8 Cong., 2 sess., 1223–1225.

[109] Samuel Harrison Smith, editor of the *National Intelligencer.*

[110] In Plumer's manuscript this marks the beginning of a new page at the top of which is the date, " March 4, 1805."

& attached to the constitution. It seems to me it was unnecessary on this occasion to make such a declaration, & thereby provoke enquiry.[111]

He is equally imprudent, but more mean, in explicitly censuring & condemning former Administrations & lavishing enconiums on himself for effecting a discontinuance of the Internal Revenues.

He complains of the abuses of the press — that the attacks on him have been licentious. And intimates in strong terms the policy of State legislatures & state Courts, correcting the proceedure. One would have thought that Mr. Jefferson after having hired such infamous wretches as Freneau,[112] Bache,[113] Duane, Callender,[114] Payne [115] & others, to defame villify & calumniate, Washington, Adams, & their associates — he would not have complained of news paper publications!

But after all it must be confessed that this man has talents — & those of the popular kind. It seems to be a great & primary object with him never to pursue a measure if it becomes unpopular. Hence it was that he abandoned the repeal of the discriminating duties — the building of a dry-dock — & the removal of Judge Chase. —

A propos of Judge Chase — I visited him this afternoon & spent the evening at his house. I never saw a family more happy — his daughters were much gratified at my visit — they are very charming girls. I was much pleased to witness the strong affection love & tenderness that mutually subsists between him & them. The Judge lives in the city of Baltimore.

---

[111] For the text of Jefferson's second inaugural speech, see Richardson, *Messages and Papers of the Presidents*, I, 378–382.

[112] Philip Freneau, editor of the New York *Daily Advertiser* and later of the *National Gazette*.

[113] Benjamin Franklin Bache, publisher of the *General Advertiser,* afterwards known as the *Aurora*.

[114] James Thomas Callender, publisher in Philadelphia of *The Political Register* and the *American Register;* later editor of the *Richmond Recorder*.

[115] Thomas Paine.

*15th.* I arrived at my Own house in Epping; & found, to my great satisfaction, my family and friends all well. I have travelled all the way in the Mail stage, & found the roads much better than I feared, & myself less fatigued than I expected.

Mr. Langdon [116] is I presume elected governor of New Hampshire for this year — A majority of the House, Senate & Council are *republicans,* alias democrats. This change will not, I beleive, convulse the State. Mr. Langdon will have I beleive a majority of about 2000 votes. He will, no doubt, appoint a great number of his creatures to be justices of the peace — profess much disinterested patriotism — & promise to do much good. But will in fact do but little either good or hurt. His greatest difficulty will be to satisfy his friends & needy dependants, who are seeking for offices he cannot grant. Could the public but consider this struggle merely to change the *person* of their governor, the public would suffer little by the *change;* but they expect a change of *measures.* This expectation imposes a kind of necessity on the elected to attempt it. In this attempt he will have much to fear & little to hope.

This change really appears less alarming to me than I expected — indeed I feel a greater degree of indifference on the subject than I thought for. I am weary of party politic's. — yet they will always exist, but under different names & principles. I expect Mr. Langdon will encrease the number of Justices — but this cannot satisfy them all. I really wish the Eastern states may be united in the great objects of national concern — & if united — they will be respected by the other portions of the Union — & their rights secured. I rejoice that federal men are to represent the State in the next Congress. Had democrats been elected they would have carried all the zeal & bitterness of party with them — Within two years much of that zeal will abate & people of that class will then feel and act more like

---

[116] John Langdon.

Men from New England than now they do. In this view of the subject I rejoice at the deep interest & active agency I had in the election of those members. I am confident that the success of that list depended much on the vigorous measures I pursued.[117]

---

[117] The Appendix which followed at this point was not copied. It contained extracts from the Senate *Executive Journal* and other documents, such as memorials, lists of treaties with the Indians, members of Congress, with birth-place and profession, etc.

# PART III.

## REGISTER: PROCEEDINGS OF CONGRESS, 1805–1807

WILLIAM PLUMER'S

REGISTER

DESIGNED TO FOLLOW HIS SECOND VOLUME OF CONGRESSIONAL
PROCEEDINGS

VOLUME I.

COMMENCING MAY 2D 1805, & ENDING APRIL 21, 1807.

# PART III.

### *May 2d 1805.*

At the last two sessions of Congress I noted several facts as they occured, & stated my opinion on several subjects. Should I attend another session I intend to pursue the same course. It will be a mean of preserving facts & opinions, which with the changes & revolution of time & of parties are rapidly hasting to oblivion. Indeed, as to many events & opinions, the world cannot suffer from the ignorance of them; unless they would consider them as beacons to avoid error & ruin.

I write not for posterity — not for others — but for myself only. I write in much haste — the facts are correct — but not the style.

. . . . . . . . . . . . . . . . . . . . . . . . . . . . . . . . . . . .

### *Friday 31st.*

Governor Strong[1] & Lt Gov Robbins[2] of Massachusetts are re-elected by small majorities — They are both federalists. In their Legislature they have a small majority of federalists in each House. In the Senate Harrisson Gray Otis was elected President by a majority of one vote only — two federal Senators were absent. In the House Timothy Bigelow was elected Speaker by a majority of fifteen votes. The town of Boston who have usually sent only six or seven Representatives, this year sent twenty-six! These are all federalists — & to them it is owing that there was when they first met a federal majority

---

[1] Caleb Strong.
[2] Edward H. Robbins.

321

in the House. There were, no doubt some members absent on the first day — These members were then *three hundred twenty three*. They are too numerous — they are too much of a mob to legislate with wisdom. I condem Boston for electing so many representatives — It is the effect of *party* — of an *expiring party* — for democracy will soon be prevalent in that State. Beside the measure will another year defeat itself — other towns will pursue the same course, & send as many representatives as they are entitled to send. This will render the House not only expensive & unwieldly, but too trifling for men of respectability. —

In Connecticut, federal majorities, & those large, still prevail.

My two much respected friends Roger Griswold & Calvin Goddard Esqrs of Connecticut have resigned their offices as representatives in the next Congress. They are men of talents information & integrity. — Tho' they are in the minority, yet their absence will be very sensibly felt. Nothing escaped the attention of the former. —

. . . . . . . . . . . . . . . . . . . . . . . . . . . . . . . . . . . .

### June 25th.

I have not received particular accounts of the proceedings of our New Hampshire legislature. John Taylor Gilman, our late governor, as was his duty, attended the election, & qualified the members of the legislature. From Nottingham to Concord he was honored by an escort. I am sorry that he suffered any of the troop to pay any part of their expences on the road, as he did for their dinners at Deerfield — At Epson he paid twenty dollars. It was enough for them to pay horse hire & loos their time. Mr. Gilman was guilty of gross inattention or of avarice. At Concord he behaved with great propriety. The gentlemen of Exeter had agreed to meet him at Watson's tavern in Epping & escort him to his own house. They notified Mr. Gilman of it & agreed on the day & hour. They notified Mr. Watson who at some considerable expence made the necessary preparations. But Mr. Gilman, accompanied by his brother Nicholas, passed by Mr. Watson's without calling, more than an hour earlier than the time appointed. The Exeter gentlemen met him two miles from his own house, & with the Academy boys escorted him home. Major Sanborn applied to me to aid him in forming an escort to wait on Mr. Gilman & accompany him through Epping; but I declined — for two reasons — Mr. Gilman is only a private gentleman — & it would encrease party spirit in this town. The major had made arrangements & several had agreed to go with him — but on my representation he dropped the project.

John Langdon is elected Governor. The whole number of votes returned was ——————— 23,443

| | |
|---|---:|
| Mr. Langdon had ——————— | 16097 |
| Mr. Gilman ———————— | 12287 |
| Scattering ————————— | 50 |

Majority of Mr. Langdon     3751

Samuel Bell is Speaker of the House of Representatives. Nathl Gilman is Treasurer. Philip Carrigain Jr is Secretary. He is a young lawyer & lives at Concord. He is a light trifling character — has more of the airs & conduct of childhood & youth than of manhood. He has for years been zealously devoted to the interest & views of the now dominant party. All the legislative caucuses for years have been held at his store & office. He is now borne into office by force not for his merit, but as a warm partizan. The appointment cannot be popular with the considerate & reflecting Democrats. Mr. Carrigain has appointed Charles Cutts his deputy. Mr. Cutts tho' far from being old is an older man & an older lawyer than the Secretary. Mr. Cutts is, & for several years has been, a representative from Portsmouth. He is a man of sense — but is indolent a lover of wine & women more than of business.

In the Senate there are 8 democrats & 4 federalists. In the House there is a majority of 40 democrats — and in the Council 4 democrats & one federalist, to wit Daniel Blasdell Esq from the County of Grafton. In the County of Cheshire there was no choice by the people of Councillor as appeared by the returns. The town clerk of Westmorland instead of returning the votes for Moses *Hale* returned them for Moses *Hall.* Hale was the federal candidate & a majority of Westmoreland voted for him but thro' the carelessness or fraud of the town clerk he returned those for Hall, a name not voted for in the County. These votes would have given a majority for Hale — but these being called scattering there was no choice — the Legislature elected Nahum Parker, a democrat. The true way for the Legislature would have been to have sent for a copy of the town record, & thereby corrected the mistake in the first return — If Hale had afterwards bro't forward this record the two Houses must have given him a seat in the Council & sent Parker home.

Gov. Langdon's speech to the Legislature is really a very empty vapid thing. In vain you look for sentiment, nervous style or well turned periods. — He is really a man of feeble mind — but he has long been in the habit of vociferating the *majesty of the people.*

On the 19th the Legislature adjourned to meet at Portsmouth the 1st wednesday of December next. The numerous applications for new banks & new turnpikes are all *postponed* to next session.

On the 20th the Gov returned to Portsmouth — The escort was numerous — A vast concourse of people welcomed him to his home.

## Sunday Nov. 17th, 1805 [3]

Late in the afternoon I left my house for the seat of Government. The regret, accompanied with tears, which my family manifested on parting with me, made the day gloomy. My wife was so much affected that she could not dine with the company. For the first time I saw my son Samuel shed tears.

At Exeter in the evening I visited Dr. Tenny [4] — found him & his wife cold, formal & unsocial. I had not been there long before O. Peabody, N Rogers & Abbot came in to spend the evening. It was apparent that my presence imposed a restraint upon them, & without regret, I very soon left them. Had I not seen Mr. Peabody here I should have called at his house, — twas a ceremony due to his conduct in lately inviting me to dine with him. I did not call upon John Taylor Gilman, & I intend never to visit him more till invited. Within a year I have several times conversed with him in Exeter but he never requested me to walk to his house. He is both unsocial & avaricious — & he never was pleased with my independence.

I studiously avoided Jeremiah Smith. Alass, how unstable are our connections! On what mistaken principles has my friendship with Smith been founded? — He was utterly unworthy of that honest confidence I have reposed in him.

The Exeter gentry have much ignorance, prejudice, partiality & vanity.

I lodged at Hutchin's tavern.

## Monday 18th.

Was the only passenger in the Stage from Exeter to Haverhill — There I found Mr. Betton [5] — he accompanied me to

---

[3] Plumer's journal from November 17 to November 27 is quoted, though in greatly condensed form, in Plumer, *Life of William Plumer*, 333–334.

[4] Samuel Tenney, representative from New Hampshire.

[5] Silas Betton, representative from New Hampshire.

Boston, where I arrived early in the evening. At Palmer's I met Mr. Nelson [6] one of the representatives in Congress from Massachusetts. The melancholly occasioned by leaving my family still clouds my mind.

### *Tuesday 19th.*

I walked up to Cambridge, three miles, to visit my son, William — found him in good spirits — & contented. I took him & his chum (Windship) to the tavern. We three sat down to a social dinner, with a cheerful glass of generous wine. My children, who are really promising, now engross my affections. Every month affords me new proofs of my encreasing affection for them. I converse with William as with a companion — I am his confident. I felt affected at parting with him. At evening I walked back to Boston — At my lodgings spent an agreeable evening with Moses Brown of Newbury Port — he was the intimate friend of my late father. He is a merchant deeply immersed in business — Money is the idol he adores.

Business & improvements encrease in Boston. Their roads are too narrow & crooked, either for the convenience, beauty or elegance. The *calamity* of a great and general fire can only relieve them from that worse curse of narrow streets. A fire in Boston would be a *partial evil* but a *general good.*

. . . . . . . . . . . . . . . . . . . . . . . . . . . . . . . . . . . . . .

### *Wednesday 20th.*

Took my seat in the Mail stage, crouded with passengers — of whom were Betton, Nelson, Thompson [7] & Tenny. In going through a narrow street in Boston we broke the pole of our carriage — fortunately no other injury happened but the loss of half an hour. The day was rainey — we arrived at *Providence*

---

[6] Jeremiah Nelson.

[7] Thomas Weston Thompson, representative from New Hampshire.

early in the evening. My spirits were much animated by meeting my friends Bourne [8] & Hunter [9] of Rhode Island. *As iron sharpeneth iron so doth the countenance of a man his friend.* Slept at Ammidons an excellent tavern — surely Mrs. Ammidon *was raised up for this very purpose.*

### Thursday 21st.

Rode to New London in Connecticut. — At Plainfield spent a few hours agreeably with my much respected friend Calvin Goddard.[10] —

The stage has afflicted me with the vertigo.

At New London, Genl Stanton [11] of Rhode Island joined a stage already too much crouded.

### Friday 22d.

Arrived at New-Haven. Here we found the Mail stage from Boston *via* Worcester — It brought Crowninshield,[12] Seaver,[13] Chandler,[14] Green [15] & others. They claimed the Mail stage from hence to New York. The *large mail* is alternately brot here from Boston by Providence & Worcester — those passengers who accompany *that* mail to New Haven have the preference in the next stage to New York — of course we had it.

### Saturday 23d.

Stage so much crouded as to be very uncomfortable — Early in the evening arrived at Rye in New York.

---

[8] Benjamin Bourn, representative from Rhode Island.

[9] William Hunter, at this time a member of the Rhode Island house of representatives, later United States senator, 1811–1821.

[10] Representative from Connecticut, March 4, 1801 to March 3, 1805; delegate to the Hartford Convention in 1814.

[11] Joseph Stanton, colonel in the Revolutionary army; United States senator from June 7, 1790 to March 3, 1793; representative from March 4, 1801 to March 3, 1807.

[12] Jacob Crowninshield, representative from Massachusetts.

[13] Ebenezer Seaver, representative from Massachusetts.

[14] John Chandler, representative from the Maine district of Massachusetts.

[15] Isaiah Lewis Green, representative from Massachusetts.

## Sunday 24th.

Arrived at the City Hotel in New York at a 11 OClock AM. I immediately entered my name in the Mail stage for Philadelphia. And having dined at one oClock I stepped into the ferry-boat & in ten minutes I crossed the North River. No one was in the stage till I arrived at Brunswic — & then only a young Briton. The day & night was stormy — but I had not a thread wet.

## Monday 25th.

At 8 OClock a.m. I arrived at Philadelphia, & but little fatigued — I escaped the croud, & in 20 hours rode near 100 miles in safety.

Here, for the first time, I became acquainted with the celebrated Mr. Sitgreaves,[16] formerly Member of Congress from Pennsylvania. I am very much pleased with the man — he is a man of talents — & of very general & extensive information — highly federal. If I have opportunity I will cultivate my acquaintance with him.

Mr. Sitgreaves enquired of me for Jeremiah Smith — after I had answered his questions respecting Judge Smith's health & scituation in life — He observed " Mr. Smith *is my friend,* but he has ever been disposed to be a time-server, & to sacrifice his principles & his friends to the phantom of popularity." I observed, as a Judge, he had given some evidence of that disposition.

The number of buildings in Philadelphia annually encrease — but their trade declines — Two reasons for this, 1st the prevalence of the *yellow fever* — 2d Their rivers are all sealed up with ice for more than 2 months in the year — & to this I may add a 3d — when there is no ice in the rivers the passage to the

---

[16] Samuel Sitgreaves, representative from Pennsylvania from March 4, 1795 to 1798; United States commissioner to Great Britain under the Jay Treaty.

Ocean by water is not good. The city of New York is equally
exposed & visited by the pestilential fever — but its passage to
the ocean is always open, easy & short. Large, long & navi-
gable rivers from a great distance in a fertile country wafts
produce to the city & carries up their merchandize in exchange.
The city & state of New York is rising with rapidity into the
first rank in the Union.

Thomas McKean is re-elected for three years more as Governor of Pennsylvania by a majority of more than 5000. His
manners & disposition are rough & unaccommodating. He was
formerly a very violent democrat, but like most of that class,
by nature a tyrant. He turned deserving federal characters
from office, & appointed violent partisians in their place. But
within a few years men more violent, & more zealous to introduce revolutionary principles & practises into the government,
have complained of his moderation. Of these Leib & Duane
hold a distinguished rank. The first is a representative in
Congress from the city of Philadelphia — the 2d is the editor
of the *Aurora* & has had much of the confidence of the President
of the United States. Leib & Duane are vile characters. This
party set up Snyder [17] for the chair. They also on all occasions
connected the necessity of *amending* their Constitution, particularly that part of it relating to the Judiciary, with the election
of Snyder. A *third party* arose in the State — they first called
themselves *Moderates* — but have now assumed the imposing
name of *Constitutionalists*. They formed committees of election
& of correspondence not only in each ward of the city but in
each County of the Commonwealth. At the head of this party
stood Alexander J. Dallas the Attorney for the United States
for the District of Pennsylvania. He is a man eminent in his
profession as a lawyer — as an advocate eloquent — his address
is insinuating & his manners courtly. He has published several
volumes of Reports of adjudicated cases in the Courts of the

---

[17] Simon Snyder; governor of Pennsylvania, 1807–1817.

United States — which do much credit to him. His style of living is too costly & splendid for any subordinate office in the U.S. to maintain. He therefore is not seeking for office — to his professional labours he looks for support.

Previous to this gubanatorial election he with the aid of Tilghman & others published a well written address to the citizens of Pennsylvania, stating in strong persuasive language the necessity of re-electing Mr. McKean to oppose the overwhelming torrent of anarchy & misrule. He assured the Federalists that there was " but a shade of difference between them & the Constitutionalists."

The federalists generally united in the election of McKean. They considered him as a better man than Snyder — they knew McKean would not change their constitution — & some of the federalists (& I think not a few) joined this party with a view of again raising themselves to power & place. A few leading federal characters however refused to act — Of this number was my much esteemed friend James Ross, Mr. Sitgreaves &c. They considered a union with these men as a prostitution of principle. — That though McKean would probably do less mischief than Snyder — yet that he who began, (in Pennsylvania) the prosecution of federal men, & who had been the most zealous & efficient supporter of wild destructive democracy, ought not to be trusted — That at all events the federalists ought not to make themselves responsible for the conduct of McKean, as they must if they voted for him — for his election depended on their votes. — That the duty of federalists was to stand still & let democracy take its own course — That if the federalists had so done the people would soon court them & call them to place — But by uniting with the third party they had reduced themselves to a subordinate rank in society — & betrayed an undue anxiety for power & place.

If the party who attached themselves to Snyder had not avowed their intention of changing the Constitution, I think they would have secured his election.

A majority of the members of the two houses of their Legislature are I beleive firmly opposed to any change in the constitution.

### Tuesday 26th.

Breakfasted at Hardy's Inn in Philadelphia Was the only passenger who took the Mail stage for Baltimore — This I did at 9 OClock AM. — Had only one *way-passenger*. At 2 OClock PM. dined at New Port in the state of Delaware. I am now so far south that the taverns bring nothing on the tables to drink, except you call & pay for it. My dinner & half a pint of wine one dollar. At half past ten OClock PM. I passed in a small row boat, with the Mail only, in 15 minutes, the Susquehannah. Supped at 11 OClock at Havre de Grass in the state of Maryland.

In the course of the day saw several fields of Indian corn standing — some people gathering it — And in the evening passed by one large company who were seated round a large heap of Corn husking it.

The United States own the line that carries the Mail from Philadelphia to Baltimore. It consists of 14 drivers, 65 horses, & 11 carriages. The drivers have $16. pr month & their expences & board. I do not know whether it is profitable to the US. At sometimes they are much crouded, at others have few or no passengers. Many persons are dissauded from travelling in the mail on account of its going all night. That circumstance is inconvenient; but then it is compensated by good drivers, lamps & the great expedition by which one travels.

There is only one other line of stages, on this road i.e. the Mail pilot. This stage left Philadelphia at 7 OClock AM. & altho' I left it two hours later I arrived at Havre de Grasse half an hour before them. At twelve OClock at night they go to bed & rise between 4 & 5 OClock in the morning, & reach Baltimore the next afternoon.

### Wednesday 27th.

At 7 OClock AM arrived at Baltimore. In 22 hours have performed a journey of more than 100 miles. I have been alone — but solitude never interrupted my happiness. Breakfasted at Evan's — at 10 OClock AM. took my seat in the mail with two other passengers for Washington —

The day pleasant, fair, & air mild. At 7 OClock PM. arrived at the seat of government. In 34 hours I have safely performed a journey of more than 150 miles, much less fatigued than I had reason to fear.

Proceeded immediately to Capt. Coyle's — He & wife were at the theatre. The children were glad to see me, & I was pleased with them. Early in the evening retired to my old bed.

### Thursday 28th.

In the morning was much pleased with the kind & affectionate manner with which I was received by my old landlord & lady. As I was the first boarder who arrived at the house, I took my choice of the chambers & bed — which for a long session is an object to me of some consequence.

Spent most of the day in my chamber — Was in good health & fine spirits.

Several of my friends visited me.

William Eaton Esq who sought the exiled Bashaw of Tripoli in upper Egypt, & who led a body of troops across the deserts and with him attacked Derne a province of Tripoli, & thereby induced the Tripolitans to make peace with the United States & release our prisoners, arrived in this city a few days since. He landed at Norfolk in Virginia. The inhabitants of Richmond gave him a public dinner. The president immediately after he came here invited him to dine. And today the inhabitants to the number of 70 or 80 gave him a splendid dinner at Stelle's Hotel. Dr. May [18] & Capt. Coyle very politely invited

---

[18] Probably Dr. Frederick May.

me to the feast; but I declined. Two reasons induced me, 1. my fatigues, & 2d, presuming that if individuals of the company undertook to invite guests, it might create some uneasiness.

This is a day of feasting in New England — that is, of thanksgiving in New Hampshire, Massachusetts Rhode Island & Connecticut.

..........................................

### Friday 29th.

At 11 OClock AM. called upon the President of the United States — tarried with him one hour. At the outer door met Mr. Madison Secy of State — he gave me his hand & very politely enquired of my health. Mr. Rhea,[19] one of the Representatives from Tennessee, was with the President. He tarried till Eliott, Fisk, & Olin [20] from Vermont came in — these I left there. I observed the President with a pencil note on a paper he had in his hand the names of his visitants.

The President was in an undress — Blue coat, red vest, cloth coloured small cloths — white hose ragged slippers with his toes out — clean linnen — but hair dissheiveled.

When I went in he was stating to Mr. Rhea the terms & conditions of a treaty just made, *but not ratified, or even laid before the Senate,* with the Creek nation of Indians, for the purchase of a tract of land in Georgia. He said, with much apparent indifference, it was the best bargain that by *fair means* could be made with them — that if our negociator had resorted to *bribery* he might have done *better.*

I had much conversation with the President — he was social & very communicative.

The report of Cannon from one of our frigates as she was coming by Alexandria in her passage up the Potomac, was

---

[19] John Rhea.
[20] James Elliott, James Fiske and Gideon Olin, representatives from Vermont.

heard. The President observed to me, that that frigate had the Tunisian Ambassador on board — that she had been three full weeks in the river unable sooner to reach this port. He said it was customary for the Government to whom Tunis sent a Minister to provide for his maintenance during the time of his residence in the nation to whom he was sent. That he had accordingly taken Stelle's old Hotel, & made a contract with him to supply the minister. That he understood the Minister had bro't with him four very fine horses which were designed as a *present* — That one of them was that valuable horse that the Dey of Algiers had lately sent as a present to the Bey of Tripoli — That altho' no person in office, can, without the consent of Congress, accept any present from any foreign prince or nation, the Government of the U.S. ought to accept these horses — At the sametime taking special care to inform the Minister that the *officers* of the US. receive no presents from foreigners. — That these horses will command such a price in the markett as will probably maintain the minister & his suit during the winter, & thereby releive the US. from that expence — That in the course of the winter the minister will probably compleat his mission.

Mr. Eliot observed that he thought Tunis paid us a mark of respect in sending an Ambassador. The President replied — They did it unwillingly — that it was a matter of necessity not of choice. That Capt. Rogers with our squadron lying before Tunis, in a peremptory manner demanded a categorical answer, to be delivered in 16 hours, what measures he would observe with the US. — That within the time prescribed the Bey replied he would send an Ambassador — But I do not know the specific objects of his mission.

I observed, it was too humiliating to the US. to be tributary to those petty Barbary powers. Mr. Jefferson replied, it was so — That the US. like China, ought not to be tributary — That the Bey of Tunis had demanded the same tribute of us, as we are now unfortunately bound by a treaty made many years since, to pay & now actually do pay to Algiers. — That he had returned a peremptory answer, that the US. would pay *no* tribute to Tunis.

I enquired of him respecting our relations with Spain. He replied that there was much difficulty with that nation — That Spain now exercised authority in some part of the country we had lately purchased — That she had actually committed hostilities upon us — that some of her troops had taken some of our people in Louisiana & still detained them as prisoners — But that he was inclined to beleive that the Spanish officers in that country were acting under orders that were revoked — but of which revocation they had not, perhaps, received official notice. That the Court of Spain was imbecile, mean & trifling — that they were both jealous & foolish — & that some of her measures were calculated only to irritate us.

I observed that it was surprising that Spain should wish a war with us — that perhaps there was not a nation in Europe with whom we could with so much ease, & so fair a prospect of success, make war, as with Spain — That her colonies in America must fall a conquest to our arms. He replied, I beleive Spain contemplates war with us — but if we are vigilant & improve the present critical moment, while Europe is convulsed, we may establish peace on favorable terms — But we have no time to lose — for should the rapid movements of Bonaparte place him in Vienna, he may there compel Europe to sign a peace on his own terms — And in that case, both France & Spain may unite their counsels & arms agt. us — But I trust our vigilance will seize & improve the present favorable moment.

From Great Britain we have *much* — much more to fear than from any other European power. The measures of the Court of London are systematic — they are persevering — they do & will greatly perplex & embarrass us.

In the West Indies great depredations have been & still are

committed upon our commerce. I observed that I had been informed, that many of our Merchant vessels had been captured by vessels unauthorized & uncommissioned by the nation under whose flag they sailed. He replied, the information is correct. I then enquired, if any nation could justly complain if our Government should send an armed force into those seas, capture & condemn those piratical cruisers? He said they could not. That he had equipped & sent some armed vessels to cruize on our own coast & protect our trade within our own jurisdiction — That he had been afraid to send any armed force into the West India seas, lest they should involve us in serious difficulties with other nations — But that he beleived, we should in defence of our commerce, be under the necessity of doing it. — That the Court of France still loudly complains to our Government against our citizens trading with Hayti, & protecting that trade with arms.

This is the substance of the conversation I had with the President — The subject I selected previous to my going there — as I conceived it more useful to me than the common subjects, of weather, health & crops, which usually engross the time of these ceremonial visits.

I called at General Eaton's lodging — as he was absent I left him my visiting card.

In the evening my much respected friend Genl. Tracy arrived — Also Mesrs Chittenden,[21] Betton and Thompson, & took lodging at the same house — the last is my chum.

### Saturday 30th.

The Tunisian Ambassador landed, under a discharge of cannon from the frigate — Genl Eaton received him on shore — There was a great collection of people present. He soon afterwards presented his credentials to the Secy of State.

Thurreau, the French ambassador is much of a brute. He

---

[21] Martin Chittenden, representative from Vermont.

has very lately most unmercifully beat & bruised his wife — 'Tis however true that she gave him the first blow. Previous to a journey he lately took to Baltimore he delivered the keys of certain rooms in his house to one of his neighbors, on his return he quarreled with him for having delivered them to his wife.[22]

### Sunday Dec. 1.

In the evening the federal Members of the House to the number of twelve met at Coyle's in a Caucus to decide for whom they should vote as Speaker. Macon & Varnum [23] are the democratic candidates — the caucus resolved they would vote for neither, but would sit up & support John Cotton Smith, a member from Connecticut. The whole number of Members is 142, of these 27 only are federal, not quite one 5th of the house — not a sufficient number to demand the yeas & nays to be entered on the journals. — I think the eastern States have an interest different from that of the southern, & I really wish we might support that interest — not indeed in such a way as would endanger the peace & happiness of the Union. In Virginia a federalist is still a Virginian; but in New England a federalist does not feel or act as a New Englandman.[24] — On this ground I think I should give my vote for Varnum were I a member — for there is no rational ground to expect the election of Smith. — This division will ensure the re-election of Macon — & will I fear add new spirit & additional bitterness to the two parties in New England.

I was present in the room where the Caucus met, I heard their observations for sometime — said nothing — but withdrew before they came to any decision.

---

[22] The marital troubles of the Turreaus were well known in Washington society; see Adams, *History of the United States,* II, 269.

[23] Nathaniel Macon of North Carolina served as Speaker from 1801 to 1807; Joseph Bradley Varnum of Massachusetts was Speaker during the Tenth and Eleventh Congresses (1807–1811).

[24] The two preceding sentences are quoted in Plumer, *Life of William Plumer,* 335.

When John Randolph, (the member from Virginia) first dined with Mr. Merry,[25] the British minister — after dinner he was asked by Merry if he would take a hand at cards — He replied — " No Sir, I do not know a king from a queen, or a *king from a knave."*

### Monday 2d.

At Eleven OClock AM. a quorum of the Senate met — The Vice President being absent Samuel Smith of Maryland was elected President pro. tem. He had 15 votes, Mr. Adams, White, & myself voted for him — 4 scattering votes It is of no use to divide on such questions. — Mr. Smith appeared somewhat embarrassed.

The House of Representatives upon the third trial, have elected Nathaniel Macon for their Speaker. The state of the vote was.

| *Candidates —* | *First ballot —* | *second —* | *third —* |
|---|---|---|---|
| More [26] | 0 | 0 | 1 |
| Holmes [27] | 0 | 0 | 1 |
| Gregg [28] | 2 | 3 | 2 |
| Dawson [29] | 10 | 7 | 3 |
| J. C. Smith | 16 | 17 | 18 |
| Varnum | 27 | 26 | 23 |
| Macon | 51 | 53 | 58 |
| | 106 | 106 | 106 |

After I commenced my journey for this place I received correct information that a few Weeks since some difference arose between Samuel Hunt Esq of Charlestown New Hampshire, late a Member of Congress, & his brother Rosswell Hunt,

---

[25] Anthony Merry.
[26] Nicholas R. Moore, representative from Maryland.
[27] David Holmes, representative from Virginia.
[28] Andrew Gregg, representative from Pennsylvania.
[29] John Dawson, representative from Virginia.

respecting *an ox chain* — From words they proceeded to blows, & Samuel was so beat bruised & wounded that his life was greatly endangered — For some time he was confined to his bed. Rosewell was indicted at the Supr. Court but I have not heard the result. Common report fixes the blame on Rosewell, & I beleive justly. Samuel is excessively mortified. He was in the city of New York a few days since.

### Tuesday 3d.

At 12 OClock this day the President sent his message to both houses of Congress by Mr. Coles his Secretary. The message is more energetic & warlike than any he ever sent to Congress. The state of the nation seems to *demand* it.[30]

The term of the Superior Court preceeding the session of the General Court [31] in which they raised Judge Smith's salary from $1000 to $1500, he agreed with Livermore & Atkins on two of the associate Judges of the same court that the application to the Legislature for raising their salaries should be *joint.* And the first notice that either of them had of Smith's seperate application was the information of his salary being raised. At the Autumn session following Atkinson & Livermore preferred a joint memorial & petition, which the Court not granting, Atkinson immediately resigned his office. —

### Wednesday 4th.

Genl Eaton spent the evening with me & the gentlemen of the mess. His company was gratifying — The accounts he gave of Egypt & his travel over the deserts with an armed force & the attack & capture of Derne were interesting. He is a man of information & great enterprize. —

---

[30] This sentence is quoted in Plumer, *Life of William Plumer*, **336.** For the text of Jefferson's message, see Richardson, *Messages and Papers of the Presidents*, I, 382–388.

[31] Of the State of New Hampshire.

Just before our late ambassador Mr. Livingston took his leave of the French Court, he observed to Talleyrand, that Genl Moreau had taken his departure for America, & that he would use his influence with the Govt that the General should be treated with attention. Talleyrand replied that it was the request of Bonaparte that the United States would not shew any marks of respect to Moreau. This information Mr. Livingston communicated to the President. And Mr. Madison the Secy of State has very recently written to Mr. Lewis govr, of New . York & to De Witt Clinton mayor of the City of N. York requesting that no particular or public notice should be taken of Moreau. The Major General, Brigadier Genl & the officers of the militia of the City & County of New York have since then invited him to attend a review of the militia. He attended & *in fact* with the Major General *reviewed* the troops. The Officers gave him a public splendid dinner, at which some toasts were drank highly honorable to Moreau.

I think favorable of Moreau's character as a frank brave soldier. But from the long established character of the french nation remarkable for duplicity, is it not possible that Moreau under the character of an exile is in fact sent here by the French Court as a spie upon the United States. Such a measure suits the character of the Emperor & his corrupt Court; but I hope better of the brave Moreau.[32]

It is a fact that when Talleyrand came to this Country [33] as an exile a few years since & subsisted on the charity of an American gentleman — at that time he was high in the favor of the French Court & sent by them as a spy upon us.

---

[32] Moreau arrived in the United States in December, 1804. He settled in New Jersey in 1806, where he resided until 1813 when he returned to Europe to assist in the campaign against Napoleon.

[33] Talleyrand was in the United States from 1793 to 1795.

## Thursday 5th.

There has been for several years an attempt to change the Judiciary system in the state of Maryland. The Justices of the Peace had jurisdion of all cases of assumpsit & debt of £ 10 & under, with the right of an Appeal to the County Court. The County Court had unlimited original jurisdiction — from their decisions on Appeal lie to the Genl Court — & from the judgts given by the Genl Court in all suits where more than £ 150 was demanded an appeal was granted to the Court of Appeals. No cause could be twice tried by Jury, unless the Court in which it was tried granted a new trial; which new trial must be in the Court in which the suit was commenced. Each of those Courts, Justices of Peace excepted, had authority to grant a new trial.

By the Constitution of Maryland these Courts were established — & that provides that if two successive Legislatures pass a bill making a change in the Constitution — that change is valid.[34] The last & present Legislature have abolished their General Court, & established the following — Justices jurisdiction as before and the right of appeal to the District Court. The district Courts each consist of three Judges learned in the law — two, 3, or 4 Counties form a district. — This Court has unlimited jurisdiction of all causes. From their judgments appeals lie to the *Court of Appeals,* which is composed of 5 Judges, to wit, the Chief Justices of each of the District Courts.

Each of these Judges are to hold their office during good behavior — To have a salary that cannot be diminished during their continuance in office.[35]

Serious attempts have been made to offset material changes in the Judiciary system in Pennsylvania — but have proved unavailing.

---

[34] Article LX; Thorpe, *Federal and State Constitutions,* III, 1701.
[35] Amendment ratified 1805; *ibid.,* 1703–1705.

In Connecticut they also wish for changes — all parties say
they are necessary — but cannot agree upon the principles.
Their lower House will not consent that the Judges should hold
their office during good behavior.

Massachusetts is dissatisfied with their system — Vermont
wishes for change — And the attempt will, the present session
of the Legislature in New Hampshire be made to abolish our
Courts of Common Pleas, and institute a County Court of one
Judge in each County.   This plan will not, I think, succeed.
No essential change can be effected but with the approbation
of Justices of the Peace.   Amend the Constitution, & give to
Justices jurisdiction of civil suits to $50 with the right of appeal
— let that appeal be to the Common Pleas — That Court to
consist of 2 Justices one to make a quorum.   Appeals in all
suits of more than $100 to lie to supr. Court.   The fees for
entries to be such as to support both Courts.   This system,
would, I think, be a real improvement.   It would injure lawyers
but promote the interest of the community — The interest of a
particular class ought never to be promoted to the injury of the
whole. —

---

The more I read the Presidents message of the 3d, the more I
approve of it — The sentiments, if I understand them, are more
noble, liberal & just than any he ever before avowed.

It seems to be the course, as soon as the President gives notice
to Congress of the time he will send his message to the two
houses, he then sends copies to the printers, so that it may be
printed immediately after it is read in Congress.

### Friday 6th.

The Senate passed the bill appropriating $250000. for the Naval
service of 1805.[36]   Note the appropriations for the support of

---

[36] The bill is one making an additional appropriation for the naval
service.   For the text, see *Statutes at Large,* II, 348.

the Navy for 1805 amounted to $1,240,000, of which $411,951..02 was appropriated " for repairs of vessels, store rent & other *contingent* expences " See Laws of US. Vol. 7. p. 246.[37]

## Saturday 7th.

In the evening Robert Smith the Secretary of the Navy called & spent an hour or two with me & the gentlemen who board at Coyle's. He is a very gentlemanly man — his manners and address are pleasant. He appeared very desirous of knowing our opinion's of the Presidents message, & of the state of the nation.

Speaking of Levi Lincoln the late Attorney General of the US. he said, he never thought him qualified for that office. That the 2d year after his appointment, Lincoln asked him whether he thought the Supreme Court would be offended if he did not attend them when in session. He said, he replied, he tho't the duties of his office required his attendance — And that the fees that an Attorney General would receive from private suitors for advice & advocating causes, would in that Court, produce annually $3000. Lincoln replied, You do not know me — I am wholly unacquainted with the laws arising in the cases that are here decided. Mr. Smith observed that he did not think that Lincoln enjoyed a moments happiness from the time he accepted of the office till he resigned it — That the heads of Departments wished him to defend the suit bro't agt Capt. Murray, but he declined — saying the US. were not interested — tho' in fact they were, & eventually suffered by his inattention to that very suit, as the law passed last session will show.

The Secretary said he had been to visit Soliman Melemelli the Tunisian Ambassador. That this being the month Ramadan, a season for fasting to the Turks, he found him on his hands & knees on a very fine skin that was spread on the carpet. That the Secretary was about to withdraw — but was told it was

[37] *Ibid.,* 310–311.

unnecessary — That he tarried till Melemelli had performed his devotians, which he did with much zeal & apparent piety — That rising from the floor he addressed the Secy in the same manner as if he had just come in from another room. That he is a Turk — was governor of a province — a man esteemed in his own country — of much influence — That his brother is first general — That he delivered in specie $17000 to the Secretary, for safe keeping, not knowing our government would submit to the practise of Europe, in supporting him while on his mission. That he invited him to dine with him, but he replied he could not eat this month untill after sunset — but came in the evening & drank coffee. That his pipe-bearer always attends him with a very long pipe — that the Ambassador, smokes very fine tobacco in all companies — That he expressed much surprize that the Americans leaving so fine a Country to make war on so distant a nation as Tunis. The Secretary said, it was the intention of the Administration to keep him here till the roads should be well settled in the spring, & then that he should travel through the great cities, Baltimore, Philadelphia, New York & embark from Boston. That this was to be done to impress his mind with a just idea of our population, wealth & importance. He said the Government were much embarrassed respecting the presents that accompanied him from the Bey & were designed for the President. If they were refused he feared it would create disgust at Tunis — If the President applied to Congress for their consent, & if that consent was obtained — it would seem necessary to reconsider the resolves of the former Congresses, who have uniformly denied our Ambassadors the liberty of receiving small presents that were presented to them on their leaving foreign courts — EG. Pinckney, Humphreys [38] & als.

---

[38] See *Annals of Congress*, 7 Cong., 2 sess., 442–443, 512; also, Humphreys, *Life of David Humphreys,* II, 305–307.

## Sunday 8th.

Turreau, the french Ambassador after his wife had been with him sometime, frequently in mid-day publicakly rode in his carriage to visit a woman of *easy virtue*. . . .

This man & his wife were at the commencement of the revolution in France of the lowest grade in society. He was a soldier — sanguinary — unfeeling as a brute — qualities which rendered him useful to Buonaparte — he rose in office till he became a general in the army — & the last year his master judged him qualified as ambassador to this country. 'Tis said his wife retains more of the habits of her rustic life & more integrity than he does — having seen much less of the world than he has. That she brings too much of the *kitchen* language & manners with her into the *parlour* — That she sometimes treats the guests in such an awkward rude manner as offends him — That for this he has several times beaten her. — I have never yet beheld a face so cruel & sanguinary as his. —

What an astonishing contrast between this man, & the late Charge des affaires who preceded him? *Pichon* was a man of talents — of information — of courtly insinuating manners, & the most pleasing address. His company was sought for with avidity! I was always pleased with him.

---

## Monday 9th.

The President sent on friday a confidential message [39] to each house of Congress, but the Senate was adjourned before it arrived. It was then read in the House with closed doors. To day it was read in the Senate in like manner. There were many papers accompanying this message. On the largest packet, it

[39] For the message, see Richardson, *Messages and Papers of the Presidents,* I, 388–390. The documents are in *American State Papers,* II. *Foreign Relations,* II, 669–695.

was written *not confidential* & these we directed to be printed. The *private* documents accompanying this message, consisted of letters from Pinckney & Monroe, our ministers at Spain, to the Secy of State & to the Spanish Minister with his reply. Letters from Armstrong, our minister at France, to our other ministers, & to Talleyrand, & his answer. The principle subject of these, relate to the boundaries of Louisiana. The difference between the claims of the US. & Spain, as it respects the territory ceded, is great indeed. France is very explicit on three points. 1. That Spain is right as to the boundaries of Louisiana, 2d That Spain is not bound to compensate us for the depredations we alledge she committed on our Commerce in suffering French vessels to carry our merchantmen into Spanish ports & their condemn them by French Consuls — & 3d in case of a war between the US. & Spain, that France will give aid to Spain. — The Court of Spain explicitly refused to make any compensation for the injury done the US. in suspending the right of deposit at New Orleans.

### Tuesday 10th.

The documents, accompanying the message communicated yesterday, not confidential, are now published. They really contain little if anything that actually charges the govt of Spain with hostile acts — 1, They relate to recent depredations on our commerce, the capture of our merchantmen — but to use the language of Mr. Jefferson on a former occasion, *these appear rather to be the unauthorized acts of individuals, than of the government.*

2d In demanding 12 pr Ct. duty on all our Vessels that pass in the river Mobile by the town of Mobile. This is a great embarrassment to our navigation in that river. But whether the Spaniards have a right to impose this duty on us, I am at present unable to determine.

3d Acts of trespass in arresting the Kempers. The testimony

as to this shews that the arrest & detention was made not by
Spaniards, but by Americans & Englishmen — The Kempers
were rescued by Lt Wilson, one of our military officers, commanding at Fort Coupee. It appears from the whole of the
papers that some *private quarrels* previously existed between
the inhabitants living on each side of the line, & that each of
these committed acts of *trespass* upon the other. Rodney, one
of the Judges of our supreme Court of Orleans, examined witnesses — examined the Kempers, & some of those men who live
under the Spanish govt & found the conduct of the three Kempers so unjustifiable, that he required each of them to give bail
" to keep the peace, especially towards the subjects of the king
of Spain, & to do no injury to any one below the line of de-
markation." [40]
p. 73. [41]

The impression that a first reading of these documents make
on my mind is, that the facts will by no means warrant us in
declaring war against Spain — That the injuries done us are
of the minor kind.

### Wednesday 11th.

Visited several of the Indian Chiefs of the Cherokee tribe
now on a visit at this place. They were all well dressed, in
our manner of dressing — Most of them were of mixt blood —
several of them have property — houses — cattle & cultivate the
soil. They live in Tennessee & the Mississippi Territory. They
expressed their pleasure at seeing me — gave me their hands &
called me father. The celebrated Col. Benjamin Hawkins
introduced me to them. He has for many years been imployed
as our Minister to the Indians, & has made many treaties with
different tribes.

A mixture of our blood with Indians, and with the negroes

---

[40] For details concerning the matter mentioned here, see documents
under preceding note.

[41] Page reference to the documents.

in the southern states, disgusting as it is, will probably take place at some future period. Indeed many instances of the kind are daily seen, as it respects the negroes.

---

In the state of Maryland, no man is allowed to marry unless he previously purchases a license, for which he pays $4. This sum is paid over to support the university.

---

The last year, after Jesse Franklin, then a senator in Congress from North Carolina, received news that he had failed in a re-election — he said to a friend of mine — " my conduct as a senator has not been so decisive as it ought to have been — This excess of liberty will prove the ruin of our Republic as it has of all who preceded us."

---

I returned a visit to Mr. Merry the British minister in the same way & manner as he visited me — i.e. by leaving my card at his house. I afterwards met him in the street, & held a very social conversation with him.

### Thursday 12th.

Yesterday Mr. Clinton the Vice President arrived in the city. I very well knew that the last year he was assured I was the writer of the address of July 1804 to the Electors of New Hampshire, under the signature of Impartialis, upon the subject of the Election of Representatives. In that address his name was mentioned not in terms very flattering to his *old age*. I therefore felt myself bound to call early & pay my respects to this aged old gentleman. He received me with attention & treated me with respect. He took occasion to tell me he had reason to beleive I was sincerely attached to the interest of

New England — & that he actually thought our habits, manners, costoms, laws & country were much preferable to the southern States. I am very confident the old gentleman will make a sorry figure as president of the Senate. Tho' he complained to me that the office was too inactive for him, yet, I fear, he will find it too laborious for his advanced age. —

The Documents accompanying the Presidents message of the 10th were laid upon our tables. These contain stronger evidence agt Spain of their encroachments upon our territory in Louisiana, than those accompanying the former message. But I think these insufficient to justify war.

Examined several maps & charts, at the office of the Secretary of State, of Louisiana, to ascertain the difference between our government & that of Spain relative to boundaries. If the construction of Spain be just it will deprive us of much more than one half of that country.

### *Friday 13th.*

The Cherokee Indian Chiefs & Warriors waited upon Soliman Melemelli the Tunisian Minister. The Minister asked them what God they worshipped. The Indians answered *The Great Spirit.* He then asked them if they beleived in Mahomed, Abraham, or Jesus Christ? They answered in neither. He then asked what prophet do you worship. They replied none. We worship the Great Spirit without an agent. Soliman then exclaimed you are all vile Hereticks. He soon after related it to Mr. Jefferson & enquired how he could prove Indians were the descendants of Adam? The President replied it was difficult.

### *Saturday 14th.*

As soon as breakfast was over I called upon General Eaton. I went thus early because I wished to converse with him alone. I really hate the croud. Found him retired — in his chamber at breakfast — apologized for my early calling — He conversed

with ease & frankness.   He said he knew Tobias Lear (formerly
of Portsmouth New Hampshire) to be a man of a little mind —
jealous — cowardly, & what was worse *false*.   Eaton said that
had not Lear, who is now Consul-General from the US. to
the Regencies of Algiers, very prematurely made a treaty with
Tripoly, the officers & crew of the frigate Philadelphia would
have been released without our paying a cent for their ransom.

That the Ex-Bashaw Hamet whom he sought in Egypt — &
who joined his forces marched thro' the desert of Lybea, attacked
& conquored Derne — is a sober man — of talents, courage &
enterprize.

That Lear was so unfriendly to this expedition, that he con-
trived to with-hold provisions from them — but they (Eaton
& officers) purchased it with their own money & upon their
credit — And had they not received official information of
peace between the US. & Tripoli — in a very few days more
they would have marched into the city & placed Hamet on the
throne, & released our unfortunate countrymen from captivity
without money or price — obtained a treaty upon our own terms
— & taught the petty Regencies of Barbary to fear & venerate
the name & authority of the United States.

That Hamet the exiled Bashaw was a very popular man in
that regency — but that his expedition thus failing — his friends
consider him as being a false fraudulent man — & that he can
never rise again.

That he tho't highly of the government of the United States
— but imputed his failure to the mean, pusillanimous selfish
conduct of Lear.   That he had no wish of coming to the United
States — That he went to Syracuse — & that he did not expect
his brother, the reigning Bashaw of Tripoli, would restore him
his wife & children, notwithstanding it was an article in Lear's
treaty.   General Eaton added — that it was confidently asserted
That there was a private understanding between the reigning
Bashaw & Lear that that article was never to be fulfilled.

General Eaton appears a brave open frank intelligent man.[42]

He said when he proposed to our Government this enterprize they considered it chimerical — he said that he was not surprised that they did so — That Commodore Morris & all other American Naval officers, except Preble, had represented, to the Government of the United States, the coast of Barbary as being much more dangerous than it really was — & those powers as more potent than they are. That Commodore Preble being a man of a strong mind & sound courage raised the veil — & dared honestly to represent those Barbary nations, & their coast to our government truly & faithfully. That he (Eaton) assured the government, that it was not for pecuniary considerations that he wished to engage in the expedition — To prove this he should not request wages or salary — his expences was all he required & this only the govt engaged to pay him. He added my account for my actual expences is now at the Treasury for ajustment — I have refused, & will continue to refuse any wages — my Expences is all I ask — If these are paid I shall return to my farm in Brimfield, Massachusetts. I am not rich — I have a small farm & I am fond of cultivating it.

He bro't with him a young Egyptian The lad is about 14 years old — is a sprightly boy — is nearly of as dark complexion as a Molatto. He has no wool — but black curley short hair. He has a servant who was a soldier under the Ex-bashaw.

He has three Arabian horses — one is a handsome mare — the others *appear* not worth more than $50. each.

At 12 OClock sat out to visit Melemelli — met him in his carriage going to the Presidents to present him with horses from the Bashaw. He took 4 horses — one has died since his arrival. Two large negroe servants preceded his carriage each leading a horse. The horses did not appear remarkable — one of them was handsome — what will the President do with them — Postponed my visit.

---

[42] Plumer later changed his opinion of Eaton; see pages 496, 522.

### Sunday 15th.[43]

I was this day informed by Orchard Cook, member of Congress from the District of Mayne, that he had within a few days seen a private letter from James Bowdoin our Minister at Madrid, in which he writes, "that the French Court would persuade the Spanish Court to settle our differences with that nation to our full content in case we would make a present of a handsome sum of money to France."

In a private conversation with Samuel Smith (a senator from Maryland) some hours afterwards Smith told me in confidence that he tho't it probable our government would purchase of France & Spain, their title to the two Florida's.

In the evening, in an after conversation with Mr. Crowninshield, (member of Congress from Massachusetts) he told me he had seen a letter from Mr. Bowdoin — that he was to leave London the 1st of October for Madrid, & that he had no doubts of his being now in Spain.

Our federal gentlemen generally decline visiting the Republican members, & so vice-versa. I visit them, converse with them — avoid disputation — & obtain some information from them. My rule is to converse generally and negatively on subjects, & ask many questions — but avoid giving direct answers when questioned myself — & on subjects not important display much frankness. I abhor duplicity — whenever I answer to a question I will answer truly — But a politician is bound to act cautiously & with much prudence.

### Monday 16th.

For the first time George Clinton the Vice President took his seat in the Senate. He is an old feeble man — he appears altogether unacquainted with our rules — his voice is very weak &

---

[43] The entry for this date is quoted in condensed form in Plumer, *Life of William Plumer*, 336.

feeble — I cannot hear the one half of what he says — he has a clumsey awkward way of putting a question — Preserves little or no order — What a vast difference between him & Aaron Burr! One would think that the *office* was made for Clinton, & not *he* for the office. This however being his first day it is to be hoped he will in time do better — though he is too old to make improvements.

———

I have a perfect & distinct recollection of Judge Arthur Livermore's coming to me one morning to dissuade me from advocating the causes of those sectaries who claimed an exemption from ministerial taxes — He told me that the *Bench* was not pleased with my conduct in that particular — & added that he supposed that information would not change it. I replied, I must decide & act as I thought proper, whether I should be so fortunate as to please or displease the Court. —

What a change since then (say six years) — now that court is astute to find reasons & excuses to exempt sectaries from the support of the Clergy.

Formerly that Court took much pains to destroy titles to land founded on Collecter's sales — they now consider much more anxiety in supporting that kind of titles. How unstable is man!

### Tuesday 17th.

General Bradley some days since gave notice he should ask liberty to bring in a bill to prohibit the importation of Negroes into the United States *after January 1808.* He yesterday offered his bill but the opposition continued till adjournment. To day the debate was long warm & animated. Mr. Adams [44] & Tracy contended that Congress were by the 1st paragraph of the 9th section of the Constitution prohibited from passing a

———

[44] Adams refers to this debate but does not mention his part in it: *Memoirs,* I, 378–379.

law upon the subject untill the year 1808. Others that we ought never to do it — that policy forbid our stirring the question. I have no doubts of our authority now to pass the law — I have none of the policy of the measure. We have too many slaves in our Country — too many born in it — Our interest is to prevent as soon as possible the importation of more. To do this, severe penalties must be inflicted on the importers. — These must be established sometime before the law can operate. To postpone the passing of the law till 1808 will necessarily delay its operation till 1809.

I went to Bradley & requested him to have the question decided by ayes & nays — He did — and on this Dr. Mitchel rose & said had the vote been taken *ore-tenus* he should have voted *against* the motion — but as the question is now to be decided by *ayes & nays* entered on the Journal he should vote *in favor of it*. The journals are imperfect notes of our proceedings — they are true — but do not contain the whole truth. If my name should appear agt. this motion, its obvious import to readers would be that I was a supporter of *slavery* — This would be false. I will therefore never suffer my fame to be attacked by these records — I will always vote when by ayes & nays for or agt a measure according as the question appears on the journal without any reference to the subject itself. I will never consent that, that brief loose & imperfect journal shall be used with the people against me. Mr. Wright said he was opposed to the measure he thought it wrong — but as the great opinion of the people was in favor of it he should record his name for it. The question prevailed by a large majority. Had not the ayes & nays been required, its certain the motion would have been negatived.

I am at no loss for Bradley's motives — The legislature of Vermont have passed a resolution upon the subject — his re-election will be effected by this measure. One of his democratic friends in the Senate said that was the only reason why

he voted with Bradley — and that, was a *strong* reason why
Tracy voted against it. My determination is to support every
measure that to me appears *right*, let the party, or the *motives*
of the man who brings it forward be ever so wrong.

### Wednesday 18th.

On the question to postpone said bill to the first monday of
December next ayes 14, noes 14 — the Vice President voted in
the affirmative, & so the bill is in fact negatived. Note this
vote was ore tenus or it would have been negatived.

General Eaton spend the evening with me — He informed me
that when he marched from Alexandria his army consisted of
600 — That he had 120 camels — took one barrel of brandy &
one of wine one of pork — the rest of his provisions were bread
& rice — That the first day he made a forced march of 40 miles
with a view of fatiguing his men so that they should not desert
— That the next day he marched 25 miles & then his men tho'
their liquors, except water was gone, did not dare desert — for
fear of wandering Arabs tc that his troops increased to 1200 &
after marching 600 miles thro' the desert of Lybea he conquered
Derne the capital of the province in which Hamet Bashaw, the
exile, had commanded — That this town contained 12000 souls.

That the character in which our government sent him was
that of *Navy Agent* — That they have settled his accounts —
paid him the wages & allowed him the rations tc of a Captain
of our largest frigates — equal to that of a Brigadier Genl.
That the whole amount of his expedition, which produced the
peace of Tripoli, cost the United States less than $42,000. That
the Government have settled his old accounts, to his satisfaction,
of expenditures tc during his Consulship to Tunis.

The General is certainly a bold brave enterprizing man —
& discovers much knowledge of human nature — but is imprudent & not fit for command.

## Thursday 19

The Senate took up the treaty with the Chickasaw nation of Indians dated July 23d 1805 [45] — In this, the Indians cede a considerable tract of land to the United States & establish boundaries. The United States to pay them $22,000. in specie; and an annuity to Chinnubbee Mingo during his natural life of $100. —

The treaty with the Cherokees, dated Oct 25th 1805 [46] — This nation cedes to the United States a considerable tract of land, & the use of two roads — The United States to pay them $14000 in cash & an Annuity of $3000 forever.

Twenty eight senators were present, I only voted against advising the President to ratify these treaties. I do not see any necessity for extinguishing the Indian claim to these lands at the present. We have more uncultivated lands for sale in the markett than we can sell. The money to purchase these lands is drawn principally from duties on the commerce of the eastern states & the benefit almost exclusively results to the southern & western states. For example the land ceded in the last treaty lies in the state of Tennessee — The United States have no land offices there for the disposal of it — If they had it may not for years be in demand — The inhabitants of that State may occupy & claim it — They are a sovereign state — & can the United States exercise jurisdiction over the soil within the limits of that State. In the last treaty the annuity is considerable, & does not depend on the good behavior of these Savages. It ought to — that would have a powerful tendency to preserve them in peace with us. As there is no pressing call for the purchase now — as our relation with that portion of the Union may not always continue, & as the state of the Union appears to demand all the money we have I felt myself bound

---

[45] See *American State Papers,* IV. *Indian Affairs,* I, 679.
[46] *Ibid.,* 697–698.

to with-hold my vote from advising to the ratification of these treaties. — It is my rule not to vote for a measure unless I am convinced of its justice & expediency. The debts & annuities we have contracted with the Indians & are still making amount to a very considerable sum. During the last year, 1804, we paid for the Indian Department $116,500. —

### Monday 23d.

The Senate, without any division, agreed to advise the President to appoint John Brackenridge, late a Senator in Congress from the State of Kentucky, Attorney General of the United States.

The treaty with the Creek nation of Indians was decided in Senate, ayes 28 & myself only in the negative. This treaty is dated Nov 14, 1805 & on the part of the US. was negociated by Henry Dearborn Secy of War. It was made in this city. It relates to the cession of nearly the same tract that was ceded by a treaty that the Senate rejected the last year. Had I considered the terms, under all the circumstances of the case, as being reasonable, I should in consequence of the convention between the United States & Georgia have tho't myself bound to vote in favor of its ratification. The treaty contains a cession of land between the rivers Oconee & Ockmulgee in the state of Georgia, to the United States — And also a right of way. The United States is to pay said tribe for eight years an annuity of $12,000. — & for ten years commencing after the expiration of said eight years a further annuity of $11,000. — And for eight years to furnish said nation with two blacksmiths & two strikers.[47]

A treaty with the Cherokees, of October 27, 1805 [48] — This is a cession of a small tract of land & the use of a road — & the United States to pay therefor $1600. For ratifying this treaty

---

[47] *Ibid.,* 698–699.
[48] *Ibid.,* 698.

ayes 26, Mr. Hillhouse & myself were in the negative. This tract of land is scituated in the State of Tennessee & as soon as the title of the Indians is extinct the State will own the land. I am unwilling to establish such a precedent. Several of the Senate, particularly, Genl Bradly, on a former day, reasoned strongly against the treaty — but today voted for it.

After the Senate adjourned, I went with Genl Eaton to visit the Tunisian *Ambassador* (for that is his title). He converses in Italian — Eaton was the interpreter. He was drest in his military robes, which, for a man, between the Savage & civilized state, were elegant & rich. He never wears a hat, but a turban made of fine white muslin. It is said it contained more than 20 yards. His cloths were of fine *scarlet* colour inwrought with much gold. His waistcoat came down to his waist, & his coat was short — it had no folds — it resembled a sailors coatee. It came up close round his neck, & the sleeves of it was so strait round his wrist, that there was on no part any appearance of his having any shirt or linnen on him. He had no breeches or pantaloons — but much cloth wound & folded on him in a loose but curious manner. He had white silk hose — yellow Morocco shoes, with goloshoes of the same kind.

He told me that he was 50 years of age — He is a large personable man — his neck is very large — his complexion is about as dark as that of a Molatto. His manners were easy & really graceful. As soon as I was announced as a Member of the Grand Divan — he bowed very respectfully — gave me his hand — & directed me to be seated. He then came up & bowed to me — He opened his elegant gold dimond snuff box, & gave me some very excellent snuff. He took his pipe which was more than four feet long & very elegant & smoked. — His room was perfumed with the essence of roses — which to me was very agreeable. His beard was 6 or 8 inches long — its colour black turning grey. His countenance is good — it bespeaks intelligence & integrity.

Soon after I was seated, his two Aid-decamps came in — they were dressed in the same manner as he was — except the colour of their Clothes; the one of them was navy blue, the other light blue. These were natives of Constantinople. Being unmarried their beards were shaved except their upper lips. His servants were all drest in scarlet. They were all large black men. In a short time he sent one of them who ordered his Italian band to play in an adjoining room upon the drum, fife tc which they did very well indeed. He said he had ordered this in honor of me who had deigned to visit him. He had eleven persons in his suit. He is a very firm beleiver in the Alcoran — he reads and expounds a lesson from it every day to his household.

Our government has, on his application, provided him with one or more women, with whom he spends a portion of the night.

On my rising to leave him he again presented his elegant snuff box and enjoined me to partake of his very fine snuff — which I did. He then gave me his hand — wished me long life & the blessings of Heaven.

A corporal's guard attend at his doors every day from daylight to dark. The government after his first arrival, found that his novel & singular appearance attracted the attention of all classes, so that he was imposed upon by even the boys & children breaking into his room — this induced them to set sentries at his doors.

### Tuesday 24th.

The treaty with the Delawares, Potawatamies, Miamis, Eelriver & Weas nations of Indians dated August 21, 1805 was read for the third time in the Senate.[49] This treaty is joint & several on the part of said nations. The said nations cede to the United States a certain tract of land. The United States give them an additional *permanent annuity,* viz to the Miamis $600 — to

---

[49] *Ibid.,* 696–697.

the Eel River $250 — to the Weas $250. — And to the Potowata-
mies an additional annuity of $500 for ten years.  And also to
said nations $4000 which was at the time of the treaty paid
them.

On the question to ratify this treaty, the ayes were 25, myself
only in the negative.

### *Friday 27th.*

The House of Representatives referred some days since the
confidential message of the President to Congress & the Documents accompanying the same to a select committee.  John
Randolph is chairman of that committee — Barnabas Bidwell [50]
is a member.  The committee are much divided.  John C.
Smith,[51] who belongs to it, informed me that the Committee
consists of 7, but that Mr. Nicholson [52] being out of town had
not met with them — That the Committee was much divided in
opinion — That Bidwell moved to pass a law appropriating 5
millions of dollars to enable the President to purchase the two
Florida's. — That Mr. Randolph was zealously opposed to this
— declared he would never consent to vote for a cent to purchase that Country — That if the President wished to obtain it,
let him negociate, & if he wants money to aid that negociation
let him explicitly say so — & thereby the responsibility of the
measure will rest as it ought on himself — That it was wrong to
obtain the approbation of the House to a measure — then form
a treaty — & thereby prematurely pledge the faith of the House
to support it — That he hoped the purchase of Louisiana would
never form a precedent. — The Committee have not reported.

It is said that the President is desirous of purchasing the
Florida's — that Mr. Gallatin [53] & Mr. Randolph are strongly
opposed to the measure.

---

[50] Barnabas Bidwell, representative from Massachusetts.
[51] John Cotton Smith, representative from Connecticut.
[52] Joseph Hopper Nicholson, representative from Maryland.
[53] Albert Gallatin, Secretary of the Treasury.

Mr. Randolph says No American Administration can support themselves in a war — that a war will damn any Admõn.

### Saturday 28th.

There is a *small* congregation of Episcopalians in this city who usually attend the preaching of Mr. McCormick. As A society they are poor. During this year they have paid some attention to music — Every sunday they have two Musicians from the Marine Corps who played upon instruments of music. For their attendance the Society paid one dollar pr day which was collected by a voluntary contribution after service. During the session of Congress their Chaplin's preach every sunday in the Representatives chamber — & Mr. McCormick & his society attend in the same place. After service was ended in the Hall on Christmas Dr. Grant gave notice that next sunday, & the first sunday in each month there would be a Contribution in the Representatives chamber for the purpose of supporting the music. On the next day after the House were in session Mr. Macon, the speaker, informed them that he " tho't contributions improper, & unless he was otherwise directed he would not suffer them." Mr. Randolph said " if there was a motion to levy a contribution he hoped it would be raised in a Committee of the whole house."

What authority has the Speaker to make such a regulation? May he not as well regulate the prayers & sermons of the Chaplin's?

### Monday 30th

The Senate adjourned early — The chiefs & warriors from twelve different tribes of Indians were introduced into the Senate preceeded by their Interpreters & several of our agents to their tribes. The Vice President took his seat, & the senators their chairs. After the Indians had walked into the Chamber & stood arranged in proper order — One of the Chiefs walked up to the Vice President took him by the hand — bowed — retired,

& then made an eloquent address to him — which was then translated & delivered orally by the interpreter to the President in the hearing of all.  The same course was followed by several other chiefs.  The substance of the address was that they had come a great away to see us — that they had been treated with much kindness — & that they were grateful for the favor shewn them in admitting them into the Great Senate Chamber of the Great Nation — & wishing us long & great happiness.  The Cherokees were dressed in our manner — very well — genteely — & hair powdered.  The *Osages* who come from the Missouri are large tall strait well proportioned men.  One of their chiefs was ruffled at the bosom & hands — all were painted — principally red — their heads shaven — except a small tuft of hair behind — their hair painted — They had rings & jewels in their ears & noses — some of them had their ears cut — most of them had feathers — strings of wampum & other trinketts.  Some had battle axes & one or two had hangers.  One of their young men was very handsome.

In the evening they had a war dance at the theatre — many members attended — I did not.

At 12 OClock at night one of the fine large Osage Chiefs who in the day was in the Senate, & who was well & uncommonly active in the dance at the theatre — died almost in an instant at his lodgings without a sigh or groan.  The other Chiefs cried & made a most grievous lamentations.  His exertions at the dance & the change of life no doubt produced the event.  I think the fatal stroke was the bursting of a vessel & occasioned by his exertions.

### Tuesday 31.

The Secy. at war directed him to be buried.  The United States gave a new suit & medal, which they had promised the Chief before he died.  The survivors drest the corpse in these & put the medal on him — The Indians then took them off & put them up with much care to carry to his family.  He has left a wife & two daughters. Col: Hawkins & Mr. Rogers, (the Chief Clerk in the War Department), followed the Corpse, & the Indians followed next in order to the Grave. They said the will of the Great Spirit of all Spirits was done & they ought to submit to it. They appeared very melancholly. From the time of his death & untill after his funeral they eat nothing.

### Wednesday January 1, 1806.

It has been the general practise from the first establishment of the Federal government for members of Congress, heads of departments, gentlemen of distinction & their ladies on the *first day of the year,* to call upon the President of the United States with the *compliments of the season.* The federalists, at their arrival in the city, this session as usual waited upon him. I know of no exception except Mr. Tracy & Mr. Dana. But the federalists in general said as they had not been invited this session to dine with him they would not this day visit him. I thot it a respect *due* from me to the *President* I therefore went — Mr. Adams, Genl. Chittenden [54] & Mr. Taggart [55] were the only federalists who attended. These are mere visits of *ceremony* — marks of respect due from the officers of the government to *its chief* — Marks of respect & decorum that I will pay, if only from the respect I *owe myself.* I will never yield implicit obedience to the will of any man or party. The course I shall pursue in life — in politics must & shall be one that my Judgment approves — not what my *friends* or *political foes* dictate. I see much to approve & much to condemn in all parties. I wish for understanding clearly to discover my duty on all questions — I have resolution to do it. This conduct has already extorted respect from men of very different politic's.[56]

---

[54] Martin Chittenden, representative from Vermont.
[55] Samuel Taggart, representative from Massachusetts.
[56] The preceding paragraph is quoted, though not in exact form, in Plumer, *Life of William Plumer,* 338.

I went to the Presidents house at 12 & tarried till 2 OClock. There was much company — brillant — & various. There were very many ladies. A great majority of both houses of Congress — All the heads of department — the subordinate officers — The Naval & marine officers — The British Minister [57] & Secretary — the French Minister Turreau — The Charge des Affaires from Sweden & Denmark — The Tunisian Ambassador — and all the Indian Chiefs — with a great concourse of respectable private characters. *NB* The senators from *Vermont* [58] did not attend — Bradley appears disgusted.

All the rooms on the lower story were thrown open. The presedent stood in the drawing room a few yards from the door, & as each person came in they made a congee to him — which he returned. In the large unfinished hall there was a full band of Music which played well & with fine effect. The side boards were numerous & amply furnished with a rich variety of wines, punch, cakes — ice cream tc. The interview was pleasant, & to me very agreeable.

### Thursday 2d.

After the Senate had been an hour in session & disposed of the business pending before them the Vice President informed the Senate that the Tunisian Ambassador had given him notice that he wished at 12 OClock to come into the Senate Chamber & pay his respects to them. A question arose how he should be received. Saml. Smith moved that a resolve pass admitting him & suit to a seat in the Chamber. Several senators objected to this as being improper. Mr. Adams said it would be establishing a precedent — That Ambassadors from the greatest nations had never received this mark of notice — that they would demand — & we must grant it or give umbrage.

Dr. Mitchel said — we had improperly in common parlance,

[57] Anthony Merry.
[58] Stephen R. Bradley and Israel Smith.

given this *half-savage* the dignified title of *Ambassador* in common with the Ministers from nations of the first rank — That we have thus established a new precedent in diplomacy — That European nations to whom the Barbary powers sent agents, never recognize them as Ministers or Ambassadors — That they negociate the business with them privately — but that they are never introduced to the Secretary of State, much less to the King. And that he was sorry that this man had been formally & in the title of an Ambassador introduced to our Secretary of State, & in the same character to the President of the United States — & by them in that character received.

Mr. Hillhouse, I consider this Tunisian in the same character as I do the Indian Chiefs — & I would treat him accordingly — I am not afraid that our conduct toward him will be drawn in as a precedent by the Minister's from civilized nations, more than that towards the savages.

Mr. Smith withdrew his motion.

Mr. Bradley moved to adjourn — 15 Senators in the affirmative — adjourned.

The Tunisian came in, attended by his two secretary's. He took the Secretary of the Senate's chair — & his Secretaries on his Right The Vice President took his seat — the Members their chair's. Mr. Thruston, a senator from Kentucky, addressed the Tunisian in Italian. The Tunisian had been into the Representatives chamber, & the House were then in debate — He said to Mr. Thruston if each Representative has a right to debate on each question it will require a year to come to a result. He seems incapable of distinguishing between making & executing of laws — between a legislative & judiciary Court. After having sat in the Senate chamber about 20 minutes he rose shook hands with the President & bid the Senate *adieu* — he retired.[59]

[59] *Cf.* J. Q. Adams, *Memoirs*, I, 380–381.

He says the western Indians are the descendants of Arabs — & are his brethern.

At a ball in this city a few days since he & those Indian Chiefs were present. They paid much attention to the ladies. The Indians were asked whether they thought their own or our American women were the handsomest? They bluntly answered the Indian women were the handsomest on earth. The same question was asked of the Tunisian — He replied " The American — they are angels in human shape — they are the proper inhabitants of Heaven. — But our women belong to Earth."

---

M. *Turreau,* the French Minister & the Secretary of Legation M. ——— [60] called & paid me a visit. I was pleased with the manners and conversation of the Secretary — they are more agreeable than those of the Minister — & the Secretary discovers the most understanding.

---

I am very strongly inclined to think that Mr. Jefferson intends to purchase the Florida's — That he has not been himself deceived as to the eastern boundaries of Louisiana though immediately after the cession, to render that purchase popular he insinuated that it included West Florida. That all the present clamour for warlike preparation, & the publication of supposed aggresions some of which purported to have been committed three years since, are now made to prepare the public mind for the purchase of the Florida's — And by that means affect an object that for years has been dear to the President. A few weeks will decide. This evening I have been assured from pretty high authority that *France* will sell & guaranty both the

---

[60] Blank occurs in Plumer's manuscript.

Florida's to us for seven millions of dollars. At present I do not see any cause for either war or purchase of territory.[61]

The fact, however, may be, that the President at the time of cession of Louisiana was as much deceived as he afterwards deceived others as to the extent of that territory — And that still considering the Florida's, particularly West Florida, as highly useful to this Country — he is still determined to acquire them.

### Friday 3d.

The Committee of the House on the *Confidential Message* reported That the President be authorized to call forth ——— of troops into service whenever in his opinion the interest of the United States require it. This report was accompanied with a chain of well connected reasoning, as I am told. It was drawn up by John Randolph. At the sametime, Mr. Bidwell offered a resolution to Appropriate ——— dollars to defray the expences incident to foreign intercourse — That is in plain English to authorize the President to purchase the Florida's. Both resolutions are made the order of the day for monday next. The House was closed.

### Saturday 4.

Visited John Quincy Adams, senator from Massachusetts.[62]

### Tuesday Jany 7, 1806.

Yesterday & today the House of Representatives have been occupied with closed doors in debating upon the resolutions offered on the 3d instant by Mr. Randolph & by Mr. Bidwell. I am told that Mr. John Randolph made two or three very able & truly eloquent speeches — That he solemnly protested he would never give his Vote to give the President a single Cent

---

[61] The above paragraph, in condensed and altered form, is quoted in Plumer, *Life of William Plumer,* 339.

[62] There is no entry under this date in J. Q. Adams, *Memoirs.*

to purchase the Florida's — That it was the height of impropriety to begin the business this way — If the President thinks it necessary for the United States to obtain the Florida's by negociation, let him open the negociation & take the responsibility of the measure upon himself — And if he forms a treaty & two thirds of the Senate advises him to ratify it — we must then decide whether we will pass the requisite Appropriation laws. But to pass the resolution now offered by the Gentleman from Massachusetts (Mr. Bidwell) is fettering the House — 'tis pledging improperly pledging the House to support a measure which when brot before them may be a sacriface of national honor & interest. — That this mode, of purchase was mean — & gave no security — that after all we may be obliged to fight for the very territory we purchased — That it would be unjust to give our gold to induce France to compel Spain to cede the Floridas to us. — That he would never consent that the wealth of the United States should be transferred to the consumptive coffers of the French treasury.

In reply to some one who observed we had better reserve our forces to chastise the injustice & insolence of Great Britain — He said — I have no doubt Great Britain has done us acts of injustice — But I have infinitely more confidence in their justice & honor than in that of France. Chastise Great Britain! How can we do it. We have a bold enterprizing seargeant at arms, who is ambitious to execute our orders — Shall we send *him* with our *Mace* in a *canoe* to Admiral Collingwood to order him to surrender the royal fleet of Great Britain?

Mr. Eppes (the son in law of the President) openly & warmly supported the idea that the House should pass an Appropriation law to enable the President to purchase the Florida's. The House adjourned without decision.

Mr. Randolph said, Great Britain may Act like a highwayman — but not as a swindler — she has never violated her faith with us. The character of France is the reverse of this. She

knew when she made the cession of Louisiana to us — that she
had solemnly promised Spain she would never alienate that
country — she knew, & our government well knew, that France
had never performed the conditions on which the treaty of Cession of Louisiana from Spain to France was founded. I mean
the treaty of St Idelphonso. France in her cession of Louisiana
to us has so described that country as to leave the limits &
boundaries uncertain — This was done by Bonaparte to give
opportunity for Spain to complain — that so France might again
interfere as a mediator & obtain from us a douceur of millions —
Purchase the Florida's — we do not purchase peace — purchase
to the Pacific Ocean & still the avarice of France will contend
with you — still you must grease the fists of Bonaparte with
your gold. " I will never consent that the asses milk of the
United States shall enrich the consumptive coffers of France —
I will never consent to give him a single cent — so help me
God! "

### Wednesday 8th

The House of Representatives again debating with closed
doors — Mr. Randolph took a view of the situation politic's &c
of Europe — & the relation they stood to us. He considered
Great Britain as the mistress & arbitress of the Ocean — That
she was able to enforce her laws relative to the trade of
Neutrals — That if we pass a non-importation bill it would
injure us infinitely more than it can Great Britain — If G^r.
Britain is governed solely by her own interest — she may find
it convenient to wage perpetual war with us — She can tax our
commerce *ad libitum* — A few frigates will block up the Chesa-
peack — Two or three more attended with a ship or two of the
line will block up the port of New York, from whence you receive more than a 4th of your Revenue — These ships will prostrate the trade of the south — Your New England fishermen from
Salem & Marblehead & Newbury Port may find employment
in privateering but their trade will be annihilated. — Talk of

frightning G. Britain with non importation Acts! Gentlemen forget that a man is at the head of that nation who is capable of arming the myriads of Russia — of creating the most formidable Confederation of force ever known — of conquering & governing a world in India — & on the Ocean of hurling defiance against the United flags of the Universe.

Can you fairly purchase the Florida's of Spain — Will she for a paltry sum of money sell you a barrior that defends her invaluable provinces — her mines of the Mexican world?

Can you evince to the world the meanness & injustice of bribing the insatiable avarice of France to *compel* Spain to cede you the Florida's?

Why wish such a Cession? Do you want a territory of barren trackless sands, so extensive that the sun can never rise or set thereon? Such extent may *ruin,* but cannot profit the United States?

———

John Smith, a senator from Ohio told me this day, that the President of the United States lately said to him — " He did not know what course to pursue with Mr. Randolph — he would never consult him — or his friends — but regardless of them all pursue his own course — That some of his measures were he thought wild & impracticable."

### Thursday 9th.

The House were debating with closed doors in Committee of the whole — on the question upon Mr. Randolph's resolution to raise troops, ayes 56 nays 70. The federalists all voted in the affirmative.

### Friday 10th.

Debate with closed doors continued — The question to appropriate a sum of money to purchase the Florida's, as pr Bidwell's resolution, after being amended so as to designate the

Object for which the same was appropriated, passed ayes about 70 nays near 60. — Mr. Randolph reasoned strongly agt the measure.

### Saturday 11th

Debate continued — but not decided.  The House have each day this week sat till near 4 OClock P.M.

### Sunday 12th.

The President, Vice President, majority of Congress & many others attended in the Representatives Chamber to hear Deborah Ripley preach.  She is neither Quaker nor Methodist; but approaches nearest the Quaker of any other Sect.  She spoke nearly an hour, & prayed fervently.  She appeared sincere — Her discourse had more of method than genius — & more scripture than logic.

---

While our company was in the *west* parlour Mr. Tucker, the Treasurer of the United States came into the entry.  John Cotton Smith who happened to be there conducted him into the *east* parlour, & informed him he would give notice to the gentlemen of the House.  Leaving the doors of both rooms open he addressed himself to Mr. Tracy & informed him that Mr. Tucker was waiting in the other room.  Mr. Tracy replied " There let him wait — what care I for that."  All this passed in language so loud that Mr. Tucker must necessarily have heard the whole.  I rose immediately went into the Treasurer shut the door & held a friendly conversation with him for 15 Minutes.  *That pink of Connecticut politeness* did not again return to the room — Mr. Tracy saw him not — Mr. Dana only came in — but tarried not.  Mr. Tucker is a gentleman of pleasing inoffensive manners.  His politic's are democratic.  But his morals are unexceptionable. — I confess I am shocked at the rudeness of Tracey & Smith — & the gross negligence of the boarders in gen-

eral. I trust in God that a difference, neither in religion or politic's, will ever make me rude & brutal to any — Especially to
men of virtue — talents — science & inoffensive lives. I could
easily see by Mr. Tucker's conversation & countenance that he
had heard the whole & felt embarrassed. I convinced him that I
felt myself gratified by his attention to me. I solicited his
stay —

I have from my early acquaintance with Mr. Tracy known him
to be *imprudant* — to use *indecent vulgar language* — which
but for his wit — would exclude him from genuine polite company — but I never knew him guilty of such insufferable rudeness as this of today. The manners & behavior of Mr. Smith
are those of a haughty overbearing man, whose talents skims
the superficies. — Mr. Dana is the polite accomplished gentleman — & certainly would not so hastily have retired from the
room but from an apprehension that Mr. Tucker & myself were
in a private consultation.

At the table found Tracy, Smith & Davenport, who are really
great bigots in religion, censure & very liberally condemn those
who attended the preaching of Miss Ripley. The former himself attended, the later avoided, & considered it as a breach of
holy time. Their language is emphatic "stand by — I am
holier than thou!"

### Tuesday 14th.

Some weeks since the Senate requested the President of the
United States to lay before them the instructions to Mr. Lear
who made the treaty with Tripoli — the instructions to Mr.
Eaton, the correspondence tc tc. Yesterday he sent to the
Senate a volume in manuscript — It has this two days occupied
their whole attention in the reading of them.[63]

There appears to be great negligence & inattention in relation
to the papers — some of them are originals — some copies — of

---

[63] See *American State Papers,* II. *Foreign Relations,* II, 695–725.

some we have duplicates — Some of them are the very same that he sent copies of with the treaty now before us — & several of the letters are the same that were published the last summer in the newspapers. Many of them in another message are sent into the House & they without reading them have ordered them printed. But the Senate read all with closed doors under an injunction of secresy. A part of them are properly *confidential*.

The greatest part of the papers are really very unimportant — contain little useful information relative to the subject. Many of the letters are merely stating the local situation of Eaton — the Exbashaw — their march thro' the desert of Lybia — the particular situation of a particular ship tc. Some of the documents are very important. They clearly show the imprudence & folly of Lear in opening at that time a negociation & making a treaty with the reigning Bashaw. There is no doubt had Eaton been supported a few weeks more, Tripoli by the joint attack of our fleet & army must have surrendered at discretion. The documents clearly shew that we basely & ungenerously deserted the Ex Bashaw — That the moment his measures operated in our favor & secured to us a peace we abandoned him & his friends to wrechedness & ruin! I cannot but despise & detest that vile wretch of a *Lear!*

---

I find some Members of Congress think we ought to declare war against Spain — At least some federalists converse in that way. From them I dissent.

There are several reasons assigned in favor of war. 1. The *Spanish aggressions on our territory*. What evidence have we of the fact. It arises, as far as I recollect from the Presidents messages to Congress & the several documents accompanying them.

The President in his message of the 3d Dec last speaking on this subject says, " Inroads have been recently made into the territories of Orleans & the Mississippi. Our citizens have been seized & other property plundered in the very parts of the former which had been actually delivered up by Spain: & this by the regular officers & soldiers of that government. I have, therefore, found it necessary at length to give orders to our troops on that frontier, to be in readiness to protect our citizens, & to repel by arms any similar agressions in future. Other details necessary for your *full information* of the state of things between this country & that, shall be the subject of another communication." p. 6.

What evidence have we that these agressions were committed by the order of the Spanish Government? A few years since when the Spanish officer, the Intendent at New Orleans, prevented us from exercising the right of Deposit at that city — the President then said those violations of our rights *were the acts of unauthorized individuals* — & yet they were the acts of *Spanish officers.* When *individuals,* but particularly when *officers,* commit acts of violance & wrong on the citizens of another nation — when the government to which those Wrong-doers belong are informed of the fact, & refuse, or unreasonably delay, to punish them — the Government then becomes answerable to the injured — & answerable to the nation to whom the injured people belong. Doth the Government of Spain avow & justify these acts? Has our Government required of them an explanation?

What are the aggressions complained of — what evidence of their existence? Their existence we learn from the documents accompanying the Message of the President of the 6th December. These principally relate to the Kempers — three brothers who have long been turbulent quarrelsome men. They had been guilty of very great outrages both in the Mississippi Territory & within the Spanish lines. They lived at Pinckneyville in the Mississippi territory — & by a party of men principally living in that territory, whom the Kempers had injured, they were taken in the night & carried within the Spanish lines & there delivered to a body of men, who it seems intended to carry them to a Spanish tribunal for trial & punishment for the crimes the Kempers had committed within the Spanish jurisdiction. But they were rescued by Capt. Wilson at Point Coupee. This assult & battery, on these old offenders, will not justify the United States in appealing to Arms! Tis too trivial!

William Flanagan Jr was arrested & carried within the Spanish line — his horse taken & sold — & himself detained for a short time. It seems that his father was accused of having murdered one *John Sharp*. The arrest, detention &c of Flanagan was irregular & improper; but for ought appears the Courts of law in the Spanish provinces are willing to do him justice. To them applications ought to be made.

From the documents accompanying the Presidents message of the 10th of Dec [64] — it appears that five Spanish soldiers in Louisiana took a horse from Andrew Chamar.

That in Sept last a detachment of Spanish soldiers arrested Francis Roban — took some horses — & attempted to take Oliver & Case. That the next morning Roban escaped from them. This statement is from his deposition — he assigns no reason for the conduct of the Spaniards. This detactment was *very small* — A corporal was the officer. I am convinced we have not the whole of this case — I think the conduct of the Spaniards in these instances improper — but will not justify us in declaring war as yet. —

Another cause of complaint is that the Spanish officer at Mobile exacts 12 pr Cent duties from our people who carry goods to down that river. If the Mobile is within their territory, as I beleive it is, I do not see any thing to prevent them from demanding the duty. I can see nothing in our treaty of October 20th 1795 that prohibits it. The mouth of the Mobile for several miles being clearly within their territory, & their being no provisions in the treaty in our favor, their claim to demand

[64] See note 39.

duties appears to me indisputable. The sources of this river are in Georgia & the Mississippi territory — but I do not see that it follows from that fact that we have therefore a right to navigate *freely* through that part of the river which is in the Spanish territory. May not each nation exact from the subjects or citizens of the others duties from ships who pass up or down the river thro' the territories of the other? May they not levy, for example, light money to support light houses &c?

Another cause of complaint is that Spain has sent troops and are erecting forts & making fortifications on our frontiers — And 'tis said that some of these are within our own limits. I cannot consider this, under the peculiar circumstances of the case as cause of war. For long before this event our government proclaimed to the world that they not only had a legal & clear title to Louisiana but that the treaty ceding that country to us did in fact & truth also include West Florida. To this last province we asserted our claim — Spain was clear that her claim to this province was just. And to be prepared to support that claim she has sent a few hundred troops & cast up a few small intrenchments. Whether she has in fact passed the line is doubtful — & if so whether ignorantly or through design, is equally uncertain. The only use we should make of this is to have troops ready in that country to protect our citizens.

Various letters I have written this session to my friends, copies of which are on file, shew my opinion, & the letter from Talleyrand to Mr. Armstrong of Dec 21, 1804, (see My Repository [65] Vol. 3. p. 58) contains strong unswerable reasons in favor of the Spanish claim respecting the boundaries, & against those set up by our Government. There really is no solid ground to support our claim to West Florida — our claim is visionary.

The most substantial cause of complaint however respecting those boundaries are said to be this, that Spain will not agree to any mode for ascertaining & settling them. The fact is,

---

[65] The *Repository* was a collection of Plumer's letters.

she contends they are all established except on the northern part, & to ascertain & settle this she is willing to agree on Commissioners — But the United States will not agree to have Commissioners at all unless they are authorized to settle each & all of the lines & boundaries. Is the object for an immediate settlement of boundaries of this desart land of such importance as to justify war?

But in fact the greatest cause of complaint against Spain is the spoilations she has committed on our Commerce. These depredations are of 3 kinds.

1 Those captures made by cruisers under French colours, in which Our vessels were taken & carried into the ports of Spain & *there* condemned by *French consuls.* Since these have happened we have made a treaty with France & released all demands we then had against the French Republic.[66] Spain contends that in relation to these captures & condemnations, France was the *principal* trespasser, & as the United States have settled & released all claims she had against France, Spain who at the most was but an *accessary,* is by that release compleatly discharged. This is certainly sound law.

2, There were other captures & condemnations made by the Spaniards from 1796 to the year 1802. This is a fact not denied by Spain. And Augt 11th 1802 the Spanish minister agreed with Charles Pinckney, our Ambassador, to submit these claims to the decision of Commissioners. Jany 18, 1803 the President laid this Convention before the Senate for their approbation. On the 3d of March following, the question was taken ayes 13 nays 9, there not being *two thirds* in favor of a ratification the question was lost. The ground on which this Convention was rejected was that it made no provision for the Captures & condemnations made by the French as aforesaid. The Executive issued fresh instructions to Mr. Pinckney — He pressed the

---

[66] For the treaty of 1800 with accompanying documents, see *American State Papers,* II. *Foreign Relations,* II, 727–773.

Spanish Government to admit said claims, but they pertinaciously refused. On the 9th of January 1804 two thirds of the Senate advised the President to ratify & approve said Convention [67] — which he did & transmitted it to the Court of Madrid. But Spain refused to ratify it on their part. After having ourselves retained this treaty this unreasonable length of time, have we any just cause of complaint against Spain for not ratifying & exchanging it on her part? A man who makes proposals to another of the terms on which he will sell his House, is not *always* bound by those proposals — If the other does not in a reasonable time accept of them, he that made them is after that not bound by them. The obligations to be binding must be mutual. The same rule will apply to nations as well as to individuals.

Still it remains a fact that we have a just claim upon Spain for compensation for these spoilations. Altho' our not ratifying the Convention with Spain in due time absolved her from all obligation ever to *ratify it* on her part — yet it has not released her from the obligation she is under to make restitution to our injured citizens for the wrongs she has done them.

A 3d description of spoilations she has committed upon our commerce has happened within the two last years. These have been principally confined to depredations committed in Cuba & near the coast thereof. Of these violations I am not fully & correctly informed. Some part of them were committed by persons sailing under the French flag — some by pirates — & others by Spaniards. Their conduct, judging by the partial evidence I have, is certainly unjustifiable.

But when we turn to her complaints against the United States, I am sorry to say I cannot fully justify our conduct. Without the knowledge & against the consent of Spain we purchased Louisiana. Before we ratified that treaty — the act of Cession

---

[67] Examination of the Senate *Executive Journal* shows Plumer's references to be correct.

— Spain exhibited her remonstrance against it — She averred that the conditions on which she agreed to cede it to France had never been performed on the part of France. And that France solemnly pledged her faith to Spain that she would never alienate the territory — & directly declared that the cession of France to us, on the part of France was founded in fraud & perfidy — yet the Government of the United States with this information ratified the treaty. Till this event took place Spain was friendly to us. From that period her disposition & conduct assumed a different direction. The placing a bad neighbour near a nation has been considered as a good cause for war. Spain considers us as a very bad neighbour — Our approach to her Provinces & rich mines alarms all her fears.

These things do not justify the conduct of Spain to us; but they mitigate the evils — they reduce them so low as to render a declaration of war on our part imprudent & impolitic. In forming an opinion we ought to examine impartially the whole case. And I hope we shall never go to war for the meer punctillio's of honor — Never but from necessity — when justice policy & interest demand it.

### *Wednesday Jany 15, 1806*

The Senate without debate agreed to give Dr. Logan liberty to bring in a bill to prohibit all intercourse between the United States & the Island of St Domingo — ayes 27 nays 7. I voted in the negative.

### *Friday 17th.*

Mr. Bidwell & Mr. Early came up with a bill that the Other House had passed appropriating $2,000,000 *towards* enabling the President to maintain the expence of the intercourse between the United States & foreign nations. This bill was passed in the House yesterday with closed doors by a majority of about 20. These gentlemen bro't it up & delivered it to us when our doors were closed — & with it a confidential message from the House stating that the object for which the bill was passed was to enable the President to purchase land from Spain — to wit the Florida's. The bill was read in the Senate with closed doors & passed to a second reading.

---

The President communicated confidentially an Extract of a letter from Mr. Monroe our Minister at London dated Oct 18, 1805 with a postscript of the 25th.[68] Mr. Monroe is of opinion that we have little ground to expect an amicable adjustment of our differences with Spain. That he has no doubts that the captures of our vessels made by British cruizers & the condemnation's of them by their Courts of Admiralty, is by order of their Government. That they are systematic & persevering in their measures — That a prospect of obtaining redress from them is feeble & distant — That an idea prevails in England that our government is too popular to act with energy, & therefore they have little to fear from us. Mr. Monroe advises that our Goverment should as it respects G. Britain and Spain act with energy and decision. He evidently discovers strong prejudices against the English nation.

As soon as the letter was read, it was said to be the request of the President, that it should be delivered to Mr. Coles, as it was the only copy they had time to make — which was done — & by him delivered to the other House.

---

The Senate advised to ratify two Indian Treaties [69] — The one with the Wyandot, Ottawa, Chipawa, Munsee, Delaware, Shawanees & Potawatamies, dated July 4, 1805. The Indians cede lands & establish boundaries. The United States to pay them

[68] For the message with accompanying documents, see *American State Papers,* II. *Foreign Relations,* II, 727–773.
[69] See *American State Papers,* IV. *Indian Affairs,* I, 695–696.

an annuity of $1000 forever. And also $16,000 to be paid by Installments. This last sum, & $175. of the Annuity is paid & secured to be paid by the Connecticut Land company tc. — to whose use most of the ceded territory reverts.

The other treaty is between the same parties & of the same date. The Indians cede to the said " Connecticut Land Company, & to the proprietors of the Half million acres of land lying south of lake Erie, called Sufferers' land " — certain tracts of land, & said companies pay to said Indians $18,916..67.

As these two Treaties were for the use of Individuals & the payments are principally made by them, & the Government is called upon to ratify their bargains, I did not feel justified in voting against the ratification and as I had some doubts, I retired to the fire side & did not answer when called. All the Senators present voted in their favor.

### Saturday 18th.

In the morning I called upon my friend Capt. O'Brian [70] formerly Consul to the Barbary powers. He is a bold brave enterprizing man. He was in the Mediterranean at the time when Barron superceded the brave Preble. And he (O'Brian) had previous to that time acted as the aid of Preble so far as related to treating with those regencies. He assured me that the fleet which Barron then had in those seas, without any aid from Eaton or Hamet Caramelli was fully sufficient to have battered down the walls of Tripoli — destroyed, or captured Hamet Jessuff the reigning Bashaw. Mr. O'Brian blames in strong language the fear & weakness of Lear. He says that almost every officer in the Navy was opposed to Lear's treaty for peace — that Barron was as feeble in mind as he was sick in body. That he has the information from unquestionable authority that at the time when Lear signed the treaty, — Hamet objected to the restoration of his brothers wife & family

---

[70] Richard O'Brien, consul at Algiers.

as the treaty provided — Lear told him that he should never be required to do it — that that article was necessary to quiet popular clamours but he never expected it should be executed. — Captain O'Brian, in confidence, added he did not think we needed the aid of the Ex Bashaw — that our own naval force without that was fully adequate.

---

Capt O'Brian waited upon me to Soliman Melimelli — we found him on the carpet prostrate in the act of worshipping his God — He received me with much ease & professions of friendship.  In the course of conversation he told me that his house, exclusive of the furniture, cost him $80,000.  His Secretary is a young but very cunning active man.  He shewed me some of his drawings & writings which were very accurate.

---

Visited the Osage Indians, & the other Chiefs from the borders of the Missouri.  All their interpretors were present. They told me that they generally beleived in the existance of ONE *Great spirit* who was able to do them much good or much hurt — but that they fully beleived he was inclined to do them good & not evil — That he had no equal — no son — no beginning, no end — no one with whom he consulted — That they never assembled to worship him — That when they die & fall to dust, like the precious seed that falls to the earth, they do not expect to perish, but to rise & live in another & better world than this.  I asked them if they beleived in revelation or in any Devil or evil spirit — They said No.  They are temperate — avoid ardent spirits.  The *Osages* are a very civil & quiet people.

They have neighboring Indian nations who resemble the ancient Tartars.

In the course of the week the Marquis D'Erujo, the Spanish Minister, came into the City. He has visited the Heads of Department; but they have not returned the visits. This very much offends him. He clamours against them. Our Administration has requested the court of Madrid to recall him. He is now considered more as a spy than a minister.[71]

---

Some days since as Genl Turreau was writing to his Government his wife came by him with a smothing iron & struck him. He rose & beat her cruelly with a large cane. She cried murder — the children & servants came in crying — instantly the Secretary of Legation raised the windows, & to drown the noise played furiously on the French horn.

---

I am now from a variety of circumstances fully satisfied that France has several ministers in disguise — spies — in this country. That nation has carried their system of espionage to great perfection. There is no nation but what feels its fatal effects.

### Sunday Jany 19, 1806

From the most correct information I can obtain it appears that nearly a year since our Government applied to the Spanish Court to recall the Marquiss D'Yuro. The causes for this were two, his inflamotory letters & opposition to the Presidents establishing a port of Entry at the Mobile — & his attempt to induce Major Jackson the Editor of the *Register* to publish certain essays in justification of the measures of Spain, & aspersing our Government. To this request the Court of Madrid

---

[71] Don Carlos Martinez Yrujo, Spanish minister at Washington, as intimated by Plumer, became *persona non grata* to the Jefferson administration. This episode, including Yrujo's relations with Jackson, editor of the Philadelphia *Political Register*, is well related in Adams, *History of the United States*, II, 258 ff; III, 184 ff.

replied — that the Marquiss had intimated that he should soon wish to return — & that they should prefer his returning upon his own motion to recalling him.

I think this is the same answer that the Court returned to a similar request made by the Administration of John Adams.

It appears not only that our Heads of departments have not returned the visits to the Marquiss — but that Mr. Madison, the Secretary of State, when visited by him, treated him with great caution & coolness & avoided conversation.  A few days after the Secy sent him a Card in which he intimated to the Marquiss that his presance at the seat of Government was not agreeable to the President — & that it would be a desirable thing for him to depart.  The Marquiss is in a rage — swears he will tarry as long as he pleases — & that he will publish to the world the proceedings & secrets of our Government.

I ought to have noted sometime since that the Administration have discontinued the guard which they at the first placed at the Tunisian Ambassadors house.  The boys & negroes no longer consider him as an object of curiosity, & therefore they do not intrude upon him.

### Monday 20th

The Senate imposed the injunction of secrecy on its members respecting the bill mentioned p. 173.[72]  This was done by a resolve.

### Tuesday 21.

The bill last read was this day again read and the question was shall this bill pass to a third reading [73] — On this question the following debate ensued

---

[72] Pages 379–380 of this volume.

[73] Of this day's debate, J. Q. Adams remarks (*Memoirs*, I, 387); "The secret bill was taken up in committee of the whole, and pressed through to the third reading with the most anxious solicitude to suppress all discussion and all enquiry."

Mr. Adams This bill places $2,000,000 of dollars at the discretion of the President. The confidential message from the other house states it is to enable him to purchase Spanish lands —

Had the President intimated to this House that he needed money I would agree to grant it altho he did not state for what purpose he required it —

But I am not willing to pass it on the grounds stated by the House of Representatives. Tis not a *useful* object.

From the Diplomatic documents it appears Spain is not disposed to sell us land —

That she is unfriendly to us — & has committed outrages against us on sea & land —

With such information what prospect of purchasing.

I hope its friends will assign reasons in favor of its passage, & not make laws without discussion.

*Mr. Anderson,* I am not yet prepared to give my assent to this bill.

*Mr. Wright,* This is for a peace establishment. Its more honorable to acquire dominion by purchase than conquest. It will not cost half so much to purchase peace & territory as to fight for it.

I hope the bill will soon pass — for if it remains with *us* I fear it will not be kept *secret*.

This is a *paltry sum* to trust to the discretion of our present Chief Majestrate.

*Mr. Mitchel,* I am in favor of this bill — False erroneous opinions have prevailed respecting the *extent* of Louisiana — We did not purchase near so much as was reported.

We purchased Louisiana, more or less — Spain always protested agt the construction that Louisiana included either or any part of the Florida's. In this she acted an open frank & honest part — she was in fact a party to the cause. The conduct of our Government in relation to this conduct of Spain was unjust & impolitic — We disregarded her just complaints relative to boundaries. We erected a port of Entry on the Mobile but with caution —

France, & with propriety, justifies this conduct of Spain.

Spain never ceded the Florida's to France — of course we have no title to them. Spain has an unquestionable right to exact duties from our vessels passing in the Mobile. 'Tis within her territory.

The raising troops — making fortifications by the Spainards, is no breach of peace — because I am confident they have been made within their own limits.

These considerations I urge to shew that we have no cause to arrange ourselves in a hostile manner against Spain.

Our Ministers at Versailles did expect when they purchased Louisiana that our Government would give such a construction (altho' they knew it would be a forcible one) to the Cession as would include the Florida's. They did expect that our Govt would forcible take possession of them — & that France would enforce our claim. But France since then has settled her differences with Spain — our army did not take the possession — & now France says, & says truly, Spain has not ceded the Florida's — & I will not give you possession.

The purchase of Louisiana small as it is, is an advantageous one. The Florida's are more important — we must purchase them. It was the Alpha & omega of our former negociation.

We are not prepared for war —

We have difficulties with France — to satisfy France we must interdict the trade with St. Domingo.

With Great Britain, I see more serious difficulties — but we must make commercial regulations — we must pass laws that will induce her to adopt better terms.

*Mr. Anderson* I am opposed to the bill not on account of its containing the principle of purchasing — but for giving the authority to borrow money — Shall we borrow when we are at the sametime representing our treasury as full & our debt as daily diminishing.

*Mr. Saml Smith,* I do not like the principle of borrowing money — but I will not restrict the Administration because I am confident nothing but unexpected necessity will ever induce them to do it. We have on several occasions given authority to the present Administration to borrow money but they have never used, & will never abuse, that authority. However I should not be willing to pass this bill without such a provision.

The bill then passed without a division to the third reading.

---

Today I had a conversation with Dr. Logan upon the subject of his bill prohibiting all intercourse between the United States & the island of St Domingo — I observed to him that the provisions of his bill could not possibly effect the object. For it only prohibited our custom house officers from clearing out any vessel to that port — when in fact, none, or scarse any, are now cleared out for it — but vessels who are trading to the islands clear out for the *West Indies generally,* & not for any *particular island.* He replied he " knew that — & it was not his intention to prohibit the trade — but only pass a bill that would please the French, which he said this bill would do — & not injure our own traders," The French cannot be deceived by such flimsey acts as these!

It is said that Turreau is much offended that our Goverment have published his letters & Talleyrands upon this subject. And 'tis added that Mr. Madison has answered Turreau's notes in which he justifies our trade to that island.

---

### Wednesday 22d.

On the 14th Dr. Mitchell speaking in Senate on the subject of the British having in the present war introduced new principles into the law of nations in relation to the commerce of Neutrals,

and there captures & condemnation of our ships & commerce —
& repelling a motion for further information from the President — said that the Secretary of State had made out a statement of the subject at large — that he had ordered it to be printed, & that it would be soon laid on our tables.  On the 16th a pamphlet of 204 pages was accordingly laid on our tables — entitled " Examination of the British Doctrine, which subjects to capture a Neutral trade, not open in time of peace." [74] This is the work of Mr. Madison.  It discovers that he has read many, & consulted more books, upon the law of Nations, in relation to the rights of Neutral commerce.  But it is evident that he is not thoroughly master of the subject.  He is often obscure & sometimes unintelligible.  He extends the discussion too far — 'tis too prolix for common use.  But the greatest lies in not stating precisely the doctrine he intends to maintain, & the points now in dispute between the Government of the United States & that of Great Britain.  This is really a great defect — & another not unimportant is, that no end or use is stated for writing this work — no system intimated by which we are to obtain redress for the wrongs committed by Great Britain.

This is a subject on which I do not pretend to much information.  But I never read a book that fatigued me more than this pamphlet has done.  That circumstance may arise from my want of information on the subject.

If I understand the difference between the United States & Great Britain it is this.  The US. contend that we have a right to bring in our ships the produce of the islands & colonies of the belligerents to our own ports & having landed them here & paid the duties on them, we then have a right to export & carry those articles, that are not contraband of war, to any of the ports of the Belligerents that are not blockaded.  Great

---

[74] Printed in full in the *Writings of James Madison* (Hunt, ed.), VII, 204–375.

Britain agrees to this doctrine with this proviso, to wit, that this circuituous trade shall be confined as it was used & practised in times of peace — or in other words that we cannot in any case even by this circuituous rout carry the productions of a belligerent colony to its mother country unless *it was a trade we used & had a right to, previous to the war.* No part of the contest respects the exportation of our own produce, or the importation of articles from any Country for our own consumption. 'Tis confined to our *Carrying trade only.*

It also *appears* from some documents, that Great Britain also requires evidence that the Colonial produce which we bring here & afterwards export to the Belligerent was brot to the US. for our own consumption & not for re-exportation. A thing very difficult to prove.

To return to Mr. Madison's pamphlet — tho' I think he discovers strong prejudice against Great Britain — tho' the work has faults — yet I think it useful — it contains many facts — &, in several instances, very justly exposes the fallacy & inconsistency of the British Courts of Admiralty.

### Thursday 23d.

On the question whether the President should be requested again to communicate to the Senate the letter of Mr. Monroe mentioned p. 174,[75] Mr. Logan said he should vote against the resolution — No man is wise at all times — the President was off his guard when he sent us that letter — it ought never to have been communicated to the Senate though under the strictest injunction of secrecy — The letter contains sentiments unfriendly to peace. If we make this application for the letter again, we shall justify the mistake & error of the President in first sending it. The President committed one error, & I will not consent to pass a vote that will approve of that, & request him to committ another. I again repeat the letter breathes a spirit of war & blood — this Senate is for peace.

---

[75] Page 380 of this volume.

### Saturday 25.

Dined with Genl Turreau the French Minister  The dinner was splendid, & the *furniture* of the table superb — more so than I ever beheld.  His servants were well dressed — His cook was richly clad.  I do not relish french cookery.  His fruit was rich & various — still more so his wine.  His guests were Genl S Smith, Mr. Thurston, Dr Logan & Myself from the Senate, — Mr J Randolph and Mr. Livingston from the House — The Marquiss D'Erujo, & Mr Facio the Spanish Secy of Legation — Mr. Peederson Swedish Charge des Affaires — Mr. Duval Comptroller of the Treasy — Mr. Petrie Secy of French Legation, & the General's private secretary.

The General received his guests very politely & attended to them with much frankness & assiduity.  Dr. Logan, with a spirit truly servile, in the hearing of several of us, told the Genl, that the bill to interdict the trade of the United States with St Domingo would pass the Senate as 21 to 7.  The General, not only sensible, of the impropreity of such language from a Senator, but its being rendered peculiarly so, from the circumstance of one of the Minority (myself) being present — & the indelicacy of rendering it the subject of conversation — would not appear to hear it — but instantly with a raised voice introduced a new topic.  This piece of politeness was due from him — He exhibited it in that graceful manner which is so common & so pleasing with the French.  Tho' I still think he has a heart devoid of morals — yet a sense of propriety — of manly pride — will often induce him to perform acts of decency & politeness to which many of our Democrats are strangers.

The Generals wife was yesterday delivered of a son.

At eight clock it was announced that coffee was ready in the Chamber — as the company walked up stairs I took my hat in the Entry.  The Genl accosted me in a very familiar style — Ah! saith he you have a saying that applies to leaving

company without ceremony, that you call "French leave"—
You must not, said he, Monsieur be permitted upon your first
dining with me to depart without coffee"—then taking me
by the Arm he very politely conducted me to the Chamber.

It was a little singular that of the small company who dined
with him this day there were men from four different nations
— & from six different American States, yet all but myself
could speak the French language. The Minister speaks our
language brokenly—his secretary fluently. The knowledge of
the French language is much more necessary & useful than
that of either Greek or Hebrew. The latter is worse than
useless—tis lumber in the mind.

In private conversation, I alternately pressed the Secy of
Legation from France & the Secy from Spain—upon the treatment that the Marquiss D'Erujo has received from the Heads
of Department. They avoided & evaded as much as they
could politely the subject. After the bottle had circulated with
great freedom, on renewing the attack, I found them, as is
usual on such occasions, more communicative. They informed
me that the Marquiss came here with a disposition to cultivate
peace on just terms with our Government—That the treatment
he had received from the Secy of State was such as precluded
the Marquiss from seeing the President—But Mr. Facio added
your laws I know—your Constitution I understand—I have
lived here nearly 12 years—& I know that Your President,
with all his power—hath no authority to send *any* man, not
the meanest malefactor, out of this Country without his consent—much less can he remove an accredited Minister against
his will from residing in any town or city, as long
as he pleaseth. Spain, said he, is willing to pay for her own
spoilations on your Commerce—but will not for those of France
—Though she regrets your purchase of Louisiana—she has
no objection to establish its just boundaries. Your claim to
West Florida has no foundation—the manner in which you
announced it was as disgusting as its foundation was futile.

In turn, as I expected, they intimated a wish to know what caused the private sessions of Congress. I replied, I was surprised at the question — but more so if they really expected an answer. However, I observed, such was the cause of business in the Senate that in all appointments the Senate proceeded with *closed doors* — this would account for our private sessions — But as to the House — I as a Senator am not to know them, & therefore cannot disclose them. — Like Free Masonry, most secrets, I presume, of public deliberate assemblies are in their nature unimportant — *the main thing* is to keep the object so far unknown as to attract notice.

## Monday 27.

I ought to have observed that in the debate in the House of Representatives, the last week, upon Mr. Sloan's [76] resolution to impose a tax of ten Dollars upon every slave that should be hereafter imported into the United States — Mr. Broom, the Member from Delaware made some severe observations on the State of South Carolina importing slaves, & its Members advocating the horrid doctrine of slavery.[77] The evening following O'Brien Smith, one of the Representatives from South Carolina, sent a note to Mr. Broom requesting an explanation. The next day in course of debate upon the same subject — Mr. Broom said he was sorry to say that the preceding day in the warmth & animation of debate he had said things improper of South Carolina & its Representatives. This fully satisfied Mr. Smith.

This is nearly the whole of three days that the Senate have spent upon the question whether they will advise the President to appoint James Wilkinson to be Governor of the district of Louisiana — & John B. C. Lucas to be one of the Judges of the Supreme Court of that territory.

[76] James Sloan, representative from New Jersey.
[77] For Broom's speech, see *Annals of Congress,* 9 Cong., 1 sess., 365–371.

The objection stated agt Mr. Wilkinson was that he was now Brigadier General of all the Armies of the US. & that it was — antirepublican to unite a civil & military office in one person — The question was decided ayes 17, nays 14.[78]

To the appointment of Lucas evidence was offered to prove him immoral — ignorant of law — tyrannical & oppressive in office — ayes 16 nays 15. Note every federalist voted for Wilkinson & against Lucas. This is the same Lucas who procured the impeachment & conviction of Judge Addison in Pennsylvania.

### *Wednesday 29th.*

The weather has for several days been very pleasant & mild indeed — Farenheits thermometer this day in the shade stood at 60 — that is 5 degrees above temperate heat. We have yet had no snow. —

In the course of conversation this day with Dr. Logan of the Senate — I asked him what course could be taken with effect to settle our differences with Great Britain — he replied " I would adopt the same measure as the Federalists did when they were in power — I would send to the Court of London — a man of talents & integrity as Envoy Extraordinary & Minister Plenipotentiary — & not trust business of such importance to a Minister [Munroe] [79] who is running from London to Paris — from Paris to Madrid — & from thence to London again — but who in fact is not resident any where."

### *Thursday 30th.*

The weather is still remarkably mild — tis warm — Farenheit's thermometer in the shade stood at 66.

Yesterday Mr. Gregg one of the Representatives from Pennsylvania moved in the other House a resolution That untill

---

[78] Jefferson had some doubts as to the propriety of the appointment of Wilkinson; Jefferson, *Writings* (Memorial ed.), XI, 112.

[79] Brackets appear in the original manuscript.

equitable & satisfactory arrangements respecting seizing our seamen & capturing our vessels shall be made between the Governments of the United States & Great Britain, it is expedient, that from & after the . . . . day of . . . . next, no goods, wares or merchandize, of the growth, product or manufacture of Great Britain, or of any of the colonies, or dependencies thereof, ought to be imported into the United States: provided, however, that whenever arrangements, deemed satisfactory by the President of the US, shall take place, it shall be lawful for him, by proclamation, to fix a day on which the prohibition shall cease. — [80]

In the Senate the bill heretofore mentioned, appropriating of $2,000,000, for foreign Intercourse — was read, Genl Bradley moved an amendment designating the object for which the appropriation was made to wit — to enable the President to obtain the free navigation of the river, the provinces of Canada, Nova Scotia & the Florida's by purchase or *otherwise.*  He said we had difficulties to adjust with Great Britain as well as Spain — That if we had a war with either, it might be important for the President to be authorized to obtain possession of said Provinces — The provinces at the east are as important to the Union as those at the west.  This amendment will conciliate the Eastern States — it does not oblige, but only authorizes, the President to act.

If the amendment is rejected I shall vote for the bill — though I consider the amendment as important. —

It will conceal the real object from Spain.

*Mr. Bayard,*  This bill gives too much discretion to the President — it does not oblige him to expend it in the purchase of lands — He may expend it in bribes if he pleases — in corrupting the Courts of France and Spain — if they are capable of further corruption.  The bill does not restrict him —

---

[80] For the text of the resolution, see House *Journal* (1804–1807), 250–251.

The Amendment is a decent cloak for passing the bill — it renders the appropriation definite.

*Mr. Anderson* The answer to this is the law we passed in Feby 1803 a similar law for a similar purpose [81] — Reads it — I am against delay. —

*Mr. Tracy* I really wish for information on this subject — I wish to know what is the true object of the bill — Is the money designed to add to the corruption of European Courts — Is it to bribe Talleyrand & his adherents?  If to purchase lands, the amendment is proper — it renders the appropriations definite. —

The $2,000,000 mentioned in the law of Feby 1803 was designed for the purchase of the Florida's — It never was applied to that use.  The appropriation was unnecessary.  If the President wishes to negociate for lands he can do it — witness his numerous Indian treaties. — The amendment would authorize an exchange — to exchange the useless unbounded swamps of Louisiana for the Florida's — Is it not of as much importance to the Union to obtain Canada & Nova Scotia as the Florida's? Is not Halifax a nest of pirates will it not soon be more vexatious to us than Algiers? —

A few years since we expended fifteen millions to purchase Louisiana — this, if a benefit, was principally so to the West & to the South — We were then told by many that they then wished to obtain Canada & Nova Scotia.  But now opposition is made to a clause merely to authorize the President to obtain it — if he thinks proper.

I am not talking for the public — not for news papers — not for my constituants — for the Galleries are closed.

The bill before us appears to me an encroachment upon execu-

---

[81] This act appropriated a sum of $2,000,000 " for the purpose of defraying any extraordinary expenses which may be incurred in the intercourse between the United States and foreign nations."  For the full text, see *Annals of Congress,* 7 Cong., 2 sess., 1560–1561 (Appendix); also *Statutes at Large,* II, 202–205.

tive measures — upon the treaty powers of the President &
Senate — particularly of the House against the Senate. Is it
designed as a pledge on the part of Congress to bind us to
approve of a treaty before it is made.

The *haste* to pass this bill looks more like a design to purchase *men in Europe* than a province in America.

Silence & hurry have ever fatally attended all we have done
relative to Louisiana — Is it still to be hurried — I wish those
who are advocates for this bill would give us reasons why it
should pass. I am anxious to know them.

*Mr. Baldwin,* I am always glad to hear bills discussed —
They produce conviction — The bill does not express its real
object — I wished to have it — but think it now impracticable
— The not confining the bill to any particular place has a
tendency to prevent local prejudices — This is in fact a contingent fund — when the Barbary affairs was pending we
granted an appropriation of a million of dollars — We did
indeed then designate it to be applied to the Barbary
powers —

The boundaries of Louisiana — are loose — the manner in
which we acquired it — & the difficulties attending it are so
great that we should purchase more — My confidence in a future
purchase is not great — still I am for making the attempt.

*Mr. Worthington,* My mind is much divided on the subject
of this bill — I think I shall vote in its favor. — I beleive the
President will make a good use of it — The purchase of
Louisiana is beneficial to each & every State — The idea of a
seperation — of a division of the Union is painful — I think of
it with horror. — The eastern frontier of the US. is strong the
South & West is feeble — We want to purchase the Florida's —
to remove our bad neighbours further from us —

I do not feel much confidence that this appropriation will
answer the purpose but I am for trying it.

I see no reason for purchasing in the East — The purchase

in the west of the Florida's are of as much importance to the eastern States, more so to their commerce, than to the southern & western States.

*Mr. Israel Smith,* The purchase of territory to the United States as such is not necessary or useful — But to remove bad neighbors & settle boundaries tis highly useful. Nova Scotia will facilitate the fishery — Canada the fur trade — In both the people are numerous & may be highly useful. To give the President power to obtain the eastern territory is as requisite as in the west. It will tend to conciliate the eastern section to the government — It will conceal the object from Spain. It leaves it to the Executive — it does not bind him.

*Saml Smith* Had the bill come from the other House with the provision contained in the Amendment I should have voted for it.

The port of Halifax in case of a War with Great Britain would prove of immense use to that nation & of equal injury to us. I ergo consider our acquiring those possessions as of great importance.

I consider the amendment as important in another respect — it authorizes the President to obtain the territory in question by purchase or *otherwise.* That last word is important — It would authorize him to send troops if necessary to repel aggressions — obtain possession of territory & thereby have the power of doing ourselves Justice.

I do not know that this bill will do us any good — the former did not — The bill is not a secret — tis known to the Foreign ministers here — tis talked off out of Doors — I think we could purchase in the markett better without it — The former law did no good — it did injury — it locked up much money — we lost the interest of it —

We did not get so much land by the former purchase as we expected — We were disappointed in it — I do not know how to vote on this amendment I am not prepared to vote for or against it — I wish time — I ergo move for a postponement till tomorrow — postponed — 17 voting in the affirmative.[82]

---

Mr. Adams, the Senator from Massachusetts has drawn up three resolutions upon our disputes with Great Britain [83]

1  That the captures & restraints imposed by that nation on our Commerce are wanton & unjust — That they are violations of the law of nations — That she has no lawful right in time of war to confine our trade to the same limits as it was in time of peace.

2.  That the President be requested to instruct our Minister at the Court of London to *demand* restitution for these outrageous injuries, & *insist* upon the same without delay. —

3  That a law be passed prohibiting the transfer of all stock in the funds & in the bank of the United States that now stands in the name & to the use of any subject of Great Britain.

I have seen the resolutions in his hands — I have given the substance of them  He has not yet offered them — He contemplates moving them in the Committee of the Senate upon that part of the Presidents message relating to aggressions on our Commerce.

The Marquiss Yrujo has published two letters, the one a letter written in December to the Secretary of State accusing the President with making inaccurate statements agt Spain in his message of the 3d of that month to Congress — The other to the Public Ministers accredited at the United States inclosing the first, giving them liberty to publish it — & complaining of the conduct of our Government to him.  Copies of these letters I now have.

---

[82] J. Q. Adams characterized this as " one of the most curious debates I ever heard in the Senate;" *Memoirs*, I, 392.

[83] The account of the framing of these resolutions and their subsequent history occupy a large portion of J. Q. Adams, *Memoirs* for several days (I, 390–400).

The note to the Secretary of State respecting the President's wish to him to retire, & the marquiss's reply, I have not seen. The latter is insolent. In it the Marquiss says, " The Envoy extraordinary and Minister Plenipotentiary of his most Catholic Majesty receives not commands from any other power but from the King his master. " What course our Government will adopt is enveloped in mystery.

### Friday 31.

The same Bill as was mentioned yesterday was again read — And the debate on the Amendment offered yesterday by Mr. Bradley was commenced by

*Mr. Anderson,* It was with difficulty that I could bring my mind to beleive that the gentleman from Vermont (Mr. Bradley) was serious.

The real object of this bill is to purchase the Florida's —

The aggressions of Great Britain on our commerce — the design of our raising 100,000 militia — the difficulty of settling our commercial affairs with that nation — render it impolitic to adopt the amendment — It will excite too much jealousy in that nation.

There is no prospect that Great Britain will sell —

We have reason to beleive the President wishes the bill to pass in the same form as it passed the other house.

*Mr. Bradley,* I am serious — The amendment will not embarrass the object intended by the original bill —

The Amendment goes to authorize the President to take by force & arms the Provinces of Canada, Nova Scotia & the Florida's. — The public message — & the public expectations — &, what is more, the state of the Union, require us to give such discretionary power to the Executive.

This authorizes the President to treat of peace — & if necessary to act offensively — I am not prepared to say we must submit tamely to injury & insult.

To the bill for calling out 100,000 of the militia, I shall move an amendment to authorize him to enlist of them a certain number for 6 or 12 months — & if this amendment is adopted he will then have power to march them into these territories — Without this amendment I doubt whether the President can march troops out of the U. States.

*Mr. Anderson*  The extent to which the gentleman carries his amendment renders it alarming. 'Tis giving the Power to the President to declare war — A doctrine unconstitutional, dangerous & extremely impolitic. The right of declaring War is in Congress they cannot delegate it to the President.

*Mr. Adams,*  I am not opposed to the primary object of the bill — in case there is a necessity for the purchase — & a probality of affecting it.

I am in favor of the Amendment because it specifies the objects for which the appropriation is to be made — The bill does not specify any object — but leaves it altogether to Executive discretion.

The former law, of Feby 1803, was accompanied with a private confidential message from the other House that those $2,000,000, was for the purchase of the Florida's — But Louisiana, not the Florida's was purchased not for two, but for $15,000,000. A similar message from the other House accompanies this bill — but what assurance have we that this money will be applied to that purpose more than the former. The amendment fixes it.

Our ministers tho't when they purchased Louisiana they also purchased West Florida. Reads confidential letter from Livingston &c to Secy of State in April 1803 — [84]

The Gentleman from New York (Dr. Mitchell) the other day

---

[84] See *American State Papers,* II. *Foreign Relations,* II, 552 ff. In a letter to Madison, under date of June 7, 1803, Livingston and Monroe stated: " We are happy to have it in our power to assure you, that, on a thorough examination of the subject, we consider it incontrovertible that West Florida is comprised in the session of Louisiana," *ibid.,* 564.

said we had no right to West Florida — I cannot absolutely say
we have no right to it — But tis proper & necessary now to fix
an object for which we appropriate — That we may not hereafter be told when we acquire the Province of Quito that it includes the Florida's.

I think the purchase of Louisiana was a good one — but I
think it improper to say that by purchasing one tract we buy
another.

I see no use of this appropriation without the amendment —
with the amendment he may negociate or act offensively — it
gives a useful double edge to the instrument.

We have come to a situation with Great Britain in which the
more we can raise her jealousies & excite her fears the better
for us. Should the President take possession of the port of
Halifax it will tend to convince GB. of our importance — & of
the ease with which we may annoy her West India possessions.

*Dr. Mitchel,* I hardly know even at this late stage of the
bill how I shall vote —

We complain of former Administrations for squandering
monies & involving us in debt. But what have we done since
we have had power — We have had & still seem to have a land
mania — I hold in my hand treaties — a volume — made with
Indians this session for the purchase of lands — A few years
since we purchased Louisiana — a world without bounds —
without limits — We gave for this $15000000 — Still we say we
have not land enough — we must buy more — we must have the
Florida's — What next — why all the Globe — why this rage —
Have we an inhabitant for every acre. At a time when our
rights on sea & land are outraged — when our commerce is
checked by captures & our territory left defenceless — why
neglect our own peace & security for the purchase of useless
provinces? — Are our resources adequate for defence & protection — & the purchase of mere provinces. The first is most
important — The last unnecessary.

I think more can be said in favor of the amendment than of the bill — As much can be said in favor of buying Canada Nova Scotia & New Brunswick as for the Florida's — The coal & plaster of Paris in these eastern provinces — their numerous inhabitants whose manners habits & language are similar to our own — are infinitely more important than the barren wastes of the Florida's —

But look at the Map of America — how easy may enemies — Indians — be bro't down from Canada upon New York —

If we owned Canada we should derive much revenue — We should be able to abolish the long line of custom house officers on the division line.

There is less extravagance in this purchase than in that of Louisiana.

There will be a union of a Country under one government which in the early days of Revolution Congress thought necessary — & in vain attempted to affect it.

When the navigation of the Mississippi was obstructed — it seemed then as if the national pulse was about to cease — we obtained it — & now we are told with like importunity — we must purchase the navigation of the Mobile *or* we are lost.

This national extravagant appetite to buy land is a disease. But if it must be indulged why not gratify it by a purchase of Provinces in the north?

He then read a letter from Mr. Livingston the Minister to himself dated Sept 1805 —

I considered Florida a part of our purchase & my advice to our Government was to take possession — & I urged that I should justify to France our conduct — for France was then disposed to do it —

France never would when we treated with her admit or deny the question whether she had a title to West Florida — the fact was France had not at that time examined how far her claims extended.

[Note, the two last paragraphs are the substance of what the Dr. read from the letter] [85]

I beleive on this subject, delay will afford us safety — We had better examine two things critically before we act — our danger from abroad & our means to repel it. And 2d what use the territory will be to us if acquired — Moved to postpone it for a fortnight — only nine rose in favor of it.

*Mr. Hillhouse,* I wish for time — for a free discussion — the measure taken in connection with our situation is important.

This is not a common subject of legislation — if we pass a law that operates unfavorably we can repeal it, but an error here has no remedy —

We cannot keep this law a secret when its passed — a knowledge of it in Spain will convince that Nation that our opposition to them is to consist in negociating — This bill has nothing effective in it — it has neither bones or sinews — The amendment gives both —

Mr. Monroe writes from London that energetic measures alone can operate on either Great Britain or Spain — The amendment holds the olive branch of peace — negociation but if these are rejected it authorizes other & more dignified measures in the last resort.

The bill in its original form is in support of the idea that Mr. Monroe says Europe has of us — That we have no energy — that our resort is to money — to buy peace tho' at the expence of our honor — to receive injury & insult — pocket it — & buy, meanly buy peace.

This bill, passed under our peculiar circumstances, will render us contemptible —

Some appear to fear amendments because it may endanger its existence in the other House. This argument goes to the very existence & use of the Senate. It destroys deliberation — it renders us useless.

---

[85] Brackets appear in the original manuscript.

But its said that it will produce delay.  What shall We suffer by it — Who wants to purchase the Florida's — I know of no competitor.

Haste in legislation is destructive to our interest, honor & safety.

I have yet heard no reason for the bill no substantial ones agt the amendment.

*Mr. McClay,*  Different subjects ought never to be combined in the same bill — The Amendment & the bill relate to Countries totally dissimilar — The Port of Halifax is of too much importance for Great Britain to sell —

We have information that Spain will for a reasonable sum sell the Florida's — The amendment ought therefore to be rejected.

Spain owns the Florida's — we want them — it would be unjust to obtain them by war — the amendment will justify war — I shall therefore vote against it — The Bill authorizes a purchase I shall therefore vote for it.

*Mr. Saml Smith,*  I do not think the British would for a trifle sell Halifax — As to Florida we have long since sent a Minister to Spain to purchase — Spain has refused to sell — I *ergo* beleive it is not more easy to purchase of Spain than of Great Britain.

From the documents it appears that Spain will not on any account sell Florida's —

I do not mean to take any part either in respect to the Amendment or the Bill.

*Mr. Kitchell,*[86] If the amendment prevails it will ruin the bill — If the principle of the amendment is good, let another bill be bro't in — but not annex it to this — Here it will embarrass us — It will exasperate Great Britain against us — We have already too many enemies — With Great Britain we must adopt more energetic measures than with France or Spain.

*Mr. Pickering,*  I will say one word — At our former purchase — New Orleans & West Florida was our object — Louisiana was meerly accidental —

---

[86] Aaron Kitchell, senator from New Jersey.

France is now triumphant in Europe — Great Britain is now contending for her existence — the pressure upon her is great — tis increasing — The Canada's are burthensome to her — Under these circumstances she may probably be induced to sell them on reasonable terms — The amendment gives the President the power to accept the terms — & If we must appropriate monies for purchasing lands the amendment renders the bill more perfect.

Amendment lost ayes 10 — nays 21.

*Mr. Bayard* The terms of the bill are too general — It is confined only to foreign Intercourse — it can never be applied to defence — its true meaning can never extend beyond ascertaining the limits of our territory.

Our lines with Spain are disputed — tis agreed these must be settled.

If West Florida is to be purchased — let it be avowed — Let us know our object —

Offers his amendment which was to apply the money to ascertain fix establish and *defend* the boundaries of our territories.

This will enable the President in case negociation fails to take possession & do ourselves justice — If this amendment prevails, & the money is applied, either our limits will be established by negociation — or the President will have authority to do it by the strong arm of the Union.

Ayes 10 — nays 20.

The question then was shall the bill pass.

*Mr. Bayard,* The question is important — because its probable it will carry the bill into a law. A little time has changed the state of public affairs — a short time may produce other & great changes. I really want information on the subject of this bill. I want time to obtain it.

If I was an enemy to the President & his Admõn I should gratify that enemity by wishing this bill to pass. Public opinion calls for more energetic measures — This bill is degrading — it will soon be so considered.

I wish to know what injury delay will occasion —

What are the specific objects to which this money is to be applied — what specific loss will a few days delay occasion? Tis said there is to be a Congress of European Powers. How does this appear — rumours in public papers. I beleive myself Bonaparte will form it in his own camp.

If a Congress in Europe what have we to do with it? Is this Money to be appropriated to buy votes — or to defray the expence of a member.

If such a Congress it will set long — If you send a member there what have you to do with it — Is it to be an auction for the sale of lands — Is Florida's to be their sold at auction — or is the question of boundaries to be there settled? No Sir, It is to settle the peace of Europe — & what have we to do with the entanglement of Europe? We have no connection with the objects of such a body. If something more material cannot be offered I see no evil from postponement — no necessity for precipitation.

I do not know from whom this bill comes — Not from the President — not from the Chancellor of the Exchequer [Mr. Randolph] [87] If the President wishes for it why does he not inform us so — why not take the responsibility of the measure.

'Tis important — our country is involved in serious difficulties with more than one nation — why lock up $2000000 when we actually need it — When it does not appear the appropriation will be useful.

We want information from the President. His public message is, perhaps, the language of a *bold patriot* — but the bill is that of a *broker*. I am therefore *bound* to beleive this measure is not agreeable to the President.

Since this bill has passed the other House the Spanish Min-

---

[87] Brackets appear in the original manuscript.

ister has here in this city grossly insulted your President. When such insults are offered will you appropriate money to buy his land — Will you treat with Spain when her humble agent is insulting your Chief in his palace. This bill looks too much like the language of a Jew broker  Have we no other spirit — no other power but to raise & pay money to the use of those whose feet are trampling upon us?  You invite the cupidity of all nations to injure & insult you.  Nations who adopt such measures accelerate their ruin.  Rome by purchase induced the Barbarians to leave her territories.  These very purchases induced their return — & terminated in the destruction of the Roman power.

This is not a time to pass this bill — Is this money to be paid to the Marquiss Yrujo — What is your dispute with Spain — are they not confined principally to the Mobile.

We are on the eve of a war with a powerful maritime Nation — it requires all our resources — why embarrass our measures & exhaust our finances at this time in such a purchase.

Of what consequence is it to us whether the boundaries are settled this year or not.  It is good policy to let them remain in statu quo & turn our undivided attention & powers to Great Britain from whom we have much to fear.

I do not see how our President can submit to the insults he has received from the Spanish Minister in his own doors. We must attend to this case —

Moved to postpone — 12 only voted in favor of it.

Motion for adjournment — lost by majority of one.

*Mr. Adair,* We are told this $2,000000 is for the purchase of the Florida's — tis to be given to a Minister — he is to treat — & if he pays the money on a bad bargain — The treaty is to be laid before the Senate  they are, tho' they dislike its terms, to advise to its ratification or loose the money.

In the former bill no use was made of the money to our advantage — I am told on good authority that when Talleyrand heared of that bill he raised the price from 10 to $15,000,000. The passage of that law shewed to him our eagerness to purchase.

I do not like the project as proposed by our ministers in Spain — they relinquish territory they ought not — And I fear men of like opinions will be sent there.

I wish to see a treaty — before we pay money for it. I shall therefore vote against the bill.

*Mr. Hillhouse* at this late hour an adjournment is refused — Gentlemen who favor the bill refuse to assign reasons in its support — They discover an uneasiness to hear any reasons agt it — But I must & will state my objections.

No money is to be drawn from the Treasury or applied to any purpose but by law. This bill applies the money to foreign intercourse, & without a violation of law he cannot appropriate a Cent to purchase territory. He may apply it to corrupt & bribe but not to purchase — such nefarious measures I will never support.

Adjourned

### Sunday Feby 2d.

John Cotton Smith said he wished the Government had authority to suppress all Newspapers — That he was now ready & willing to enter into a private association to affect that object.

### Monday 3d.

I have taken considerable pains to make up my mind upon the subject of fortifying our ports and harbors. This is a subject that is now pending before both Houses. Most of the federal Gentlemen appear zealous in favor of the measure — but I am strongly inclined to think I shall vote against it. 1st. Because I do not think that the whole revenues of the United States for any one year would be equal to erecting fortifications to each of our ports and harbors so as to be able each of them to defend themselves against the attack of a single 74 gun ship.

And if any defence is made, it could not be less than this — if it is to answer any valuable purpose of actual defence. Whoever will turn his attention to the Map of our Country — whoever will examine a seaboard of 1700 miles in extent must be satisfied of the fact that the *whole amount* of our revenue for any one year would be inadequate to the purpose. But if *necessity* required it the revenues of ages ought to be mortgaged for the purpose.

2. I can see no necessity whatever for the measure — I have not satisfactory evidence that any Nation will attempt to invade us. I think it is altogether improbable that such an event will happen.

And 3d It would not only cost an immense sum to make the fortifications & provide the requisite artillery ammunition &c — but by erecting them you would entail to posterity a very considerably *annual tax* for there support. For the works when once erected, & the artillery provided, must be preserved & maintained.

The question on the $2,000000 bill was again bro't up before the Senate —

*Mr. Hillhouse.* I wish some gentleman would inform me how this money can be drawn out of the Treasury & applied to the purchase of the Florida's.

The Constitution has provided that no money shall be drawn from the Treasury but by law directing the object & design for which its drawn. This is a wise provision.

How can you draw money appropriated for *foreign intercourse* to be applied to a *land speculation*. This bill is therefore I presume to be passed to enable the Executive to bribe & corrupt the agents of European powers.

With Barbarians we advance money, but not with civilized nations, untill after a treaty is ratified.

This bill will raise the price of Florida.

It may alarm G Britain, because it is furnishing France &

Spain, her enemies, with money — This is giving aid to one of the Belligerents — & may be a cause for war.  The purchase of land may be only the pretext, but the object of paying the money may be only to aid one of the Belligerents.  This doctrine deserves much attention, in our present critical situation with Great Britain.

Your President has been grossly insulted by the Spanish Minister, would you appropriate money to enable him to induce the Marquiss to leave your Country — Would it not be better to pass a law authorizing your President to carry him out of your country.  The case is somewhat similar — Spain has insulted you by aggressions on your territory — claiming your lands — instead of repelling these encroachments you bribe her Officers — you buy land with a view of buying peace.

The President does not wish this law — tis impossible — because it is opposed to his public messages — they all speak a different language.  He cannot have a public mind — at variance with his private Communications! -

If you bribe France to coerce Spain to sell Florida, you do an act as immoral as to hire a highway robber to rob a traveller.

Your territory is already too extensive for your population. It weakens your force — why then extend it.  You do not want the land — It can afford no aid to your Commerce —

You have a bill for appropriating of $2,000000 for militia — Your ports & harbors ought to be fortified, & your Navy encreased.  Have you money for these purposes & for the purchase of the useless sands of Florida?

*John Smith of Ohio,*  The only information I have is from the house of Representatives — I have none from the President or heads of Department, that the object of this bill is to purchase the Florida's.  I knew not how, or from whence the House obtained their information — but I beleive it correct.

I think the object is important — The acquisition of the Florida's is important — There is a valuable harbor there.  The lands have much pine & live oak timber — The free navigation of the Mobile is as important as that of the Mississippi — It runs through a rich valuable territory —

In 6 years Mr. Washington had authority to loan $27,000,000. In three years Mr. Adams $13,000,000 — In 5 years Mr. Jefferson has had authority for less than $5,000,000. Why therefore complain of trusting his discretion. His predecessors had more — they nor he have not abused it.

No evidence of fraud — The appropriation is general — but I think may be applied to purchase the Florida's.

France has a right to purchase Florida of Spain — & we of France — This is no violation of neutrality with England — Tis like purchasing goods of England.

*Mr. Saml Smith,* I think we are told by the President we have in the treasury a surpluss of a Million of dollars. If we now pass this bill Will it not take one million from the eight millions which we are bound by law to appropriate for the payment of our debts — for let gentlemen remember we have not yet this session — this year — made that necessary appropriation.

*Mr. Tracy,* If you pass this bill now you cannot meet your other demands — you cannot meet those which we are bound to appropriate for payment of our debts — Unless the President borrows — the money — Do Gentlemen pretend this call is so pressing as to render it necessary for the President to open new loans.

If we are to pass this bill, because the other House has done it — we are useless.

The Presidents speech shews a million surpluss, the bill requires two millions — G Britain will soon have the knowledge of both. It will cripple us in their estimation to see us engaged in a land speculation — & that on the system of borrowing money.

I beleive a majority of the Senate are in heart opposed to

the bill — but the fear of opposing the other house — of damping the spirit of purchasing territory — will I fear insure its passage.

The other day we were told the President was waiting for the passage of the bill, that he might send of the money. If so your Treasury cannot pay off your debt as you engaged.

If the *bill* only is to be sent — you will injure the purchase — it will shew our anxiety to obtain the land — & will raise the price.

If we buy — France will do as they did in the sale of Louisiana — She obtained as much in money as if she had not obliged us to pay for her spoilations on our own Merchants. We gave her price — paid Own Merchants & relinquished our claims on France for them. This manner of proceeding served to bribe our merchants — silenced their opposition agt. that Treaty. The same course is now to be pursued. —

This bill can do no good — It gives no authority to purchase — The President has the power. It will lock up the money — though the President will never use it — It reduces him to the necessity of borrowing on interest — It will & must raise the price. 'Tis a useless nefarious bill.

*Mr. Worthington,* The Florida's are important & we must obtain them. We shall have money enough — if not we can borrow.

*Mr. Kitchel,* This is a favorable time to purchase — Spain is oppressed & needs money.

*Mr. Adams* [88] I have no objection to our obtaining the Florida's. But I must vote agt the bill — because no reason has been assigned that renders it necessary.

If reasons do not exist for passing a bill it ought not in any case to pass.

The recommendation of the other House — no reason for us to pass it.

---

[88] Adams states (*Memoirs*, I, 400): "I made a very incoherent speech, without order and without self-collection."

The President recommends in Message of Dec 3d the surpluss of the money in the Treasury to be applied to means of defence — Reads page 11. of that message.

West Florida I consider as our own — we have bo't & paid for it — But the other House by this appropriation relinquish it — for they never would appropriate $2000000 for East Florida. Our Country will never be content to purchase the same land twice. —They ought not.

Refers to the Correspondence of Livingston & C Pinkney — who then advised to the taking actual possession of the very land we now are to purchase.

It was stated in Oct 1803 by a senator (Genl Dayton) that in New Orleans he was assured by the French Commandant or Prefect that he intended to take possession of both the Florida's — that he considered the title of France under the treaty of St Idelphonso to the Florida's as compleat.

$2,000000 for East Florida is extravagant — its object therefore is both — & ergo wrong — as it cedes our just claim.

This bill opens a door to bribery & corruption — to improper speculations — There is a vast deal of diplomatic skill in France. Under a Convention with France, a french minister may acquire much money — It difusses new sources for corruption & speculation in our own Country — The former Convention has created much uneasiness which is now unfolding itself.

*Mr. Saml Smith* The discussion of this day presents the bill in a new aspect. It seems that the money is instantly to be drawn from the Treasury & be placed in the hands of our Minister who is to treat —

States that this appropriation will affect that for the paymt of our debt.

Reads the last page of Message Dec 3d. —

What will you do for defence of our harbors I would borrow — but I fear it will with others have a powerful effect in voting against defence of the harbors &c.

I want time to enquire — Moved for an adjournment — 17
voted to adjourn — carried.

After we had been about half an hour in debate with closed
doors upon this confidential bill it was discovered that there
was a spectator in the gallery.  The man was there it appeared
very innocently — He stood behind one of the pillars when the
door was locked.  He was a man of little information — a
countryman.  During the time he was in the gallery the bill
was read at full length.

### Wednesday 5th.

The bill to prohibit intercourse with St Domingo being the
order of the day for its second reading Mr. Bayard previously
moved a resolution requesting the President to lay before Senate
the answer that the Secretary of State returned to the French
Minister's notes &c on the subject.  The Senate negatived the
motion.  Dr. Mitchel told me the reason why those who wished
the bill to pass had agreed to negative the call for papers, was
the knowledge that Mr. Madison's answer contained a vindication of our right to trade to that island — & that if it was
produced it would have a powerful tendency to prevent the
passing of the bill.

### Thursday 6th Feby 1806.

*The Confidential bill under consideration.*

*Saml Smith.*  It is probable there will be a *surpluss* from
the revenue of two millions of dollars for the year 1805, instead
of one, as stated by the President in his message of Dec 3d.
This information I have from the Secy of Treasy.  It is contemplated if the bill passes to send only one million — & a
loan to be made in Holland for the other.  I think the Finances
of the United States are able to meet this bill. —

The sums appropriated for the support of the Govt & the
$8,000,000 for the payment of public debt have the priority over

all other appropriations — And if any defalcation happens will fall on this bill.

It is the course at the Treasury that when any defalcation happens for the Secy of Treasy to state all the Appropriations — the dates of the laws — and then the Pres't without being bound by dates of the laws — determines on which Appropriation law the defalcation shall fall.

*Mr. Adair*, I have objections to the bill that I cannot state — I am not at liberty —

The bill is unconstitutional — on account of the appropriation being so indefinite — The President might under this law expend the money in support of armies —

The Constitution authorizes one senator more than a third to reject a treaty — this bill will destroy that important right — for it may pass by a majority of only one — The money may be by a minister paid to purchase a Province & when the treaty is returned you *must* ratify or lose the money. This doctrine is too dangerous — We may have a President in whom we may have little confidence — Why destroy our means of security.

*Mr. Adams* moved That a Committee be raised to consider this bill & examine the treaty ceding Louisiana to us, April 30. 1803 & the documents to enquire & report whether by that treaty we have acquired a title to West Florida. I am satisfied our claim to this Province is good — This bill virtually relinquishes our claim to it —

It is impossible to suppose any man can be so extravagant as to give for East Florida $2,000,000. In the private instructions given by our Govt two years since to our Ministers they were prohibited from giving more than $667,000 dollars for it.

These documents (accompanying the treaty of Cession April 30, 1803) was unknown to the House — hence its more important to the Senate who have them to make the enquiry.

*Mr. Anderson* I am sorry the motion is made at so late a period.

There is nothing in the bill that shews the money is to purchase West Florida.

If we maintain our claim for West Florida we must expect war from France.

*Mr. Wright,* It is the *treaty* — not the opinion of our ministers that must decide whether we own West Florida —

Are we to distrust the President?

*Mr. Bayard,* The object of the motion is to ascertain as far as we are able the boundaries of the territory we purchased of France April 30, 1803 — If from this investigation it should be evident that we own W. Florida — a less sum than two millions will be necessary — Are we in such a situation that renders it necessary that we should legislate in the dark & without information — Do Gentlemen fear information — will it defeat their favorite bill — Let them declare —

*Mr. Saml Smith* I see no use in a reference — I formerly thot West Florida was included in the cession of Louisiana — But I now have strong doubts of the fact — this therefore induces me to favor a new negociation —

If the Committee report W. Florida is ours — if they convince us of the fact — will that convince Spain — We must either treat or fight with Spain — or leave our boundaries unsettled. I know we can with arms take possession — but I doubt the right — I *ergo* am in favor of negociation — & agt a committee.

*Mr. Pickering* — We want necessary information. In 1804 The President himself declared W. Florida was ours — he declared it to me

[*Mr. Adams* reads letters from Monroe & Livingston in 1803 — communicated to Senate Oct 1803 — confidentially.] [89]

They had no doubt of our title

*Mr. Mitchel,* I am unwilling to vote agt obtaining information — but in this case I must — 'Tis too late — There are

---

[89] See note 84. The brackets appear in the original manuscript.

doubts of our title to W. Florida. The report of a Committee cannot remove them. Spain is positive that her title is good — a Committee therefore can do no good. 'Tis better to buy it a second time than fight for it. If we have bo't it of France, we must now buy it of Spain. We have lately done so with Indian tribes. The fact is France had no title to W. Florida yet we bo't it of her, altho' Spain at that time protested agt. it. — This Committee would delay the bill a long time — & in the end do no good.

I am *now* much more inclined in favor of passing the bill — & therefore agt the motion.

*Mr. Tracy* It was my wish, & my request at an early hour to have it committed — It was then refused — Gentlemen say in purchasing Louisiana we acted with too much haste — yet the same precipitation is now practised — Why this fatal haste in every act of our's that relate to that Country?

If a million of dollars can obtain a settlement of our claims with Spain if that is to pass thro' France still I am willing to raise it.

I wish to know the President's design in having this bill pass. A Committee can obtain that — If that Committee do not promptly attend & report the friends of the bill can & will discharge them. — But you are never to suppose a Committee will delay unnecessarily.

Reads the Confidential message of Dec 6th [90] to shew that the President did not want money for negociation but to raise & pay troops — but not for a *formal war.*

*Mr. Saml Smith,* I do not recollect that this Message was ever read in Senate — This Message is the foundation on which the bill rests. It will justify the measure — till now I have been in the dark & so has the Senate.

*Mr. Tracy —* The message contemplates force not money for

---

[90] The message bears the date of December 6 but was received by the Senate on December 9; *Annals of Congress,* 9 Cong., 1 sess., 18–19.

a treaty — for treaty he needed not the aid of Congress — He can without us proceed —

After a debate of near three hours — ayes 8 — nays 23.

---

The question on the passing of the bill —

*Mr. Pickering,* We are not distressed for want of land — our population is so scattered that we have no strong *point* anywhere.

He offers a resolution for a call for papers from the President relative to instruction to Mr. Monroe &c for the former purchase & what evidence of title he has in his possession to West Florida &c.

*Mr. Israel Smith* I have always been clear that we had, & still have, no title to W. Florida — The Ibberville is the boundary —

7 only voted in favor of the motion.

At Three OClock motion for adjournment denied 13 only in favor.

Motion for the passage of the bill.

*Mr. Bayard,* The subject is of great magnitude — it may ultimately require $10,000,000.

This is jeopardizing the peace of the Country —

Scarsely has the dust settled under the feet of your Ministers to Spain since they demanded their passports — before you again come forward to negociate with the same nation & on the same subject.

But if negociation is necessary there is no need of this bill — Our claim on Spain for her spoilations on our Commerce far exceeds the value of the Florida's —

Our Government claims damages for the suspension of the right of deposit at Orleans. Are not these sufficient without money.

But, Sir, there is another point of importance — if you make a new treaty for the purchase of this territory — do you not necessarily waive your right for the preceeding claims.

This bill must necessarily raise the demand for the territory — tis therefore imprudent & impolitic in us to pass it.

This is not the Presidents measure — for all his communications to us are directly against it. — The President asks for force in his message of 6th Decr — I would give it to him — It is the correct ground — tis manly — & demands our support.

It is on the recommendation of the other House. I think I discover a strong reluctance in Gentlemen agt mending the bill from a fear if sent to that House again that it would not pass — They would reject it.

I am willing to trust the President when necessary — but here I see no reason — no necessity for it.

We once trusted him with $2,000,000 to purchase Orleans — & West Florida — we then had no view beyond it — But under that indefinite confidence — he purchased Louisiana & involved us in a debt of $15,000,000. Will you again blindly pursue a similar course? Yet your President tells you in that same message of Dec 6, for your $15,000,000 you have only Orleans & a *string of land* upon the Missisipi.

What hands are you likely to fall into the same you did before. Beware of the diplomacy of France — It will deceive you.

What is your object — you have land enough — more than you want — But you want the navigation of the Mobile. Is your want so great so pressing as imperiously to compel you to obtain it *now?*

This bill contains no constitutional appropriation — 'tis an abuse of words. The design of the constitution in requiring appropriations to be made by law was to limit & specifically designate the objects for which the money was to be applied.

" Foreign intercourse " extended only to support your Ambassadors — or at most to pay tribute to Barbary powers —

untill the $2,000,000 bill which passed in 1803 — But you now render appropriations useless — You do this at your hazard — What the very men who were once so boisterous in complaining agt former Admõns for not being particular in appropriations. This line of conduct may be fatal to those now in power. A few years may place them in the minority. I beg them sincerely to consider what will be the consequence if Your President under an Appropriation for foreign intercourse should apply it to buy land?

I remember a great clamour made by those now in power agt taking money where there was not a specific Appropriation. I mention this in due time — that if you think proper you may now remedy the evil by mending your bill.

Is this money to go to Spain — Do you beleive if we did not fear France the bill would pass? If you pay it to France — you pay it as a bribe — for all agree she has no title to the land in question. You may call it a douceur — a present — you cannot change the nature of things — but still it will be bribery — it will be corruption. Are honorable gentlemen prepared to go this length. I have done my duty — I now feel as indifferent as others to its fate.

[Note Mr. Bayard was up one hour.] [91]

Mr. Sumpter called for an adjournment — 16 in favor carried.

---

The President made a confidential Message. It enclosed a letter from Mr Monroe our Minister at London of Nov 26, 1805 to our Secy of State, announcing that he had received a letter from Lord Mulgrave the British Secy of State upon the subject of their spoilations upon our Commerce. Mr. Monroe adds that there was a prospect of our complaints agt. that Government terminating favorably.

---

[91] Brackets appear in the original manuscript.

Lord Mulgrave's note to Mr. Monroe was dated 25th Nov. he apologizes for not returning an answer sooner — by saying that the subject was important — & he had caused it to be referred to those best acquainted with it for their examination & report, which he had not yet received — and presumed that Mr. Monroe would not complain of the delay when informed that it was the intention of the Ministry fully to investigate the subject & then return an answer thereon.

## Friday 7th.

The Confidential bill was at twelve OClock again called up, & the doors closed — The question was on its passing —

*Mr. Sumpter,* If the object be to purchase the Florida's I think it unnecessary. At *this time* I think the US. better without that country than with it. That country has a sea-coast of near 500 miles — It is accessible to shipping — our seacoast is already too extensive for our means of defence — If it should be inhabited we must protect them however sparse —

This is near Cuba — & exposed —

This coast will be favorable to smuggling.

Has our peace in that quarter been disturbed? No — it has not — nothing has happened there to alarm even our timid fears. We have nothing to fear from its present inhabitants.

This Country is now a barrier to us.

If the object is to settle our boundaries the sum is too large.

The acquisition of that country will be injurious. to us.

'Tis unusual to vest Ambassadors with such sums —

The measure is at variance with the messages of the President & the communications from all our Ministers.

I will never legislate in the dark — When I have examined & made up my mind on a subject I always intend, regardless of the opinions of others, to vote in such manner as justice, & the honor & interest of my country require. On this bill I think it my duty to say I am bound in conscience to vote against it — Neither justice or policy require such a law.

*Mr. Pickering,* I have been much gratified — If Spain requires duties on the Mobille we can impose similar ones on her.

The President has not communicated in any message to the Senate that he wishes such a law. 'Tis too undignified a course for him to communicate his opinion in such an indirect manner as by private conversations with individual senators. And I am sorry to say that from the decõns of so many senators I am compelled to beleive the fact.

We have *official* information that Spain peremptorily refused a few months since to cede the Florida's — Must we not then beleive this appropriation is for bribes to France.

Was not Spain offended at our having Louisiana — She views us as a jealous unwelcome neighbor.

Are we willing to take a cession of Spain — humble depressed Spain — carried by all-powerful France. —

Will Talleyrand serve us for nought — ? He is the most corrupt Minister in Europe. He has become rich — immensely rich — He has made Nations tributary to his coffers — He has heretofore required douceurs from us. If thro' his agency we are to obtain this territory — he must be *bribed.*

We know the character of our Minister there — His conduct in relation to claims under the treaty of April 30 1803 is well known, particularly in relation to Nichlin & Griffith — he was guilty of such base conduct as has tarnished his fame — [92]

[States that case] [93]

What line of conduct then are you to expect from him — And we have no reason to beleive we shall soon have another minister at that Court.

---

[92] The minister referred to was John Armstrong. Nicklin and Griffith were the owners of the ship *New Jersey,* illegally captured under the authority of France, and partly compensated for from the Louisiana fund. For the correspondence in the case, see *American State Papers,* II. *Foreign Relations,* II, 774–775.

[93] Brackets appear in the original manuscript.

Two years ago we were told the purchase of Louisiana would secure peace with Spain — We are now told we must purchase the Florida's or we must have war.

If Spain is now compelled to cede the Florida's — The cession will be void both in a moral & political view. 'Twill be the cause of future war, should Spain be able.

The land is barren & steril — the ports are unnecessary — they will be burthensome.

Whenever, we want if ever, we should want them, we can then obtain them.

*Mr. Tracy,* I *will* speak my mind freely — I dislike the bill — & I am glad that a spirit of it encreases in this House —

This bill is not *secret* — I am very well convinced its *known* to the Spanish Minister —

One objection to the bill is its total *uncertainty*.

Mr. Tracy moved to strike out *two* Million & insert *one*. Mr. Bayard called for a division — first on striking out.

One million is more than the state of our Country — & of our treasury — can afford.

The aggressions on our Commerce may render many of your most mercantile houses unable to pay their bonds for duties.

Why require two millions for this purpose —

The other House say this is done " to *commence* the negociation with more *effect.*" This is plain language — & must we give *bribes* to that amount.

We are immediately to send a $1,000,000 in *specie* out of our Country — This is a serious object.

*Saml Smith* I will set the gentleman right — 'Tis to be in bills — in coffee & sugar —

*Mr. Tracy* Then we are to turn brokers — I hope its not the coffee & sugar of St Domingo — What security have you the British will not capture it — Are the US. to insure it — If Bills of Exchange — there will be a loss.

Your cities & ports require your money to fortify them.

Can your President & Secy of Treasy give such a precedency & priority to appropriations as the Gentleman from Maryland (S. Smith) the other day stated. 'Tis not correct — 'Tis a language not warranted by law — 'tis a violation of law — 'tis establishing an iniquituous system of *favoritism.*

ayes 13 — nays 18.

*Mr. Tracy* then moved an amendment declaring that this money should be applied to purchase certain lands from Spain — [94]

*Mr. Israel Smith.* It appears to me the great object of the Executive is not to obtain an appropriation of money — but to gain the opinion of the Congress whether they wish he should obtain the Florida's.

Ayes 9 noes 20.

Question on the passage of the bill —

*Mr. Tracy* 'Tis now late (half past 4) I see the majority are disposed to sit — I shall make no apology for rising. There is one view of the subject I wish to take of it — It is the one stated by the Gentleman from Kentucky (Mr. Adair) — But I wish to present that idea in a stronger point of view — I mean the treaty-making power —

If one more than a third of the Senate vote agt. a treaty, it cannot be ratified — But what are we doing — We are admitting a principle — a precedent destructive of the constitutional right that is vested in a minority of the Senate. The House of Representatives pass a bill authorizing the President to give millions to make a particular treaty — a majority of one in the Senate agree in the passage of the bill — A treaty then is made by law. Is not this bill an encroachment — is it not destroying that check which the Constitution established. I really

---

[94] The amendment proposed the purchase " from the Spanish Government of their territories lying on the Atlantic ocean and Gulf of Mexico, and eastward of the river Mississippi; " *Annals of Congress,* 9 Cong., 1 sess., 87.

wish gentlemen to reflect upon it — If our government is to be long supported it is to be done in this house.

Tis in the nature of popular houses — the Representatives — to make encroachments —

Mr. Bradley moved a postponement 12 only rose — lost.

The question then recurred shall the bill pass — At 5 OClock it passed. Those who voted in favor of it were, Anderson, Baldwin, Condit, Fenner, Gaillard, Howland, Kitchill, Maclay, Moore, Smith of Maryland, Smith of New York, Smith of Tennessee, Smith of Vermont, Thruston, Turner, Worthington, and Wright.

Those who voted against it were Adair, Adams, Bayard, Gilman, Hillhouse, Pickering, Plumer, Stone, Sumpter, Tracy & White.

Ayes 17, noes 11.

Bradley, Mitchell, Logan & John Smith of Ohio avoided the house previous to the Call [95] — Giles & Jackson were sick & unable to attend. Just one half of all the Senate voted in favor of the bill.

Untill Samuel Smith of Maryland ascertained the fact that the Government in case the bill passed would purchase bills upon Europe for one million of Dollars — & that he might draw to a certain amount bills payable several months hence & have the money immediately advanced to him — he was strenuously opposed to the bill. He will now have the use of many thousands of dollars for six, perhaps 12, months, without interest — Alas for poor human nature!

John Smith of New York, said to me they were heartily sorry the bill was ever bro't into the Senate — But since it was they must pass it — or publish to the world that the President has not a majority of the Senate in his favor!

---

[95] J. Q. Adams, (*Memoirs*, I, 403–404) makes a similar statement.

### Saturday 8th.

A friend shewed me this day, *in confidence*, the last correspondence between the Secy of State & the Marquiss Yrujo. I could not with propriety request a copy — The substance however is as follows. On the 15th Jany Mr. Madison wrote to the Marquiss stating that he in the name of the President had last April requested the Court of Madrid to recal him — That that Court returned for answer that the Marquiss had himself requested liberty to return — & they should prefer his return under his own request to that of recalling him — That the President being informed of his arrival at the seat of Govt of the US. was displeased thereat — & requested him to retire — from the city but that at this inclement season of the year the President would not insist upon his embarking for Spain — But, at all events should expect him to leave the Country the approaching spring — That the US. would receive his successor.

The next day, the 16 Jany, The Marquiss returned an answer, That he did not come to the city of Washington to hatch treason or devise plots against the govt. of the United States. That he came peaceably & innocently — in discharge of his duty as an accredited Minister of Spain — That he was at a loss to conjecture what just offence he had given to the Government of the United States — unless in the affair of Major Jackson more than a year since respecting the publication of certain writings — That he tho't he had long since satisfactorily explained this matter to the Secy of State — That he would now only observe that Jackson being by profession & occupation a *printer*, he was of course a *liar*, & therefore not entitled to credit in what he had said upon the subject — But That if Jackson's declarations were to be credited, What must the people think of the President — for Jackson had published many matters & things of and concerning Mr. Jefferson, derogatory of his character as a man, & highly injurious to his reputation as a statesman.

The Marquiss not receiving any reply on the 19th of the same month, he sent another note to the Secretary — In which he said that he considered the treatment he had received as a direct violation of the rights of diplomatic characters — That he should communicate to all the foreign Ministers near the United States copies of the correspondence that had taken place between him & the Govt of the US. — That the Minister plenipotentiary of his Catholic Majesty would not receive instructions but from his sovereign — That he should remain in the city of Washington as long as he thought the duty he owed to the king his master required his stay — & as long as should suit his convenience & inclination — & not leave the Country till ordered so to do by the King his master, whose orders on all occasions he should cheerfully obey. [96]

In a private confidential conversation this day with Genl Saml Smith — he told me — That the President was immediately, to send the whole of the $2,000,000, appropriated in the bill of yesterday, to France — That the real object & design was to expend it in *bribes* — but that should the purchase be made the sum so expended will form a part of the consideration & be deducted therefrom — That it is a fact well known that if you mean to succeed in the Courts of France or Spain you must make use of money — That a man discovers his ignorance who thinks he can succeed without it. —

That a special Minister will not be sent from hence to France — but that Mr. Bowdoin, the Minister to Spain, will be associated with Mr. Armstrong now at France — That the latter has no knowledge of money affairs — that he can write well — that his speculations are ingenious — but he is not a practical man — not a man of business.

---

[96] Parts of these letters were quoted by Adams, *History of the United States*, III, 185–188. The letters are given in full in *Annals of Congress*, 9 Cong., 1 sess., 1221–1223 (Appendix).

That the *act of yesterday* has thrown an immense responsibility on the President — That he will find difficulty in trusting so much money to any Ministers — That this measure will endanger his popularity.

## *Monday 10th.*

The federalist appear to me not only imprudent — but much more than that — To day at our lodgings Mr. Pickering of the Senate & Col. Talmagdge (of Connecticut) of the House said they were in favor of a measure, " because they beleived it would *embarrass* Mr. Jefferson, the President." Mr. Tracy of the Senate & Mr. Betton (of New Hampshire) of the House, to day said " they voted in favor of a claim upon the Treasury of the United States not so much because they thought it just as that they wished to drain the Treasury " — And both of them have repeatedly said, in my hearing they wished a majority would vote for claims they tho't unjust, so that the administration might feel the evil of an empty treasury. I must own I never felt a disposition to wish success to a measure in Congress I tho't wrong. Whenever I wished success, it was because I judged it right & proper, & my vote followed my wish. Rigid Federalists I think are bad members of Congress. Their prejudices govern more than their reason — Such men ought not to be vested with Legislative power.

This day James Jackson, the senator from Georgia, was tapped, & four gallons of water was drawn from him. At the commencement of the session although he was weak & sickly there was no appearance of a dropsy. He has for some weeks past used but to no useful purpose, the *Fox glove*. He has been very intemperate — ardent spirits have ruined him.

## *Thursday 13th.*

In a conversation with Dr. Logan of the Senate upon the resolution respecting negociating with Great Britain upon

Compensating us for the spoilations on our commerce — I observed to the Dr. I should vote agt. it, because the President was vested with power to negociate & I fully beleived he did not wish to involve us in a war. The Dr. replied — " I have no confidence in the President — he will not negociate unless we resolve it is necessary — He has shamefully neglected the interest of this country by not making a treaty with Great Britain years ago — He has sacrificed our interests by sending such a feeble & improper man as Monroe to the Court of London."

And in the course of debate in the Senate upon this resolution this day, Saml Smith said he had no doubt but that the President had the power to negociate as fully without the resolution as with it. But every body knows the clamour & dust that was raised agt. Jay's treaty with Great Britain — That the President he feared still felt the impulse those impressions made on his mind — & he was confident he would not treat with that nation unless the resolution passed — That it would endanger his popularity — That he was sorry the President had four years ago neglected to make a commercial treaty with Great Britain when it was compleatly in his power to have made one on good terms — And that it was errant nonsense to talk of regulating commerce with other nations by laws — The object could never be attained but by negociation.

When walking home with Genl Smith he told me he had waited on the President & pressed upon him the necessity of sending an Envoy Extraordinary to the Court of London — But he said the president preserved a cautious silence on the subject — & fully convinced him that if the resolution does not pass, the President will prove too timid to negociate with effect.

### Friday 14th

On Wednesday last the Senate took into consideration the report of their Committee upon that part of the Presidents message relating " to the spoilations of our Commerce on the high seas, & informs us of the new principles assumed by the British courts of admiralty, as a pretext for the condemnation of our vessels in their prize courts." This report contains three distinct resolutions. On that day the first resolution was unanimously adopted. It was in the following words, " Resolved, That the capture & condemnation, under the orders of the British government, & adjudications of their courts of Admiralty, of American vessels & their cargoes, on the pretext of their being employed in a trade with the enemies of Great Britain, prohibited in time of peace, is an unprovoked aggression upon the property of the citizens of these United States, a violation of their neutral rights, & an encroachment upon their national independence."

The debate on the second resolution engrossed most of the time of yesterday & to day.[97] The resolution as reported by the committee is in the following words.

" Resolved, That the President of the United States, be requested to *demand & insist upon the restoration of the property of their citizens, captured & condemned on the pretext of its being employed in a trade with the enemies of Great Britain, prohibited in time of peace; & upon the indemnification of such American citizens, for their losses & damages sustained by these captures & condemnations: & to* enter into such arrangements with the British government, on this & all other differences subsisting between the two nations, (& particularly respecting the impressment of American seamen,) as may be consistent with the honor & interests of the United States, & manifest their earnest desire to obtain for themselves & their citizens by amicable negociation, that justice to which they are entitled."

Various motions to commit, & to amend this resolution were

---

[97] The debates on these resolutions are printed with unusual detail in *Annals of Congress,* 9 Cong., 1 sess., 90–112.

made. The motions to commit were lost by a majority of one. The motion to strike out all the words *italized* was negatived ayes 13, nays 16. The motion to strike out the words " and insist upon — upon " was carried by a majority of one. The question to adopt the resolution was carried ayes, 23 nays 7. Those who voted in the negative were Adair, Bradley, Plumer, Smith of Vermont, Stone, Sumter, & Thruston. The motives that influenced & produced this result were various.

My own reason for voting in the negative were That this subject is altogether of an Executive nature & our rules & practise require that we should when on Executive business sit with *closed doors* — & that our proceedings when we act in our Executive capacity should be kept on a seperate and distinct book (Rule 25).[98] But we did *not* sit in our Executive capacity, or enter our proceedings on our Executive book — We deliberated & voted with open doors — & we entered our proceedings on our Legislative journals — And as such it was usurping upon the prerogatives of the President.

This is introducing a new & unnecessary principle into our government. In no case, on the subject of treating with a civilized Nation, have the Senate ever on *their motion* ever underken to instruct or request the President to negociate with any civilized nation. President Washington, did, indeed, soon after the organization of the Government come into the Senate Chamber, &, I think, in one or two instances, send in messages, requesting their opinion whether they would advise him to treat upon certain *specific propositions,* which he submitted to them.[99] And even those, I think, related to treaties with Indian tribes & the Barbary powers. The practise, till

---

[98] Rule IV, sec. 2 of the Standing Rules of the Senate says: " The legislative, the executive, the confidential legislative proceedings, and the proceedings when sitting as a Court of Impeachment, shall each be recorded in a separate book."

[99] See the *Journal of William Maclay,* 128–132; also Hayden, *The Senate and Treaties. 1789–1817.* where the question of treaty procedure is discussed.

now, has been uniform & unvarying for the President to make up by his minister the articles of the treaty & then submit it to the Senate for their consideration, & if two thirds of them advised & consented to its ratification, he was then at liberty to ratify the same. The words of the constitution on this subject are "He (the President) shall have power, by & with the advice & consent of the Senate, to make treaties, provided two-thirds of the Senators present concur."[100] This early & unvaried exposition of the constitution, appear to me the most correct & just.

This will appear more evident when you pursue the subject in its consequences. If it is the *duty* of the Senate to resolve that negociations shall be opened with any nation — it certainly then follows that it is the bounden duty of the President to negociate — for no other branch of the government can treat with any Nation but the President. And if the Senate, as matter of right, have the authority to resolve when & with whom Negociaiton shall be made — they have an equal right to prescribe the principles & draw up the precise articles. The minister is only to be the bearer; & if the nation to whom he is sent refuses to agree to them — The negociation is at an end — or protracted till new ones are proposed — & so on at the expense of much time money & real injury. Indeed in many cases treaties would never be well formed — & in some cases a treaty could never be made. But the fact is no part of the Constitution will justify the Senate in such an assumption of power.

When the Senate pass such a resolution they have no means of executing it. They cannot compel the President to conform to it. 'Tis useless —

But what is still worse, it is mischievous — It removes the just weight of responsibility from the President. It no longer leaves him answerable for his conduct — relating to the inter-

---

[100] Article II, sect. 2., cl. 2.

course with other nations. Everything that removes from or weakens in public Officers their responsibility renders the people more insecure & unsafe.

Tis the duty of the President to manage our exterior relations — 'Tis his exclusive right not only to nominate ambassadors, but to instruct them how & upon what principles they shall form treaties.

I would not encroach on this right — I would not pass a vote that should in this indirect manner arraign & censure him. If his conduct merits censure — meet the subject openly & directly. Pass a vote of censure if propriety & policy require it.[101]

I have plenary evidence that Mr. Jefferson has no wish or desire to involve this Country in a war. It is & long has been his intention to negociate — But the secret is, he himself wished these resolutions to pass — He wished to remove from himself to the Senate the responsibility of a Commercial treaty with Great Britain. He knew the former one (Jays) had occasioned much clamour & had rendered A former administration unpopular. He therefore wished the Senate to place him in a situation that should not only justify, but render it necessary, for him, to treat.

This business has been by Mr. Jefferson, & his friends in the Senate, managed with great address. Worthington & Moore [102] till within five minutes of taking the final question this morning publickly declaimed agt the second resolution not only as to its form but to its principles. Gaillard [103] after the question was called whispered to me that he thot his duty required him to vote against it — Yet all of them voted for the resolution.

The federal Gentlemen were all of them zealous for the measure. They wished to place the President in a situation in which he should not only be bound to treat but to adopt Jay's treaty

---

[101] The remainder of the entry for this date is given in condensed form in Plumer, *Life of William Plumer*, 339–340.

[102] Andrew Moore, senator from Virginia.

[103] John Gaillard, senator from South Carolina.

— to perpetuate a treaty that the President & his exclusive friends had branded with every odious epithet.  They wished to drive the majority to adopt such measures, or they themselves did agt this same majority in the year preceding Jays treaty to wit to abandon Congressional commercial arrangements, to a treaty. —

I ought previous to this to have said that the spirit of the two resolutions are at variance with each other — When critically examined they appear absurd & ridiculous.  The true spirit of them may *justly* be comprized in these words —

Whereas the capture & condemnation of *American vessels* & there cargoes by *Great Britain* is an *unprovoked aggression* upon the property of the citizens of the *United States,* a *violation* of their *Neutral rights,* & an encroachment upon their *national independence:*

Therefore, resolved, That the President of the United States be requested to make arrangements with the British government by *demanding* & *earnestly desiring* them *Amicably to negociate!*

I never like voting for abstract resolutions — They Never do much good — but generally produce evil. But such was the rage in favor of the first resolution that to gratify my friends more than myself I consented to vote for it.  I think it would have been better not to have moved it.

### Monday 17

Thermometer in the shade at 58 — snowed much of the day tho' much disolved — yet evening there was three inches of snow.  This is the first time the ground has been covered with snow this winter in Washington.

The Spanish Minister has at length published in the United States Gazette, a federal News paper, at Philadelphia, his correspondence with the Secretary of State.  These letters I stated in a former part of this Journal.  They are copied in my

*Repository* Volume 3d page **203**. The Marquiss certainly is imprudent & impudent.[104]

## *Tuesday 18th*

All the snow dissolved, & sidewalks on Capitol hill dry.

## *Thursday 20th*

The bill interdicting the trade to St Domingo passed the Senate by a large majority. It is evident the *threats* of the French government produced the measure. My vote was against it. Neither justice — policy or interest required the sacrifice. Several of the Senators from the southern States declared that almost the only reason that reconciled them to the bill was the fatal influence that the independence of the Haytians would have on their own slaves. I think they misjudge — for if those blacks are by us deprived of supplies they will visit our coasts, & thereby gain access to the slaves in the south. If France subjugates them, 'tis more than probable some of them will flee to the southern states.

## *Friday 21.*

The following gentlemen being at Coyle's conversing on the events of the war in Europe Mr. J C. Smith proposed, & with his pencil noted the question & answers — In the order following. Question, " Where is Bonaparte this evening? "

*Mr. Plumer,* In France, if living, & not a prisoner.

*Mr. Pitkin,*[105] In Italy.

*Mr. Tracy,* Has made peace, or is negociating.

*Mr. Hillhouse,* Dead on the field of battle.

*Col. Talmadge,*[106] Severely drubbed & run off to France.

---

[104] The conduct of Yrujo led J. Q. Adams to draft a bill to prevent the abuse of privileges and immunities enjoyed by foreign ministers; *Memoirs,* I, 407. The bill was reported, February 20 (*Annals of Congress,* 9 Cong., 1 sess., 116); was debated at length, March 3 (*ibid.,* 145–161); and defeated, March 9 (*ibid.,* 165–166).

[105] Timothy Pitkin, representative from Connecticut.

[106] Benjamin Tallmadge, representative from Connecticut.

*Mr. Davenport*,[107] Beaten — sued for peace & now negociating.

*Mr. Sturges*,[108] On his way to Petersburg a prisoner.

*Mr. Pickering*, In *cul de sac* — Burgoyned — or fled to France with a small corps of horse.

*Mr. Harper*,[109] Sadly defeated & made his way to France.

*Mr. J. C. Smith*, Victorious.

*Mr. Dana*, In the Tyrolese, or on the frontiers of France.

I have as a matter of curiosity noted these answers, & will, if I recollect, when the news arrives, state the fact.[110]

### Saturday 22

Aaron Burr has been several times in this city this session. He came here a few days since from Charleston. He dined this day with the President of the United States.

### Monday 24

Appointed William Cranch first judge of the District Court of Columbia vice Mr. Kilty resigned.

Pierpoint Edwards of New York Judge of the District of Connecticut vice Mr. Law deceased.

I this day dined with the President of the United States — He was *absent* & appeared in low spirits — oppressed with anxious care — conversed but little. I had much conversation with Mr. Cole's his private secretary — He is a pleasant, companionable — gentlemanly man. In the hours of conviviality he communicated to me much useful knowledge, upon subjects, on which I pressed him, with all my address.

The President observed to me that he feared Congress would

---

107 John Davenport, Jr., representative from Connecticut.
108 Lewis Burr Sturges, representative from Connecticut.
109 Possibly Robert Goodloe Harper.
110 Napoleon was in Paris. His victory at Austerlitz occurred December 2, 1805, and the campaigns against Prussia were not undertaken until the latter part of 1806.

be obliged to be in session sometime not so much on account
of *business,* as to wait the great events that are taking place in
Europe.

### Thursday 27.

It seems that *half joes* are, & for more than a year have been,
coined from North Carolina gold by a mercantile house in
Baltimore. A majority of the Senate, agt my opinion, have
decided that Congress has no authority to prohibit an unauthorized individual from exercising the highest act of soveignty,
*coining money!* [111]

General Turreau, the French minister, in private circles,
expresses strong dissatisfaction with the law interdicting our
commerce with St Domingo — 1. Because it does not require our
merchants previous to their obtaining a clearance to give bonds
with *sureties* that they will not trade with that island. 2.
Because it does not subject the merchant to a penalty in case
he sells his *ship* to persons for the use of the Haytians — And
3d because it does not restrain our citizens who reside *without
the United States* from trading to that island.

### Friday 28th.

I do not know that I have given any account of one of the
most foolish absurd & unjust bills ever bro't into the Senate.
The bill brot in by Mr. Wright *for the protection of American
seamen.* It declares the act of impressing an American seaman
to be *piracy* — It gives to those seamen who oppose impressment
a bounty of $60 — It provides that in case any seamen im-
pressed by the British (for the bill is confined to them) should
suffer death, that the President should retaliate on any British
subject — That each impressed seamen shall have $60 pr month

---

[111] Plumer is referring to the striking out of a section of the bill
imposing a penalty for counterfeiting foreign coins *not current* by law.
J. Q. Adams held that " the Constitution only empowered Congress to
punish for counterfeiting the *current* coin." *Memoirs* I, 416. For the
full text of the section, see *Annals of Congress,* 9 Cong., 1 sess., 143.

for his detention — These wages & bounties to be recovered by suit from any debt due from any American citizen to a British subject — or any property belonging to any British subject where-ever it may be found — And it declares so much of our treaty with Great Britain no longer obligatory as is opposed to the bill.

Jany 16, Mr. Wright gave notice that he should ask liberty to bring in this bill. On the 20th he obtained permission & the bill was read [112] — And from *meer sport,* against my vote, the bill passed to a second reading. On the 29th of the same month the Senate resumed the consideration of it — & Mr. Wright made a speech of two hours — which has since been published in the Universal Gazette (the Court paper) & the Aurora. No reply was made to this speech. The consideration of the bill was further postponed. On the 31st. the senate referred the bill to a committee of five, of whom Mr. Wright was chairman. *February 10th* The committee reported the bill *without amendment.* This is the report that Committees make in two cases, 1st where the principles of the bill & its details are correct — And 2d in cases where they think the principles inadmissable, & that the bill ought not to pass. The latter case governed the committee, each of whom, except Mr. Wright, were clearly of opinion that the bill ought to be rejected. On the *14th of Feby* it was made the order of the day for tuesday — On the *21st* it was moved to postpone it to the first monday of Dec next, ayes 10 nays 19. Different motives produced on different minds a very different result. I voted against the postponement because I wished to meet the subject *directly* & negative it — others voted for postponement because they wished *indirectly* to negative it. It was again referred to a committee of five. Sam Smith was chairman, but Wright was of the Committee. A few days since this last committee reported amendments. One was to strike out the whole of the first bill except

---

[112] See *ibid.,* 55–57.

the enacting clause, and report a substitute more general but as obnoxious as the first. The first part of the report, that of rejecting Wright's bill, was agreed — but the first section of the new bill was also rejected, & after an animated debate of most of the day — this title and enacting clause was again referred to a new committee of seven to fill up with a new bill.

It was apparent, this day, that the friends of this new bill, intended to let it be negatived without debate. But such was the imprudence of Adams, Bayard, Hillhouse & Pickering that they provoked debate. This excited warmth & too much passion. Mr. Pickering is honest, but passionate, & imprudent. His passions often produce as fatal consequences to society as the wickedness of other men. His manners & habits are too abrupt & disgusting. To day, in the absence of Mr. Wright, & in .debate, his reflections were personal & very gross. If he advocates an opinion he generally does it fatally, & arms some of the Senate against him. I really wish he had more prudence — & would content himself with voting only.

The unfortuante course this business has taken, ought to warn gentlemen against the danger of voting to have bills pass to a 2d reading, & to committees, *for the sake of amusement.* Legislative business is too serious for sport!

### Sunday March 2d.

In Pennsylvania, at Lancaster, Dickson a printer has been indicted, convicted, fined $500 & ordered to be imprisoned 3 months for publishing a libel of & concerning Gov. McKean. The purport of it was that he had caused certain offices (prothanatory of a County &c) to be offered to *Wertz* one of the senators, on condition that he would support certain measures. From various publications &c I am induced to beleive the publication was in its substantial parts *true.* McKean is a hasty imprudent man. The majority of the Senate depended on one man — *Wertz* was a young unsuspecting man — naturally vain but frank. The most likely to be tempted — especially as some *doubts* existed respecting his political creed. This same Govr. by removing one of his friends, from the Senate, to wit Mr. Gamble, whom he appointed auctioneer in Philadelphia, created the necessity, as some of his creatures, say, to secure the vote & influence of Wertz in his favor. This Dickson was tried in Lancaster while the Legislature was sitting, & while *Wertz* was present — but neither the Commonwealth or the Respondent called upon Wertz as a witness. The trial took up all saturday & *sunday*. As soon as sentence was pronounced agt *Dickson,* his friends in the *Legislature,* with others, immediately raised the $500 & funds to support him in prison in a higher style than he lived at home. From his prison he is now writing for the Gazette.

---

For a long time it has been bandied about from New Hampshire to Georgia in the News papers &c that *Aaron Burr* was to be appointed Envoy Extraordinary & Minister plenipotentiary to Great Britain. I have Myself given no credit to the relation. Mr. Jefferson has no confidence in him. He knows him to be capable of the darkest measures — a designing dangerous man.

Mr. Burr has been most of the winter travelling from Philadelphia to Charleston — & spending time in this city.

Attempts have been made in New York to form a coalition between the Clintonians & the *Burrites.* The latter have been anxious, & they have confidently affirmed that the Union has been established. The ostensible reason for this measure has been to form a party to prevent the re-election of Governor Lewis in that State. But the true motive with *Burr* has been to give himself importance. This pretended union, for such I have ever considered it, has created in some of the Virginians & southern men a jealousy that the *real object* of the union is to secure the election of either old George Clinton, or his nephew

DeWit Clinton, as president of the United States. This jealousy operates in the mind of Mr. Jefferson unfavorably for Mr. Burr.

On the 18th of last month some Clintonians & Burrites met in New York — vowed friendship to each other — & drank much wine & many toasts. At this meeting Theodorus Bailey, the postmaster (a Burrite) & Wm Smith, the Naval officer, presided as presidents. The proceedings of this meeting was announced as plenary evidence of the union of the two parties.

On the 25th of February last at a numerous meeting of the Clintonians in New York of which the following is a copy of their proceedings as by them published.

" At a general meeting of the republican citizens, unusually numerous, convened at Martling's long room on tuesday evening, Feby 25th, in consequence of various reports & publications tending to induce beleif that a coalition or union had been formed between the Republican party in this State, & the *Burrites*, derogatory to the honor & interest of the Republications.

" Thomas Farmar Esq in the chair;

" 1 Resolved, That it is inconsistent with the honor & dignity of the republican party in this state to enter into any bargain, treaty, or alliance with any other party whatever.

" 2 Resolved, unanimously, That it would not only be degrading to us, but injurious to the republican interest, silently to submit to what any person or persons may attempt to do unauthorized by the great body of republicans.

" 3, Resolved unanimously, That this meeting do not acknowledge the proceedings of a meeting of certain persons at Dyde's Hotel, on the 18th inst. as the act of the Republican party; but expressly disavow & disapprove of the same.

" 4, Resolved unanimously, That *Aaron Burr* does not, & *ought not,* to possess the confidence of the Republican party.

" Resolved unanimously, That the Republicans of this State are willing at all times to receive as friends such of their political opponents as may shew by their conduct that they have adopted Republican principles.

" Resolved, That the proceedings of this meeting be published in the Merchantile Advertizer & in the American Citizen.

> " Thomas Farmar, Chairman
> " Ichabod Prall, Secretary."

I consider Governor Lewis as a useful governor. Whether he will next year be re-elected is uncertain. There is no state in the Union in which the Elections are governed by so few men as in New York.

### Monday 3.

The question was this day taken to advise the President to ratify a treaty made Dec 30th 1805 with the Piankeshaw Indians. I was the only senator who voted in the negative.

This treaty contains on the part of the Indians a cession of a tract of land to the United States. Mr. Worthington stated to the Senate that was *about* 12 miles wide & *about* 90 long.

The United States are to pay to the Indians an additional annunity of $300. And at the signing of the treaty paid them $1100.[113]

### Tuesday 4th.

Genl Wilkinson in a letter to his friend a few days since says " Of all *rogues* a Connecticut rogue is the *greatest*."

Henry Dearbon, Secretary of War, sometime since observed to me, " That he never knew a Connecticut man but what was cunning & knavish."

Tho' I have not much respect for these two men yet I am obliged to say the people of that State have more cunning, more art, hypocrisy & meanness than those of any other State. This opinion is the result of much information on the subject.

All the members in Congress board with me. They have much

---

[113] See *American State Papers*, IV. *Indian Affairs*, I, 704–705.

vanity — they are continually puffing each other in the grossest, &, to me, in a manner, truly, disgusting. Davenport, Smith & Talmage under the mark of religion would destroy every man that differs from them. They serve their God on sundays & the rest of the week they serve themselves — & are not squeamish at doing it At the expence of truth, & justice. Hillhouse is cunning & covetous & mean. Tracy has talents — wit & literature — but his manners are rude & his conversation indelicate. Dana is a belles lettres scholar — more liberal & just — not a slave to money a man of no pleasures — but imprudent. Mosely is a man of wit & pleasantry — liberal in his sentiments — yet sometimes peevish & fretful. Pitkin a man of words — Sturges loves wine & women more than business — Yet he is not an idle man — or is he often intoxicated by the love of either wine or women.

In Connecticut, in almost every town, there are meeting houses, stocks & whipping posts. Articles for which they find much use.

### Wednesday 5.

I have been very much entertained this day in attended to Mr. John Randolph's speech in the house of Representatives upon Mr. Gregg's resolution to prohibit intercourse with Great Britain.[114]

Mr. R. displayed much eloquence. He certainly is an able speaker. His language is very appropriate & forcible. He was decidedly opposed to the resolution — as being unjust & impolitic. He considered Great Britain as now contending for her existance — as fighting the battles of the civilized world against Bonaparte Who is usurping the dominion of the world. That Great Britain & the United States are the only commercial nations — That this resolution is designed to injure Great Britain & the United States & to aid the tyrannic measures of France.

---

[114] See *Annals of Congress,* 9 Cong., 1 sess., 537–574.

That the present administration of the United States is weak & feeble — that it has neither efficiency or system —

That Madison's defence of our Neutral rights, as contained in the pamphlet, entitled " Examination of the British doctrine " &c see p. . . . [115] is not only weak & feeble but destroys the very ground it attempts to support.

That our carrying trade is much of it fraudulent & not worth fighting for.

It was the most bitter, severe & eloquent phillippic I ever heard. I really wish I had a correct copy of it. There will appear in the Newspapers the substance of it — but not its spirit & highly finished eloquence, elegance, & well turned periods — The stenographer cannot relate them.

### Thursday 6th.

Mr. Randolph has this day occupied two hours in the house on the same subject — The attention of crowded galleries were fixed upon him — The senators left their chamber & listened to his eloquence.

He made many just pertinent and noble observations upon his subject — Was uncommonly severe on the President & on Mr. Madison's feeble obscure book.[116]

Mr. Randolph has passed the rubicon, neither the President or Secretary of State can after this be on terms with him. He has set them & their measures at defiance.

He is an eloquent — bold majestic speaker — but too desultory.

He added today to the list of his complaints, that some of our public Minister's, particularly Armstrong was *unfaithful.* That the fact was known to the President — but why he was not recalled he could not tell, unless the Minister & his connections were too powerful.

---

[115] Blank in the original manuscript.
[116] See *Annals of Congress,* 9 Cong., 1 sess., 592–605.

## *Friday 7.*

Mr. Adams sometime since brought into the Senate a bill to authorize the President in certain cases to send foreign Ministers out of the Country.[117] On a former day Mr. Adams made a very able argument, clothed in elegant language & delivered in an impressive manner, in support of the bill. I had myself doubts upon the propriety & expediency of the law — my doubts arose from the single question whether the Constitution & law of Nations did not in fact authorize & warrant the President in pursuing the same course as the bill did. The examination of the subject left me doubting, to remove these doubts on a subject of so much importance to the Nation I was willing to pass the bill, & voted for it. But the bill was negatived by a large majority. The reasons on which many of them voted, as they stated, was that no law was necessary — the President already had the power. But I am confident that some of the majority voted agt. it, because the President had without any statute authority directed the Spanish Minister, Yrujo, to depart from this District — & had taken measures relative to his leaving the United States — they therefore considered the bill as an indirect censure upon the President. Mr. Adams did not so intend it. He is a very honest man — tho' a man of violent prejudices.

## *Saturday 8th.*

The Senate not sitting I attended as a spectator in the House. Gregg's resolution under consideration. James Eliott of Vermont spoke in favor of it near two hours — It was a long time, half an hour, before I could determine whether he was for or against it. His speech wanted animation — his argument logic, & his facts, truth.

Mr. Williams of South Carolina made a concise but eloquent

---

[117] See note 104.

speech against it — He presented in a strong point of view the principal arguments against the resolution. He is a young man.

Mr. Bidwell of Massachusetts closed the argument. He was in favor of the resolution & reasoned more logically than Eliot. He is a man of industry — And in point of talents, I think, superior to any representative from that State. He has much of the confidence of the President — & of course, from that circumstance, & his being a new Member — the federalists affect to contemn & despise him. He is a man not to be despised as it respects his talents & information or as a public speaker — But from the little I have seen of him, he appears to have a small portion of the milk of human kindness flowing in his veins.

The severe philippic that John Randolph pronounced agt. this resolution — agt the President & Mr. Madison, has bro't some members in favor of the measure, who, I beleive, would otherwise been opposed to it. I find that Thomas. M. Randolph & Mr. Eppes, the president's sons in law, appear very anxious for its passage. They & many of the members now seem to lose sight of the principles & consequences that must flow from the resolution.

They now say if it does not pass Mr. Randolph will obtain a triumph over the Administration. And to avoid this, it now appears that the Government think they must use its influence to carry a measure they did not approve. Nicholson's resolution, a partial prohibition of imports extending to particular specific Articles was their measure. The President & Mr. Madison both said previous to the commencement of this debate that Nicholson's resolution must be adopted, & that Gregg's was too extensive. The President said to Mr. Adams if Nicholson's resolve was not adopted we must abandon the carrying trade.

## *Sunday 9.*

In the 61st volume of my collection of *State papers* & in the 3d volume of my manuscript Repository may be seen the letters of Mr. Armstrong our minister to France relating to the claim of the owners & insurers of the ship New Jersey. It seems that the Insurance office at New York sometime sent a remonstrance to the President of the United States expressing in strong terms their disapprobation of the doctrine avowed & the conduct persuued by Mr. Armstrong. In consequence of this, Mr. Madison on the 25th of August, by order of the President, wrote Mr. Armstrong a letter on the subject disapproving the opinion given by the minister. And the President at the same time informed the Insurance office of his having ordered Mr. Madison thus to write, & added he had full confidence in the integrity of the Minister.[118]

## *Tuesday 11th.*

On the 7th I stated that I had reason to beleive that the principal reason why Mr. Adams's bill respecting *Foreign Ministers* failed was because the Administration feared the bill would be considered as a censure for what the President had done in relation to requesting the Marquiss to retire from the city &c without any statute law.

To day Mr. Adams told me, that not knowing that the Administration had proceeded so far with 'Yrujo, previous to his bringing in the bill — he informed Mr. Madison what he intended to do. Mr. Madison approved of it — said it was necessary & very proper.

Mr. Worthington soon after the bill was bro't in applied to the President — he declared he approved of the bill — & added that had there been such law in force, he would before this time have sent the Spanish minister out of the United States.

---

[118] See note 92.

But it seems the measure was abandoned by administration & the bill as has been seen was rejected by a large majority.

I have satisfactory evidence that Mr. Merry, the British Minister, & Genl Turreau, the French ambassador, intimated to our government their wishes that the bill might not pass into a law.

Mr. Adams assured me to day that Mr. Merry remonstrated with him against the bill — And that Genl Turreau entreated him not to press the subject.[119] That the former said that without a statute law the President had no authority in the case. That if the law passed he might abuse his power to the great injury of diplomatic characters. Turreau said he considered this bill as giving no other authority than what the laws of nations gave — but beleived without this law the President would never exercise the power of sending away a foreign minister — And therefore it was important to them that the bill should not pass.

I consider Mr. Merry as a feeble inefficient man — he has considerable knowledge of man & the forms of business —& is easy polite and very civil — But is neither the scholar or man of talents.

Genl Turreau ha's more talents but less science — His manners have more of the soldier than the courtier — & yet he is civil & attentive.

" Foreign ministers, are," as Mr. Randolph justly expressed it, " priveledge spies."

### Wednesday 12.

I have for sometime been convinced that speeches in the Senate in most cases have very little influence upon the Vote. I beleive that in 19 cases out of 20 they do not change a single vote. For this inefficiency there are various causes. All our

---

[119] Adams gives a detailed account of his conversation with Turreau; *Memoirs,* I, 410–412.

documents, communications, reports bills & amendments are printed & laid on our tables & those of us who examine subjects for ourselves & do not vote on the faith of others, reads, & examine & form opinions for ourselves. Having read & examined a subject — we converse with each other & freely exchange our sentiments — This not only confirms or changes the opinion of some, but fixes the vote of others who never give themselves the trouble of examination. Some Senators are implicitly led by the administration — Others have their file leader. When a senator is making a long set speech the chairs are most of them deserted & the vote is often settled in a conversation at the fire side. The conversation is there often so loud as to interrupt the senator who is speaking — for our Vice-President has not the talents requisite for a good presiding officer. Under these circumstances it is often difficult for a man, who knows he is not attended to, to deliver an able & eloquent argument. It is a damper too strong for my nerves — To this add we have no stenographer, & seldom any hearers in the galleries. When the speeches of senators are printed in Newspapers, the speakers are obliged to submit to the drudgery of writing them themselves, which is a severe task. I speak none — at least for this & the last session — & yet my influence on many subjects is not confined to my own vote. I am industrious in all private circles — I openly & frankly express my opinions & assign my reasons. And I have frequently plenary evidence that my brother senators, of all parties, have much confidence in my opinion. For I am influenced by no party views.[120]

In the other House it is different — galleries are usually attended, frequently crouded, with spectators — Always one, often two, stenographers attend, & their speeches are reported in the gazettes. The house is more numerous — several of them absolutely depend upon their file leaders to direct their vote —

---

[120] *Cf.* Plumer, *Life of William Plumer*, 341–342.

Yet I beleive even in that House there are few votes changed
by the public arguments of the members.

There are indeed a few subjects where discussions, in each
house, are useful — where they not only influence the decision
but absolutely govern the vote.

### *Saturday 15th.*

Early this morning I called upon Mr. Clinton the Vice President & conversed with him in private for the space of two
hours.  I owe it to him — I owe it to myself — to say that
the more I see & know of this man the more highly he rises
in my estimation.  He is an old man — time has impaired his
mental faculties as much as it has the powers of his body.  He
is too old for the office he now holds; little as are its duties —
he is from age rendered incapable of discharging them.  He
cannot preserve order — He frequently forgets the state of
business before the Senate — he reads deliberately but his voice
is too feeble to be distinctly heard.  And he assured me that
the sitting three hours in the Chair at a time was extremely
fatiguing to him.  But there is something venerable in his
appearance — There is that pleasing cheerfulness — that easy
access — that flow of good humour — & docile manners, that
are so seldom found in men of his age — & which renders him,
to me, a very interesting companion.  He appears honest.

He informed me that he had not seen Aaron Burr for this
four years.  That he considered him as having great talents —
but as a designing, intriguing, dangerous man.  That his party
in New York are composed of but few & those not influential.
That the Meeting of the Club in the city of New York on the
18th of February (see p. 319) [121] in which Theodorus Bayley
was chairman was meerly accidental as it respected Bayley &
others — That it was planned by Burr — that the real efficient
Burrites had made previous arrangements — That they had

---

[121] Pages 441–442 of this volume.

drawn up their toasts — & while they were at their cups they pressed the good & unsuspecting Bayley to take the chair — That this meeting the Burrites required no terms — no conditions but only that they might be again received into the fold of Republicanism — But before the scene closed Burr was toasted & his merits eulogized. That this being published in the News papers very much alarmed the Republicans in that state — That a meeting soon after was informally called of the most substantial Republicans of the city, at which were present 1500 — For their resolves disapproving of Burr see p. 319 [122] — That the Mr. *Farmar* who presided at the last meeting is A man of great wealth — much integrity — of easy manners, & universally esteemed by men of all parties who know him.

That Mr. Bayley & others who attended the first meeting sent in a letter apologyzing for his attendance & conduct at the first meeting — acknowledging that they had been imposed upon —

The Vice President observed that it was considered in New York, (by those he said who, were in the habit of approving duels) that Genl Hamilton was under no obligation to have accepted Burr's challenge — 1. Because no time, place, or particular word was alledged when & where the offensive accusations were made. & 2d That too much time had elapsed between the conversation complained off & the giving of the challenge.

That Burr's intention to challenge was known to a certain club *Irwin* &c before it was to Hamilton — That this circumstance induced many to consider it more like an assassination than a duel.

That after Burr had slain him — the unremitted censure & pursuit against him was by many considered as partaking of persecution — That this circumstance created especially in the southern States, a number of friends to Mr. Burr.

---

[122] Pages 441–442 of this volume.

That Mr. Jefferson has had no inclination, or the most distant intention, of appointing Mr. Burr minister to any foreign Court. That he himself has caused these reports relating to this subject to be circulated & printed in the News papers in each state to give himself importance in the eyes of the people. —

Mr. Clinton said he had been well acquainted with John Armstrong, our minister at France, from his childhood. That he beleived him an honest man. That in the revolutionary army, & since the peace, in the States of Pennsylvania & New York he had held many honorable and highly important offices — That he had discharged the duties of them with fidelity — That his reputation as an honest man was unblemished. That he had no avarice — that money was never an object with him. That while he was Governor of New York he appointed Mr. Armstrong as a senator of the United States to supply a vacancy. That he did this altho' Armstrong married the sister of Chancellor Livingston — a family with whom he (Mr. Clinton) was not on very friendly terms.

The Vice President in the course of conversation observed that President Adams having, against the will of the strong federalists, sent a special mission to France, & effected a peace,[123] came very near preventing the election of Mr. Jefferson to the Presidency. For added he had we not previous to this named Mr. Jefferson for president we should have supported Mr. Adams.

That the quarrel between Mr. Adams & General Hamilton arose from that mission. That Hamilton considered negociation at that time degrading — & *ergo* broke with Adams. That this conduct lessened the number of Hamilton's friends in New York.

That Hamilton was a great man — a great lawyer — a man

---

[123] William Vans Murray, Oliver Ellsworth and W. R. Davie concluded on September 30, 1800, a Convention of Peace, Commerce and Navigation with France. Ratifications were exchanged at Paris, July 31, 1801, and the convention was proclaimed December 21, 1801.

of integrity — very ambitious — & was very anxious to effect, that ruinous measure, a *consolidation of the States.*

### Sunday 16.[124]

It seems now to be agreed amongst those called the *Court party* that Mr. Jefferson is not to be a Candidate at the next presidential election. I consider the disclosure of this fact as one of the most imprudent acts of Mr. Jefferson's public life. It is letting down his importance — *Most men shun — but all seek the rising sun.* The office of President has a vast weight of patronage attached to it. But as soon as its known that the incumbant at the end of the term is to return to private life — a vast multitude that would be his advocates — trumpeters of his fame — turn their attention to his successor — & make a merit of blaming — censuring — & perhaps, defaming the incumbent. A President if he intends to decline a re-election ought not to disclose the fact to his bosom friend — untill the eve of the election. Mr. Jefferson has now near three fourth's of his term to continue in office!

The more critically & impartially I examine the character & conduct of Mr. Jefferson the more favorably I think of his integrity. I am really inclined to think I have done him injustice in not allowing him more credit for the integrity of heart that he possesses. A city appears very different when viewed from different positions — & so it is with man. Viewed in different situations — different times — places — circumstances — relations & with different dispositions, the man thus examined appears unlike himself. My object is truth — I write for myself — I wish not — I am determined not — to set down ought in malice, or to diminish anything from the fact.

The result of my investigation is that Mr. Jefferson has as much honesty & integrity as men in the higher grades of society

---

[124] Part of the entry for this date is given in condensed form in Plumer, *Life of William Plumer,* 342–343.

usually have — & indeed I think more. He is a man of science. But he is very credulous — he knows little of the nature of man — very little indeed. He has travelled the tour of Europe — he has been Minister at Versailles. He has had great opportunities to know man — but he has neglected them. He is not a practical man. He has much knowledge of books — of insects — of shells — & of all that charms a virtuoso — but he knows not the human heart. He is a closet politician — but not a practical statesman. He has much *fine sense* but little of that *plain common sense* so requisite to business — & which in fact governs the world.

These observations on his character are founded on facts that have fallen within my own View.

An infidel in religion [125] — but in every thing else credulous to a fault!

Alas man is himself a contradiction! I do not however mean to insinuate that Mr. Jefferson is a model of goodness. He has too much cunning. Still I repeat the errors of his administration proceed more often from the head than the heart. They partake more of credulity than of wickedness. Examine his whole life with a view to this fact & you will meet with proof in almost every official act.

Permit me to mention that no one circumstance tended so much to his elevation as the *great confidence* General Washington reposed in him. Washington did this with a full & perfect knowledge of him. They were both Virginians. His conduct during & after the revolution was known to Washington. And altho' Jefferson was publickly opposed to the adoption of the Constitution of the United States yet Genl Washington when called to administer the government gave to Mr. Jefferson the most important confidential office under him, that of *Secy of State*. This office Mr. Jefferson held as long as he wished.

---

[125] See Jefferson's statement of religious principles in Mrs. Smith's *The First Forty Years of Washington Society,* 126–128.

Mr. Washington did not withdraw his confidence from him while in office. The approbation of Washington, under these circumstances, is honorable.

I do not myself so implicitly yield to the opinion of Mr. Washington as some men do. Still I think his approbation is worthy of great notice. It renders popular, the man on whom it has been conferred, to a certain extent.

It seems that Mr. Jefferson & his friends wish that Mr. Madison should succeed to the presidency. John Randolph is agt. Madison — & the avowed advocate of James Monroe.

Mr. Madison has some talents — but he wants nerve — timid & inefficient — in short he is not a practical man. — And that is a declaration that he is not qualified for the office.

Mr. Monroe, is I beleive honest — a man of plain common sense — practical — but not scientific. His conduct in France in the time of their revolution partook of the derilium of the times. It was censurable.

He was an aid in our revolutionary army to Baron Stuben, or Lord Sterling.[126] He was well known to Genl Washington — & was by him honored with the important office of Minister plenipotentiary to the Court of France in a critical time.

But really it is too soon to talk of electing another President. 'Tis unnecessarily involving the Union in turmult. I have no hesitation in saying I prefer Monroe to Madison.

Mr. Jefferson is too timid — too irresolute — too fickle — he wants nerve — he wants firmness & resolution. A wavering doubtful hesitating mind joined with credulity is oftentimes as injurious to the nation as a wicked depraved heart.

### Monday 17th

On the 28th of last month Mr. Jefferson sent a message to the Senate in which he nominated John Armstrong & James

---

[126] Monroe served on the staff of William Alexander, popularly known as Lord Stirling.

Bowdoin to be commissioners plenipotentiary for settling all unlawful captures made by Spain & for settling the boundaries on both sides of the Mississippi.

Note, Mr. Bowdoin is the minister resident at Spain & Mr. Armstrong at France. The special object for which *this* appointment is made, is, in fact, to purchase the Florida's. These commissioners are to have $2,000,000 that we have appropriated the last month on the subject of foreign intercourse, at their disposal. To the appointment of Bowdoin there was no objection — He is not a great man — but I beleive a practical man — whose integrity is not questioned.

The opposition to Armstrong was great. The subject has occasioned much animated debate. The opposition arose from his Conduct as minister in France under the Louisiana fund. It was principally from his conduct relating to the owners & underwriters upon the ship *New Jersey* & her cargo.[127] A statement of that case & his letters respecting it is in my *State papers* Vol. 61, & in my *Repository* Vol. 3.

The strange, absurd & illegal doctrine, for which he contended proves either gross ignorance or fraud. Either of which disqualify him for the office. He is a man of considerable genius — a good scholar & an eloquent writer. But not a man of business — not a practical man. I am strongly induced to beleive that his misconduct in this case proceeded more from the wickedness of the heart than the error of the head.

This day the question was taken in the Senate by ayes & noes — *Ayes* Mr. Baldwin, Bradley, Condit, Howland, Kitchill, Maclay, Mitchell, Moore, Smith of New York, Smith of Ohio, Smith of Tennessee, Smith of Vermont, Thruston, Turner, Worthington. *Noes.* Mr. Adams, Anderson, Bayard, Gaillard, Gilman, Hillhouse, Logan, Pickering, Plumer, Smith of Maryland, Stone, Sumter, Tracy, White, Wright. Ayes 15 nays 15 — The Senate being equally divided, Mr. Clinton the Vice President was requested & voted in the affirmative.

---

[127] See note 92.

Mr. Adair [128] when the question was called absconded. Had he been *obliged* to vote, it would have been in the negative.

Last saturday Mr. Clinton told me he intended not to take his seat in the Senate this session. But I apprehended they found it necessary & prevailed on him to attend. Soon after the vote was decided, which was near the hour of adjournment, he informed the senate, he should leave the city on wednesday & should not attend in Senate again this session.

The state of opinion in the Senate is surely an unpleasant one to Mr. Jefferson. 'Tis now said, *in confidence,* that the price for the Florida's is to be $7,000,000. If that sum is given — will *two thirds* of the Senate ratify it? If they do ratify will it not render the advocates of the measures odious to the people? If large sums are expended in *douceurs,* in France & Spain & no treaty of cession obtained, will not the failure be fatal to the influence of the President & his advisers?

Perhaps in relation to Armstrong I ought to have added — That after he had been induced to allow a part of the claim of those interested in the *New Jersey* he only allowed such a sum as was equal to the sum the *ship* was appraised at & the interest thereon. The ship was insured — so that at last his decision did not impair or contradict his opinion to Marbois that *underwriters* ought not to recover anything.

His friends in the Senate have said that he knowing the fund was insufficient to answer all the demands apportioned it — & in fact allowed Nicklin & Griffith, the New-Jersey claimants, more than their proportion. But it was in evidence that the claimants of the Pigore, to whom Waddel was agent, received their *whole demand* except the interest. And Waddel has said nothing would have been obtained had he not agreed & afterwards actually did pay 25 pr Cent upon the sum allowed. The claims of Swon & Barnet, which were very large, & doubtful whether they were embraced by the treaty, were allowed.

---

[128] John Adair, senator from Kentucky.

Note all the bills on the Louisiana fund were drawn on our treasury by Mr. Armstrong. There is too much reason to beleive that as soon as Mr. Livingston, who, with Monroe, made the treaty — had thro' the agency of others purchased up the claims on the French treasury — he returned to New York — And was succeeded as Minister, by, his brother-in-law, Mr. Armstrong.

### Tuesday 18th.

At Capt. Coyle's where I now board there are 16 of us. This is too many — We have too much noise — for Dana is as rude as a boy — very talkative — a voice harsh & loud as Stentor — In each chamber there are two lodgers — This is very inconvenient. 'Tis difficult to obtain an hour's quiet — all is noise. But there is another evil which to me is much more serious. The Gentlemen are all rigid federalists — Pickering, Tracy, Davenport are violent — & I dare not invite a gentleman to call upon me whose politic's are different, lest these violent inmates should treat him with rudeness & insult. The consequence is I am necessarily restrained from visiting many of the Gentlemen with whom I wish to cultivate an acquaintance. An interchange of sentiments tends to correct one's own errors — & leads us to think more favorably of others. The few federalists in Congress seldom, if ever, visit & of course do not receive visits, but only from each other. They therefore not only strengthen each others prejudices — but they encrease them — & remain ignorant of many things important to know. It is my intention the next session to board in a house in which no other person boards — & if I cannot obtain such a house on the Capitol Hill that is good — I will take a large chamber in the Hotel to myself. I can then visit & receive visits from whom I please — & the noise of the company at the Hotel will seldom if ever exceed that at my present lodgings. Besides two beds in a chamber is offensive — With

an inmate your papers are too much exposed or you must
constantly be on your guard. I beleive I have kept mine
secret. —

### Wednesday 19th

At four OClock this morning died in this City my friend
*James Jackson* one of the Senators from Georgia. He was very
unwell when he arrived here on the 9th day of December last.
He attended his duty in the Senate untill the 7th day of
January last. On that day he made a few observations against
the claim of the *Yazoo* purchasers — which he ever considered
as founded in *fraud & villainy of the deepest die.*[129] . . .

Genl Jackson was in the 50th year of his age. He had been
governor of Georgia, & senator of the United States for many
years. He was neither poor nor rich.

He was a man of strong passions, & of course of strong
prejudices — but he was a man of honor — & of strict integrity.
Though his conversation sometimes bordered on the extravagant — yet his company was pleasant & agreeable. I never
knew him quibble, evade a question, or conceal his opinion.
He was open frank & undisguised. His language expressed
the feelings & sentiments of his heart.

Being a man of honor he had fought several duels, I do not
recollect that he ever killed a man. He received a wound the
effects of which he always felt.

It is to be regretted that for several of the last years of his
life he indulged with too much freedom in the use of ardent
vinous liquors. These no doubt shortened his days.

This morning as soon as the Journals of the Senate were
read, Mr. Baldwin rose & announced the painful event of the
death of his colleague. The Senate directed the Secretary to
give notice thereof to the House of Representatives — who
immediately adjourned. The Senate unanimously resolved

---

[129] See note 125, Part I.

that they would for thirty days go in mourning, by wearing crape round the left arm, as a token of their respect & esteem for the deceased. That they would attend his funeral — Appointed a committee to make the necessary arrangements for the funeral — & then immediately adjourned.

I did not visit the deceased during his sickness — He was very unwilling to admit any person into his chamber except his son — indeed he refused it. I own his death affects my heart! For three preceeding sessions I never failed a single week of walking several times with him.

He has left four children.

### Thursday 20th.

General Jackson was this day burried at Rock-hill-creek-Church — about five miles from the Capitol. His body was laid by the side of his " friend Jone's." [130]

The procession commenced at Stell's Hotel, The House at which he died. The Italian band of music belonging to the Marine Corps led — Next followed the Marine corps in their Uniforms with their arms reversed — Jackson's Physician, & the Chaplins of Congress — The Herse — the mourners — Pall bearers — Committee of Arrangements — Senate — Heads of Departments — House of Representatives — Free Masons — & citizens. The Band played the *dead March in Saul* — The scene was solemn & rendered peculiarly so by the excellency of the music. There was more than 40 Carriages The day was remarkably unfavorable — The wind N. E. cold and rainy. The masons marched near a mile & then fell off. Not more than 20 carriages reached the grave — There was not I think more than 50 members of Congress — Two federalists only besides myself attended. Cursed be the spirit of the party! Its blind baleful malevolent degrading effects ceases not with

---

[130] Probably James Jones, representative from Georgia to the Sixth Congress, who died in Washington, January 13, 1801, and was buried there.

the grave — This gross *negligence* to the remains of an honest man roused my indignation.

When we arrived within about 200 yards of the Grave — the Marine formed — the Band played a solemn dirge — the corpse was carried — the mourners & gentlemen who attended walked through to the grave. The corpse was deposited in the earth. — Dr. Gant in his usual cold monotonous manner read the church service. The band played — & then the Marine corps marched around the grave with their arms reversed forming a hollow square — they then formed on the east side of the grave in two ranks — they then fired in good order & with great dispatch three vollies.

The procession left Stelle's little past 12 OClock and I reached my home a little past five. I was not well when I left home, & though the day was unfavorable I could not refrain from this last tribute of respect to the memory of my deceased friend — & to his son. I rejoice I did it. I feel the better for the act.

The mourners who rode together in the carriage was the General's son & his negro — Mr. Baldwin the senator — Mr. Early & two or three other of the Representatives from that State. They were all affected — The poor negro wept the loss of a good master. And when the corpse was taken from the Herse, William the son was much affected — he shed a few tears — he trembled much — but soon discovered much fortitude. I conversed a few moments with him. He discovered a grateful heart for the respect Congress manifested to the memory of his dear departed parent. — With this young gentleman I am very much pleased. His attention by day & night to his father during his sickness was constant & unremitted. He is in his 19 year — has taken a degree at college — & was at the William & Mary College in Virginia reading law, when his father requested his attendance on him. He appears intelligent, sensible & amiable.

### Monday 24th.

This day the President sent to each House of Congress, alternately, A letter from Mr. Monroe minister at London. It was the original letter, & he requested it might be immediately returned. It was read & handed back again to Mr. Cole's his private secretary. The letter was dated the 28th of January. It affords ground to beleive that the Court of London is relaxing her system in relation to our neutral trade. That the ministry in that nation will be disposed to accomodate matters between the two countries — but the change was then so recent upon the death of *Pitt*,[131] that Mr. Monroe, had not received information what course they intended to pursue.

The Federalists censure the President for sending the original — They say copies ought to have been sent & left with each House. I differ from them. Communications to such numerous bodies cannot long remain secret — And to publish the state & progress of a negociation while it is pending, is very injurious. Perhaps the most correct course would have been for the President to have sent a *confidential message* to Congress stating that he had correct information purporting &c — To this mode it might have been said that he ought to have given us not the *substance*, but the *whole* of the information. The fact is men who are disposed to find fault will never want occasion to complain.

### Friday 28th

This day a bill passed the Senate to aid the claims of those who have long been known under the Name of the *Yazou speculators*.[132] Ayes 19 nays 11. I was in the negative, & the only man in New England that voted against it. I am

---

[131] Pitt died January 23, 1806. In this connection, see J. Q. Adams, *Memoirs*, I, 395, where the possible effect of Pitt's death on British foreign policy is discussed.

[132] See *Annals of Congress*, 9 Cong., 1 sess., 208.

thoroughly convinced that this business was conceived in iniquity — bro't forth & supported in every stage of it in fraud of the deepest dye — That the United States are neither bound by the principles of law, equity or sound policy to afford them any aid. And though deserted by every man in New England & by every Federalist in the Senate, I never gave a vote with more thorough conviction of its propriety than against this bill. And I regret, not for myself, but the principle, that I was in the minority.[133]

### Saturday 29th

The Bill aforesaid was read [134] — & Mr. Nelson from Maryland moved to *reject it*. On this question a debate of near three hours ensued.[135] On this question Mr. J Randolph said many severe things against the claim & against the gentlemen who advocated it. Previous to the question Mr. Gouldsborough, a new Member & a Federalist from Maryland rose and declared he was unable to make up an opinion upon the subject & requested to be excused. Mr. Randolph expressed his wishes that his request should be granted. A majority voted in his favor. Upon this Mr. Kelly, also a new federal member from Pennsylvania, made the same declaration & request. Mr. Randolph again expressed his desire to grant the request — But a majority refused. Mr. Kelly then moved to reconsider the vote excusing Mr. Gainsborough.[136] The motion prevailed — Every federalist in the House voted for reconsideration, & against excusing Mr. Gouldsborough. He then rose & declared he would neither leave his seat or vote on the question the rule of the House to the contrary notwithstanding. The vote was taken by nominal call & Mr. G. answered to his

---

[133] *Cf.* Plumer, *Life of William Plumer,* 343.
[134] In the House of Representatives.
[135] See *Annals of Congress,* 9 Cong., 1 sess., 906–921.
[136] Goldsborough.

name but refused to say either aye or nay. The House took no notice of his conduct.

On the question to reject the bill ayes 62 nays 56. Every federalist voted in the negative — and only two men, Olin of Vermont & Seaver of Massachusetts, from the New England States voted to reject this iniquituous bill. Mr. Randolph said the weight of the *Executive* pressed upon the house in favor of the bill. I think he was not correct — He ought not, I think. to have extended that remark further than to Mr. Madison, the Secretary of the Treasury [137] & to Mr. Granger the Post-master General. Both of the sons in law of the President voted to reject the Bill.

As soon as the bill was rejected Genl Thomas asked for leave to make a report — The question of adjournment was called for & negatived. Mr. Randolph then rose & said a few days since he gave notice to the house of the death of that venerable patriot, Genl Jackson a senator from Georgia. On that information the House then immediately adjourned. It was a declaration that that worthy patriot had often made, that as soon as the Yazou claims should be rejected by Congress he should be reconciled to death. Mr. Randolph said he considered the vote just passed as the resurrection of the deceased senator — & from that principle he again moved an adjourn-ment. 68 members voted in the affirmative — carried.

## *Monday 31.*

The House of Representatives have been the whole of the day debating with closed doors upon the question whether the injunction of secrecy shall be taken off in relation to the busi-ness they have transacted this session with closed doors upon the subject of purchasing the Florida's. Mr. Randolph advo-cated the question for giving publicity to the proceedings. He displayed much energy eloquence & biting sarcasm. He ex-

---

[137] Albert Gallatin.

plicitly declared that the Administration contemplated sending away the two million of dollars & making the purchase, & trusting to Congress to confirm it. But that it was finally ruled that some members in the Confidence of the Executive should bring forward a bill for the purchase —

That Mr. Madison had at the Commencement of the session explicitly told him That we must pay money to France, or be prepared for war with both France & Spain. —

Mr. Randolph most explicitly declared That most of the evils which the United States now suffered proceeded from the measures of the Executive — & from the weak feeble and pusillanamous spirit of the keeper of the Cabinet — the Secretary of State.

At five OClock the question was taken & carried by a majority of 6 or 8 in favor of publishing the proceedings.[138]

The Federalists all voted in the affirmative — though they took no part in the debate. They calculate that the publicity of the measure will damn the popularity of the President. In this I think they are mistaken. The public mind has been roused by the publications of hints innuendoes &c in the News papers to expect something much more important — And the first exclamation of the people after reading the proceedings will be — *Is this all?*

Note Farenheit's Thermometer in the shade in Coyle's entry at 3 OClock PM stood **72**.

### April wednesday 2d

At nine OClock this morning I visited the President of the United States. I was with him in a room alone for more than an hour. I went on purpose to converse on political subjects, not on weather, roads &c.

I informed him that a report was circulating with much

---

[138] See House *Journal* (1804–1807), 454–459 (Supplemental Journal).

industry that in the treaty that Mr. Lear had made with the Bashaw of Tripoli, there was a secret article — a private agreement, that the United States, would not insist upon the Bashaw's giving up the wife & family of Hamet Caramalli. He assured me the report was not only utterly false — but that there was in fact no foundation for any suspicion of the kind. You must, said he, as a senator know that *in fact* no such secret article exists — for you have the treaty before you — And nothing can make a part of the treaty but what is agreed to by two thirds of the Senators present. And you may rest assured that Mr. Lear neither gave any written assurances to the Bashaw — or ever intimated to him, that the United States would not insist on Hamet's family being delivered up. So far from it, that the reigning Bashaw has been uniformly told that this article must be literally & fully performed. He added, I have since I received the treaty, issued new orders & given explicit directions to Mr. Lear to demand the fulfilment of that article from Joseph Bashaw.

I informed the President that some of the Senators were anxious to prevent the ratification of the Treaty — But that I should myself vote in favor of it. He replied he did not know that it was in contemplation of any one to reject the treaty. He thought it was a good one, & ought by all means to be ratified.

He then said he expected the question of ratification would be postponed to the next session. I observed my impressions upon that question were unfavorable to a postponement. That I had formerly, on the Convention with Spain, voted in favor of postponing to a subsequent session — That in consequence of that delay, Spain considered herself released from all obligation to ratify on her part — & so the convention was lost. He replied that would not be the case in regard to this treaty. That if the Senate would postpone it to the next session he would take care that Joseph Caramalli should be duely informed that the reason why the treaty was not ratified, was because he had not restored to his brother Hamet his wife & children. As soon as we ratify this treaty it is compleat — no further act of the Bashaw is requisite to give it effect.

I observed that perhaps another reason might induce to the measure of postponement. The " Meditteranean fund," raised by the 2½ pr Cent advalorem duty &c established by the law of March 25, 1804,[139] was to cease in three months after peace with Tripoli, unless war with some of the other Barbary powers should then exist. And Government may need for *other purposes* this fund. I think I did not vote for that law — but it being established, and as I beleive, unnecessary changes in our revenue laws, are always injurious to the community — I have no hesitation in saying that if the Government will intimate that they need the money arising from this fund for any other purpose I will vote to continue by law the duties.

He replied, just before the meeting of Congress I had a consultation upon the subject of this fund with Mr. Gallatin & others. It appears that these duties amount to about the same sum as the duties on salt. I then proposed to Mr. Gallatin for his consideration whether it would not be expedient to repeal the duty on salt, & continue by a permanent law the 2½ pr Ct duties. After fully considering the state of our finances, the state of Europe & our connection with that country it appeared to me improper to make any changes, & therefore I was silent, upon the subject, in my Message to Congress. The session is now too near an end to pass a law to continue the 2½ pr. Ct. &c duties. The postponement of the treaty will effectually answer that purpose — the continuance of the duties.

I then observed that as I had no objection to doing that *indirectly* which I was willing to meet & do *openly & directly*, I did not know but I should vote for the postponement of the treaty to the next session — if I could be assured that such a

---

[139] Approved March 26, 1804; see *Statutes at Large,* II, 291–292.

measure would not endanger our peace with Tripoli. He unequivocally assured me it would not.

I observed, that the Report made by a Committee of the Senate, of whom Genl Bradley was Chairman, upon the application of Hamet Caramalli, was very extraordinary. That I thought it was incorrect in principle, & false as to facts. That the documents referred to by the Committee would not support the inferences they had drawn from them. [The report is dated March 17, 1806  See my *State Papers* Vol. 62].[140]  The President replied, the principles contained in that report are unsound, and the facts are false. The documents will not support the statements — They cannot be supported by testimony.  The Senate ought to pass a vote to disapprove & reject the report. It appears that Mr. Eaton wishes to blast the reputation & destroy the character of Commodore Barron & Mr. Lear to raise his own importance. I presume there is an intimacy — a connection between Bradley & Eaton — & this connection has lead Mr. Bradley into errors.

The Government of the United States never authorized any man to co-operate with Hamet in any way agt. the reigning Bashaw, or any longer, than the United States should find it for their interest so to do.

The character of Mr. Lear is good, fair and unblemished. We thought, & still beleive, it was a very fortunate circumstance for the United States that we could prevail upon him to accept the office of Consul-General upon the Barbary coast. And I hope in his absence the Senate will not approve of a report calculated to wound his fame.

A story has been circulated, & I was yesterday requested to explain it, that Mr. Lear while private Secretary to President Washington, was induced to a breach of trust. That he candestinely procured & forwarded me the correspondence that

---

[140] Brackets appear in the original manuscript. The report is given in full in *Annals of Congress,* 9 Cong., 1 sess., 185–188.

passed between the General & myself. This story is false in every part, & has been raised & circulated to injure Mr. Lear. The last letter I ever wrote to Genl Washington was in July 1796. In August following I received a partial answer — & not untill May 1798 I recd a full one — & this was the last letter I had from him. I yesterday examined my files & read the letters.

I enquired of him whether any definite arrangements had been made with the Tunisian ambassador? He replied, This man demanded the restoration of a vessel or two that we had taken from his master. The Secretary of State was directed to inform him that altho' we considered the vessels as lawful prize yet as a proof of our friendship for the Bey & Regency of Tunis we would direct them to be restored. His answer was His master wanted money & tribute. He was informed the United States would never submit to either.

I observed I felt a degree of humiliation in seeing so much attention paid by our Government to that half savage, half Brute — whom we had deigned to receive in the dignified character of an Ambassador from Tunis. He replied it was unavoidable — That it was our interest to preserve peace with those Barbary powers — and to attain that end we must pass unnoticed the irregular conduct of their ministers.

I asked when & how he was to return home? He answered, it was our intention he should embark from Boston. We wished him to travel from hence through Baltimore, Philadelphia & to Boston, that he might have some knowledge of our population, strength, wealth & means of maintaining our rights & government. But tho' he wishes the journey, yet he has abandoned it. It would be inconvenient to transport his baggage — it would be expensive & attended with some risque. We shall in about a month send him from hence in some provision vessel, that we must send into the Mediterranean seas.

I do not think there is any danger of Tunis declaring war

against us. Her trade is considerable her means to protect it feeble. It is easy for us to blockade her coast & cut off her trade.

We must keep one frigate & some smaller armed vessels constantly in those seas. A war with Tunis would add but little to the expence of our naval armament. The prizes we should take would nearly defray the whole expence of the war.

I enquired what are our prospects of settling our differences with Great Britain? He answered they are very flattering indeed. I have not the smallest doubt upon that subject — all will be accomodated in such a manner as ought to give us entire satisfaction.

I asked, how are our affairs with Spain? He answered they are well. The Marquiss de Yrujo has done, & is still doing, everything in his power to embroil us with his nation. But he will not succeed. I expect that in all May he will voluntarily return with his family to Spain. Should he delay it — effectual measures will be taken to hasten his departure.

I regret that the House of Representatives have so soon published the object for which they made the appropriation of the $2,000,000. Its publicity was not necessary. It can do no good & it may do evil. That House is however responsible for its own measures.

I then observed that our form of government appeared to me better calculated for the management of our own internal concerns than to regulate our relations with other nations. He replied Your observation is perfectly correct — our constitution is a peace establishment — It is not calculated for war. War would endanger its existence.

I asked him if he apprehended any danger from France? Observing that a century had not produced such an extraordinary character as Bonaparte. He replied he is indeed an astonishing man. I think his views are vast, & his means of attaining them are great. It appears to me his design is to establish a federation of kings in Europe, & place himself as Emperor at their head. He is the soul that will direct & controul all their movements. Prussia must yield to his views. With England I think he will make peace — He will then attend to his Navy — that will be encreased. With the United States he has no quarrel — our peace he will not disturb. I was sorry to hear that Mr. John Randolph made such severe irritating observations in the House upon Napoleon & France. They were altogether unnecessary. I hope the French Court will take no notice of them — But I fear they will. Mr. Randolph's late conduct is very astonishing, & has given me much uneasiness. I do not know what he means.

This is the substance of our conversation. It is faithfully narrated, & in nearly his own language. He appeared pleased with my visiting him.

---

The President sometime since nominated Samuel Hammond for the office of Lt Col. commandant in the army of the United States. He had no rank as an officer in the army of the US. He was the last year appointed as civil & military officer in Louisiana. In the Senate two objections were made to the appointment, 1 That he ought not to be appointed to this office, because he was not the next officer in rank. 2nd He was appointed in 1793 as a Brigadier General by Genet for an expedition against Spanish America — & accepted the office & that at a time when we were at peace with Spain. Both objections procured votes against him. The last operated conclusively against him in my mind, & would without the other have directed my vote. His character & conduct, save in that instance, appears to be fair — a man of prudence & courage. But I will never do an act that shall in any measure justify such conduct. As a punishment — as a caution & warning to others, in like cases to offend — I will with-hold an office from him who may be otherwise qualified. The ayes & noes on the question to advise to his appointment were

*Ayes* Mr. Adair, Baldwin, Condit, Kitchel, Logan, Maclay, Mitchel, Moore, Smith of New York, Smith of Tennessee, Smith of Vermont, Thruston.

*Noes* Mr. Adams, Anderson, Bayard, Bradley, Gaillard, Gilman, Hillhouse, Howland, Pickering, Plumer, Smith of Maryland, Smith of Ohio, Stone, Sumter, Tracy, Turner, White, Worthington, Wright.

Ayes 12   Noes 19 [141]

### April 3d 1806.

John Q Adams of the Senate informed me, to day, in confidence — that Mr. Madison the Secretary of State the last evening spent half an hour with him — pressing the necessity of ratifying the treaty with Tripoli — pointing out the danger & evil consequences, to the United States, that would flow from a rejection.[142] I mentioned to Mr. Adams, in like confidence, what the President had said upon the postponement of the treaty to the next session — And asked him how he could reconcile the conversation of the President with that of the Secretary? He said he thought they were irreconcileable — That there was no such thing as placing confidence in these men.

The Senate after a long debate upon the *inaccuracy* & misstatements in Bradley's report in relation to Hamet Caramalli [143] — & upon the bill brought in for his releif, by a majority of one, recommitted them with the documents to the same Committee, with the addition of Mr. Adams & Sumter, two senators who were strenuously opposed to the former report.

In a conversation I had this day with Henry Dearborn the

---

[141] See Senate *Executive Journal* (1805–1815), 30–31.

[142] J. Q. Adams mentions this conversation with Madison; *Memoirs,* I, 426.

[143] *Cf. ibid.,* 426–428.

Secy of War — he assured me that at the time Mr. Lear was appointed the Government tho't themselves under great obligation to Mr. L. for accepting the office of Consul General on the Barbary coast. That the office is important — That much depends on his integrity — that the accounts of the Consuls on that coasts must generally be passed without vouchers. That Mr. Lear's character is still unimpeached. That Mr. Eaton is uncandid in his conduct towards Lear.

That the Tunisian Ambassador is a very avaricious, cunning swindling man — That it is for our interest & for our honor to send him away as soon as may be convenient.

Nicholas Gilman, my colleague, assured me he knew William Eaton — that he was a haughty assuming imprudent man. That he beleived him personally brave — well calculated to command a company — but not an army. Said he had seen him at Steele's come down & publickly in the entry in a most boisterous manner swear at Steele's servants, & horsewhip, strike & abuse them, because they did not bring him his breakfast in season — swaring that he would cut their throats in case any man in the house had his meals before he had. This character I think is just.[144]

Mr. Spaulding, a Representative from Georgia assured me that the present administration was down & could never rise again. That Mr. Jefferson was unpopular south of the Potomac. That John Randolph was determined to oppose the President & support the election of Mr. Monroe for the next Presidency. That Mr. Madison had few friends & less popularity even in Virginia. That south of that he had no popularity — that he was considered as an inefficient character. That Mr. Monroe's popularity was great south of this. I think Mr. Spaulding is too sanguine & 'tis too soon, it endangers the peace of the Country, to commence electioneering for the next presidential election! But alass, it cannot be prevented.

---

[144] *Cf.* note 42.

There is one subject on which the President on the 2d instant expressed his opinion fully to me that I omitted to note. It is in relation to the defence of the territory of Orleans. This is contained in a bill reported by Mr. Worthington, Chairman of a committee of the Senate March 21.[145]   The substance of this bill is that 2,000,000 of acres of land in Louisiana; " in the territory of Orleans between the Achafalaya, the Red river, & a meridian line passing by the fort at Nachitoches " be surveyed & divided into townships & lots — That every alternate lot (160 acres) shall be given to any free able bodied male who is not an inhabitant of the territory of Orleans or of the Mississippi, on condition he will live thereon & cultivate the same . . . . years & " renders . . . . years of military service in the militia of the United States, within the territories of Orleans or Mississippi, & on the usual conditions & emoluments of the regular soldiers of the United States."

The President observed to me that he considered this bill as one of the most important now pending in Congress.   That no part of the US. was so much exposed as Louisiana — That it was absolutely necessary to provide means for its defence — That near half of its present inhabitants were such that they could not be depended on in case of an invasion.   That it would be impolitic & expensive to raise a standing army — That it was very doubtful whether the militia from the States would consent to march & tarry there any time — That we had not the means of compelling them — That the climate of that country would prove unfavorable to the health & lives of our Militia — That after the revolutionary war we gave lands as bounties to those soldiers who served in that war.   These lands are to be given as bounties — If you pass the law able bodied

---

[145] Worthington introduced the measure on March 6, 1806. It was passed to the third reading by the deciding vote of the president of the Senate. On April 4, further consideration was postponed until the next session and the bill was dropped. See Brown, *Constitutional History of the Louisiana Purchase*, 163–165.

men will go into that country will settle there — become inured to the climate — will have an interest in defending it.

I asked him if there was reason to beleive proper characters could be found who would go & live there upon those conditions. He replied there were — That a respectable gentleman had assured him he would for 10 pr Cent in lands procure a brigade of men to settle there.

I observed my impressions upon the subject were unfavorable to the bill — He said he really hoped I would consent to give it my vote. I replied it appeared to me to be establishing a new principle in our government — that it would be in fact introducing the feudal system — a system of military tenures — That I was not yet prepared to give my assent to such a law — That I could not without more time satisfy myself how far it would effect our constitutional & legal system — That I feared the danger of suddenly introducing such important changes into our government.

Note, I had a conversation with Mr. Brackenridge [146] on monday — from him I learnt he had drawn the bill — & was very anxious for its passage.

### Friday 4.

The bill last read was postponed to the next session.

Mr. Worthington told me, that in a conversation he had with the President — he told him that none of his favorite measures had been adopted this session — That the bill for classing the Militia had been rejected — That the bill authorizing a detachment from the militia had not yet passed [147] — That this bill for the defence of Orleans territory would not pass — And he then added, with tears running down his face — " The people expect I shall provide for their defence — but Congress refuse me the means."

---

[146] John Breckinridge, Attorney General of the United States.

[147] This bill was passed, however, being approved April 18, 1806; *Statutes at Large*, II, 383–384.

Note this same Mr. Worthington is a strange man   He may deny this — But he has told the same to Genl Bradley — But, he, again, is still more equivocal!

This same Bradley told me, he really hoped that Delaware, Connecticut & Massachusetts would maintain their federalism. That he was sick & heartily satiated with democracy. That Mr. Jefferson was a visionary man — never qualified for the presidency — That we must now turn our attention to an eastern man — That Rufus King would make a good president — that Burr a better. That Mr. Jefferson had explicitly told him he would not be a candidate at the next election.

A Committee of 5 was some days since appointed upon the bill granting a bridge over the Potomac. Dr. Mitchel was chairman. This day he reported to the Senate that the Committee had directed him to report it without amendment. Two of the Committee assured me that they had not only not directed him to do it — but that they had not had even time to examine the subject & had come to no resolution. Before the bill was half read thro' in the Senate the Dr. rose & moved two amendments!

### Saturday 5th

The House of Representatives have been most of the day debating whether they would publish the *Confidential* Message of the President of the 6th December last.[148]   They debated without method or order — & of course were involved in many questions of order. This proceeding, tho' relating to confidential business, was public. It ought to have been private. I think the Message ought not to be made public. It will disclose the views of our government unnecessarily to France & Spain. Confidential messages ought not to be published but with the consent of the President. It has been a fault of our

---

[148] Concerning the purchase of the Floridas, see *Annals of Congress,* 9 Cong., 1 sess., 946–955.

government in giving too much publicity to their proceedings. The House adjourned without a decision.

### Sunday 6th.

Aaron Burr is still in this city. He visits little, & is seen but by few. I have not waited upon him. He intended to have been elected member for the House of Representatives in Congress from the State of Kentucky. But the arrangements were not seasonably made. Their laws do not require that the Member at the time of his election should be an inhabitant of the State. If he cannot before the next election obtain a better office — He is then to attend Matthew Lyon thro' all the county Courts & become acquainted with the people. Lyon is to be elected, & then resign — & Burr to be set up, as his successor. Burr to be raised to office by the patronage of Matthew Lyon! *How are the mighty fallen!*

This information I had in *confidence* this day from my worthy friend Martin Chittenden the brother in law of Lyon, from whom he received it. I will never disclose it — Till time unfolds it — & then not my informer — or the plan.

Paid a visit to Varnum, Crowninshield, Bidwell, Fisk, Elliot & Olin — expressed my disapprobation of the publishing the presidents confidential message — & the passage of the non-importation bill. They treated me with great civility. Varnum said the federalists had heretofore made much complaint against Virginian influence — yet in the House to a man voted on all important questions with John Randolph. I told him on some questions I was sorry they did — particularly in making their proceedings public — That if that question should be raised in the Senate I should vote against it.

Varnum said Randolph had not more than 20 adherents in the House except the Federalists — That on all great questions the Republicans would unite except R. & his feeble band. To this Bidwell & Crowninshield assented.

## Tuesday 8th.

The Senate spend most of the day debating the question moved by Genl Bradley that the further consideration of the treaty with Tripoli be postponed to the next session —

*Ayes*  Mesrs. Adair, Anderson, Bradley, Howland, Pickering, Smith of Ohio, Tracey, White, Worthington, Wright.

*Noes*  Mesrs. Adams, Baldwin, Condit, Gaillard, Gilman, Hillhouse, Kitchel, Logan, Maclay, Mitchel, Moore, Plumer, Smith of Maryland, Smith of New York, Smith of Tennessee, Smith of Vermont, Stone, Sumter, Thruston, Turner.

Ayes 10  Noes 20.

A report has circulated for some time in the city that Mr. Brackenridge the Attorney General has not the confidence & friendship of Mr. Jefferson. Genl Adair, one of the Senators from Kentucky, is the friend & intimate of the Attorney Genl. — I stated to him the report. He said he had often heard it — but beleived it was not true. For the President professed much friendship for Mr. B. & had oftentimes consulted him on *particular subjects*. But said Mr. Adair, the President wants nerve — he has not even confidence in himself — For more than a year he has been in the habit of trusting almost implicitly in Mr. Madison. Madison has acquired a compleat ascendancy over him. I observed that I considered Mr. M. as an honest man — but that he was too cautious — too fearful & timid to direct the affairs of this nation. He replied that is my opinion of the man.

I observed that the spirit manifested in the other House was such as appeared to me subversive of our government. He said it was alarming — But added, John Randolph's measures will be popular — they are daily becoming so with the people in the south & in the west. I observed that the republicans considered his number of adherents to be in the House only twenty. He answered, That is a great many considering the shortness of the time since Mr. Randolph has abandoned the Administration. I answered an enemy dispised often proves dangerous. He replied Mr. Randolph has great talents, & he will crumble down this administration. I beleive Mr. Jefferson, said he, is honest.

This was the substance of a private conversation I had this day with Genl Adair. From the acquaintance I have had with him, I consider him an upright & honest man. Tho' not a man of a strong mind or extensive information. He always on all subjects appears very candid.

### Wednesday 9th.

Yesterday Mr. Tracy moved to strike out certain articles, such as appropriations for laying out a particular road, out of the general Appropriation bill — because he said there was no previous law authorizing the making of the road. In an hour after, he reported a bill appropriating money for the salaries of Clerks — & in that bill introduced the very same provision, as he had objected to in the other bill. Yesterday at his request the Senate in committee of the whole struck out many items from the general appropriation law — To day he moved & voted for the restoration of most of them. His bill respecting clerks, which he said was the fruit of much attention — he to day suddenly on the suggestion of another materially changed. He has too many whims & caprices as well as imprudence for the file leader of a party!

### Thursday 10th.

. . . . . . . . . . . . . . . . . . . . . . . . . . . . . . . . . . . . . .

This evening Wm. Eaton Esq (alias the *Arab* Genl) set down with us to supper at our lodgings. He was told what he well knew before that the Senate had postponed the bill for the releif of Hamet Caramalli to the next session. He then said with much warmth " a majority of the Senate have sold the

honor of their country." I observed he had assumed great
liberties — but that I trusted the Senate would act agreeable
to the conviction of their own minds — uninfluenced by the
opinions of others. That for one he would most assuredly find
I should.

I beleive I did not the other day note, That Mr. Eaton speaking of Mr. Adams the senator, said " That man has sold the
honor of his country."

### *Friday 11.*

After we breakfasted this morning I mentioned to the Gentlemen boarders at the table that I considered Mr. Eaton's accusation against the majority of the Senate — " That they had sold
the honor of their country " — as being highly improper &
wholly unjustifiable — That considering Mr. Eaton knew that
I was in that majority whom he so wantonly & unjustly censured — his conduct was an outrageous violation of good breed-
ing. That this was heightened by being made at my lodgings
to which he was invited by some of my brethren. That I had
no objection to Mr. Eaton's being invited to our table — but
requested that when any gentleman invited him, he would be
so obliging as to give me previous notice — for that I would
retire & not again dine or drink tea with Mr. Eaton in this house.
They all seemed to agree in expressing an opinion that Mr.
Eaton's conduct was improper & unjustifiable.

---

In debate in the Senate, upon the bill authorizing the President of the United States to make a detachment from the militia
when he should think necessary — General Adair said — He was
fully convinced that before the commencement of the next session the President would be obliged to make a detachment
from the militia to defend the southern & western States &
Louisiana.

Mr. Gilman told me that he beleived the President was an honest man — but he wanted firmness — That Mr. Madison was much more timid — & yet he governed the President — That he consulted the other heads of department but little — That Genl Dearborn, the Secy of War, thought the measures of the President were too feeble — that he thought he was afraid to take the responsibility of proper measures upon him — That he trusted too much in governing Congress by an indirect and secret influence.

Mr. Adams told me he had been offered if he would act as a lawyer before the Committee of Claims — or in Congress, a large sum to obtain a law allowing the demand. He spurned the offer with indignation! This has not been the case with all my acquaintances — I have too much reason to fear that some gentlemen who are so anxious in supporting Eaton's & Caramalli's claims are interested in the success.

### Saturday 12th.

At 12 OClock the debate commenced with closed doors upon the question of ratifying the treaty made by Mr. Lear with the Bashaw of Tripoli, & ended at 6 OClock in the evening. This treaty was printed & laid on our tables more than four months ago. Mr. Jefferson's intention was to have it postponed to the next session under the plausible pretext of the Bashaw's not having given up the wife & children of Hamet Caramanly, but in fact for the sake of continuing the Meditteranean fund. Some days since I told Mr. Baldwin, a confidential friend of Mr. Jefferson, that such indirect & crooked policy would & ought to damn the Administration.

The debate today was animated — but most of it foreign to the subject. The conduct of Eaton, of Hamet Caramanly & their feeble expedition to Derne — the conduct of Commodore Barron — of Lear & their motives was the principle topic of debate. But in fact the only question was, is the treaty such a one as is for the honor & interest of the United States — is it a good one. To me it was evident that it is a good treaty, & that we are bound by the principles of justice & the welfare of our Country to ratify it.

We have been too much in the habit of attempting to amend — & to delay the ratification of treaties. The Convention with Spain was delayed so long before we ratified it, that Spain refused & justly to ratify the same. The last treaty with G Britain we ratified with an amendment — That nation refused to accede to it. Both these treaties to our injury were lost. We shall in this way suffer in the estimation of other nations. We attempted to amend our last treaty with France — & we suffered by it.

Mr. Wright moved an amendment to the resolution of ratification. The amendment was to ratify the treaty *on the condition that the wife & children of Hamet should be delivered up to him.* On the amendment, the question was, shall the amendment stand part of the resolution

Ayes  Mr. Adair, Hillhouse, Pickering, Smith of Maryland, Smith of Ohio, Tracy, White, Worthington, Wright.

Nays Mr. Adams, Mr. Anderson, Baldwin, Condit, Gaillard, Gilman, Howland, Kitchell, Logan, Maclay, Mitchell, Moore, Plumer, Smith of New York, Smith of Tennessee, Smith of Vermont, Stone, Sumter, Thruston, Turner

Ayes 9  Noes 20.

Mr. Smith of Ohio then moved to postpone the further consideration of the resolution untill the 2d tuesday of December next. On this question the ayes were, Adair, Pickering, Smith of Maryland, Smith of Ohio, Tracy, White, Worthington & Wright. The question was lost. The question was then taken on ratifying the Treaty —

Ayes Mr. Adams, Anderson, Baldwin, Condit, Gaillard, Gilman, Howland, Kitchell, Logan, Maclay, Mitchell, Moore, Plumer, Smith of Maryland, Smith of New York, Smith of Tennessee, Smith of Vermont, Stone, Sumter, Thruston, Turner.

Nays Mr. Adair, Hillhouse, Pickering, Smith of Ohio, Tracy, White, Worthington, Wright.

Ayes 21 noes 8.

After 4 OClock Wright & Pickering exercised the patience of the Senate with long dry & tedious speeches. A large majority of the Senate have made up their opinion upon the subject — and nothing new or interesting being contained in their speeches we withdrew to the fireside & spent our time cheerfully & left them to talk & read documents, we had before examined, to the empty chairs. At sometimes, for ten minutes, there was not but four senators within the bar. Six several times they moved the President to adjourn for the want of a quorum. As soon as the motion was made we took our chairs, negatived it, & then immediately withdrew. Gentlemen who profess to speak to convince those who hear them, must have a strong inclination for continuing debate with closed doors — when the seats are deserted. These few gentlemen seem to think that no others ever read documents, examine cases or principles — or take the trouble of forming an opinion.

### Tuesday 15th

Some few days since the President removed Wm. Smith from the office of Naval Officer of the city of New York. His connection with Miranda in the Leander expedition is assigned as the cause of removal. This morning Mr. Adams showed me a long letter from Mr. Smith upon the subject of Miranda. His project is to revolutionize the province of Carracas — a portion of the Spanish possessions in South America. In this letter col. Smith states that early last winter Miranda disclosed his project to him & requested Col Smith to accompany him. Smith said he held an office under the authority of the United States & that he could not be absent unless he obtained permission from the President or Secretary of State — and intimated to Miranda that as he was going to Washington & intended a con-

fidential disclosure of some part of his projects to the President
& Mr. Madison — it would be well for him to sound them upon
the subject of his (Smith's) accompanying him in the expedition.
That Miranda came to Washington visited the President and
Mr. Madison — From Washington he wrote Mr. S. informed
him he had made a disclosure of his project — That he had
requested permission for Mr. S. to accompany him — but that
the Secy said he could give none — That the government could
not interfere or take any notice of the business. That he dined
with the President & Secy at their houses. After Miranda's
return to New York, he wrote a letter to the President & enclosed the history of Chili — And in the letter mentions his
expedition. He also wrote a letter to Mr. Madison. Copies
of these was delivered by Miranda to Mr. Smith, & by him
copied literally into this letter to Mr. Adams. Col. Smith says
that Gelston the Collector of New York knowing the arrange-
ment — men, arms &c that was on board the Leander — Yet he
granted a clearance. Gelston is suffered to remain in office —
but he (S.) tho' he has on all occasions done his duty — yet he
is removed — He is made a sacrifice by the Executive, to keep
up an appearance that the Govt. did not approve of Miranda's
measures. This is the substance of the letter as near as I can
recollect.[149]

Note, Mr. Smith & others are indicted at the Court of the
US. New York for being concerned in Miranda's plot. The
trial is put off till July. Smith made affidavit that Mr. Madison
is a material witness & that he expects to be able to procure
him.

---

The Senate today passed the bill prohibiting the importation
of certain goods & wares and merchandize from Great Britain

---

[149] *Cf.* Adams, *History of the United States* III, 189–192. See the
debate in the House on this subject, *Annals of Congress,* 9 Cong., 1 sess.
1085–1094; also, J. Q. Adams, *Memoirs,* I, 436–440.

after the 15th day of November next. The impolicy of this measure I have stated in several of my letters, copies of some of which are on file. Some days since the friends of the bill on the 2d reading made an amendment excepting " black bottles " from the prohibition. To day the Senate struck out the amendment — & Mr. Wright said if any amendment was made it would endanger the passage of the bill in the other House. My own opinion is the bill would pass the House at this time but not with so large a majority as formerly.

### *Wednesday 16.*

The Senate ratified a treaty made with the Cherokee Indians, January 7. 1806. They cede certain lands to the United States. The United States pay them $10,000; build a grist mill — & an annuity of $100 to Black Fox, a Chief, during his life.[150]

The Indian treaties ratified this session obliges us to pay them about $100,000 — & annuties of $18,400. — The expence of making these treaties is not less than $30 or $40000 more.

### *Wednesday* [151] *April 17, 1806.*

Sometime since the House of Representatives on the motion of Mr. Clark of Virginia appointed a committee to enquire into the conduct of Gideon Granger the Postmaster General, & to report whether he had so misbehaved as to require an impeachment. To day the Committee reported that the shortness of the session would not permit them to make the necessary enquiry & that the subject be postponed to the next session.[152]

There are two charges whispered against him. 1 That he has made use of his office as well as personal influence to induce Duane, to support, in the Aurora, the *Yazou Claim.* 2 That

---

[150] Text of the treaty in *American State Papers*, IV. *Indian Affairs*, I, 704.

[151] Thursday.

[152] See *Annals of Congress*, 9 Cong., 1 sess., 244–245.

he refused to make a contract with a federalist of good character & who had undoubted security for its performance, to carry the mail in a certain route in Connecticut for one dollar fifty Cents pr mile — but gave a democrat the same contract at *four Dollars* per mile.

It is said that Mr. Granger did this last act in conformity to the special direction of the President.

### Friday 18.

Yesterday Dr. Logan moved & obtained a resolve of the Senate requesting the President to communicate to the Senate the correspondence & proceedings between the Government & the Bey of Tunis. To day the President made the communication. It was enclosed in a message — *not marked confidential* — It was read in the Senate with open doors — Several persons were in the gallery. The papers consisted of a correspondence between the Secretary of State & Sidi Solimon Mellimella, the Bey's Minister now at this place. Mellimella states the proceedings of Dr. Davis late Consul at Tunis as being not only rude & insulting but false & deceitful — That Commodore Rogers had without any just cause captured one or two of his vessels — blockaded his port — & required the Bey to recal a threat he had uttered against the Americans — That the Commodore gave the Bey but 36 hours to return an answer — That Davis detained this letter 20 hours — That the Bey had in consequence of these abrupt proceedings sent him here — That the vessel captured was not of great value not more than $4000 — but *for the honor* of the Tunis flag his master had ordered him to demand the restoration — That his master expected trieniel presents from the United States.

The Secy replied That altho' the President considered the capture as fully authorized by the laws of nations — yet to evince his love of peace & shew his disposition to preserve our friendship with the Bey of Tunis, he had ordered the vessel in question to be restored. — That as to tribute the United States could not submit to pay any. —

Mellimelli replied, Tribute must be paid to his Master by the United States — or that which is equivalent, presents. That the great Republic of France has lately sent them rich presents of Naval stores — & 40 carpenters who have been & still are employed in building them ships — That the US. is a great nation & have much, very much, naval stores — & that of this he requested only a small portion.

The Secy replied to him the United States would not pay him a single Cent.

Mellimelli, entreated tribute as a mark of respect to his master. He said if he succeeded in his mission God would have all the glory — but if he failed he should suffer by that failure the forfeit of his life — which on his return would be taken from him by his master. From a view to his own personal safety he therefore intreated favor.

The Secy said No tribute — no presents would be given, let the event be what it may.

Mellimelli replied he should return very soon to his master, & in one year after, or in *one month* if the United States preferred that, the Bey his master would declare war in due form.

Thus ended the communications by the Secy's assuring him that the US. were not to be terrified by threats of war — That we were ready to meet it.

These communications were made on the part of Mellimelli orally — They were taken down in Arabic read to him — he assented to their correctness by signing the same — Translations of them were sent to us.

After they were read, Dr. Logan moved to have them published — Mr. Anderson opposed it — & moved a reference of them to a committee, to wit Baldwin, Logan & Israel Smith.

## Saturday 19th.

Mr. Baldwin moved to have the doors closed — They were done — he then read a report — That the papers aforesaid be returned to the President — & that he be requested to renew negociation with the Tunisian Minister to compromise our differences with that regency. Mr. Adams objected to receiving or acting upon the report with closed doors [153] — Over-ruled. It was then moved to strike out all that relates to a renewal of negociation — Carried ayes 19, noes 9. I was in the affirmative. The vote to return the papers was carried without a division.

Genl Smith, the President pro. temp. stated that in a conversation he had with the President that morning — he told him it was his intention to have sent the papers under an injunction of secrecy.

In the President's message to *Congress* this week upon the ratifying of the Tripolitan treaty — he publickly stated as a reason why the Meditteranean fund should be continued — the great probability of a war with Tunis.

Had the President directly asked the opinion of the Senate whether they would advise to a renewal of negociation with Tunis, I should have had no objection to answering in the affirmative. For I think our conduct to that Regency not perfectly correct — That a meditteranean war will be a curse to us. But I am unwilling in this indirect way to take the responsibility upon us. It ought to rest with the President. He cannot declare war — he may recommend it — He can negociate.

The President nominated James Monroe & William Pinkney of Maryland as Commissioners & Envoys plenipotentiary to the Court of London to adjust our differences & wrongs committed on the high seas & other seas, & to establish principles of navigation & commerce between the United States & the United Kingdom of Great Britain & Ireland.

[153] *Cf.* J. Q. Adams, *Memoirs,* I, 434–436.

Mr. Pickney was formerly commissioner at London under the British treaty. He was then, & his friends now, say he is still a federalist. He has this year been appointed by the Legislature of Maryland, attorney General of that State. He is a man of talents & integrity — He will probably be very acceptable to the British ministery. Some zealous republicans censure the President for nominating him. They say he ought not to have appointed a federalist. I think it a stroke of sound correct policy.

The bill to repeal the duty on salt — & to continue the Meditteranean fund one year was taken up. That part relating to salt was struck out ayes 16 nays 9. I was in the affirmative — The bill thus amended passed to a 3d reading.

### *Monday 21.*

The Senate met at 10 OClock this morning & the bill last mentioned as amended passed the Senate — And the House agreed to the amendment notwithstanding there was only 11 against repealing the duty on salt when that House first passed the bill.[154] Thus the Senate by their firmness have saved the duty on salt — & continued the Meditteranean fund another year. The Government actually wanted the money arising from both these sources — tho' they had not firmness enough to say so explicitly. This duty reaches all classes of people & tends to render the revenue more *equal* than it would otherwise be. All changes in revenue operate injuriously upon a portion of the community. They ought not to be made but for substantial causes. The state of the nation at this time forbid repealing duties. We are appropriating money for defence, & at the same time by repealing this duty we are cutting off one of the sources from whence the money must come. To repeal the duty now would be popular — but to restore it — & very soon we must restore it — would occasion clamour. I doubt the policy of

---

[154] Approved April 21, 1806; see *Statutes at Large,* II, 391.

repealing anyone of our duties. When the state of the nation will justify it — we may reduce them — And then when circumstances require it, raise it. But every new article added to the list of dutied ones — always will create complaint.

This attempt to repeal the duty on salt was in the House a mere scramble for popularity. Richard Cutts, from the district of Maine, told me he voted for it — but tho't it wrong — he said the people clamored for it — And he trusted to the Senate to negative it.

The bill to pay all the witnesses who attended the trial of Judge Chase's impeachment passed.[155]

Appropriations for an Indian treaty is lost. The House annexed two paragraphs rendering it penal for any person to settle on the lands purchased of the Indians, unless the settlers had title under the United States — & authorized the President to raise the militia to remove them. This was designed by John Randolph to prevent the Yazou claimants from entering. 'Tis abominable to tack such provisions to an appropriation law. 'Tis virtually annihilating the Senate, in this case — They struck it out by a large majority. The House departed from their usual decorum. They refused to confer —but instantly adhered — The Senate promptly met them in adherence & the bill was lost. Tis a good provision in the constitution of Maryland that prohibits their Legislature from adding any thing to an appropriation law.

In the evening Thomas M. Randolph, the presidents son in law, in debate speaking of the conduct of John Randolph said, he was leaky — had revealed secrets — had excited clamour — Thomas said he was not afraid of powder, ball, pistol & steel — that he was ready to use them — & insinuated doubts respecting the courage of John — alluded to the affair with Dana. John soon sent a messenger to Thomas. They met in committee

---

[155] Approved April 21, 1806; *Annals of Congress,* 9 Cong., 1 sess., 1272 (Appendix); *Statutes at Large,* II, 389–390.

room — John said his observation were not intended for him. Thomas went into the House — And publickly said to the House he had accused John under improper impressions, & he regreted the doing of it — And so it ended. —

Congress adjourned at 11 OClock PM. It has been a tedious day — We have passed many laws.

### *Tuesday 22*

Too much fatigued to commence my journey. Visited the President. He said he did not think Congress need meet sooner than December. Said if a commercial treaty should be made with Great Britain the merchants might continue to import goods from that country. The Secy of the Treasury might issue orders to the Collectors to store their goods so imported & deliver up the keys & when Congress met they might repeal & annul the law. The principle that a people should be invited to violate a law because it will probably be repealed, seems to me incorrect.

Mr. Adams told me that Rufus King might have been appointed minister to London instead of W. Pinkney — but King would not accept if his power should be restricted to certain principles. The Admõn said it must be restricted. — He said he would, tho', with reluctance, — undertake the mission, if they would leave him unfettered with particular restrictions — He would take the responsibility of the measure upon himself. It would then rest with the President & senate ultimately to approve or reject the treaty thus made.

Upon particular enquiry into the political tenets of Wm Pinckney — it is doubtful whether he is a federalist or Republican. He has for several years been a Commissioner in London acting under our late treaty with Great Britain. In that situation he had no occasion to disclose his political tenets. He is now Attorney General of Maryland — appointed by a democratic Admõn. When the question was taken in the Senate upon his present appointment, Dr. Mitchel rose & requested information as to his character & abilities. The Dr knew both, from reputation, to stand fair. Mr. Wright rose & said he knew Mr. Pinkney — he was a well read lawyer — a good scholar — a man of much information & of splendid talents — but — but (shrugging up his shoulders) his politic's are, to speak most favorably, of the doubtful kind. The vote in senate was pretty full — no one voted in the negative. I am told that some of the senators, had contemplated to negative the nomination. 'Tis certain that Samuel Smith would have been gratified by being himself sent on this mission.

### Wednesday 23

Last evening at 11 OClock PM took my seat in the mail stage — at 10 this morning arrived at Baltimore. The business & population of this city is increasing with astonishing rapidity. The young ladies of this place make the greatest display of beauty, neatness and elegance of dress that I ever beheld.

### Thursday 24.

Yesterday at one OClock P.M. left Baltimore & arrived in Philadelphia at 10 OClock this morning. The stage travelled all the night. Yesterday was taken in one net at one draught an astonishing number of fish. I saw several cartloads of them. They were drawn out of the Susquehannah at Havre de Grass. There were 185000 Alewives & 500 shad. This information I had from a gentleman of integrity who was present & saw them counted. The Alewives were sold at two dollars pr 1000.

### Saturday 26

Yesterday at One OClock in the afternoon I left Philadelphia in the stage & this morning at 7 I arrived in the city of New York very much fatigued — but principally owing to the want of sleep.

During my stay in Philadelphia I was much surprised at the striking contrast between the young ladies of Philadelphia & Baltimore. The former appear too solemn & gloomy. There was a general meeting of the Quakers in Philadelphia yesterday. I saw hundreds of the young ladies of that sect altho' they were dressed in their silks & appeared neat — yet the gloom on their countenances wasted & destroyed their beauty. That religion is not divine that is founded in the destruction of the innocent pleasures & amusements of life. 'Tis vile superstition, & tho' it may correct some errors it produces more.

At nine OClock I again took the stage.

### Sunday 27

At one OClock this morning I arrived at New Haven. Sleep was welcome & refreshing. In travelling I endeavor to avoid the company of Congressmen — because their quantity of baggage incommodes me — sometimes obliges me to have mine bound outside of the stage & exposed. But a greater advantage arises from being able to meet with intelligent strangers. Yesterday I rode with & to day spent my time with a modest well informed Frenchman — John Bossuier of Philadelphia. After becoming acquainted with him — He told me he was a native of Provence. That his father was a Judge — That he was in their ill-fated revolution elected a member of their Convention but declined accepting the appointment. He was from that circumstance arrested thrown into prison & condemned as an Aristocrat to the gullatine — His property was all confiscated & sold — The death of Roberspeire saved his father's life. This man, the son, fled poor the West Indies & then to America — sat up trade, & acquired property. He is now about retiring to a plantation in Orleans territory he purchased for $15000 & 33 negroes. He finds trade uncertain — & means to secure what property he has.

He assured me he had letters from his friends in France complaining of the tyranny of Napoleon — that his system of taxation was oppressive.

Mr. Bossuier says he was a classmate with Moreau — That he is a great good & amiable man. That Napoleon respects but fears him.

That Genl Turreau sprang from the lowest grade of society — That Mrs. Turreau was of the same grade — That by the horrid practises of the revolution her first husband acquired wealth & died — That Turreau married her — that having risen from a common soldier to a general & from that to an ambassador — he now despises & beats his wife — That she displays her vulgar habits & rude illiberal manners & morose disposition.

Mr. Bossuier says he was one of 44 who left France to live in Martinique — That at the end of the year two only of them survived — That this was owing to their too free use of spirits & of women — that the latter was most fatal. He says that the climate will prevent Napoleon from conquering St Domingo.

He says Turreau is proud haughty & mean — confirmed the story of his acquiring the furniture of Pichon in the manner I have formerly mentioned. He adds that the latter is learned — wise & and very amiable.

I ought sometimes since to have mentioned that the account of William Eaton for his services & expenditures as Consul to Tripoli in 1801 &c are yet unsettled. In March last the Comptroller of the Treasury reported a ballance due from Mr. Eaton of —— $40,803..79. That in Mr. Eaton's account the charges he had suspended amounted to . . . $46,701..29 These were composed of the following items

The detention of the Anna Maria.................. 3,800 —
Cash paid to the Sapatapa, the minister of Joseph
Caramanli, the reigning Bashaw.................. 10,131..78
Services of the Carolina with dispatches to
Tripoli & Gibralter............................... 2,135 —

Detention &c of the Gloria...................... 19,166..67

. Antonio Porcello's daughter...................... 6,921..46

sundries ........................................ 4546..38

46,701..29

That the United States had charged him with $22,000 for monies Commodore Morris had been compelled to pay for him in that country. That Eaton had contracted certain debts in Tripoli — that when Morris went on shore the Bashaw ordered him arrested & confined untill he paid Eaton's debts.

The money paid for the redemption of an Italian girl had no connection with his consulship — & the US. ought not to pay it.

The money paid to the Sapatapa was for a bribe to the Minister to aid Eaton in his connection with Hamet Caramanli — The minister betrayed him to the Bashaw — & so the project failed. But the Bashaw compelled Eaton to pay the bribe. I hope the United States will never admit a charge agt. their treasury founded on monies paid by our Consul to bribe the Minister of the Prince to whom the Consul was sent, to aid in the cause of the rebellion & treason agt that government! 'Tis a principle too vile & too dangerous to admit of a moments consideration.

A few weeks before the close of the session Eaton presented his claim to Congress — It was referred to the Committee of Claims of whom his abject friend John C. Smith was chairman. After those two had held many private consultations — Smith called his committee together & prevailed on them to direct him to report a bill authorizing the Accounting officers of the treasury under the direction of the Secy of *State* to settle said accounts upon the principles of justice & *equity*. Those officers have authority to settle his account upon legal principles — why introduce equity? This would destroy all responsibility in our agents abroad. If their accounts may thus be settled you have no hold on them — no security agt. 'em. If you introduce it in one case you must in all. Why did he not suffer his account to be settled by the proper officers of the treasury & if he had other equitable claims — for those let him appeal to the equity of Congress. If the claim was well founded he would succeed.

I have little doubt the Govt has proceeded in some of those transactions upon principles which cannot be justified — They therefore wish a *private* settlement. I found Mr. Madison desired it.

The friends of Eaton — & I am sorry to say, the federalists to a man, Mr. Adams & myself excepted, not only unite in his favor, but consider that too much cannot be done for him. They purposely delayed the business to near the close of the session — would not have the bill printed — & expected in the hurry of more important business, this would pass unnoticed — The last day but one of the session it passed to a 3d reading by a majority of only 2 or 3. Its friends suffered it to rest — in this inchoate state.[156]

I cannot consider Mr. Eaton so favorably as I used to. There are many things that tend to prove him an imposter. He is continually vaunting of the glory of his expedition — complaining at Lear for making a treaty so soon & depriving him of conquering Tripoli. And yet if the state of that little affair is examined it will be found trivial in its operations & not affording a single prospect of success. In Derne he & the Ex Bashaw had 300 men — most of them unarmed — Joseph Caramanly had there thousands in arms, & as soon as Eaton's men marched out they were either slain or prisoners. If they marched to Tripoli they must travel round the bay of Sidra a distance of more than 700 miles. The whole of this country was inhabited with a barbarous fierce and warlike people. But Eaton said if they could reach Bengazi they should there be re-inforced. This was a distance of 110 miles — But how could they get there — they

---

[156] Eaton's claims for compensation for pecuniary losses were not allowed. The State of Massachusetts, however, granted him 10,000 acres of land.

had not the means — & when there, there was no certainty of aid. The prospect existed but in the expectation of the sanguine projector! Eaton knew that Commodore Barron was limited in the aid he should offer to Hamet to $20,000. That sum he had already expended. The conduct of Barron & of Lear deserve praise — that of Eaton censure. It is unfortunate for our Country that the credulity of Jefferson led him to aid this wild projector. He seems now convinced of his error — but is afraid to correct it in a manly way. The Rashness of Eaton has been termed *bravery*. The populace have huzzaed him — federalists have been extravagant in their enconiums. It has answered with them the double purpose of strengthing their party — & affording them another opportunity of attacking the Administration. Delay may save the country money & some credit — It must now rest till another session — It will then be more cooly & fairly examined.

### Monday April 28, 1806.

Rode this day to Springfield — Was accompanied for a few miles in the Stage with a very *learned* sensible intelligent young lady. She discovered much talent & information — was modest — social & manners agreeable. She travelled no further than Hartford — Did not discover her name, but conjecture she was a daughter of Col. Wadsworth.[157] Was much pleased with her — I am much more pleased with the company of ladies than formerly.

### Tuesday 29th

Was fortunate in my company — from Worcester to Boston Miss Abigail Clark of North Hampton accompanied me. She is sensible & agreeable but not well read. The lady of yesterday is the best compainion; but Miss Clark will make the best wife. At Cambridge I was unable to see my son William — he was not at his chamber — Wrote him from Boston.

---

[157] Probably Peleg Wadsworth, representative from Massachusetts.

### Wednesday 30th

Arrived at my home — received a cordial welcome from my family. Found my wife weak feeble & much emaciated. The great change gave me a considerable shock — There is great appearance of a rapid decline — but little cough tho' great debility.

### Thursday May 15.

Visited, this week, my friends & acquaintance at Portsmouth. Was received with cordiality & treated with much attention. Waited upon Govr Langdon — was treated with much politeness by him. The rage of party appears to have spent its force in this State — All is now calm & tranquil. The Republicans have prevailed — Langdon is re-elected without a real rival — a large majority of the legislature are of that party. The federalists are silent quiet & submissive. The violent Democrats are obliged to own that the change of men has produced but little change in the public measures. The greatest is an unnecessary encrease of Justices of the peace — & of these many would never have attained commissions but for the rage of party.[158]

In Portsmouth, where party spirit hath raged with wanton violence, all is calm. The enquiry in the election of town officers is now who is best qualified — not who is of a particular party. Several federalists are elected as town officers. It is in politic's, as in religion, party cannot subsist in either without opposition. Moderation is a great useful virtue to society.

### Wednesday 21.

This day returned from Cambridge with my son William. Visited several of my friends.

---

[158] *Cf.* Plumer, *Life of William Plumer*, 345–346.

### Wednesday June 4 1806.

Accompanied my son again to Cambridge College. Spent the night at the house of the Revd Dr. Jedediah Morse at Charlestown — Was pleased with him — He is a rigid Calvinist — A man of much industry — Has written much — is studious — diligent — but has little originality. His writings discover more of the labour of a compiler than of an author.

He solicited me to write the General history of our government. Such a work well executed would be useful — and had I leisure I would commence the undertaking. I have many materials, but want many more.

### Thursday [June] 5th.

At half seven accompanied the Doctor to the State prison in Charlestown — It was the hour of prayer & he officiates as chaplin. There are near 50 of the convicts. They all came into a chamber assigned for that purpose. They are most of them likely active men — none I beleive exceed 50 — most of them are under 30 years of age. They were clothed in blue & red — half of each garment was of different colors. Several of them wore chains on their legs. They were civil & attentive during the hour of worship. I was much affected at seeing such a number of well formed intelligent men banished from society & immured in such a gloomy prison. Their crimes have rendered their punishment necessary.

This is a large & very strong prison. It is built of stone — The yard is spacious — I visited all its rooms apartments & cells — & all the work shops. The prisoners were civil. They are industrious. They labour in various of the useful trades — such as blacksmiths, shoemakers & tailors. Some of them are ingenious.

I doubt whether it will answer the expectation of the Legislature. The expence attending it is a serious object. The building & out buildings cost about $140,000 — & the salaries and wages of the officers & men who govern & attend it are considerable. Dr. Morse appears very anxious for its welfare — He devotes much of his time & attention to these unfortunate men. He preaches every sunday with them after the afternoon service is done in his society.

Visited Boston. The legislature of Massachusetts is now in session. They have returns of 481 members for the House of Representatives. Such a numerous house is but a tumultuous mob. 'Tis an error that must be reformed. They have been 8 days in session. The Republicans have a majority of about 50 in the House & 2 in the Senate. The choice of a governor is not yet declared. I am convinced that the dominant party will bring in James Sullivan as governor. His character is bad. Caleb Strong is a fair & amiable man & is the candidate supported by the federalists. He had a small majority, say 300 out of 75000 votes. But the returns from several towns will be rejected. A joint committee of the Legislature have reported against several returns. Some they reject for informality — Some they set down as scattering votes because the name of Strong is mispelt — altho' no doubts *can* exist for whom they were given. This report leaves no choice by the people — According to that Govr Strong wants 14 votes of a majority. I consider this report as the voice of the dominant party. The committee is their organ. In the moment of exultation & triumph the voice of reason, of moderation & propriety is not heard by a political party.

I discovered much bitterness & animosity in both parties. They do not treat each other with civility. Boston is now a Vast pile of combustibles, & a spark may produce a flame that would end in mobs & spread blood & destruction through its streets. Tis an eventful period in the history of Massachusetts. I feel anxious for its peace.

There is no doubt a majority of the people in the commonwealth are democrats. The choice of senators & representatives is proof of the fact. The personal popularity of Strong gave him the majority over the unpopular Sullivan. Cursed be the demon of party that hurries a people to prefer a vicious to a virtuous man.

In the choice of a President of the Senate John Bacon had after several trials a majority of one. He was formerly a representative in Congress. He is a man of talents but too metaphisical for a useful legislator. He was once an ordained Clergyman.

In the House for a speaker Perez Morton had 257. Timothy Bigelow (a federalist) 204. Morton's private character is not good. He is a lawyer — a sensible cunning man.

### *Saturday 7th.*

I have spent two days with my friends at Salem. This town is the victim of religious and political dissentions. They multiply houses of worship — They croud into them with zeal to serve the Lord; but with hearts full of bitterness and hatred against those who do not subscribe to their creed.

Their political disputes have destroyed much of the blessings of society. Members of the same family pass by each other without speaking — Many go so far as to dismiss their truckmen mechanics & seamen who differ from them in politic's. This is the case with both parties. They are governed by their feelings, not their reason. In point of numbers the two great political parties are nearly equal. This renders them more violent. In talents, information, integrity & wealth the federalists have a decided superiority.

This evening the Legislature had not declared or chosen a Governor. The Senate by a majority of one or two have adopted the report of the joint committee.

The federalists declare that in case Sullivan is thus unfairly declared Governor, those of them who are members of the Legislature will enter a protest against the proceedings & *secede.* At Boston & Salem I used my utmost endeavors to persuade them to abandon such an idea. To me it appears to be a spirit of disorganization — of insubordination & tumult subversive of all government. It will operate unfavorably to the seceders & their party with the people. Each Legislator is charged not only with the general interests of the State but with particular & local concerns, which they are not at liberty to abandon. The conduct of the dominant party is unreasonable & unjust, yet, I think cannot justify a secession. I hope the federalists will abandon the wild project.

Both the Federalists & Republicans in the Legislature have each a caucus at Boston almost every night. At these each party settles the most important questions.

### Monday 9th.

Spent the day at Newbury Port — party spirit does not rage here as at Boston & Salem — altho' it has imbittered much of the sweets of society. The parties are not here so equal as in the other towns. The federalists have a clear decided majority.

Religious fanaticism abounds in this town.

There are two or three facts relative to the report of the joint committee of the Massachusetts Legislature that I have not noticed.

The town of Lynn returned 357 votes for *James Sulvan* as governor these were set to the name of *James Sullivan.* The committee reported that they be taken from his column & set under the name of James *Sulvan.* They say that Strong had 36,692 votes Sullivan 36031, James *Sulvan* 357, & Wm Heath 85. That these are the four persons who had the highest number of votes & are the candidates for the office of Governor. By the constitution of that commonwealth when there is no choice of Governor the House of Representatives are to elect 2 persons

out of the 4 candidates having the highest number of votes &
send their names to the Senate, who are to elect one of those
two to be Governor.   There can be [no] doubt that the Lynn
votes were given for Sullivan the omission of *l* & *i* notwithstanding.   *Sulvan* is an ideal name. — No such man was ever voted
for by the people — no such man exists.   If this report is accepted, as no doubt it will be, the House will be deprived of a
constitutional right of selecting from *four real* candidates nominated by the people.   They will be confined to three.   But
should the House set up Sullivan & *Sulvan* the Senate will have
but one real candidate — they will have no election, no choice,
their votes must be for Sullivan, or an ideal man.   But what
renders this report still more unjust and absurd, is, they say,
" in the town of Otisfield there were given 27 votes for *James
Sullan* as governor."   These votes the committee say " should
be taken from the votes set against the name of James Sullivan
& placed in a seperate column & counted as *scattering votes.*
Why give a real name to *Sulvan* & not to *Sullan?*   Why place
the former in a column by itself & the latter under an head without name but with the general designation of *scattering?*

The constitution of Massachusetts requires that the town clerk
in the presence of the selectmen & with their assistance shall
in open town meeting sort & count the votes given for governor,
form a list of the persons voted for — make a fair record of the
same in the town books, & a public declaration thereof in said
meeting; & shall in the presence of the inhabitants seal up
copies of the said list attested by him & the selectmen & send
it to the Secretary's office.   In the town of Parsonsfield a majority of the votes were for Mr. Sullivan.   The committee report
" That there is among said returns a list from the town of Parsonsfield, on the margin of which is written the words following,
to wit; *N. B. by reason of the town clerk being sick, this was
not sealed up in meeting;* but the committee are of opinion, that
the words aforesaid are not in the hand writing of either of the

selectmen or townclerk of Parsonsfield, & is no part of said
return, but an interpolation thereon, & that the same list ought
to remain on said schedule."

This return was signed by the town clerk & two selectmen,
the town clerk being one of the two selectmen. One of the selectmen is a member of the House of Representatives & was in his
seat. A federal senator moved to send for him as a witness not
to contradict but to explain the return. A democratic senator
retired. On the question of sending for the Representative the
senate divided ayes 19 nays 19 Mr. Bacon, the president voted
in the negative. And the report was accepted. Had this return
been rejected Strong would have had a majority.

### Monday June 16, 1806.

The spring & summer thus far have been very cold & dry.
The prospect for a good crop of hay is very small indeed. The
last evening was nearly cold enough for a frost. This day has
been very fair — scarse a cloud to be seen. There was 20 minutes past twelve a total eclipse of the sun. The total obscurity
continued two minutes & a half. It was so dark in my chamber
that I was unable to read. Eight stars appeared visible & two
or three of them very bright & brilliant. The air was very cold
— chilly.

On the 11th instant the disputed election of Massachusetts
was settled in their House of Representatives. The report of
the joint committee was under debate, Mr. King, a republican
moved to postpone it — Carried — Mr. Bigelow then moved to
reject the votes from Lincolville because it did not appear in
the return when the votes were given — carried unanimously.
Mr. Bacon moved that the return from Cambridge which from
the date of the certificate (April 29) appeared not to have been
sealed in the meeting, should be rejected — carried unanimously.
The report of the Committee was recommitted, & they soon
reported, That Caleb Strong had a majority of the votes for

Governor & Wm Heath for Lt. Govr. The report was unanimously agreed to by both the House & Senate. And on the 12th Govr Strong was qualified.[159] Mr. Heath declined — alledged old age as the cause. Previous to the decisions of the House six or seven of the republican members declared publickly in the House that they were fully convinced that Strong was elected by the people & they never would consent any other man should be governor for this year. This declaration, with the fears excited by the Federalists avowing their intention of receding, & the still, to them, more alarming fear least the people should disapprove of their conduct prevented them from bringing Sullivan to the chair. I very much approve of the result. It will produce another year of quiet & safety in that great commonwealth. And I sincerely hope that before another election the zeal & bitterness of both parties will moderate. And that the people will see much of the contest is not for principle, not for public measures, but a controversy for office.

The 14th the Court elected Levi Lincoln, Wm Eustis, Daniel Kilham, Samuel Fowler, Thomas Hazard Jr, Marshall Spring, Benja. J Porter, Nathan Weston & Wm Wedgery as Councillors. Each of them are republicans, & opposed to Govr Strong. This will be an unpleasant year to him.

Thomas J Skinner, treasurer & Jona L Austin secretary. Both democrats.

### Wednesday 25th.

The weather since the eclipse has been most of the time very cold for the season. Wind W & NW. On the 20th in the morning there was a very fine moderate shower. In the evening a moderate shower attended with some thunder & lightning. The 21st the wind was NW & very high & in the evening a frost. The ground is very dry indeed — we shall have very small crops

---

[159] A brief account of the disputed election is given in Bradford, *History of Massachusetts*, III, 92–93. Sullivan was elected governor in 1807.

of hay — And in many places the worms have very much injured the Indian Corn, & what remains is low.

On the 20th the Legislature of New Hampshire adjourned to May next. I have had little opportunity of knowing what they have done. I think however it is fortunate they have done so little.

The votes for Governor were as follows —

| | |
|---|---:|
| John Langdon | 15,277 |
| Timothy Farrar | 1720 |
| John T. Gilman | 1553 |
| Jeremiah Smith | 902 |
| Oliver Peabody | 866 |
| Scattering | 255 |
| | 20573 |

Clement Storer president of the Senate; Samuel Bell Speaker of the House; Philip Carrigain Jr Secretary — & Nathl Gilman treasurer.

Nahum Parker is elected my successor in the Senate of the United States. I felt no anxiety for a re-election. I studiously avoided saying anything upon the subject — even to my most intimate friends. No doubt much of this indifference proceeded from a full persuasion that a man so moderate in his politic's as I am could not be elected. — I am too much of a federalist to have republican votes, & too much of a Republican deeply to interest federalists in my favor.

The Governor in his speech notices the great unanimity in the votes of the people — the encrease of harmony — recommends that when the Constitution is revised they so change the time of election as to have but one session a year — That other pieces of artillery be provided for the artillery companies — That a fine be imposed on each soldier who is not on muster days provided with the proper accroutrements — And a permanent seat of Government be established & the necessary buildings erected.

### Saturday 28th.

Wind N.W. fair cold & dry — The last night there was so much frost as to kill the tops of brakes in low land.

### Friday July 4th.

On the 1st in the night was a considerable shower attended with much lightning & some thunder. Since then the wind has been at N.W. high & cold.

The thunder shower on the 8th of last month was considerable & very extensive. Three persons were killed in one house in the County of Cheshire in this State — Two in Lebanon in the District of Mayne — & two near Providence in Rhode Island.

Within a few days one or two small shocks of an earthquake has been felt in the District of Mayne. We have had many days, & more evenings, that have been *cloudless.*

To the great misfortune of *drought,* is now added that of grass-hoppers. They are small but numerous.

### Friday July 11, 1806.

On the 8th was a very fine shower with thunder & lightning. This day & even. a very considerable shower. The weather cold —

Hay is selling at Portsmouth from $25 to 30 dollars pr ton.

### Thursday July 17.

Began my haying. Weather still dry.

### Tuesday July 22d

On the 19th was a very considerable fall of rain — Yesterday a shower — to day showery & cloudy.

Hay is now selling at Exeter at $20 — at Portsmouth from $20 to 22 Dollars pr ton.

I have for some time wished to see a full and impartial history of the government of the United States. There are several histories of several of the States — some of the revolution; but none of the Government. A history of the administration of our government, its laws, — of the presidents — heads of departments — of Congress particularly eminent members of it, the judiciary — our connection with foreign powers — negociations — treaties — our connection with the Indian tribes — purchases of lands of them & of France — our commerce & revenue — would, if well executed, be a very useful work. There are many things in relation to this subject that are little known that would be useful to future statesmen. About two months since the thought occured to me to undertake the work. I have, perhaps, as many materials as almost any man — but still I want many more. It is a great & laborious task. It requires much research & investigation — indefatigable industry, & patient labour to render it useful to others and honorable to myself. It requires, I fear, more time than the short period to which my life may be protracted. If well executed it would be an imperishable monument that would perpetuate my name more effectually than anything I could do. It would exist when columns of marble are dissolved & crumbled to dust. If ill executed, it would tarnish & destroy much of the little fame I have acquired.

Most of the historic performances published in the United [States] were written with too much haste. They contain many errors & inaccuraries as to fact — & the style & composition is loose & slovenly. They fall infinately short of the true style & dignity of history. The system of geography & volumes of gazetter's, published by the industrious Dr. Morse [160] are of this number. The Doctor, tho' industrious, has too many vocations —

---

[160] Jedidiah Morse published the *American Universal Geography; The American Geography;* and *The American Gazeteer.*

Sullivan's history of Maine [161] is loose, & incoherent — tis a jumble of fact & fable — It contains too many little trifling incidents. Tho' he is a man of application & industry, yet owing to his professional business & to his natural inaccuracy — every page is stampt with haste — with blunders confusion & perplexity. Trumbulls Connecticut [162] is written in the style of a low dull Chronicle — It relates too many little trivial events.

Hutchinsons Massachusetts,[163] Minot's continuation,[164] Belknaps New Hampshire,[165] William's Vermont,[166] Smith's New York [167] & New Jersey,[168] Jeffersons Virginia [169] & Ramsey South Carolina,[170] hold a more distinguished rank. American literature suffered a great loss in the early death of *Minot,* & a severe stroke by the inebriety of *Ramsey.* [The last was not so] [171]

I have spent most of this day on ruminating on this undertaking — And it has, *now,* for the first time, occurred to me, that it would be advisable to extend the work so as to embrace a general history of the United States, to commence from the first discovery of America by the Europeans — & the biography of eminent Americans. But when I reflect on its extent & immense labour, I shrink from the task. A library must be read & critically examined. Everything that has been published on the subject should be attentively perused. I have the laws of

---

[161] James Sullivan, *History of the District of Maine.*
[162] Benjamin Trumbull, *Complete History of Connecticut, from 1630 to 1764.* 2 vols.
[163] Thomas Hutchinson, *History of the Colony [and Province] of Massachusetts Bay.* 3 vols.
[164] G. R. Minot, *Continuation of the History of the Province of Massachusetts Bay, from the Year 1748 to 1765.* 2 vols.
[165] Jeremy Belknap, *History of New Hampshire.* 3 vols.
[166] Samuel Williams, *Natural and Civil History of Vermont.*
[167] William Smith, *History of the Late Province of New York, from its Discovery to 1762.* 2 vols.
[168] Samuel Smith, *History of the Colony of Nova Caesaria, or New Jersey.*
[169] [Thomas Jefferson], *Notes on the State of Virginia.*
[170] David Ramsay, *History of South Carolina, from its First Settlement in 1670, to the Year 1808.* 2 vols.
[171] Brackets appear in the original manuscript. The bracketed note evidently was a later addition.

the United States — I have more than 100 volumes of the Journals of Congress & State papers including the reports of Committees of Congress & heads of department. I have three or 4 volumes of Manuscripts & as many of letters containing many useful and necessary facts. I have most of the histories of the several States that have been published in this country — Many volumes of Newspapers. I still want many others — some of whom I think I cannot obtain — at least it will be difficult.

It will require much time & labour — & I have a weak & feeble constitution. Virgil devoted 12 years in composing the Eneid — & Gibbon 20 years in making his Roman history.

I have a sick wife, to render whose life happy, both inclination & duty unite. I have a young promising family of children to whose education I am bound by affection & the most sacred principles to devote a considerable portion of my time. My eldest son, who promises to be a man of science, is now in his 18th year. He is at Harvard college — this is the first year he has been there. I did not wish to have him enter early. I was desirous he should while acquiring, know the importance & value, of knowledge.

The work will be attended with much expence and if I should live to compleat & publish it — the *copy right,* will perhaps never renumerate it. My property is of the value of near $50,000, a considerable portion of this is in uncultivated lands that instead of being productive is a large annual charge. My homestead is in good repair — but not productive. The residue of my estate is in Banks, Marine Insurance offices, evidences of the public debt of the United States & private securities. The care of my property is every year requiring less of my time & attention. This property I have all but about $3000 acquired by the unremitted industry of less than 18 years unwearied application to the business of my profession as a lawyer, & to the use of my money.

I live a prudent, frugal, retired country life. I expend annually from 12 to \$1500 including the education of my children. My life is a life of temperance. I am not a man of pleasure — I am not fond of pomp or parade. My life has been a life of industry & application. — And It is now chiefly divided between my pen & my books.

I am no scholar — I am not even master of the English grammar — & I cannot read any other language. It requires much time to express my ideas on paper so as to satisfy myself — Tho' I find I compose with more & greater facility than formerly.

I am greatly deficient in geography and subjects of general science. This will prove a great impediment to my progress in this contemplated work.

I am quite undertermined whether I shall pursue this project or not. I am conscious that the most busy life is the most happy. When my term in Congress expires, which will be next March, I shall then decide ultimately. If I do not commence historian, I may most probably return to the bar, & with renewed avidity again enter upon the noisy, active bustle of that profession. Should that be the case, I shall probably remove to Portsmouth, for the sake of giving my children a better education, & of enjoying more & better society. I have a strong reluctance to returning to the bar. I dislike the drudgery & fatigues of the business — And I am not ambitious of wealth. The many materials I have collected, & that without a view to my writing any history — there being no one, of the kind I contemplate — the use it may be to mankind — the prospect of acquiring fame with posterity — seem to unite in urging me to the task. If I begin it is my first resolution not to be in haste to publish — But to write with candour, & faithfully narrate facts, & truly delineate characters.

Since my return from Congress I have employed all my leisure hours in recording & correcting my letters, which I have brot up within ten years of this time — recording the notes &

extracts from books I formerly read — reports of pleas & cases
in Courts of law — & of essays & select pieces. To each of
these alternately I devote a week. Of this I have much to do
— It now engrosses all my leisure hours, except evenings in
which I read. This business I shall continue till I return to
Washington. I shall also continue to make arrangements &
collect materials for the history.

I have some doubts in what manner to write whether to attempt the dignity of history & divide my work into books &
chapters; or write in the more familiar style of letters. The
last is the easiest & perhaps is that species for which I have
the greatest talent. But why speak of manner when I have
not even determined to commence the work.

. . . . . . . . . . . . . . . . . . . . . . . . .

### Friday [August] 22d

I have attended the Court of Common Pleas this term —
though I have been successful in my suits — still the business
is not pleasant to me — tis too fatiguing for my slender constitution. My health will, if nothing else, prevent my return
to the practise of Law.

### Monday 25th.

This was the election of Members of Congress for this State.
I attended & voted myself for Wm King Atkinson, Josiah Bart-
let, Samuel Bell, Caleb Ellis & Ben. J Gilbert — honest men
& true — Men that I should not be ashamed to meet in the
Council of my Nation — They will not be chosen. The Democratic list will prevail — feeble as they are — Each of them will
gain most votes where least known. My tickett is of both
parties but all of them are moderate but firm men. There is
a great apathy & indifference to the election — I attempted to
influence no man — I asked no man to vote — In this town 43
votes were all.

. . . . . . . . . . . . . . . . . . . . . . . . .

### Monday [September] 22d.

The votes of Representatives of this State in the next Congress of the US. have been returned, & the result is That Clement Storer had 5695, Daniel M Durrel 5123, Jedediah Kilburn Smith 5773, Francis Gardner 5677, & Peter Carlton 5695 votes & are chosen. The present members had the following number of votes to wit Samuel Tenny 3685, Caleb Ellis 3625, David Hugh 3596, Thomas W Thompson 2838, Silas Betton 2825 votes. The scattering votes were considerable but I have not ascertained their number.

At the election in 1804, the present members, had, I think, rising 12,000 votes each. There now appears a spirit of indifference on the subject. I regret that men devoid of talent, information, & respectability, should be called to represent the State in the Supreme legislature of the Nation.

. . . . . . . . . . . . . . . . . . . . . . . .

### Wednesday [November] 12th.

Early last winter Mr. Jefferson & his confidential friends at Washington gave information that he would again be a candidate for the Presidency. Just before Congress adjourned his intimate friends whispered that they beleived he might be persuaded to stand candidate for another term — From that time, I pronounced to my friends, that he was not only willing, but anxious, to secure a re-election.

In September Duane, & a few others, in Philadelphia procured meetings of the Republicans in the different wards in that city, who passed resolutions approving of Mr. Jefferson's administration, & expressing their anxious wishes for him to stand Candidate. They appointed a committee to address the president on the subject. A few weeks since the same proceedings have been had in the City of New York. These are to sound the public mind — & I presume that Mr. Jefferson was consulted & approved of the measure before it was whispered in the streets of Philadelphia or New York.

More than two years & a quarter yet remain of the present term — & yet the incumbent is looking forward to a re-election. What firmness, or system, can we expect from a Chief Majestrate who has a re-election so often & so much in view? — I do not love the man who is wholly regardless of publick opinion — But I despise him who will sacrifice his own well informed Judgmt to the clamour of the populace — I love, I venerate, I idolize, the public officer, who takes the necessary measures to obtain correct information what the public interest requires of him, & who with prudence but inflexible firmness discharges his duty. Such a man, tho' not displeased with public approbation, will enquir is a measure just & necessary, not will it render me popular? I do not love that popularity that is sought for; but I love that which follow the man & is the result of virtuous actions.

How few men have integrity & nerves to serve the people agt the will and pointed opposition of the populace? — There are *moments* in which public opinion is wild. — How small is the chance of such a ruler in a popular election agt a cunning time serving candidate? This circumstance alone forms a strong objection to our form of Government.

### Saturday Even Nov 15.

I have packed up my things — & tomorrow noon intend to set out for the seat of government. It is now a cold storm of rain — wind N.E. & high. —

### Sunday 16

Last night fell 4 Inches of snow.

### Register [172]

---

[172] This marks the beginning of Plumer's *Register* for the second session of the Ninth Congress (December 1, 1806–March 3, 1807).

### Wednesday Nov 26, 1806.

I arrived at the city of Washington in good health — an account of my journey I have related in a letter to my wife.

### Thursday 27.

Took my lodging at the house of Frost & Quinn — visited Georgetown.

### Friday 28.

Reports have for some time circulated from one end of the United States to the other, that Aaron Burr, late Vice President, with others, in the western States are preparing gun boats, provisions, money, men &c to make war upon the Spaniards in South America — that his intention is to establish a new empire in the western world — & that he contemplates forming this Empire from South America & the western States of North America —

Yesterday the President of the United States issued a proclamation, which is made public today. It states, " That information has been received that sundry persons, citizens of the United States, or residents within the same, are conspiring & confederating together to begin & set on foot, provide & prepare the means for a military expedition or enterprize agt. the dominions of Spain, that for this purpose, they are fitting out & arming vessels in the waters of the United States, collecting provisions, arms, military stores, & other means, are deceiving & seducing honest & well meaning citizens, under various pretences, to engage in their criminal enterprizes, are organizing, officering & arming themselves for the same, contrary to the law in such case made & provided." — It requires, all persons concerned in such conspiracy to withdraw from the same, & cease all further proceedings therein — And it requires all officers to be diligent in searching, arresting & bringing such offenders to condign punishment — & to seize all vessels, arms,

military stores, or other means provided or providing for such
expedition ——

There are many things reported agt Mr. Burr — some of
them too foolish for him to be guilty off.

Wm. Eaton has certified, That, Mr. Burr last winter desired
him (Eaton) to accept of a commission under Burr — That
Burr told Eaton that Genl Wilkinson was second in command
— & under him, & that Eaton should be third.   This is not the
language of the cunning cautious wily Burr.   He would never
use such language to a man so imprudent, wild, & raving as
Eaton.

Burr is capable of much wickedness — but not so much folly.

### *Saturday 29th.*

Paid my respects to Mr. Jefferson the president.

He told me that the drought in Virginia this year exceeded
anything of the kind he ever knew — That large rivers had
ceased to run — & that there was not more than half a crop of
Indian corn. —

He said he had no doubt that preparations were making in
the Western States to form an expedition against Spanish America — That the conspirators were building from 12 to 15 gun
boats near Marietta in the Ohio — That he presumed they were
now launched — That provisions to a considerable amount was
collected — That the contractor of the Stage leading to Pittsburgh had given information, that in the course of a few days,
more than a 100 active young men had gone on toward that
country — That another contractor, on a different rout, said
he had seen more than ten times that number — That these
men were of a class superior to the common labouring people.

It was my intention to have been particular in my enquiries
into this subject; but the servant announced that the Secretary
of the Navy was in the other room. — I conceived it proper, &
I rose bowed & retired.

At Philadelphia, 3 things were stated to me — 1. That Burr had spent some time in that city — & had been observed frequently visiting in a private manner the Marquiss De Yrujo. 2d That a few of his confidential friends had given dinners to a particular class of young enterprizing men of good families — That Burr was present.   3d — That 2 or 3 young men presented an affidavit to the Chief Justice of Pennsylvania Tilghman stating that Burr had made overtures to them to engage in a secret expedition — But Tilghman declined swaring them — alledging he did not think himself authorized to issue a warrant to arrest Mr. Burr — But said he would communicate the information to the Secy of State.

This information was given me by Ceasar Augustus Rodney Esq;[173] who called to see me at my lodgings.

Some few years since, during the time when Mr. Burr was Vice President, I used to visit him, in Washington, frequently — He several times invited me to his table — He always entertained his company well — his manners were those of the finished gentleman.  I never dined at any house with more pleasure than at his lodgings.  This was in the early part of the winter of 1804; when the Republicans had decided he could not be their candidate for the office of Vice President.  He & his friends had then announced him as candidate for the office of Governor of New York.

At this time Timothy Pickering, James Hillhouse, myself & others, dined with him one day.  Mr. Hillhouse unequivocally declared that it was his opinion that the United States would soon form two distinct & seperate governments — On this subject Mr. Burr conversed very freely — & the impression that his observations made on my mind, was, that he not only

---

[173] Caesar Augustus Rodney, representative to the Eighth Congress; one of the managers who conducted the impeachment trial of Judge Samuel Chase; Attorney General of the United States from January, 1807 to December, 1811; in later life a member of the House of Representatives and the Senate; died in Buenos Aires in 1824, while acting as minister plenipotentiary to Argentina.

thought *such an event would take place — but that it was neces-sary it should.* — To that opinion I was then a convert. I well recollect, that on my return to my lodgings, I carefully recollected every sentiment & even expression that were used by Mr. Burr, upon that subject. And after critically analyzing his conversation there was nothing that he said that necessarily implied his approbation of Mr. Hillhouse's observations.

In after visits I became more particularly attentive to the language of Mr. Burr — & I found he possessed the talent of making an impression of an opinion upon the subject, on the person with whom he conversed, without explicitly stating or necessarily giving his sentiments thereon. In every thing he said or did, he had a design — & perhaps no man's language was ever so apparently explicit, & at the same time so covert & indefinite.[174]

### *Sunday 30th.*

In a conversation this day with Abraham Baldwin a senator from Georgia — & a member of the Convention who formed the Constitution of the United States — he said that, Genl Washington at that time, in a morning's walk, told him he did not expect the constitution would exist more than 20 years.

He said, That the convention was more than once upon the point of dissolving without agreeing upon any system. Many beleived they had no authority to report a new system, but only propose amendments to the old articles of Confederation. Some were for a government of energy embracing many objects of legislation — but others to have a more limited authority & to extend to fewer objects. All were better pleased with it when the propositions were reduced to form & connected together than they expected. All the members present, except three signed it — these were Elbridge Gerry of Massachusetts, George Mason & Edmund Randolph of Virginia.

---

[174] *Cf.* Plumer, *Life of William Plumer,* 283 ff., where (p. 295), Plumer's words are quoted, but with a condensation of the original.

Mr. Baldwin observed That after the instrument was engrossed & ready to be signed, Genl Washington then President of the convention rose, with his pen in his hand — & observed, That his duty as presiding officer, & his inclination had united in preventing him from taking an active part in the interesting debates of that body — That doubts might exist whether *he approved* of the instrument, or only signed it by order of the Convention — he tho't it his duty to remove these doubts by explicitly declaring That tho' he did not consider it a perfect system — yet he approved of it as a man, & as a delegate from Virginia. — There was however one feature in it he wished, even at this late hour, might be changed — It was the only favor he had, or would ask of the Convention — That was the representation of the States — 40,000 souls he tho't too high a number for a representative. — A state, who has from 70 to 100 representatives in its Legislature, will if this principle is retained have not more than 2, 3, or 4 representatives in the House of Representatives in Congress. This principle, to him, appeared antirepublican — He wished the convention would strike out 40, & insert 30,000 — To this the Convention unanimously agreed.[175] ——

### Monday Dec 1.

A motion was made in the House of Representatives, that the standing Committees should be appointed by ballot, and not by the Speaker. The house divided on the question ayes 42, nays 44. The federalists voted in the negative.

### Tuesday 2d.

The President of the United States this day communicated his message to Congress.[176] . . .

---

[175] *Cf. Debates in the Federal Convention of 1787* reported by James Madison (Hunt and Scott, editors), 579.

[176] Plumer's summary of the message is here omitted. For the full text, see Richardson, *Messages and Papers of the Presidents,* I, 405–410.

This message, will, I think, prove a popular one. The administration certainly deserve well of their country in their paying off so much of the public debt.

In the note I made, Nov 29th, of my visit to the President, I ommited to observe that he said, That he was anxious to have some enterprizing merchantile Americans go on to the river Columbia & near the Pacific ocean, & settle the land there.[177] That they might easily engross the fur & peltry trade with the Indians — which he conceived would soon be very lucrative — That he beleived no European nation claimed either the soil or jurisdiction — That he was informed by Capt. Lewis it would Meet with the approbation of the Indians living in that country — But the President — added that he doubted whether it would be prudent for the government of the United States to attempt such a project — because their concerns & business with Indian tribes are of vast extent and subject us to considerable expense.

### Wednesday 3d.

The President of the US. sent a message to Congress,[178] in which he states, " That the negociation between the United States & Great Britain, is proceeding in a spirit of friendship & accomodation which promises a result of mutual advantage " — " That we find, by the communications of our plenipotentiaries, that a temporary suspension of the act of the last session, prohibiting certain importations, would, as a mark of candid disposition on our part, & of confidence in the temper & views with which they have been met, have a happy effect on its course." ——

The President concludes by saying — " I cannot, therefore, but recommend the *suspension* of this act for a reasonable time, on considerations of justice, amity, & the public interests."

This Non-Importation act ought never to have passed — &

---

[177] Astoria was founded in 1811.
[178] See Richardson, *Messages and Papers of the Presidents*, I, 411.

it seems to me — that instead of a *suspension* it ought now to be *repeal* of the law. That to suspend its operation, will still be considered by the British Court, as holding it up as a threat & menace. The most manly & dignified course would be at once to repeal the law — And it appears to me that every reason that operates in favor of a suspension operates with equal force for a repeal. But it is said with the Government, as with an individual, it requires an exertion to confess, we have erred and done wrong — we must re-trace our course. The pride of Administration will not be so much wounded by suspending, as it would by repealing, the law.

### Thursday 4.

Some few days since Genl Turreau, the French Ambassador, privately hired some French sailors to come to his house in the night to take his wife & carry her on board a French frigate then at Annapolis, but bound to France. They came seized the woman — bound & gagged her — but her child alarmed a Maid whose attachment to her mistress induced her to run into the streets — & by crying murder, with a strong voice — raised so many of the sovereign people as rescued Mrs. Turreau from the grasp of the sailors. The General himself appeared at the window, & threatened the people he would discharge his pistol at them, if they did not release his wife. But they refused — & in turn threatened to destroy him — He retired — & they carried off his wife in triumph. They have since sent to him to support her — but he refuses, as says report.

There is no doubt she came to this Country much against his will — She did not come in the same ship with him. There was a report that the ship in which she came was lost. I well recollect enquiring of him of the fact, & of his saying — " I fear it is so, for I had 30 boxes of furniture in the ship."

'Tis disgraceful that such a man should be the representative of a nation! 'Tis degrading both to the nation who sends, & to the nation who receives such a minister!

### Friday Dec 5.

Dr. Park of Boston has a few days since published in his Repertory, a statement purporting to be the conversation of Mr. Burr with William Eaton the last winter — & of Eaton's giving information to the President.[179] It appears that Mr. Eaton declares this statement published by Park to be correct. From this we are informed, That Burr disclosed to Eaton his intention to attempt a seperation of the western states from the Union, & to invade Mexico — & invited him to join in the project — And yet in this same statement, revised by Eaton himself, we are told that Eaton represented Burr as a dangerous man in this country, & tho' a traitor — yet he (Eaton) recommended the President to appoint him (Burr) minister either to London or Madrid — for says Eaton " if Burr is put upon his honor he would act with fidelity." After this what opinion ought a man to form of Mr. Eaton?

There are contradictory accounts of Eaton's declarations published. I do not beleive his relations either in this or his Mediterranean expedition. He is too light, too fleeting, too unsteady a man to gain my beleif — I very much question the soundness of his heart & the correctness of his head — both are distempered.[180]

### Saturday 6th.

I recollect that near the close of the last session, walking one evening with General Bradley — he told me, *he beleived Eaton would be a member of the next Congress.* Soon after this, I confidentially told Mr. Ely the member from that District that I had heard Eaton was to be ran against him. He told me he gave no credit to it. Ely is a federalist from Massachusetts. A few weeks preceeding the election, an anonymous printed address to the Electors of that district, was circulated in the

[179] See Boston *Repertory,* November 25, 1806.
[180] Compare with Plumer's earlier impression of Eaton, page 351.

district, recommending Mr. Eaton as well qualified to represent them in Congress. In the address was a letter purporting to be written & signed by Eaton, wrote to a friend, in which he declares himself to be of *no party in politics* — & intimates that if elected he would serve. Mr. Eaton has always professed himself a warm federalist. This letter he has never denied to be genuine. It disgusted many of the Federalists — He had a very few votes — The party thot it a trick — & Mr. Ely was re-elected. It was said that this circular of Eaton's was printed in Connecticut under the direction of Alexander Woolcott [181] — I think it was printed at Vermont, or in Walpole New Hampshire, under Bradley's care.

### Sunday 7.

I am much pleased with my accomodations. I board with Frost & Quinn on Capitol Hill, about 80 rods from Congress hall. I have a very convenient chamber, in front of the house on the second story, to myself. The house is neat & clean — good bed — good table — & thus far the servants appear good. There are now only six members of Congress besides myself, & Mrs. Tenney,[182] who are boarders. We all eat at one table — We eat in a large chamber — which is our parlour, & in which we meet for conversation, & to receive company. Although the house is a hotel, no person is admitted into our parlour but with our consent. The house is still & quiet. none of the lodgers are noisy — each is sober. All are federalists.

It has not been usual for the Host to provide any liquors for his guests — Our's however sets half a pint of brandy & gin, each day, on the dining table. — Of which we do not drink more than half. At every other place at which I have boarded in this city, the boarders have formed into a club & appointed a steward to provide spirits & wine. But here no person of the

---

[181] Probably Dr. Alexander Wolcott, brother of Oliver Wolcott.
[182] Wife of Samuel Tenney, representative from New Hampshire.

Mess has mentioned it. I have myself purchased a Demijohn of Madeira wine; London particular — which I keep in my closet in my own room — give it to my friends who visits me — & drink of it there myself.

Frost & Quinn have made great preparation for boarders — but have few — They must suffer by the undertaking. Mrs. Frost told me they had expended $4,000 for furniture for the house — & they have many servants, & pay high rent — & appear to have but little transcient company at their hotel. — There price for members of Congress, two in a chamber, is $10. pr week. There are more boarding houses on the Hill than there ever were before — at some of them, the price, two in a room, is $8 pr week. —

### Monday 8.

Some days since Mr. Tracy laid a resolution on the table requesting that the President of US. would communicate to the Senate such correspondence &c from our Minister's in London as he should think proper relative to the Act passed last session prohibiting the importation of certain articles from Great Britain. To day the resolution was after debate, negatived — Tracy, Hillhouse, Bradley, Pickering & White only voted in the affirmative.[183] I voted agt the resolution, because 1, I wanted no official information to convince me of the fitness & propriety of either suspending or repealing said law. The nature of the subject did not require it. 2, The President in his message says our Minister's are of opinion that the suspension of the Act is necessary to aid their negociation & he also explicitly recommends it. In a case like this I am bound to beleive them — & do not think it necessary that I should see their reasoning on the subject. 3, I think it pernicious that the correspondence of our ministers should be communicated upon a negociation *that is pending.* The doctrine *That a Re-*

---

[183] *Cf. Annals of Congress,* 9 Cong., 2 sess., 18–19.

*public has no secrets,* is false & absurd — it ought not to be countenanced by any man.

The federalists say that the British ministers will not treat untill this act is suspended. The Republicans deny this. My curiosity as a man is strong to read the correspondence — but my duty as a senator compelled me to vote against its being communicated to the Senate.

After the vote was taken Mr. Giles said to me, in confidence he was *certain* (intimating he had seen the correspondence) that there was nothing in the letters from our Envoys that conveyed an idea that the British government required the suspension of the Law as a condition precedent — But they contained this idea, to wit, That if the American government had confidence in the sincerity of the British, & did not mean that Act should be considered as a threat they (Congress) would suspend the law. —

## *Tuesday 9th.*

The motion, (p. 521) [184] That the standing committees should be appointed by ballot, was bro't forward to prevent John Randolphs being chairman of the committee of ways & means. The Speaker, who appoints the committees, is friendly to Randolph — Indeed the latter governs the former. Soon after it was determined that the committees should not be chosen by ballot, & previous to their being appointed, Mr. Randolph had a conversation with the Speaker. The Speaker did not appoint him one of that committee — Joseph Clay of Philadelphia was the man first named. By the rules of the House, if a committee do not appoint a chairman, the man first named is of course chairman. The next day Mr. Garnet,[185] the intimate friend of Mr. Randolph, who was member of that committee, requested the House to excuse him from that service. His request was

---

[184] Page 519 of this volume.
[185] James Mercer Garnett, representative from Virginia.

granted. The Speaker appointed John Randolph in his room. The committee met, & unanimously elected him their chairman.

## *Wednesday 10th.*

At the last session of Congress it was expected that the south wing of the Capitol would be so far finished as that the House of Representatives would be able to sit therein. The walls are up, & the roof is nearly laid over, but not finished. There are no windows put in. — The inside work is very far from being done. This wing will be an elegant & superb building when finished. It appears very strong & substantial. There is no wood in it till you come up to the roof. The lower story, most of which is under ground, is covered with Arches made of brick. The second story is formed by arches of brick — but much larger than those in the first — On the tops of the arches in the second story is to be laid the floor for the hall in which the Representatives are to sit. From, and on, the outside of this hall, stand large stone pillars the tops of which support the roof, together with arches of brick, thrown over from the outside of the building to the stones laying across the top of these pillars.

To this wing are three stair cases. Two of them are from the bottom of the building to the top. The steps are of stone — the outer end is the smallest, & forms a very handsome column. They are winding stairs & the most elegant I ever saw.

Between two pillars, & at the top of them over the Speakers seat, but a little back of his chair, is the figure of a large eagle with his wings extended. It is carved out of a rock, & is well executed. It is the work of an Italian.

I never saw so large a building that appears to have so little room in it. The arches in the first & second story, are several of them designed as rooms to deposit papers in. I think they will not only be too dark, but that they so much exclude the

air, as will render them so damp & moist as to destroy the ink
& paper.

The north wing of the Capitol was finished in a most shame-
ful manner.  Dr. Thornton,[186] who superintended it, knew little
of architecture — was incapable of designing it properly — &
was, deserving, of more censure for his gross inattention to the
manner in which it was executed.  The building now leaks so
much that in every storm that falls, the water leaks down into
every room.  It not only renders it damp & unhealthy, but
keeps the minds of members, during every storm, in a state
of fear & uneasiness, least the wall, which is thick & high, should
fall on them & either maim or kill them.  I own I have sat for
hours in my chair rather uneasy.  The falling of water once
obliged me to leave my seat.  The last session at the door of
the Representatives chamber, just after they passed, there fell
near 500 ℔ weight of plaistering.  This week the members of
that house have been so much alarmed for themselves, that they
have suspended their business, & requested their Speaker to
examine the wall, & take measures to render it secure.

### *Thursday 11th.*

The Legislature of the State of Vermont in their last autumn
session have agreed to, & sent an Address, to Mr. Jefferson expressing their wishes that he would condescend to be a candidate
for the next presidential election.

General Bradley, of the State, said to me this day, " That it
was time to have some other man president — That Mr. Jefferson's influence in Congress was irresistable — that it was alarming — That if he should recommend to us to repeal the Gospels
of the Evangelist, a majority of Congress would do it."

---

[186] William Thornton, physician, architect, and first head of the patent
office.  The latter post he held from 1802 until his death in 1827.

### Friday 12th.

The Senate this day passed the bill sent from the House, to suspend, the non-importation law of last session, till July next — with an amendment that the President be authorized further to suspend it till Dec next, if to him it shall appear necessary.

To day received European intelligence, that I have for some time expected, that Napolean has defeated, & in short, destroyed the Prussian army — & is in possession of Berlin. Prussia is now subject to his will — The Emperor of France is the wonder & astonishment of the world. His name is a host — The world trembles before him. The rapidity of his movements are really astonishing! Who can set limits to his conquests! This man is now able to disturb the repose of the world! Europe bows submission to his will — England however is not yet conquered, tho' I fear one season more, will render her a province to France. I think Bonaparte will find it difficult to conquer Russia. There, I trust, his empire will be bounded. Tis fortunate for us that a vast ocean seperates America from Europe. This, I hope, will prove a barrier against his great power.

He is the idol of his vast army — & in his army *merit, alone,* is the qualification for promotion. This has done much, much indeed, in rendering that army invincible. Some of his bravest generals are from the most obscure & illiterate families. He seeks with avidity for merit, & rewards it promptly, & with vast liberality. The British have long practised upon the same principle in their navy; & it has become the terror of the world. A contrary principle seems to have been adopted by them as respects their armies. In the British army I do not recollect a single great distinguished officer. It may not be attainable for any nation, at the same time, to have the greatest & best army & navy. There union in one nation would too much endanger the peace & security of the world.

The French nation is now subject to a military government.

They are now literally a nation of soldiers. — And their vast resources & physical force is directed by a single mind — By a man who will crumble all the confederacies of Europe to dust. — His object seems to be clear — tis to render Europe a federative government — a government not republican but monarchical — a government of kings subject to his will. And his prospects for success are surely too flattering. Within a short time he has dissolved the Germanic constitution — & established a number of tributary kings, in what he calls the *Confederacy of the Rhine.* And 'tis not difficult to see what use he will make of his late successes against Prussia.

How very different has been the fate of Miranda! Tis near a year since he sailed from New York, elated with the prospect of revolutionizing the provinces of Caraccas. In this he has failed — From the main he sailed to Barbadoes — He dared not land, least sheriffs should arrest him for debt. A few days since he landed at Trinadad with his little army in a most deplorable condition. The merchants met & petitioned the government to compel him to leave the island. The Gov[r]. pledged himself he should carry on no offensive operations, but by his orders. Many of Miranda's followers are young enterprizing men — of good families — they are now scarsely able to get bread to eat. They execrate their leader. I pity them — their expectations were too sanguine — they were deceived. — Miranda was too precipitate — he is bold & enterprizing — He may yet rise to consequence — such restless spirits very often do. The British have recently conquered Buenos Ayres [187] — they may yet turn their arms agt. Caraccas & Mexico — & in that case Miranda would be highly useful to them. I think he is better qualified for subordinate, than supreme command.

My notes this evening have been more prolix than usual. My *Register* ought to have been called the *Waste* book — for I write

---

[187] The city of Buenos Aires was captured by a small British force in June, 1806, but was soon retaken by the Argentinians.

in too much haste — I have not time to correct my style & composition. I need not register this fact — Whenever I read these pages I shall have plenary evidence of it.

### Monday Dec 15, 1806.

Mr. Erskine,[188] his Britannic Majesty Minister plenipotentiary, & Mr. Dearborn secretary of War, visited me, by leaving cards at my lodging.

### Tuesday 16th.

General Bradley told me this day, in confidence, that he was well acquainted with Mr. Burr's designs & movements in the western States. — That I might be assured there was nothing treasonable — or tending to a seperation of the western States.

That long before the king of Spain had ceded Louisiana to France, he granted to Baron Bastrop a tract of land thirty miles square, of immence value, in that province — That this grant was made on condition of Bastrop having a certain number of settlers thereon within a certain term — That the king on his part was to furnish the settlers with rations for a certain number of years. That an after agreement was made between the grantor & grantee prolonging the term for procuring settlers. That at the time when the country was ceded to the United States the settlement duties were far from being performed — That sometime after the cession to the United States Bastrop conveyed the premises to one Lynch, either of Virginia or Kentucky  That Lynch was to pay him a certain sum by installments — That he made one payment — & then conveyed the land to a certain number of men of whom Burr was one. That after this conveyance from Lynch to Burr &als a suit was commenced in the Federal court in the Orleans territory by Bastrop agt. Lynch, in chancery, praying that Lynch might be compelled to

---

[188] David Montague Erskine succeeded Merry as British minister at Washington.

pay him the money promised & damages, or that the land might be decreed to him again. Lynch made answer to the bill, in the nature of a disclaimer, stating that he had no interest in the premises — but that previous to the commencement of the suit he had conveyed all his right & title to A B & others, naming them. The court, without notifying A B &als, gave judgment that Bastrop should have the land again. That Burr & his associates, 30 in all, are of opinion that the judgment does not conclude any person but Lynch — that they, not being privy to it, are not effected by it — That the associates had a meeting the last summer in the State of New York — That Genl Curtis of Vermont, Samuel Hunt of New Hampshire are associates — That two or three very wealthy men in New York are of the number — That he intended to have been one himself. That he went to the place of meeting but was too late. That the greatest fears of the associates are, that Bastrop will take actual possession, & forcably hold it — That to prevent this they have procured men — provisions & boats, & mean immediately to take possession — That Burr is the *Conductor Generalis* of this expedition — That this tract is of immense value — & that the associates will make fortunes. He said That Alston,[189] Burr's son in law, speaker of the Assembly in South Carolina, had advanced $70,000 — That large sums had been advanced by others.

I then observed, if it was necessary to expend so much money, I doubted whether the speculation would be profitable to the associates. He said the great number of young men who had engaged to go on as settlers made it necessary — but that there were in that country other grants of extensive tracts that they intended to take up. Upon my representing that the preparations of the associates appeared disproportionate to the professed object — Bradley appeared confused & embarrassed.

He told me that the District Judge & Atty of Kentucky, after

---

[189] Joseph Allston, who married Burr's daughter Theodosia.

complaint filed by the latter & process requested agt Burr —
were confidentially told by Mr. Burr what his real object in all
this preparation was — & that disclosure was the real cause of
the witnesses not being examined before the grand jury, agt
Burr — & not the absence of one of them as stated in the Newspapers.

How much of this relation is correct I cannot tell — I never
place implicit confidence in Bradley's information. I know he
was intimate with Burr — & if he is capable of friendship, I
should say he was the friend of that man.

If Burr designed a division of the States, or the conquest of
Mexico, or both — a speculation in land, would be an excellent
pretext under which to cover the preparation.

### *Wednesday 17.*

The Senate, without division, advised to the appointment of
Brockholst Livingston of New York as associate justice of the
Supreme Court of the United States in the room of William
Patterson deceased. Livingston was a Judge of the Superior
Court in the State of New York — He supports the reputation
of an able lawyer & good judge. I beleive the appointment will
be generally approved. Altho' no court has been held for sometime the President in the recess appointed him. His commission
issued on the 8th of last month. This would entitle him to
salary from that time. Genl Bradley said to me, had Livingston lived in Vermont, & my colleague in New York, the latter
would have been appointed. Great states will have a commanding influence on a President who intends to stand, candidate for a re-election.

The Speaker of the House stated that he had received an
anonymous letter, directed to the House — that the writer calls
himself a foreigner — & requests that the letter might be read
with closed doors. Mr. Newton [190] moved to have it lay on the

---

[190] Thomas Newton, Jr., representative from Virginia.

table — Mr. Early [191] to have it burnt — Mr. Bidwell [192] hoped no order would be taken with it — His wish was gratified.

The letter was postmarked, *Philadelphia* — It intimates that Napolean intends to invade the United States — recommends raising an army, and placing Moreau at the head of it. — says, his next letter shall be from Bordeau.

This day returned visits by cards to Mr. Erskine & Mr. Dearborn. The most polite mode is to let the coachman, when you arrive at the door, take your card, & give it to the servant of the gentleman whom you visit. You make no enquiry for the gentleman.

### Thursday 18th.

General Turreau, & Mr. Petry, first secretary of Legation, paid me visits this day, by leaving cards. The General's card was the small piece of a common playing card. I am told that all his visiting cards, this session are in that style. The English minister's are elegant with handsome copper plate engraving.

In conversation with Gideon Granger I asked him, if the account published in the newspapers of November last, of his taking down William Eaton's conversation respecting Aaron Burr — & of Eaton's susbcribing the same, was true? He replied it was true — & he had delivered the paper, or a copy of it. (I cannot say which) to the President of the United States.

Mr. Granger appears anxious to have people beleive he is not friendly to Mr. Burr. He shewed me a letter from the western country stating that Burr near Pittsburgh was fitting a number of boats, collecting men & provisions. — He, Granger, ordered a Clerk to transcribe a paragraph from this letter. That paragraph was afterwards (for this conversation was on saturday) on monday last published in the " National Intelligencer."

---

[191] Peter Early, representative from Georgia.
[192] Barnabas Bidwell, representative from Massachusetts.

*Friday 19th.*

Went in the evening to the Theatre to see Manfredi., wife, daughters & son dance on the tight rope — ballance — & perform other feats — price one dollar. I was much pleased with them — They were very nimble — discovered much art in ballancing — great agility & muscular force. I do not think my time or money mispent — There were about 150 persons present — many of whom were members of Congress — About a dozen ladies present.

*Saturday 20th.*

Visited, by cards, Genl Turreau & Mr Petry.

Weather very warm for the season — snow nearly dissolved — roads wet and muddy. Robins & blue birds singing. —

David Stone, one of the senators from North Carolina, has always come early in the session & had his name entered on the journal — & in the course of a very few days, without obtaining leave from the Senate, has returned to his own house. This session he tarried but a *few days* — obtained a considerable sum of money for his travel & attendance & then left the city. He will no doubt before the close of the session return — & receive his pr diem from the commencement to the end of the session. It is not now the practise, for senators who absent themselves, to ask liberty of absence. If they did that, their diurnal pay would cease — but now their wages continues as well when absent as present. The practise is, I think, dishonorable.

Genl Samuel Smith of Maryland appeared the first or 2d day — remained in town two days only, & then returned to his family.

*Sunday 21.*

In a conversation with John G. Jackson, one of the Representatives of Virginia, He told me that the taxes levied upon the inhabitants of that State, by their Legislature were as high as

they dared to impose — that the burthens were very considerable
— That as a State they were always in debt — That the demands
on their Treasury exceeded the appropriations made by the
legislature — & that the appropriations always, by far, exceeded
the money on hand.

There roads, he told me, were very bad — but at such a time
as the present, a thaw, they were dangerous — & in the night
impassable — That on their great roads, waggoners would often
throw down the fences & for miles, to the great injury of the
proprietors, travel through the inclosures.

He added that the tax for the support of roads was a kind of
capitation tax — for that it was of the same amount to a poor
as to a wealthy man.

I am myself inclined to think it is more expensive to make &
keep in repair a good road in Virginia or Maryland than it is in
New England.   In the latter, the steady cold of more than three
months in the year, renders repairs, during that period, unnecessary — except sometimes making paths through the snow.   Nor
does the thaws of spring greatly injure the roads; for a few days
the travelling is bad — but soon the roads settle, become firm
& good.   But, in these southern states the frosts are often, but
continue for a few days only.   Every thaw renders their roads
wet, muddy, founderous & rutty — & require frequent & considerable repairs to render them good.   There rains, are, I beleive, more frequent than with us in the east — their rivers and
rivulets rise much more rapidly — And their hills are more
washed and gullyed than in New England.

Mr. Granger, the postmaster general assured me, that for
sometime he had been obliged to send out, at a considerable
expence, men & horses into Virginia, to seperate the letters
from the Newspapers, in the western mail — in order to
have them in season.   The state of things in the western
states rendered this necessary at this juncture.

In a conversation I had, a few days since, with Mr. Gallatin, he told me that not many weeks since he rode from here to Annapolis, on the great public road in his Chaise — That his son a little boy was with him — that he had to get out of his Chaise 37 times to open gates. That the proprietors of the land through which the road ran declared themselves unable to fence it — That these gates were not turnpike gates but put up by the owners of the lands to save the expence of fencing out the road. I think from Washington to Annapolis is about 50 miles only.

The roads in Maryland are generally bad — yet their state treasury, unlike that of Virginia, is rich — & their taxes small.

Yesterday Mr. Findlay,[193] a representative from Pennsylvania, received & delivered an anonymous letter to the President. The purport of it was That Aaron Burr was collecting men & arms with rapidity — & unless efficacious measures were promptly taken & vigorously persued by the Government against him, he would soon be a formidable & dangerous enemy.

At little past twelve the President had all the heads of department at his house, where they remained till near evening. All that I have yet learnt of the result is that dispatches were immediately sent by Expresses into the western country. Government appear to me to want the necessary information. They ought long before this time to have known the actual state of things in that country. This state of incertitude is painful, & to the government disgraceful. If Burr has treasonable designs agt the United States, they ought to have been known, & crushed in embryo. If it is private speculation in lands — the public ought to know it — & be quiet.

Robert Smith, Secy Navy, said yesterday to Genl. Bradley, as he this day informed me, " That he was satisfied Burr was connected with a foreign power, who supplied him with money."

---

193 William Findley.

### *Monday 22d*

It seems that the Executive some days since issued peremptory orders to seize the boats, provisions &c that belong to Burr & his partizans — & to prevent them from descending the Ohio — & to seize & arrest certain persons in the western states.

### *Tuesday 23d.*

This day Robert Smith, the secretary of the Navy paid me a visit by leaving his card at my lodgings.

It has been the practice of Congress to print the journals of their proceedings, the messages of the president, the reports of the heads of departments — of committees — board of commissioners of the Sinking fund — &c &c &c. Of each of these there has always been printed supernumerary numbers, that is, more than one for the President, Vice President, each senator & representative & head of departments, who are regularly furnished with them. These spare copies, & such copies as the members leave in their drawers at the end of the session, are in the recess carried up in the large lumber room over the senate chamber.

When I came here in Dec 1802, I was informed that each member of Congress was entitled to each document if he would take the trouble of selecting them. I accordingly began — selected & removed a considerable number, when I received a message indirectly from John Beckly clerk of the House of Representatives, in whose custody the key of the chamber was, that those documents were the property of the United States, & that members of Congress had no right to them. A few days after I found one of his favorites, a member of the House selecting a number of those papers. I then renewed my search & in the course of the session procured a trunk of them, which I sent home. This session I have bro't on a list of those I obtained formerly — & have now re-examined the whole mass

that remained in the chamber.  I have obtained all the journals
of Congress from 1774 to this time, except the Journal of the
Senate of their first session — and a great many documents —
more than 70 volumes — but not a compleat sett.  Some of
those I have are of little value — but my object was to get all
— not having time to discriminate the useful & important from
the useless & trivial.

The key is now kept by Mr. Kearney the librarian, who
owes his appointment to Beckley.  To the librarian I owe many
thanks for his politeness & attention.  I have every day, sundays excepted, this month spent two hours in that chamber.
Near the close of it — the last day, I discovered a disposition
in Beckley to withhold the key from me.  The librarian was
deprived of it.  I went to Beckley requested, and he with great
reluctance gave it to me.  I was aware that my spending so
much time in this business would induce other gentlemen to
procure documents — & that the doors would soon be shut
against us all — I therefore pursued & closed my search as soon
as time would admit.

I have procured a large box of these documents for the Massachusetts historical Society — & a large trunk of them for my
inquisitive friend Ichabod Tucker Esq of Salem.  With the
society they will long be preserved & rendered useful.  Mr.
Tucker contemplates a compilation of facts relative to this
Country — in which these documents will aid him.
Neither of these two collections of documents are half so large
& extensive as mine — tho' as much so as I was able to make
them.

The documents, principally, lay on the floor without any order
— covered & mixed up with dirt, plaster and rubbish.  They
are much diminished since 1802.  The water, in every rain that
falls, runs thro' the roof & wets these papers.  They will soon
be destroyed — They are trodden under foot by workmen — for
in the same room are a great quantity of glass in basketts with

straw — window sashes &c. The new edition of the Journals of the old Congress, which the United States, have lately purchased are in the same situation. It is really a pity that documents, some of which are so valuable, should be suffered thus wantonly to be destroyed.

The quantity of water on the papers, the dirt & filth in the chamber, has rendered it unhealthy. And I greatly rejoice that I have fulfilled the task I imposed upon myself — & that I have rescued so many useful papers from inevitable ruin.

At the session of 1803 I found it was the practise of the Secretary of the Senate to pay for the binding of the journals and documents. Since that period I have had about 40 or 50 volumes bound at the expence of the United States. This practise has not been adopted by the Clerk of the House.

## *Wednesday 24th.*

At the second election of President and Vice President Aaron Burr had one vote. Rufus King & Burr were then members of the Senate. Genl Bradley told me this day, that at the time when he first heard of it — he asked King if he believed that vote was given with the consent of Burr? King replied, " You do not know Mr. Burr — Nothing will satisfy that man but the throne of God! "

We have this day received information from Ohio — from which it appears that in consequence of a communication from the President of the United States, thro' the Secy of State, to Mr. Tiffin the governor of Ohio, the govr had made a confidential communication to the legislature of that State — who with closed doors passed a law authorizing him to arrest persons suspected to be carrying on an expedition unfriendly to the United States — & to seize & detain any boats containing provisions arms or ammunition suspected to belong to such persons. — In consequence of this the governor caused ten boats or batteau's lying at Marietta to be seized. It is said these belonged to Burr.

The accounts add that Blanherhassett[194] & Comfort Tyler
have fled — That one Cassett, of Ohio is arrested charged with
giving a bounty of ten dollars to enlist men for Burr.

Other accounts, from Kentucky — state that Mr. Davies the
Atty of that District had again requested a grand jury — That
one was called — & he with from 10 to 15 witnesses appeared
& were sworn and examined before said jury in support of a
bill or bills of Indictment drawn against Aaron Burr & John
Adair (late senator in Congress) charging them with forming
a design to invade the Spanish dominions in America — to
seize Orleans & Louisiana — form an empire in the west &c.
To this the grand jury return to the Court that they have no
evidence of such a design being formed by either of said men,
acquit them honorably — and even eulogize them.

I am still at a loss to know what Burr is doing — & to what
object he is driving.

As a conspirator — or as a politician — he has a fault — he
is too cunning — too secret — even in business where frankness & openness would not injure him. The reputation of being
a *cunning* man, is enough to blast any man's popularity — It
at once renders him an object of suspicion. Burr's lawful business always appears enveloped in mystery. This trait in his
character is strong, & marks all his conduct.

Query, If a statesman was to be open & frank on unimportant
subjects — & cautious, reserved, & secret, on those of great
magnitude — would he not succeed better than if he was on
all occasion to be silent & secret?

Samuel Smith of Maryland again took his seat in the Senate.

### Thursday 25th December 1806.

Last session we passed, at the request of Napoleon, a law
suspending all commercial intercourse with St. Domingo.[195]

---

[194] Harman Blennerhassett, implicated in the Burr conspiracy.
[195] Approved February 28, 1806; see *Statutes at Large*, II, 351–352.

This law to continue one year. Genl Saml Smith (Maryland) told me today, That Genl Turreau said, That as a Minister he could not interfere and request the repeal of said law — but as a man he would say its repeal would not be displeasing to him or to his court — for that since that law has existed, the trade of that country has almost entirely fallen into the hands of the British, who are, in general so well armed as to bid defiance to French privateers.

The Library of Congress consists of something less than 2000 volumes of different books. Many of which are very useful — and to many gentlemen of Congress afford not only much amusement in this *desert-city*, but information. The Librarian, a few days since told me, that Nathaniel Macon, the speaker of the House, said he thought it a useless expence, & wished the law establishing the institution was repealed — That he would cheerfully give his portion of it to any member. The Librarian told me he never knew Mr. Macon to take a book from the library — that he certainly had not taken any one this session.

### Friday 26th

Returned my visit to Robt. Smith by leaving my card at his house.

The last night & this morning it rained — At ten it cleared away warm — at three oClock, in the shade outside of the house, Farenheits thermometer stood at 61. There is a softness & agreeable feeling in the air of this climate that to me is highly delightful.

Thomas Truxton, known by the name of Commodore Truxton, once an officer in our Navy — & who had a long correspondence with the Secretary of the navy in the course of last summer, in which he absurdly contended against his own letter that he had not resigned his office of Captain in the Navy. This correspondence was published in Smith's universal gazette. This man is vanity's eldest legitimate son. In the course of this month he wrote a confidential letter to Judge Washington in which he says that Aaron Burr *last summer*, in the month of *August* made overtures to him — requested he would accept the office of Admiral of his (Burr's) fleet. In this letter he authorizes Judge Washington to shew it to Genl Dearborn, Secretary of War. Washington accordingly did. And I am informed that since then Truxton has written a similar letter to one of the heads of department.

Among a great number of questions that crowd upon the mind, in revolving this communication, are these — 1. If Burr did in fact make this proposal to Truxton in August — why did the latter delay *for four months* informing the government of such a treasonable design? 2d Where is Burr's fleet — a bankrupt in fortune & in character? If the British, French or Spanish are combined with Burr would they make him an Admiral — would they do more — would they give Burr the high authority of appointing an Admiral for their Navies?

Governor Wilkinson, the general of our army — the man who has long been in habits of intimacy with Burr, sometime since has, I am told by Mr. Giles in confidence, written a letter to the Secretary of War in which he says a large sum of money I think, $200000, was offered him by a friend (say Swartout) of a man once high in office (meaning Burr) if he (Wilkinson) would use his influence with the army of the United States to attack the spanish dominions & to effect a seperation of the western states from the Union.

I never had much confidence in the integrity of this same general. I do not know what offers may have been made him to betray his trust. But it is singular that the subtil cunning Burr should develope his treasonable designs to such men as James Wilkinson, Thomas Truxton & William Eaton! Three vainer men I never saw — Hasty, imprudent, unguarded men — incapable of retaining a secret. If Burr has made, or authorized any of his associates to make, those overtures to these men, he has acted unlike himself.

### Saturday 27.

Col. Tayloe returned my visit by leaving a card at my lodging.

Dined with the President of the United States — tarried in the evening & drank coffee — & had much conversation with him.

My usual course, when invited to dine with him, is to converse very little with him, except on the weather & such common topics, untill I come to the dining table, nor even then untill after the more substantial dishes are disposed off — & we have drank a glass or two. I do *not* mean, that the President is under the influence of wine — for he is very *temperate*. But as I am generally placed next to him — & at that time the company is generally engaged in little parties eagerly talking — & thereby gives him & me More freedom in conversation — & even two glasses of wine oftimes renders a temperate man communicate.

He told me  That Blannerhast, (mentioned p. 584) [196] had fled — That he is reputed to be a man of property, worth $100,000. — That he owns & lives on an island in the State of Virginia, adjoining the river Ohio — That the governmental agents are in possession of full evidence to convict him of being engaged in the conspiracy. But he tho't not enough agt the arch traitor Burr.

That he did not believe either France, Great Britain or Spain were connected with Burr in this project — but he tho't the marquiss de' Yrujo was — That he had advanced large sums of money to Mr. Burr — & his associates. But he beleived Yrujo was duped by Burr.

That last winter at the time when both those men were in the city, Mr. Burr frequently said the Administration were bound in support of their own honor & dignity, as well as that of the Country, to send him home immediately. And yet at

---

[196] Page 540 of this volume.

that very time there was scarce a single night but what, at a very late hour, those two men met & held private consultations. I have since then ascertained the fact.

That it is also highly probable that there was a secret understanding between Miranda & Burr.

That Ogden [197] of New York, on whom many of the bills of Burr & his associates were drawn, is not the same man with whom Miranda was concerned [198] — but the two Ogden's are kinsmen. That neither of them are wealthy — yet the bills drawn on them are promptly paid.

That Alston, who is speaker of the Assembly in South Carolina had been with his wife to visit his father-in law, Mr. Burr — & had indorsed bills for him to the amount of $25,000. That Alston is reputed to be a man of great wealth.

That Genl Wilkinson was at the date of his last dispatches at New Orleans fortifying the city — & that he had ordered his army to follow him — That the general apprehended the city would be attacked by Burr — by land — & on water by vessels suited to such an enterprize. — I asked the president who was to supply the naval force. He replied he could not tell — nor could Wilkinson give a satisfactory account — but that W. seemed to intimate Miranda.

That Burr had a confidential agent at New Orleans — Swartout of New York — brother to the late marshal of that name. That Wilkinson had ferretted out of Swartout all Burr's plans.

That there was no room to doubt of the integrity, firmness & attachment of Wilkinson to our government. And as little room to doubt of the loyalty & attachment of the western people to the union — That he, himself, had no doubt the conspiracy would be crushed, extensive as it was, with little trouble & expense to the United States.

---

[197] David A. Ogden.
[198] Samuel G. Ogden was the owner of the ship *Leander,* hired by Miranda for his filibustering mission. In this connection, see *Annals of Congress,* 9 Cong., 1 sess., 1085–1094.

That the French government would expect Congress to revive & continue the law passed at the last session to prohibit our commercial intercourse with St Domingo — That he was surprised at the measure & conceived the prohibition had already operated favorably to their enemy the English — That he beleived supplies were, under English colours, sent from the United States to that island — & if the law should be continued the supplies would be still furnished in that way — That the prohibition would injure us, the allies of France, & benefit Great Britain, their enemy.

He said he was actually astonished at the falshood & licentiousness of the *press* — That he did not beleive of 100 paragraphs contained in news papers that they would average more than one that was strictly & literally true — And he *darkly* intimated that some restraint ought to be by law imposed upon them. I observed, That the constitutions & forms of government established by the people of the United States, had given to the printers of News papers, by declaring *their presses should be free, & by prohibiting the legislatures from infringing that freedom,* a degree of importance far beyond their natural rank in society. That I thot it impracticable to pass a law that would effectually restrain its licentiousness & at the same time not impair its constitutional freedom. That public opinion must regulate it — That the very circumstance of the press being considered as the vehicle of slander & falsehood, would in proportion as that opinion prevailed, render News paper slander & falsehood harmless. That public prosecutions agt printers for slander could never correct the evil, so long as public opinion supported the printer and condemned the prosecution. I asked of what use was the Indictment conviction fine & imprisonment in the case of the Commonwealth of Pennsylvania agt Dickson for a libel agt Gov$^r$ McKean the last winter — when a majority, or near that, of the legislature in a few days after gave Dickson a public dinner at his prison, honored him with their company as guests — & paid the fine & costs of prosecution — And when to this is added — that the county of Lancaster soon after elected him their treasurer?

The President replied, he beleived my opinion was correct — That individuals who are injured should be secured in their right to prosecute printers for the injury they suffer from libels — & leave the residue of the evil to be corrected & punished by public opinion.

I stated as my opinion that Napolean would eventually govern Europe — that in Prussia, as it respected the great mass of *Prussian people,* whether Napolean or Frederick William should be their king, was not to them an important question — It would to them, be only a change of masters, in case Napolean should succeed. That I beleived if he conquered Europe, he would have enough to do to govern it without thinking of troubling us. — That president replied he had no fear of the French emperor's having any design agt us — That whenever he shall have settled Europe to his mind, he will then turn his attention & effect the conquest of St Domingo. Perhaps it will be well for Europe that he should conquer the whole of it. For then at his death it will suffer changes highly beneficial to itself & the world.

I asked the President if he expected the purchase of the Florida's would be made, so as to be communicated to Congress during the present session? He answered, Certainly not — But had Napolean been in Paris he had no doubt the purchase would have been effected. That if we can once obtain those provinces he should not then doubt, but that that single acquisition would insure to the United States another term of 20 years peace. I replied I thot we ought to preserve peace as long as possible.

He told me that he had taken great pains to ascertain what each year of our revolutionary war cost the United States including the money paid and services actually performed by the States individually — That he found it averaged during that war about $15,000,000 in good specie — That in this sum was not included either the property destroyed by the enemy or the depreciation of the paper money.

It appears to me that Mr. Jefferson is growing hard of hearing — that deafness is approaching upon him. I observed him several times to bend his head to listen — & he enquired what I had said. Age has some effect upon him.

He always renders his company easy & agreeable. His table was well furnished — good dinner — rich & various desert — but his wine, except Madeira & Hermitage, not good.

### Monday Dec 29, 1806.

This day Henry Clay, the successor of John Adair for this session, was qualified & took his seat in the Senate. He is a young man — a lawyer — his stature is tall & slender. I had much conversation with him, & it afforded me much pleasure. He is intelligent, sensible & appears frank & candid. His address is good & manners easy.[199] So much for the first impression — I hope a further & more intimate acquaintance, will not weaken, but add force, to these favorable impressions.

He told me that Aaron Burr was present at the District court in Kentucky when Mr. Davies made the second attempt to indict him for a conspiracy agt the Spanish dominions & for attempting &c to effect a disunion of the United States. — That at this second time he told Mr. Burr that it was possible that there might be something in the nature of his enterprize that would militate against his (Clay's) duty as a senator — & therefore it would be improper for him to engage as his council. Mr. Burr replied That he was guilty of no hostile measures against the United States or any power in amity with them.

Mr. Clay then said to me here is a letter Mr. Burr wrote & sent to me upon the subject. I read it with attention — it is dated the first day of this month. I did not request Mr. Clay to permit me to take a copy of it. The substance of it I will now state —

---

[199] Quoted in Plumer, *Life of William Plumer*, 351.

As you (Mr. Clay) are now called to a high office, a member of the national council — you may be impressed with an idea that your engaging in my defence may interfere with your duty as a senator. To remove this impression, I think it proper for me explicitly to state to you — That I have issued no commissions — enlisted no men — purchased no arms or military weapons — or has any man raised men or procured arms for me by my consent or with my knowledge.

That I have no hostile intention agt. any power in amity with the United States.

That I have no idea of attempting to seperate any one or more States from the Union, or from the residue of the States.

That the object of my pursuits are lawful & right — That it is not political, or any way connected with politics — but is a mere private personal speculation.

That I have consulted several officers of the United States thereon, & they approved of my measures — That my object, is, "*I beleive*" known to the Administration, & that they have looked upon it with *complacency.*

The foregoing is I beleive the substance of the letter — Tis not his language but I think it conveys every idea contained in it.[200]

Mr. Clay told me, that Mr. Davies, the district Atty, was zealous in carrying on the prosecution agt. Mr. Burr — That the grand jurors were gentlemen of the first respectability in that State. That they were near two days engaged in the examination of witnesses & investigating the subject — That they were unanimously of opinion that Mr. Burr was wholly & altogether innocent of the crimes whereof he was accused — He said but one opinion prevailed in that State as far as he could collect it — & that was in favor of Mr. Burr.

He said there was no disposition in Kentucky to attack, in

---

[200] The letter is printed in the *Works of Henry Clay* (Federal ed.), IV, 13–14.

this manner, the dominions of Spain — or to secede from the government of the United States. Their people were strongly attached to the Union.

Mr. Clay said his own opinion was that Mr. Burr was unjustly accused. That if there was any evidence agt him he had not been able to discover it.

That he knew Mr. Burr was interested in the tract of land in Louisiana — called "Bastrops Grant" — he had examined his title with attention — & intimated he thot it legal.

That he had heard Mr. Burr say, that the Marquiss de Yrujo was an enemy to the United States — & was a man not to be trusted.

Mr. Clay said he asked Mr. Burr why he did not contradict in the News papers the accounts that was published against him? He replied his enemies were industrious, & intent upon his ruin. That he had published nothing — & if he should commence the work it would be endless & unavailing — That time would set all things right.

Mr. Clay said he passed through Chilicothe (in Ohio) just at the time when Gov' Tiffin had issued his orders to seize the batteau's at Marietta  That Harman Blannerhasett & Tyler had fled — that they had acted imprudently he had no doubt — but not in flying — for such was the state of public opinion in Chilicothe that innocence was no security — that accusation founded on mere suspicion, was in fact equivolent to conviction & condemnation — That a mania had seized the public mind in that place.

He told me that Burr assured him he owned only two boats or batteaus. —

Genl Smith of Maryland told me that some gentlemen at Baltimore had enquired & found Burr had drawn bills upon gentlemen in Baltimore Philadelphia & New York to the amount of $80,000 — that they were selling at a discount of ten pr cent, & difficult to find purchasers at that price.

Mr. Giles told me that the President assured him that he was in possession of two letters written by Mr. Burr to two officers of different regiments in the western states — in which Mr. Burr requested them to have their regiments ready .to march with him to Mexico — for that a war with Spain was inevitable — & that he should be employed by the President to command an army agt. that country. I asked Mr. Giles in what state those officers lived? He said he could not tell.

Genl Saml Smith told me, That the Administration knew what Burr's object was — That it was first to seize New Orleans — He said that Genl Wilkinson had intimated to Swartout, Burr's agent, that he would join Burr — that having in this way obtained all the information he could, he had then communicated it to the President — That the Executive was in possession of a vast body of documents relative to Burr's expedition.

---

John Q. Adams shewed me a letter he this day received from his wife at Boston, in which she writes him that Wm. Eaton was then at Boston — that he was frequently in a state of intoxication — that the better sort of people avoided him — & that he was going out of fashion there.

### Tuesday 30th.

I have never seen the President of the United States when he rides horseback, which is almost every pleasant day, that I am here accompanied with a servant. He sometimes has his private secretary, Mr. Coles, with him — but generally rides alone. I do not know the cause of this singularity — for gentlemen of rank & consequence here are usually attended when they ride, by their servants — It may proceed from affectation — & it may arise from other causes. The appearance ill accords with the dignity of the Chief of a great nation.

Mr. Coles, his secretary, is a gentlemanly man in his dress, address & manners. He bears a considerable likeness in stature form & features to the president.

Last saturday, Gideon Olin, one of the representatives from Vermont, told me that a few days before he left home Comfort Tyler was at his house, made some enquires relative to certain claims, &c. That since Olin's arrival in this city he has had information by letter from a well informed correct man in that State, that Tyler at the time aforesaid had secretly attempted to enlist 50 men on an enterprize not then to be explained — That each man was to take a weeks provision & $30, & march to the lake, & there they would be provided for. Tyler did not, its understood, succeed.

Mr. Giles informed me that a son of Genl. Neville,[201] who lives at or near Pittsburg, had gone down the river to join the Expedition. That the General had written to the President that his son had gone without his consent, & that he had written to him to return. That another respectable gentleman had a son gone in the same manner & without his knowledge & consent. This man also wrote the President stating the fact — But not content with this he pursued from 20 to 30 miles down the river & overtook his son. He make use of his parental authority & persuasion to have his son return — but all was unavailing — The young man said, *he would join the standard of Burr.*

Note, These are almost the only two young men of respectable families in Pittsburg & its vicinity, that I have had information of moving in this expedition. Young Neville, I was told, by Mr. Hamilton, representative from that District in Congress, has never been quiet, steady & contented since he was a second in the duel of last winter, in which one of the principals was killed.

The affairs of Burr are still involved in mistery — I cannot

---

[201] Probably Presley Neville, an officer in the Revolutionary army, who resided at Pittsburg from 1792 to 1818.

develope them. The people & government of Ohio consider him as a traitor, & would arrest & hang him, if they could catch him. But in Kentucky he is accused — witnesses are produced — a grand jury of their first characters investigates his conduct, & honorably acquit him — & the people of the first rank in society of both sexes are giving him the most sumptious & elegant entertainments ever given in that state to any man.

### Wednesday 31.

The Senate passed the Naval appropriation bill for 1807 — It appropriates for the next year the sum of $800,000..50.

Dec 9. 1805, John Adair of Kentucky took his seat in the Senate of the United States. He was elected to supply the vacancy occasioned by John Brackenridge's resignation — who was appointed Attorney General of the United States. The term for which Mr. Adair was elected would have expired the 3d of next March.

Mr. Adair did not come this session — The legislature of Kentucky met last month — At the first of this month the question of choosing a senator to Congress for six years from the 3d of March next was taken up. Mr. Adair offered himself as a candidate — He attended their legislature. Mr. Pope,[202] a member of their legislature, also offered himself for the same office — & was anxious to succeed. After 3 or 4 ballottings Mr. Pope obtained a majority of 7 or 8 votes. The report here, was that Adair lost the election in consequence of his being considered attached to Mr. Burr. Mr. Clay, this day informed me, that Adair's supposed connection with Burr did not lose him a single vote. He said, That Adair was never popular — that Pope was always so — & had a great advantage over Adair by being a member of the legislature who elected the senator.

The next day after Pope's election, Genl Adair told Clay that as he did not possess the confidence of the Legislature he would

---

[202] John Pope, senator from March 4, 1807 to March 3, 1813.

no longer represent them in the Senate of the United States — & he accordingly sent in his resignation.

I have no doubt he was mortified at losing the re-election. In an elective government, no man, I think, ought to be chagrined at loosing an election. It is the duty of every citizen to wait the calls of his country — & when elected to office to discharge the duties enjoined — And when the term of service expires, return with complacency & mingle with the mass again. For myself, I can very sincerely say, I feel thus disposed.

From the acquaintance I had, the last session, I am led to beleive Genl Adair is a man of candor & integrity — though, perhaps, too much opiniated. He is not a man of strong mental powers — He is ambitious — & is not destitute of vanity.

The Executive have received official information from General Wilkinson that he & the Commander of the Spanish forces have agreed that the river Sabine shall be the temporary line between the United States & the Spanish dominions, so long as friendly negociations shall continue between the two nations.[203]

General Wilkinson has himself returned to New Orleans & his army are following him. He is busily employed in fortifying the city. This information will be published in the Universal Gazette of tomorrow, or the next day, under the head of a letter to the Secretary of War.

### Thursday Jany 1, 1807.

At twelve OClock, the usual hour, I attended the President's levee. The day being pleasant there was a great concourse of people. The Vice President many senators, representatives, heads of departments, foreign ministers, ladies, gentlemen strangers, gentlemen of the vicinity — & several Indian Chiefs with their wives & children, attended.

---

[203] For correspondence between Wilkinson and Antonio Cordero, commander-in-chief of the troops of Spain on the eastern frontier of the province of Texas, see *American State Papers*, II. *Foreign Relations*, II, 803–804.

The senators Bradley & Smith of Vermont, Pickering of Massachusetts, Hillhouse & Tracy of Connecticut & McClay of Pennsylvania — & the Representatives Dana, Dwight & Pitkin of Connecticut, & several others did not appear.

There was a great plenty of ice creams, apple pies, cakes, & a variety of wines. I tarried till two OClock in the afternoon — at which time very few visitors remained.

In the evening, for a second time, I attended at the theatre Manfredi's exhibition. They perform with great agility. The whole was closed with a grand Indian dance — the war dance, & the Calumet dance. There were about six or 8 Indian chiefs on the floor — The squaws did not join — they remained in the boxes. I was not pleased with these savage dances — There music, the drum & singing, was not pleasant — & the attitude, gesture & motions of the dancers were not graceful. They were however regular in keeping time & discovered muscular strength. One of the Indian thighs legs & feet were bare but highly painted.

The Mundane chief who lives near 2500 miles from this, at near the head of the Missouri, & who came with Capt. Lewis, tho' on the floor, took no part in the exercise. He is a *white Indian,* at least he is of a lighter complexion than many of our own people. He was dressed well, but had many ornaments on. Both his dress & ornaments were American. His wife looks more like a northern Indian. One of his sons, a lad of ten years, is of a fair complexion.

### *Friday 2d.*

Mr. H. Clay in the Senate, in prefacing his motion for a committee to take into consideration the propriety of revising the Judiciary establishment of the United States — said that the suits now pending in the District Court of Kentucky exceeded 400 — that a majority of them were on the Chancery side of the Court — & that a majority of the suits related to titles of land. He appears to be an easy, graceful & eloquent speaker.

### Saturday 3.

On the first instant Wm. Thornton an acting Justice of the peace in this District was so obliging as to loan me the original statement of facts made by him & justice Gardner at the time when Genl Turreau attempted forceably to send his wife out of the Country, as is stated p. 529.[204]  This statement I have copied into my Repository, Vol.[205] . . . p. 279.  Today I returned the original to Dr. Thornton.  He told me  That at the time when Madame Turreau parted from her husband — she then told the General that she was treated in the most cruel & ungrateful manner — That he well knew that at the time when she married him he was charged with crimes — & that she freely gave him all her property to exonerate him from his embarrassments.  To this he made no reply.  I asked Thornton if it was true — he said it certainly was.

I asked the Dr. if the General had sent the small trunk to his wife.  He answered — " so far from doing that he has had the *meanness* to open it & to rifle it of 100 dollars of her money that was in it."

The Dr. said that the General engaged to pay his wife for her seperate maintenance whilst she remained in the United States £200. sterling per annum — That Mrs Turreau a few days since told him the Genl had paid her only 20 or 40 dollars — & that she was now living with her infant child at Georgetown upon charity.

The Dr. shewed me a copy of a very free letter he wrote the General reminding him of his promise to support his wife.  He told me he had received no answer — but that the General said the Dr. was a busy meddling impertinent fellow — & was very angry.  The Dr. said he had advised Mrs. Turreau to write the General a very civil letter requesting the means of sub-

---

[204] Page 521 of this volume.
[205] The number of the volume is left blank in the manuscript.

sistence — & that if he neglected it for any length of time to cause a narrative of his scandalous conduct to be published from one end of the Continent to the other — & that he would aid & assist her therein.

The Executive of the United States very prudently take no notice of this transaction. It would be improper, on every account, that they should even be considered as knowing of such an event. But it is worthy of notice, that while Dr. Thornton, *a justice of the Peace,* is assuming airs of importance in acting & writing to Turreau upon this subject, the *wives of the heads of Department* do not think it prudent even to visit Mrs. Turreau. Mrs. Dearborn, the wife of the Secretary of war, the other day said to Mrs. Tenney, " I should like to call upon Madame Turreau, but I fear Bonaparte would be offended." Mrs. Dearborn is a plain, unpolished, but honest woman. And I am confident this declaration proceeds from the deliberations of the Executive & not from her own cogitation. This shews the fear our government have of the displeasure of Napolean.

---

This Justice Thornton is the keeper of the Patent office — who records all those inventions, & titles of books for whom patents & certificates of copyrights do issue. With him a set or volume of each book is lodged, & the model or drawing of each piece of mechanism, for which a patent has issued. His office is a room in the same building in which the War & Post office is kept. The floor & shelves are covered with models thrown together without any order or regularity. The books lie in an irregular confused pile on shelves & window stools covered with dust. The room is too small for the purpose; but a little money & labour would procure a convenient & useful book case, & arrange the models & drawing in order. This Dr. Thornton ought to do — he has too long been guilty of great negligence.

### Sunday 4th

The Legislature of Virginia have passed a law extending the jurisdiction of single majestrates to all sums between 10 & 20 dollars, with the right of appeal.

The House of Delegates of that State at their present session passed by a large majority a resolution approving of the Conduct of the Administration of the Government of the United States at the last session of Congress in relation to the management of our public affairs with foreign nations. It was understood that this resolution was designed not only to approve of the conduct of the President but to censure the conduct & measures of John Randolph & his friends. The resolution was sent to the Senate for their concurence — A motion was there made to postpone its consideration to 31st March next ayes 11 nays 10 — This is a virtual rejection because at that time the senate will not be in session.

### Monday 5th.

I have seen it several times stated in the News papers that orders on the Treasury of Virginia are sold at a discount of fifteen pr Ct. I enquired of Mr. Giles, of the senate, to day what was the fact. He replied, it sometimes happened — but seldom. That there taxes were usually paid in October — a few months previous to this, persons in want of cash sometimes sell the orders they hold agt the treasury at a discount of from 6 to 15 pr Cent. That it sometimes happens that the demands on the Treasury exceed the appropriations, then orders also may be purchased at a discount.

He said that such was the state of society in Virginia, that no News paper could be supported that was a vehicle of slander & attacked the reputation of individuals. That altho' Callender in his Recorder violently attacked the Administration of Adams — yet because he published slander agt individuals his paper fell in a few months; notwithstanding the politic's of Callender were highly popular in that state, — & notwithstanding a few individuals with a design to aid that party, took & paid for 250 of his papers. Ritchie,[206] the editor of the Richmond Enquirer, continued Mr. Giles, is a young gentleman of talents — but too precipitate in approving or censuring men & measures — he has too much literature for the editor of a News paper — it soars too high for the mass of readers — Altho' this paper is in high repute with our well informed men — yet because a few months since it commenced attacks upon the private character of Individuals — several of the customers withdrew, & Ritchie was assured, unless he reformed, his paper must fall. This we consider as the true mode of correcting the licentiousness of the press.

The apparent candor & great frankness of Mr. Giles render him a pleasing companion.

### Tuesday 6th.

Uriah Tracy, senator from Connecticut, a few days since told me — That the last session M. Turreau the French minister visited him — that he returned the visit in the usual style of leaving his card. That other senators received invitations from Turreau to dine with him — but he had none. That not knowing but what the servant might neglect to give the card to his master & he be taxed with incivility, a few weeks after in a conversation with Turreau in the Capitol he informed him that he had returned the visit but was unfortunate in doing it at a time when the General was absent. Turreau replied he had received the card. Mr. Tracy told me Turreau had not called upon him this session altho' he beleived he had on each of the other senators. Tracy imputed this to the part he had taken in favor of the British politic's & against the French.

The Senate passed the bill making military appropriations

---

[206] Thomas Ritchie, editor and publisher of the Richmond *Enquirer* for forty years.

for the present year. The amount was $913,654..55. Of this sum $106,000. is for the Indian department.

At the last session Congress appropriated $5000, of which 1000 was to be annually expended in purchasing books & maps for the use of Congress. To make the purchases they appointed, for the last year, a committee of three members from each house. Dr. Mitchel of New York was one of this committee. He has purchased more than 100 volumes. — Of this number is a volume entitled the "Secret history of St. Cloud." [207] It contains a great number of anecdotes of Napolean & his court; which represents him in the most unfavorable point of view — It paints him as a devil incarnate. Mr. *Parish,* formerly our Consul at Hamburg, & who has spent much time at Paris — & has in fact been an agent for Napolean, a few months since said in my hearing at Mr. Sheafe's,[208] *That it was a collection of stories that are whispered in the coffee-houses & vilest taverns of Paris —* but he added, *some of them are founded in fact.* I consider the book as a mere catch penny business — & extremely improper to belong to the library of Congress.

A few years since Napolean complained to the British government, for permitting certain scandalous publication against him in England. About a year since he complained to our Government for permitting certain toasts to be drank on board a Merchant ship at New York that aspersed his character. A few months since he tried Palm, a German printer, by a court martial, for publishing slander. He was convicted & executed.[209] With a prince so potent as Napolean, so much alive to, & so jealous of, his own reputation — & with whom we are

---

[207] Probably Stewarton, *Secret History of the Court and Cabinet of St. Cloud. In a series of letters.* Anon.

[208] Probably James Sheafe former representative and senator from New Hampshire.

[209] A Nuremberg bookseller, Palm, published and circulated a pamphlet written by one Yelin of Ansbach, entitled, "Germany in her Deep Abasement." Palm was arrested and shot in Braunau on August 25, 1806. The execution of Palm caused a storm of indignation to sweep over Germany.

in amity — it certainly is improper & impolitic to suffer such a book to constitute a part of the Congressional library. I am not for crouching servilely to the conqueror — I would not tamely yield the rights of my country to gratify his unbounded ambition. But I would never by an act that is improper unnecessarily wound his pride, & tempt him to reek his vengeance on my country.

To day I went to the Librarian & asked him if that book belonged to the library. He answered it did not. I told him I had seen it on the *written* additional catalogue. He replied, *It once belonged to the library — but Dr. Mitchel had withdrawn it.* I answered, I approve of that. He said, *no book in the library was in so much demand — It was constantly out — & in the course of a week it was several times read — The number who took it for the week, read it, & lent it to others.* Such a currency has scandal, especially when its shafts are directed against a great man.

I then went to Dr. Mitchel & asked him if that book belonged to our library. He said it did not. I replied that I was pleased that it did not — that I thought it an improper book for such a library. He rejoined, *The bookseller by mistake packed it up in the chest with the other books.* How unwillingly we are to own our errors, & how natural to charge them upon others?

I am satisfied that Genl Bradley remonstrated & complained to Mitchel against this book — & in consequence of it, the latter withdrew it.[210]  . . .

-sired this party as *Mackeanites* — for in fact the appelation is almost exclusively applied only to those who were in favor of the election of Thomas Mc Kean as governor of that State. And the term *Snyderites* to those who supported *Simon Snyder* as a candidate for the Gubanatorial chair.

---

[210] A page and a half have been torn from the manuscript at this point, causing the succeeding paragraph to be somewhat incoherent.

To day as I was sitting in my Chair [——] [211] the last number of our Dr. [————] [212] with so much haste, as to be very incorrect.

To me he was always very civil and attentive, & I used to converse with him with much ease & satisfaction. He appeared to me an honest man — but of strong passions. He had more of violence than of art — more of passion than of hypocrisy — He boldly announced his object, & openly directed his measures to its attainment. Such a character cannot but have warm friends & bitter enemies. His virtues exceeded his vices — He did much more good than evil to the world. And I regret his early removal from it.

The Legislature of Maryland have requested Mr. Jefferson to suffer his name to be used as a candidate at the next presidential election.

A meeting of the inhabitants of this city has been held & a vote passed for the same purpose.

### Thursday 8th.

At ten OClock this morning waited upon the President of the United States — tarried one hour. I went with an intention of communicating to him my design of writing the *history of the United States,* & requesting of him some documents. Found him alone; but having myself enquired of him for news from the westward — the conversation continued till company & other engagements precluded me from introducing my design.

The President assured me he had no doubt of Burr's traiterous designs agt the United States — That if he was arrested & a trial postponed for a short time he thot evidence might be collected to convict him.

That he hoped Blannerhassett, C. Tyler, & Swartout (brother to the late N. York marshal) would be arrested.

---

[211] Manuscript torn.
[212] Manuscript torn.

He added Burr had a *second* in this place who is acting the part of a *spy* upon government — It is improper to name him — agt. him the proof is insufficient. [Is not this *Clark* the Delegate from New Orleans?] [213]

That he had recd information that John Adair (late senator) had gone down the Ohio — supposed to join Burr.

That they had evidence of Bannerhassett's mortgaging his island for $50,000 — & receiving $30,000 in money — That a dozen young men had come to the island — that a majestrate had arrested them; but upon examination imprudently released them — That they immediately after took Brannerhassetts wife & children, & in a boat descended the Ohio.

That Alston, Burr's son in law, had indorsed bills for Burr to the amount of $80,000.

That John Wood had this morning sent him (the president) a prospectus of a News paper to be printed in this city — & called the *Atlantic world* — & requested his subscription — but he refused. That in this paper Wood pledged himself to demonstrate the innocence of Burr.

That he had no doubt Wood was in the employ & received pay from Burr.

After I rose, in a low voice, I observed, I would call another time when he was more at leisure & spend 15 minutes. He replied at any time when you find it convenient.

Note, This John Wood is the author of the history of " Adam's Administration " [214] — late one of the editor's of the paper called the " Western World ". He is a vile infamous lying fellow.

There is one or two ideas the President stated that I have omitted — He said That the Legislature & people of Ken-

---

[213] Brackets appear in the original manuscript. Daniel Clark, delegate from New Orleans to the Ninth and Tenth Congresses.

[214] For the story of the suppressed history of the Adams Administration, see McMaster, *History of the People of the United States*, II, 471–472.

tucky did not discover that zeal to aid the views of Government that he expected — That it appeared that his proclamation was recd on the 16th or 17th of Decr — That it was not inserted in the Palladium of the 18th — That it only appeared in the " Western World ", Burr's own paper.

That he had no doubts of D'Yrujo's being the dupe of Burr — that he had furnished Burr with money to effect a revolt in the western States — That he (the President) expected that as most of Burr's flotilla was now seized, he would flee to Mexico — That the Spaniards would raise him to a military command — which, he feared, would prove very injurious to the United States.

I have been told tho' I cannot vouch for its correctness, that Burr gave John Wood $1500 to suppress the *history of Adams's Admōn* — That Wood had previously sold the *history* to a printer who refused to return the copy — It was then published — Wood upon this published a pamphlet of the *history of the suppression*. The *last* publication aided the sale of the *first*. And it is said the whole business of the *suppression* was a meer piece of finess. But of this I have not satisfactory evidence. And tis certain that we sometimes overate the art of cunning men.

The question in the Maryland house of delegates to address Mr. Jefferson to stand candidate at the next presidential election — ayes 34 nays 20.

General Walton,[215] a representative from Kentucky has just arrived from that State. He told me he saw John Adair a few days since, & in a conversation he observed to him that it was reported *he was connected with Burr*. Adair replied, *My enemies have raised that report*. Walton answered, It is no

[215] Matthew Walton.

matter from whom the report came, the only question is, *is it true* Adair contented himself with saying, *It is the report of my enemy.*

### Friday Jany 9th 1807.

The Legislature of Ohio have requested one of their senators [216] in Congress to resign his seat. In their address to him they say he has been guilty of *great negligence* in not attending to his duty in this city. The statement is true. — He has frequently been absent — he has not attended this session. It does not appear that he has returned an answer. The proceeding of the legislature is singular — And query, what can a State, do, if a Senator neglects to attend? Perhaps, the only remedy is for the Senate themselves, in such a case, to expel the member for breach of their rules in not attending his duty.

### Saturday 10th

Mr. Foster his Britannic Majesty's Secy of Legation visited me by leaving his card.

### Sunday Jany 11, 1807.

In the last month D. Cassett, a trader of Whelan in Pennsylvania, travelling in the State of Ohio, was arrested by order of Govr Tiffin at Chilicothe upon the charge of being concerned in *Burr's conspiracy* — & held to bail in the sum of $10,000. When he was bro't before the Court he demanded immediate trial. A grand jury was summoned. Judge *Tod* in his charge to the jury advanced the alarming doctrine — *that altho Mr. Casset's character stands fair in society — yet that so far from creating a presumption of his innocence, is a strong circumstance against him — for such men will be more*

---

[216] John Smith. Smith was later accused of complicity in the Burr conspiracy, and a motion to expel him from the Senate failed by one vote. He resigned, April 25, 1808.

*readily trusted with the secret of such schemes.* [See Scioto Gazette Dec 18, 1806] [217] What! is, not a fair untarnished reputation a pledge to society that the possessor will not commit crimes of the deepest dye? Does the habitual practise of the moral & social virtues afford no security to the individual? Do his virtues qualify him for the commission of crimes? Alass there are moments in which frenzy seizes even courts of Judicature — when prejudice & popular clamour hurries judicial tribunals to violate first principles & to trample with impunity on long established usages.

The grand jury consisted of 22 men, 10 of whom were for finding a bill agt Casset & 12 for acquiting him. The court then *admonished* Casset & dismissed him.

Some of the Ohio papers accuse Henry Clay, the senator from Kentucky with being employed as the standing counsel of Aaron Burr — & taking improper measures to vindicate him.

Mr. Clay is a young lawyer of considerable eminence. He came here as senator for this session only — His clients who have suits depending in the Supreme Court of the US. which is to sit here next month gave him a purse of $3,000 to attend to said suits. He would not be a candidate for the next Congress. He tho't it would materially injure his business. But it was very convenient, & a money getting business, to him, to attend this session.[218]

The 2d day of last month a 2d grand jury was at the request of Mr. Daviess the District Atty brot into the District Court of Kentucky before Judge Inness to enquir into the conspiracy of Aaron Burr. Mr. Daviess said all the witnesses were not in — 2 were absent — he was not ergo ready to proceed. Burr was personally present. Clay & Allen his councel contended that the Grand jury being sworn & charged had a right to meet

---

[217] Brackets appear in the original manuscript.

[218] This paragraph and the short one concerning Clay, under date of January 12 following, are quoted by Plumer, *Life of William Plumer*, 351–352, as appearing together in the manuscript.

at such times as they pleased — & that they were not the mere machines of the District Attorney. The judge declared the grand jury had a right untill discharged, to retire to their chamber & proceed to enquire of any matters within the sphere of their duty. They went to their chamber & after sometime returned into Court, & reported they had nothing to present. Mr. Daviess informed the Court that the next day he should have something to lay before them. The court adjourned & ordered the jury to attend the next day.

*Dec* 3. In the Court Mr. Daviess called the foreman to him, handed him a paper, & said it was an indictment agt Gen. John Adair. Before the jury retired Mr. D. said he should claim it as a right to go into the room with the jury. This right was strenuously opposed by Clay & Allen. Mr. Burr said he had courted enquiry — he had assisted Mr. D. in collecting the witnesses — That he had been many years attorney general of New York, but had never attempted to claim the right of examining witnesses before the grand jury; nor did he ever meet with a precedent that would justify it in all the books he had read — That the Atty ought to be satisfied with the choice of the witnesses he would send to the jury — That grand juries were designed to shield & protect the reputation of a citizen from the arm of power — but if the doctrine of the Atty prevailed, it would become an engine of oppression — That if one party went in the other ought —

The judge decided agt. the claim of Mr. D. as being without precedent, & of dangerous example.

*Dec* 4. The jury returned the bill agt Gen. Adair, "Not a true bill." Mr. D. handed the foreman an indictment agt Mr. Burr. They withdrew.

*Dec* 5. The jury without any order from the Court sent for John Wood & Street, the editors of the Western World. They came into Court & were sworn & sent to the jury. In the afternoon the jury returned the bill agt Mr. Burr, "Not a true bill " — with a special report — stating the innocence of Burr & Adair.[219]

These proceedings added much to the distinction & influence of Burr. The inhabitants of Frankfort afterwards gave him a public splendid dinner.

I think the decision of Judge Inness in denying the District Atty the right of going before the Grand Jury & examining of the witnesses & stating of the law, was unsound & erroneous. In New Hampshire, Massachusetts & Vermont the invariable practise has been for the Attorney Generals to attend the witnesses before the grand jury whenever they pleased. The institution of grand jurors is to guard & protect the Community, the State, against the crimes of offenders, as well as to shield the innocent when accused.

---

In the month of November last a charge was made in the Legislature of Kentucky, that Benjamin Sebastian, one of the judges of their highest courts of law, had for several years received a pension from the Spanish government. This charge was referred to a select committee. Pending the reference the judge resigned. The committee pursued their enquiry. The facts were, That the Spanish governor of Louisiana, Genl Miro, & also the baron Carondelet, in 1793 secretly made overtures to Sebastian, Harry Innes (the District judge aforesaid) Murray, Nicholas &als, to establish a convention respecting the navigation of the Mississippi — The Governor appointed Gayoso his agent who was to meet these conspirators agt the American government. Many of The people of Kentucky had formed democratic societies — a union with the Spanish government was contemplated. Genl Wilkinson & John Brown late senator

---

[219] For Henry Clay's connection with Burr, and the legal proceedings here described by Plumer see McElroy, *Kentucky in the Nation's History,* 279–314; also, in greater detail, Marshall, *History of Kentucky* (2nd ed.), II, 393–412.

were concerned.   Before the business was compleated the treaty
of the United States arrived.   Carondelet then informed he
could proceed no further.   In consideration of the *personal
services of Sebastian to Spain* — a pension of $2000 pr. annum
was settled by the Spanish governor upon Sebastian.   This was
considered as an annual pension during life.   There was plenary
evidence, accompanied with Sebastian's confession, that it had
been actually paid for several years.

There was also full proof that these men had consultations
with the Spanish officers As late as the year 1797 — long after
the treaty of Spain with the United States was established.
That they then conspired agt the laws and government of the
United States — attempted to regulate commerce with a foreign
government, & establish one of the limits & boundaries of the
Union.

One of Sebastians friends in New Orleans, whom he had
authorized by letters to receive the pension, died.   His executor
upon receiving & examining the papers disclosed the transaction.

Of the number of witnesses examined by this committee was
Judge Innes.   He states his being concerned in these criminal
Affairs, & discovers much anxiety least his connection with it
should make impressions unfavorable to his reputation.   His
anxiety will not, cannot, & ought not, to prevent it.   His conduct was base traiterous & wholly unjustifiable.   He pretends
the reason why he did not disclose it was because he feared
John Adams would send a standing army into Kentucky.   In
1793 Washington, not Adams, was president.   But on this
principle, why has he been wholly silent for the last five years,
during the Administration of Jefferson, who was never suspected
as being friendly to standing armies? [220]

---

[220] For an account of the intrigues above described, see Butler, *A
History of the Commonwealth of Kentucky* (1834) 243–252, 320–326;
McElroy, *Kentucky in the Nation's History,* 200–210.   A number of docu-
ments bearing on the case will be found in Wilkinson's *Memoirs,* II,
Appendix.

What a disgrace to the United States that such a man should be permitted to hold the office of a Judge under their authority? That he should have the powers & authorities not only of a district, but circuit, Judge of the Union. A man, from his own testimony, guilty of a conspiracy with Spain, agt the United States is acting as judge in the case of the United States against Burr charged with a like conspiracy. The decisions of a judge thus circumstanced is not entitled to our confidence. He ought to be removed from office. I really think the constitution of the United States would be more perfect, if it authorized two thirds of each house of Congress, by a concurrent & joint resolution to remove any judicial officer from office when in their opinion it should appear necessary. In cases of confirmed inability, arising from sickness or old age, to discharge the duty of office — would be good cause of removal. But not cause of impeachment — that can only extend to crimes & high misdeamenors.

The Kentucky Committee have published their report, which includes copies of the testimony. It is in the Aurora & Baltimore Federalist of this month. These, in a time of more leisure, I will re-examine.

### Monday 12th.

Soon after the acquital of Mr. Burr, a number of the inhabitants of Frankfort gave a public dinner & ball to Mr. Burr. Judge Inness, & John Brown & all his family were present.

A few days after a more splendid dinner & ball was given to Mr. Daviess the District Attorney; & which was much more generally attended.

All parties, & all classes of people who are informed, appear to distrust Genl Wilkinson the commander of our armies. They are apprehensive he will support the cause of Aaron Burr. His friends, distrust him — their confidence in him is not for his virtues — but they hope his *interest* will restrain him from committing treason.

This day Henry Clay senator from Kentucky, & Matthew Clay his uncle representative from Virginia joined our lodgings. They are republicans & I am glad they have come. I dislike this practise of setting up such a partition wall agt members of Congress, because one party are federalists & the other Republicans. The more we associate together the more favorable shall we think of each other.

### Tuesday 13th.

Dr. Samuel Tenney is a representative from New Hampshire. He is a native of Essex in Massachusetts. He had a collegiate education, & was bred to the practise of physic. Was a physician & surgeon in our revolutionary army for some considerable time. He is a large tall personable man. He lives in Exeter — married Tabitha Gilman. Since he lived in that town he has practised physic a very little but for several years not any. His knowledge of diseases & remedies is very limited. He has kept a small store of English goods & medicine — has boarded one, two or three scholars that belonged to the Academy. Governor Gilman, who would not appoint a man to office that lived out of Exeter, so long as he could find a man in that town of his junto, appointed Tenny judge of probate for the county of Rockingham tho little acquainted with the laws. He was member of the convention for revising the State constitution. He has been member of the House of Representatives in Congress for . . .[221] years (see Journals).

He is a dull heavy moulded, indolent man — as destitute of wit, humour & vivacity as lead is of elasticity. He is a man that reads much more than he studies. He *reads* to kill time — but is too indolent to investigate a subject. His conversation is languid & unentertaining — He is credulous — & oftimes relates the most absurd & improbable stories as facts,

---

[221] Blank in the original manuscript. Tenney served from December 8, 1800 to March 3, 1807.

e.g. such as That he knew Revd David Jewitt, a very strong healthy man, who eat a hearty breakfast at eight oclock in the morning, yet actually *died of hunger* for want of his dinner before one O'clock in the afternoon of the *same day*. I have heard him relate this story and aver its truth a number of times. Yet he & his wife delight to dwell upon Mr. Jefferson's credulity & story telling. He is not rich. Yet has sufficient property to live in a handsome style.

. . . . . . . . . . . . . . . . . . . . . . . . . . .

### Wednesday 14th

The legislature of Georgia have addressed the President requesting he would stand candidate for one more presidential election.

Genl Bradley yesterday informed me that when he presented a similar address from the legislature from Vermont to the President early this session, he informed him that if he had any reply to Make to the Legislature he would with cheerfulness communicate it. The president replied if he made any to the Address he would enclose it to Genl Bradley. The General assured me he had not yet received any.

The President in his Message to Congress of Dec 2d considering the fullness of the treasury recommends that the impost on salt, a necessary of life, be repealed, & that the Mediterranean fund, levied chiefly on luxuries, be continued for a short time.

Mr. Gallatin the Secretary of the Treasury in his letter of the 18th December to Mr. Randolph the Chairman of the Committee of Ways & means, says " *If no other expences whatever* shall be incurred, but such as are already actually authorized by law, neither the salt tax nor the Mediterranean fund are any longer wanting. — Under existing circumstances, I should think it consistent with prudence to continue the *last* one year longer."

Yesterday the House passed, almost unanimously, a law repealed the duty on salt, on making allowances to ships &c employed in the fishery, & continuing the Meditteranean fund one year longer. To day the bill passed without opposition to a second reading in the Senate.

I afterwards observed to Mr. Giles that the last year, I voted agt repealing the duty on salt, & for the continuance of the Mediteranean fund because I thot we needed the money — but that I now had doubts respecting the continuance of the impost on salt. That the President, who certainly must be presumed to know the state of our finances & the nation had recommend the repeal of the duties on salt — had declared we did not want the money arising from those duties — That the Secretary of the Treasury fully concurred with him in opinion. That I felt an aversion to unnecessary charges in our revenue system, because they must produce partial evils. But when such high officers of government, possessed of the most ample means of information, recommended the change — I was strongly induced to change my own opinion.

Mr. Giles replied he was opposed to repealing the duty on salt, & in favor of continuing the Mediteranean fund — because he beleived we really needed both. He said the state of the nation demanded a full treasury. Our differences with Great Britain were not, as we knew, compromised — With Spain we had serious evils to combat — They could not be settled but by the sword, or the purchase of territory — & in the *west* we are threatened with conspiracies & insurrection. He had, he said, told the President that he was opposed to discontinuing any of our revenues — That the President still averred *he tho't the duty on salt was unnecessary* Mr. Giles added, he was convinced, That the presidents aversion to taxing the necessaries of life had led him into this error. And he added, as to Mr. Gallatin, his prejudices were always violent agt the salt duty — & its repeal would be popular in Pennsylvania. For himself he would never be influenced by popular considerations.

In a conversation afterwards with Genl Samuel Smith — He said to me, I have bro't in a bill to make a very considerable addition to the standing army — The senate have to day passed it to a second reading — This will add much to the expences of government — And *I know* that this additional army-force is what the *president wishes*  And it is damned nonsense to augment the charges of government & at the sametime to cut off the means necessary for its subsistance.  I will vote against repealing the duty on salt, & for continuance of the Meditteranean fund.

In a conversation with General Bradley He unquivocally declared, that he hoped to God if the duty on salt was repealed Burr would seize New Orleans — That the recommendation of the President in this case proceeded from mere motives of personal popularity, & not from a conviction that it was necessary — That the President had long discovered his design to avoid on every popular question, all responsibility — That he beleived the President did not wish us to repeal the duty on salt — That he recommended it beleiving, It would give him popularity, & trusting that the Senate would negative it.  That yesterday a member of the House told him he had voted for the repeal — That he dare not do otherwise — for if he had, he should have hazarded his re-election — but begged him (General Bradley) for God's sake to negative the bill.  The general added, to me, I almost despair of long supporting our government — The President is failing he is growing old — If he gains a re-election — before his next expires, his administration will be overthrown.

I have not yet made up a definitive opinion what vote to give upon the question of repealing the duty on salt.  The consideration of popularity will have no influence in forming my opinion.  And tho' it is right, as it respects the administration, if they adopt measures meerly to gain popularity that they should be taken in their devices & reap the fruit of their own doings — Yet it will be wrong for me to adopt such a line of conduct as will punish them; but at the same time injure my country. My present impressions are that I shall vote against repealing the duty on salt. I am inclined to think the present state of our affairs will not warrant us in lessening our revenue. If more money is collected than is necessary to support government & pay $8,000,000 of our debt — Let the Secy of Treasury, or Commissioners of the sinking fund be authorized to expend the surpluss, in redeeming our debt by purchasing it at par or the price in the market.

I live on friendly terms with all parties — I meet & converse freely with all — To a federalist I never repeat what republicans say to me — or to a republican what the federalists communicate. They perceive this — it has given them confidence in me. My credit as a *party-man* with the federalists is gone. They know I will do nothing for them for the sake of making opposition to the administration, or supporting their party. John Q. Adam's attachment to me encreases in the same ratio as Timothy Pickering's decreases. The prejudices of Pickering are often times too strong for his reason.

### Thursday 15th

Genl Bradley said to me, The presidents of the United States have taken more pains to acquire popularity than to promote the interest of the United States. This was the case with General Washington — This is the case with Mr. Jefferson. He is now catching at every thing that he thinks will aid his popularity. The last year the house, by a great majority, passed a bill to repeal the duty on salt. This year he recommends it. Last year I bro't in a bill to prohibit slavery [222] — It did not pass. — This year in his message he seizes the subject — presses it upon Congress — & means to deprive me of the honor of the measure, by taking it to himself.

---

[222] See Plumer's entry under date of December 17, 1805, p. 353.

This evening my colleague, Nicholas Gilman, told me, That Mr. Jefferson a few days since informed him, That the last winter Aaron Burr made several visits to him — & requested that as he was out of employ that the President would give him an appointment as minister to some foreign court. That at the last visit, Mr. Burr pressed the subject — The President then replied to him — You once had my confidence — the people & myself have now lost that confidence they had in you — I cannot therefore gratify you with an appointment. Burr then intimated to the President, that he would find he had it in his power to do Mr. Jefferson much injury.[223]

---

I have this day seen letters from Genl Wilkinson from New Orleans — in which he states That young Swartout as the agent of Burr had requested him to join Burr — to use his influence with the officers — & that Swartout had offered him $100,000, & assured him he should be second in command. Wilkinson adds he now came to a determination to throw off the mask arrest Swartout & als & put them under a military guard.

### Thursday 16th.

To day I had a long & free conversation with Buckner Thruston senator from Kentucky relative to the conduct & character of Harry Innes District Judge of that State. Mr. Thruston assured me that Judge Innes is a man of a fair irreproachable character — of an amiable disposition — of easy manners — but rather indolent. That he is a native of Virginia — That Washington was well acquainted with him, & appointed him to the office of Judge immediately after that state was admitted into the Union.

This Mr. Thruston is himself a native of Virginia — He was educated to the profession of the law — & is a man of science

---

[223] Quoted in Plumer, *Life of William Plumer,* 348.

— Is a good Greek & Italian scholar. Is a man of an amiable disposition — his manners are refined — His feelings exquisitely delicate — is subject to hypocendriacal complaints, &, of course, at different times appears very different & unequal. He assured me to day, that was he once attacked with rudeness in a news paper publication he would retire to private life. He is not like his late colleague, Brackenridge, or his present fellow Clay, *effective man*. He very seldom takes an active part in the Senate — & when he does come forward in debate, he does not appear to advantage. But his vote expresses the sentiment of his heart. He is an honest upright man. At the time when he was elected senator he was then, & for years had been, a judge of one of their courts of law.

The Legislature of Ohio have elected their governor Tiffin as a senator for the next six years in the room of Thomas Worthington. Tiffin was formerly a Methodist or Baptist preacher. Worthington is a cunning designing man — Has more talent than integrity — Tho' his talents are not of the first class — yet he is effective, industrious and intriguing. I always suspect evil from this man — His disposition is malevolent — & I rejoice at the decline of his popularity. It is said he will run for the gubanatorial chair at the next Autumn election. He is a native of Virginia — was formerly a deputy sheriff in that State. He is deeply engaged in land speculations — & owns much unimproved land in the western world.

The House of representatives have this day passed two resolutions. — The one requesting the President to transmit to them such information as he shall think proper relative to the conspiracy in the western world. And the second what measures he has taken to suppress it.[224] These resolutions were bro't forward & supported by John Randolph. I think it was imprudent to pass these resolutions. It is too soon to require a

---

[224] See *Annals of Congress,* 9 Cong., 2 sess., 334–359, for the debate on Randolph's resolutions.

disclosure of the information the President possesses — & the measures he has taken. Much of the information that the Executive has, are confidential letters from individuals. I know the fact from him. These ought not to be communicated — for tho' sent under an injunction of secrecy, they will transpire. One hundred & forty men cannot, & will not keep a secret. Their publicity will prohibit men from giving information — Their contents will be known to the conspirators. If the president makes a partial communication, Congress will not have a *view of the whole ground* — & his measures will subject him to censure, & perhaps contempt. A disclosure of the measures he has taken to suppress the conspiracy — may defeat the measures. I have not heard the arguments for or against the resolutions. These are my own immediate impressions on the subject. And they are such as would have induced me to have voted against the resolutions. Few men have a stronger inclination for information than I have; yet curiosity ought not to be gratified at the hazard of our security — It is to be presumed that if the President tho't the communication proper he would have made it without being requested — as he well knew the anxiety of Congress to be informed. And as he requires no law to be passed to aid his measures there is no *official* necessity of the information.

### Saturday 17th.

Wm. B Giles, today, assured me that the following facts might be depended on — That last autumn when Aaron Burr arrived at Nashville, State of Tennessee he called upon Genl Andrew Jackson — told him that a war between the United States & Spain was inevitable — That he (Burr) should have a command in the army & requested the General to have his brigade in readiness. A short time after this, Genl Jackson [225] wrote a letter to Mr. Jefferson informing him that he had three

---

[225] Andrew Jackson. For Jackson's connection with the Burr conspiracy, see Bassett, *Life of Andrew Jackson,* I, 43–49.

regiments that would be ready to march on short notice whenever required. The President was surprized at the information & requested information. The General explained — & the President undeceived him. And Jackson was in a rage agt. Burr.

As soon as the President issued his proclamation [226] [See p. 510] [227] A friend & confident of Burr's rode express with a copy & delivered it to him in Kentucky some days sooner than it arrived by the mail. In four days after Burr rec'd it he rode from Frankfort in Kentucky over the mountains to Nashville, a distance of 300 miles. He immediately called upon Jackson & shewed him the proclamation & assured him, it was agreed between him & the President that such a proclamation should be issued — but that the President had committed an error — & issued it sooner than the time prefixed. Jackson was again duped.

Mr. Giles added, Genl Jackson is a man of talents & information — was formerly a member of Congress.[228]

-----

On the 12th the house of *Delegates* of the State of Virginia agreed to an Address to Mr. Jefferson (ayes 102, nays 63). In it they say " we *most earnestly request,* that you, will consent to be considered as a candidate, at the next election, to fill the presidential chair." The impropriety of this address is handsomely stated in the *Richmond Enquirer* of the 13th.

### Sunday Jany 18, 1807.

On the 13th the Senate of Virginia rejected the address to Mr. Jefferson (see p. 701 [229] which had been adopted by the house of delegates) ayes 15, noes 5.

[226] See page 515.

[227] Page 515 of this volume. Brackets appear in the manuscript.

[228] Andrew Jackson served as a representative from Tennessee from December 5, 1796, to March 3, 1797; elected to the Senate, he served from September 26, 1797, until his resignation in April, 1798.

[229] Page 578 of this volume.

### *Monday 19th*

David Stone again took his seat in the senate. He is now elected by the legislature of North Carolina a judge of their supreme Court of law.

Mr. Giles made a very able speech agt. the bill to erect a bridge from this city over the Potomac. He was on the floor two hours — & discovered extensive information & much ingenuity. His manner is conciliating. He is a man of much talent — & maintains the appearance of much candor.

### *Tuesday 20th*

The question was this day called up whether the Senate will advise the President of the United States to appoint Ceasar Agustus Rodney Attorney General of the United States? [230] Samuel Smith of Maryland with warmth contended That the question ought to be postponed to a future day — intimated that he thought he was not qualified for the office — was not a correct lawyer. The motion to postpone was negatived. On the question of advising to the appointment all the senators rose in the affirmative except, Adams, Hillhouse, Smith of Maryland, Pickering, Tracy & Worthington. Mr. White said it gave him pleasure when he heard the nomination — for he thought him well qualified for that office. Mr. Bayard was absent. I voted in favor of the appointment — tho' I think a better lawyer, a man of more talent — of more liberal views a man more efficient & of extensive information might have been found. Tho' not best, yet beleiving him qualified, he had my vote.

He is an industrious, fair minded, pleasant man. Has a talent of using common place observation to great advantage. He is modest persuasive unassuming. There is nothing haughty, imperious or assuming in his manners & deportment. He has not

---

[230] *Cf.* Senate *Executive Journal* (1805–1815), 48.

the legal knowledge of Parsons,[231] Dexter [232] or Dallas [233] — not
the science of Adams [234] or Rawle,[235] or the great commanding
talents & efficiency of Bayard [236] or Martin.[237]

I omitted to state that a few days since the Senate passed a
bill supplementary to the law establishing the military establishment of the United States for raising in addition to the present
peace establishment one regiment of infantry & one battalion of
cavalry — & authorizes the President in certain events to augment each company of the peace establishment to one hundred.
Genl Smith of Maryland bro't forward the bill — upon the
ground of our territories being extended by the acquisition of
Louisiana.[238] It passed the Senate without a division.

## *Wednesday Jany 21, 1807*

I omitted to notice that on the 18th Genl Moore a senator
from Virginia, while the bill to prohibit the importation of
Slaves was under consideration, rose & stated that he had a communication to make to the Senate, that from its delicacy &

---

[231] Probably Theophilus Parsons, noted jurist of Massachusetts; member of the Massachusetts convention to ratify the Constitution, which he
actively supported; from 1806 until his death in 1813, chief justice of the
supreme court of the State. A collection of his opinions was published
under the title, *Commentaries on the Laws of the United States.*

[232] Probably Samuel Dexter, representative from Massachusetts, 1793–
1795; senator, December 2, 1799 until June, 1800, when he resigned to
become Secretary of War under President John Adams. He served as
Secretary of the Treasury from December 31, 1800, until the inauguration
of Jefferson.

[233] Alexander James Dallas, United States district attorney for the
eastern district of Pennsylvania, 1801 to 1814; Secretary of the Treasury
under President Madison.

[234] John Quincy Adams.

[235] William Rawle of Philadelphia, noted as a jurist and author of
numerous legal and literary works.

[236] James Asheton Bayard.

[237] Luther Martin of Maryland, delegate in the Continental Congress,
1784–1785; member of the Federal constitutional convention; attorney
general of Maryland, 1778–1805, and from 1818 to 1820. Martin appeared
as counsel for the defence in the impeachment trial of Judge Samuel
Chase, and for Aaron Burr in the latter's trial at Richmond in 1807.

[238] The bill was introduced by Smith, January 5, and passed, January 16.

importance he thought should be made with closed doors, & under an injunction of secrecy. The doors were closed. He then read certain resolves of the legislature of Virginia upon the subject of procuring some place to which they could send such negroes as should become dangerous. These resolves passed Dec 31, 1800, Jany 16, 1802 & Jany 22, 1805.[239] It was stated that there were certain letters accompanying them. These were not read. — It was agreed they should lay on the table for the inspection of members. No vote was passed injoining the Members of the Senate to keep them secret. Nor have we any rule that obliges any senator to consider them as secrets. The 27 rule [240] of the Senate requires the galleries to be cleared on the motion of one senator seconded by another, & provides that *during the discussion* of such motion, the doors shall remain shut — but does not prohibit the members from disclosing it after the discussion is ended. The 36th. rule declares " all confidential communications, *made by the President of the United States* to the senate, shall be by the members thereof kept inviolably secret; & *all treaties* which may hereafter be laid before the Senate, shall also be kept secret, untill the Senate shall, by their resolution, take off the injunction of secrecy." [241] These are the only rules that apply to the case.

Mr. Giles told me, the resolutions were passed by the Virginia legislature with closed doors — & had never been published.

I applied to Mr. Otis to borrow the papers to bring to my lodgings but he said he could not consent to my reading them out of the Senate chamber or his office — but if Mr. Giles would take them, I might borrow them of him. I then asked the Secretary for the papers, he gave them to me, & I carried them to Mr. Giles, informed him of what had passed between the Secy & myself, & asked him if he had any objection to my taking

---

[239] See *American State Papers. Miscellaneous*, I, 464–467.
[240] *Cf.* Rule XXXV of the present standing rules of the Senate.
[241] *Cf.* Rule XXXVI, sec. 3 of the present rules.

them to my lodging — he said *none.* I have taken copies of them — see Repository, vol. . . . ,[242] page 294 &c  These I will keep secret — no person shall see them.

In the course of the proceedings of the Senate upon the bill to erect a bridge over the river Potomac in the district of Columbia, the memorial of the Applicants, memorials against the bridge, letters to private gentlemen stating reasons for & agt the bill — certificates from individuals &c had been received & printed.  Of these was a letter from Theodore Burr, an architect, in which he states his Opinion in favor of a pile bridge.  Yesterday Mr. Giles moved to read a certificate from the same Mr. Burr — read & ordered to be printed.  In this certificate Mr. Burr explicitly states his opinion that such bridge could not stand if built over that river.  This day Mr. Bayard stated that he held certificates from Mesrs Lewis,[243] Renssellaer [244] & Uri Tracy,[245] members of the other House, stating declarations made by said Burr upon the subject of the bridge contradicting his last certificate.  To the reading of these there was a pointed opposition from Adams Giles &als — ayes 17, nays 15.  After they were received & read Mr. Giles moved that Mr. Burr should be examined on oath at the bar of the Senate.  This was opposed as improper — as unprecedented in the Senate — as leading to dilema's — to delay — that it would compel us to hear other witnesses upon a subject within our own view — that we had no rules established for the examination of witnesses.  The vice President said he had doubts whether the question was in order — & requested the opinion of the Senate thereon — After long debate upon the question of order, the Senate (32 senators being present) were equally divided.  The Vice President then decided that Mr. Giles's motion was not in order.[246]

---

[242] Number of the volume not given in the manuscript.
[243] Joseph Lewis, Jr., representative from Virginia.
[244] Killian K. Van Rensselaer, representative from New York.
[245] Uri Tracy, representative from New York.
[246] *Cf. Annals of Congress,* 9 Cong., 2 sess., 38.

Note it was observed by most of those who voted that Mr. Gile's motion was not in order, That he was at full liberty to send in a letter or certificate to the Senate explaining his views & conduct. — Of this number I was one.

Wm Eaton, (improperly called Genl Eaton) has been several days at the house at which I board — He dines &c at the same table with me. I make no conversation with him, & converse little on any subject in his hearing — I set a guard upon my lips — for so irregular wild & confused is his mind that I think every man that converses with him or in his hearing is in danger of being *misrepresented by him.*

I heard him say to day, That last winter Aaron Burr repeatedly pressed him to join his standard — That Burr offered to make him second in command — That Burr said that Congress should either declare themselves for his measures or he would expel them from the Capitol — That Burr said he would kill Tom. Jefferson — That he would make him (Eaton) his first Executive officer. Eaton added, That he had never disclosed this to any man till this week & now he had communicated it to the President.

The more distant the time, the more distant from Burr, & the louder public opinion is expressed agt Burr — the fuller & stronger are the declarations of Eaton against the accused.

### Thursday 22d

The President in answer to the resolution of the House of Representatives of the 16th, (see p. 696) [247] communicated a message to both houses upon the subject of Aaron Burr's conspiracy.[248] It is printed — to it I refer. How Genl Wilkinson could with any degree of certainty decypher A Burr's letter to him, written in cyphers, unless Burr had previously communi-

---

[247] Page 576 of this volume.
[248] For the message and accompanying documents, see *American State Papers. Miscellaneous,* I, 468–471.

cated to him the *key,* I cannot tell.  If Burr had previously given him the *key,* when was it?  And did Wilkinson give Burr assurances?

If W. had the key has he given the President information of it, & when?

I am confident the letter is not accurately stated — it sounds more like Wilkinson's letter than Burr's.  There more things contained in it than is *necessary* — somethings quite irrelevant — E.g. *that his daughter would accompany him.*  Burr's habits have been never to trust himself on paper, if he could avoid it — & when he wrote — it was with great caution.

Alexander Hamilton, who fell by his shot, once said to an acquaintance of mine, (*Jona Mason Esq*) [249] " The talents of Mr. Burr are over-rated — the world will ere long know it — His arguments at the barr were concise — his address was pleasing, his manners were more, they were facinating.  When I analized his arguments I could not discover in what his greatness consisted.  But his ambition is unlimited."  Mr. Mason stated these observations of Hamilton to me this day.  If Wilkinson's communications are correct, Burr either discovers want of talent, discernment & prudence — or a mania, a phrenzy, has seized his mind.  W. is not an accurate correct man.

This evening Dr. Erick Bollman & Mr. Swartout were brot to this city.  They were arrested by order of Genl Wilkinson at New Orleans, & sent by water under a military guard to this place.  Bollman is the man who attempted the release of the Marquiss de la Fayette from the prison at Magdeburg.[250]  He

---

[249] Jonathan Mason, senator from Massachusetts, November 14, 1800 to March 3, 1803; representative from March 4, 1817 to May 15, 1820. J. Q. Adams notes in his *Memoirs* (I, 445) that Mason was in Washington at this time.

[250] The attempt to rescue Lafayette from the Austrian prison at Olmutz was made by Dr. Bollman and Francis K. Huger, of South Carolina.  Lafayette was set free and had nearly reached the Austrian border when he was recaptured and returned to his dungeon.  He was finally freed, September 27, 1797, as a result of the victories of Napoleon Bonaparte.

is of German extraction — a genteel pleasant man.  He married at Philadelphia — his wife is dead — but he has a family there.

### *Friday 23d.*

At twelve OClock this morning Mr. Giles moved that the doors of the Senate be closed.  It was done.  He then moved a resolution, That a committee should be appointed to bring in a bill to suspend for a limited time the Habeas corpus Act.  He then stated Burr's rebellion, & adduced the message & documents of yesterday, as proof of its existance — as sufficient cause to pass such a bill.  And as two of the principle actors were now in this city in custody of the Military power — to prevent their escape, & to secure others who may be arrested in more distant parts of the Union, he hoped the Senate would dispense with their rules & pass the bill this day.[251]

He also observed that these two men, would, he presumed, be used as witnesses against Col Burr the prime mover.

*Mr. Bayard* said he had doubts as to the necessity or propriety of passing this bill.  That the evidence to prove a rebellion, so far as he had heard it, appeared inconclusive — That if a rebellion had existed in the west the bubble was burst — it had terminated — That the writ of Habeas corpus is the great palladium of our liberties — That a *suspension* of this, leaves our persons subject to the whim & caprice of Judges —

That on this subject the constitution is explicit & imperative.  " The priveledge of the writ of habeas corpus *shall not be suspended,* unless when in cases of rebellion or invasion the *public safety* may require it."  (Const. Art. I, Sect. 9)  I do not think the *public safety* at this time requires this measure.  Individual liberty is not to be endangered but to preserve the security of the nation.

---

[251] Rule XIV of the Standing Rules of the Senate requires that " every bill and joint resolution shall receive three readings previous to its passage, which readings shall be on three different days, unless the Senate unanimously direct otherwise."

That the principal object seems to be to hold Bollman & Swartout in custody — And the object of detaining them has been announced, that they may bear witness against Mr. Burr.

Let us enquire — Can these men be witnesses? are they competent? They are themselves principals in the rebellion — they are associates in guilt with Burr — if we beleive the documents. But the President can pardon them — Agreed — But this will not make them witnesses — they must be *willing witnesses* or they cannot testify at all. For if they testify agt Mr. Burr, they must necessarily disclose & avow their own guilt — The 5th Art. of amendment to the constitution, expressly declares " That no man shall be *compeled,* in any criminal case to be a witness *against himself.*

But will you pass this bill for the sake of holding these individuals to trial. It is contrary to the sound principles of law, to consider these men criminals — they are prisoners. Untill after trial and conviction, such is the charity of the law, it always considers the accused *as innocent.*

You again reply we will hold them as witnesses agt. Burr. What grounds have you to beleive you will arrest Col. Burr? I have no hesitation, in saying, from my knowledge of that man, that he would prefer instant death to a trial before your Judiciary tribunal. He will never submit to such a process.

The object avowed by the mover as the ground on which to pass a bill is too small, too limited, to justify a measure of such vast importance. Your law must be general — it must extend to every part and portion of the Union. It may endanger the liberty of thousands of unoffending citizens. — Can you limit its effects — can you prevent the shock it will give the public mind — Can you say it will not affect your public credit — or the transactions & credit of your merchants?

That the great & primary powers of government ought never to be exercised but on great & important occasions. If you exercise them unnecessarily, your law will be disregarded — & the dignity of government will be prostrated.

*Mr Giles,* I am sorry the gentleman from Delaware (Mr. Bayard) has imputed so limited an object to me as the confinement or punishment of two men — Tis not for or agt. them that I move this resolution.   Rebellion exists — it is not confined to a single state — Men disaffected to your government are connected as parties & actors in this opposition, in this rebellion — who live in each State almost of your Union.   I fear the capture of a few provision boats on the Ohio has not destroyed this rebellion.

*Mr. Adams.*   I am in favor of the resolution.   Tho' I consider the writ of Habeas Corpus as the great palladium of our rights in common and ordinary cases — yet on extraordinary occasions I beleive its temporary suspension is equally as essential to the preservation of our government & the priveledges of the people.

*Mr. Smith* (of Maryland) I am no lawyer — but I have no hesitation in saying rebellion exists in the United States.   I have recd, since this debate began, a letter from the Commander of your armies (Genl Wilkinson) from New Orleans of the 25th ult — He writes, Burr has many friends in New Orleans — That one of your judges [Workman] [252] in that territory is suspected of being in the conspiracy — That he granted Ogden a writ of habeas Corpus & immediately released him without notice altho' he knew he was confined by his order — That he had declared that man to be a fool who had power & did not use it to obtain a better order of things. — Mr. Smith then read a part of the letter.                                                                          ¶

He said, He tho't the law should be general & extend to every part of the Union — That the scene of action is at New Orleans, a remote part of our country — That this is a preventive measure — That the same evidence is not requisite as to convict & punish — That we ought to act & not debate till the usurper assumes our seats & makes us his prisoners.

*Mr. Bayard,* My doubts arise from constitutional principles.

---

[252] Brackets appear in the original manuscript.

I am not disposed to countenance insurrection, — aid rebellion, or favor its patrons. I beleive Col. Burr has actually contemplated rebellion — but I do not see the evidence of his overt acts.

I request honorable Gentlemen not to act with too much precipitancy. I entreat them to recollect that legislation ought never to be the effect of feeling but of cool disspassionate reason. These feelings that now appear to influence us are honorable — they arise from love of country — but remember that in such moments legislatures have been hurried on to enact laws that have formed precedents dangerous to freemen.

He feared the present resolution would pledge the Senate to pass the bill when reported. He wished them to consider the bill in its details without being tramelled by a previous vote to support its principles. He therefore moved that the resolution be so amended as that the committee be directed to enquire into the expediency of suspending said writ — & to be authorized to report by bill or otherwise. After some few remarks — the resolution as amended was agreed to without a division. Mesrs Giles, Adams & Smith of Maryland were appointed the committee — & had liberty to meet during the sitting of the senate.

At a little past one OClock the Committee retired. At three they reported a bill which suspended the writ of Habeas corpus for all commitments made by warrants from the President of the United States, by officers directed by him, or the first Executive Majestrate in each State & territorial Governments, for offences against the constitution & penal laws of the United States — for the term of three months.

The debate upon this bill continued untill near five OClock — The description of offences were made more limited — They were restricted so as to include only treason, misprision of treason, rebellion & other high crimes and misdemeanors immediately affecting the peace and neutrality of the United States.

Mr. Bayard well observed That the bill as reported would be

a suspension of the writ for the smallest offence known to our laws. — That these are numerous, & some of them of the lighter kind.

Some of the Senators moved to have added previous to the words *on complaint,* the word *oath.* This was done & for the purpose of giving greater security to the liberty of the individual — not considering that this very amendment, being part of the description of cases, took away the suspension from persons committed on lawful process — & left it to others — when in fact it ought to have been silent as to the lawfulness or unlawfulness of commitment.

I voted for the bill — because I thought the state of things required such a suspension — & because I do not think much, if any, evil will result from the law.

John Q Adams was *passionately zealous* for its passage.[253] Samuel Smith, (whom rumour has heretofore declared as devoted to Burr) discovered much anxiety to have the bill passed. Henry Clay told me he thot there was no occasion for the bill but the delicate situation in which, he was (late councillor for Burr) would not only prevent him from opposing it, but oblige him to vote for it — which he did.[254]

Genl Smith gave an informal information by note, to the Speaker stating That the Senate were debating with closed doors on a measure that would probably pass this day & require the concurrence of the House. At 4 OClock however the house adjourned to monday next.

I can see no reason why this business was transacted with closed doors — But as I have no objection to doing all our business that way, I did not, or did any one, object.

The circuit Court for the District of Columbia is in term.

---

[253] *Cf.* J. Q. Adams, *Memoirs,* I, 445–446; also *Annals of Congress,* 9 Cong., 2 sess., 44. Plumer's is the only extended account of the debate on this important subject.

[254] The statement concerning Clay is quoted in Plumer, *Life of William Plumer,* 352.

The President of the United States presuming the bill aforesaid would this day have passed into law, gave verbal instructions to Mr. Jones the district Attorney, that He should move the Court for a warrant against Bollman & Swartout. He accordingly moved for a Bench warrant. The court adjourned this day without deciding the motion.

### Sunday 24th.[255]

Dr. Bollman very anxiously solicited the officer having charge of him to request the President of the United States to permit him to a private interview with the President. The officer after much importunity, consented to communicate the request to the Secretary of War — He informed the President — who sent for Bollman, — who was with the President some considerable time. The result has not transpired.

Today Mr. Caldwell moved the District Court for a writ of Habeas Corpus to bring up Mr. Swartout. The motion was opposed by Mr. Jones. The Court granted the writ returnable on monday next.

I ought to have mentioned that the bill suspending the writ of Habeas Corpus passed yesterday the Senate by the votes of all the senators present except 3 or 4. Two senators only were absent — Anderson & John Smith of Ohio. — I ought also to observe that if any one senator had been strenuously opposed the bill, by our rules, could not have been read a 2d time on the same day.

### Monday 26th.

This morning Genl S. Smith by order of the Senate went to the bar of the House of Representatives (their gallery being previous cleared) & communicated to them a message of the Senate accompanying said bill — informing them we had passed it with closed doors, & desiring they would proceed in like manner & concur with us.

---

[255] Saturday.

The bill was read, & the House almost immediately took off the injunction of secrecy. And on the first reading of the bill the motion was to *reject it*. The debate on this motion took up the whole day — The motion prevailed, — If I did not mistake the numbers, it was, ayes 113 nays 19.[256]

On information of this the Senate immediately took off from its members the injunction of secrecy.

There cannot now remain any doubts of Burr's seditious & treasonable designs — unless multitudes, & some of those having the best means of information, have conspired to establish falshood. I was myself a long time an infidel — my knowledge of his talents & cunning, & to my views, the impracticability of success, induced me to disbeleive the whole. But the evidence establishes his treason And on a closer investigation the chance of his success appears more probable. I have no doubt but that the Marquiss de Yrujo was duped by Burr. The marquiss had no doubt induced the Spanish commander to march his troops to the Sabine, to give employment to Wilkinson — & thereby draw our feeble army from New Orleans, & leave that city unprotected. Burr had *reason* to beleive Wilkinson would aid him, at least in *an indirect manner*. Some of the officers of our *little* navy were devoted to Burr. The traitor had thousands of men of the idle, disaffected, & men of desperate fortunes, devoted to his plans. Had not his flotilla at Marietta &c been seized by order of the govt. of Ohio — Had not that state & Kentucky turned out their militia, ere this time Burr would have had New Orleans in his possession — & the plunder of the millions of dollars of the Bank of the United States at that city would have induced thousands to have joined his standard. For many of the people of Orleans territory were only waiting for his appearance. The Spanish army from the hope of again recovering Louisiana would have joined his standard. He might then, after being reinforced from the United States, have thrown off

---

[256] *Cf. Annals of Congress*, 9 Cong., 2 sess., 402–425.

the mask, as it respected Spain, & seized by his rapid movements Mexico & its treasures. This was an object suited to his ambition. And who can now say, his plans are rendered abortive. I hope they are.

But such a state of things yet exists, as to me, would, & does, justify the suspension of the writ of Habeas Corpus. That writ is designed to secure our rights — but its temporary suspension in such a state of things will most effectually secure its object — *public security.* Laws and rules are made to promote & preserve peace & justice — but public security and justice are not to be sacrificed to the shrine of *law & rules.* This would be sacrificing the object to the means.

When the danger of this rebellion is past — when our feelings, our bitter feelings subside, — when time has rendered the transactions less important — Wilkinson himself will probably fall a victim. He will be harrassed by suits — by prosecution, by those whom he has arrested — whom he has imprisoned & transported — Govt. may then let rigid law operate to his ruin. His duplicity will then be punished — that duplicity will render him, perhaps justly, odious to the Government he now supports. But if in a time of rebellion & public danger you do not support your Commanders, you will render them timid, & palsy their nerves. I admire the attachment to rights — I venerate the motives that lead men into these errors — still the errors may be fatal — A mistaken zeal for liberty — for theoretic liberty has often endangered the security of nations.

### Tuesday 27th.

To day Col. Wharton made return to the District Court on the writ of Habeas Corpus that he held Bollman and Swartout prisoners by virtue of the Orders of his Superior Officer — & bro't the prisoners into Court. The Court ordered them into the custody of the Marshal of this district. And assigned tomorrow for the argument relative to their liberation.

*Jany 27, 1807.*

This day John Smith of Ohio took his seat in the Senate.

### Wednesday 28th.

The Vice President preserves very little order in the Senate. If he ever had, he certainly has not now, the requisite qualifications of a presiding officer. Age has impaired his mental powers. The conversation & noise to day in our lobby was greater than I ever suffered when moderator of a town meeting. It prevented us from hearing the arguments of the Speaker. He frequently, at least he has more than once, declared bills at the *third* reading when they had been read but once — Puts questions without any motion being made — Sometimes declares it a vote before any vote has been taken. And sometimes before one bill is decided proceeds to another. From want of authority, & attention to order he has prostrated the dignity of the Senate. His disposition appears good, — but he wants mind & nerve.

### Thursday 29th

The Senate were engaged for more than a week the last session upon a bill passed by the other House granting liberty to certain persons to erect a toll bridge from this city over the river Potomac. On the question then to its passage to a third reading ayes 17, nays 11. After it was read a third time a motion was then made to postpone it to Decr then next, under the pretext that there was not then time to discuss it — & the want of information. The motion prevailed ayes 19, nays 10.

At this session the business was taken up *de novo* — the House of Representatives without much division passed a similar bill. It came to the Senate this session — It was refered to a committee, who reported it without amendment — memorials & counter-memorials — letters, certificates & dispositions to a considerable number were published on the subject by the order of the Senate. The bill at the second reading was debated for more than a week — A motion was then made to postpone it to the first monday of December next. Under the old pretext want of time & want of information. The debate on this question has taken up several days  It was very irregular — the Vice President allowed the speakers for & agt the motion to go fully into the merits of the bill. Mr. U. Tracy said he was in doubt how to vote upon the merits of the bill, & made declarations, which I have conclusive evidence, that he knew were not facts. Not ten minutes before he rose he told me at the fire side he was decided in Opinion, no bridge ought to be built over the river. The more I see & know of this man, the less confidence I have in his integrity. Under the mask of sanctity he practices much deception.

On this bill Mr. Giles discovered more art, intrigue & deception than I was aware he was capable of practising. He really descended from that dignified frank & manly course he usually pursues. He descended to the meaness of discoloring & misrepresenting facts. It presented a trait in his character he had never before exhibited to me.

Mr. Bradley ridiculed the motion in a strain of wit & pleasantry equal to anything of the kind I ever witnessed.

The irony & sarcasm of Mr. Milledge,[257] from Georgia — (late their governor) was keen & pointed. His sentiments are manly frank & open, & his manners those of a polished gentleman. He appears to have the intregity of his predecessor, the late Genl. Jackson, but none of his roughness.

Genl Moore of Virginia, from the decõn of Mr. Giles that their Legislature would remonstrate agt the bill at the next session, yesterday said that altho' he was in favor of the bridge, he should vote for the postponement. To day he observed to

---

[257] John Milledge, appointed to fill the vacancy caused by the death of James Jackson, took his seat December 11, 1806.

the Senate he had reviewed the subject — tho' he did not wish
to be subject to a charge of inconstancy, yet he never would, to
avoid that imputation, vote agt the conviction of his own mind.
He was now satisfied the bill ought not to be postponed — &
he should vote agt. it.

Mr. Clay of Kentucky made an eloquent speech agt the
motion — As a speaker he is animated — his language bold &
flowery — But he does not reason with the force & precision of
Bayard. But he is prompt & decisive.[258]

Genl Smith of M. told me privately that the true ground
that induced them to wish a postponement to next session was
that he knew several of us who would vote for the bridge would
not be senators at the next Congress. —

The question for postponement was carried ayes 17, nays 16.

What most surprizes me is that senators who are perfectly
satisfied that the bill ought to pass, yet voted to postpone it. Of
this number are Logan and Mitchel. Mitchel is always easy
pleasant and accomodating, but has no nerve — no firmness
— Consistency is no trait in his character.

The conduct of Logan is surprizing. He is a warm partizan
for the bridge — His term expires with this session — & he well
knew that Andrew Gregg his successor, the last year in the House
voted agt the Bridge. I attribute Logan's conduct on this occasion to his personal friendship to Genl Mason, whose lucrative
ferry would be materially injured by the bridge. Logan is not
a great man — his views are limited.

Fenner & Howland of Rhode Island are men of little minds —
unstable — They were in favor of the bridge — but voted for
postponement.

Adams and Pickering were zealous for postponement. Their
real zeal was transformed into so great a passion & so much
anger that they were utterly unable to speak.

I do not consider the object as important, I was in favor of

---

[258] *Cf.* Plumer, *Life of William Plumer*, 353.

the bridge I voted agt the postponement, & so I should have done had I been agt the bill. I always wish to meet an object directly. I take pains to form an opinion — & will not shrink from the responsibility of acting.

I should not have been thus particular had not the conduct of the Senators, given on this occasion, new views of their character.

I have seen men in a single day pass an important bill, the suspension of the Habeas Corpus — but after weeks debate postpone a bill for erecting a bridge over a small stream under the flimsy pretext of gaining more information. The want of time & information is not true.

### *Friday Jany 30, 1807*

The Court have this day decided that Bollman & S. Swartout shall be committed to goal upon the warrant for high treason without bail or mainprize. The Court were divided upon this question Fitshugh and Duchett were in favor of commitment, Cranch C. J. e contra.

Swartout is a fine genteel intelligent young man of about 30. His situation excites my commisseration. Bollman's countenance & previous conduct makes an impression on my mind less favorable to him.

There certainly never was a rebellion more unjustifiable than this of Burr's. There is no oppression — no rights invaded — not even a single statute that is the subject of general complaint in even a district or village.

The prison in which Bollman & S. Swartout are committed in this city is constantly guarded, night & day, by an officer & 15 soldiers of the Marine Corps. The government are apprehensive that the arts & address of *Bollman,* who affected the liberation of the Marquiss la Fayette from the strong prison of Magdeburge, may now find means to liberate himself.

During the long argument in Court respecting the confinement of these men, notwithstanding the vast croud who gazed

upon them, they appeared collected & firm — & Swartout was
much at his *ease;* but when the Court decided that they must
be *imprisoned without bail,* his countenance changed.  He said
to a friend near him " An innocent man is now doomed to bear
the horrors & disgrace of imprisonment."

## Monday Feby 2d.

Mr. Otis was elected Secy of the Senate at their first session
& has continued such ever since.  He was formerly a member of
Congress, from Massachusetts, under the old confederation.
There has been several attempts to remove him from his present
office.  I think I have stated the attempt of Mr. Wright some
sessions since.[259]  Genl Bradley a few days since informed me
that previous to that motion a caucus of the republican senators
was holden — of which he was appointed Chairman.  That at
this caucus the question of removing Otis from office was long
debated — And that if a majority were in favor of removal,
each individual member of the caucus in the Senate, whatever
his private opinion might be, should support their resolution.
Genl Jackson & Smith of Vermont vehemently opposed the doctrine and removal.  Jackson declared he would not be bound by
such a vote.  Dewit Clinton insisted upon a vote being taken
to remove Otis.  Bradley declared the motion was not in order
— That he had long been acquainted with caucuses — That the
great object was to settle principles — not the election, or removal, of men to or from office — That the only exception to
this rule, arises from its vast importance, the election of president & vice president of the United States — That a majority
of the Senate are republicans — & of course can in their senatorial capacity prescribe their own rules & elect their own
officers. — That it is derogatory to the dignity of a senatorial

[259] See pages 81–83.

caucus to take a vote for the removal of Otis —And that at all events he would not suffer such a vote to be taken. Clinton then said they would appoint another Chairman; Bradley told them, even caucuses were bound by rules — & before another chairman could be chosen, this caucus must be dissolved & another called — & then a new chairman might be elected. They broke up divided & irritated, Bradley recommended to Otis to give the printing business to Duane & secure his influence. This was done — & the question in the senate, to choose a new Secretary, was negatived.

Otis was formerly federal — But he never had the qualifications that are requisite for a good Secretary. His composition is not elegant — his statements are not always accurate — they are sometimes incorrect in fact, & often blundering & obscure. But what is worse, in appearance, he has no dignity, & is a very bad reader. The Federalists have been desirous at different times to get rid of him — & some of the Republicans dislike him. With a view of removing him he was formerly appointed a Commissioner under the Bankrupt law — but he would not accept it.

His son Harrison Gray Otis of Boston, at the close of Mr. Adam's administration was a member of the House of Representatives in Congress.[260]  He was a violent federalist, & very often pronounced severe phillippic's agt. the republicans. The secretary was alarmed least the Senate should afterwards visit the violance of the son on the father. He once remonstrated with Harry — told him his speeches would soon remove him from office. His son replied he should be sorry to be even the innocent occassion of such a loss — but he had done no more than what he thot his duty — & a sense of duty would induce him to pursue the same course.

The Secretary is now past sixty years of age. He has a salary of $2000 pr annum. Tarries at this city but a *very few* days

---

[260] Otis served from March 4, 1797 to March 3, 1801.

longer than Congress. His compensation is nearly double to that of a senator. His duty is easy — he has always, at the least, two clerks under him, who discharge, by far the greatest part, of his duty, as secretary. To the principal Clerk $1300, & to the other $1000 pr annum salary is given.

His office is not kept in the most regular manner. In vain do you look for a sett of even those documents that have been printed. Although he has been secretary from the first so negligent has he been as not to have a single full sett for the office.

His records are kept in a blind confused manner. In his *secret* journals are documents that are *public*. He is timid to a fault. A few years since to *one* in the minority he was afraid to entrust anything — To one in the majority he would trust everything. He has refused me papers to carry to my chamber — and has afterwards privately requested me to desire some Senator to call on him for them — & then for me to borrow them from that Senator. Such conduct is mean & despicable — but as my object was information I never would appear to notice it — Especially as *I knew* he did not distrust my integrity. But was influenced by fear of losing his office.

With all his clerks his office is neglected — & the official communications made to the Senate for several years are not yet recorded.

---

On saturday evening died in this city, & this day was buried, General Levi Casey, one of the Representatives in Congress from the State of South Carolina. Mr. Casey had been for —— [261] years a member of Congress. He was a Colonel in our revolutionary army — A brave enterprizing officer under General Sumpter — And from the little acquaintance I had with him, appeared to be a fair, upright, honest man. I spent half an hour

---

[261] Blank in the original manuscript. Casey served from March 4, 1803 until his death.

with him in the Senate Chamber ten days before he died. He died of a pleurisy — This fever at this place at this season of the year is fatal to people who come from a warmer clime. He was in his 58 year, & when I last saw him appeared in a state of good health. He met death with the resolution & firmness of a brave man — undismayed. He has left a numerous family to bewail their loss. Its probable the first information they receive of his sickness will relate to them his dissolution. He has left his family in easy affluent circumstances. He was buried at Georgetown with the honors of war. — Congress adjourned on receiving the information of his death — The House voted to wear mourning, that is crape on the arm, for him. Many members of Congress, the Marine Corps &c attended the funeral. It was so late, so cold & windy, I was afraid of exposing my health too much, & *ergo* did not attend.

### Wednesday 4th.

The House of Representatives in the State of Georgia have unanimously passed a resolution, "requesting that Thomas Jefferson will devote *four years* more of his life to the service of his country, in order more permanently to establish those principles of political liberty which is the boast & glory of republican America." The Executive department agreed to this address.

This morning I spent an hour or two with Mr. Jefferson the President at his house. Most of the time we were alone. I visited his library —at least that part of it which is in the Presidoliad. He informed me that the principal part of his books were at his own house in Montecella. I observed he had taken care to have his News papers bound and lettered, he replied he had — they contained some things worthy of notice but he considered them as vehicles of slander & falsehood — That no reliance could be placed on them. That he beleived

Smith's paper [262] of this city was the most correct, but even that is sometimes very erroneous — And he had requested the editor to be vigilant in correcting, & frank in avowing his errors, when he discovered them.

I informed the President that I had for some time contemplated writing the history of the United States — That it was my intention to state facts & delineate characters fairly & impartialy — That I hoped to execute the work in such a manner that the *reader* should not be able to ascertain, from the work, to what sect or party I belonged. That I did not contemplate gain as my object — but to preserve facts the knowledge of which were daily passing from us — That I hoped the work would be honorable to my country — That I intended to devote years to its accomplishment — And hoped it would remain, when executed, a monument not disgraceful to Myself.

While making these observations, with great freedom — I observed the countenance of the President repeatedly changed. At some moments there was the appearance of uneasiness and embarrassment — at others he seemed pleased — He alternately looked at me, & then fixed his eyes on the floor. I could perceive his mind was agitated with different emotions.

He enquired of me at what period I contemplated to commence the work. I replied I had not definitely settled that question — but should commence as early as the revolution.

I observed to him that my object in this morning's visit was to inform him that I wanted certain information — particularly in relation to our affairs with the European nations — & to request his aid. He said he was not only willing, but desirous, of making some communications — That he had from the commencement of the revolution to the present time, with very little interruption, been employed in the service of his country. That had he preserved copies of the letters he had written, they

---

[262] The *National Intelligencer,* edited by James Harrison Smith.

would of themselves, form a narrative of the most interesting events during that period.

That for several years past, having a letter press, he had preserved copies of his letters — That the best collection of State papers, previous to the Constitution, that is published are contained in the "American Museum" & the "Columbian Magazine."

I told him I was particularly anxious to obtain extracts from the correspondence of our ministers at foreign courts as far as it would be proper. He replied these are all recorded in volumes in the office of the Secretary of State. That he saw no objection to my having free access, & making extracts from, them, in all cases were the negociation was "*Wound up.* — & in particular those under the former administrations." That he would make a point of consulting the Secretary of State upon the subject. I observed to him that I presumed our negociations with the Barbary powers were of such a nature as that it would not be improper for me to have the perusal of them. He said I certainly might have them.

He enquired of me when I should commence the work. I replied soon after my return. He said his present engagements to the duties of his office gave him no leisure — It engrossed his whole attention & employed all his time — But in two years more he should be entirely at leisure & that he would then contribute to such an undertaking. He very clearly & emphatically conveyed the idea to me that it was his present intention to decline a re-election — the addresses from the people & the legislatures to the contrary notwithstanding.

I really wish I could fully ascertain the impressions that this visit made on the President. If I am not wholly deceived, the subject matter was not only wholly unexpected — but embarrassing to him. I think from his conversation — his manners & countenance he disapproved of the project — & yet it was apparent that he was anxious to conceal that disapprobation.

### Friday Feby 6th 1807.

James Turner one of the senators from North Carolina informed me this day, that in a conversation he had with the President, he took the liberty to ask him Whether he would gratify the general wishes of the people, by standing candidate for another presidential term. He said Mr. Jefferson assured him that he had made up his mind not to permit his name to be used as a candidate — That Genl Washington had established a precedent, of standing only for *two elections* — That it was a precedent which he thot was obligatory upon himself — & from which he could not depart. That he has himself uniformly advocated the principle of rotation in high offices. That he thot the Constitution defective because it did not contain that principle. That at the first election he and & Aaron Burr had an equality of votes — That he is now convinced that had Mr. Burr succeeded, he would have taken measures to have prolonged his term — That the most effectual method he can take to discountenance the idea, & prove the sincerity of his profession of rotation in office, will be, now he has the power, to imitate the great Washington, & not suffer himself to be a third time a candidate.

---

The last evening there fell about two inches of snow — It was cold. This morning the wind was N. W. & the atmosphere hazy. At twelve the wind blew a perfect hurricane, & so continued for several hours. Several brick buildings were unroofed — & two four wheeled carriages on Capitol hill were blown over on a plain good road, & much injured. It was with some difficulty I could walk 100 rods from the Capitol to my lodging. Some gentlemen were blown agt. the side of houses & bruised. It was the strongest wind I ever witnessed. The day was cold, & the night is now severe.

## Monday 9th

A few days since John Q. Adams received a letter dated Paris Sept 1806 without any signature. It was postmarked *Norfolk, Virginia.* He shewed to me before he read it, & desired me to look at the direction & postmark — I did it & then left him. To day I enquired of him respecting the letter & its contents. He said he would *in confidence* disclose it to me. The letter he said was written by *Pichon* (late *Charge d'affaires* from France to the United States) He then stated a number of circumstances that conclusively proved that fact. The writer said that the familiarity, that had existed between his family & Mr. Adams during his stay at Washington — The confidence he had in him — The information of his having resigned his seat in the Senate for the professorship at Harvard College, & therefore no longer a public man — had induced him thus to address him — He said that when he left France for the United States that invaluable work, " The defence of the American Constitutions," [263] by your father (John Adams) was by men then in power in France condemned as political heresy — as advocating a system of govt too energetic for the security of liberty — That this induced him to read & study it with attention — That the result on his mind was the entire approbation of the book. That on his return to France, to his great surprize, he found men who formerly condemned but now high in authority, approved of the work. [Mr. Adams said he thought that Pichon, among others, alluded to Talleyrand] [264] He then proceeds, to intimate, to Mr. Adams, *that the Govt of France contemplated a crusade to the United States.* And adds this I communicate in confidence — my name is not to be mentioned — I write to you as a *private gentleman* — and commit my letter to *your discretion.*

---

[263] *A Defence of the Constitutions of Government of the United States of America against the attack of M. Turgot in his Letter to Dr. Price, dated the twenty-second day of March, 1778.*

[264] Brackets appear in the original manuscript.

Mr. Adams after again enjoining confidence on me — and after my assuring him I would not mention the subject to any one — said, At first he had thot's of communicating the substance of the letter to Mr. Jefferson — but as the letter was written a month before Napolean's expedition to Prussia was known in France, he conceived, Pichon was probably mistaken as to the *crusade* to this Country — That if a measure of that kind was intended or in preparation in France our minister must be blind and stupid not to have gotten scent of it & communicated it to our Executive — And that the circumstance of the letter being written to him in confidence as a private citizen, & not as a senator — ought to restrain him.

I approved of his conduct.

In the course of the day I communicated to Mr. Adams pretty fully my intention of writing the history of the United States. Stated to him an outline of my plan — of my collection of materials — of the deficiency & difficulty of obtaining certain information respecting the early, & also the more modern part, of the work — particularly the correspondence of our ministers at Foreign Courts — That without these the history must be trivial & unworthy of notice — And requested him to grant me a perusal of his correspondence — & expressed an anxious wish to peruse those of his fathers during his various & highly important missions.

He replied with much frankness — I am much gratified at your undertaking — Such a work is necessary & I hope you will persevere, & compleat it. I will with pleasure give you my correspondence. It is contained in 3 Vols. of letter paper. It was not an interesting period. I replied the doctrine of *free ships making free goods,* was considered with great ability. He said that subject gave an interest to the discussion.

I think, said he, my father will give you the perusal of his correspondence. It is voluminous — 12 or 14 volumes.

With you I think the correspondence of our ministers both at home & abroad is important — indeed is essential.

At what period will you commence?

I answered I had not settled that question. Two periods have presented themselves — 1, the discovery of the Country — 2d the commencement of the revolution. He said adopt Hume's mode — He began his history with the Stuart family — brot it down to their revolution published it — & then wrote & published the earlier parts. Commence your work with the revolution write and publish a volume — Then begin at the period in which the European's discovered this country. The early part of the history of the Country is important. I request you will not abandon it. A good one has never been written of our country.

I mentioned to him that I had imparted my intention &c to Mr. Jefferson, & requested Mr. Adams would not communicate it — He said he would not — I then observed to him the surprize that it excited & different passions that were touched in the President. Mr. Adams replied, The President cannot be a lover of history — there are prominent traits in his character, & important actions in his life, that he would not wish should be delineated, & transmitted to posterity.

I told him how far he had given me assurances of aid — & that I intended to wait on the Secretary of State this week upon the subject. He replied, Mr. Madison cannot wish you success — He will suffer in history — His project not to make peace but only as Count Vergennes should dictate — his willingness to abandon the fisheries — & relinquish a considerable portion of our territory is proof of the fact.

He recommended to me to procure & examine the " Remambrancer " 3 Vols — & " Prior Documents " 1 Vol. published by Almond in London in 1775, 6 & 7.[265]

---

[265] John Almon compiler. *The Remembrancer, or Impartial repository of public events;* and *A collection of interesting, authentic papers, relative to the dispute between Great Britain and America,* the so-called " Prior Documents ".

## Tuesday 10th.

After an absence of 10 days Samuel Smith again took his seat in the Senate.

## Wednesday 11th.

In a conversation with Saml H. Smith I accidently mentioned to him my idea of writing the history of the U.S. He said he should advise agt publishing that part of it which is the most important, *our own times,* write it & leave directions to have it a posthumous work. That if I published it while living I must necessarily give mortal offence — & must retire from the world. He added he knew of several who are engaged in the same work — Most of whom he presumed would never proceed — but some would — particularly Joel Barlow Esq.[266]

Barlow is a man of considerable science — a poet — Has been an Agent in France — he is a friend of Mr. Jefferson & will, if industrious, have the necessary information. This will not restrain me.

------

When the bill was first debated on the subject of preventing intrusions by tresspassers upon lands of the United States, Timothy Pickering advocated the principles of the bill, and said its details were correct. In ten minutes after he was told it would have an unfavorable effect upon the Yazou claim. He replied, I did not think of that — I will stand by my friends, & will oppose the bill at all events. And on the question to pass the bill this day voted against it.

## Thursday 12th.

Mesrs Lewis, Tilghman, Hopkinson & Rawle, eminent lawyers of Philadelphia, assured me that Mr. C. A. Rodney's business as a lawyer, was not in their opinion the last year worth $300.

------

[266] Joel Barlow made extensive preparations for a history of the American revolution. His epic " The Columbiad " was issued in 1807.

Previous to his appointment as Attorney General of the United States, some of his friends, who pretended to have the means of information, assured me his professional business was worth $10,000 pr Annum. They were mistaken.

Note Mr. Rodney lives in Philadelphia — & those gentlemen are men of integrity.

---

Mr. Coles, the Presidents private secretary, yesterday told me that John Randolph did not this session visit Mr. Jefferson — That he appeared studiously to avoid the President. That there was no friendship subsisting between John Randolph & Thomas Man Randolph.

### Friday 13th.

Yesterday morning the blue-birds and robbins sang at my window.

The day & the last night was very rainy — a great fall of water. Weather mild as May, this morning — foggy.

Henry Clay, the senator from Kentucky, is a man of pleasure — very fond of amusements — gambles much. He told me that one evening he won at cards $1500 — that at another evening he lost $600 — He is a great favorite with the ladies — is in all parties of pleasure — out almost every night — gambles much here — reads but little. Indeed he said he meant this session should be a tour of pleasure.

He has talents — is eloquent but not nice or accurate in his distinctions — He declaims more than he reasons. He is genteel polite & pleasant companion. A man of honor & integrity.[267]

---

Samuel White, senator from Delaware told me that he himself never plays cards not even for a Cent. This is a man of highly polished manners.

[267] *Cf.* Plumer, *Life of William Plumer,* 353.

Genl Samuel Smith, senator from Maryland told me that he thought more highly of the people than he used formerly to do — That they had more virtue than he expected — more firmness — & more information — That to effect a revolution in Baltimore, from federalism to democracy, he had spent much time — harangued the people — treated them — purchased & distributed news papers pamphlets &c — That in this business he had expended in actual money more than $5000 — That the change of politic's in that city produced a similar change in the State.

---

The account that James Sullivan in his history of the " District of Mayne " gives of Moffat's burning the town of Portland, is incorrect.  Genl Ligthgow who was a native & lived & died in that district, just before his death was preparing to review & expose the many errors of that history.  He said that Moffit demanded of the inhabitants the delivery of a small number of old arms that belonged to the king.  To this, a number of the elderly inhabitants were violently opposed — The denial was so peremptory, & accompanied with so much bitterness & insolence, as exasperated him — & in this moment of anger he burnt the town.  The Revd Mr. Gardner of Boston informed me, in Nov last, that he had this information a few years since from Genl Ligthgow.

---

On the 21st of Nov last, Napolean, at Berlin, made a decree, declaring, " That the British islands are in a state of blockade — That all commerce & correspondence with them is prohibited — That every ware house, all merchandize or property whatever belonging to an Englishman are declared good prize — That the commerce of English merchandize is prohibited — all merchandize, the produce or manufacture of England or her colonies, is declared to be good prize.  No vessel coming directly from

England or her colonies, or having been there since the publication of this decree, shall be admitted into any port. Every individual, a subject of Great Britain, of whatever rank or condition, who is found in countries occupied by our troops or those of our allies shall be made a prisoner of war."

---

In a conversation I this day had with the French Minister, Turreau, I observed to him, I was apprehensive that the decree though designed to operate agt Great Britain only would materially injure our commerce. He replied we had nothing to fear on account of that decree — That he had received dispatches from his Court expressly declaring that the decree was not to affect the United States — & that the Emperor was determined to respect their interest & observe the convention subsisting between the two nations.

I am informed the same assurances were given to our minister at the French Court.

It seems the English courts of Admiralty, eg. at Jamaica, have taken & condemned some of our ships for going into french ports & disposing of their cargo therein.

The commercial interest is much alarmed at this state of things — & not without cause.

---

Genl Bradley & Mr. Giles both have once & again assured me That they are satisfied, That Genl Washington actually recd the British treaty while Congress was in actual session — that he considered the public mind as not prepared to receive it — & therefore would not communicate it to the Senate — but waited & called a special session of the Senate some months afterwards. I called on them for the evidence — they said they could not prove the fact. — I confess there is some reason, but no conclusive evidence, to conjecture this was the case. I have examined the Executive & public Journals of the Senate. I will state the fact I there find.

The treaty with Great Britain was dated Nov. 19, 1794.

Mr. Jay's letter, inclosing the treaty, was of the same date.[268] In it he expresses a strong wish that it might be ratified by the President & Senate and returned to him early in the spring — as he should then return, & should be desirous of bringing it back ratified.

Congress met Nov 3d 1794 & sat till March 3d 1795.

On the 3d of sd March the President issued a summons requiring each Senator to attend on the 8th day of June then next.[269]

On said 8th of June he sent a message to the Senate, inclosing the treaty — He says, " the treaty with Great Britain was on the 7th of March *delivered to the secretary of State*." [270] The senate sat till the 26th of June,[271] & advised to the ratification of the treaty.

The next session of Congress was Dec 7, 1795. On the 8th of that month the President in his message had not recd the *ratified* treaty.

May 6, 1796 The President approved of the bill making appropriations to carry the treaty into effect. [272]

From the date of Mr. Jays treaty to the time it was *delivered* to the Secy of State was three months & 18 days. This was certainly a long time for a passage. It does not indeed appear what day the letter & treaty left England — but it is to be presumed it was very soon after it was written — As the State of the Union, well known to Mr. Jay, & his anxiety would induce him to send it as soon as possible.

---

[268] See *American State Papers*, I. *Foreign Relations, I,* 503–504.
[269] *Cf.* Senate *Executive Journal* (1789–1805), 177.
[270] *Cf. ibid.,* 178.
[271] *Cf. ibid.,* 191–192.
[272] See *Annals of Congress,* 4 Cong., 2 sess., 2898–2899 (Appendix); *Statutes at Large,* I, 459.

## Saturday 14th.

On the 29th of last October the Revd Dr Spring of Newbury
Port (Massachusetts) informed me that he was chaplin to the
brigade, that was detached from the American army, & that
marched under the command of Genl Montgomery, to attack
Quebec. That they were 31 days on the march thro' the wilderness — suffered much fatigue & endured many privations. That
Aaron Burr was a volunteer in this expedition — That Genl
Montgomery made Burr his aid. — That as soon as the General
fell, the American army fled in great consternation — That Burr
returned back alone & attempted, amidst a shower of musquetry,
to bring off on his shoulder, the body of Montgomery — But
the general being a large man, & Burr small, & the snow deep,
prevented him — That this attempt of Burr's gave him much
eclat with our army.

---

Mr Hopkinson of Philadelphia told me that some years since,
I think 1780, the Legislature of Pennsylvania passed a law
declaring the *children of all negroes* that should be born in that
State, after *that time* should as soon as they arrived to the age
of 28 years *be free.*[273] That at the present time he thinks there
is not more than 100 slaves in the State. But he adds the free
negroes in the city are idle & immoral — That there are some
thousands of them in the city — that they live by stealing —
that the servants in gentlemen's houses steal provisions, liquors
& clothing which they carry to there houses — That many of
the houses are of bad fame — That a large portion of the offenders for petit larceny in the city are of this description —
That when they grow sick they are supported by the corporation
— That the City pauper tax annually exceeds $100,000. That

---

[273] See *Laws of the Commonwealth of Pennsylvania* (Carey and Bior-
nen), II, 246–251; also, Locke, *Anti-Slavery in America, 1619–1808,* 77–78.

many of their negroes dress richly & have two or three houses of public worship — tho' they profess religion, yet they are immoral.

For this month we have had a great accession to our boarders in the house in which I live. The Supreme Court of the United States is now in term. Ingersoll, Tilghman, Rawle, Hopkinson & D'Ponceau, of Philadelphia, Harper, Mason & Key of Maryland, Marshall of Kentucky &c able lawyers & well informed, gentleman, attending Court — are lodgers with us. To these add a number of very respectable gentleman who transciently call. Being in all between 20 & 30 upon an average at the dining table. This forms a company intelligent & highly agreeable — Tho' sometimes we are subject to a little croud & bustle. But to me these are meerest trifles when contrasted with the information & pleasure I receive from them.

Even Wm Eaton seems to be awed into respect & self government — He has been very peaceable quiet & well behaved — except one morning he appeared quite intoxicated — & even then he was not rude — though foolish.

### Thursday Feby 19, 1807.

This day I attended in Senate four hours. My health is much restored. We recd a message & documents from the President. By it & them we are informed 1, That a treaty is agreed on by our ministers with Great Britain.[274] 2 A declaration from *Decres* Minister of French Marine to Genl Armstrong that the decree of Napolean of the 21st Nov was not to affect the Commerce of the United States.[275]

Note, *Decres,* informs Mr Armstrong that he was not the proper officer to whom Armstrong should have applied upon this subject — The prince of Benevento (Talleyrand) was the man.

---

[274] The ministers were James Monroe and William Pinkney; see *American State Papers,* II. *Foreign Relations,* II, 805.
[275] See *ibid.,* 805–806.

*Decres* gives his *own opinion* — He was not, as to this subject the organ of the Nation.

3. That Col. Burr on the 18th Jany surrendered himself to the highest court of law in the Mississippi territory for trial. That he has " 9 boats & 100 men, & the major part of these are boys, or young men just from school." A guard was sent to examine the boats. This information is from Cowles Mead.[276]

### Friday 20th

Attended the Senate 5 hours — Tho' not perfectly well — My mind has not recovered its tone & firmness for business.

My friend Henry Clay gave me the perusal of a letter of two sheets of letter paper, from Genl John Adair, late Senator from Kentucky, addressed to the Senators & Representatives from Kentucky. Dated on board a Schooner in Chesepeake Bay, some day this week. I twice read it with great attention.

The substance of it is as follows —

Genl Adair, avers — That he never wished a seperation of the United States —

That he never joined with Aaron Burr or aided him in any plot whatever, " or his infamous co-intriguer, Wilkinson."

That he did indeed, last autumn receive a letter from Genl Wilkinson — That it was dated Sept 28th 1806 & postmarked the 29th — That in this letter W. says *Dear Adair, The time is now come to subvert the Spanish government — That 5000 light troops would conquer Mexico — That your military talents are requisite — That unless you fear to join a Spanish intriguer* (meaning myself) *come immediately That without your aid I can do nothing.*

Adair says, that soon after he recd said letter, he wrote Wilkinson an answer, which must have reached him by the 1st of Dec. — That he assured Wilkinson *He* (Adair) *was too old*

---

[276] Cowles Mead, secretary of the Mississippi Territory, acting governor; see *ibid., Miscellaneous,* I, 478.

*for military service — That he was incumbered with a family —*
*That the United States had not declared war agt Spain — That*
*he did not beleive they would — & That he could not violate*
*the laws of his country by levying war agt a power in amity*
*with it.*

Adair states that the objects of his present journey to New
Orleans — That he had at some post on the river 3000 gallons
of whiskey — a Debt of $1500 due at the city to collect — 2
boat loads of provisions which he had ordered down to sell —
& some negociations to make respecting lands — That his business was purely personal & private. That he was accompanied
with only one servant — That immediately after he had taken
lodgings at New Orleans, a captain with 100 soldiers by an order
of Genl Wilkinson arrested him — That they would not suffer
him to dine altho the provision was ready on the table — or to
take some medicine with him, for he was then sick — That they
would not even permit him to give direction, respecting his
horses which cost him $700 in Kentucky — or take all his cloth-
ing with him — That he was hurried on board a boat — carried
down a river — then sent on board another — & from thence
shipt into a schooner for Baltimore under a military guard —
That during the voyage he suffered much from the sciatic, from
the inclemency of weather, want of accomodations & from sea
sickness — That they deprived him of pen ink & paper. — That a
stranger on board had furnished him with them to write this
letter — That the same stranger of his own accord had assured
him he would, the instant he landed at Baltimore, procure a writ
of Habeas Corpus for him.

That he had fought and bled for his country — and that he
now demands protection agt the wanton oppression of one in
high office acting under color of authority from that very
country.

The foregoing is the substance of the letter.

I have information from Baltimore on which I can depend —

That Joseph H. Nicholson, judge of one of the circuit courts of Maryland, issued a writ of Habeas Corpus — That the Military officer who had Adair in custody bro't up Adair & Ogden & said he held them under military orders from Genl Wilkinson his superior officer — who had directed him to carry them to Washington — & that he was instructed to say that a sealed packett in his possession, given him by the general, contained the evidence of the prisoner's guilt — but that he should obey his orders, which were peremptory, to deliver it to the Secretary of War only.   Judge Nicholson immediately liberated both Adair and Ogden, there being no evidence against either of them.

Adair was bro't to Baltimore in the schooner Thatcher, arrived there on the 17th — was 25 days from New Orleans.   On the 18th was liberated as above.

John Randolph says within a few days he has seen a letter from Genl. Wilkinson written to a friend in this city that contains this idea,   That altho' Aaron Burr's treasonable plans are supprest — he will soon revive them — To prevent which, its best to *take him off* — & that he has provided 2 or 3 men who are well qualified to effect that laudable service for their country.

The plain english of which is   That Wilkinson has men in pay to *assassinate* Burr!

Dr. Erick Bollman told me this day   That Swartout assured him that in Burr's letter to Wilkinson in cypher there is mention made of a letter from Wilkinson to Burr with comments on it. Note,   That tho' W. swears that the translation he has given of this letter is substantial correct — he altogether omits this part of it.

Bollman told me, That for some days previous to his arrest, Wilkinson had borrowed Swartouts gold watch — After S. was arrested he sent a note to W. requesting him to deliver up his watch — but W. took no notice of the request.   Whether he wished to retain it as plunder taken from an enemy — or to prevent Swartout from obtaining by means of the watch the conveniences and comforts of life is uncertain. Either of which motives are base enough to damn the wretch!

Bollman says at New Orleans he lived in retirement — was not connected with the people — meddled with no man's business — was quiet and inoffensive — That Wilkinson knew this — visited him — As to being a spy to Burr, there was nothing to disclose — That such was the vanity & folly of Wilkinson that he himself daily published in the New Orleans News papers his apprehension of Burr's measures, & what means he had adopted to defeat them.

### Saturday 21.

In the communications from Genl. Wilkinson to the government upon the subject of Burr's conspiracy he represent Bollman as an artful, subtil, dangerous intriguing man — & long acquainted & versed in such measures. But Swartout as being a young inexperienced amiable man — & that he felt so tender of him as to caution him not to say anythng to him that would criminate himself.

Now observe the conduct of Wilkinson to these two men. He causes both of them to be arrested; but by different officers, & sent to this place. Bollman was arrested by Lt. Wilson, — and was allowed to take his bed with him — & Wilson was ordered by Wilkinson to advance him money to any amount he should require not exceeding $200, to render his passage & situation afterwards comfortable.

Swartout was arrested by Lt. . . .[277] & was not permitted to take his clothing — was refused his own watch — And so far was the Lt from being ordered to advance him even a cent of money, that he was positively directed to put him *in chains*. Swartout Assured the officer that he would never submit to that degradation — that he would die sooner than be chained. The officer replied he had once been a prisoner in chains to the Spaniards,

---

[277] Blank in the original manuscript.

& felt the disgrace & galling weight of chains — & would, in that particular, venture to violate his orders — No chains should therefore be imposed upon him.

Swartout was hurried into a boat crossed the river & lodged for several days & nights in a poor inhospitable shed — & deprived of the necessaries of life. In a few days he was ordered to march with the men. He enquired of the Officer where he was going? The Lt. replied he was ordered not to give him any information. Swartout said you are ordered to murder me, & I had as well die here as in the woods — & leapt over the railing. The Lt drew up his file of six men & ordered them to shoot him. The soldiers directed their guns at him & snaped them, but owing to the great rain, 3 of the guns flashed in the pan, & the other's would not take fire. The men pursued & took him. But for the wetness of the powder this unfortunate young man must have be murdered in very deed.

If Adair, Alexander, Bollman, Ogden & Swartout, were in fact traitors — they were not convicted — they were but prisoners, & in contemplation of law were presumed innocent — and ought to have been treated with humanity — with respect and with the attention due to men of their talents & rank in society. Adair in particular was well known to Wilkinson — he had recently held offices of great importance, & sustained a fair moral character. But this vain intriguing haughty infamous Wilkinson, deprived them of the rights which our laws guarantee even to common *convicted* malefactors.

For the case of Alexander I refer to his address published a few days since in the News papers.

Wilkinson has done more to destroy our little feeble military establishment, than its bitterest enemies have been able for years to effect. The President ought instantly to remove him from his two offices of Gov of Upper Louisiana & commander of the army. If he does not do it, Wilkinson will damn him & his administration. Thomas M. Randolph told me he tho't Wilkinson must be removed or his father in law (Jefferson's) administration would fall.

The public indignation seems now to be transferred from Burr to Wilkinson. And I expect in a few days to hear that the former has been tried & legally acquited.

It is now very apparent Wilkinson himself has *created* much of the alarm, & has greatly exaggerated the force & importance of Burr. I think Burr's object was the Mexican provinces — not a seperation of the Union. And I rejoice the bill to suspend the writ of Habeas Corpus did not pass into a law. I hope I shall never again consent to the passing an important law in haste.

The Supreme Court of the United States have this day, upon the Habeas Corpus, after long debate & much consideration, discharged Bollman & Swartout from prison. They are now at large.

Four judges only sat — & on some important points they were equally divided. Judge Livingston [278] returned to New York to a sick & melancholly family. Judge Cushing [279] has not attended Court this term — He is now confined to a sick bed at Stelle's. Tis really wrong that that old gentleman should hold this high office, the duties of which he is utterly unable to discharge — & receive a salary for services he cannot perform His nonattendance has occasioned great delay — & the continuance of many suits — to the great expence & injury of many suitors. There ought to be a power in Congress to remove such incurables from the bench of justice.

---

No men in the Senate have discovered more anxiety to prevent, the bill from the House, passing into a law, *to repeal the*

---

[278] Brockholst Livingston.
[279] William Cushing of Massachusetts. Cushing sat on the bench from 1789 to 1810.

*duty on Salt* than Bradley, & Smith (of Maryland).  They declared their conviction that the Govt wanted the money arising from this source — & that salt was a proper subject to collect a duty from.  They both made long speeches agt the repeal — but when the question was yesterday taken by ayes & nays, Smith voted *in favor of the repeal.*  Bradley indeed voted *agt the repeal* — but as soon as the question was carried not to repeal, he moved to amend the bill by reducing the duty from 20 to 12 Cents per bushel.  In this he succeeded.  He then moved further to amend the bill by adding a clause *to repeal the whole of the duty on salt from & after the 31st day of December next.*  This was negatived by a small majority.  When will men have sufficient sense of propriety as to know that *consistency* is one of the most valuable traits in the character of the statesman!

### Sunday 22d.

Humphry Marshall of Kentucky had been a boarder at the same house with me for this 3 weeks.  He is cousin to John Marshall chief Justice of the Supreme Court of the United States — & married the C. Justice's sister.  Humphry is a man of plain good sense & had acquired considerable information.  He is a native of Virginia — He was senator in Congress from Kentucky in 1795, & one that voted in favor of the ratification of Jay's treaty.  Soon after his return from that session to Kentucky, the people, to express their indignation at him for his vote upon that subject, rose in a mob (countenanced by John Brown) surrounded his house, seized his person, & hurried him down to the edge of a large muddy pond, & were upon the point of plunging him into the pond.  At which he observed to them that he was informed it was the practise of persons, previous to their being baptized to relate their experiences — & he hoped that before he was immersed they would grant him that priviledge.  They desired him to proceed — He addressed them in a speech of half an hour with so much wit & pleasantry, that they huzza'd him — omitted the rude ceremony — & conducted him to his house with every mark of respect that such a rabble was capable of manifesting to him.

He told me last evening, that he was well acquainted with Genl Wilkinson — That he was vain — deceitful — intriguing, & the most *corrupt man* he ever knew. That the people of Kentucky held him in so much detestation that he did not beleive a single company of their militia would, on any occasion, serve under him.

He also informed me that very early in the last year Mr. Daviess the district Atty of Kentucky opened a confidential correspondence with Mr. Jefferson, the President, upon the subject of Burr's conspiracy. That in his first & second letters he named Burr, Wilkinson, and several others. That in the president's first answer to Mr. Daviess he said, he felt the necessity & propriety of keeping the communication a secret, yet as one of the persons implicated (meaning Wilkinson) was acting a highly responsible part under the Secretary of War he had taken the liberty of shewing the letter, in confidence, to him.

Mr. Marshall added that Mr. Daviess, as a friend, had shewn him copies of his two letters to the President — & also the answer from the President to Mr. Daviess. That he is confident he saw the last letter & the copies of the first two as early as April last. [280]

I think the President says, in his message to Congress, upon the subject of Burr's conspiracy, that the first information he had upon the subject was as late as September or October last.[281]

---

[280] The facts here related by Humphrey Marshall to Plumer concerning Burr were later narrated at greater length by Marshall in his *History of Kentucky* (2d ed.), II, 385–396. Volume I, covering the period to 1791, appeared in 1812 but no second volume was issued until the second edition made its appearance in 1824.

[281] The latter part of September according to Jefferson's message.

In a conversation I had yesterday with Gideon Granger he assured me he was determined before the next session of Congress to resign his office of Postmaster General — & resume the practise of law in either Boston or the city of New York for a few years to enable him to educate his sons — & then retire & live on his lands in the State of Ohio.

## *Monday 23d.*

My colleague, Mr. Gilman, this day informed me, That the President had unequivocally assured him that he was fully resolved not to be again a Candidate for the Presidency.

Mr. Gilman then said, Mr. Madison will be our next president — & he is a *Quid or third party man.*

He also added, " I do not all together approve of the conduct of Mr. Jefferson — His great object is popularity — He bends the interest of his country too much to that — hence, & hence only, it is that he recommends the repeal of the duty on salt."

---

' Tis now a week since Thomas M. Randolph has been a boarder in the same house with me. Rumour was bussy in assigning the cause — for he had always boarded with Mr. Jefferson his father in law. It was said he & the President had quarrelled. This is not true for he speaks of the President with great cordiality — visits him often & dined at his house with him on saturday. Its said he and his brother [282] Eppes has quarrelled — I doubt this. I think he boards here to save the inconvenience of riding or travelling so far — But this is conjecture.

He always eats in his own room — He has never once dined in company since he has boarded with us.

He is a bashful timid man — Is — a pleasant agreeable com-

---

[282] Brother-in-law.

panion — a man of study — much devoted to books. Being on good terms I called & spent an evening with him last week.

In conversation with him respecting Adair, I mentioned his letter & his account of a letter of the 28th Sept from Wilkinson. Mr. Randolph replied, " I am confident that the President some months since shewed me a letter from Wilkinson with a copy of this very letter to Adair, & Adair's answer."

This fact renders Wilkinson still more contemptible in my mind. What is the commander of our Armies to assume & write in the style of a *friend* to men of rank & importance & persuade them to join with him in an expedition agt. a power in amity with the United States — with a view that he may betray the very man whom in the guise of a friend he attempts to seduce? The wretch that is capable of such baseness & villainly is not fit to be trusted by any man.

I spoke to Mr. Randolph freely my opinion of Wilkinson. He told me he was confident that Wilkinson would endanger the very existence of the Presidents authority — And that he had advised to his removal from office. That doubts were raised as to the method of removal — The conduct of former Presidents had been examined — It was found that two officers in the Navy had been, under former administrations, removed by the President. But no instance could be found of removal from office, by a President of the United States of a high military officer.[283] He tho't the law had not provided for the trial of the Genl by Court martial — And that for the House to impeach & the Senate to try him, would be a long tedious procedure.

I replied the President of the United States had an unquestionable right to remove him, & expressed my wishes that he would not delay to exercise that authority.

That his conduct would soon destroy our military establish-

[283] *Cf.* C. R. Fish, " Removals of Officials by Presidents of the United States," in *Annual Report* of the American Historical Association, **1899,** I, 67–86.

ment entirely.  Mr. Randolph said no friend of his country could justify, & ought not to apologize, for his conduct.

## Tuesday 24.

This morning I went paid a visit to Genl John Adair now in this city.  He appeared much pleased with the attention I paid him.  I thot it my duty to shew him in his present situation this mark of my respect and esteem.  I really consider him an honest respectable man.

He narrated to me the events of his journey & voyage from home to this place, with great ease & simplicity.

He said he had no opportunity, while at New Orleans to speak to Genl Wilkinson.  That before he had an opportunity to dine, Col. Kingsbury with a 100 soldiers came to the house at which he had put up — And in a gentlemanlike manner informed him that he knew the duty of a military officer was to obey the commands of his superior — That he had orders from Genl Wilkinson, which he was sorry to have received, but which he was bound to execute.  That he must consider himself a prisoner.

That he was then taken & delivered up to an officer with a file of men — put into a boat & carried down the river 25 miles, & landed the other side of the river, & placed under a tent in a swamp.  That they tarried in this place six days, & should have suffered from hunger, had not some of the men accidently killed a deer — on which they subsisted.

That the officer who had him in custody was ordered, by Wilkinson, not to speak to him.  But that he was treated by the officer with civility, & allowed to walk in the woods where he pleased.

That after his arrest, but before he left the city, a considerable number of the officers of the army, called at his door in the house in which he was, gave in their Names, & very politely enquired of him if there was anything in their power they could do for him?

That after the six days he was carried down the river, & under custody of Lt. Luckett he was shipped aboard the schooner Thatcher for Baltimore. That Wilkinson's orders to the Lt. was peremptory to carry him to Baltimore, & deliver him to some military officer there who would carry him to the Marine barracks in this city. That he must retain him a close prisoner at all events — & that if any civil officer should attempt to take him by a writ of Habeas Corpus, he should resist such officer with force & arms. He saw & read the orders.

That the Lt. treated him with much attention & civility — That had a civil officer come with a writ of Habeas Corpus — he would have used his influence not to have it served untill he should be delivered over to some other officer — for he did not wish to subject him to censure.

That at Baltimore he was by the Lt. dld over to the commander of the fort at that city. That a stranger, who was a passanger with him on board the schooner, without his request, applied to Judge Nicholson for a writ of Habeas Corpus — That no evidence whatever was produced agt him — & the Judge discharged him.

That yesterday he arrived in this city — that he had not called upon the President or Secy of War — That he had sent a note to the Atty Genl of the United States, informing him he was in this city — & requesting to know if any accusation was made agt him — & by whom — averring his innocence — & his willingness to submit to an investigation of his conduct. The Atty returned a verbal answer, he knew of no charge agt him — but would make the requisite enquiry & return him an answer this day.

The General in plain but with unequivocal language declared his innocence — & his attachment to this country.

He said he tho't he knew Genl Wilkinson — but that his present conduct was so wild & ruinous that he considered him as a *deranged man.*

I asked him what he considered as the motive that induced him to order his arrest? He replied a few days before my arrival at Orleans the Genl at a public table declared I was marching to the city at the head of 2000 hostile troops. On my arrival I contradicted this report. His pride was wounded — & I became his victim.

There are no men in Kentucky attached to Burr — before I left that State he could not procure men, for high wages to row down his boats.

The genl also informed me that a very few days before his arrival at Orleans, Wilkinson had this very Lt. Luckett arrested on the charge of being an accomplice with Burr — That after detaining him in arrest 14 days — without an enquiry or trial, he released him from arrest — & ordered him into his custody.

It is a fact that he appointed sometime since Ensign Mead as the officer to bring to this city, one of the persons accused of being in league with Burr — And at the same time sent on sealed orders by Mead himself to have him arrested as soon as he arrived as being a party in Burr's conspiracy. Mead delivered his prisoner & the packett — & was immediately after arrested. See Meads statement & defence a few days since published in the News papers.

Wilkinson seems destitute of common sense — & lost of all sense of propriety.

---

When Mr. W. Giles (senator from Virginia) was informed last saturday, That the Supreme Court of the United States had unanimously discharged & liberated Bollman & Swartout — he declared he would bring forward in the Senate an amendment to the Constitution prohibiting that Court from having any jurisdiction in criminal prosecutions.

---

When I informed him to day that I had visited Adair — he intimated that it was improper.

He said, he tho't Wilkinson had acted rightfully, & that he must be supported.

Mr. Giles told me, That Genl Washington declined laying a copy of Jays ratified treaty before the House of Representatives, alledging that he had not the ratified copy under the sign manual of King George. Had he at that period sent that Copy the House would then have refused to make the necessary appropriations to carry it into effect. But after three weeks Washington's influence prepared the House to approve of it — & then without waiting for the original he communicated the same copy to the House.

Examine his message to Congress at the opening of that session & the journal of the House.[284]

Mr. Giles also assured me That General Gunn, then a senator from Georgia, declared to John Brown of Kentucky, That he had strong reasons, which he could not resist, to vote for the ratification of that treaty — That those reasons, & not the conviction of his own mind, compelled him to do it. That the strong reasons were assurances from Rufus King that if he would vote for the treaty — their party would ratify & confirm the *Yazou claim.* — This fact said Giles I can prove. — But, added, Mr. Giles, Gunn was deceived by the smooth language & sybtle insinuations of Mr. King — for King never made such assurances — for he was opposed to the Yazou claim — He only made insinuations which the ardent mind of Gunn appreciated beyond their true meaning — Gunn was deceived.

I think upon the subject of the Yazou claim there was a resolution brought in by Mr. King at that or the next session.[285] Examine the journals upon the subject.

---

[284] See Richardson, *Messages and Papers of the Presidents,* I, 182–186 (especially p. 183).
[285] King sent his resignation to the Senate, May 23, 1796, having accepted the appointment as minister to Great Britain.

For several days the Senate have been employed in debate upon a bill " Authorizing the sale & grant of a certain quantity of public land, to the Chesapeake & Delaware Canal company." This canal Company is formed by acts of incorporation from the States of Delaware, Pennsylvania, & Maryland. The canal is to run from the river Christiana to the Elk river — & is to be large enough to carry ships of more than 100 tons. The object of this bill was for the United States to grant to the company a tract of unlocated land, say 200,000 acres, in the State of Ohio and in the Indiana Territory. The company were not to sell said land for a less sum pr acre than what the US. sell. The United States to receive as many shares of stock in said Canal Company as said land would amount to.

When I first contemplated this subject I was inclined to oppose it — But when I considered its great importance — the use & value of it to the nation especially in case of an invasion — The great facility it would give in conveying the productions of the country to the markett — The immense importance of inland navigation — with what care & expence all well informed nations have attended to the making and improving of canals — The immense tracts of unlocated lands the United States possess not yet disposed off, not less than 300,000,000 acres on this side the Mississippi — & the wilderness world in Louisiana — That our treasury is overflowing, & our national debt rapidly wasting away — as fast as the terms of payment will permit — the bill met with my hearty approbation, as well calculated to aid a great & important & highly useful national object.

Mr. Bayard, White & Clay supported the bill with great ability & much eloquence. See an account of the debate in the Gazettes.[286]

*Mr. Adams* was violent in his opposition He considered it as a revenue bill & ought not to have originated in the Senate.

---

[286] White's speech is reported in full in *Annals of Congress,* 9 Cong., 2 sess., 80–87.

As laying a foundation for more fraud & collusion than *Yazou-ism* itself — That it would form a league of States — of senators — who would combine to sacrifice public interest to that of individual States — & as an opening wedge for other speculations & grants of public lands.[287]

*Mr. Hillhouse,* That turnpike roads & canals would invite invaders & aid their movements agt us.

*Mr. Tracy* That the whole of the public lands were pledged for the redemption of the public debt — That to appropriate any part of it to this object would be a violation of public faith pledged to our creditors.

Not considering that, this was never the understanding of the pledge — That all our revenues beyond the support of Govt. are also pledged — That the true meaning of this pledge is only to give sufficient funds for the payment — That Congress have always understood that the pledge as it respects the lands is qualified with an implied reservation that gives them authority to appropriate a portion of lands to such objects as the nation requires — Hence grants of lands have been made to officers & soldiers of the army — to Nova Scotia refugees — to schools, academies &c.

But on the motion to postpone to the next session the bill a small majority was in favor — altho' a majority of the Senate were in favor of passing the bill.   There is really something insiduous in this business of postponing — The minds of some men shirk from responsibility — They are averse to business.

Saml Smith opposed the bill — but would not vote agt it, because as he privately said to me the Legislature of Maryland had given a charter to the Company.

He said he considered its object to build up Philadelphia as a commercial city at the expence of Baltimore.

We are doing much by protecting duties, drawbacks, light

---

[287] *Cf.* J. Q. Adams, *Memoirs,* I, 460–461.

houses, beacons, &c to aid our merchants — ought we not to do something to aid agriculture?

. . . . . . . . . . . . . . . . . . . . . . . . . . . . . . . . . . . . . . . .

### Thursday 26th

A day or two since the Senate sent the bill to repeal the duty on salt &c with this amendment, that the repeal be confined to the repeal of *part* of the duty on salt, to wit, to reduce the duty from 20 to 12 Cents per bushel — The House to day departed from its usual rule in cases of disagreement & instead of *insisting* on their bill they voted  That they would *adhere* & refused a conference on the disagreement — Some of their Members rudely declared in debate they would not submit to the decision of the Senate — that the Senate had no right to make amendments.  The bill was returned, & the Senate voted to adhere 15 to 13.  I was in the affirmative.  For I will never yield the right that the Senate have to amend or reject bills.  The consequence is the Meditteranean fund will cease after this session.  The repeal of the duty on salt, & the continuance of the two & a half pr Cent ad valorem duty ought never to have been joined in the same bill.

Genl Bradley who at first opposed the duty on salt, after this bill was rejected, gave notice that tomorrow he should ask liberty to bring in a bill to suspend the law repealing the duty on salt.  He is determined to run in this scramble for popularity.

This evening Capt Ranken of the Marine Corps invited Mrs Frost & myself & Mr. Nelson [288] & Miss C Frost to spend the evening at his house — & attend at the baptism of his infant son. We attended — Judge Bushrod Washington & lady were the sponsors or godfather or godmother.  The ceremony was performed by Mr McCormick an Episcopal clergymen — He made use of the cross ie. he drew a cross with his finger with Water

---

[288] Probably Jeremiah Nelson, representative from Massachusetts.

over the face of the child. Man is a supertitious animal —
superstitution seem inherent in his nature. Wise men may laugh
& ridicule it — but fools, the mass of mankind — will retain &
adore it! I will neither quarrel or imitate them.

Capt Ranken informed me, that during the time that Bollman
& Swartout were in goal, he in turn attended as officer three or
4 days. That he found the prisoners very polite & gentlemanly
men — That after the Supreme Court had on writ of Habeas
Corpus liberated & discharged them — he presumed they must
be considered as innocent at least in contemplation of law. And
he invited S. Swartout, & his brother who was in the city, with
Judge Washington & lady, to drink tea one evening at his house.
They attended — News of this reached the President — he was
offended at Ranken — mentioned it to the Secretary of the
Navy — who wrote to Ranken censuring him as guilty of a
great impropriety, in inviting men accused as traitors to his
house. Are the sound maxims of law to be reversed? Is accusation and conviction to be considered as synonymous? And is
a man, an officer, to be publicly censured, for an act of common
civility towards the accused, even after he is liberated & set
at liberty by the highest court in the Union?

I did not think my self disgraced in dining at my lodgings
with Dr. Bollman — or degraded in visiting Genl Adair —
though some censure me for so doing.

### Friday 27th

A motion was made in the House of representatives to Appoint a Committee upon the subject of repealing the duty on
salt & continuing the Meditteranean fund. John Randolph opposed it on the ground that the House had once this session
passed upon the subject, & that the Senate had rejected the bill
— & it was more than probable would again reject it — & therefore would be humiliating, and, in fact, prostrating the dignity
of the House at the feet of the Senate. He pronounced a most

severe phillipic upon the Senate, & upon the advocates of the present motion.[289]   It was however carried agt. him, & a Committee appointed.

### Saturday, Feby 28, 1807.

This day I communicated my intention of writing history, to Mr. Gallatin Secy of the Treasury.  He very promptly offered his aid to furnish any materials in his department.  He said in a few instances there were some inaccuracies in some of the official reports from that department.  These he would point out to me — and also select such documents as were correct & material.

I mentioned to him my having read his treatise on finance. He said he beleived the work was correct — That document No. 10 was the most important part as it contained an account of monies paid in Holland for the foreign debt that is not stated in the accounts of the Treasury department.[290]

I asked him if had examined Sam Blodget Jr *Statistical Manual of the United States,*[291] published the last year.  He said he had not fully done it — but he had so far examined it as to perceive errors in the tables — & advised me not to rely on it — but resort to the reports of the heads of Department on all subjects on which they had reported.  That Blodgetts table of *specie* in the U.S. was very incorrect, particularly in 1802 in which he makes a decrease from the proceeding year of $1,000,-000; when in fact in that year there was a great encrease — That the encrease in that year at the bank of the United States alone exceeded in actual specie $300,000.

I well recollect that specie that year was unusually plenty.

---

[289] See *Annals of Congress,* 9 Cong., 2 sess., 641–642, 650–653.

[290] For the full text of Gallatin's *Sketch of the Finances of the United States* (1796), see *Writings of Albert Gallatin,* (Adams, ed.), III, 73–199, with additional tables.

[291] See Bryan, *A History of the National Capital,* for a short sketch of the early career of Samuel Blodgett.

The President nominated Meriweather Lewis, late Captain in the Missouri expedition to be governor of the Territory of Louisiana. This nomination is a removal of Genl Wilkinson from the office of Governor of that territory. I am pleased with his removal — The interest of the country required it.

Note the Grand jury at the Supreme Court in the Orleans territory have presented the late arrests & conduct of the General, as illegal & as acts of public oppression. Judge Workman has stated to the Legislature that the functions of the civil authority were suspended by the arbitary acts of the Military power — & that he adjourned his Court *sine die.*

That legislature had secret sessions, at which Genl Wilkinson was admitted to make communications. The result has not reached me.

The President had also nominated Thomas Todd of Kentucky to be a Judge of the Supreme Court of the United States. This nomination is founded upon a law of Congress passed this session adding another judge to that Court.[292] He is said not to be a great lawyer. He is brother in law to Judge Innes, & is now a judge of their Supreme Court of that State.

Lewis is I think tolerable well qualified for Governor of Louisiana — & I think I shall advise to his appointment.

The President also nominated Lt [293] . . . Clark of the artillery to be Lt. Colonel of the regiment of Infantry *vice* Col Cushing promoted last year. Clark is a brave man, & I beleive his moral character is fair. He was a lieutenant under Capt Lewis in the late exploring expedition to the Pacific Ocean. I regret that this nomination is made — for there are several older deserving officers in the army of superior grade to Clark. In times of peace prior rank, especially when qualified, ought always to have the preference. This raising of inferior Officers in the Army or Navy over the heads of superiors, must produce discontent quarrels & resignations of the officers.

---

[292] Act of February 24, 1807; see *Statutes at Large,* II, 420–421.
[293] William Clark. Blank appears in the original manuscript.

At four OClock the Senate adjourned to 7. Did little business in the evening sitting. Mr. Clay moved to sit tomorrow, sunday — the ayes & nays being required on this question — The friends of the motion did not like to vote on record in favor of it — & to avoid that adjourned to monday next.

The House of Representatives sat from 10 OClock AM. till after midnight. They had a disorderly tumultuous session in the evening. They again passed a bill to repeal the duty on salt & to continue the Meditteranean fund. The majority was less than on the former bill — See their journal.[294]

I am much fatigued — This long attention to business has affected me — I am weary. I will tomorrow in letter to my wife give some further account of this days proceedings.

### Sunday March 1

The Heads of Department visit few members of either House. Mr. Madison for this two or three years past has entirely omitted even the ceremony of leaving cards at their lodgings. He invites very few to dine with him.

Mr. Gallatin leaves no cards, makes no visits — scarce ever invites a Member to dine — or has even tea parties — Mrs. Gallatin is a domestic wife & averse to company. He is himself frugal and parsimonious — Is very inattentive & negligent of his person & dress — his linen is frequently soiled, & his clothes tattered.

Genl Dearborn leaves cards for all the members — invites few to dine — some to tea parties. He has taken care to avoid company by living in a remote part of George Town.

Robert Smith leaves cards with all the members — invites few to tea, & scarse any to dine.

These gentlemen do not live in a style suited to the dignity of their offices.

Mr. Clinton, always comes to the city in his own carriage,

---

[294] House *Journal* (1804–1807), 623–632.

accompanied by one of his daughters, & a servant. He is immensely rich — but lives out at board like a common member — keeps no table — or invites anybody to dine. A style of living unworthy of the 2d officer in our government.

He is old, feeble & altogether uncapable of the duty of presiding in the Senate. He has no mind — no intellect — no memory — He forgets the question — mistakes it — & not infrequently declares a vote before its taken — & often forgets to do it after it is taken — Takes up new business while a question is depending.[295]

---

In some of my manuscripts I have stated things upon the relation of Uriah Tracy, senator of Connecticut. From a more perfect knowledge of the man I am convinced, he seldom states things truly. He is too wild, too extravagant — & has too strong a prejudice — & too much disposed to exaggerate & misrepresent to be entitled to full credence. The rage of *party* has preverted his mind, & blinded him to truth.

### Monday March 2d

The Minister from Great Britain, Mr. Erskine, to the United States, is a young inexperienced man, of feeble intellect — & very ignorant. He appears altogether unacquainted with the law & usuages of Nations, & even of the statute & common law of his own country — tho' he pretends to have been bred a lawyer — & has inscribed on the pannels of his coach " *Trial by Jury.*" His actions & conversation are puerile — There is no dignity in his person, manners or observations. He married some years since in Philadelphia, a young lady of that city, who was then at school. She was the daughter of Genl Cadwallader. She appears to have an amiable disposition — but wants talent & animation.

---

[295] This description of the department heads and the Vice President is quoted, but in condensed form, in Plumer, *Life of William Plumer,* 353–354.

As an instance of Mr. Erskine's ignorance of the law of Great Britain, I heard him say that in a civil suit brought by an individual to recover damages, for libellous publication, the defendant could not give, under any plea whatever, the truth of the publication in evidence. The reverse of this is the law & constant practise of that country.

His father is an eminent lawyer, & ranks high at the British bar. He now holds the dignified office of Lord chancellor of Great Britain.

The French minister, Genl Turreau, is a man of little learning & slender talents. Of a ferocious disposition, and brutal manners.

The Marquiss D Yrujo, the present unacknowledged minister from the Court of Madrid, is far superior in talents, science, knowledge of law, of the world, & application to either of the other two ministers. He is artful, intriguing & indefatagible. His enemies under-rate his talents. He is not, however, a man of first rate talents — but is above mediocrity.

It is surprizing that the great nations of Europe, France, Great Britain & Spain, should send such feeble characters as ministers plenipotentiary to the United States. It is either proof that *favoritism* to particular families & persons govern these Courts — or that they consider the United States as of little consequence to them.

The bill repealing the duty on salt & continuing the Mediterranean Fund came down from the House. It was read — It was objected to be out of order — The President of the Senate asked the advice of the Senate — a majority of the Senate decided it was in order to receive it. It was read & a great majority voted it should pass to a second reading. Mr. Turner [296] moved to have it read a 2d time — several members objected. He then moved to dispense with the rule — The President decided that question out of order. He then moved to reconsider the rules

---

[296] James Turner, senator from North Carolina.

of the Senate — The motion was laid on the table, for to be acted upon tomorrow.

Abraham Baldwin, senator of Georgia, lies at the point of death. In my letter to my daughter of this day I have given an account of him.

At five OClock PM. the Vice President gave notice that he should not again attend the Senate this session — Adjourned to 7 OClock this evening.

In the evening Saml Smith of Maryland was elected President pro. tem. of the Senate.

The Senate, without division advised to the appointment of M. Lewis to be gov. of Louisiana.

Thomas Todd to be a Judge of Supreme Court of the United States.

Upon the nomination of Lt Wm Clark to be Lt Colonel of the army of the United States an opposition was made, that he was not the next officer in rank. All agreed he was a man of a fair character & approved bravery. That those officers of superior Rank were well qualified for this office. On this question the ayes & nays were —

*Ayes* Bradley, Clay, Condit, Kitchel, Logan, Mitchel, Smith of Tennessee, Smith of Vermont, Thruston. 9, ayes

*Nays* Adams, Bayard, Fenner, Gaillard, Giles, Gilman, Hillhouse, Howland, Maclay, Milledge, Moore, Pickering, Plumer, Reid, Smith of Maryland, Smith of New York, Smith of Ohio, Tracy, Turner, White. nays 20.[297]

At 10 OClock the Senate adjourned.

Seth Hastings, a representative from Massachusetts, this day recd information of the sudden death of one of his children. He appeared to take no notice of it — He attended the House — dined with the company, & conversed as merrily as if no such event had happened. I admire the man who bears affliction with fortitude — but the man who has no sensibility — who is

---

[297] *Cf.* Senate *Executive Journal* (1805–1815), 54.

lost to parential ties, & social feelings, must be a wretch indeed.
His heart is hard as adamant & cold as Greenland ice. Trust not
such a man. Hastings is unsocial — he avoids society. He is
mulish, an obstinate wrong headed man.

### Tuesday March 3d 1807

I omitted to mention that Paul Dudley Sargeant of the District of Mayne was sometime since nominated by the President to be Collector of one of the Ports in that District. Mr.
Adams stated that this man had some years since been indicted
& convicted by a Court of law as guilty of extortion in office.
That the house of Representatives of that State had voted to
address the Gov to remove him from the office of Judge of A
County Court — That the Senate of that Commonwealth refused to concur in the resolution to remove him — upon the
idea that he was guilty of a *crime* (extortion) & ought to be
impeached. The Senate of the United States yesterday negatived the nomination.[298]

The Senate this day suspended their rule requiring a bill to
be read on three different days — ayes 15, nays 10.[299] Those
in the affirmative were a minority of all the Senators but a
majority of those present. I *think,* this is the first instance in
which the Senate have ever suspended their rules.[300] This was
done to pass the bill repealing the duty on salt & to continue
the Meditteranean fund. That bill was taken up & passed. I
consider the suspension of the rule so long established as more
ruinous to the order of the Senate than any act I have ever witnessed within its walls. The constant importunity & ill temper
of Mr. Turner, on this occasion was disgusting — It however
affended his friends more than those who differed from him.

---

[298] *Cf. ibid.*

[299] See *Annals of Congress,* 9 Cong., 2 sess., 104–105.

[300] The Senate suspended this rule in order to pass the bill suspending
the privilege of the writ of habeas corpus; see page 590.

The ordinance for the government of the territory of the United States northwest of the river Ohio, passed July 13, 1787 — provides, That the Legislative Council shall consist of five persons — That the house of representatives of that Territory shall nominate ten persons out of whom Congress shall appoint the five councillors — And that whenever a vacancy shall happen in the council by death or removal from office the said house shall nominate two persons, & Congress shall appoint one of them a councillor. Laws of Congress Vol. 2. p. 541.

Congress, March 2, 1805 by statute declared by legislative council for the territory of the Orleans territory shall be appointed in conformity to said ordinance — Laws of Congress Vol. 7. p. 281.[301]

The House of Representatives of Orleans territory nominated to the President ten persons, five of whom to compose their Legislative council. At the last session the President nominated 5 of them to the Senate. The Senate advised to the appointment of four of them; but the 5th, John W Gurley, they negatived. The president commissioned the four & gave, information to the House of Representatives of the Territory. At their then next session, they nominated two other persons to the President, & he in the recess of the Senate appointed one of them, Julian Poydrass, to be councillor. On the 6th [302] of last December the president nominated Poydrass to the Senate. Feby 4, 1807,[303] the Senate took up the nomination. Mr. Tracy contended, That the nomination ought to be negatived because Poydrass was not one of the ten named in the first nomination made by the House of Representatives from Orleans — & that this was not such a vacancy as is contemplated in the ordinance, the office having never been filled.

---

[301] See *Statutes at Large*, II, 322–323.

[302] The nomination of Poydrass was communicated to the Senate, December 15, 1806; see Senate *Executive Journal* (1805–1815), 44.

[303] *Ibid.*, 49.

There was no objection to the character or qualifications of Poydrass.

It was postponed to this day — & on the question of advising to the appointment — ayes 13, nays 9.[304] I voted in the affirmative. I think that as soon as the five persons were nominated from the first list, the list was at an end — That the President by electing of 5 virtually rejected the other 5. — That if it was of doubtful construction two authorities, the President & House of Representatives in Orleans had decided it — the Senate ought to abide by their decions, especially as their rejecting it would virtually compel the President to nominate one whom he did not approve — & would at the same time nullify his right & enlarge their own authority.

Bradley & Tracy said some severe unhandsome personal things of each other with great passion, in the debate.

I tarried till after ten — till all the business was done in the Senate, except waiting for information from the President that he had nothing further to communicate. I should have tarried till the hour of adjournment — but I found my heart too full to take a final farewell of my friends. The Senate adjourned before 12 OClock, at night.

I part with the honors and emoluments of office without regret or disgust. I have done my duty — I have acted according to the convictions of my own heart. And what I most regret, is the parting with men whose friendship I highly prize — many of whom I shall never behold again.

See my letters to my wife & children written about this time — & perhaps tomorrow.

### *Wednesday March 4, 1807.*

Abraham Baldwin died today at ten in the morning, aged 53. Ten days ago he told me that for 18 years he had not been absent from the Senate. I regret that I cannot attend his fu-

---

[304] *Ibid.*, 54–55.

neral tomorrow. He is to be buryed at Rock Hill church by the side of his late friend James Jackson — who died in this city about 11 months since.

I called upon the President this morning to take leave of him. He received me very cordially.

He told me he had not received the treaty with Great Britain — but that Mr. Erskine the British minister had received a copy of it — & had politely sent it to him — The President said he disapproved of it — for it contained no stipulations for the protections of American seamen — nothing to prevent their being impressed. That had he recd the treaty ten days ago he should not have laid it before the Senate [305] — That from some letters he received from our ministers some time since he was apprehensive they would make a treaty without such stipulation — That in February new instructions was sent to them upon this subject with positive assurances that no treaty would be ratified unless provision was made to secure the right of our seamen — That our ministers were ordered to open a new negociation upon the subject.

That he did not expect our negociations with Spain for the Florida's would proceed untill Napolean returned to France.

That he expected Aaron Burr had a trial in the Mississippi territory and was acquitted. But that Wilkinson had orders to arrest him & send him to this city — & he presumed he was now on his way as a prisoner for W. had many spies around Burr. But that he feared he would be discharged the Courts being inclined to construe the law too favorably for the accused & too rigidly agt. the Government. That it was difficult to say, where he ought to be tried — but on the whole tho't in the State of Virginia — And there the judges were Marshall, who had already, in the case of Bollman & Swartout, given an unfavorable opinion — And that Griffin district Judge was a poor creature.

---

[305] The immediately preceding sentences are quoted in Plumer, *Life of William Plumer*, 347.

The President bid me a very polite farewell, & Mr. Giles who was present, a very affectionate one.

Thomas Man Randolph who is still at Frost's is very sick, & much I fear his sickness will terminate fatally.[306] I think he has much to fear from his physicians. They seem to me to load & oppress him with medicine. He is an amiable man. I am certain he came here *not* from any dissatisfaction with Mr. Jefferson as has been reported. But I beleive from a quarrel with Mr. Eppes his brother in law. No man could pay greater attention or discover more anxiety for Mr. Randolph than Mr. Jefferson has. Mr. Eppes has not visited him in his illness.

One thing appeared singular — Mr. Randolph is not a military man — yet he has a pair of pistols & sword laying on the mantle piece in his chamber at this house.

I have frequently visited him.

---

Little progress has been made the last year in building up the city of Washington. Few new houses have been erected. The south wing of the Capitol is a great addition — tis not yet finished. It will be elegant & strong — but the Representatives chamber will be hard to speak in, & the accomodations for spectators bad — & the large lobby out of sight of the speaker — & of course the spectators will be noisy.

There are many buildings whose brick walls are mouldering in ruins. It looks like a deserted city. Two things have contributed to retard the growth of the city  1. The attempt to build it all up in its various parts at once, instead of concentrating the buildings. 2 The failure of Greenleaf, Morris & others, the first undertakers.[307] The workmen were defrauded of their wages. This had prevented mechanics from coming here. —

---

[306] He died at Monticello, June 20, 1828.

[307] Robert Morris, James Greenleaf and John Nicholson were the principal promoters whose failure is here referred to; see Bryan, *A History of the National Capital*, I, 298.

### March 5, 1807

I ought yesterday to have stated  That Mr. Jefferson when speaking of the treaty with G.B. observed that the decōn made by the British Commissioners at the time of signing the treaty & which I understood was in writing & dld. to our Commissioners, purported that it was the understanding of the King that the United States should to a certain extent make a common cause agt France — & that the king reserved to himself the right of making retaliation upon neutrals in case Napolean's decree of Nov 21 should be enforced & Neutrals would not arm agt it — That is, I presume, of declaring France in a state of blockade.

I also ought to have observed that Mr. Jefferson said our Ministers had early in the winter intimated that they should sign a treaty even in case they could not fully provide for the rights of seamen — if other provisions should be fully satisfactory.  This occasioned the instructions of *January* as mentioned yesterday.

At 7 OClock am left Washington — at 9 OClock fell 4 Inches of snow to day — P.M. arrived at Baltimore.  roads bad

. . . . . . . . . . . . . . . . . . . . . . . . . . . . . . . . . . . . . . . .

John Q Adams was with me in the stage on my journey.[308] He gave me much information of his living in Europe — the manners & characters of the Europeans.  He is a man of much information — but too formal — his manners are too stiff & unyielding — he is too tenacious of his opinions.[309]

---

[308] In J. Q. Adams, *Memoirs,* there is no entry for this date.

[309] Plumer's entries from March 7 to April 21 concern personal matters primarily and are omitted here.

# INDEX

Abel, Annie H., "History of Events resulting in Indian Consolidation West of the Mississippi," in *Annual Report of the American Historical Association,* 137 *n.,* 138 *n.*

Adair, John, opposes foreign intercourse bill, 407–408, 415; avoids voting, 457, 457 *n.;* opinion of Jefferson, 478–479; on militia bill, 480; implicated with Burr, 540, 562, 563–564; resigns from Senate, 552–553; indictment, 566–567; denies complicity with Burr, 614–615; liberated, 616; treatment, 618; letter, 623; story of arrest, 624–626; vote, 425, 431, 472, 478, 482; mentioned, 631.

Adams, Henry, *History of the United States,* 337 *n.,* 383 *n.,* 427 *n.,* 484 *n.*

Adams, John, franking privilege, 303; amount of loans, 411; quarrel with Hamilton, 452; convention with France, 452, 452 *n.;* mentioned, 100 *n.,* 269 *n.,* 280, 316, 384, 568; *A Defence of the Constitutions of Government of the United States of America,* 604, 604 *n.*

Adams, John Quincy, on election of President, 21, 21 *n.,* 38, 41; on protection of seamen, 34–35; favors majority rule on questions concerning constitutional amendment, 36; on popular and federative principles of government, 43–44; on presidential succession, 45; on government of Louisiana, 73; moves amendment to Constitution concerning Louisiana, 75–76; on salary bill, 90; opposes opening Senate chamber to ladies, 92; on personnel of court of impeachment, 98, 98–99, 148; resolutions concerning

government of Louisiana, 103–104; on granting Orleans territory delegate to Congress, 108; on slavery, 114, 126, 130, 353–354; opposes Louisiana government bill, 143–146; criticises minutes of impeachment court, 157, 158; criticises proceedings in Pickering trial, 161–162; favors postponement of Pickering trial, 170–171, 174; describes Pickering trial as mock trial, 175; on procedure in impeachment trial, 240; favors hearing petition concerning slavery, 250; as to military discipline, 261; opposes amendment to Creek treaty, 262; favors Creek treaty, 265–266; on franking privilege, 302, 305; vote in Chase trial, 309; opposes admitting Tunisian ambassador to seat in Senate, 364; opposes bill placing money at discretion of President, 385; resolutions on disputes with Great Britain, 398; on appropriation for foreign intercourse, 400–401; opposes foreign intercourse bill, 412–413; on title to West Florida, 415; bill concerning foreign ministers, 445, 447; Merry and Turreau remonstrate with, 448; on treaty with Tripoli, 472; criticised by Eaton, 480; refuses offer to present claims to Congress, 481; letter concerning Miranda, 483–484; opposes executive session, 488; discusses appointment of minister to London, 491; letter concerning Eaton, 550; friendship for Plumer, 574; favors suspension of habeas corpus act, 587, 588, 589; on Potomac bridge bill, 595; receives warning of danger from Napoleon, 604–605; advises Plumer concerning writing of

# UNIVERSITY OF MICHIGAN STUDIES

## HUMANISTIC SERIES

General Editors: FRANCIS W. KELSEY AND HENRY A. SANDERS

Size, 22.7 × 15.2 cm. 8°. Bound in cloth

VOL. I. ROMAN HISTORICAL SOURCES AND INSTITUTIONS. Edited by Henry A. Sanders, University of Michigan. Pp. viii + 402. $2.50 net.

### CONTENTS

1. THE MYTH ABOUT TARPEIA: Henry A. Sanders.
2. THE MOVEMENTS OF THE CHORUS CHANTING THE CARMEN SAECULARE: WALTER DENNISON.
3. STUDIES IN THE LIVES OF ROMAN EMPRESSES, JULIA MAMAEA: Mary Gilmore Williams, Mt. Holyoke College.
4. THE ATTITUDE OF DIO CASSIUS TOWARD EPIGRAPHIC SOURCES: Duane Reed Stuart, Princeton University.
5. THE LOST EPITOME OF LIVY: Henry A. Sanders.
6. THE PRINCIPALES OF THE EARLY EMPIRE: Joseph H. Drake, University of Michigan.
7. CENTURIONS AS SUBSTITUTE COMMANDERS OF AUXILIARY CORPS: George H. Allen.

VOL. II. WORD FORMATION IN PROVENÇAL. By Edward L. Adams, University of Michigan. Pp. xvii + 607. $4.00 net.

VOL. III. LATIN PHILOLOGY. Edited by Clarence Linton Meader, University of Michigan. Pp. vii + 290. $2.00 net.

Parts Sold Separately in Paper Covers:

Part I. THE USE OF IDEM, IPSE, AND WORDS OF RELATED MEANING. By Clarence L. Meader. Pp. 1–111. $0.75.

Part II. A STUDY IN LATIN ABSTRACT SUBSTANTIVES. By Manson A. Stewart, Yankton College. Pp. 113–78. $0.40.

Part III. THE USE OF THE ADJECTIVE AS A SUBSTANTIVE IN THE DE RERUM NATURA OF LUCRETIUS. By Frederick T. Swan. Pp. 179–214. $0.40.

Part IV. AUTOBIOGRAPHIC ELEMENTS IN LATIN INSCRIPTIONS. By Henry H. Armstrong, Beloit College. Pp. 215–86. $0.40.

VOL. IV. ROMAN HISTORY AND MYTHOLOGY. Edited by Henry A. Sanders. Pp. viii + 427. $2.50 net.

Parts Sold Separately in Paper Covers:

Part I. STUDIES IN THE LIFE OF HELIOGABALUS. By Orma Fitch Butler, University of Michigan. Pp. 1–169. $1.25 net.

Part II. THE MYTH OF HERCULES AT ROME. By John G. Winter, University of Michigan. Pp. 171–273. $0.50 net.

## THE MACMILLAN COMPANY

Publishers          64–66 Fifth Avenue          New York

Part III. ROMAN LAW STUDIES IN LIVY. By Alvin E. Evans. Pp. 275–354. $0.40 net.

Part IV. REMINISCENCES OF ENNIUS IN SILIUS ITALICUS. By Loura B. Woodruff. Pp. 355–424. $0.40 net.

VOL. V. SOURCES OF THE SYNOPTIC GOSPELS. By Rev. Dr. Carl S. Patton, First Congregational Church, Los Angeles, California. Pp. xiii + 263. $1.30 net.

---

Size, 28 × 18.5 cm.   4to.

VOL. VI. ATHENIAN LEKYTHOI WITH OUTLINE DRAWING IN GLAZE VARNISH ON A WHITE GROUND. By Arthur Fairbanks, Director of the Museum of Fine Arts, Boston. With 15 plates, and 57 illustrations in the text. Pp. viii + 371. Bound in cloth. $4.00 net.

VOL. VII. ATHENIAN LEKYTHOI WITH OUTLINE DRAWING IN MATT COLOR ON A WHITE GROUND, AND AN APPENDIX: ADDITIONAL LEKYTHOI WITH OUTLINE DRAWING IN GLAZE VARNISH ON A WHITE GROUND. By Arthur Fairbanks. With 41 plates. Pp. x + 275. Bound in cloth. $3.50 net.

VOL. VIII. THE OLD TESTAMENT MANUSCRIPTS IN THE FREER COLLECTION. By Henry A. Sanders, University of Michigan. With 9 plates showing pages of the Manuscripts in facsimile. Pp. viii + 357. Bound in cloth. $3.50 net.

Parts Sold Separately in Paper Covers:

Part I. THE WASHINGTON MANUSCRIPT OF DEUTERONOMY AND JOSHUA. With 3 folding plates. Pp. vi + 104. $1.25.

Part II. THE WASHINGTON MANUSCRIPT OF THE PSALMS. With 1 single plate and 5 folding plates. Pp. viii + 105–349. $2.00 net.

VOL. IX. THE NEW TESTAMENT MANUSCRIPTS IN THE FREER COLLECTION. By Henry A. Sanders, University of Michigan. With 8 plates showing pages of the Manuscripts in facsimile. Pp. x + 323. Bound in cloth. $3.50 net.

Parts sold separately in Paper Covers:

Part I. THE WASHINGTON MANUSCRIPT OF THE FOUR GOSPELS. With 5 plates. Pp. vii + 247. $2.00 net.

Part II. THE WASHINGTON MANUSCRIPT OF THE EPISTLES OF PAUL. With 3 plates. Pp. ix, 249–315. $1.25 net.

VOL. X. THE COPTIC MANUSCRIPTS IN THE FREER COLLECTION. By William H. Worrell, Hartford Seminary Foundation.

Part I. THE COPTIC PSALTER. The Coptic text in the Sahidic Dialect, with an Introduction, and with 6 plates showing pages of the Manuscript and Fragments in facsimile. Pp. xxvi + 112. $2.00 net.

Part II. A HOMILY OF CELESTINUS ON THE ARCHANGEL GABRIEL AND A HOMILY OF THEOPHILUS ON ST. MARY THEOTOKOS, FROM MANUSCRIPT FRAGMENTS IN THE FREER COLLECTION AND THE BRITISH MUSEUM. The Coptic Text with an Introduction and Translation, and with plates showing pages of the Manuscript in facsimile. (*In press.*)

## THE MACMILLAN COMPANY

Publishers          64–66 Fifth Avenue          New York

Vol. XI. Contributions to the History of Science.

Part I. Robert of Chester's Latin Translation of the Algebra of Al-Khowarizmi. With an Introduction, Critical Notes, and an English Version. By Louis C. Karpinski, University of Michigan. With 4 plates showing pages of manuscripts in facsimile, and 25 diagrams in the text. Pp. vii + 164. Paper covers. $2.00 net.

Part II. The Prodromus of Nicolaus Steno's Latin Dissertation Concerning a Solid Body Enclosed by Process of Nature within a Solid. Translated into English by John G. Winter. University of Michigan, with a Foreword by Professor William H. Hobbs. With 7 plates. Pp. 165–283. Paper covers. $1.30 net.

Part III. Vesuvius in Antiquity. Passages of Ancient Authors, with a Translation and Elucidations. By Francis W. Kelsey. Illustrated. (In preparation.)

Vol. XII. Studies in East Christian and Roman Art. By Charles R. Morey, Princeton University, and Walter Dennison. With 67 plates (10 colored) and 91 illustrations in the text. Pp. xiii + 173. $4.75 net.

Parts sold separately:

Part I. East Christian Paintings in the Freer Collection. By Charles R. Morey. With 13 plates (10 colored) and 34 illustrations in the text. Pp. xiii + 86. Bound in cloth. $2.50 net.

Part II. A Gold Treasure of the Late Roman Period. By Walter Dennison. With 54 plates and 57 illustrations in the text. Pp. 89–175. Bound in cloth. $2.50 net.

Vol. XIII. Documents from the Cairo Genizah in the Freer Collection. Text, with Translation and an Introduction by Richard Gottheil, Columbia University. (In preparation.)

Vol. XIV. Aspects of Roman Law and Administration.
Part I. The Master of Offices in the Later Roman and Byzantine Empires. By Arthur E. R. Boak, University of Michigan. Pp. x + 160. Paper covers. $1.00 net.

Vol. XV. Greek Themes in Modern Musical Settings. By Albert A. Stanley, University of Michigan. (In press.)

Vol. XVI. Nichomachus of Gerasa: Introduction to Arithmetic. Translated into English by Martin Luther D'Ooge, with Studies in Greek Arithmetic by Frank Egleston Robbins and Louis Charles Karpinski. (In preparation.)

## SCIENTIFIC SERIES

Size, 28 × 18.5 cm. 4°. Bound in cloth

Vol. I. The Circulation and Sleep. By John F. Shepard, University of Michigan. Pp. ix + 83, with an Atlas of 63 plates, bound separately. Text and Atlas, $2.50 net.

Vol. II. Studies on Divergent Series and Summability. By Walter B. Ford, University of Michigan. Pp. xi + 194. $2.50

# THE MACMILLAN COMPANY

Publishers          64–66 Fifth Avenue          New York

# UNIVERSITY OF MICHIGAN PUBLICATIONS

## HUMANISTIC PAPERS

General Editor: EUGENE S. McCARTNEY

Size, 22.7 × 15.2 cm. 8°. Bound in cloth

LATIN AND GREEK IN AMERICAN EDUCATION, WITH SYMPOSIA ON THE VALUE OF HUMANISTIC STUDIES. Edited by FRANCIS W. KELSEY. Pp. x + 396. $1.50.

THE PRESENT POSITION OF LATIN AND GREEK, The Value of Latin and Greek as Educational Instruments, the Nature of Culture Studies.

SYMPOSIA ON THE VALUE OF HUMANISTIC, Particularly Classical, Studies as a Preparation for the Study of Medicine, Engineering, Law and Theology.

A SYMPOSIUM ON THE VALUE OF HUMANISTIC, Particularly Classical Studies as a Training for Men of Affairs.

A SYMPOSIUM ON THE CLASSICS AND THE NEW EDUCATION.

A SYMPOSIUM ON THE DOCTRINE OF FORMAL DISCIPLINE IN THE LIGHT OF CONTEMPORARY PSYCHOLOGY.
(*Out of print; new edition in preparation.*)

THE MENAECHMI OF PLAUTUS. The Latin Text, with a Translation by JOSEPH H. DRAKE, University of Michigan. Pp. xi + 130. Paper covers. $0.60.

THE LIFE AND WORKS OF GEORGE SYLVESTER MORRIS. A CHAPTER IN THE HISTORY OF AMERICAN THOUGHT IN THE NINETEENTH CENTURY. By R. M. WENLEY, University of Michigan. Pp. xv + 332. Cloth $1.50 net.

THE SENATE AND TREATIES, 1789–1817. THE DEVELOPMENT OF THE TREATY-MAKING FUNCTIONS OF THE UNITED STATES SENATE DURING THEIR FORMATIVE PERIOD. By RALSTON HAYDEN, University of Michigan. Pp. xvi. + 237. Cloth $1.50 net.

---

Size, 23.5 × 15.5 cm. 8°. Bound in cloth.

WILLIAM PLUMER'S MEMORANDUM OF PROCEEDINGS IN THE UNITED STATES SENATE, 1803–1807. Edited by EVERETT SOMERVILLE BROWN, University of Michigan. Pp. xii + 673. Cloth. $3.50.

## THE MACMILLAN COMPANY

Publishers                    64–66 Fifth Avenue                    New York

"One of the most helpful books for teachers of American history which has been produced in the last generation." HARRY E. BARNES, *Clark University.*

# NEW VIEWPOINTS IN AMERICAN HISTORY

BY

## ARTHUR M. SCHLESINGER

PROFESSOR OF HISTORY IN THE UNIVERSITY OF IOWA

THE object of the present work is to bring together and summarize in non-technical language, some of the results of the researches of the present era of historical study and to show their importance to a proper understanding of American history. It seems unnecessary to say that the interest aroused by the World War in Americanization work makes it important that all citizens of the republic should learn what the historians have to say about the past of their country: Americanization must begin at home. History teachers in the public schools may also find in this volume a short cut to a rather extensive literature inaccessible to most of them. It is the further hope of the author that graduate students venturing forth into the field of American history for the first time may find this book useful in suggesting the special interests of the present generation of historians and some of the tendencies that seem likely to guide historical research for some years to come. It has not been my primary purpose to celebrate the names of the men and women who have cleared the new trails; but an effort has been made in the notes at the end of each chapter to render due acknowledgment. — *From the Preface.*

### CONTENTS

Price $2.40

## THE MACMILLAN COMPANY

Publishers      64–66 Fifth Avenue      New York

*A new volume of great historical importance*

# THE McKINLEY AND ROOSEVELT ADMINISTRATIONS, 1897–1909

BY

## JAMES FORD RHODES, LL.D., D.Litt.

FEW historians can lay claim to such a spontaneous and vigorous style as James Ford Rhodes. The book opens with the excitement of the presidential campaign of 1896, takes up and makes live again the Spanish War, the Venezuela dispute of 1902, the Hay-Pauncefote treaties leading to the building of the Panama Canal, the Russo-Japanese Treaty Conference, Roosevelt's prosecution of the trusts, and the other events of the time to which the country thrilled.

CHAPTER I. Introduces Mark Hanna and follows his political career through the meeting of McKinley, the intimacy that formed over the coin question and his aid in McKinley's campaign and election.

CHAPTER II. Deals with the arranging of the Cabinet and the trouble involved.

CHAPTER III. Presents the Cuban question giving public opinion and McKinley's stand.

CHAPTER IV. The Spanish War chapter beginning with the battle of Manila and ending with the destruction of the Spanish Fleet.

CHAPTER V. Gives the main provisions in the Protocol, some personal glimpses of J. P. Morgan and John Hay, and ends with an explanation of the Boxer Uprising in China.

CHAPTER VI. Carries us through the Presidential Campaign of 1900, the stock panic and the assassination of McKinley.

CHAPTER VII. Opens with a discussion of the situation in Puerto Rico, Cuba and the Philippines, followed by character sketches of Root, Taft, Forbes and Coolidge.

CHAPTER VIII. Begins the Roosevelt administration and describes his New England tour.

CHAPTER IX. Includes Roosevelt's dealing and settlement of the Anthracite coal strike and his views of the Venezuela question, the Alaska Boundary Dispute and the size of the British Navy.

CHAPTER X. Covers the discussions about the Panama Canal, including the Hay-Pauncefote treaties, the Hay-Herran treaty, the Panama Revolution, and the Hay-Bunau-Varilla treaty.

CHAPTER XI. Roosevelt's ability is contrasted with that of Hanna.

CHAPTER XII. Records the status of the Republican Party, the result of the election of 1904 and the St. Louis Fair.

CHAPTER XIII. Brings us to the Russo-Japanese War and includes some salient mentions of the Morocco Affair and the Algeciras Conference.

CHAPTER XIV. Discusses the different matters of legislation in 1905 such as the Railroad rate, the Hepburn Bill, the Senate Bill, and the Pure Food laws.

CHAPTER XV. Clearly elucidates the president's efforts during the panic of 1907 and his actions in regard to Irrigation.

CHAPTER XVI. Gives us some sidelights on Roosevelt's opinion of the navy and the Japanese question.

CHAPTER XVII. Has for its background the Republican Convention of 1908 across which come the figures of prominent men: Taft, Lodge, Morton; but most conspicuous among these is Roosevelt.

THE McKINLEY AND ROOSEVELT ADMINISTRATIONS, 1897–1909

BY JAMES FORD RHODES, LL.D., D.Litt.

*Illustrated with portraits of prominent men of the time*

**Probable Price $5.00**

## THE MACMILLAN COMPANY

Publishers          64–66 Fifth Avenue          New York

**DATE DUE**